Our Best Recipes

Volume Three

Jean Wickstrom

Library of Congress Catalog Number: 78-55774
ISBN: 0-8487-0489-4

Manufactured in the United States of America

Our Best Recipes
Volume Three

Editor: Karen Phillips Irons
Cover Design and Illustration: Thomas F. Ford
Photographs: Charles Beck (pages 2, 24, 130, 276);
Jerome Drown (title pages, pages 34, 60, 138, 156,
218, 238, 304); Kent Kirkley (page 202);
Phillip Kretchmar (page 110); Taylor Lewis (pages
82, 88, 284).
Illustrations: *Southern Living* Editorial Art Staff

Southern pound cakes have a reputation of being
some of the most delicious ever made. Million Dol-
lar Pound Cake (page 81) and Butterscotch-Mocha
Pound Cake (page 80) are just two of the favorites.

CONTENTS

★ indicates the Editors' favorite recipes.

INTRODUCTION

When many people think about Southern food, images of country ham, turnip greens, and cornbread come to mind. Southern food is these things, but it's more—much more. Whether they are serving crispy fried chicken or an elegant she-crab soup, Southerners love food and entertaining.

The recipes in *Our Best Recipes, Volume Three* appeal to the varied tastes and interests of Southerners. We trust that you will enjoy serving these recipes to your family and guests as well.

It is no exaggeration to say that this cookbook would not be possible without the readers of *Southern Living*. We believe that a magazine, the food section of which is dedicated to Southern cuisine, can find its best source of ideas from its readers. Since our first issue in 1966, virtually all of the recipes which we have published have come from our readers. Thousands of our readers share their favorite recipes with us monthly. These recipes are prepared in our test kitchens by our staff of home economists. Each recipe is judged for taste, cost, ease of preparation, and appearance.

Only the best recipes are selected for publication in *Southern Living*. From those that were published in 1976-77, we have selected for this cookbook the ones we consider to be the most taste-tempting and appealing. Of these, we have starred special recipes which we feel are our very best as Editors' Choice.

Our Best Recipes, Volume Three is not only for the experienced cook but for the novice as well. Our recipes range from the quick-and-easy to gourmet fare, but all have a special touch and flair that will delight your family and friends. Whether your taste runs to traditional Southern food or cosmopolitan cuisine, we hope these recipes will become some of your favorites.

Jean Wickstrom

Jean Wickstrom, Foods Editor

Southern Living

Our Best Recipes
Volume Three

Jean Wickstrom

OXMOOR HOUSE, INC. • BIRMINGHAM

Appetizers, Snacks, and Sandwiches

Whether served as the prelude to a meal or the meal itself, appetizers, snacks, and sandwiches are all-around pleasers. With these favorites you get additional bonuses; they are easy to prepare, easy to serve, and easy to eat.

Appetizers are the taste-tempting canapés, dips, spreads, and other hors d'oeuvres that add a special flair to parties. The appetizers served before a dinner should be quite light and just enough to whet the appetite.

Snacks, on the other hand, are the pick-up nibbles that are enjoyed between meals, after school, and before bedtime. Your choice can be as simple as a piece of fruit, an assortment of cheese and crackers, or a mixture of nuts.

Sandwiches can be a complete meal or served as a hearty snack. Sandwich sizes vary from a big hero to the tiny tea sandwich; they can be made with a variety of breads and served plain or toasted, hot or cold.

Party Antipasto Tray

- ½ medium-size head iceberg lettuce
- 1 small head endive
- 1 (3½-ounce) package thinly sliced pepperoni
- 1 (4-ounce) package thinly sliced Genoa salami, quartered
- 1 (3-ounce) package thinly sliced Italian ham
- 1 (15-ounce) can garbanzo beans, drained
- 1 (2-ounce) can anchovies with capers, drained
- 1 (8-ounce) jar peperoncini, drained
- 1 pound cherry tomatoes
- Radishes
- Carrot sticks
- Ripe olives
- Green olives
- 8 ounces provolone cheese, cubed
- Dressing

Shred lettuce and part of endive. Combine shredded salad greens; toss well and spread over bottom of serving tray.

Make a border of remaining endive leaves around edge of tray. Arrange meats, vegetables, and cubed cheese on top of shredded salad greens. Serve with Dressing. Yield: about 10 to 12 servings.

Dressing:

- 2 tablespoons water
- ¼ cup wine vinegar
- 1 cup salad oil
- 1 tablespoon olive oil
- 1 clove garlic, crushed
- 1 teaspoon ground oregano
- 1 teaspoon basil
- ¼ teaspoon thyme
- Salt and pepper to taste (optional)

Combine all ingredients; mix well. Let stand several hours at room temperature. Yield: about 1½ cups.

A savory marinade and the flavor of grilling make these Party Barbecued Shrimp (page 4) especially appealing.

Creole Shrimp Tarts

2   *pounds shrimp, cooked, peeled,*
deveined, and chopped
½   *cup finely chopped green onion tops*
½   *cup finely chopped parsley*
½   *cup mayonnaise*
¼   *teaspoon cayenne pepper*
1   *teaspoon lemon juice*
1   *garlic clove, minced*
½   *cup finely chopped mushrooms*
Tart Shells
Pimiento strips
Capers
Paprika

Combine shrimp, onion, parsley, mayonnaise, cayenne pepper, lemon juice, garlic, and mushrooms; stir well. Spoon mixture into baked Tart Shells.

Garnish with pimiento strips, forming a circle; place a caper in center of each circle. Sprinkle with paprika. Yield: 24 appetizers.

Tart Shells:

1   *(3-ounce) package cream cheese,*
softened
½   *cup butter or margarine, softened*
1   *cup all-purpose flour*
½   *cup sesame seeds*

Combine cream cheese and butter; blend well. Add flour and sesame seeds, mixing well. Chill 1 hour. Shape into 2 dozen 1-inch balls.

Press dough on bottom and sides of greased tart or muffin tins. Bake at 325° for 20 minutes. Cool. Remove from pan. Yield: 24 tart shells.

Party Barbecued Shrimp

1   *clove garlic, crushed*
½   *teaspoon salt*
½   *cup salad oil*
¼   *cup soy sauce*
½   *cup lemon juice*
3   *tablespoons finely chopped parsley*
2   *tablespoons finely chopped onion*
½   *teaspoon pepper*
2   *pounds large shrimp, peeled*

Combine first 8 ingredients to make marinade; mix well. Place shrimp in a shallow dish; add marinade. Cover and refrigerate 2 to 3 hours.

Thread shrimp onto cocktail skewers. Broil or grill over medium heat about 3 to 4 minutes on each side. Serve with cocktail picks. Yield: 15 to 20 appetizer servings.

Cajun Chafing Shrimp

6   *cloves garlic, finely chopped*
½   *cup olive oil*
1   *cup melted butter or margarine*
½   *cup hickory-flavored barbecue sauce*
1   *cup chili sauce*
¼   *cup Worcestershire sauce*
¼   *cup lemon juice*
2   *lemons, sliced*
1   *tablespoon basil*
1   *tablespoon oregano*
¼   *cup liquid smoke*
2   *tablespoons parsley flakes*
½   *teaspoon cayenne pepper*
Hot sauce to taste
Salt and pepper to taste
4   *pounds medium-size shrimp, peeled and*
deveined

Sauté garlic in olive oil. Add remaining ingredients except shrimp; simmer 15 minutes, stirring occasionally. Pour over shrimp; bake at 300° for 20 minutes or until shrimp begins to turn pink. Cool; then refrigerate several hours for seasonings to blend.

Before serving, reheat shrimp, and transfer to a chafing dish set on low heat. Have toothpicks handy for serving. Yield: 10 to 12 servings.

Blue Cheese Shrimp

1   *(3-ounce) bag crab boil*
2½   *pounds shrimp*
About 2 tablespoons salad oil
1   *medium-size onion, thinly sliced*
Salt and pepper to taste
6   *ounces blue cheese, crumbled*
Crackers

Place crab boil bag in a large saucepan with 4 to 5 quarts water; bring to a boil. Add shrimp; return to boil, and boil 1 to 2 minutes. Drain, cool, and peel shrimp.

Toss shrimp with oil to coat lightly. Combine shrimp with remaining ingredients except crackers; mix thoroughly. Cover and refrigerate 2 days, stirring often. Serve with crackers. Yield: about 8 servings.

Snappy Shrimp Marinade

½ cup melted butter or margarine
⅓ cup Worcestershire sauce
2 teaspoons garlic puree
1 teaspoon rosemary, finely crushed
1 teaspoon cayenne pepper
1 teaspoon salt
1 teaspoon pepper
½ teaspoon celery salt
1 teaspoon olive oil
1½ pounds medium-size shrimp, peeled

Combine all ingredients except shrimp in a saucepan; simmer 10 to 15 minutes. Cool slightly; add shrimp. Cover tightly, and marinate in refrigerator 3 to 8 hours.

Spread shrimp in a single layer in a shallow baking dish; pour marinade over shrimp. Bake at 400° for 18 to 20 minutes or until done. Yield: 6 to 8 appetizer servings.

Remoulade à la St. Tammany

1 cup mayonnaise
¼ cup salad oil
2 tablespoons dry mustard
1 tablespoon chopped green onion
1 tablespoon chopped celery
1 tablespoon chopped parsley
1 tablespoon horseradish
1 tablespoon vinegar
1 teaspoon paprika
½ teaspoon salt
½ teaspoon Worcestershire sauce
Dash of hot sauce
Cooked shrimp or crabmeat
Shredded lettuce

Combine all ingredients except shrimp and lettuce in blender container; blend until smooth. Chill thoroughly, and serve with shrimp or crabmeat on a bed of lettuce. Yield: about 1½ cups.

★ Coquille St. Jacques

3 tablespoons all-purpose flour
1 teaspoon salt
⅛ teaspoon white pepper
6 tablespoons butter or margarine, divided
2 cups half-and-half
¼ cup finely chopped onion
½ pound scallops, sliced and halved
½ cup chopped fresh mushrooms
½ pound shrimp, cooked, peeled, and deveined
⅓ cup white crabmeat or 1 (6-ounce) package frozen crabmeat, thawed and drained
3 tablespoons dry white wine or dry vermouth
4 dozen (1-inch) patty or pastry shells

Combine flour, salt, and pepper. Melt 4 tablespoons butter in top of a double boiler over boiling water; gradually add flour mixture, blending well.

Remove top of double boiler from boiling water, and place over direct heat; gradually add half-and-half, stirring constantly until mixture reaches boiling point. Return double boiler to boiling water, and cook 5 minutes.

Melt 2 tablespoons butter in skillet. Add onion and scallops; sauté 5 minutes. Add mushrooms, and sauté 3 minutes. Stir sautéed vegetables and scallops, shrimp, crabmeat, and wine into cream sauce; heat thoroughly.

Serve as filling for patty shells. Yield: 48 appetizer servings.

Italia Caponata

 1   *(9¼-ounce) can tuna, drained and*
     flaked
 ⅓   *cup pitted black olives, sliced*
 ⅓   *cup stuffed green olives, sliced*
 1   *(2-ounce) jar sliced pimiento, chopped*
 1½ *tablespoons capers*
 1   *tablespoon lemon juice*
 ⅛   *teaspoon minced garlic*
 ¼   *teaspoon pepper*
 2   *teaspoons Worcestershire sauce*
 1   *(6½-ounce) jar marinated artichoke*
     hearts, drained and quartered
     Lettuce
     Commercial Italian salad dressing
     (optional)

Combine first 10 ingredients, mixing well; cover and refrigerate at least 2 hours. Serve on lettuce with Italian dressing, if desired. Yield: 6 servings.

Crabmeat Bites

 1   *(7-ounce) can crabmeat*
 ½   *cup butter or margarine, softened*
 1   *(5-ounce) jar sharp process cheese*
     spread
 ¼   *teaspoon garlic salt*
 ¼   *teaspoon seasoned salt*
 1½ *teaspoons mayonnaise*
 1   *(12-ounce) package English muffins*

Combine first 6 ingredients, blending well. Chill. Split muffins in half; spread with cheese mixture. Cut each muffin half into quarters. Yield: 4 dozen bites.

Ginger Meatballs

 1½ *pounds ground beef*
 1   *(4½-ounce) can deviled ham*
 ¾   *cup all-purpose flour, divided*
 ¾   *teaspoon ground ginger, divided*
 ½   *to ⅔ cup half-and-half*
 7   *tablespoons soy sauce, divided*
 6   *tablespoons melted butter or margarine*
 2   *cups water*

Combine ground beef, ham, ½ cup flour, and ½ teaspoon ginger in a large bowl; mix well. Gradually add half-and-half and 3 tablespoons soy sauce, stirring well to make a smooth, pastelike mixture.

Shape into 1-inch balls. Brown well in butter; drain and reserve drippings. Place meatballs in chafing dish to keep warm.

Combine remaining ¼ cup flour and ¼ teaspoon ginger with drippings in skillet. Cook, stirring constantly, until smooth and bubbly. Stir in water and remaining 4 tablespoons soy sauce. Cook, stirring constantly, until thickened. Pour over meatballs. Serve with toothpicks. Yield: about 85 (1-inch) meatballs.

Zesty Meatballs

 1   *pound ground round steak*
 ½   *teaspoon onion salt*
 ¼   *cup water*
 ½   *cup fine breadcrumbs*
 1   *egg*
 ½   *cup firmly packed brown sugar*
 1   *(15-ounce) can tomato sauce*
     Juice of 1 lemon
     Lemon slices
     Parsley

Combine meat, salt, water, breadcrumbs, and egg; mix well, and shape into small balls. Set aside.

Combine sugar, tomato sauce, and lemon juice in a saucepan; simmer about 3 minutes. Add meatballs, and continue to simmer 45 minutes.

Transfer to a chafing dish set on low heat. Garnish with lemon slices and parsley. Yield: about 3½ dozen meatballs.

Barbecue Pork with Petite Buns

 1   *(4-pound) boned, rolled pork loin roast*
 1   *clove garlic*
     Spicy Barbecue Sauce
 30 *to 40 (2-inch) cocktail buns*

Rub pork roast with garlic. Place roast in a 450° oven; reduce heat to 350°. Allow 30 minutes per pound or 2 hours for roasting. Chill well, and slice very thin. Place in a shallow baking dish; add Spicy Barbecue Sauce. Bake at 325° about 30 minutes or until bubbly. Serve in a chafing dish. Spoon onto buns. Yield: 30 to 40 servings.

Spicy Barbecue Sauce:

- 4 *cups catsup*
- ¾ *cup butter or margarine*
- 2 *cups vinegar*
- ½ *cup Worcestershire sauce*
- ½ *cup steak sauce for seasoning and cooking*
- ¼ *cup thick, rich, spicy steak sauce*
- ⅓ *cup tarragon vinegar*
- 2 *cups sherry*
- *Hot sauce to taste*
- *Salt and pepper to taste*
- ¼ *teaspoon onion salt*
- ¼ *teaspoon garlic salt*

Combine all ingredients in a large saucepan; simmer until butter is melted. May be prepared ahead and stored in refrigerator. Yield: about 2½ quarts.

Deviled Ham Puffs

- 1 *(8-ounce) package cream cheese, softened*
- 1 *egg yolk, beaten*
- 1 *teaspoon onion juice*
- ½ *teaspoon baking powder*
- *Salt to taste*
- ¼ *teaspoon horseradish*
- ¼ *teaspoon hot sauce*
- 2 *(2¼-ounce) cans deviled ham*
- 24 *(1-inch) bread rounds*

Combine cream cheese, egg yolk, onion juice, baking powder, salt, horseradish, and hot sauce; blend until smooth. Stir in deviled ham.

Toast bread lightly on one side; spoon about a teaspoonful of ham mixture on untoasted side of bread. Place on a cookie sheet, and bake at 375° for 10 to 12 minutes or until puffed and lightly browned. Serve hot. Yield: 2 dozen puffs.

★
Party Ham Biscuits

- 2 *cups all-purpose flour*
- ¼ *teaspoon salt*
- 2½ *teaspoons baking powder*
- 3 *to 4 tablespoons shortening*
- ¾ *cup buttermilk*
- ½ *teaspoon soda*
- *Butter or margarine, softened, or mustard*
- *Thinly sliced ham*

Combine flour, salt, and baking powder; cut in shortening until mixture resembles fine crumbs. Combine buttermilk and soda; stir into flour mixture, blending well.

Roll out dough to ¼-inch thickness on a floured surface; cut with a small biscuit cutter. Place on a lightly greased baking sheet; bake at 500° for 7 to 8 minutes, or until slightly golden. Remove biscuits quickly to a large towel. Slice each in half with a sharp knife; spread lightly with butter. Let cool.

Trim fat from ham; set ham aside. Sauté fat over medium heat; discard fat, reserving drippings. Cut ham with small biscuit cutter used for biscuits; fry ham quickly in ham drippings over low heat.

Assemble biscuits and ham slices sandwich-style. Place biscuits on baking sheet; bake at 450° for 4 to 5 minutes or until golden. Yield: 2 dozen biscuits.

Pickled Wieners

- 4 *(1-pound) packages frankfurters*
- 2 *large onions, thinly sliced*
- ¾ *cup sugar*
- 2 *tablespoons salt*
- 1 *teaspoon pepper*
- ¼ *cup ground cumin*
- 1 *(4½-ounce) bottle pepper sauce*
- 4 *cups white vinegar*

Slice each frankfurter into 3 pieces; combine with onion, and set aside. Combine remaining ingredients in a saucepan; bring to a boil, and boil about 3 minutes. Pour over frankfurters and onion. Cover tightly. Refrigerate several days before serving. Yield: 8 dozen wiener bites.

Swiss-Stuffed Mushrooms

2 *pounds fresh mushrooms*
Salt
¼ *cup butter or margarine*
1 *cup fine, dry, white breadcrumbs*
1 *cup shredded Swiss cheese*
2 *eggs, beaten*
2 *teaspoons dried parsley flakes*
2 *teaspoons crushed dillweed*
1 *teaspoon grated lemon rind*
¼ *cup lemon juice*

Wash mushrooms; drain. Remove stems, and set aside. Sprinkle inside of caps with salt.

Chop stems fine; sauté in butter over medium heat 3 to 4 minutes. Add remaining ingredients except mushroom caps, mixing well. Spoon mixture into mushroom caps.

Place mushrooms on ungreased baking sheet; bake at 350° for 5 to 8 minutes or until thoroughly heated. Serve hot. Yield: 12 to 16 servings.

Note: These may be made ahead of time and refrigerated until ready to bake.

Clam-Stuffed Mushrooms

24 *large fresh mushrooms*
⅓ *cup melted butter or margarine*
1 *(8-ounce) can minced clams, drained*
3 *tablespoons sliced green onion*
1 *tablespoon chopped parsley*
¼ *teaspoon salt*
⅛ *teaspoon pepper*
⅛ *teaspoon garlic powder*
¾ *cup mayonnaise*
½ *teaspoon prepared mustard*

Clean mushrooms with a damp cloth; remove stems, leaving caps intact. Set mushroom caps aside.

Chop mushroom stems; sauté in butter 10 minutes. Add clams, onion, parsley, salt, pepper, and garlic powder; sauté 5 minutes. Stuff mushroom caps with clam mixture. Place in a lightly greased baking dish; chill.

Combine mayonnaise and mustard; top each mushroom cap with mayonnaise mixture. Bake at 350° for 10 to 15 minutes. Yield: 6 to 8 appetizer servings.

Bacon-Cheese Fingers

1 *cup shredded Swiss cheese*
8 *slices bacon, cooked and crumbled*
3 *to 4 tablespoons mayonnaise*
1 *tablespoon grated onion*
½ *teaspoon celery salt*
10 *slices day-old sandwich bread, crusts removed and cut into thirds*

Combine first 5 ingredients; blend well. Spread cheese mixture over each piece of bread. Bake at 325° for 10 minutes. Yield: 30 appetizers.

Bacon-and-Rye Balls

1 *pound bacon*
1 *(8-ounce) package cream cheese, softened*
¼ *cup evaporated milk*
1 *cup fine rye breadcrumbs*
2 *teaspoons finely chopped onion*
1 *teaspoon Worcestershire sauce*
¾ *to 1 cup chopped parsley*

Cook bacon until crisp; drain and crumble. Combine bacon, cream cheese, milk, breadcrumbs, onion, and Worcestershire sauce; mix well. Chill 2 hours, and shape into 1-inch balls; roll each in parsley. Yield: about 2 dozen balls.

Smoked Sausage Appetizers

3 *(20-inch) link sausages*
Justin's Barbecue Sauce

Place sausage on smoker. Prick sausage with fork while it cooks to allow fat to drain out. Smoke about 20 minutes. Cut sausage in bite-size pieces, and serve with Justin's Barbecue Sauce. Yield: about 6 dozen appetizer servings.

Justin's Barbecue Sauce:

  2 *medium-size onions, chopped*
  ¾ *cup melted margarine*
1½ *cups firmly packed dark brown sugar*
  1 *(24-ounce) jar prepared mustard*
  1 *(4-ounce) bottle liquid smoke*
  2 *tablespoons garlic powder*
  2 *(26-ounce) bottles catsup*
  1 *(7-ounce) bottle Worcestershire sauce*
  ¾ *cup lemon juice*
     About 5 cups water

Sauté onion in margarine in large saucepan. Add brown sugar, mixing well. Add remaining ingredients; bring to a boil and simmer over low heat 30 minutes, stirring occasionally. Yield: about 4 quarts.

Note: This sauce stores well in the refrigerator and may be used for chicken, ribs, steaks, or hamburgers.

★
Marinated Cocktail Vegetables

  1 *pound carrots, peeled and sliced in long strips*
  ½ *head cauliflower, broken into flowerets*
  ½ *cup cider vinegar*
  1 *tablespoon sugar*
  2 *tablespoons grated onion*
  4 *tablespoons salad oil*
  1 *teaspoon salt*
  1 *teaspoon dry mustard*
     Chopped parsley

Chill carrots and cauliflower in ice water; drain, and pat dry. Combine remaining ingredients except parsley; simmer 5 minutes. Cool.

Place chilled vegetables in a shallow dish; pour marinade over all. Chill at least 4 hours; drain. Arrange on platter, and sprinkle with parsley. Yield: about 8 servings.

Ribbon Bologna Wedges

  1 *(5-ounce) jar cream cheese with olives and pimiento, at room temperature*
12 *thin slices bologna*
  ¼ *cup finely chopped pecans*
     Sliced stuffed olives

Spread each slice of bologna with cream cheese; sprinkle with pecans. Make 2 stacks of bologna, with 6 slices in each. Cover with plastic wrap; chill.

At serving time, cut each stack into 16 wedges; garnish with sliced stuffed olives, and insert a colored toothpick in each wedge. Yield: 32 wedges.

Garlic Cocktail Olives

  1 *(7-ounce) jar pimiento-stuffed green olives, drained*
  1 *(7½-ounce) can pitted ripe olives, drained*
  1 *tablespoon chopped fresh parsley*
  1 *clove garlic, crushed*
  3 *tablespoons olive oil*
     Salt and pepper to taste

Combine all ingredients; cover and chill several days. Before serving, remove garlic and let olive mixture stand at room temperature several hours. Yield: about 2 cups.

Fresh Melon Delight

  ½ *cup orange juice*
  ½ *cup lime juice*
  2 *tablespoons sugar*
  2 *teaspoons grated orange rind*
  2 *teaspoons grated lime rind*
  8 *cups melon balls*
  1 *(12-ounce) can lemon-lime carbonated beverage*

Combine first 6 ingredients; chill several hours. Just before serving, add carbonated beverage. Yield: about 10 to 12 servings.

★
Jalapeño Cocktail Pie

2   *or 3 jalapeño peppers, seeded and chopped*
1   *pound sharp Cheddar cheese, shredded*
6   *eggs, beaten*

Sprinkle peppers in a well-greased 9-inch square pan; cover with cheese. Pour eggs over cheese. Bake at 350° for 30 minutes or until firm. Cool and cut into 1-inch squares. Yield: about 6½ dozen squares.

Danish Delight

1   *(8-ounce) can refrigerated crescent dinner rolls*
1   *(4¾-ounce) can chicken spread*
2   *teaspoons lemon juice*
⅛   *teaspoon garlic salt*
⅛   *teaspoon ground oregano*
⅛   *teaspoon horseradish*

Separate dough into 4 rectangles; pinch perforations to seal. Cut each rectangle lengthwise and crosswise to form 4 small rectangles.
    Combine remaining ingredients; blend well. Place a teaspoonful of filling on each rectangle; fold over, and seal edges with a fork.
    Place appetizers on a lightly greased cookie sheet; bake at 350° about 10 to 12 minutes or until golden. Yield: 16 appetizers.

Salmon Tomato Bites

12   *cherry tomatoes*
1   *(7¾-ounce) can red salmon, drained and flaked*
¼   *cup mayonnaise*
1   *tablespoon finely chopped celery*
1   *tablespoon finely chopped onion*
Salt to taste
Monosodium glutamate to taste
Paprika or parsley flakes

Cut a slice from top of each tomato; scoop out pulp, leaving shells intact. Invert tomatoes to drain. Reserve pulp for soups or sauces.

Combine salmon, mayonnaise, celery, onion, salt, and monosodium glutamate; blend well. Spoon mixture into tomato shells; chill. Sprinkle with paprika. Yield: 1 dozen bites.

Chili-Cheese Dip

1   *medium-size onion, finely chopped*
3   *slices bacon, chopped*
1   *pound process American cheese, cubed*
1   *(15-ounce) can chili without beans*
1   *(10-ounce) can tomatoes with hot peppers, chopped*
Corn chips

Sauté onion and bacon until onion is tender. Stir in remaining ingredients except corn chips; heat until bubbly, stirring well. Serve warm with corn chips. Yield: about 3½ cups.

★
Curry Mayonnaise

2   *cups mayonnaise*
2   *teaspoons curry powder*
2   *teaspoons lemon juice*
2   *teaspoons grated onion*
2   *teaspoons sweet pickle juice*

Combine all ingredients, mixing well. Chill. Serve with vegetables: uncooked snow peas, sliced yellow squash and zucchini, radishes, sliced cucumbers and uncooked turnips, carrot sticks, and cooked artichokes. Yield: 2 cups.

Hollowed Rye Cheese Dip

1   *round loaf rye or pumpernickel bread, unsliced*
1   *cup stale beer*
3   *(6-ounce) rolls process cheese with garlic*
2   *ounces blue cheese, crumbled*
½   *teaspoon hot sauce*
¾   *teaspoon Worcestershire sauce*
1   *small onion, minced*
1   *tablespoon butter or margarine*

Hollow out bread using a spoon, leaving a 1-inch shell. Break bread that has been removed into bite-size pieces.

Combine remaining ingredients in the top of a double boiler. Cook, stirring frequently, until melted and smooth. Pour hot cheese mixture into bread shell. Serve at once with bread pieces as dippers. Yield: about 8 servings.

Hot Cheese and Crab Dip

   1   (10-ounce) package sharp natural
        Cheddar cheese, cubed
   1   (8-ounce) package process American
        cheese, cubed
  ⅓   cup milk
   1   (6-ounce) package frozen crabmeat,
        thawed and drained
  ½   cup dry white wine
       Crackers

Combine cheese and milk in top of a double boiler; place over hot water, stirring until cheese melts. Shred crabmeat; stir into cheese along with wine. Transfer to a chafing dish set on low heat. Serve with crackers. Yield: 3 cups.

Chili Dip

   1   pound ground beef
  ½   medium-size onion, chopped
   1   (16-ounce) can refried beans
   2   cups hot catsup
   3   teaspoons chili powder
   1   teaspoon salt
   1   green onion, chopped
  ½   cup chopped black olives
  ½   cup shredded Cheddar cheese
       Corn chips

Brown beef and onion in a skillet; drain off drippings. Add beans, catsup, chili powder, and salt to skillet; mix well. Bring to a boil; reduce heat, and simmer 20 to 30 minutes. Spoon into a fondue pot. Top with green onion, olives, and cheese. Keep warm. Serve with corn chips. Yield: about 3 cups.

Spicy Cream Cheese Dip

   1   (8-ounce) package cream cheese,
        softened
  ¼   cup picante sauce
       Juice of ½ lemon
       Salt and pepper to taste
       Corn chips, tortilla chips, potato chips, or
        crackers

Combine first four ingredients, blending well. Serve with corn chips, tortilla chips, potato chips, or crackers. Yield: about 1 cup.

Beef 'n Bacon Dip

   2   (2½-ounce) packages dried beef,
        chopped
  ½   pound bacon, cooked and crumbled
  ½   pound shredded sharp Cheddar cheese
  ¼   cup chopped pimiento
   1   (14½-ounce) can tomatoes, drained and
        finely chopped
   1   cup mayonnaise
       Party rye bread

Combine all ingredients except rye bread, mixing well. Spoon into a 1-quart casserole, and bake at 325° for 15 minutes or until cheese melts. Serve with party rye bread. Yield: about 3 cups.

★
Avocado Dip

   6   ripe avocados, peeled and quartered
   1   medium-size Spanish onion, minced
   1   large tomato
   2   tablespoons hot sauce
   1   tablespoon Worcestershire sauce
       Chips

Combine all ingredients except chips in container of electric blender. Blend until smooth. Serve with chips. Yield: about 5 cups.

Note: Reserve 2 or 3 seeds from avocados. Place in dip to prevent mixture from darkening.

Chicken Spread

>   3   *pounds chicken breasts*
>   1   *(8-ounce) package cream cheese,*
>   *softened*
>   2   *tablespoons mayonnaise*
>   ¾   *cup chopped pecans or walnuts*
>   1   *tablespoon grated onion*
>   2   *tablespoons sweet pickle juice*
>   1   *cup finely chopped celery*
>   ⅛   *teaspoon curry powder*
>   *Salt and pepper to taste*
>   *Green and ripe olives*
>   *Parsley*
>   *Cherry tomatoes*
>   *Twist of lemon*
>   *Crackers*

Cook chicken in salted water to cover until tender. Remove from broth, reserving broth; cool. Bone chicken, and grind or chop fine.

Combine cream cheese and mayonnaise, beating well. Add pecans, onion, pickle juice, celery, curry powder, salt, and pepper; stir until well blended. Combine chicken and cream cheese mixture; blend well. Add ¼ to ½ cup chicken broth to desired consistency. (Mixture will thicken when chilled.)

Spoon spread into an 8-inch cakepan; chill. Unmold and garnish with green and ripe olives, parsley, cherry tomatoes, and twist of lemon. Serve with crackers. Yield: about 4 cups.

Note: Chicken will be more moist if cooked and boned the day before using and placed in the broth to chill.

Deviled Canapé Spread

>   1   *(8-ounce) package cream cheese,*
>   *softened*
>   ¼   *cup mayonnaise*
>   1   *hard-cooked egg, minced*
>   1   *teaspoon prepared mustard*
>   *Few drops of hot sauce*
>   1   *teaspoon Worcestershire sauce*
>   1   *teaspoon horseradish*
>   2   *tablespoons minced stuffed olives*
>   1   *(4½-ounce) can deviled ham*
>   *Sliced stuffed olives*
>   *Pumpernickel or rye bread*

Beat cream cheese until fluffy; blend in next 8 ingredients. Chill. Garnish with sliced olives. Serve with pumpernickel or rye. Yield: about 2 cups.

Oyster Spread

>   2   *(8-ounce) packages cream cheese,*
>   *softened*
>   ¼   *cup milk or evaporated milk*
>   2   *to 3 tablespoons mayonnaise*
>   1   *tablespoon lemon juice*
>   1   *tablespoon Worcestershire sauce*
>   *Dash of hot sauce*
>   *Salt to taste*
>   2   *(3.66-ounce) cans smoked oysters,*
>   *minced*
>   *Paprika*
>   *Chopped parsley*

Combine first 7 ingredients; blend well. Stir in oysters, and refrigerate several hours. Sprinkle with paprika and parsley before serving. Yield: about 3 cups.

Shrimp Spread

>   1½ *pounds cooked, peeled shrimp*
>   1   *small onion, chopped*
>   1   *(8-ounce) package cream cheese,*
>   *softened*
>   ¼   *cup mayonnaise*
>   *Juice of 1 lemon*
>   1   *teaspoon Worcestershire sauce*
>   ⅛   *teaspoon hot sauce*
>   *Dash of cayenne pepper*
>   *Salt to taste*
>   6   *tablespoons butter or margarine, melted*
>   *Parsley*
>   4   *cooked, peeled shrimp*
>   *Toasted bread rounds*

Combine first 10 ingredients in container of electric blender; blend until smooth. Refrigerate 24 hours before serving. Garnish with parsley and remaining shrimp. Serve with toasted bread rounds. Yield: 1 quart.

Corned Beef Spread

1   (12-ounce) can corned beef
1   (8-ounce) package braunschweiger
½   cup mayonnaise
3   tablespoons vinegar
3   tablespoons instant minced onion
1½ teaspoons dry mustard
   Crackers or party rye bread

Combine first six ingredients, mixing well. Serve with crackers or party rye bread. Yield: about 3 cups.

Smoked Oyster Log

1   (8-ounce) package cream cheese, softened
1½ tablespoons mayonnaise
1   teaspoon Worcestershire sauce
   Dash of garlic powder
   Dash of onion powder
   Dash of salt
1   (3.66-ounce) can smoked oysters, drained and chopped
   Dried green onion
   Crackers

Combine cream cheese and mayonnaise; blend well. Stir in next 4 ingredients. Spread ¼ inch thick on waxed paper. Chill at least 30 minutes.

Spread oysters on cream cheese mixture, and roll up jellyroll fashion. Roll log in dried green onion. Chill overnight. Cut in ½-inch slices. Serve with crackers. Yield: about 2 dozen slices.

Paprika Cheese Rolls

½   pound process American cheese, shredded
1   (3-ounce) package cream cheese, softened
⅓   cup chopped pimiento-stuffed olives
¼   teaspoon onion powder
   Dash of ground red pepper
1   tablespoon commercial sour cream
   Paprika
   Melba toast rounds

Combine American cheese and cream cheese, blending until smooth. Stir in olives, onion powder, red pepper, and sour cream. Shape into three 4-inch rolls.

Sprinkle paprika heavily on waxed paper. Roll each cheese roll in paprika, coating well. Wrap each roll in foil; refrigerate several hours. Cut into thin slices, and serve on melba toast rounds. Yield: three 4-inch rolls.

★
Party Cheese Mousse

2   envelopes unflavored gelatin
1½ cups beef broth
1   large clove garlic, crushed
¼   teaspoon curry powder
   Salt and pepper to taste
4   (3-ounce) packages cream cheese, softened
   Pimiento strips
   Parsley
   Crackers

Sprinkle gelatin over beef broth in a saucepan; let stand until softened. Place over medium heat, stirring until gelatin is dissolved; cool completely.

Combine gelatin mixture, garlic, curry powder, salt, and pepper in container of electric blender; blend 30 seconds. Cube cream cheese; add a small amount at a time to blender, blending until smooth.

Pour mixture into a 3-cup mold. Refrigerate until firm, at least 3 hours. Unmold; garnish with pimiento and parsley. Serve with crackers. Yield: 3 cups.

Cheese Layer Mold

1 *(8-ounce) package cream cheese,*
  softened
3 *tablespoons blue cheese*
1 *(8-ounce) can crushed pineapple,*
  drained
½ *cup chopped pecans*
Dash of ground ginger
1 *(3-ounce) package cream cheese,*
  softened
¼ *cup milk*
½ *pound mild Cheddar cheese, shredded*
6 *slices bacon, cooked and crumbled*
1 *teaspoon grated onion*
¼ *teaspoon hot sauce*
Crackers

Combine 8-ounce package cream cheese, blue cheese, pineapple, pecans, and ginger; blend well. Pack into a 4-cup mold; chill.

Combine 3-ounce package cream cheese and milk; blend well, and add next four ingredients. Spread over first layer in mold. Refrigerate several hours; unmold. Serve with crackers. Yield: one 4-cup cheese ball.

Cheese Salmon Ball

1 *(7¾-ounce) can red salmon, drained*
  and flaked
1 *(8-ounce) package cream cheese,*
  softened
1 *tablespoon lemon juice*
2 *teaspoons grated onion*
1 *teaspoon horseradish*
¼ *teaspoon salt*
¼ *teaspoon liquid smoke*
Chopped parsley

Combine all ingredients except parsley. Shape into a ball; roll ball in parsley. Yield: 1 cheese ball.

Belgian Pâté

1 *(8-ounce) roll braunschweiger, softened*
1 *(8-ounce) package cream cheese,*
  softened
¼ *cup finely chopped onion*
6 *slices bacon, cooked and crumbled*
2 *tablespoons minced parsley*
2 *teaspoons Worcestershire sauce*
Party rye bread

Combine braunschweiger and cream cheese until well blended; add remaining ingredients except rye bread, mixing well. Serve on party rye bread. Yield: about 2 cups.

Note: Pâté improves if refrigerated at least 1 day before serving.

★
Chicken Liver Pâté

1 *pound chicken livers*
½ *cup melted butter or margarine*
2 *medium-size onions, chopped*
3 *hard-cooked eggs, divided*
Salt and pepper to taste
Parsley
Crackers

Sauté livers in butter over low heat until lightly browned; remove livers from pan and set aside. Sauté onion in butter. Cut 2 slices of egg; reserve for garnish. Place remaining eggs, livers, onion, salt, and pepper in container of electric blender; blend for 30 seconds.

Pat mixture into an oiled 2-cup mold; chill about 4 hours. Unmold and garnish with parsley and egg slices. Serve with crackers. Yield: about 2 cups.

Peach Jerky

2½ *pounds fresh peaches*
2 *to 4 tablespoons sugar or to taste*

Line two 15- x 10- x 1-inch pans or two cookie sheets with clear plastic wrap; fasten edges with cellophane tape.

Wash peaches. Plunge in boiling water for 30 seconds; remove with a slotted spoon, and place in cold water. Remove skins, and slice enough peaches to make 5 cups.

Place peach slices in a saucepan; add sugar. Bring peaches to a boil over medium heat, stirring constantly. Pour into container of electric blender, and puree. Cool to lukewarm.

Pour puree into prepared pans, spreading evenly to ⅛-inch thickness. Keep fruit clean by stretching cheesecloth over pans without touching surface. Set outside in sun to dry.

Drying time will depend on humidity and sunlight, and can vary from 8 to 24 hours. Bring indoors overnight, and continue drying the second day.

Jerky is dry when it can be peeled off the plastic; do not leave in sun longer than needed. Roll the sheets of jerky, still on plastic wrap; seal with additional plastic wrap.

Jerky may be stored 1 month at room temperature, 3 months in refrigerator, or 1 year in freezer. Yield: two 15½- x 10-inch sheets.

Note: Follow same procedure for Plum Jerky, using 5 cups sliced plums.

To make Spicy Jerky, add 1 teaspoon of one of the following spices to 5 cups sliced fruit before cooking: ground cinnamon, allspice, ground cloves, or ground nutmeg.

To make Nutty Jerky, add ½ cup chopped nuts and/or ½ cup flaked coconut to 5 cups cooked fruit before pureeing.

Cheese Wafers

    2   cups shredded Cheddar cheese
    ½   cup butter or margarine, softened
    1   cup all-purpose flour
    1   teaspoon salt
    ¼   teaspoon ground red pepper
    ¾   cup finely chopped nuts

Combine cheese and butter in a mixing bowl; beat well. Add flour, salt, pepper, and nuts; mix well. Divide dough in half; shape each half into a 1- x 8-inch roll. Wrap in waxed paper, and chill at least 2 hours.

Slice rolls into ¼-inch wafers. Bake at 400° for 5 to 7 minutes. Yield: about 6 dozen wafers.

★ Southern Cannon Balls

    1   pound hot bulk sausage
    2   cups shredded sharp Cheddar cheese
    2   cups biscuit mix
    2   tablespoons grated onion
    1   tablespoon poultry seasoning

Combine all ingredients, mixing well. Roll into walnut-size balls. Place on an ungreased baking sheet and bake at 400° for 15 minutes. Drain on paper towels. Serve hot. Yield: about 48 balls.

★ Pecan Snacks

    1   tablespoon corn oil
    2   cups pecan halves
    ½   teaspoon onion powder
    ½   teaspoon garlic salt

Heat corn oil in a heavy skillet over moderate heat. Add pecans, onion powder, and garlic salt; stir constantly 1 minute. Remove from heat, and drain on paper towels. Yield: 2 cups.

Homemade Crackers

    4   cups all-purpose flour
    1   teaspoon salt
    2   tablespoons sugar
    ¼   cup butter or margarine
        About 1¼ cups milk
        Melted butter or margarine
        Additional salt

Combine flour, 1 teaspoon salt, and sugar; cut in ¼ cup butter. Stir in enough milk to make a stiff dough. Roll dough to ⅛-inch thickness on a lightly floured surface. (If dough is too elastic, let it rest 15 minutes.) Cut into desired shapes with cookie or pastry cutters.

Place crackers on lightly greased cookie sheets, and pierce with a fork. Bake at 400° for 15 minutes or until golden. Brush with melted butter, and sprinkle lightly with additional salt. Yield: about 10 dozen 2- x 1-inch crackers.

Date-Stuffed Cheese Balls

1   *pound pitted dates*
2   *cups shredded Cheddar cheese*
½   *cup butter or margarine, softened*
1   *cup self-rising flour*
1   *teaspoon paprika*

Cut dates in half; set aside. Combine cheese and butter in a mixing bowl. Stir in flour and paprika, and blend thoroughly. Chill dough 15 minutes. Put about 1 teaspoon of dough around each date half to form a ball.

Place balls 3 inches apart on a lightly greased baking sheet; chill well. Bake at 400° for 15 to 20 minutes. Yield: about 4 dozen cheese balls.

Note: Cheese balls may be frozen before or after baking. If baked, cool thoroughly before freezing.

Cheese Chips

1   *cup finely crushed potato chips*
½   *cup shredded Cheddar cheese*
2   *(4½-ounce) cans deviled ham*
1   *cup all-purpose flour*
¼   *teaspoon red pepper*

Combine all ingredients, mixing well. Shape mixture into a 9-inch roll; chill well. Cut into ¼-inch slices. Bake at 425° about 10 minutes. Yield: 3 to 4 dozen.

★ Swedish Nuts

1   *cup whole blanched almonds*
½   *cup butter or margarine*
2   *egg whites*
1   *cup sugar*
Dash of salt
1   *cup walnut halves*
1   *cup pecan halves*

Spread almonds on a cookie sheet. Roast at 325° until lightly browned, about 15 to 20 minutes, stirring occasionally; cool. Melt butter in oven in a 13- x 9- x 2-inch baking pan.

Beat egg whites until stiff; add sugar and salt, and continue beating until very stiff. Fold in almonds, walnuts, and pecans; spread nut mixture in baking pan over melted butter.

Bake at 325° about 30 minutes or until mixture is browned and all butter is absorbed, stirring and turning every 10 minutes to cook evenly. Yield: about 4 cups.

Spiced Walnuts

1   *cup sugar*
1   *teaspoon salt*
2   *teaspoons ground cinnamon*
½   *teaspoon ground nutmeg*
¼   *teaspoon ground cloves*
½   *cup water*
2½   *cups walnut halves*

Combine sugar, salt, and spices in a heavy saucepan; stir in ½ cup water. Cook, stirring constantly, over medium heat until sugar dissolves; cook to soft ball stage (230°). Remove from heat, and stir in walnuts. Stir until until mixture becomes creamy.

Spread on waxed paper, and separate nuts with a fork. Cool. Yield: 2½ cups.

Fried Devil Dogs

1   *egg, slightly beaten*
½   *cup milk*
1   *tablespoon salad oil*
¾   *cup all-purpose flour*
½   *teaspoon salt*
½   *teaspoon baking powder*
½   *teaspoon dry mustard*
⅛   *teaspoon red pepper*
8   *frankfurters, cut into 1-inch pieces*
1   *cup fine dry breadcrumbs*
Hot salad oil

Combine egg, milk, and oil. Combine flour, salt, baking powder, mustard, and pepper; stir into egg mixture.

Dip frankfurters in batter, and roll each in breadcrumbs. Cook in deep hot oil until browned. Drain on paper towels. Yield: about 32 appetizer servings.

Spiced Pecans

  1   *egg white*
  1   *teaspoon water*
  ¾   *cup sugar*
  1   *teaspoon salt*
1½ *teaspoons ground cinnamon*
  ½   *teaspoon ground cloves*
  ½   *teaspoon ground nutmeg*
  2   *cups pecan halves*

Beat egg white and water lightly; set aside. Combine sugar, salt, and spices. Dip pecans in egg white mixture, then in sugar mixture. Place on a greased baking sheet. Bake at 275° for 30 minutes. Yield: 2 cups.

Toasted Pecans

½ *cup melted butter or margarine*
3 *cups pecan halves*
Salt to taste

Pour butter over pecans, stirring to coat well. Arrange pecans in a single layer on a baking sheet; sprinkle with salt. Bake at 275° about 1 hour; stir occasionally. Yield: 3 cups.

★
Luncheon Crab Sandwich

  2 *English muffins*
  1 *(7-ounce) package frozen crabmeat,*
     thawed and drained
  4 *slices tomato*
Salt and pepper to taste
  ⅓ *cup finely chopped celery*
  1 *teaspoon lemon juice*
Mayonnaise
  4 *slices Cheddar cheese*

Split English muffins, and broil until lightly browned; top each half with a fourth of crabmeat. Place a slice of tomato on each, and sprinkle with salt and pepper.

    Combine celery, lemon juice, and enough mayonnaise to make a spreading consistency; spread over tomato slices. Top with cheese slices, and broil until cheese melts. Yield: 2 to 4 servings.

★
Hot Brown Sandwich

  ¼ *cup butter or margarine*
  ½ *cup all-purpose flour*
  ½ *teaspoon salt*
  ⅛ *teaspoon white pepper*
  1 *cup turkey broth or chicken broth*
  1 *cup milk*
  ½ *cup grated Parmesan cheese*
  8 *slices bread, toasted*
Sliced turkey
Paprika
  8 *slices tomato*
  8 *slices bacon, cooked*
Parsley

Melt butter, and stir in flour; cook over low heat, blending until smooth. Stir in salt and pepper. Gradually add broth and milk; cook, stirring constantly, until smooth and thickened. Add cheese; simmer about 10 minutes. (Sauce will be thick.)

    Place 2 slices toast on each of 4 ovenproof plates. Place turkey on each slice of toast; cover with sauce, and sprinkle with paprika. Top each with 1 slice tomato and 1 slice bacon. Bake at 400° for 10 minutes or until sauce is bubbly. Garnish with parsley. Yield: 4 servings.

Deluxe Sandwiches

  6 *slices boiled or baked ham*
  6 *slices cooked turkey or chicken*
  6 *slices process American cheese*
12 *slices bread*
1½ *cups milk*
  3 *eggs, beaten*
  ½ *teaspoon salt*
  ¼ *teaspoon pepper*
  ¼ *cup melted margarine*
  ¼ *cup salad oil*

Place 1 slice ham, 1 slice chicken, and 1 slice cheese on each of 6 slices of bread; top with remaining bread.

    Combine milk, eggs, salt, and pepper. Dip each sandwich into egg mixture; brown on both sides in combination of margarine and oil. Serve hot. Yield: 6 servings.

Devonshire Sandwiches

18   slices bacon
½   cup all-purpose flour
2   cups milk
½   pound Cheddar cheese, shredded
1   teaspoon dry mustard
6   slices bread
12   thin slices chicken or turkey breast
¼   cup grated Parmesan cheese

Cook bacon; drain, reserving ¼ cup drippings. Combine flour and reserved drippings over low heat, blending until smooth. Gradually add milk; cook until smooth and thickened, stirring constantly. Add Cheddar cheese and dry mustard, stirring until cheese melts.

Place 3 slices bacon on each slice of bread, and top with 2 slices of chicken. Place in a 13- x 9- x 2-inch baking pan; cover with cheese sauce, and sprinkle with Parmesan cheese. Bake at 350° for 10 minutes or until bubbly. Yield: 6 sandwiches.

Hot Turkey Sandwiches

2   tablespoons all-purpose flour
2   tablespoons melted margarine
1   cup milk
½   teaspoon salt
Dash of pepper
Softened margarine or mayonnaise
4   slices toast
Sliced cooked turkey or chicken
4   slices Cheddar cheese
Paprika to taste
4   slices process American cheese
3   slices bacon, cooked and crumbled

Combine flour and margarine; place over low heat, blending until smooth. Gradually add milk; cook, stirring constantly, until smooth and thickened. Add salt and pepper; set aside.

Spread a small amount of margarine on each piece of toast; place in a shallow pan. Arrange turkey slices on each piece of toast, and top with Cheddar cheese. Spoon sauce over cheese, and sprinkle with paprika; broil until bubbly.

Top each sandwich with American cheese; sprinkle with paprika, and return to broiler until cheese melts. Sprinkle with bacon. Yield: 4 servings.

Smoked Turkey Sandwich

⅓   cup finely chopped turkey
1   tablespoon mayonnaise
1   teaspoon prepared mustard
6   dill pickle slices
1   slice whole wheat bread, toasted
¼   cup shredded sharp Cheddar cheese
Garlic powder

Combine turkey, mayonnaise, and mustard. Place pickles on toast; top with turkey mixture. Sprinkle with cheese and garlic powder; broil sandwich until cheese is bubbly. Yield: 1 serving.

Swiss-Tuna Grill

1   (6½-ounce) can tuna, drained and
       flaked
½   cup shredded Swiss cheese
½   cup finely chopped celery
2   tablespoons finely chopped onion
¼   cup mayonnaise or salad dressing
¼   cup commercial sour cream
Dash of pepper
12   slices rye bread
Softened butter or margarine

Combine tuna, cheese, celery, onion, mayonnaise, sour cream, and pepper, stirring gently to mix. Spread between slices of bread to make sandwiches. Spread soft butter on outer sides of sandwiches, and brown on both sides in skillet over medium heat. Yield: 6 sandwiches.

Hot Ham and Chicken Sandwiches

2 *(.675-ounce) envelopes instant cream of chicken soup mix*
1 *cup boiling water*
1 *(8-ounce) package process cheese spread, cut into cubes*
1 *(2½-ounce) jar sliced mushrooms, drained*
1 *(10-ounce) package frozen broccoli*
4 *thin slices boiled ham*
4 *thin slices cooked chicken*
4 *slices whole wheat bread, toasted*

Combine soup mix and water in top of double boiler; stir in cheese until melted. Add mushrooms. Set aside and keep warm.

Cook broccoli according to package directions; drain, and set aside. Place 1 slice of ham and 1 slice of chicken on each slice of bread. Top with stalks of broccoli.

Pour cheese sauce over sandwiches; serve warm. Yield: 4 servings.

Creamy Chicken Filling

2 *(5-ounce) cans boned chicken, undrained*
⅓ *cup whipping cream*
½ *cup finely chopped almonds*
¼ *cup salad dressing*
1 *teaspoon dry mustard*

Combine all ingredients, blending well. Store in refrigerator. Yield: about 2 cups.

Raisin Sandwich Spread

1 *egg*
1 *cup sugar*
Juice and rind of 1½ lemons
1 *teaspoon butter or margarine*
1 *cup ground raisins*
1 *cup mayonnaise*
Thin sliced whole wheat bread

Beat egg until light colored. Combine egg, sugar, lemon juice and rind, and butter in a medium saucepan. Cook over low heat, stirring constantly, until thickened. Cool. Stir in raisins and mayonnaise. Cool thoroughly. Spread on whole wheat bread. Yield: about 2½ cups.

Cheesy-Bacon Sour Cream Sandwiches

1 *(8-ounce) carton commercial sour cream*
½ *cup mayonnaise*
1 *cup shredded Cheddar cheese*
2 *to 4 slices bacon, cooked and crumbled*
¼ *cup wheat germ*
¼ *cup chopped toasted almonds*
1 *tablespoon chopped green onion tops*
¼ *teaspoon salt*
Rye bread

Combine first 8 ingredients, and blend well. Spread on bread. Yield: 2 cups filling.

Onion Brunch Squares

1 *large onion, chopped*
1 *tablespoon melted margarine*
1 *(8-ounce) carton commercial sour cream*
¼ *teaspoon salt*
½ *teaspoon dillweed*
1 *teaspoon prepared mustard*
1¼ *cups shredded Cheddar cheese, divided*
1 *(8½-ounce) package corn muffin mix*
1 *egg, beaten*
⅓ *cup milk*
1 *(8¾-ounce) can cream-style corn*
¼ *teaspoon hot sauce*

Sauté onion in margarine until tender. Combine sour cream, salt, dillweed, mustard, and ½ cup cheese; add to onion, stirring well.

Combine corn muffin mix, egg, milk, corn, and hot sauce; mix well. Spoon batter into a greased 8-inch square pan; spread onion mixture over batter, and sprinkle with remaining cheese.

Bake at 400° for 25 to 30 minutes or until firm in center. Cut into squares to serve. Yield: 6 servings.

Dried Beef Sandwich Filling

2   *(2½-ounce) packages dried beef, ground*
1   *(16-ounce) can stewed tomatoes*
½   *pound process cheese spread*
2   *eggs, beaten*

Combine beef, tomatoes, and cheese in a saucepan; heat, stirring frequently, until cheese melts. Add eggs; cook, stirring constantly, until thickened. Chill until firm. Store in refrigerator. Yield: about 4 cups.

Pimiento Cheese

1   *tablespoon all-purpose flour*
2   *tablespoons sugar*
1   *tablespoon vinegar*
1   *teaspoon dry mustard*
1   *egg, beaten*
1   *tablespoon butter or margarine*
1   *pound process American cheese*
1   *(4-ounce) jar pimientos, chopped*
2   *tablespoons mayonnaise*
Salt and pepper to taste

Combine first 6 ingredients in a small saucepan; cook over low heat until thickened, stirring constantly.

Remove from heat; pour over cheese, and mash to blend ingredients. Add pimientos, mayonnaise, salt, and pepper; mix well. Store in refrigerator. Yield: about 2½ cups.

Garden Medley Sandwiches

2   *tomatoes, finely chopped*
1   *cucumber, peeled and finely chopped*
1   *cup finely chopped celery*
1   *small onion, finely chopped*
1   *green pepper, finely chopped*
1   *envelope unflavored gelatin*
¼   *cup cold water*
¼   *cup boiling water*
1   *teaspoon salt*
2   *cups mayonnaise*
Whole grain bread

Drain vegetables on paper towels. Soften gelatin in cold water; add boiling water, and stir

until gelatin is dissolved. Add salt and mayonnaise, mixing well; stir in vegetables. Chill at least 4 hours.

Cut crusts from bread, and spread with vegetable mixture. Top with bread, and cut each sandwich into quarters. Yield: 4 to 5 cups filling.

Round Steak Sandwiches

4   *medium-size cubed steaks*
2   *tablespoons salad oil*
2   *tablespoons all-purpose flour*
1   *cup water*
1   *(10¾-ounce) can golden mushroom soup, undiluted*
Salt and pepper to taste
Garlic salt to taste
2   *tablespoons sherry*
4   *onion rolls or hamburger buns*

Brown steaks in hot oil; remove from skillet and set aside, reserving pan drippings. Add flour to drippings, stirring until smooth; cook until bubbly. Gradually add water, stirring until smooth; add soup, seasonings, and sherry, mixing well.

Return steaks to skillet; cover and simmer over low heat 1½ hours or until steaks are tender. Serve on rolls with gravy. Yield: 4 sandwiches.

★
Reuben Sandwiches

16   *slices rye or pumpernickel bread*
¼   *to ½ cup butter or margarine, softened*
About ¾ cup commercial Thousand Island dressing
8   *slices corned beef*
8   *slices Swiss cheese*
About 2½ cups sauerkraut, well drained

Spread one side of each slice of bread with butter. Place 8 slices of bread, buttered side down, on a lightly greased griddle or skillet; spread Thousand Island dressing on top side. Top each slice with corned beef, cheese, and sauerkraut.

Spread Thousand Island dressing on unbuttered side of remaining bread slices. Place these, dressing side down, on top of sandwiches. Grill slowly until cheese melts and bread browns; turn and grill other side. Yield: 8 servings.

Celebration Sandwich Loaf

  1 (16-inch) loaf white bread, unsliced
Butter or margarine, softened
Fillings
  3 (8-ounce) packages cream cheese, softened
  ½ cup mayonnaise
Minced parsley

Trim crust from sides and top of bread. Slice loaf horizontally into 5 equal slices. Place bottom slice on serving platter or tray. Spread with butter; cover with one of the Fillings.

Spread remaining slices on both sides with butter. Place one buttered slice of bread on top of Filling and bread on tray; cover with another Filling. Repeat layers until all Fillings are used and loaf is reassembled. Chill.

Beat cream cheese and mayonnaise until smooth. Frost top and sides of loaf with cream cheese mixture. Chill. Garnish with parsley before serving. Yield: about 12 servings.

Ham Filling:

  1½ cups ground cooked ham
  ⅓ cup pickle relish
  1 tablespoon prepared mustard
  ½ cup mayonnaise

Combine all ingredients. Chill. Yield: about 2½ cups.

Tuna Filling:

  1 (6½-ounce) can tuna, drained and flaked
  ⅓ cup sliced ripe olives
Salt and pepper
  ¼ cup mayonnaise

Combine all ingredients. Chill. Yield: about 2 cups.

Egg Filling:

  6 hard-cooked eggs, chopped
  1 tablespoon chives
  2 tablespoons chopped pimiento
Salt and pepper
  ¼ cup mayonnaise

Combine all ingredients. Chill. Yield: about 2 cups.

Chicken Filling:

  1½ cups ground cooked chicken
  ⅔ cup crushed pineapple, well drained
  ¼ cup chopped green pepper
  ⅓ cup mayonnaise

Combine all ingredients. Chill. Yield: about 2½ cups.

Corny Sandwich Squares

  1 (8-ounce) package cornbread mix
  1 (8¾-ounce) can cream-style corn
  2 eggs
  2 tablespoons milk
  1¼ cups shredded American cheese, divided
  1 pound ground beef
  ¼ cup catsup
  2 tablespoons sweet pickle relish
  ¼ cup grated Parmesan cheese
  ¼ cup water
  1 tablespoon cornstarch
  1 (16-ounce) can stewed tomatoes, diced
  1 teaspoon Worcestershire sauce

Combine cornbread mix, corn, eggs, milk, and ¾ cup American cheese; stir until blended. Spread half of batter in a greased 8-inch square baking dish; set aside.

Brown ground beef. Drain; add catsup and relish. Spread mixture over batter; sprinkle with remaining ½ cup American cheese and Parmesan cheese. Top with remaining batter. Bake at 350° for 35 minutes.

Combine water and cornstarch in a saucepan; stir in tomatoes and Worcestershire sauce. Cook over medium heat, stirring constantly, until thick. Let sandwiches stand 5 minutes before cutting into squares; serve topped with sauce. Yield: about 6 servings.

Mushrooms Magnifique

> 1   *medium-size onion, chopped*
> 1   *pound fresh mushrooms, thinly sliced*
> 2   *tablespoons butter or margarine*
> *Salt and pepper to taste*
> *Chopped parsley*
> *Paprika*
> 1   *tablespoon lemon juice*
> 1½ *cups commercial sour cream*
> 6   *slices Canadian bacon*
> 3   *English muffins, halved and toasted*

Sauté onion and mushrooms in butter until tender. Add salt, pepper, parsley, paprika, lemon juice, and sour cream; place over low heat until warm. (Do not allow to boil.)

Fry Canadian bacon, and place on muffin halves. Spoon sauce over bacon. Serve immediately. Yield: 6 servings.

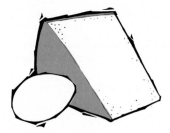

Mexican Heroes

> 1½ *pounds ground beef*
> ½   *cup chopped onion*
> 1   *(8-ounce) can tomato sauce*
> 1   *(1¼-ounce) package taco seasoning*
> 6   *hamburger buns, split and toasted*
> 12 *tomato slices*
> ¾   *cup shredded Cheddar cheese*
> ¾   *cup shredded lettuce*
> 6   *tablespoons chopped stuffed olives*
> 2   *onion slices, separated into rings*

Sauté beef and onion until lightly browned; drain. Stir in tomato sauce and taco seasoning; simmer about 5 minutes.

On bottom of each bun, place about ½ cup meat mixture, 2 slices tomato, and 2 tablespoons cheese. Bake at 375° for 5 minutes or until cheese melts. Top with 2 tablespoons lettuce, 1 tablespoon olives, and onion rings; close with bun tops. Yield: 6 sandwiches.

Great Guacamole

> 4   *avocados, peeled and chopped*
> 2   *tomatoes, chopped*
> ¼   *cup chopped onion*
> 1   *teaspoon lemon juice*
> 1   *tablespoon mayonnaise*
> ¼   *teaspoon hot sauce*
> 1½ *teaspoons salt*
> *Chips*

Combine all ingredients in container of an electric blender. Blend until smooth. Chill. Serve with chips. Yield: about 3 cups.

Note: Reserve 1 or 2 seeds from avocados. Place in dip to prevent mixture from darkening.

Zippy Blue Cheese Ball

> 2   *(2-ounce) packages blue cheese or Roquefort*
> 1   *(8-ounce) package cream cheese, softened*
> ¼   *teaspoon onion powder*
> 1   *tablespoon chopped green pepper*
> 1   *tablespoon chopped pimiento*
> ½   *cup chopped toasted walnuts*
> *Parsley*

Combine cheese, and mix until well blended. Add onion powder, green pepper, and pimiento; mix well. Chill until firm enough to handle.

Shape mixture into a ball, and coat with walnuts. Garnish with parsley, and serve with crackers. Yield: one 12-ounce cheese ball.

Oyster-Stuffed Cherry Tomatoes

> 18 *cherry tomatoes*
> 1   *(8-ounce) package cream cheese, softened*
> 1   *tablespoon chopped chives*
> 2   *teaspoons Worcestershire sauce*
> 1   *(3.66-ounce) can smoked oysters, drained and chopped*
> *Salt and pepper to taste*
> *Chopped parsley*

Cut a thin slice from tops of tomatoes; carefully scoop out pulp, leaving shells intact. Reserve pulp for use in soups and sauces.

Combine cream cheese, chives, Worcestershire sauce, oysters, salt, and pepper; blend well. Fill tomato shells with cream cheese mixture. Garnish each tomato with parsley. Yield: 1½ dozen.

Party Cheese Ball

2 *(8-ounce) packages cream cheese, softened*
1 *(8-ounce) package sharp Cheddar cheese, shredded*
1 *tablespoon chopped pimiento*
1 *tablespoon chopped green pepper*
1 *tablespoon finely chopped onion*
2 *tablespoons Worcestershire sauce*
1 *teaspoon lemon juice*
Dash of cayenne
Dash of salt
Finely chopped pecans

Combine cream cheese and Cheddar cheese, blending well. Stir in remaining ingredients except pecans. Shape into a ball, and roll in chopped pecans. Chill. Serve at room temperature. Yield: about 3 cups.

Pineapple Nibblers

1 *(8-ounce) package cream cheese, softened*
1 *(15 ¼-ounce) can pineapple chunks, drained*
1 *cup finely ground pecans*
1 *head crisp lettuce*

Gently press a small amount of cream cheese around each pineapple chunk. Roll each in ground nuts. Spear with toothpicks and stick into head of lettuce. Yield: about 36 balls.

Orange Almonds

1½ *cups whole blanched almonds, lightly toasted*
1 *egg white, slightly beaten*
¾ *cup powdered sugar*
1½ *teaspoons grated orange peel*
Dash of ground nutmeg

Combine almonds and egg white; set aside. Combine remaining ingredients. Drain almonds, and stir into sugar mixture until well coated. Spread on a greased baking sheet. Bake at 250° for 20 to 30 minutes or until coating is dry and nuts are crisp; stir occasionally. Yield: 1½ cups.

Cool Sandwich Delight

2¼ *cups minced chicken or turkey*
¼ *cup minced sweet or dill pickles*
3 *hard-cooked eggs, minced*
½ *cup minced celery*
½ *cup minced apple*
¼ *cup chopped pimiento*
¾ *cup salad dressing or mayonnaise*
Salt and pepper to taste

Combine all ingredients; mix well. Use as a sandwich filling or serve on a lettuce leaf. Yield: about 4 cups.

Chicken Salad Balls

1 *cup chopped cooked chicken*
1 *tablespoon chopped onion*
2 *tablespoons chopped pimiento*
Dash of hot sauce
½ *cup salad dressing or manonnaise*
1 *cup chopped pecans*

Combine all ingredients, mixing well; chill several hours. Shape into l-inch balls. Yield: about 2 dozen.

Beverages

Sometimes a beverage can provide just the lift you need to wake you up, cool you off, perk you up, or warm you up. Hot coffee, both instant and perked, can be served around the clock. Soothing, warming Café au Lait or Hot Mocha can be in your mug in a minute using one of our instant mixes. For a refreshing coffee punch, add some ice cream, a spice, or ice.

Tea can be just as versatile as coffee. Hot or iced, minted or spiced, it makes a great nightcap or party punch. For a summertime thirst quencher, serve a sparkling fruit punch or an icy slush. And don't forget eggnog for the holidays—spiced with nutmeg, spiked with brandy, or flavored with orange and coffee.

When an unexpected visitor drops in, beverages such as these make entertaining easy. Many of them can be made ahead or on the spur of the moment.

Indian Punch

    2 cups sugar
    4 cups water
    Juice of 4 lemons
    1 cup strong tea
    1 tablespoon vanilla extract
    1 tablespoon almond extract
    1 quart ginger ale, chilled

Combine sugar, water, and lemon juice in saucepan. Place over low heat and boil 3 minutes; cool. Stir in tea and flavorings. When ready to serve, add ginger ale; serve over ice. Yield: 3 quarts.

Rosy Punch

    1½ cups sugar
     2 cups boiling water
     4 cups cranberry juice
    ⅓ cup lime juice
     2 cups orange juice
     6 cups ginger ale, chilled
    Lime slices

Dissolve sugar in boiling water; cool. Stir in cranberry juice, lime juice, and orange juice; chill thoroughly. Add ginger ale at serving time. Garnish with lime slices. Yield: 3½ quarts.

Vodka Slush

    1 (6-ounce) can frozen orange juice
       concentrate, thawed and undiluted
    2 (6-ounce) cans frozen lemonade
       concentrate, thawed and undiluted
    2 (6-ounce) cans frozen limeade
       concentrate, thawed and undiluted
    1 cup sugar
    3½ cups water
    2 cups vodka
    2 (28-ounce) bottles lemon-lime
       carbonated beverage, chilled

Combine the first 6 ingredients, mixing well. Freeze 48 hours, stirring occasionally. For each serving, spoon ¾ cup frozen mixture into a tall glass; fill with carbonated beverage. Serve at once. Yield: about 16 (8-ounce) servings.

Vodka Slush, a mixture of vodka and fruit juices, is made ahead and stored in the freezer. You'll find this delicious drink on page 25.

Sunshine Punch

  1 *(46-ounce) can orange-pineapple juice, chilled*
  1 *(28-ounce) bottle ginger ale or lemon-lime carbonated beverage, chilled*
    Orange slices
    Lemon slices

Combine juice and ginger ale in a punch bowl. Serve over ice cubes, and garnish with orange and lemon slices. Yield: 8 servings.
   Note: For delicious variations, 1 pint of pineapple sherbet or vodka to taste may be added to punch.

Cranberry Punch

  1 *pound fresh cranberries*
4½ *to 5 quarts water, divided*
2¼ *cups sugar*
 ¾ *cup or 1 (6¾-ounce) container hot cinnamon candies*
  2 *whole cloves*
  1 *(12-ounce) can frozen orange juice concentrate, undiluted*
    Juice of 3 lemons

Carefully sort and wash cranberries; cook in 1 quart water until skins burst (about 5 minutes). Strain off juice, and set aside.
   Combine 1 quart water, sugar, candies, and cloves; heat, stirring until candies have dissolved.
   Combine cranberry juice, sugar mixture, orange juice, and lemon juice, and 2½ to 3 quarts water; stir well. Chill or serve over ice. Yield: about 5 quarts.

Sparkling Punch

  1 *(6-ounce) can frozen lemonade concentrate, thawed and undiluted*
  1 *(8-ounce) can crushed pineapple, undrained*
  1 *(10-ounce) package frozen strawberries, thawed and undrained*
  3 *quarts ginger ale, chilled*

Combine all ingredients except ginger ale in container of electric blender. Blend at high speed 30 seconds or until smooth. Just before serving, stir in ginger ale. Yield: about 4 quarts.

Slush Punch

3½ *cups sugar*
  6 *cups water*
  2 *(3-ounce) packages mixed fruit-flavored gelatin*
  1 *(46-ounce) can pineapple juice*
  1 *quart orange juice*
 ⅔ *cup lemon juice*
  2 *(28-ounce) bottles ginger ale, chilled*

Combine sugar and water in a large saucepan; bring to a boil, and simmer 3 minutes. Stir in gelatin, pineapple juice, orange juice, and lemon juice. Ladle into wide-topped freezer containers, leaving 1-inch headspace. Cover tightly and freeze.
   To serve, partially thaw juice mixture at room temperature (about 5 hours). Place in punch bowl, and stir with a fork to break up ice chunks. Add ginger ale. Yield: about 1½ gallons.

Fruit Punch Slush

  6 *ripe bananas*
  1 *(6-ounce) can frozen lemonade concentrate, thawed and undiluted*
  1 *(12-ounce) can frozen orange juice concentrate, thawed and undiluted*
  1 *(46-ounce) can pineapple juice*
  3 *cups water*
  2 *cups sugar*
  2 *(64-ounce) bottles lemon-lime carbonated beverage, chilled*
    Orange slices

Combine bananas and fruit juice concentrates in container of electric blender; blend until smooth.
   Combine banana mixture, pineapple juice, water, and sugar in a large mixing bowl; mix well. Pour into plastic freezer containers or molds. Freeze. To serve, thaw until mushy; add carbonated beverage. Garnish with orange slices. Yield: 6 quarts.

Banana Slush

3   medium-size bananas, mashed
1   cup sugar
1   (20-ounce) can crushed pineapple,
      undrained
Juice of 2 lemons
2   cups undiluted frozen orange juice
      concentrate
2   cups ginger ale

Combine banana and sugar; blend well. Stir in remaining ingredients, and freeze until firm. Thaw slightly to serve. Yield: 6 to 8 servings.

Mock Pink Champagne

½   cup sugar
1½ cups boiling water
2   cups cranberry juice
1   cup pineapple juice
½   cup orange juice
2   (7-ounce) bottles lemon-lime carbonated
      beverage, chilled

Dissolve sugar in boiling water; cool. Stir in fruit juices; chill. Just before serving, add lemon-lime carbonated beverage. Yield: 14 servings.

Orange Shake

1   cup fresh orange juice
¼   to ½ cup instant nonfat dry milk solids
1½ tablespoons sugar
2   to 3 drops vanilla extract
½   cup crushed ice

Combine ingredients in container of electric blender; blend until frothy. Serve immediately. Yield: about 2 cups.

Lime Punch

3¼ cups pineapple juice
½   gallon lime sherbet, softened
3   (28-ounce) bottles ginger ale, chilled

Combine juice and sherbet. Add ginger ale just before serving. Yield: about 3½ quarts.

Patio Blush

½   cup frozen orange juice concentrate,
      thawed and undiluted
¼   cup lemon juice
¼   cup maraschino cherry juice
¼   cup honey
1   (28-ounce) bottle ginger ale, chilled
1   pint pineapple sherbet

Combine fruit juices and honey; mix well. Pour equal amounts in 4 tall chilled glasses. Fill three-fourths full with ginger ale; top with a scoop of pineapple sherbet. Yield: 4 servings.

Pineapple 'n Ice Cream Punch

1   (46-ounce) can pineapple juice, chilled
1½ pints vanilla ice cream, softened
1   pint orange sherbet, softened
3   cups ginger ale, chilled

Combine all ingredients except ginger ale. Beat at low speed of electric mixer until well blended. Pour mixture into punch bowl. Just before serving, add ginger ale. Yield: about 30 (4-ounce) servings.

Angel Frost

2   (10-ounce) packages frozen sliced
      strawberries, divided
2   (6-ounce) cans frozen pink lemonade
      concentrate, undiluted and divided
2   cups water, divided
1   quart vanilla ice cream, divided
2   (7-ounce) bottles lemon-lime carbonated
      beverage, chilled

Combine 1 package strawberries, 1 can lemonade, 1 cup water, and ½ quart ice cream in container of electric blender; blend until thick and smooth. Pour into punch bowl. Repeat with remaining strawberries, lemonade, water, and ice cream. Add to punch bowl.

Carefully pour lemon-lime beverage down side of punch bowl; mix gently. Yield: about 11 cups.

★ Mint Tea

      2   quarts boiling water
     10   individual-size tea bags
    1½   to 2½ cups sugar
           Fresh mint sprigs
           Juice and rind of 1½ lemons

Combine water, tea bags, sugar, 10 mint sprigs, and juice and rind of lemons; cover and steep 30 minutes to 1 hour. Strain and cool. Serve over ice. Garnish each glass with a sprig of mint, if desired. Yield: 2 quarts.

★ Sunny Cider

      8   cups apple juice
      2   cups orange juice
      3   cups pineapple juice
           Orange slices
           Maraschino cherries

Combine juices; chill. Serve garnished with orange slices and cherries. Yield: 12 to 15 servings.

★ Orange Breakfast Drink

     ⅓   cup frozen orange juice concentrate,
           thawed and undiluted
     ½   cup milk
     ½   cup water
     ¼   cup sugar
     ½   teaspoon vanilla extract
      5   or 6 ice cubes

Combine all ingredients in container of electric blender. Blend until smooth. Serve cold. Yield: 2 cups.

Surprise-Surprise

      1   quart Dr Pepper, divided
      1   quart milk, divided
           Vanilla ice cream
           Frozen whipped topping, thawed (optional)
           Maraschino cherries (optional)
           Chopped nuts (optional)

Combine 2 cups Dr Pepper and 2 cups milk in container of electric blender; blend at low speed 5 seconds. Pour into chilled wide-mouthed glasses to within ½ inch of rim.

Repeat procedure with remaining Dr Pepper and milk; pour into glasses. Place one scoop of ice cream in each glass. Garnish with whipped topping, cherries, and chopped nuts, if desired. Yield: 6 to 8 servings.

Note. Cola carbonated beverage or root beer may be substituted for Dr Pepper.

Rum-Cranberry Punch

      2   cups light rum
     ½   cup sugar
      1   (12-ounce) can frozen orange juice
           concentrate, thawed and undiluted
      1   (32-ounce) bottle cranberry juice,
           chilled
      1   (28-ounce) bottle ginger ale, chilled
           Orange slices
           Strawberries

Combine rum, sugar, orange juice, and cranberry juice. Just before serving, add ginger ale and ice cubes. Garnish with orange slices and strawberries. Yield: about 2½ quarts.

Note: Substitute pineapple juice for rum, if desired.

Open-House Punch

    2½   cups bourbon
      1   (6-ounce) can frozen orange juice
           concentrate, thawed and undiluted
      2   (6-ounce) cans frozen lemonade
           concentrate, thawed and undiluted
     ⅔   cup lemon juice
      7   (10-ounce) bottles lemon-lime
           carbonated beverage, chilled
           Lemon slices
           Mint

Combine bourbon, orange juice, lemonade, and lemon juice; stir well. Add carbonated beverage and ice cubes. Garnish with lemon slices and mint. Yield: 3 quarts.

Bubbling Champagne Punch

1½   cups sugar
1½   to 2 cups lemon juice
2   (4/5-quart) bottles Sauterne
1   (4/5-quart) bottle pink champagne
1½   cups sliced strawberries

Combine sugar and lemon juice; stir until sugar is dissolved. Chill. Pour over ice into punch bowl. Add Sauterne and champagne; gently stir to mix. Garnish with strawberries. Yield: about 3½ quarts.

Rum Party Punch

2   (12-ounce) cans frozen lemonade concentrate, thawed
1   (46-ounce) can pineapple-orange drink
1   (32-ounce) bottle cranapple juice
About 2 cups rum
Orange slices

Prepare lemonade according to container directions; stir in pineapple-orange drink, cranapple juice, and rum. Serve over ice, and garnish with orange slices. Yield: 4 quarts.
   Note: Substitute ginger ale for rum, if desired.

Tart 'n Tangy Fruit Cooler

1   (6-ounce) can frozen orange juice concentrate, undiluted
1   (6-ounce) can frozen lemonade concentrate, undiluted
¾   cup lemon-lime carbonated beverage
¾   cup rum or gin
6   ice cubes, crushed
1   pint vanilla ice cream, softened

Combine all ingredients in container of electric blender, and blend until smooth. Yield: about 6 servings.

Sangría Southern

1   lemon, thinly sliced
1   orange, thinly sliced
1   lime, thinly sliced
Sugar
1   jigger Triple Sec or other orange liqueur
1   (4/5-quart) bottle dry red wine
1   cup club soda, chilled
Additional lime slices

Remove seeds from sliced fruit; place slices in glass pitcher, and add 1 to 2 tablespoons sugar. Do not add too much sugar until wine has been added. Allow to stand a few minutes.
   Add Triple Sec to sliced fruit; stir with wooden spoon, bruising fruit to extract juices. Add wine; more sugar may be added, if desired. Chill. Just before serving, add club soda. Serve over ice, and garnish with additional lime slices. Yield: 6 to 8 servings.

Banana Smasher

1   (6-ounce) can frozen orange juice concentrate, undiluted
¼   cup light rum
⅓   cup powdered sugar
1   banana, sliced
About 3 cups crushed ice

Combine all ingredients in container of an electric blender. Blend until smooth. Yield: 4 servings.

Bloody Mary Mix

2   (46-ounce) cans plus 1 (12-ounce) can cocktail vegetable juice
Juice of 10 lemons
¼   to ½ cup Worcestershire sauce
10   drops of hot sauce
1½   tablespoons ground celery seeds
2   tablespoons salt
Vodka to taste (optional)

Combine all ingredients except vodka; chill. Add vodka, if desired. Yield: 10 to 12 servings.

Hawaiian Party Drink

1   *(46-ounce) can pineapple juice*
1½   *cups vodka or rum*
       Coconut Syrup

Combine all ingredients; stir well, and serve over ice cubes. Yield: 8 cups.

Coconut Syrup:

1½   *cups flaked coconut*
¾   *cup water*
½   *cup light corn syrup*

Combine coconut and water in a saucepan; simmer over low heat, uncovered, 20 minutes. Let stand 15 minutes. Drain well, reserving liquid; discard coconut. Combine reserved liquid and corn syrup, stirring well. Yield: about 1 cup.

Mint Juleps

About 25 sprigs fresh mint, divided
1   *cup sugar*
1¾   *cups water*
2   *quarts bourbon*

Bruise 15 mint sprigs well (bruise by rubbing between palms of hands). Combine bruised mint, sugar, water, and bourbon in a crock or glass container; stir to dissolve sugar. Cover and let stand 4 to 6 hours.

Remove mint from bourbon mixture. Fill glasses with shaved ice; add bourbon mixture. Garnish each drink with a mint sprig. Serve with straws. Yield: about 20 (4-ounce) juleps.

Whiskey Sours

1   *(6-ounce) can frozen lemonade*
       concentrate, thawed and undiluted
½   *(6-ounce) can frozen orange juice*
       concentrate, thawed and undiluted
1¼   *cups bourbon*
¾   *to 1 cup water*
1½   *cups lemon-lime carbonated beverage*

Combine all ingredients, and freeze until slushy. Yield: about 4 cups.

Frosty Pink Lady

3   *cups pineapple juice, chilled*
¾   *cup gin*
¼   *cup grenadine*
       Juice of 1 lemon

Combine all ingredients, and mix well. Shake with crushed ice, and strain into cocktail glasses (may be served over crushed ice, if desired). Yield: 6 to 8 servings.

★ Superb Brandy Alexanders

½   *gallon vanilla ice cream*
½   *cup brandy*
¼   *cup crème de cacao*

Combine all ingredients in container of electric blender; blend well. Yield: about 5 cups.

★ Kahlúa Velvet Frosty

1   *cup Kahlúa or other coffee-flavored*
       liqueur
1   *pint vanilla ice cream*
1   *cup half-and-half*
⅛   *teaspoon almond extract*
       About 1½ cups crushed ice

Combine all ingredients in container of electric blender. Blend until smooth. Yield: about 6 servings.

★ Coffee Punch

1   *pint milk*
2   *quarts strong coffee, cooled*
2   *teaspoons vanilla extract*
½   *cup sugar*
1   *quart vanilla ice cream, softened*
½   *pint whipping cream, whipped*
       Ground nutmeg

Combine milk, coffee, vanilla, and sugar; blend well. Place ice cream in a punch bowl; pour in coffee mixture. Top with whipped cream and nutmeg. Yield: about 3½ quarts.

Christmas Coffee Punch

1¼ *cups sugar*
  1 *gallon strong coffee*
  1 *pint whipping cream, whipped*
  1 *pint vanilla ice cream, softened*
  1 *pint chocolate ice cream, softened*

Stir sugar into hot coffee; chill thoroughly. Fold in whipped cream and ice cream just before serving. Yield: about 5 quarts.

Hawaiian Iced Coffee

  2 *tablespoons cocoa*
  6 *cups hot strong coffee*
Sugar to taste
  1 *quart milk*
  1 *pint vanilla ice cream, cut into 1-inch cubes*
  1 *teaspoon vanilla extract*

Combine cocoa, coffee, and sugar; stir until well mixed. Cool. Add milk. Put ice cream into a punch bowl; pour coffee mixture over ice cream. Stir in vanilla. Yield: about 25 servings.

Cardamom Coffee

  8 *cups freshly brewed hot coffee*
 12 *cardamom seeds, crushed*
  1 *orange, thinly sliced*

Combine all ingredients, and simmer 5 minutes. Strain and serve hot. Yield: 8 (1-cup) servings.

Spiced Mocha

½ *cup whipping cream*
  1 *tablespoon instant coffee powder*
  3 *tablespoons sugar*
½ *teaspoon ground cinnamon*
¼ *teaspoon ground nutmeg*
Dash of ground cloves
  6 *tablespoons chocolate syrup, divided*
Hot coffee
  6 *cinnamon sticks (optional)*

Combine whipping cream, instant coffee, sugar, ground cinnamon, nutmeg, and cloves; chill several hours. Whip mixture until stiff.

Spoon 1 tablespoon chocolate syrup into each of 6 coffee mugs. Fill with hot coffee, stirring well. Top each with a generous spoonful of spiced whipped cream. Serve with cinnamon sticks, if desired. Yield: 6 servings.

Hot Mocha Mix

  2 *cups sugar*
  2 *cups instant nonfat dry milk solids*
  2 *cups nondairy creamer*
  1 *cup cocoa*
½ *cup instant coffee powder*
Marshmallows or whipped cream (optional)

Combine first five ingredients, and mix well. To serve, place 2 tablespoons mix in a cup. Add 1 cup boiling water, and stir well. Top with a marshmallow or whipped cream, if desired.

Store mix in an airtight container. Yield: enough mix for about 50 (8-ounce) servings.

Deluxe Hot Chocolate

  3 *(1-ounce) squares unsweetened chocolate*
½ *cup water*
½ *cup sugar*
Pinch of salt
½ *cup whipping cream, whipped*
  1 *teaspoon vanilla extract*
Hot milk

Combine chocolate and water in a saucepan; heat, stirring constantly, until chocolate is melted. Stir in sugar and salt; boil 5 minutes, stirring constantly. Cool. Fold in whipped cream and vanilla. Store in a covered jar in refrigerator.

To serve, use 1 tablespoon chocolate syrup to each cup of hot milk; mix well. Yield: about 20 servings.

Orange Wassail

1 *cup sugar*
1 *cup water*
1 *dozen whole cloves*
2 *cinnamon sticks*
3 *quarts orange juice*
1 *(32-ounce) bottle cranberry juice*

Combine sugar, water, and spices in a saucepan; simmer over low heat 10 minutes. Discard spices. Add juices to syrup. Heat and serve. Yield: 4 quarts.

Café au Lait Mix

½ *cup nondairy coffee creamer*
½ *cup sugar*
⅓ *cup instant coffee powder*

Combine ingredients in a small mixing bowl, blending well. To serve, place 1 tablespoon mix in a cup. Add 4 ounces boiling water, and stir well. Store mix in an airtight container. Yield: enough mix for 20 (4-ounce) servings.

Café Viennese:

1 *tablespoon Café au Lait Mix*
1 *tablespoon Cognac*
Dash of ground nutmeg

Place ingredients in a cup. Add 4 ounces boiling water. Stir well. Yield: 1 (4-ounce) serving.

Café Mexicano:

1 *tablespoon Café au Lait Mix*
1 *tablespoon Kahlúa or other*
   coffee-flavored liqueur
Dash of ground cinnamon
1 *teaspoon grated semisweet chocolate*

Place ingredients in a cup. Add 4 ounces boiling water. Stir well. Yield: 1 (4-ounce) serving.

Mocha Java:

1 *tablespoon Café au Lait Mix*
1 *tablespoon crème de cacao*
1¼ *teaspoons hot cocoa mix or instant*
   chocolate malt mix

Place ingredients in a cup. Add 4 ounces boiling water. Stir well. Yield: 1 (4-ounce) serving.

Spiced Percolator Punch

2¼ *cups pineapple juice*
2 *cups cranberry juice*
1¾ *cups water*
½ *cup firmly packed brown sugar*
3 *sticks cinnamon, broken*
1 *tablespoon whole cloves*
1½ *teaspoons whole allspice*
¼ *teaspoon salt*

Pour juices and water into an 8-cup percolator. Place remaining ingredients in percolator basket. Perk 10 minutes over heat or through complete cycle of electric percolator. Serve hot. Yield: about 1 quart.

Hot Cider Punch

2 *cups water*
1 *tablespoon ground ginger*
1 *tablespoon ground nutmeg*
6 *whole cloves*
6 *whole allspice*
2 *(2-inch) sticks cinnamon*
1 *gallon apple cider*
3 *cups sugar*
1½ *cups firmly packed brown sugar*

Combine water and spices in a large saucepan; cover and bring to a boil. Boil 10 minutes. Add apple cider and sugar. Simmer over low heat 10 minutes, stirring frequently. Serve hot. Yield: about 5 quarts.

Hot Tea Punch

2 quarts strong tea
1 (6-ounce) can frozen lemonade
    concentrate, undiluted
2 sticks cinnamon
¼ cup honey
½ cup sugar

Combine all ingredients and simmer 10 minutes. Serve in mugs. Yield: 10 to 12 servings.

Eggnog

1 (32-ounce) carton commercial eggnog
12 eggs, separated
1½ cups sugar
1 quart milk
1 quart whipping cream
Bourbon to taste

Pour commercial eggnog into a 4-cup ring mold or ice cube trays; freeze.

Beat egg yolks and sugar until thick and light colored; chill. Stir in milk, whipping cream, and bourbon. Fold in stiffly beaten egg whites. Serve from punch bowl with eggnog ring or in glasses with eggnog cubes. Yield: about 35 (½-cup) servings.

Fluffy Orange Eggnog

6 eggs, separated
Salt
½ cup plus 1 tablespoon sugar, divided
3 cups whipping cream, divided
2 cups milk
1 cup orange juice
Grated orange peel
Ground nutmeg

Combine egg yolks, dash of salt, and 3 tablespoons sugar in a large bowl; beat with an electric mixer until lemon colored. Beat in 1 cup whipping cream and milk. Stir in orange juice.

Beat remaining 2 cups whipping cream; fold into milk mixture. Combine egg whites, dash of salt, and remaining 6 tablespoons sugar; beat until stiff, and fold into milk mixture. Serve chilled; garnish with orange peel and nutmeg. Yield: 24 (½-cup) servings.

★ Christmas Eggnog

10 eggs, separated
1¾ cups sugar
4 cups milk, scalded
½ pint whipping cream, whipped
½ cup brandy
¼ cup light rum
Vanilla extract (optional)
Ground nutmeg

Beat egg yolks. Combine yolks and sugar in top of a double boiler; gradually add milk. Cook, stirring constantly, until mixture coats a spoon. Remove from heat; chill well.

Beat egg whites until stiff; fold egg whites and whipped cream into custard. Stir in the brandy and rum. Chill several hours. Add vanilla, if desired, and sprinkle with nutmeg. Yield: about 24 (½-cup) servings.

Spiced Coffee Eggnog Punch

2 cups very strong coffee
1½ sticks cinnamon, broken
6 whole cloves
6 whole allspice
2 (32-ounce) cartons commercial eggnog
1 tablespoon vanilla extract
½ pint whipping cream, whipped
1 quart vanilla ice cream, softened
Ground nutmeg

Combine coffee, cinnamon, cloves, and allspice in a saucepan; simmer 15 minutes. Strain and chill.

Combine eggnog, vanilla, and coffee mixture in a large bowl; chill. Fold in whipped cream. Spoon ice cream into a punch bowl; pour eggnog mixture into bowl, and stir. Sprinkle with nutmeg. Yield: about 20 (½-cup) servings.

Breads

Biscuits and cornbread are the mainstays of many a meal in the South, but abiding by this tradition doesn't mean our bread assortment is dull.

Recipes for good ole buttermilk and baking powder biscuits will always be popular, but for those who want variety, there are sweet potato biscuits and rye biscuits. Cornbread can be in the form of pones, sticks, muffins, and hush puppies, and we also flavor it with cheese, corn, onion, sour cream, and chiles.

Other popular quick breads span the spectrum from waffles and pancakes to muffins and fruit bread. Of course, yeast breads don't go unnoticed either. Homemade yeast rolls are just as much a part of Sunday dinner as they ever were, but we also enjoy French bread, English muffins, Swedish limpa, and German stollen.

Apple Butter Bread

    2   cups self-rising flour
    ¼   cup sugar
    1½ teaspoons ground cinnamon
    2   eggs, beaten
    ¾   cup apple butter
    ¼   cup melted butter or margarine
    2   tablespoons apple juice
    ½   cup chopped nuts
    ½   cup raisins

Combine flour, sugar, and cinnamon; set aside. Combine eggs, apple butter, butter, and apple juice; add to flour mixture, blending well. Stir in nuts and raisins. Pour into a greased 9- x 5- x 3-inch loafpan. Bake at 350° for 55 minutes. Cool 10 minutes before removing from pan. Yield: 1 loaf.

These homemade breads will leave lasting memories long after the bread is gone: (clockwise from top) Sally Lunn (page 53), Plaited White Bread (page 59), New Orleans French Bread (page 51), Black Bread (page 53), and Whole Wheat Sourdough Bread (page 52).

Banana Tea Bread

    ½   cup butter or margarine, softened
    1⅓ cups sugar
    2   eggs
    ¼   cup commercial sour cream
    2   tablespoons light rum or milk
    1   teaspoon almond extract
    2   cups all-purpose flour
    1½ teaspoons baking powder
    ½   teaspoon soda
    ¼   teaspoon salt
    1   cup mashed ripe bananas
    1½ cups chopped pecans
        Powdered sugar (optional)

Combine butter and sugar in a large mixing bowl; cream until light and fluffy. Add eggs, sour cream, rum, and almond extract, mixing well. Combine flour, baking powder, soda, and salt; add to creamed mixture alternately with mashed bananas, mixing well after each addition. Stir in pecans.

Pour batter into a greased 9- x 5- x 3-inch loafpan. Bake at 350° for 1 hour and 10 minutes or until done. If loaf gets too brown, cover with aluminum foil. Remove from pan; cool. Sprinkle loaf with powdered sugar, if desired. Yield: 1 loaf.

Nutritious Banana Bread

½   cup butter or margarine, softened
⅓   cup sugar
⅓   cup honey
2   eggs, slightly beaten
1¾ cups all-purpose flour
¼   cup wheat germ
1   teaspoon soda
3   ripe bananas, mashed
½   cup chopped pecans (optional)

Cream butter, sugar, and honey until light and fluffy; add eggs, beating well. Combine flour, wheat germ, and soda; add to creamed mixture alternately with bananas, mixing well after each addition. Stir in pecans, if desired.

Spoon batter into a greased 9- x 5- x 3-inch loafpan. Bake at 350° for 40 to 45 minutes or until done. Yield: 1 loaf.

Apricot-Prune Bread

½   cup finely chopped dried apricots
½   cup finely chopped dried prunes
1   egg, beaten
1   cup buttermilk
3   tablespoons salad oil
1   cup bite-size shredded wheat cereal
2   cups all-purpose flour
1   cup sugar
2   teaspoons baking powder
½   teaspoon salt
½   teaspoon ground cinnamon
⅛   teaspoon ground cloves
½   cup chopped nuts

Wash apricots and prunes in warm water; drain well, and pat dry on paper towels. Set aside.

Combine egg, buttermilk, oil, and cereal; set aside. Combine dry ingredients. Stir in prunes, apricots, and nuts. Add cereal mixture; stir just until all ingredients are moistened. Mixture will be stiff. Spoon evenly into a greased and floured 9- x 5- x 3-inch pan. Bake at 350° for 65 minutes. Remove from pan and cool on a wire rack; wrap and store overnight before cutting. Yield: 1 loaf.

Apricot-Nut Bread

2½ cups all-purpose flour
1   cup sugar
3½ teaspoons baking powder
1   tablespoon plus 1 teaspoon grated orange peel
3   tablespoons salad oil
½   cup milk
¾   cup orange juice
1   egg, slightly beaten
1   cup finely chopped pecans
1   cup finely chopped dried apricots

Combine all ingredients in a large bowl; mix until well blended. Pour into a greased and floured 9- x 5- x 3-inch loafpan. Bake at 350° for 55 to 65 minutes. Cool 10 minutes in pan; remove from pan. Yield: 1 loaf.

Tangy Citrus Bread

3   cups all-purpose flour
1   tablespoon baking powder
1   teaspoon salt
¼   teaspoon soda
¼   cup firmly packed brown sugar
¼   cup salad oil
1   egg, beaten
1   cup orange marmalade
½   cup orange juice
¼   cup lemon juice
1   teaspoon lemon rind
1   cup chopped walnuts
¼   cup orange marmalade, warmed

Combine flour, baking powder, salt, and soda; set aside. Combine sugar and salad oil; add egg, mixing well. Stir in 1 cup marmalade, orange juice, lemon juice, and lemon rind. Add dry ingredients, blending until smooth; stir in nuts.

Pour batter into a well-greased 9- x 5- x 3-inch loafpan. Bake at 350° for 50 to 55 minutes or until done. Remove from pan, and place on wire rack.

While bread is warm, pierce top with a fork, and drizzle with ¼ cup marmalade. Yield: 1 loaf.

Strawberry Bread

3 cups all-purpose flour
1 teaspoon salt
1 teaspoon soda
1 tablespoon ground cinnamon
2 cups sugar
3 eggs, well beaten
1¼ cups salad oil
2 (10-ounce) packages frozen sliced
   strawberries, thawed and drained
1¼ cups chopped pecans
Red food coloring (optional)

Combine flour, salt, soda, cinnamon, and sugar. Make a well in center of dry ingredients; add eggs and oil, stirring only until dry ingredients are moistened.

Stir in strawberries and pecans. Blend in food coloring, if desired.

Spoon batter into 2 lightly greased 8- x 4- x 2⅝-inch loafpans. Bake at 350° for 1 hour or until bread tests done. Let stand overnight before slicing. Yield: 2 loaves.

Apple Fritters

1½ cups all-purpose flour
1 tablespoon sugar
2 teaspoons baking powder
½ teaspoon salt
2 eggs, beaten
⅔ cup milk
1 tablespoon salad oil
3 cups peeled, finely chopped apples
Hot salad oil
Powdered sugar

Combine dry ingredients in a bowl; add eggs, milk, salad oil, and apples. Stir just until moistened.

Drop batter by spoonfuls into ½-inch hot oil. Cook until golden brown (about 3 to 4 minutes on each side); drain. Roll fritters in powdered sugar. Yield: about 3 dozen fritters.

Date-Nut Bread

½ cup firmly packed brown sugar
½ cup sugar
2 tablespoons margarine, softened
1 egg
1 cup evaporated milk
½ cup water
3 cups all-purpose flour, divided
2½ teaspoons baking powder
1 teaspoon salt
2 tablespoons chopped crystallized ginger
¾ cup chopped dates
⅓ cup chopped walnuts or pecans

Combine sugar, margarine, and egg; beat well. Stir in milk and water. Combine 2¾ cups flour, baking powder, and salt. Add to sugar mixture; blend well.

Combine ginger, dates, and walnuts; sprinkle with remaining ¼ cup flour. Stir into batter. Pour into a greased and floured 9- x 5- x 3-inch loafpan. Bake at 350° for 1 hour or until bread tests done.

Cool in pan 5 minutes; turn out on wire rack to finish cooling. Wrap securely and store 1 day before slicing. Yield: 1 loaf.

Lemon Tea Bread

½ cup butter or margarine, softened
2 eggs, beaten
½ teaspoon salt
1½ cups all-purpose flour
1 teaspoon baking powder
1 cup sugar
Juice and grated rind of 1 lemon
Glaze

Combine first 7 ingredients, mixing well. Spoon batter into a greased 9- x 5- x 3-inch loafpan. Bake at 350° for 1 hour. Spread Glaze over warm loaf. Chill. Yield: 1 loaf.

Glaze:

¼ cup sugar
Juice and grated rind of 1 lemon

Combine all ingredients, mixing well. Yield: about ¼ cup.

Pumpkin Bread

2   cups cooked, mashed pumpkin
1   cup sugar
1   cup firmly packed brown sugar
½   cup salad oil
1   egg
2½   cups all-purpose flour
½   teaspoon salt
½   teaspoon ground cinnamon
½   teaspoon ground cloves
¼   teaspoon ground nutmeg
2   teaspoons soda
1   cup chopped walnuts

Combine pumpkin, sugar, oil, and egg in a large mixing bowl; beat well. Combine remaining ingredients except walnuts; add to pumpkin mixture, mixing well. Stir in walnuts. Spoon into a 9- × 5- × 3-inch loafpan. Bake at 350° for 1 hour and 40 minutes. Yield: 1 loaf.

Walnut-Mincemeat Lace

1   (13¾-ounce) package hot roll mix
½   cup chopped walnuts
1   teaspoon cornstarch
¼   cup orange juice
1   tablespoon brown sugar
1   cup prepared mincemeat
⅓   cup chopped walnuts
¼   cup chopped candied cherries
½   cup powdered sugar
2   to 3 tablespoons half-and-half
     Candied cherries
     Walnut halves

Prepare hot roll mix as directed on package; stir ½ cup walnuts into dough. Cover and let rise in a warm place until doubled in bulk (about 40 minutes).

Combine cornstarch and orange juice in a small saucepan; cook over low heat, stirring constantly, until thickened. Stir in brown sugar, mincemeat, ⅓ cup walnuts, and ¼ cup chopped cherries; set aside.

Roll dough into a 14- x 10-inch rectangle on a floured surface. Spoon mincemeat filling lengthwise down center third of rectangle. Slit dough at 1-inch intervals along each side of filling. Fold strips at an angle across filling, alternating from side to side.

Cover and let rise in a warm place about 30 minutes. Bake at 350° for 30 minutes. Cool.

Combine powdered sugar and half-and-half, blending until smooth. Spoon over braid. Garnish with cherries and walnuts. Yield: 8 to 10 servings.

Potato Biscuits

½   cup instant mashed potato flakes
1   teaspoon sugar
2   tablespoons butter or margarine,
       softened
1   cup hot water
⅓   cup cold water
3   cups biscuit mix

Combine potato flakes, sugar, butter, and hot water; mix well. Add cold water and biscuit mix, stirring until well blended. Add more water if necessary to make a soft dough. Turn out on floured surface, and knead about 10 times.

Roll dough out to ½- to ¾-inch thickness; cut with a 2-inch biscuit cutter. Place on an ungreased baking sheet; bake at 450° about 10 minutes or until lightly browned. Yield: about 1 dozen biscuits.

Sweet Potato Biscuits

1   egg, slightly beaten
1   cup cooked, mashed sweet potatoes
¼   to ½ cup sugar
2   tablespoons butter or margarine,
       softened
3   tablespoons shortening
     About 2 cups self-rising flour

Combine egg, sweet potatoes, sugar, butter, and shortening in a mixing bowl; mix well. Stir in enough flour to make a soft dough. (Dough will be softer than regular biscuit dough.)

Turn out on a floured surface; knead lightly a few times. Roll to ¼-inch thickness; cut with a 2-inch biscuit cutter. Place on an ungreased baking sheet and bake at 350° about 15 minutes. Yield: about 1½ dozen (2-inch) biscuits.

Note: Use ¼ cup sugar if potatoes are naturally sweet and juicy.

Baking Powder Biscuits

    2   cups all-purpose flour
    ½   teaspoon salt
    3   teaspoons baking powder
    5   tablespoons shortening
    ⅔   cup milk

Combine flour, salt, and baking powder; cut in shortening until mixture resembles coarse meal. Add milk, stirring until blended well. Turn dough out onto floured surface; knead lightly 3 or 4 times.

Roll dough to ½-inch thickness; cut into rounds with a 2½-inch cutter. Bake at 425° for 15 minutes or until golden. Yield: 1 dozen biscuits.

Ever-Ready Rye Biscuits

    2   cups buttermilk
    1   cup salad oil
    ¼   cup sugar (optional)
    2   packages dry yeast
    4   cups self-rising flour, divided
    1   cup rye flour, sifted

Combine buttermilk and oil in a large mixing bowl; add sugar, if desired. Stir well. Combine yeast, 1 cup self-rising flour, and rye flour, stirring to mix; set aside.

Add 2 cups self-rising flour to buttermilk mixture; mix well. Gradually add yeast mixture, mixing well. Gradually add remaining 1 cup self-rising flour to make a stiff dough. If too stiff, add a few drops of warm water. Knead lightly.

Roll dough out on a lightly floured surface to ½-inch thickness; cut into rounds with a 2-inch cutter. Bake at 425° for 10 to 12 minutes or until lightly browned. Yield: about 5 dozen biscuits.

Note: This dough will keep up to 2 weeks if covered tightly and stored in refrigerator.

Old-Fashioned Buttermilk Biscuits

    2   cups all-purpose flour
    2   teaspoons baking powder
    ¾   teaspoon salt
    ¼   teaspoon soda
    ¼   cup shortening
    1   cup buttermilk

Combine dry ingredients; cut in shortening until mixture resembles coarse cornmeal. Add buttermilk, stirring until well mixed. Turn dough out onto floured surface, and knead lightly 3 or 4 times.

Roll dough to ¼-inch thickness; cut into rounds with a 2½-inch cutter. Bake at 475° for 10 minutes or until golden. Yield: 14 biscuits.

Onion-Cheese Muffins

    3   cups biscuit mix
    1   teaspoon onion salt
    ¾   cup shredded Cheddar cheese
    1   (3½-ounce) can French-fried onions,
        crumbled
    1   egg
    1   cup milk

Combine all ingredients in a large bowl; beat 1 minute. Fill medium-size greased muffin pans two-thirds full. Bake at 400° about 15 minutes. Serve warm. Yield: 12 to 16 muffins.

Blueberry Gems

    2   cups self-rising flour
    1½ cups sugar
    2   eggs, slightly beaten
    1   teaspoon vanilla extract
    ½   cup salad oil
    ½   cup milk
    1   cup blueberries

Combine flour and sugar in a large bowl; set aside. Combine eggs, vanilla, oil, and milk. Make a well in the center of dry ingredients; pour in liquid ingredients. Stir just until mixed. Fold in blueberries; stir 1 minute.

Spoon batter into greased muffin pans, filling about half full. Bake at 375° for 25 minutes. Yield: about 2 dozen muffins.

Bacon Cornettes

12 slices bacon
1 cup self-rising flour
1 cup self-rising cornmeal
¼ cup sugar
2 eggs, well beaten
1 cup milk

Cook bacon until crisp; drain and crumble, reserving ¼ cup drippings. Combine flour, cornmeal, and sugar. Add eggs, milk, and reserved bacon drippings; stir until moistened. Stir in crumbled bacon. Spoon batter into greased muffin pans, and bake at 425° for 20 to 25 minutes. Yield: 1 dozen muffins.

Sesame-Corn Muffins

¼ cup all-purpose flour
3 tablespoons sugar
½ teaspoon salt
¾ teaspoon soda
1 cup cornmeal
¼ cup sesame seeds
½ cup wheat germ
1 egg, slightly beaten
1 cup buttermilk
⅓ cup salad oil

Combine flour, sugar, salt, soda, cornmeal, sesame seeds, and wheat germ in a mixing bowl; set aside. Combine egg, buttermilk, and oil; stir into flour mixture.
Spoon batter into greased muffin pans, filling two-thirds full. Bake at 350° for 20 minutes. Yield: about 1 dozen muffins.

Virginia Orange Muffins

2 cups all-purpose flour
4 teaspoons baking powder
¼ teaspoon salt
3 tablespoons melted butter or margarine
2 eggs, beaten
1 cup milk
½ to ¾ cup firmly packed light brown sugar
Juice and grated rind of 1 orange

Combine flour, baking powder, and salt. Add butter, eggs, milk, and sugar; stir until moistened. Stir in orange juice and rind. Spoon batter into greased muffin pans, and bake at 400° for 20 minutes. Yield: 1 dozen muffins.

Wheat Germ Muffins

1½ cups all-purpose flour
¼ cup sugar
2 teaspoons baking powder
1 teaspoon salt
1 cup wheat germ
¼ cup light molasses
1 egg, well beaten
¾ cup milk
¼ cup melted butter or margarine

Combine flour, sugar, baking powder, salt, and wheat germ. Combine remaining ingredients; add to dry ingredients, stirring just until moistened. Spoon into greased muffin pans, filling two-thirds full. Bake at 400° for 20 minutes. Remove from pan at once. Serve warm. Yield: 1 dozen muffins.

Whole Wheat Muffins

2½ cups whole wheat flour
½ cup sugar
⅛ teaspoon salt
2 teaspoons baking powder
½ teaspoon soda
1 cup buttermilk
1 egg, slightly beaten
2 tablespoons melted shortening

Combine dry ingredients in a mixing bowl; make a well in center of mixture. Add buttermilk, egg, and shortening; stir just enough to moisten dry ingredients. Fill greased muffin pans two-thirds full. Bake at 425° for 20 minutes. Yield: about 1 dozen muffins.

Country Sausage Muffins

    ½ pound bulk pork sausage
    1 cup all-purpose flour
    1 cup self-rising cornmeal
    1 (2-ounce) jar chopped pimiento, drained
    1 (8-ounce) carton French onion dip
    ½ cup milk

Brown sausage, stirring to crumble; drain well, reserving 2 tablespoons drippings. Combine flour, cornmeal, sausage, and pimiento; add reserved drippings, onion dip, and milk. Stir just enough to moisten dry ingredients.

Fill greased muffin pans two-thirds full. Bake at 425° for 20 to 25 minutes or until golden brown. Yield: 1 dozen muffins.

Ever-Ready Bran Muffins

    2 cups boiling water
    2 cups 100% bran cereal
    2½ cups sugar
    1 cup plus 3 tablespoons shortening
    4 eggs
    2 teaspoons salt
    5 teaspoons soda
    4 cups buttermilk
    6 cups all-purpose flour
    4 cups 40% bran flakes cereal

Pour boiling water over 100% bran cereal; set aside. Cream sugar, shortening, and eggs until light and fluffy; stir in salt, soda, buttermilk, and 100% bran mixture; set aside.

Combine flour and bran flakes; add to first mixture, mixing well. Cover and store in refrigerator until ready to use (will keep up to five or six weeks).

When ready to bake, spoon batter into greased muffin pans, filling two-thirds full. Bake at 400° about 20 minutes. Yield: about 5½ dozen muffins.

Oatmeal Muffins

    1   cup regular oats, uncooked
    1   cup buttermilk
    ⅓   cup butter or margarine, softened
    ½   cup firmly packed brown sugar
    1   egg
    1   cup all-purpose flour
    1   teaspoon baking powder
    ½   teaspoon soda
    1   teaspoon salt

Combine oats and buttermilk; let stand 1 hour. Cream butter and sugar; add egg, and beat well. Combine flour, baking powder, soda, and salt; stir into creamed mixture. Add oat mixture, mixing well.

Fill greased muffin pans two-thirds full. Bake at 350° for 20 to 25 minutes. Yield: 10 to 12 muffins.

Butter Muffins

    2   cups Muffin Mix
    1   tablespoon sugar
    1   egg, slightly beaten
    ¾   cup milk

Combine Muffin Mix, sugar, egg, and milk. Stir just to moisten. Fill well-greased muffin pans two-thirds full. Bake at 425° for 20 to 25 minutes or until lightly browned. Yield: 1 dozen muffins.

Muffin Mix:

    5½ cups all-purpose flour
    4   tablespoons baking powder
    ½   cup sugar
    1½ teaspoons salt
    ½   cup butter or margarine, softened

Combine flour, baking powder, sugar, and salt; cut in butter until mixture resembles cornmeal. Store, tightly covered, in refrigerator until ready to use. Yield: about 6 cups.

Corn Sticks

1¼ cups yellow cornmeal
⅔ cup all-purpose flour
¼ cup sugar (optional)
1 tablespoon baking powder
½ teaspoon salt
1 egg, beaten
1 cup milk
¼ cup salad oil

Combine dry ingredients. Add egg, milk, and oil; mix lightly. Pour batter into 2 well-greased corn-stick pans. Bake at 425° for 12 to 15 minutes or until golden brown. Yield: 14 corn sticks.

Fried Corn Pone

1 egg
2 tablespoons sugar (optional)
1 tablespoon baking powder
1 teaspoon soda
1 teaspoon salt
2 cups cornmeal
1¾ cups buttermilk
1 tablespoon salad oil

Combine egg, sugar (if desired), baking powder, soda, and salt; beat well. Stir in cornmeal and buttermilk. Cover bottom of a heavy skillet with 1 tablespoon salad oil, and place over medium heat.

Drop batter into hot skillet, using ¼ cup batter for each corn pone. Turn corn pones over when brown. (Add more oil to skillet if needed.) Yield: about 1 dozen corn pones.

Hush Puppies

1¾ cups white cornmeal
1½ teaspoons salt
1 teaspoon baking powder
½ teaspoon soda
1 egg, beaten
1 cup buttermilk
¼ cup finely chopped onion
Shortening or salad oil

Combine dry ingredients; add egg and buttermilk, mixing lightly. Stir in onion.

Drop batter by tablespoonfuls into deep hot fat (360°); fry only a few at a time, turning once. Cook until hush puppies are golden brown (3 to 5 minutes). Drain well on paper towels. Yield: 1½ dozen hush puppies.

Mexican Cornbread

1 cup yellow cornmeal
½ teaspoon salt
½ teaspoon soda
⅓ cup melted shortening
1 (8-ounce) carton commercial sour cream
1 (8-ounce) can cream-style corn
2 eggs, beaten
1 cup shredded Cheddar cheese
1 (4-ounce) can chopped green chiles, drained

Combine cornmeal, salt, and soda; blend well. Stir in shortening; add sour cream, corn, and eggs, mixing well.

Spoon half of batter into a greased, heated 8- or 9-inch heavy skillet. Sprinkle with cheese and chiles; cover with remaining cornbread mixture.

Bake at 375° for 35 to 40 minutes or until golden brown. Yield: about 6 to 8 servings.

Wheat Germ Cornbread

1 cup all-purpose flour
½ cup sugar
5 teaspoons baking powder
1 teaspoon salt
1 cup cornmeal
¾ cup wheat germ
2 eggs, well beaten
1½ cups milk
⅓ cup salad oil
1 teaspoon vanilla extract

Combine flour, sugar, baking powder, salt, cornmeal, and wheat germ in a mixing bowl; set aside. Combine remaining ingredients, blending well; add to dry ingredients, stirring just enough to moisten. Pour into a greased 9- x 9- x 2-inch pan. Bake at 400° for 30 minutes. Yield: about 9 servings.

Mississippi Spoonbread

1 *cup cornmeal*
2 *cups milk*
3 *tablespoons butter or margarine*
1 *teaspoon salt*
3 *eggs*
Additional butter

Place cornmeal in a saucepan; gradually add milk, stirring until smooth. Bring to a boil over medium heat, stirring constantly. Remove from heat; add 3 tablespoons butter and salt, stirring until butter is melted. Cool. Add eggs, one at a time, beating well after each addition.

Pour batter into a well-greased 1½-quart casserole. Bake at 350° for 40 to 50 minutes. Serve immediately with butter. Yield: 6 to 8 servings.

Cheese Spoonbread

1⅓ *cups instant nonfat dry milk solids*
3¾ *cups water*
1 *cup cornmeal*
1½ *teaspoons salt*
4 *eggs, separated*
¼ *cup butter or margarine*
1 *teaspoon baking powder*
1½ *cups shredded Cheddar cheese*

Combine dry milk solids and water in a 2-quart saucepan; add cornmeal and salt. Cook over medium heat, stirring constantly, until mixture comes to a rolling boil; remove from heat.

Beat egg yolks well. Add a few spoonfuls of hot mixture to yolks; then stir into hot mixture. Blend in butter, baking powder, and cheese.

Beat egg whites until stiff; fold into cornmeal mixture. Pour into a hot, greased 2-quart baking dish. Bake at 400° for 40 to 45 minutes. Serve at once. Yield: 6 to 8 servings.

Onion Supper Bread

½ *cup chopped onion*
2 *tablespoons butter or margarine*
1 *(6-ounce) package cornbread mix*
½ *cup commercial sour cream*
½ *cup shredded sharp Cheddar cheese*

Sauté onion in butter until tender but not browned. Prepare cornbread mix according to package directions; spoon into lightly greased 8-inch square pan, and sprinkle with onion.

Combine sour cream and cheese; spoon over onion. Bake at 400° for 25 minutes or until lightly browned. Let stand a few minutes; then cut into squares. Yield: 9 servings.

Sopaipillas

1¾ *cups all-purpose flour*
2 *teaspoons baking powder*
1 *tablespoon sugar*
1 *teaspoon salt*
2 *tablespoons shortening*
⅔ *cup milk*
2 *cups hot salad oil*
Honey
Cinnamon sugar

Combine flour, baking powder, sugar, and salt in a large mixing bowl. Cut in shortening with pastry blender or fork until mixture resembles cornmeal. Add milk, mixing just until dough holds together in a ball.

Turn out onto a lightly floured surface; knead gently, about 1 minute, until smooth. Cover dough, and let rest for 1 hour.

Roll into a 12- x 15-inch rectangle with a floured rolling pin; dough should be 1/16 to 1/8 inch thick. Cut into 3-inch squares or 2- x 3-inch oblongs.

Heat oil in a saucepan to 370° to 380°. Drop a few pieces of dough at a time into the oil, turning at once so they will puff evenly. Turn back over, and brown both sides. Drain on paper towels.

Serve hot with honey and cinnamon sugar. Yield: about 20 sopaipillas.

Swedish Timbale Cases

    2 *eggs, slightly beaten*
    2 *teaspoons sugar (optional)*
    ½ *teaspoon salt*
    1 *cup all-purpose flour*
    1 *cup milk*
    Salad oil

Combine eggs, sugar (if desired), and salt. Add flour to egg mixture alternately with milk, beating at low speed of electric mixer. Refrigerate batter at least 1 hour.

Pour 1½ to 2 inches of salad oil in a skillet; heat to 370°. Heat timbale iron in hot oil 1 minute. Drain excess oil from iron, and dip into batter; be careful not to coat top of iron with batter.

Return iron to oil 20 to 30 seconds or until timbale case is golden brown. Remove case from iron with a fork, and turn upside down on paper towel to drain.

Reheat iron in oil, and repeat procedure for each case. Yield: about 2 dozen timbales.

Note: Cases may be filled with meat salads, sauces, or sweet fillings. Omit sugar for nonsweet fillings.

Carrot Bread

    2   *cups all-purpose flour*
    2   *teaspoons soda*
    2   *teaspoons ground cinnamon*
    ½   *teaspoon salt*
    1½ *cups sugar*
    ½   *cup flaked coconut*
    ½   *cup chopped walnuts*
    3   *eggs, beaten*
    1   *cup salad oil*
    2   *teaspoons vanilla extract*
    2   *cups grated raw carrots*

Combine dry ingredients; stir in coconut and nuts, and set aside. Combine eggs, oil, and vanilla; add carrots and dry ingredients, mixing well.

Spoon batter into 2 greased 9- x 5- x 3-inch loafpans. Bake at 350° for 1 hour or until bread tests done.

Invert pans on wire racks, and cool slightly; then remove pans. When cold, wrap loaves tightly and store overnight before slicing. Yield: 2 loaves.

Green Onion French Bread

    2 *loaves French bread*
    1 *cup melted margarine*
    2 *tablespoons parsley flakes*
    ¾ *cup finely chopped green onion*

Slice bread horizontally almost through loaf, leaving one side like a hinge. Combine margarine, parsley, and onion. Spoon mixture inside loaves; wrap in heavy-duty aluminum foil. Place on grill until well heated. Yield: 8 servings.

Parmesan Croutons

    4 *(¾-inch-thick) slices bread*
    ¼ *cup melted butter or margarine*
    2 *teaspoons grated Parmesan cheese*

Remove crust from bread, and cut bread into ¾-inch cubes. Brush or drizzle with butter, tossing lightly to distribute evenly. Sprinkle with cheese, and toss again.

Spread cubes in a single layer on a generously buttered cookie sheet. Bake at 350° for 10 minutes or until dry and lightly browned. Yield: about 4 cups.

Note: To make bread rounds to use as appetizers or with soups and salads, cut bread slices with a 3-inch round cutter; brush with butter, and sprinkle with Parmesan cheese. Toast as directed for croutons.

Seasoned Breadcrumbs

    About 8 slices bread
    1 *(3-ounce) can grated Parmesan cheese*
    1 *teaspoon parsley flakes*
    1 *teaspoon garlic salt*

Place bread on a baking sheet, and bake at 250° for 40 to 45 minutes or until bread is dry but not brown. Break bread into pieces, and place in container of electric blender; process until fine crumbs are formed. Measure out 2 cups crumbs.

Combine 2 cups breadcrumbs with cheese, parsley, and garlic salt. Mix well. Store crumbs in a tightly sealed container until ready to use. Yield: about 2¾ cups.

Note: For buttered breadcrumbs to use as casserole toppings, combine ½ cup bread-crumbs with ¼ cup melted butter or mar-garine; toss well.

Boston Brown Bread

1½   cups raisins
1½   cups boiling water
1   cup firmly packed brown sugar
4   teaspoons shortening
1   egg
1   teaspoon molasses
1   teaspoon salt
2   teaspoons soda
2⅔   cups all-purpose flour
½   cup chopped pecans

Combine raisins and water in a small bowl; set aside to cool. Combine brown sugar, shortening, egg, and molasses; beat well. Stir in salt, soda, flour, and raisin mixture. Stir in nuts. Spoon into four greased 16-ounce cans. Bake at 350° for 1 hour or until done. Cool slightly before removing from cans. Yield: 4 small loaves.

Apple Whole Wheat Waffles

2   cups whole wheat flour
½   teaspoon salt
1   tablespoon sugar
1   tablespoon baking powder
½   teaspoon ground cinnamon
½   teaspoon ground nutmeg
¼   teaspoon ground cloves
⅔   cup dry milk solids
2   eggs
⅓   cup salad oil
1   teaspoon vanilla extract
1   medium-size apple, cored, peeled, and
        chopped
1¾   cups apple juice

Combine first 7 ingredients. Place remaining ingredients in container of electric blender; blend until apple is pureed. Combine liquid ingredients and dry ingredients, mixing well. Bake in a preheated waffle iron. Yield: 8 waffles.

Note: This recipe is especially good served with Cinnamon Cream Syrup (see Index).

French Waffle Toast

6   eggs, beaten
1   cup half-and-half
¼   cup melted butter or margarine
      Pinch of salt and pepper
3   drops Worcestershire sauce
3   drops hot sauce
2   tablespoons sugar
½   cup maple-flavored syrup
      Pinch of ground cinnamon
½   teaspoon ground nutmeg
1   (16-ounce) loaf French bread, sliced
        thick

Combine all ingredients except bread in a large mixing bowl; beat well about 2 minutes. Dip slices of bread one at a time in the batter, coating well. Let drain; place on waffle iron preheated to 375°. Cook about 2 minutes or until brown.

Leftover batter can be stored in refrigerator 10 days. Yield: 10 to 12 servings.

Sour Cream Waffles

1 *cup all-purpose flour*
1½ *teaspoons sugar*
¼ *teaspoon salt*
¼ *teaspoon soda*
1 *egg, separated*
1 *(8-ounce) carton commercial sour cream*

Combine flour, sugar, salt, and soda. Stir in egg yolk and sour cream, mixing lightly.

Beat egg white until stiff; fold into batter. Bake in preheated waffle iron. Yield: 4 waffles.

Light Buttermilk Pancakes

1 *cup all-purpose flour*
1 *tablespoon sugar*
1½ *teaspoons baking powder*
½ *teaspoon salt*
½ *teaspoon soda*
1 *cup buttermilk*
1 *egg, beaten*
1 *tablespoon salad oil*

Combine dry ingredients. Combine remaining ingredients; add to dry ingredients, stirring just until flour is moistened. (Batter will be lumpy.) Bake on hot griddle. Yield: 4 to 5 servings.

Bran-Cheddar Pancakes

2 *eggs, beaten*
1 *tablespoon salad oil*
1¼ *cups buttermilk*
1 *cup pancake mix*
½ *teaspoon baking powder*
2 *tablespoons 100% bran cereal*
⅓ *cup shredded sharp Cheddar cheese*

Combine eggs, oil, and buttermilk, mixing well. Stir in pancake mix and baking powder. Add bran cereal and cheese, stirring just enough to distribute throughout batter.

For each pancake, pour about ¼ cup batter onto a hot, lightly greased griddle. Turn pancakes when tops are covered with bubbles and edges look cooked. Yield: about 4 servings.

Butterscotch Coffee Cake

1 *(18½-ounce) package yellow cake mix*
1 *(3⅝-ounce) package butterscotch pudding and pie filling mix*
4 *eggs*
⅔ *cup salad oil*
¾ *cup water*
½ *cup sugar*
1 *tablespoon cocoa*
1 *teaspoon ground cinnamon*

Combine cake mix, pudding mix, eggs, salad oil, and water; mix at medium speed of electric mixer 10 minutes. Spoon batter into a greased and floured 10-inch tube pan.

Combine sugar, cocoa, and cinnamon; mix well. Sprinkle over batter. Use a knife to carefully cut through batter once in a wide, zigzag course. Bake at 350° for 1 hour and 10 minutes or until done. Yield: one 10-inch coffee cake.

Cranberry Coffee Cake

2 *cups all-purpose flour*
3 *tablespoons baking powder*
¾ *teaspoon salt*
½ *cup sugar*
5 *tablespoons butter or margarine*
1 *egg, beaten*
½ *cup milk*
2½ *cups fresh cranberries, halved*
Topping

Combine flour, baking powder, salt, and sugar; cut in butter with a pastry blender until crumbly. Combine egg and milk; stir into dry mixture, mixing well.

Spread batter in a greased 8-inch square baking dish. Sprinkle cranberries over top of batter. Sprinkle Topping over cranberries. Bake at 375° for 35 to 40 minutes or until done. Serve warm. Yield: about 8 servings.

Topping:

¼   cup all-purpose flour
½   cup sugar
3   tablespoons butter or margarine

Combine flour and sugar in a small bowl. Cut in butter with pastry blender until crumbly. Yield: about ¾ cup.

★
Christmas Stollen

1   cup milk
1   cup melted butter or margarine
½   cup water
5¼   cups all-purpose flour
¼   cup sugar
1   teaspoon salt
2   packages dry yeast
2   eggs, beaten
½   teaspoon grated lemon rind
½   teaspoon grated orange rind
½   cup seedless raisins
½   cup chopped candied fruit
½   cup chopped nuts
3   tablespoons butter or margarine, softened
½   cup sugar
1   tablespoon ground cinnamon
1   cup powdered sugar
2   to 3 tablespoons water or milk
¼   teaspoon vanilla extract
     Candied cherry halves

Combine milk, 1 cup melted butter, and ½ cup water in a small saucepan; place over low heat just until lukewarm.

Combine flour, ¼ cup sugar, salt, and yeast in a large mixing bowl; stir in warm milk mixture and eggs, mixing well. Add lemon and orange rind, raisins, fruit, and nuts; mix well. Cover dough, and refrigerate overnight.

Place chilled dough on a floured surface; roll into an 18- x 12-inch rectangle; spread with 3 tablespoons soft butter. Combine ½ cup sugar and cinnamon; sprinkle over butter.

Beginning with long edge, roll up dough jellyroll fashion, pinching edges to seal; if ends are smaller than remainder of roll, trim off about 1 inch. Place roll on a large greased cookie sheet, and shape into a ring (it should resemble a large doughnut). Brush ends of roll with water, and pinch together to seal.

Using kitchen shears, make cuts in dough every inch around ring, cutting two-thirds of the way through roll at each cut. Gently turn each piece of dough on its side, slightly overlapping the previous piece.

Let rise in a warm place, uncovered, 1 hour. Bake at 350° for 25 to 30 minutes or until golden brown.

Combine powdered sugar, 2 to 3 table-spoons water, and vanilla; drizzle over hot ring. Decorate with candied cherry halves. Yield: 12 to 16 servings.

Fresh Apple Coffee Cake

1   cup sugar
½   cup shortening
1   egg
1½   cups all-purpose flour
1   teaspoon soda
1   teaspoon salt
½   cup strong coffee
2   cups peeled, chopped apple
2   tablespoons all-purpose flour
⅓   cup firmly packed brown sugar
1   teaspoon ground cinnamon
½   cup chopped pecans

Cream sugar and shortening until light and fluffy; beat in egg. Combine 1½ cups flour, soda, and salt; add to creamed mixture, alternately with coffee, mixing well.

Combine apple with 2 tablespoons flour; stir into batter. Pour batter into a greased 10- × 6- × 2-inch baking dish. Combine brown sugar, cinnamon, and pecans; sprinkle over batter. Bake at 350° for 40 minutes. Yield: 8 servings.

★
Almond Swirl Ring

  1   *cup milk*
  6   *tablespoons butter or margarine*
 ⅓   *cup sugar*
 ½   *teaspoon salt*
  3   *to 4 cups all-purpose flour, divided*
  1   *package dry yeast*
  1   *egg, beaten*
 ⅓   *cup sugar*
  2   *tablespoons butter or margarine,*
      softened
 ½   *cup ground almonds*
 ¼   *teaspoon almond extract*
  1   *cup powdered sugar*
  2   *to 3 tablespoons milk or water*
    Candied cherry halves
    Whole blanched almonds, toasted

Combine milk, 6 tablespoons butter, ⅓ cup sugar, and salt in small saucepan; heat just until warm (115° to 120°). Combine 2 cups flour with yeast; add warm milk mixture and egg. Beat well. Add enough remaining flour to make a soft dough.

Turn dough out on a floured surface, and knead 3 to 5 minutes; shape into a ball. Place in a greased bowl, turning to grease top. Cover; let rise in a warm place free from drafts until doubled in bulk (about 1 hour). Punch dough down, and let rise 10 additional minutes.

Place dough on a floured surface, and roll into an 18- x 12-inch rectangle. Combine ⅓ cup sugar, 2 tablespoons butter, ground almonds, and almond extract; blend well, and spread over dough. Starting with long edge, roll dough up jellyroll fashion; pinch edges together to seal.

Place roll on a greased cookie sheet; shape into a ring, and pinch ends together to seal. Using kitchen shears or a sharp knife, make a cut every inch around ring (cut should go two-thirds of way through roll). Gently pull slices out and twist, overlapping slices slightly. Cover; let rise in warm place free from drafts until doubled in bulk (about 45 minutes).

Bake at 375° for 20 to 25 minutes. Combine powdered sugar and 2 to 3 tablespoons milk to make a glaze; drizzle over hot ring. Garnish with candied cherries and almonds. Yield: 16 to 20 servings.

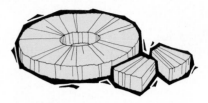

Pineapple Tea Ring

   1   *(15¼-ounce) can crushed pineapple*
  ½   *cup firmly packed brown sugar*
   2   *tablespoons cornstarch*
   1   *egg, beaten*
  ½   *teaspoon ground cinnamon*
   1   *package dry yeast*
  ½   *cup warm water (105° to 115°)*
   1   *tablespoon sugar*
 2½   *cups biscuit mix*
   1   *cup 100% natural cereal with raisins*
      and dates
    Icing
    Maraschino cherries (optional)
    Pecan halves (optional)

Drain pineapple, reserving 1 tablespoon juice for Icing. Combine pineapple, brown sugar, cornstarch, egg, and cinnamon in a saucepan. Cook over low heat, stirring constantly, until thickened. Cool.

Dissolve yeast in warm water. Stir in 1 tablespoon sugar and biscuit mix, beating vigorously. Turn dough out onto lightly floured pastry cloth or board; knead about 20 times or until smooth. Let dough rest 5 to 10 minutes.

Roll dough into a 16½- x 9½-inch rectangle; spread with pineapple filling, and sprinkle with cereal. Roll up jellyroll fashion, beginning at long side. Place on a greased baking sheet; join ends.

With kitchen shears, clip about two-thirds of way through roll at 1-inch intervals. Turn each cut on its side. Cover and let rise in a warm place about 1 hour. Bake at 375° for 20 to 25 minutes or until browned. Drizzle with Icing while warm. Decorate with maraschino cherries and pecans, if desired. Yield: 8 to 10 servings.

Icing:

1 *cup powdered sugar*
1 *tablespoon pineapple juice*
½ *teaspoon vanilla extract*

Sift powdered sugar into small bowl. Add pineapple juice and vanilla; blend until smooth. Drizzle over hot tea ring. Yield: about ½ cup.

Old-Fashioned Oatmeal Delight

⅔ *cup milk*
¼ *cup sugar*
1 *teaspoon salt*
¼ *cup melted margarine*
1 *package dry yeast*
¼ *cup warm water (105° to 115°)*
1 *egg, beaten*
1 *tablespoon grated orange rind*
1 *cup uncooked regular oats*
   About 2½ cups all-purpose flour
   Softened margarine
⅓ *cup apricot preserves*
⅓ *cup red raspberry jam*

Scald milk; stir in sugar, salt, and melted margarine. Cool to lukewarm.

Sprinkle yeast into warm water, and let stand 5 minutes; then stir well to dissolve yeast. Add to milk mixture. Stir in egg, orange rind, oats, and enough flour to make a soft dough.

Turn dough out onto a lightly floured board; knead about 8 to 10 minutes or until smooth and elastic. Place in a greased bowl, turning to grease top. Cover and let rise in a warm place about an hour or until doubled in bulk.

Punch dough down and divide in half. Roll out half the dough to form a 12- x 9-inch rectangle; brush with margarine and spread with apricot preserves. Roll up jellyroll fashion, beginning at long side. Place roll, seam side down, on a greased baking sheet; draw the ends together to make a ring.

With kitchen shears, clip about two-thirds of way through roll at 1-inch intervals. Turn each cut on its side. Repeat procedure with remaining half of dough, using raspberry jam for filling.

Cover and let rise in a warm place about 1 hour or until doubled in bulk. Bake at 350° for 30 to 35 minutes. Yield: two 9-inch coffee cakes.

Speedy Danish Coffee Cake

1 *package dry yeast*
¼ *cup warm water (105° to 115°)*
2 *cups all-purpose flour*
4 *tablespoons sugar, divided*
1 *teaspoon salt*
1 *cup butter or margarine*
1 *egg, beaten*
1 *teaspoon vanilla extract*
   Fruit Filling

Dissolve yeast in warm water; set aside. Combine flour, 2 tablespoons sugar, and salt; cut in butter with a pastry blender. Combine yeast mixture, egg, and vanilla; stir into flour mixture, blending until smooth.

Place dough on a floured surface, and roll into a 14- x 10-inch rectangle. Place in a greased 11- x 7- x 2-inch pan; allow extra dough to hang over sides of pan. Spread Fruit Filling over dough, and fold overhanging dough over fruit.

Sprinkle dough with remaining 2 tablespoons sugar. Bake at 375° for 30 minutes; reduce heat to 300°, and bake 15 to 20 minutes or until lightly browned. Yield: about 6 servings.

Fruit Filling:

⅔ *cup cooked, chopped prunes*
⅔ *cup cooked, chopped apricots*
1 *(8-ounce) can crushed pineapple, undrained*
½ *cup sugar*
1½ *tablespoons quick-cooking tapioca*

Combine all ingredients, mixing well. Yield: about 2⅓ cups.

Cream Cheese Braids

  1 *(8-ounce) carton commercial sour cream*
  ½ *cup sugar*
  1 *teaspoon salt*
  ½ *cup melted butter or margarine*
  2 *packages dry yeast*
  ½ *cup warm water (105° to 115°)*
  2 *eggs beaten*
  4 *cups all-purpose flour*
     Cream Cheese Filling
     Glaze

Heat sour cream over low heat; stir in sugar, salt, and butter; cool to lukewarm. Sprinkle yeast over warm water in a large mixing bowl, stirring until yeast dissolves. Add sour cream mixture, eggs, and flour; mix well. Cover tightly; refrigerate overnight.

The next day, divide dough into four equal parts; roll out each part on a well-floured board into a 12- x 8-inch rectangle. Spread one-fourth of Cream Cheese Filling on each rectangle; roll up jellyroll fashion, beginning at long sides. Pinch edges together, and fold ends under slightly; place the rolls seam side down on greased baking sheets.

Slit each roll at 2-inch intervals about two-thirds of way through dough to resemble a braid. Cover and let rise in a warm place, free from drafts, until doubled in bulk (about 1 hour). Bake at 375° for 15 minutes. Spread with Glaze while warm. Yield: 4 (12-inch) loaves.

Cream Cheese Filling:

  2 *(8-ounce) packages cream cheese,*
     softened
  ¾ *cup sugar*
  1 *egg, beaten*
  ⅛ *teaspoon salt*
  2 *teaspoons vanilla extract*

Combine cream cheese and sugar in a small mixing bowl. Add egg, salt, and vanilla; mix well. Yield: about 2 cups.

Glaze:

  2 *cups powdered sugar*
  4 *tablespoons milk*
  2 *teaspoons vanilla extract*

Combine all ingredients in a small bowl; mix well. Yield: about 1 cup.

Poppy Seed Coffee Cake

  ⅓ *cup poppy seeds*
  1 *cup buttermilk*
  1 *cup butter or margarine, softened*
1½ *cups sugar*
  4 *eggs*
2½ *cups all-purpose flour*
  2 *teaspoons baking powder*
  1 *teaspoon soda*
  ½ *teaspoon salt*
  1 *teaspoon vanilla extract*
  ⅓ *cup sugar*
  1 *teaspoon ground cinnamon*
     Powdered sugar

Combine poppy seeds and buttermilk; soak overnight in refrigerator.

Cream butter and 1½ cups sugar until light and fluffy. Add eggs, one at a time, beating after each addition. Combine flour, baking powder, soda, and salt. Add vanilla to buttermilk mixture.

Add dry ingredients and buttermilk mixture alternately to creamed mixture, beginning and ending with dry ingredients. Spoon half the batter into a well-greased 10-inch tube pan or Bundt pan.

Combine ⅓ cup sugar and cinnamon; sprinkle over batter. Top with remaining batter; bake at 350° for 1 hour or until coffee cake tests done. Cool in pan for 10 minutes; turn out and dust with powdered sugar. Yield: one 10-inch coffee cake.

Caraway Bread

1¼ *cups warm water (105° to 115°)*
  1 *package dry yeast*
  2 *tablespoons shortening*
  1 *tablespoon sugar*
  2 *teaspoons salt*
  3 *cups all-purpose flour, divided*
  2 *tablespoons caraway seeds*
     Melted butter or margarine
     Coarse salt

Combine warm water and yeast; add shortening, sugar, salt, and 1½ cups flour. Beat at medium speed of electric mixer 2 minutes. Add remaining 1½ cups flour and caraway seeds, mixing well. Cover with cloth, and let rise 45 minutes.

Stir batter down; then beat 25 strokes by hand. Spoon batter into 2 well-greased 1-pound coffee cans. Let rise, uncovered, 45 minutes.

Bake at 375° for 30 to 40 minutes or until golden brown. Remove from cans immediately, and place on wire racks to cool. While still warm, brush tops with melted butter and sprinkle with coarse salt. Yield: 2 loaves.

New Orleans French Bread

  2 *tablespoons shortening*
  1 *tablespoon sugar*
  1 *tablespoon salt*
  1 *cup boiling water*
  1 *cup cold water*
  1 *package dry yeast*
5½ *to 6 cups all-purpose flour, divided*
    Egg White Glaze

Combine shortening, sugar, salt, and boiling water in a large bowl; stir occasionally to melt shortening. Add cold water, and allow mixture to cool to 105° to 115°. Sprinkle yeast over liquid mixture; let stand 5 minutes, and stir to dissolve. Gradually beat in 4 cups flour; add enough remaining flour to form a stiff dough.

Turn dough out onto a floured surface, and knead until smooth and elastic (about 5 minutes). Place in a well-greased bowl, turning once to grease top. Cover with a damp cloth. Let rise in a warm place, free from drafts, 1 to 1½ hours or until doubled in bulk. Punch down; cover. Let rise 30 minutes or until doubled in bulk.

Turn dough onto a floured surface; knead slightly to press out gas bubbles; shape into a 14- to 16-inch cylinder on a greased baking sheet. Cover; let rise until doubled in bulk.

Cut ¼-inch deep slashes in top of loaf with a sharp knife; brush with Egg White Glaze. Bake at 375° for 40 to 50 minutes or until golden brown. Remove from baking sheet; cool on wire rack. Yield: 1 loaf.

Egg White Glaze:

  1 *egg white*
  2 *tablespoons cold water*

Combine egg white and water, beating until frothy. Yield: glaze for 1 loaf.

Dilly Bread

    1 *package yeast*
  ¼ *cup warm water (105° to 115°)*
    1 *cup creamed cottage cheese*
    2 *tablespoons sugar*
    1 *tablespoon minced onion*
    1 *tablespoon melted butter or margarine*
    2 *teaspoons dillseeds*
    1 *teaspoon salt*
  ¼ *teaspoon soda*
    1 *egg*
2¼ *to 2½ cups all-purpose flour*
      Softened butter or margarine

Soften yeast in warm water; set aside. Heat cottage cheese to lukewarm in a saucepan. Combine cottage cheese, sugar, onion, melted butter, dillseeds, salt, soda, and egg in a large bowl. Stir in yeast. Add flour to make a stiff dough; beat well.

Cover and let rise in a warm place until doubled in bulk, about 50 to 60 minutes. Stir down dough. Spoon into a well-greased 2-quart round baking dish. Let rise in a warm place until doubled in bulk, about 30 to 40 minutes. Bake at 350° for 30 to 40 minutes or until golden brown. Brush with softened butter. Yield: about 8 servings.

Whole Wheat Sourdough Bread

1½ cups boiling water
½ cup shortening
1 package dry yeast
1 teaspoon sugar
1 egg, well beaten
½ cup sugar
½ teaspoon salt
1 cup Sourdough Starter, at room
    temperature
3 cups all-purpose flour, divided
2 cups whole wheat flour

Combine boiling water and shortening in a large bowl; allow to cool to 105° to 115°. Add yeast and 1 teaspoon sugar; let stand 15 minutes. Add egg, ½ cup sugar, salt, Sourdough Starter, and 2½ cups all-purpose flour; beat at medium speed of electric mixer 3 minutes. Gradually stir in ½ cup all-purpose flour and whole wheat flour.

Turn dough out on a floured surface, and knead about 5 minutes or until smooth and elastic. Place dough in a greased bowl, turning to grease top. Cover with plastic wrap. Let rise in a warm place, free from drafts, 1½ to 2 hours or until dough is doubled in bulk.

Divide dough in half, and place on a floured surface. Roll each half into an 8- x 18-inch rectangle. Roll up, beginning at narrow edge; as you roll the dough, press firmly to eliminate air pockets. Pinch seams and ends together to seal. Place seam side down in 2 well-greased 9- x 5- x 3-inch loafpans.

Cover and let rise until doubled in bulk. Place in a cold oven. Bake at 400° for 15 minutes; reduce heat to 350°, and continue baking 20 minutes or until loaves sound hollow when tapped. Remove from pans; cool on wire racks. Yield: 2 loaves.

Sourdough Starter:

1 package dry yeast
3 cups warm water (105° to 115°)
3½ cups all-purpose flour

Combine yeast and water; set aside 5 minutes. Gradually add flour, beating at medium speed of electric mixer until smooth. Cover with plastic wrap. Place in a warm spot, free from drafts, until bubbles appear on surface (about 24 hours). If starter has not started to ferment after 24 hours, discard it and start over.

Stir starter well; cover and return to warm place. Let stand 2 days or until foamy.

Stir well, and pour into an airtight glass container. Store in refrigerator. Stir before using, and allow to come to room temperature. Yield: about 4 cups.

Note: Starter may be stored in refrigerator several weeks, but it should be used weekly. If not used regularly, add 1 teaspoon sugar, stirring well. This will keep yeast active.

★
Swedish Limpa

2 packages dry yeast
¼ cup warm water (105° to 115°)
2 cups medium rye flour
½ cup dark molasses
¼ cup firmly packed brown sugar
⅓ cup shortening
1 tablespoon salt
1 tablespoon caraway seeds
4 ounces candied orange peel, chopped
3 cups hot water
2 tablespoons sugar
7 to 8 cups all-purpose flour

Dissolve yeast in warm water. Combine rye flour, molasses, brown sugar, shortening, salt, caraway seeds, and orange peel in a large bowl. Add hot water, and mix well; cool to room temperature, and stir in yeast mixture and sugar. Gradually add flour, beating well after each addition.

Turn dough out on a floured surface; coat dough lightly with flour. Cover and let rest 15 minutes. Knead until smooth and elastic (about 8 to 10 minutes). Place dough in a well-greased bowl, turning to grease top. Cover and let rise until light (about 45 minutes). Turn out on floured surface and knead until elastic.

Divide dough into quarters, and shape into round loaves; seal seam well. Place on greased baking sheets, seam side down. Cover; let rise in a warm place until doubled in bulk. Bake at 350° for 40 minutes. Lightly grease crust to prevent cracking. Cool on wire racks. Yield: 4 round loaves.

Onion-Herb Batter Bread

½ cup milk
1½ tablespoons sugar
1 teaspoon salt
1 tablespoon butter or margarine
1 package dry yeast
½ cup warm water (105° to 115°)
2¼ cups all-purpose flour
1 tablespoon instant minced onion
½ teaspoon dillweed
½ teaspoon fines herbes
Melted butter or margarine
Salt

Scald milk in a small saucepan. Remove from heat and add sugar, salt, and butter, stirring until dissolved. Set aside until mixture becomes lukewarm.

Dissolve yeast in warm water in a large bowl. Stir in lukewarm milk mixture. Stir in flour, onion, dillweed, and fines herbes. Cover and let rise until tripled in bulk, about 45 minutes. Beat dough vigorously 30 seconds.

Spoon dough into a greased 9- x 5- x 3-inch loafpan. Bake at 350° for 50 to 60 minutes or until done. Remove from pan; brush crust with melted butter, and sprinkle lightly with salt. Cool on wire rack. Yield: 1 loaf.

Sally Lunn

1 package dry yeast
¼ cup warm water (105° to 115°)
¾ cup warm milk
½ cup butter or margarine, softened
⅓ cup sugar
3 eggs, well beaten
4 cups all-purpose flour
1 teaspoon salt

Combine yeast and water in a small bowl; let stand 5 minutes. Stir in milk. Cream butter and sugar until light and fluffy in a large bowl; add eggs, blending well.

Combine flour and salt; add to creamed mixture alternately with milk mixture, beginning and ending with flour. Mix well after each addition. (Batter will be very stiff.) Cover and let rise in a warm place free from drafts about 2 hours or until doubled in bulk.

Spoon batter into a well-greased 10-inch tube pan or Bundt pan. Cover and let rise in a warm place free from drafts until doubled in bulk. Bake at 350° for 50 to 60 minutes. Remove from pan; cool on wire rack. Yield: one 10-inch ring.

★ Black Bread

1 package dry yeast
2 cups warm water (105° to 115°)
2 tablespoons sugar
2 teaspoons salt
2 tablespoons shortening, melted and cooled
4 to 5 cups all-purpose flour, divided
3 tablespoons dark molasses
3 cups rye flour
1 tablespoon caraway seeds
1 tablespoon dillseeds
Melted butter or margarine

Dissolve yeast in warm water in a large bowl. Add sugar, salt, shortening, and 3 cups all-purpose flour; beat well. Add molasses, rye flour, caraway seeds, and dillseeds. Stir in enough additional all-purpose flour to form a stiff dough.

Turn dough out on a floured surface, and knead until smooth and elastic (about 8 to 10 minutes). Place in a well-greased bowl, turning to grease top. Cover and let rise in a warm place, free from drafts, until doubled in bulk.

Divide dough in half, and shape each half into a smooth ball. Place each ball on a greased baking sheet, and lightly press to flatten bottom. Cover; let rise in a warm place, free from drafts, until doubled in bulk. Bake at 400° for 30 minutes or until loaves sound hollow when tapped. Brush hot loaves with melted butter. Remove from baking sheets; cool on wire racks. Yield: 2 loaves.

Calas

1   *package dry yeast*
½   *cup warm water (105° to 115°)*
1½ *cups well-cooked rice (short grain is best)*
3   *eggs, beaten*
¼   *cup sugar*
1¼ *cups all-purpose flour*
½   *teaspoon salt*
¼   *teaspoon ground nutmeg*
    Salad oil
½   *cup powdered sugar*
1   *tablespoon ground cinnamon*

Dissolve yeast in warm water. Mash rice grains while hot with the back of a spoon; cool to lukewarm.

Combine yeast and rice, mixing well; cover and let rise in a warm place overnight. In the morning, add eggs, sugar, flour, salt, and nutmeg to rice mixture, beating until thoroughly mixed.

Heat 3 inches of salad oil in a skillet to 375°; drop batter by tablespoonfuls into hot oil, and cook until golden brown, turning once. Drain well on paper towels.

Combine powdered sugar and cinnamon; sprinkle over hot calas, and serve immediately. Yield: about 2 dozen calas.

Raisin Cinnamon-Swirl Bread

1   *cup raisins*
1⅓ *cups milk, divided*
1   *package dry yeast*
½   *cup sugar*
1   *egg, beaten*
¼   *teaspoon salt*
½   *cup melted butter or margarine*
1   *teaspoon cardamom*
4   *cups all-purpose flour*
2   *tablespoons sugar*
2   *tablespoons ground cinnamon*
1   *egg white, lightly beaten*

Cover raisins with water, and soak until plump. Scald ⅓ cup milk; cool to lukewarm. Sprinkle yeast in milk, and stir until yeast is dissolved. Combine 1 cup milk, sugar, egg,

salt, and butter in a large bowl; mix well. Stir in yeast mixture. Combine cardamom and flour; gradually add to milk mixture, stirring until a soft dough forms.

Turn dough out on a lightly floured board; knead until smooth and elastic. Place in a greased bowl, turning to grease top. Cover and let rise in a warm place until doubled in bulk (about 1 hour).

Punch dough down; place on a lightly floured board, and roll into a 14- x 12-inch rectangle. Combine sugar and cinnamon; sprinkle over dough. Drain water from raisins, and sprinkle over cinnamon mixture. Roll up jellyroll fashion.

Place roll on a greased baking sheet, seam side down. Cover and let rise 35 minutes. Brush dough with egg white. Using a sharp knife, slash top of dough at 2-inch intervals. Bake at 350° for 30 to 40 minutes. Yield: 1 loaf.

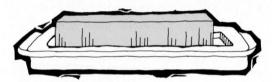

Light Cornbread

1   *cup milk*
6   *tablespoons sugar*
2   *teaspoons salt*
½   *cup butter or margarine*
½   *cup warm water (105° to 115°)*
2   *packages dry yeast*
2   *eggs, beaten*
3½ *cups all-purpose flour*
1¾ *cups yellow cornmeal*

Combine milk, sugar, salt, and butter; heat until milk is scalded and butter is melted. Cool to lukewarm.

Combine warm water and yeast, stirring until yeast is dissolved. Add milk mixture, eggs, flour, and cornmeal; beat until well mixed (about 2 minutes). Batter will be stiff.

Spoon batter into 2 greased 8-inch round cakepans or 2 greased 9- x 5- x 3-inch loafpans. Cover; let rise in a warm place until doubled in bulk (about 1 hour). Bake at 375° for 30 to 35 minutes. Cool on wire racks. Yield: 2 loaves.

★
Monkey Bread

1 *cup milk*
1 *cup butter or margarine, melted and divided*
¼ *cup sugar*
1 *teaspoon salt*
1 *package dry yeast*
3½ *cups all-purpose flour*

Combine milk, ½ cup butter, sugar, and salt in a saucepan; heat until butter is melted. Cool to 105° to 115°; stir in yeast until dissolved. Place flour in a large bowl; make a well in flour and pour in liquid mixture. Stir until blended.

Cover and let rise until doubled in bulk, about 1 hour and 20 minutes. Turn dough out on a floured surface. Roll ¼ inch thick. Cut into 3-inch squares. Dip each square into remaining butter.

Layer squares in a 10-inch tube or Bundt pan. Let rise until doubled in bulk, about 30 to 40 minutes. Bake at 375° for 30 to 40 minutes. Yield: about 6 servings.

Hard Rolls

1 *package dry yeast*
¼ *cup warm water (105° to 115°)*
1 *tablespoon sugar*
2 *tablespoons salad oil*
1 *teaspoon salt*
¾ *cup water*
4 *cups unbleached flour, divided*
2 *egg whites, stiffly beaten*
Cornmeal
2 *egg yolks*
2 *tablespoons water*

Dissolve yeast in ¼ cup warm water; set aside. Combine sugar, oil, salt, and ¾ cup water in a large bowl; add 1 cup flour, and beat well. Blend in yeast mixture and egg whites. Stir in remaining flour.

Turn dough out on a floured board; knead 10 minutes. Place in a greased bowl, turning once to grease top. Cover and let rise in a warm place until doubled in bulk (about 50 minutes). Punch down; cover and let rise until doubled (about 50 minutes).

Divide dough into 24 pieces; cover and let stand 10 minutes. Shape into balls. Grease a large baking sheet; sprinkle with cornmeal. Place rolls 2½-inches apart on prepared sheet. Cover and let rise about 30 minutes.

Combine egg yolks and 2 tablespoons water; brush on each roll. Place a large flat pan of boiling water on lower shelf of oven. (This makes the rolls crusty.) Place baking sheet on shelf above water. Bake at 450° for 10 to 15 minutes. Yield: 2 dozen rolls.

Sweet Potato Rolls

3 *cups whole wheat flour*
3 *cups all-purpose flour*
2 *packages dry yeast*
1½ *cups warm water (105° to 115°)*
⅓ *cup firmly packed brown sugar*
1¼ *teaspoons salt*
½ *cup butter or margarine, softened*
2 *eggs*
1 *(9-ounce) can sweet potatoes, undrained*

Combine flour, mixing well. Combine yeast and warm water in container of electric blender; process to dissolve yeast.

Add sugar, salt, butter, eggs, sweet potatoes, and 1 cup flour to yeast mixture; blend until smooth. Place remaining flour in large bowl; add yeast mixture, mixing to make a soft dough.

Turn dough out on a lightly floured board; knead about 5 minutes or until smooth and elastic. Place in a greased bowl, turning to grease top. Cover with plastic wrap, and refrigerate 6 hours or overnight.

About 1 hour before baking, divide dough in half. On a lightly floured surface, roll out each half into a 16-inch circle about ¼ inch thick. Cut each circle into 16 wedges; roll up each wedge, beginning at widest edge.

Place wedges on greased baking sheets with the point on bottom. Cover and let rise in a warm place about 30 minutes or until light. Bake at 350° for 15 minutes. Yield: 32 rolls.

★ Pan Rolls

¾   *cup sugar*
¾   *cup shortening*
1   *cup boiling water*
2   *packages dry yeast*
1   *cup warm water (105° to 115°)*
2   *eggs, slightly beaten*
6   *to 7 cups all-purpose flour, divided*
1   *teaspoon salt*
1   *teaspoon baking powder*
½   *teaspoon soda*

Cream sugar and shortening until light and fluffy. Add boiling water, mixing thoroughly; set aside to cool.

Dissolve yeast in 1 cup warm water; set aside. Add eggs to cooled shortening mixture, mixing well; stir in yeast mixture. Combine 5 cups flour with salt, baking powder, and soda; add to yeast mixture, and mix well. Turn dough out on a well-floured surface; knead in enough remaining flour until dough is no longer sticky.

Roll dough into 1½-inch balls in hands, and place in 2 greased 9-inch round cake-pans. Cover and let rise in warm place until doubled in bulk (about 1½ hours). Bake at 400° for 20 minutes or until golden brown. Yield: about 3 dozen rolls.

Note: Dough may be stored in refrigerator until ready to use; brush surface with salad oil, and place in a covered container.

Soft Pretzels

1   *package dry yeast*
1½   *cups warm water (105° to 115°)*
4   *cups all-purpose flour*
1½   *teaspoons sugar*
¾   *teaspoon salt*
1   *egg white*
Coarse salt (table salt may be substituted)
Mustard (optional)

Dissolve yeast in warm water. Combine flour, sugar, and salt; add yeast mixture, and mix until well blended. Turn out onto a lightly floured surface, and knead until smooth and elastic (about 5 minutes).

Using kitchen shears dipped in flour, cut dough into 18 pieces; roll each into a ball. With floured hands, roll each ball between hands to form a rope about 14 to 16 inches long and about ½ inch in diameter; twist each into a pretzel shape, and place on a lightly greased baking sheet.

Beat egg white until frothy, and brush on each pretzel; sprinkle with salt. Bake at 400° for 15 minutes or until lightly browned. Serve warm or cold with mustard, if desired. Yield: 1½ dozen pretzels.

Hot Cross Puffs

1   *package yeast*
¼   *cup warm water (105° to 115°)*
1   *cup sugar, divided*
1   *teaspoon salt*
1   *cup warm milk (105° to 115°)*
4   *cups all-purpose flour, divided*
3   *teaspoons ground cinnamon, divided*
¼   *teaspoon ground nutmeg*
2   *eggs*
¼   *cup salad oil*
¾   *cup raisins or currants*
1   *cup powdered sugar*
2   *tablespoons water or milk*

Soften yeast in warm water in a large bowl. Add ¼ cup sugar, salt, milk, 2 cups flour, 1 teaspoon cinnamon, and nutmeg; beat until smooth. Stir in eggs, oil, and remaining 2 cups flour; beat until shiny and smooth. Stir in raisins. Cover and let rise until doubled in bulk (about 1 hour).

Stir down. Fill greased muffin pans one-third full. Combine remaining ¾ cup sugar and 2 teaspoons cinnamon. Sprinkle 1 teaspoon sugar mixture over each puff. Cover and let rise until doubled in bulk (about 1 hour).

Bake at 375° for 15 minutes or until done. Remove from oven; cool. Combine powdered sugar and water, mixing well; spoon over each puff, forming a cross design. Yield: 2 to 2½ dozen puffs.

Bran Rolls

1 *cup boiling water*
1 *cup 100% bran cereal*
¾ *cup shortening*
¾ *cup sugar*
1 *package dry yeast*
1 *cup warm water (105° to 115°)*
1¼ *teaspoons salt*
2 *eggs, beaten*
About 6 cups all-purpose flour

Combine boiling water, cereal, shortening, and sugar; set aside. Dissolve yeast in warm water; add salt and eggs. Combine cereal mixture and yeast mixture in a large mixing bowl. Stir in enough flour to make a soft dough.

Place dough in a greased bowl, turning to grease all sides; cover and refrigerate overnight.

Punch dough down, and turn out on a lightly floured board; knead lightly. Roll dough into 1½-inch balls, and place in 3 greased 9-inch pans. Cover; let rise in a warm place until doubled in bulk (about 2 hours). Bake at 375° for 10 to 12 minutes or until browned. Yield: about 4 dozen rolls.

Note: Dough may be made into rolls without refrigerating overnight. Turn out onto a lightly floured board; knead lightly. Shape as directed; cover and let rise in a warm place about 1 hour. Bake as directed.

Whole Wheat Rolls

1 *cup milk*
¼ *cup sugar*
1 *teaspoon salt*
¼ *cup shortening*
1 *package dry yeast*
¼ *cup warm water (105° to 115°)*
1 *egg*
2 *cups whole wheat flour*
1½ *cups all-purpose flour*
Melted butter

Scald milk; stir in sugar, salt, and shortening. Cool mixture to lukewarm. Sprinkle yeast in warm water; stir until yeast is dissolved. Add milk mixture, egg, and whole wheat flour, beating until smooth. Add all-purpose flour to make a soft dough.

Place in a greased bowl, turning to grease top. Cover and let rise in a warm place 1½ to 2 hours or until doubled in bulk.

Punch dough down; turn out on a lightly floured board. Roll half of dough into a circle about 10 inches in diameter and ¼ inch thick. Cut into 12 wedges, and brush with melted butter.

Roll each wedge tightly, beginning at wide end. Seal points. Place on greased baking sheets with point underneath; curve into crescent shape. Repeat with remaining half of dough. Cover and let rise 45 minutes to 1 hour or until doubled in bulk.

Bake at 400° about 10 to 12 minutes or until browned. Yield: about 2 dozen rolls.

★
English Muffins

1 *cup milk*
3 *tablespoons shortening*
1½ *teaspoons salt*
3 *tablespoons sugar*
1 *package dry yeast*
¼ *cup warm water (105° to 115°)*
1 *egg, beaten*
4¼ *cups all-purpose flour, divided*
Melted shortening

Scald milk, and stir in shortening, salt, and sugar; cool to lukewarm. Sprinkle yeast into warm water; stir well, and add to milk mixture. Add egg and 2 cups flour, mixing well.

Turn dough out on a lightly floured board; knead in remaining flour until smooth and elastic. Place in a large greased bowl, and brush with melted shortening; cover and let rise in a warm place about 1½ hours.

Turn dough out on a lightly floured board, and roll to ¼-inch thickness. Cut with a 3½-inch round cutter, and place on an ungreased baking sheet. Let rise in a warm place about 45 minutes or until doubled in bulk. Bake at 325° about 8 minutes on one side; turn muffins, and bake about 8 minutes on other side. Yield: about 1 dozen muffins.

★ Orange Rolls

    1   *package dry yeast*
    ¼   *cup warm water (105° to 115°)*
    1   *cup sugar, divided*
    1   *teaspoon salt*
    2   *eggs*
    ½   *cup commercial sour cream*
    ½   *cup melted butter or margarine, divided*
    3½ *cups all-purpose flour*
    2   *tablespoons grated orange rind*
        Glaze

Sprinkle yeast into warm water in a large mixing bowl, stirring well; add ¼ cup sugar, salt, eggs, sour cream, and 6 tablespoons butter. Gradually add 2 cups flour, and beat until smooth. Knead in remaining flour.

Turn dough out onto a lightly floured board, and knead 5 minutes or until smooth and elastic. Put in a greased bowl, turning to grease top. Cover and let rise in a warm place, free from drafts, until doubled in bulk (about 1½ to 2 hours). Punch dough down; turn out onto a lightly floured board, and knead lightly.

Roll half of dough into a 12-inch circle about ¼ inch thick. Combine remaining sugar and orange rind. Brush dough with 1 tablespoon melted butter; sprinkle with half of orange-sugar mixture. Cut dough into 12 wedges. Roll up each wedge, beginning with wide end and rolling toward point. Repeat procedure with remaining half of dough.

Place rolls, point side down, in 3 rows in a greased 13- x 9- x 2-inch pan. Cover and let rise in a warm place, free from drafts, about 1 hour. Bake at 350° for 20 minutes or until golden brown. Top with Glaze. Yield: 2 dozen rolls.

Glaze:

    ¾   *cup sugar*
    ½   *cup commercial sour cream*
    2   *tablespoons orange juice*
    ½   *cup margarine*

Combine all ingredients in a saucepan; place over medium heat, and bring to a boil. Boil 3 minutes, stirring constantly. Pour over warm rolls. Yield: about 1½ cups.

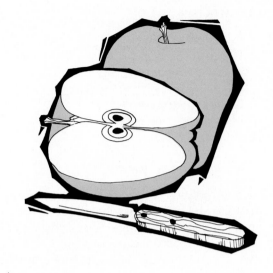

★ Butterhorns

    4   *cups all-purpose flour*
    1   *teaspoon salt*
    1   *package dry yeast*
    ½   *cup butter or margarine*
    ¾   *cup shortening*
    3   *egg yolks*
    1   *(8-ounce) carton commercial sour cream*
    1   *teaspoon vanilla extract*
        Powdered sugar
        Meringue Filling
        Butter Frosting

Combine flour, salt, and yeast; cut in butter and shortening until the mixture resembles coarse cornmeal. Beat egg yolks; blend in sour cream and vanilla. Stir yolk mixture into flour, mixing thoroughly.

Divide dough into 4 equal parts, and shape each into a ball. Chill thoroughly.

Lightly sprinkle a pastry cloth or board with sugar. Work with one pastry ball at a time, keeping others chilled.

Roll each ball into a 12-inch circle, and cut into 12 wedge-shaped pieces. Spread each wedge with Meringue Filling; roll up, starting at large end. Place 1-inch apart on a lightly greased cookie sheet. Place point of each roll down so it will not unroll, and curve into a crescent. Bake at 375° for 12 minutes or until lightly browned. Spread with Butter Frosting while hot. Yield: 4 dozen butterhorns.

Meringue Filling:

    3   *egg whites*
    1   *cup sugar*
    1   *teaspoon vanilla extract*
    ½   *to 1 cup finely chopped nuts*

Beat egg whites until stiff; add sugar and vanilla, and beat 2 to 3 minutes. Blend in nuts. Yield: 2½ to 3 cups.

Butter Frosting:

    2   *cups powdered sugar*
    ¼   *cup melted butter or margarine*
    ¼   *cup milk*
    ¼   *teaspoon salt*
    2   *teaspoons vanilla extract*
    1   *(3-ounce) package cream cheese
        (optional)*

Combine all ingredients, and beat thoroughly. Yield: about 2 cups.

Note: For variety, ½ cup of plumped raisins may be added to the filling, or a peeled apple wedge may be placed inside each Butterhorn. If desired, frosting may be tinted different colors.

Plaited White Bread

    1   *package dry yeast*
    2   *cups warm water (105° to 115°)*
    ⅓   *cup sugar*
    2   *teaspoons salt*
    1   *egg, well beaten*
    6 to 7 *cups all-purpose flour, divided*
    3   *tablespoons salad oil*

Combine yeast, warm water, sugar, salt, and egg in a large bowl; set aside 5 minutes. Gradually add 3 cups flour, beating well. Add salad oil and 3 to 4 cups flour to form a stiff dough.

Turn dough out on a floured surface, and knead until smooth and elastic (5 to 8 minutes). Place in a well-greased bowl, turning to grease top. Cover with plastic wrap. Let rise in a warm place (85°), free from drafts, 1½ to 2 hours or until doubled in bulk.

Punch dough down, and divide into thirds. Shape each third into a 14- to 16-inch rope. Place ropes on a greased baking sheet, and firmly pinch ends together at one end to seal. Braid ropes together (see photo), and pinch loose ends to seal.

Cover; let rise in a warm place, free from drafts, until doubled in bulk. Bake at 350° for 20 to 25 minutes or until lightly browned. Yield: 1 loaf.

Wheat Germ Bran Bread

    1   *cup milk, scalded*
    1   *cup water*
    6   *tablespoons honey or sorghum*
    6   *tablespoons salad oil*
    1   *tablespoon salt*
    2   *eggs*
    2   *packages dry yeast*
    ¼   *cup warm water (105° to 115°)*
    ½   *cup unprocessed bran*
    ½   *cup wheat germ*
    ½   *cup whole wheat flour*
    About 4 to 5 *cups unbleached flour*

Combine milk, 1 cup water, honey, oil, salt, and eggs in a large bowl; mix well. Dissolve yeast in ¼ cup warm water; add to milk mixture. Stir in bran, wheat germ, and whole wheat flour; mix well. Stir in enough unbleached flour to make a soft dough.

Turn dough out on a floured surface, and knead about 10 minutes or until smooth and elastic. Place dough in a greased bowl, turning to grease top. Cover with a damp towel. Let rise in a warm place, free from drafts, 1½ to 2 hours or until doubled in bulk.

Divide dough in half, and place on a floured surface. Roll each half into an 8- x 18-inch rectangle. Roll up, beginning at narrow edge; as you roll the dough, press firmly to eliminate air pockets. Pinch seams and ends together firmly to seal. Place dough, seam side down, in 2 well-greased 9- x 5- x 3-inch loafpans.

Cover and let rise until doubled in bulk. Bake at 350° for about 30 minutes or until loaves sound hollow when tapped. Remove from pans, and cool on wire racks. Yield: 2 loaves.

Cakes and Frostings

The good thing about cakes is that you don't need to have a reason to bake them. Of course, there are always birthday cakes, wedding cakes, and fruit-cakes, but more often cakes are baked "just in case company drops in" or just because someone "feels like it."

One of the most popular cakes in the South is the pound cake. Originally made with a pound each of butter, flour, eggs, and sugar, this fine-textured cake can be flavored with everything from nuts and spices to fruits and chocolate. However, the plain butter version is hard to beat.

Cupcakes, tube cakes, layer cakes, and loaf cakes—we have them in every flavor imaginable. Bake one for your next dessert party, birthday, or covered-dish dinner. Or bake one just because you feel like it.

Apricot Refrigerator Cake

  1 *(6-ounce) package dried apricots*
  2 *cups water*
  1 *cup butter or margarine, softened*
  2 *cups sifted powdered sugar*
  4 *eggs, separated*
Juice and grated rind of 1 lemon
  ¾ *cup sugar*
  3 *dozen ladyfingers, split*
Whipped cream
Toasted coconut

Combine apricots and water in a saucepan; cook, uncovered, until apricots are tender (about 20 minutes). Puree apricots in electric blender, or press through a sieve (there should be about 1½ cups pulp); cool.

Cream butter and powdered sugar until light and fluffy; add egg yolks, and beat well. Add apricot pulp, lemon juice, and lemon rind; mix well.

Beat egg whites until stiff, gradually adding ¾ cup sugar; fold into apricot mixture. Line bottom and sides of a 9- or 10-inch springform pan with ladyfingers. Spoon one-third of apricot mixture over ladyfingers, and top with another layer of ladyfingers; repeat layers, and top with remaining third of apricot mixture. Chill overnight.

Remove sides of pan. Garnish cake with whipped cream and toasted coconut. Yield: 10 to 12 servings.

Apricot Cake

  2 *cups sugar*
  2 *cups self-rising flour*
  3 *eggs*
  1 *(7¾-ounce) jar apricot baby food*
  1 *cup salad oil*
  1 *teaspoon ground cinnamon*
  1 *teaspoon ground allspice*
  1 *cup chopped pecans*

Combine all ingredients in a large mixing bowl; mix until well blended. Pour into a well-greased and floured 10-inch tube pan or Bundt pan. Bake at 350° for 1 hour or until done. Yield: one 10-inch cake.

Traditional desserts like these highlight a Southern Christmas: (clockwise from top) Holiday Coconut Cake (page 64), Tipsy Cake (page 70), Charlotte Russe (page 115), Ambrosia (page 112), and Kentucky Bourbon Cake (page 80).

Angel Food Cake

13   *egg whites*
¼   *teaspoon salt*
1½   *teaspoons cream of tartar*
2   *cups sugar*
1½   *cups sifted cake flour*
½   *teaspoon almond extract*
1   *teaspoon vanilla extract*

Beat egg whites and salt until foamy. Add cream of tartar; beat until stiff, but still moist.

Sift sugar and flour separately seven times each. Lightly fold sugar into egg whites. Carefully fold in flour. Add almond and vanilla extracts.

Spoon batter into an ungreased 10-inch tube pan. Bake at 325° for 50 minutes. Invert cake; cool 1 hour or until completely cold. Yield: one 10-inch cake.

Banana-Nut Cake

1   *cup shortening*
3   *cups sugar*
4   *eggs*
¼   *cup buttermilk*
2   *tablespoons vanilla extract*
3   *cups all-purpose flour*
1½   *teaspoons soda*
¼   *teaspoon salt*
6   *small or 4 large bananas, mashed*
1½   *cups chopped pecans*

Cream shortening and sugar until light and fluffy. Add eggs, one at a time, beating well after each addition. Add buttermilk and vanilla; blend thoroughly until smooth.

Combine flour, soda, and salt; add to creamed mixture. Add bananas and pecans, mixing just until blended.

Spoon batter into a greased and floured 10-inch tube pan. Bake at 325° for 1 hour and 30 minutes or until cake tests done. Yield: one 10-inch cake.

Banana Split Cake

1   *cup margarine, divided*
1½   *cups graham cracker crumbs*
2   *cups powdered sugar*
2   *eggs*
1   *teaspoon vanilla extract*
3   *or 4 bananas, sliced*
1   *(20-ounce) can crushed pineapple, drained*
1   *(9-ounce) carton frozen whipped topping, thawed*
½   *cup chopped pecans or walnuts*

Melt ½ cup margarine, and add to graham cracker crumbs. Mix well, and pat into a 13- x 9- x 2-inch pan.

Combine sugar, eggs, ½ cup softened margarine, and vanilla; beat until smooth and creamy. Spread over graham cracker crust. Add a layer of banana slices and pineapple; spread whipped topping evenly over fruit. Sprinkle with nuts. Refrigerate until set. Yield: 12 to 15 servings.

Blueberry Cake

1   *cup butter or margarine, softened*
2   *cups sugar*
3   *eggs*
3   *cups all-purpose flour*
1½   *teaspoons baking powder*
⅛   *teaspoon salt*
¼   *teaspoon mace*
½   *cup milk*
2   *cups blueberries*
2   *teaspoons sugar*
2   *teaspoons all-purpose flour*

Cream butter and 2 cups sugar until light and fluffy. Add eggs, one at a time, beating well after each addition. Combine next 4 ingredients; add to creamed mixture alternately with milk, beating well after each addition.

Coat blueberries with 2 teaspoons sugar and 2 teaspoons flour; fold into batter. Pour into a greased and floured 10-inch tube pan or Bundt pan. Bake at 350° for 70 to 80 minutes. Yield: one 10-inch cake.

Filled Carrot Cake

    2 *cups sugar*
    3 *cups all-purpose flour*
    1 *teaspoon soda*
    ¼ *teaspoon salt*
    2 *teaspoons ground cinnamon*
    1½ *cups buttery-flavored salad oil*
    1 *teaspoon vanilla extract*
    3 *eggs, beaten*
    1 *cup crushed pineapple, well drained*
    1¾ *cups grated raw carrots*
    ¼ *cup peeled, grated apple*
    1 *cup chopped pecans*
       Frosting

Combine sugar, flour, soda, salt, and cinnamon; set aside. Combine oil, vanilla, eggs, pineapple, carrots, and apple; beat well. Stir in dry ingredients and pecans.

Spoon batter into 3 greased 8-inch cake-pans. Bake at 350° for 25 to 30 minutes. Cool 10 minutes in pans; remove from pans, and cool completely. Spread Frosting between layers and on top and sides of cake. Yield: one 3-layer cake.

Frosting:

    ½ *cup butter or margarine, softened*
    1 *(8-ounce) package cream cheese, softened*
    1 *(16-ounce) package powdered sugar*
    1 *cup chopped pecans*

Combine butter and cream cheese; cream until light and fluffy. Add sugar, mixing well. Stir in pecans. Yield: enough frosting for one 3-layer cake.

Carrot Cake

    4 *eggs, beaten*
    1¼ *cups salad oil*
    2 *cups grated raw carrots*
    3 *cups all-purpose flour*
    3 *teaspoons baking powder*
    2 *teaspoons soda*
    2 *teaspoons ground cinnamon*
    ½ *teaspoon salt*
    2 *cups sugar*
    ½ *cup chopped pecans*

Combine eggs and oil, mixing well; stir in carrots and set aside. Sift dry ingredients three times. Add to carrot mixture gradually, mixing well. Stir in pecans.

Pour batter into a greased 10-inch tube pan. Bake at 350° for 65 to 75 minutes. Yield: one 10-inch cake.

Peanut Butter Cupcakes

    ½ *cup chunky peanut butter*
    ⅓ *cup butter or margarine, softened*
    1½ *cups firmly packed brown sugar*
    2 *eggs*
    1 *teaspoon vanilla extract*
    2 *cups all-purpose flour*
    2 *teaspoons baking powder*
    ½ *teaspoon salt*
    ¼ *teaspoon ground cinnamon*
    ¾ *cup milk*
       Peanut Butter Frosting
       Finely chopped peanuts

Combine peanut butter and butter; beat until creamy. Add brown sugar, and mix well. Add eggs, one at a time, beating well after each addition. Stir in vanilla.

Combine dry ingredients; add to peanut butter mixture alternately with milk, beginning and ending with dry ingredients. Beat mixture well after each addition.

Spoon batter into lightly greased muffin cups, filling two-thirds full. Bake at 350° for 20 minutes. Remove from pan to cool. Frost with Peanut Butter Frosting, and sprinkle with chopped peanuts. Yield: about 20 cupcakes.

Peanut Butter Frosting:

    ⅓ *cup chunky peanut butter*
    2 *cups sifted powdered sugar*
    1 *teaspoon vanilla extract*
    2 *teaspoons honey*
    4 *to 5 tablespoons milk*

Combine all ingredients, and beat at low speed of electric mixer until light and fluffy. Add 1 more tablespoon milk, if needed, to make spreading consistency. Yield: enough frosting for 20 cupcakes.

Chess Cake

    ½ cup butter or margarine
    1 (1-pound) package light brown sugar
    1 cup sugar
    4 eggs, separated
    2 cups all-purpose flour, divided
    2 teaspoons baking powder
    ¼ teaspoon salt
    1 teaspoon vanilla extract
    1 cup chopped pecans

Melt butter; cool. Blend in sugar, beaten egg yolks, 1½ cups flour, baking powder, salt, and vanilla. Combine remaining flour and pecans; stir into sugar mixture. Beat egg whites until soft peaks form; fold into batter.

Spoon batter into a lightly greased and floured 13- x 9- x 2-inch pan. Bake at 325° for 45 minutes. Cut in squares to serve. Yield: 18 to 20 servings.

★
Holiday Coconut Cake

    ⅓ cup shortening
    ⅓ cup butter, softened
    1¾ cups sugar
    3 cups cake flour
    3½ teaspoons baking powder
    ¾ teaspoon salt
    1⅓ cups milk
    2 teaspoons vanilla extract
    4 egg whites
    Lemon Filling
    Fluffy Frosting
    Freshly grated coconut

Cream shortening, butter, and sugar until light and fluffy. Sift together flour, baking powder, and salt; add to creamed mixture alternately with milk, beating well after each addition. Stir in vanilla. Beat egg whites until stiff, and fold into batter.

Pour batter into 3 greased and floured 8-inch cakepans; bake at 350° for 30 minutes. Cool completely. Spread Lemon Filling between layers. Frost top and sides of cake with Fluffy Frosting, and sprinkle with coconut. Yield: one 8-inch layer cake.

Lemon Filling:

    1 cup plus 2 tablespoons sugar
    ¼ cup cornstarch
    1 cup plus 2 tablespoons water
    2 egg yolks, slightly beaten
    2 tablespoons butter
    3 tablespoons lemon juice
    1 tablespoon grated lemon rind

Combine sugar and cornstarch; gradually stir in water. Cook over medium heat, stirring constantly, until mixture thickens and boils. Boil 1 minute.

Slowly stir a small amount of the hot mixture into egg yolks; add to hot mixture in saucepan. Boil 1 minute longer, stirring constantly. Remove from heat and continue stirring until smooth. Stir in butter, lemon juice, and rind. Cool. Yield: about 2 cups.

Fluffy Frosting:

    1 cup sugar
    ⅓ cup water
    ¼ teaspoon cream of tartar
    2 egg whites
    ½ teaspoon vanilla extract
    ½ teaspoon almond extract

Combine sugar, water, and cream of tartar in a heavy saucepan. Cook over low heat without stirring until syrup spins a 6- to 8-inch thread.

Beat egg whites until soft peaks form. Continue to beat egg whites, and slowly pour in syrup mixture. Add flavorings; beat well. Yield: enough frosting for one 8-inch cake.

Cherry Snow Valentine Cake

    2 cups sifted cake flour
    1¼ cups sugar
    3½ teaspoons baking powder
    1 teaspoon salt
    ½ cup shortening
    ⅞ cup pineapple juice
    1½ teaspoons almond extract
    1 teaspoon vanilla extract
    3 egg whites, unbeaten
    Cherry-Almond Frosting

Combine flour, sugar, baking powder, and salt in a mixing bowl. Add shortening, pineapple juice, and flavorings; beat 2 minutes at low speed of electric mixer. Scrape bowl. Add egg whites, and beat 2 minutes on high speed.

Spoon batter into 2 greased and lightly floured 8-inch cakepans. Bake at 350° for 25 to 30 minutes or until cake tests done. Chill layers completely; then split each. Spread Cherry-Almond Frosting between layers and on sides and top of cake. Chill before serving. Store in refrigerator. Yield: one 8-inch layer cake.

Cherry-Almond Frosting:

    1 *envelope unflavored gelatin*
   ¼ *cup cool water*
    1 *(8-ounce) jar maraschino cherries,*
          undrained and finely chopped
   ½ *cup sugar*
   ⅛ *teaspoon salt*
   ⅓ *cup finely chopped blanched almonds*
   ½ *teaspoon almond extract*
   ¼ *teaspoon vanilla extract*
    1 *pint whipping cream, whipped*

Place gelatin and water in top of double boiler; let stand 5 minutes. Place over boiling water, and stir until gelatin is completely dissolved. Remove from heat; add cherries, sugar, and salt. Chill until slightly thickened.

Stir nuts and flavorings into gelatin mixture; fold in whipped cream. Yield: about 4 cups.

Fresh Pear Cake

    2 *cups sugar*
    3 *eggs, well beaten*
   1½ *cups salad oil*
    3 *cups all-purpose flour*
    1 *teaspoon soda*
    1 *teaspoon salt*
    1 *teaspoon vanilla extract*
    2 *teaspoons ground cinnamon*
    3 *cups thinly sliced, peeled pears*
       Powdered Sugar Glaze

Combine sugar, eggs, and oil; beat well. Combine flour, soda, and salt; add to sugar

mixture, 1 cup at a time, mixing well after each addition. Stir in vanilla, cinnamon, and pears.

Spoon batter into a well-greased 10-inch Bundt pan or tube pan. Bake at 350° for 1 hour. Remove from pan, and allow to cool; top with Powdered Sugar Glaze. Yield: one 10-inch cake.

Powdered Sugar Glaze:

   1¼ *cups sifted powdered sugar*
     2 *to 4 tablespoons milk*

Combine ingredients, blending until smooth. Yield: about ½ cup.

Fig Cake

   ½ *cup butter or margarine, softened*
    1 *cup sugar*
    3 *eggs*
   ½ *teaspoon vanilla extract*
    2 *cups all-purpose flour*
    1 *teaspoon soda*
    1 *teaspoon ground cinnamon*
    1 *teaspoon ground nutmeg*
    1 *teaspoon ground cloves or allspice*
    1 *cup buttermilk*
   1½ *cups fig preserves with juice, chopped*
   ½ *cup chopped nuts*
   ½ *cup coconut (optional)*
    1 *cup raisins (optional)*

Cream butter and sugar until light and fluffy; add eggs, one at a time, beating well after each addition. Stir in vanilla.

Combine flour, soda, and spices; add to creamed mixture alternately with buttermilk, mixing well after each addition. Stir in figs and nuts; add coconut and raisins, if desired.

Spoon batter into a greased and floured 10-inch tube pan or Bundt pan. Bake at 350° for 50 minutes or until done. Yield: one 10-inch cake.

Maple-Flavored Gingerbread

2½   cups all-purpose flour
1½   teaspoons soda
  1   teaspoon ground cinnamon
  1   teaspoon ground ginger
  ½   teaspoon ground cloves
  ½   teaspoon salt
  ½   cup shortening
  ½   cup sugar
  1   egg
  ½   cup molasses
  ½   cup maple-flavored syrup
  1   cup hot water
     Whipped cream

Combine flour, soda, spices, and salt; set aside. Cream shortening and sugar until light and fluffy. Add egg, beating well. Gradually beat in molasses and syrup. Add dry ingredients alternately with hot water, beating well after each addition.

Pour batter into a greased 13- x 9- x 2-inch pan. Bake at 350° for 30 minutes or until done. Cool thoroughly in pan. Serve with whipped cream. Yield: 16 servings.

Soft Gingerbread

  1   cup sugar
  1   cup dark molasses
  ½   cup butter or margarine, softened
  1   cup boiling water
  3   cups all-purpose flour
  1   teaspoon ground ginger
  1   teaspoon ground cinnamon
  1   teaspoon ground cloves
  2   teaspoons soda
  2   eggs, well beaten

Cream sugar, molasses, and butter until fairly smooth. Stir in boiling water. Combine dry ingredients; add to molasses mixture gradually, blending well after each addition. Stir in eggs.

Spoon batter into a greased 13- x 9- x 2-inch baking pan. Bake at 350° for 35 to 45 minutes or until gingerbread tests done. Yield: 16 servings.

Honey Spice Cake

  1   cup honey
  1   cup sugar
  2   cups raisins
2½   cups water
  1   cup shortening
1½   teaspoons ground cinnamon
1½   teaspoons ground cloves
  1   teaspoon salt
  3   cups all-purpose flour
  2   teaspoons soda
     Topping

Combine honey, sugar, raisins, water, shortening, spices, and salt in a medium saucepan. Bring to a boil; boil 3 minutes. Cool. Stir in flour and soda, blending well.

Pour batter into a greased 12- x 8- x 1¾-inch pan. Bake at 350° for 1 hour or until done. Spread Topping over cake; broil cake 3 minutes or until coconut is toasted. Yield: 12 (3-inch-square) servings.

Topping:

  ⅓   cup butter or margarine, melted
  ⅓   cup honey
  ⅓   cup firmly packed brown sugar
  ½   cup chopped pecans
  ½   cup coconut

Combine all ingredients in a small saucepan; heat through. Cool 5 minutes. Spread on hot cake. Yield: about 1½ cups.

Mincemeat Cake

  1   (28-ounce) jar mincemeat
  1   (15-ounce) box raisins
  2   cups chopped pecans
  1   tablespoon vanilla extract
  ½   cup butter or margarine, melted
  2   cups sugar
  3   eggs, separated
1½   teaspoons soda
  ¼   cup water
  3   cups all-purpose flour

Combine mincemeat, raisins, pecans, and vanilla; set aside. Combine butter, sugar, and egg yolks; beat well. Dissolve soda in water, and add to butter mixture. Stir in flour and mincemeat mixture. Beat egg whites until stiff; fold into mincemeat mixture.

Line bottom of a 10-inch tube pan with heavy brown paper; grease paper and sides of pan. Spoon mixture into pan. Bake at 275° for 2 hours and 10 minutes or until cake tests done.

Cool cake slightly; remove from pan and remove paper. Cool thoroughly. Wrap in aluminum foil and store in a cool place several weeks. Yield: one 10-inch cake.

Molasses Pudding Cake

2¼ cups all-purpose flour
¾ cup sugar
1½ teaspoons ground cinnamon
¾ teaspoon ground nutmeg
¼ teaspoon salt
⅓ cup butter or margarine, softened
¾ cup molasses
1½ cups water
1 teaspoon soda
Orange Sauce

Combine flour, sugar, cinnamon, nutmeg, and salt; cut in butter with a pastry blender until mixture resembles coarse meal. Pat 1 cup of mixture in a greased 8-inch square pan; set aside.

Combine molasses, water, and soda; spoon half over mixture in baking pan. Sprinkle 1 cup remaining flour mixture over liquid. Spoon on remaining molasses mixture, then remaining flour mixture.

Use a fork to cut gently through batter in a wide, zigzag course, creating a marbled effect; be careful not to disturb bottom crumb layer. Bake at 350° for 50 minutes or until top is set. Serve with Orange Sauce. Yield: about 8 servings.

Orange Sauce:

½ cup sugar
1 tablespoon cornstarch
1 cup boiling water
2 tablespoons orange juice
¼ teaspoon grated orange peel

Combine sugar and cornstarch in a saucepan; blend well. Stir in remaining ingredients. Cook over medium heat, stirring constantly, until thickened. Yield: about 1¼ cups.

★
Sweet Potato Cake

1½ cups salad oil
2 cups sugar
4 eggs, separated
4 tablespoons hot water
2½ cups sifted cake flour
3 teaspoons baking powder
¼ teaspoon salt
1 teaspoon ground cinnamon
1 teaspoon ground nutmeg
1½ cups grated raw sweet potato
1 cup chopped pecans
1 teaspoon vanilla extract
Coconut Filling

Combine oil and sugar in a large mixing bowl; beat until smooth. Add egg yolks; beat well. Stir in hot water. Combine dry ingredients; blend into sugar mixture. Stir in potato, pecans, and vanilla, blending thoroughly. Beat egg whites until stiff; fold into batter.

Spoon mixture into three greased 8-inch cakepans. Bake at 350° for 25 to 30 minutes. Remove from pans; cool on wire racks. Spread Coconut Filling between layers and on top of cake. Yield: one 8-inch layer cake.

Coconut Filling:

1 (13-ounce) can evaporated milk
1 cup sugar
½ cup butter or margarine
3 tablespoons all-purpose flour
1 teaspoon vanilla extract
1 (3½-ounce) can or 1⅓ cups flaked coconut

Combine milk, sugar, butter, flour, and vanilla in a saucepan. Cook, stirring constantly, over medium heat until thickened, about 12 minutes. Remove from heat; stir in coconut. Beat until thickened and cooled. Yield: enough filling to fill and top one 8-inch layer cake.

Pumpkin Cupcakes

   1   *cup all-purpose flour*
   2   *teaspoons baking powder*
   ¼   *teaspoon salt*
   ½   *teaspoon ground cinnamon*
   ⅛   *teaspoon ground cloves*
   ¼   *cup shortening*
   ⅔   *cup sugar*
   1   *egg*
   ½   *cup cooked, mashed pumpkin*
   2   *tablespoons milk*
       Lemon Glaze

Combine first 10 ingredients in a bowl; mix well. Spoon into greased muffin cups, filling about two-thirds full. Bake at 350° about 30 minutes. Cool 5 minutes; drizzle with Lemon Glaze. Serve warm. Yield: 10 to 12 cupcakes.

Lemon Glaze:

   1½   *tablespoons melted butter or margarine*
   ½   *cup powdered sugar*
        About 1 tablespoon lemon juice
   ⅛   *teaspoon grated lemon peel*

Combine butter and powdered sugar; add lemon juice, stirring until smooth. Add more lemon juice, if needed, to make proper consistency. Stir in lemon peel. Yield: enough glaze for 10 to 12 cupcakes.

Fresh Orange Cake

   2¼   *cups cake flour*
   1½   *cups sugar*
   2   *teaspoons baking powder*
   ¼   *teaspoon soda*
   1   *teaspoon salt*
   ½   *cup melted butter or margarine*
        Grated rind of 1 orange
   ⅔   *cup milk*
   ⅓   *cup fresh orange juice*
   2   *eggs*
   1   *(16½-ounce) can lemon frosting*
        Orange slices
        Additional grated orange rind

Combine dry ingredients; set aside. Combine butter, rind of 1 orange, milk, and orange juice. Add 1 cup liquid mixture to dry ingredients; beat 2 minutes at medium speed of mixer. Add remaining liquid and eggs; beat 2 minutes.

Spoon batter into 2 greased and floured 9-inch cakepans. Bake at 350° for 30 minutes. Cool and frost with lemon frosting. Garnish with orange slices and grated orange rind. Yield: one 9-inch cake.

Old-Fashioned Jellyroll

   ¾   *teaspoon baking powder*
   ¼   *teaspoon salt*
   4   *eggs (at room temperature)*
   ¾   *cup sugar*
   ¾   *cup all-purpose flour*
   1   *teaspoon vanilla extract*
       Powdered sugar
   1   *cup jelly (any flavor)*

Grease a 15- x 10- x 1-inch pan; line with waxed paper, and grease lightly.

Combine baking powder, salt, and eggs in a mixing bowl. Beat at medium speed of electric mixer until well mixed. Add sugar gradually, beating until thick and light colored; fold in flour and vanilla.

Spread batter evenly in prepared pan. Bake at 400° for 13 minutes or until cake springs back when gently pressed.

Sift powdered sugar in a 15- x 10-inch rectangle on a linen towel. Turn cake out on sugar, and peel off waxed paper. Trim off crisp edges of cake, if necessary.

Starting at narrow end, roll up cake and towel together. Cool on wire rack, seam side down.

Unroll cake; spread with jelly, and reroll. Place seam side down on serving plate; sprinkle with additional powdered sugar, if desired. Yield: 8 to 10 servings.

Pumpkin Roll

3 *eggs*
1 *cup sugar*
⅔ *cup cooked, mashed pumpkin*
1 *teaspoon lemon juice*
¾ *cup all-purpose flour*
2 *teaspoons ground cinnamon*
1 *teaspoon baking powder*
½ *teaspoon salt*
1 *teaspoon ground ginger*
1 *teaspoon ground nutmeg*
1¼ *cups powdered sugar, divided*
1 *(8-ounce) package cream cheese,*
   softened
¼ *cup butter or margarine, softened*
½ *teaspoon vanilla extract*

Beat eggs 5 minutes at high speed of electric mixer. Gradually add sugar, beating well. Stir in pumpkin and lemon juice.

Combine flour, cinnamon, baking powder, salt, ginger, and nutmeg; add to pumpkin mixture, and blend well. Spoon batter into a greased and floured 15- x 10- x 1-inch jellyroll pan, spreading evenly to corners. Bake at 375° for 15 minutes.

Turn cake out onto a towel sprinkled with ¼ cup powdered sugar. Beginning at narrow end, roll up cake and towel together, jellyroll fashion; cool.

Combine 1 cup powdered sugar, cream cheese, butter, and vanilla; beat until smooth and creamy. Unroll cake, and spread with filling. Roll cake up again; chill, seam side down. Yield: about 10 servings.

Surprise Cupcakes

½ *cup butter or margarine, softened*
6 *tablespoons sugar*
6 *tablespoons brown sugar*
½ *teaspoon vanilla extract*
1 *egg*
1 *cup plus 2 tablespoons all-purpose flour*
½ *teaspoon salt*
½ *teaspoon soda*
Surprise Topping

Cream butter and sugar until light and fluffy; add vanilla and egg, beating well. Combine flour, salt, and soda; add to creamed mixture, blending well.

Spoon 1 rounded tablespoonful of batter into each of 16 paper-lined muffin tins. Bake at 375° for 10 to 12 minutes; remove from oven. Prepare Surprise Topping, and spoon 1 rounded tablespoonful over each cupcake; return to oven, and bake 15 minutes longer. Cool in pan 10 minutes; remove to wire rack to complete cooling. Yield: 16 cupcakes.

Surprise Topping:

½ *cup firmly packed brown sugar*
1 *egg*
⅛ *teaspoon salt*
½ *teaspoon vanilla extract*
1 *(6-ounce) package semisweet chocolate*
   morsels
½ *cup chopped nuts*

Combine brown sugar, egg, salt, and vanilla; beat until smooth and thick. Fold in chocolate morsels and nuts. Yield: topping for 16 cupcakes.

Chocolate Nut Cupcakes

⅓ *cup shortening*
1 *cup sugar*
1 *egg*
2 *cups all-purpose flour*
½ *teaspoon salt*
2½ *teaspoons baking powder*
¾ *cup milk*
1 *teaspoon vanilla extract*
1 *(6-ounce) package semisweet chocolate*
   morsels
½ *cup chopped walnuts*
1 *(16½-ounce) can milk chocolate frosting*

Cream shortening and sugar until light and fluffy; add egg, beating well. Combine flour, salt, and baking powder; add to creamed mixture, and mix well. Add milk, vanilla, chocolate morsels, and nuts; mix well.

Spoon batter into lightly greased muffin cups, filling two-thirds full. Bake at 375° for 20 minutes. Remove from pan; cool. Frost with chocolate frosting. Yield: 1½ dozen cupcakes.

Whole Wheat Spice Cake

    1   cup boiling water
    1   cup quick-cooking oats
    ½   cup butter or margarine, softened
    1   cup honey
    2   eggs, well beaten
    1   cup whole wheat flour
    ½   cup all-purpose flour
    2   teaspoons baking powder
    ½   teaspoon salt
    ½   teaspoon ground cloves
    2   teaspoons ground cinnamon
    ¼   cup instant whole wheat cereal
    ¼   cup sesame seeds
    ¾   cup raisins
    1   cup chopped dates
    1   cup chopped pecans
    1   (14-ounce) can sweetened condensed
        milk
    1   (6-ounce) package semisweet chocolate
        morsels

Combine boiling water and oats; set aside for 25 minutes. Cream butter and honey until smooth; add eggs and oats, mixing well. Stir in flour, baking powder, salt, cloves, cinnamon, cereal, sesame seeds, raisins, and dates.

Pour mixture into a greased 13- x 9- x 2-inch pan. Bake at 350° for 35 minutes or until done. Combine pecans, condensed milk, and chocolate morsels; spread over hot cake. Return to oven 8 minutes. Cool. Yield: about 15 servings.

Tipsy Cake

    6   eggs, separated
    1½   cups sugar, divided
    1   teaspoon vanilla extract
    1½   cups all-purpose flour
    1½   teaspoons baking powder
    ½   teaspoon salt
    4½   tablespoons cold water
    2   cups sherry
    1   cup apple jelly, divided
    1¼   cups sliced almonds, toasted
          Custard
          Whipped Cream Frosting

Beat egg yolks until light; gradually add ¾ cup sugar, beating until thick and lemon colored. Add vanilla.

Combine flour, baking powder, and salt; add to egg mixture alternately with water, mixing well.

Beat egg whites until foamy; gradually add remaining ¾ cup sugar, beating until stiff peaks form. Fold egg whites into cake batter until thoroughly mixed.

Pour cake batter slowly into an ungreased 10-inch tube pan; bake at 350° for 25 to 30 minutes. When cake is golden brown and begins to pull away from sides of pan, test for doneness with a toothpick. When cake is done, invert pan on a wire rack and let cool completely; then remove from pan.

Split cake into 2 layers; place each layer on a platter. Drizzle 1 cup sherry over each layer; cover loosely with waxed paper and let sit for 1 day.

Next day, spread bottom layer of cake with ½ cup apple jelly and sprinkle with ½ cup almonds; top with a layer of Custard. Place top layer of cake on top, and repeat layers of jelly, almonds, and Custard. Cover cake with plastic wrap and refrigerate 1 more day.

When ready to serve, frost cake with Whipped Cream Frosting, and sprinkle with remaining ¼ cup almonds. If desired, serve with any remaining Custard and Whipped Cream Frosting. Cake will keep up to 1 week when stored in refrigerator. Yield: about 20 servings.

Custard:

    1½   cups sugar
    ¼   cup all-purpose flour
    ⅛   teaspoon salt
    6   eggs, beaten
    1   quart milk, scalded
    2   teaspoons vanilla extract

Combine sugar, flour, and salt in top of double boiler; add eggs and beat well. Gradually add milk, stirring constantly, until well blended. Place over boiling water and cook, stirring constantly, until mixture thickens and coats spoon.

Remove from heat and cool; stir in vanilla. If custard is not smooth, strain through a sieve or process in blender. Chill thoroughly. Yield: about 6 cups.

Whipped Cream Frosting:

1 pint whipping cream
3 tablespoons sugar
2 teaspoons vanilla extract

Whip cream until it begins to thicken. Gradually add sugar and vanilla, and continue beating until stiff peaks form. Yield: about 4 cups.

★
Belgian Mocha Cake

2½ cups sugar, divided
3 tablespoons water
2 (1-ounce) squares unsweetened chocolate
¾ cup butter or margarine, softened
1 teaspoon vanilla extract
4 eggs, separated
2¼ cups sifted cake flour
½ teaspoon soda
½ teaspoon salt
1 cup milk
1 teaspoon cream of tartar
Mocha Frosting
Grated chocolate (optional)

Combine ½ cup sugar, water, and chocolate in a heavy saucepan; place over low heat, stirring until chocolate is melted. Remove from heat; cool.

Combine remaining 2 cups sugar and butter; beat until light and fluffy. Stir in vanilla. Add egg yolks, one at a time, beating well after each addition. Stir in chocolate mixture.

Combine flour, soda, and salt; add to creamed mixture alternately with milk, beating well after each addition. Beat egg whites until frothy; add cream of tartar, and beat until stiff peaks form. Fold into batter.

Grease three 9-inch or four 8-inch round cakepans; line with greased waxed paper, and dust with flour. Pour batter into prepared pans, and bake at 350° for 25 to 30

minutes. Cool thoroughly on wire racks. Spread Mocha Frosting between layers and on top and sides of cake. Store in refrigerator; may be frozen. If desired, garnish with grated chocolate before serving. Yield: 12 to 16 servings.

Mocha Frosting:

1½ cups butter, softened
2 to 2¼ cups powdered sugar, divided
1 tablespoon instant coffee powder
¾ teaspoon cocoa
¾ teaspoon hot water
2 egg yolks
1 to 1½ tablespoons almond extract
2 tablespoons rum

Cream butter and 1½ cups powdered sugar until light and fluffy. Combine coffee, cocoa, and water; stir into creamed mixture. Add egg yolks, and beat 5 minutes. Stir in almond extract and rum. Add enough of remaining sugar to make spreading consistency (frosting gets quite firm when refrigerated). Yield: enough for one 8- or 9-inch layer cake.

Cocoa Angel Food Cake

11 egg whites
⅛ teaspoon salt
1 teaspoon cream of tartar
1 cup minus 3 tablespoons all-purpose flour
3 tablespoons cocoa
1½ cups sugar
1 teaspoon vanilla extract

Combine egg whites and salt; beat until foamy. Add cream of tartar, and beat until stiff. Combine flour and cocoa; sift 3 times. Sift sugar 3 times. Fold sugar gently into egg whites with a spatula or whisk; fold in flour mixture and vanilla.

Pour batter into a 10-inch tube pan. Put into a cold oven; set temperature at 350°, and bake about 45 minutes. Invert pan to cool. Do not remove from pan until cake is cold. Yield: one 10-inch cake.

Chocolate-Beet Cake

2 *teaspoons lemon juice*
1 *cup grated cooked beets*
2½ *cups all-purpose flour*
1 *teaspoon salt*
2 *teaspoons soda*
2 *cups sugar*
½ *cup cocoa*
1¼ *cups melted butter or margarine*
4 *eggs, beaten*
2 *tablespoons honey*
½ *cup milk*
2 *teaspoons vanilla extract*
Cream Cheese Frosting

Sprinkle lemon juice over beets; set aside. Combine next 10 ingredients in a large mixing bowl; stir in beets. Beat 2 minutes at medium speed of electric mixer. Pour into a greased 13- x 9- x 2-inch pan. Bake at 350° for 40 minutes. Cool. Frost with Cream Cheese Frosting. Yield: 12 to 15 servings.

Cream Cheese Frosting:

2 *to 3 tablespoons half-and-half*
1 *(3-ounce) package cream cheese,*
   softened
1 *teaspoon vanilla extract*
Pinch of salt
1 *(1-pound) package powdered sugar*
Chopped pecans (optional)

Combine half-and-half, cream cheese, vanilla, and salt. Add powdered sugar, beating until fluffy. Spread over cooled cake. Sprinkle with chopped pecans, if desired. Yield: enough frosting for one 13- x 9- x 2-inch cake.

Mahogany Cake

1 *cup butter or margarine, softened*
2 *cups sugar*
4 *eggs*
4 *cups all-purpose flour*
1½ *cups buttermilk*
2 *teaspoons soda*
1 *cup chocolate syrup*
2 *teaspoons vanilla extract*
Frosting

Cream butter and sugar until light and fluffy. Add eggs, beating until well blended. Add next 5 ingredients; beat at medium speed of electric mixer until well blended and smooth.

Pour batter into a greased 10-inch tube pan. Bake at 350° for 50 to 60 minutes. Cool in pan 10 minutes; remove from pan and cool completely before frosting. Yield: one 10-inch cake.

Frosting:

2 *(1-ounce) squares unsweetened*
   chocolate
1 *cup boiling water*
1 *cup sugar*
3 *tablespoons plus 1 teaspoon cornstarch*
¼ *teaspoon salt*
3 *tablespoons butter or margarine*
1 *teaspoon vanilla extract*

Melt chocolate in boiling water in a heavy saucepan. Combine sugar, cornstarch, and salt; stir into chocolate mixture. Cook over medium heat, stirring constantly, until thickened. Remove from heat; stir in butter and vanilla. Cool to lukewarm, and spread on cake. Yield: about 1½ cups.

Surprise Chocolate Cream Cake

1 *(3⅛-ounce) package vanilla pudding*
   and pie filling
2 *cups milk*
2 *cups all-purpose flour*
1 *teaspoon soda*
1 *teaspoon baking powder*
½ *teaspoon salt*
½ *cup butter or margarine, softened*
1 *cup sugar*
2 *eggs*
2 *(1-ounce) squares unsweetened*
   chocolate, melted
1 *teaspoon vanilla extract*
¾ *cup buttermilk*
½ *cup chopped pecans*
Chocolate frosting or powdered sugar

Prepare pudding and milk according to package directions; cool completely. Set aside.

Combine flour, soda, baking powder, and salt, mixing well; set aside. Cream butter and sugar until light and fluffy; beat in eggs. Blend in chocolate and vanilla. Add flour alternately with buttermilk, beginning and ending with flour; beat well after each addition. Stir in pecans.

Spread half of batter into a greased 13- x 9- x 2-inch pan. Spoon pudding evenly over batter. Spread remaining batter over pudding. Bake at 350° for 40 minutes. Cool cake completely.

Frost with a chocolate frosting or sprinkle with powdered sugar. Yield: 12 to 15 servings.

Rainbow Ice Cream Cake

    1   *quart strawberry ice cream, softened*
    1   *quart pistachio ice cream, softened*
    1   *(18½-ounce) package chocolate cake mix*
    2   *envelopes whipped topping mix*
    1   *tablespoon light rum (optional)*

Line an 8-inch cakepan with plastic wrap, and quickly spread half the strawberry ice cream evenly over bottom; cover with plastic wrap, and quickly spread with half the pistachio ice cream. Repeat procedure with remaining ice cream. Freeze until firm.

Prepare cake mix according to package directions. Spoon batter into 3 well-greased and floured 8-inch cakepans. Bake at 350° for 15 to 20 minutes or until cake tests done. Cool.

Place serving plate in freezer to chill. Place 1 layer of cake on serving plate, and top with a layer of strawberry ice cream and a layer of pistachio ice cream; repeat procedure, and top with remaining layer of cake.

Prepare whipped topping mix according to package directions; add rum, if desired, beating well. Frost cake with whipped topping. Serve at once. Yield: one 8-inch cake.

Note: Ice cream layers may be prepared several days ahead. Cake can be assembled, without frosting, and stored in freezer. Frost just before serving.

Holiday Log Cake

    ¾   *teaspoon baking powder*
    ¼   *teaspoon salt*
    4   *eggs, at room temperature*
    ¾   *cup sugar*
    ¾   *cup all-purpose flour*
    ¼   *cup cocoa*
    1   *teaspoon vanilla extract*
    2   *to 3 tablespoons powdered sugar*
    1   *pint sweetened whipped cream*
    Chocolate Frosting

Grease a 15- x 10- x 1-inch pan; line with waxed paper and grease lightly. Set aside.

Combine baking powder, salt, and eggs in mixing bowl; beat at medium speed of electric mixer. Add sugar gradually, beating until thick and light colored. Fold in flour, cocoa, and vanilla.

Spread mixture evenly into prepared pan. Bake at 400° for 13 minutes or until surface springs back when gently pressed.

Sift 2 to 3 tablespoons powdered sugar in a 15- x 10-inch rectangle on a linen towel. Turn cake out on sugar; remove waxed paper from cake. Trim crisp edges, if necessary. Starting with the short end, carefully roll cake and towel, jellyroll fashion. Cool thoroughly on wire rack. Unroll; spread with whipped cream, and reroll. Chill. Frost with Chocolate Frosting. Yield: 8 to 10 servings.

    Chocolate Frosting:

    3   *(1-ounce) squares unsweetened
          chocolate*
    ¼   *cup butter or margarine*
    1   *tablespoon instant coffee powder*
    Dash of salt
    ⅓   *cup boiling water*
    About 2½ cups sifted powdered sugar
    Candied cherries

Melt chocolate in top of a double boiler; blend in butter, coffee, salt, and boiling water, stirring until smooth. Cool to lukewarm. Stir in about 2½ cups powdered sugar to make a spreading consistency. Spread frosting evenly over cake. Mark with tines of a fork to resemble bark of a tree. Decorate with candied cherries. Refrigerate until serving time. Yield: about 1½ cups.

★
Perfect Chocolate Cake

    1   cup cocoa
    2   cups boiling water
    1   cup butter or margarine, softened
    2½ cups sugar
    4   eggs
    1½ teaspoons vanilla extract
    2¾ cups all-purpose flour
    2   teaspoons soda
    ½   teaspoon baking powder
    ½   teaspoon salt
        Filling
        Frosting

Combine cocoa and boiling water, blending until smooth; set aside to cool.

Combine butter, sugar, eggs, and vanilla; beat at high speed of electric mixer until light and fluffy (about 5 minutes). Combine dry ingredients; add to sugar mixture alternately with cocoa mixture, beating at low speed of electric mixer and beginning and ending with dry ingredients. Do not overbeat.

Pour batter into 3 greased 9-inch cakepans. Bake at 350° for 25 to 30 minutes. Cool in pans 10 minutes; remove from pans, and cool completely. Put layers together with Filling, and spread Frosting over top and sides.

Serve at once, or refrigerate until needed. Yield: one 9-inch layer cake.

    Filling:

    ½   pint whipping cream
    ¼   cup powdered sugar
    1   teaspoon vanilla extract

Combine all ingredients in a bowl; whip until thick. Chill. Yield: about 2 cups.

    Frosting:

    1   (6-ounce) package semisweet chocolate
            morsels
    ½   cup half-and-half
    1   cup butter or margarine
    2½ cups powdered sugar

Combine chocolate morsels, half-and-half, and butter in a saucepan; place over medium heat, stirring until chocolate is melted. Remove from heat; blend in powdered sugar. Set saucepan in ice, and beat until frosting holds its shape. Yield: about 3 cups.

Super Fudge Cake

    1   (4-ounce) bar milk chocolate
    ½   cup boiling water
    1   cup butter or margarine, softened
    2   cups sugar
    4   eggs, separated
    1   teaspoon vanilla extract
    2½ cups all-purpose flour
    1   teaspoon soda
    ½   teaspoon salt
    1   cup buttermilk
        Chocolate Frosting

Combine chocolate and boiling water in a small bowl, stirring until melted; cool. Cream butter and sugar until light and fluffy. Add egg yolks, one at a time, beating well after each addition. Add chocolate mixture and vanilla; mix well.

Combine flour, soda, and salt; add to creamed mixture alternately with buttermilk, beating well after each addition. Fold in stiffly beaten egg whites.

Pour batter into 3 greased and floured 9-inch cakepans. Bake at 350° for 30 minutes or until done. Cool and frost with Chocolate Frosting. Yield: one 9-inch layer cake.

    Chocolate Frosting:

    ¾   cup butter or margarine
    2   cups sugar
    ½   cup cocoa
    ½   cup milk
    1   teaspoon vanilla extract

Melt butter over low heat in a medium saucepan; add sugar, cocoa, and milk. Cook, stirring constantly, until sugar dissolves. Bring to a boil over medium heat; boil 2 to 3 minutes. Remove from heat, and add vanilla. Cool completely; then beat until spreading consistency. Yield: enough for one 3-layer cake.

★
Milky Way Cake

      6 (1-ounce) chocolate-covered
           malt-caramel candy bars
      ½ cup butter or margarine
      2 cups sugar
      1 cup shortening
      4 eggs
   2½ cups all-purpose flour
      1 teaspoon salt
   1½ cups buttermilk
      ½ teaspoon soda
      1 teaspoon vanilla extract
         Chocolate-Marshmallow Frosting

Combine candy bars and butter in a heavy saucepan; place over low heat until melted, stirring constantly.

Combine sugar and shortening; beat until creamy. Add eggs, and continue beating until light and fluffy. Combine flour and salt; combine buttermilk and soda. Add dry ingredients to creamed mixture alternately with buttermilk mixture, beating well after each addition. Stir in vanilla and candy bar mixture.

Pour batter into 3 greased and floured 9-inch cakepans. Bake at 350° for 30 minutes or until done. When layers are completely cool, frost with Chocolate-Marshmallow Frosting. Yield: one 3-layer cake.

Chocolate-Marshmallow Frosting:

      2 cups sugar
      1 (13-ounce) can evaporated milk
      ½ cup butter or margarine
      1 (6-ounce) package semisweet chocolate
           pieces
      1 cup marshmallow cream

Combine sugar, milk, and butter in a heavy saucepan; cook over medium heat until a small amount dropped in cold water forms a soft ball. Remove from heat, and add chocolate pieces and marshmallow cream; stir until melted. Yield: enough frosting for one 2-layer cake.

Japanese Fruitcake

      1 cup butter or margarine, softened
      2 cups sugar
      4 eggs
      3 cups all-purpose flour
      1 tablespoon baking powder
      1 teaspoon ground cloves
      1 teaspoon ground allspice
      1 teaspoon ground cinnamon
      1 cup milk
      1 pound chopped candied fruit
      ½ cup raisins
      ½ cup chopped nuts
         Coconut Filling

Cream butter and sugar until light and fluffy. Add eggs, one at a time, beating well after each addition. Combine flour, baking powder, and spices. Add to creamed mixture alternately with milk; beat well after each addition. Add fruits and nuts; mix well.

Pour batter into 4 greased and floured 9-inch cakepans; bake at 325° for 25 to 30 minutes or until cake tests done. Cool completely. Spread Coconut Filling between layers and on top of cake. Yield: one 9-inch layer cake.

Coconut Filling:

      3 cups sugar
      2 tablespoons all-purpose flour
   1½ cups milk
         Juice and grated rind of 3 lemons
      1 fresh coconut, grated, or 2 cups flaked
           coconut

Combine sugar and flour in a saucepan; gradually stir in milk. Bring mixture to a boil; cook, stirring constantly, until thickened. Remove from heat, and stir in lemon juice, lemon rind, and coconut. Cool completely before spreading on cake. Yield: enough filling for four 9-inch layers.

★
Light Fruitcake

1½ cups butter, softened
1½ cups sugar
 1 tablespoon vanilla extract
 1 tablespoon lemon extract
 7 eggs, separated and at room
     temperature
 3 cups all-purpose flour
1½ pounds (about 3 cups) candied yellow,
     green, and red pineapple
 1 pound (about 2 cups) candied red and
     green cherries
 ¼ pound (about ½ cup) candied citron
 ½ pound (about 1½ cups) golden raisins
 3 cups pecan halves
 1 cup black walnuts, coarsely chopped
 ½ cup all-purpose flour
    Additional candied fruit and nuts
 ¼ cup brandy
    Additional brandy

Make a liner for a 10-inch tube pan by draw-ing a circle with an 18-inch diameter on a piece of brown paper. Cut out circle; set pan in center, and draw around base of pan and inside tube. Fold circle into eighths, having the drawn lines on the outside.

Cut off tip end of circle along inside drawn line. Unfold paper; cut along folds to the outside drawn line. From another piece of brown paper, cut another circle with a 10-inch diameter; grease and set aside. Place the 18-inch liner in pan; grease and set aside.

Cream butter and sugar until light and fluffy. Stir in flavorings. Beat egg yolks. Al-ternately add egg yolks and 3 cups flour to creamed mixture.

Combine candied fruit, raisins, and nuts in a large mixing bowl; dredge with ½ cup flour, stirring to coat well. Stir mixture into batter. Beat egg whites until stiff; then fold into bat-ter.

Spoon batter into prepared pan. Arrange additional fruit and nuts on top, if desired. Cover pan with greased 10-inch brown paper circle, placed greased side down. Bake at 250° for 2½ to 3 hours or until cake tests done. Remove from oven. Take off paper cover, and slowly pour ¼ cup brandy evenly over cake; cool on wire rack.

Remove cake from pan; peel paper liner from cake. Wrap cake in brandy-soaked cheesecloth or clothlike disposable wiper. Store in an airtight container in a cool place 3 weeks. Pour a small amount of brandy over cake each week. Yield: one 10-inch cake.

Note: Cake may be baked in 4 (9- x 5- x 3-inch) paper-lined loafpans. Bake at 250° for 1½ hours or until done.

Old-Fashioned Light Fruitcake

 1 cup butter or margarine, softened
2¼ cups sugar
 6 eggs
 3 tablespoons brandy flavoring
 4 cups all-purpose flour
 ½ teaspoon baking powder
1½ teaspoons salt
1½ teaspoons ground cinnamon
 1 teaspoon ground nutmeg
1½ pounds (about 6 cups) coarsely chopped
     pecans
1½ pounds (about 4 cups) mixed candied
     fruit and peel, chopped
 1 (15-ounce) package golden raisins
    Honey
    Additional candied fruit and nuts
     (optional)

Cream butter and sugar until light and fluffy. Add eggs, one at a time, beating well after each addition; stir in brandy flavoring. Com-bine dry ingredients, pecans, candied fruit, and raisins; mix well. Add fruit mixture to creamed mixture, blending well.

Spoon batter into a well-greased 10-inch tube pan or two 9- x 5- x 3-inch loafpans lined with brown paper. Bake at 275° for 2½ to 3 hours. Brush top with honey 30 minutes be-fore cake is done; then decorate top with additional candied fruit and nuts, if desired.

Remove from oven when cake tests done; when completely cool, wrap cake tightly in aluminum foil. Store several weeks to allow flavors to mellow. Yield: one 10-inch cake or 2 loaves.

Southern Date Cake

1½ cups seedless raisins
1½ cups chopped dates
 2 cups sugar
 2 cups boiling water
 5 tablespoons shortening
 3 cups all-purpose flour
 2 teaspoons ground cinnamon
 1 teaspoon ground cloves
 1 teaspoon soda
 ½ teaspoon salt
 1 cup chopped walnuts or pecans

Combine raisins, dates, sugar, water, and shortening in a saucepan; simmer over low heat 20 minutes, stirring occasionally. Cool.

Combine flour, cinnamon, cloves, soda, and salt; add to date mixture, blending well. Stir in walnuts.

Spoon batter into a well-greased and floured 10-inch tube pan. Bake at 325° for 1 hour and 50 minutes. Yield: one 10-inch cake.

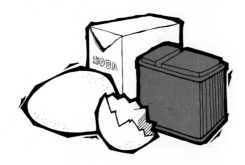

Orange-Glazed Cake

 1 cup sugar
 ½ cup shortening
 2 eggs
 2 cups all-purpose flour
 ½ teaspoon baking powder
 ½ teaspoon soda
 ½ teaspoon salt
 ⅔ cup buttermilk or sour milk
 ½ cup chopped raisins
 ½ cup chopped dates
 ½ cup crushed pineapple, drained
   Grated rind of 1 orange
   Juice of 1 orange
 ½ cup sugar

Combine ½ cup sugar, shortening, and eggs; beat until smooth. Combine flour, baking powder, soda, and salt; add to creamed mixture alternately with buttermilk, mixing well after each addition. Add raisins, dates, pineapple, and orange rind, mixing well.

Pour batter into a greased 10-inch tube or Bundt pan. Bake at 350° for 45 to 50 minutes or until done.

While cake is still hot, combine orange juice and ½ cup sugar; drizzle glaze over cake. Remove cake from pan when cool. Yield: one 10-inch cake.

Miniature White Fruitcakes

 ¾ cup butter or margarine, softened
 1 cup sugar
 5 eggs
 2 cups all-purpose flour
 1 teaspoon cream of tartar
 ¼ teaspoon salt
 ½ teaspoon soda
 ½ pound (about 1¼ cups) red and green candied cherries, chopped
 ½ pound (about 1¼ cups) yellow and green candied pineapple, chopped
 ½ pound (about 1¼ cups) mixed candied fruit and peel, chopped
 ½ pound (about 1½ cups) white raisins
 2 cups fresh or frozen shredded coconut
 2 cups chopped nuts
   Additional candied fruit and nuts (optional)

Cream butter and sugar until light and fluffy. Add eggs, one at a time, beating well after each addition. Combine dry ingredients. Combine fruit and nuts in a large bowl; add about 1 cup dry ingredients, mixing well. Add remainder of dry ingredients to creamed mixture, and mix well; then stir in fruit mixture.

Spoon batter into well-greased miniature Bundt pans or loafpans, filling about three-fourths full. Bake at 350° for 20 to 25 minutes or until done. Cool; decorate with additional candied fruit and nuts, if desired. Yield: 8 to 10 miniature fruitcakes.

Lemon-Nut Cake

  1 *pound butter or margarine, softened*
  2 *cups sugar*
  6 *eggs, separated*
  1 *(3-ounce) bottle lemon extract*
  1 *teaspoon soda*
  1 *teaspoon warm water*
  5 *cups all-purpose flour*
  3 *cups chopped pecans*
  1 *(15-ounce) package golden raisins*

Cream butter and sugar until light and fluffy. Add egg yolks, beating well; stir in lemon extract. Dissolve soda in warm water; add to creamed mixture along with flour, blending well. Stir in pecans and raisins. Beat egg whites until stiff, and fold into batter.

Pour into a greased and floured 10-inch tube pan or two 9- x 5- x 3-inch loafpans. Bake at 300° for 2 hours or until cake tests done. Yield: two loaves or one 10-inch cake.

Applesauce Christmas Cake

  ½ *cup shortening*
1¾ *cups sugar*
  1 *egg*
1½ *cups applesauce*
  1 *teaspoon soda*
2½ *cups all-purpose flour*
  1 *teaspoon baking powder*
  ¾ *teaspoon salt*
  2 *teaspoons ground cinnamon*
  1 *teaspoon ground cloves*
  2 *teaspoons ground nutmeg*
  2 *tablespoons molasses*
  1 *teaspoon vanilla extract*
  1 *cup raisins*
  ¼ *cup chopped walnuts*
    Frosting

Cream shortening and sugar until light and fluffy. Beat in egg. Combine applesauce and soda; beat into creamed mixture. Combine flour, baking powder, salt, and spices; add to applesauce mixture. Stir in molasses, vanilla, raisins, and walnuts.

Line the bottom of a 10-inch tube pan with waxed paper; grease and flour sides of pan.

Spoon batter into pan. Bake at 350° for 50 to 60 minutes.

Let cool in pan 10 minutes; then remove cake from pan. When completely cool, spread top of cake with Frosting. Yield: one 10-inch tube cake.

    Frosting:

  1 *tablespoon milk*
  4 *tablespoons butter or margarine*
1½ *cups powdered sugar*
  ¼ *cup chopped walnuts*
  ¾ *teaspoon vanilla extract*

Heat milk and butter in a saucepan until hot, but not boiling. Beat in sugar. Stir in walnuts and vanilla. Yield: about 1 cup.

Pecan Pound Cake

  1 *cup butter or margarine, softened*
  3 *cups sugar*
  6 *eggs, separated*
  3 *cups sifted cake flour*
  ¼ *teaspoon soda*
  1 *(8-ounce) carton plain yogurt or*
      commercial sour cream
  2 *to 4 cups chopped pecans*

Cream butter and sugar until light and fluffy. Add egg yolks, one at a time, beating well after each addition. Set aside about ¼ cup flour. Combine remaining flour and soda; add to creamed mixture alternately with yogurt, beating well after each addition. Fold in stiffly beaten egg whites. Dredge pecans in reserved flour, and fold into batter.

Spoon batter into a greased and floured 10-inch tube pan or Bundt pan. Bake at 300° for 1½ hours. Cool 15 minutes before removing from pan. Yield: one 10-inch cake.

Ginger Pound Cake

  1 *cup butter or margarine, softened*
  1 *cup sugar*
  2 *cups all-purpose flour*
  2 *teaspoons ground ginger*
  5 *eggs, slightly beaten*
  1 *cup light mild-flavored molasses*
 ½ *cup commercial sour cream*
 ½ *teaspoon soda*
  2 *tablespoons warm water*
    Powdered sugar

Combine butter and sugar; cream until light and fluffy. Combine flour and ginger; add to creamed mixture, blending well. Combine eggs, molasses, and sour cream; add to flour mixture, beating well. Dissolve soda in water; add to batter, mixing well.

Pour batter into a greased and floured 10-inch tube pan. Bake at 325° for 1 hour or until done. Cool 10 minutes before removing from pan. Sprinkle with powdered sugar. Yield: one 10-inch cake.

Easy Pound Cake

   1 *cup butter or margarine, softened*
1¾ *cups sugar*
   5 *eggs*
  ½ *teaspoon almond extract*
   2 *cups all-purpose flour*

Combine butter and sugar until light and fluffy; add eggs, one at a time, beating well after each addition. Add almond extract. Stir in flour, mixing well.

Spoon batter into a greased and floured 9- x 5- x 3-inch loafpan. Bake at 350° for 1 hour and 10 minutes or until cake tests done.

Let the cake cool in loafpan 10 minutes before removing to a wire rack. Yield: 1 loaf.

Crispy Pound Cake

   3 *cups all-purpose flour*
   3 *cups sugar*
   9 *eggs*
1½ *cups shortening*
1½ *teaspoons lemon or almond extract*

Combine all ingredients in a large mixing bowl; blend until smooth. Beat on medium speed of electric mixer 10 to 15 minutes or until very fluffy. Spoon batter into a greased 10-inch tube pan or Bundt pan. Bake at 300° for 1 hour and 25 minutes or until done. Yield: one 10-inch cake.

Lemon-Orange Pound Cake

 ½ *cup shortening*
 ½ *cup butter or margarine, softened*
  2 *cups sugar*
  6 *eggs*
  3 *cups all-purpose flour*
 ½ *teaspoon salt*
 ½ *teaspoon soda*
  1 *teaspoon baking powder*
  1 *cup buttermilk*
  1 *teaspoon vanilla extract*
  1 *teaspoon lemon extract*
    Glaze
    Sprigs of mint
    Orange and lemon slices

Cream shortening, butter, and sugar until light and fluffy; add eggs, one at a time, beating well after each adddition.

Combine flour, salt, soda, and baking powder; add to creamed mixture alternately with buttermilk, beginning and ending with dry ingredients. Beat well after each addition; stir in flavorings. Pour batter into a well-greased 10-inch tube pan or Bundt pan. Bake at 350° for 1 hour.

Using a toothpick, punch holes in cake while hot; drizzle with Glaze. Garnish with mint, orange slices, and lemon slices. Yield: one 10-inch cake.

    Glaze:

   1 *tablespoon grated lemon rind*
   1 *tablespoon grated orange rind*
   3 *tablespoons orange juice*
   3 *tablespoons lemon juice*
1½ *cups powdered sugar*

Combine all ingredients, and blend well. Yield: about 1½ cups.

Milk Chocolate Pound Cake

    1 *cup butter or margarine, softened*
   1½ *cups sugar*
    4 *eggs*
    8 *(1⅛-ounce) milk chocolate candy bars,*
       melted
    1 *cup buttermilk*
   2½ *cups all-purpose flour*
       Pinch of salt
    ¼ *teaspoon soda*
    1 *cup chopped pecans*
    1 *(5½-ounce) can chocolate syrup*
    2 *teaspoons vanilla extract*
       Powdered sugar (optional)

Cream butter and sugar until light and fluffy. Add eggs, one at a time, beating well after each addition. Add melted candy bars and buttermilk, and mix well.

Combine flour, salt, and soda; add to chocolate mixture, mixing well. Add pecans, chocolate syrup, and vanilla, blending well.

Spoon batter into a greased and floured 10-inch tube or Bundt pan. Bake at 325° for 1 hour and 15 minutes or until done. When cake is cool, sift powdered sugar over cake, if desired. Yield: one 10-inch cake.

Butterscotch-Mocha Pound Cake

    1 *(6-ounce) package butterscotch-flavored*
       morsels
    2 *tablespoons instant coffee powder*
    ¼ *cup water*
    1 *cup butter or margarine, softened*
   1½ *cups sugar*
    3 *cups all-purpose flour*
    ½ *teaspoon soda*
    ¼ *teaspoon salt*
    ¾ *cup buttermilk*
    4 *eggs*

Combine butterscotch morsels, coffee powder, and water in top of a double boiler, stirring until smooth; set aside.

Cream butter and sugar until light and fluffy. Stir in butterscotch mixture. Combine flour, soda, and salt. Add to creamed mixture

alternately with buttermilk, beating well after each addition. Add eggs one at a time, beating after each addition.

Pour batter into a well-greased and floured Bundt or tube pan. Bake at 350° for 55 to 60 minutes. Cool 10 to 15 minutes before removing from pan. Yield: one 10-inch tube cake.

Kentucky Bourbon Cake

    2 *cups sugar*
   1½ *cups butter, softened*
    6 *eggs*
    ½ *cup molasses*
    4 *cups all-purpose flour*
   2½ *teaspoons baking powder*
    2 *teaspoons ground nutmeg*
    1 *(15-ounce) box raisins*
    1 *cup chopped candied pineapple*
    1 *cup chopped candied cherries*
    1 *cup orange marmalade*
    2 *pounds chopped pecans (about 8 cups)*
    1 *cup bourbon*
       Additional candied cherries (optional)

Cream sugar and butter until light and fluffy; add eggs, one at a time, beating well after each addition. Add molasses, and mix well.

Combine flour, baking powder, and nutmeg; set aside. Combine fruits, marmalade, and pecans in a large bowl; add 1 cup flour mixture and toss to coat fruit. Add remainder of flour mixture to creamed mixture alternately with bourbon; mix well. Stir in fruit and nuts.

Grease one 10-inch tube pan or two 9- x 5- x 3-inch loafpans; line with greased heavy brown paper. Spoon batter into pan, and cover with greased brown paper. Bake at 250° for 2½ to 3 hours or until done. Do not overcook. Cool completely. Garnish with additional candied cherries, if desired.

Wrap cake in a cloth that has been soaked in bourbon; place in a container and seal, or wrap in aluminum foil. (Storing cake in refrigerator makes for easier slicing.) Yield: one 10-inch cake or two loaves.

Million Dollar Pound Cake

    3 *cups sugar*
    1 *pound butter, softened*
    6 *eggs, at room temperature*
    4 *cups all-purpose flour*
    ¾ *cup milk*
    1 *teaspoon almond extract*
    1 *teaspoon vanilla extract*

Combine sugar and butter; cream until light and fluffy. Add eggs, one at a time, beating well after each addition. Add flour to creamed mixture alternately with milk, beating well after each addition. Stir in extracts.

Pour batter into a well-greased and floured 10-inch tube pan. Bake at 300° for 1 hour and 40 minutes or until cake tests done. Yield: one 10-inch cake.

Heredity Pound Cake

    3 *cups cake flour*
    ½ *teaspoon baking powder*
    1½ *cups butter or margarine*
    2½ *cups sugar*
    1½ *cups (6 to 7) eggs*
    ¼ *cup milk*
    2 *teaspoons vanilla extract*
    ½ *teaspoon orange extract*
    3 *tablespoons butter or margarine, melted*
    3 *tablespoons sugar*

Let all ingredients stand at room temperature 15 minutes. (If butter is used, let stand 1 hour.) Sift flour and baking powder together; set aside.

Cream 1½ cups butter and 2½ cups sugar on medium speed of electric mixer until light and fluffy. Reduce speed to low; add 1 egg, and beat well. Sprinkle 2 tablespoons flour mixture over batter; beat well. Repeat process until all eggs have been added.

Combine milk and flavorings; add milk mixture and remaining flour alternately to batter, beating well after each addition. Pour into a greased and floured 10-inch tube pan. Bake at 350° for 50 to 60 minutes or until golden and a crack forms around top of cake.

Brush top of cake with melted butter; sprinkle with 3 tablespoons sugar. Cover pan tightly with aluminum foil, and let stand 30 minutes. Remove foil and cool completely; remove from pan. Yield: one 10-inch cake.

Chocolate Pound Cake

    1 *cup butter, softened*
    ½ *cup margarine, softened*
    3 *cups sugar*
    5 *eggs*
    3 *cups all-purpose flour*
    ½ *teaspoon baking powder*
    ½ *teaspoon salt*
    ½ *cup cocoa*
    1 *cup milk*
    1 *teaspoon vanilla extract*
    Butter Cream Frosting

Cream butter and margarine until smooth; add sugar and beat until light and fluffy. Add eggs, one at a time, beating well after each addition.

Combine dry ingredients, and add to creamed mixture alternately with milk and vanilla. Spoon batter into a well-greased 10-inch tube pan or Bundt pan. Bake at 325° for 1 hour and 15 minutes or until done.

Cool; spread with Butter Cream Frosting, and decorate as desired. Yield: one 10-inch cake.

Butter Cream Frosting:

    ¾ *cup margarine, softened*
    1 *(3-ounce) package cream cheese, softened*
    Pinch of salt
    1 *(16-ounce) package plus ½ cup powdered sugar*
    ¼ *to ½ cup milk*
    1 *teaspoon vanilla extract*

Cream margarine and cream cheese until light and fluffy. Add salt and sugar, a small amount at a time, beating until smooth. Slowly beat in just enough milk to make mixture spreadable; add vanilla. Yield: enough for one 10-inch cake.

Cereals and Grains

Cereals and grains, especially rice and grits, contribute substantially to Southern diets. Though somewhat bland by nature, these two staples lend themselves to a variety of preparation methods.

Grits can be boiled, baked, or fried, and bacon, cheese, or mushrooms can be added. Serve rice with butter or gravy, or toss it in countless other combinations. Then use the leftovers in croquettes, or eat them with cream and sugar. If most of the rice produced in this country is consumed in the South, it isn't at all surprising—most of it is grown here, too.

For those who like granola, we've included recipes for making it at home—crispy, toasty, whole-grain goodness made with nature's ingredients. Make it with fruit or with nuts.

Oriental Cheese Rice

      3 tablespoons melted butter or margarine,
            divided
      3 tablespoons all-purpose flour
    1½ cups milk
      ½ teaspoon salt
      2 cups shredded Cheddar cheese
      ½ cup chopped green pepper
      1 cup chopped celery
      1 medium-size onion, chopped
      3 hard-cooked eggs, coarsely chopped
      ¼ cup chopped pimiento
         Hot cooked rice

Combine 2 tablespoons butter and flour; cook over low heat until bubbly. Gradually add milk; cook, stirring constantly, until smooth and thick. Season with salt. Add cheese, stirring until melted.

Sauté green pepper, celery, and onion in 1 tablespoon butter. Add to sauce along with eggs and pimiento; stir gently. Serve over hot rice. Yield: 6 servings.

You'll never want plain rice again when you taste these dishes: Okra Shrimp Creole (page 145), Rice Pudding with Marmalade Sauce (page 124), and Polynesian Rice Salad (page 270).

Wild and Dirty Rice

      1 cup chopped celery
      ¾ cup chopped green pepper
      3 cloves garlic, minced
      3 tablespoons chopped parsley
      5 green onions, chopped
      1 large onion, chopped
      ½ cup olive oil
    1¾ cups uncooked wild rice
      ¼ cup long grain rice, uncooked
      2 (4-ounce) cans sliced mushrooms,
            drained
      4 cups hot chicken broth
    1½ cups finely chopped cooked chicken
            giblets
      1 cup finely chopped cooked chicken
      ½ cup slivered almonds, toasted
      1 tablespoon salt
      1 teaspoon black pepper
      ¼ teaspoon cayenne pepper
      ½ teaspoon poultry seasoning

Sauté vegetables in olive oil until tender; add remaining ingredients. Pour into a lightly greased 3-quart casserole. Cover and bake at 250° for 1 hour and 15 minutes. Yield: 8 to 10 servings.

Baked Rice

1   cup uncooked long grain rice
¼   cup melted butter or margarine
2   chicken bouillon cubes
3   cups boiling water
2   tablespoons chopped parsley

Sauté rice in butter until lightly browned, stirring frequently. Spoon into a 2-quart casserole.

Dissolve bouillon in water; pour over rice. Cover and bake at 350° for 45 minutes or until rice is tender. Sprinkle with parsley. Yield: 4 servings.

Green Rice

1   cup chopped green onion
1   green pepper, chopped
¼   cup butter or margarine, melted
2   cups uncooked long grain rice
4½ cups beef or chicken broth
1   cup chopped parsley
Salt and pepper to taste

Sauté green onion and green pepper in butter until tender; add rice, and stir until rice is well coated with butter, about 5 minutes. Add broth; cover and cook 25 minutes or until rice is tender. Stir in parsley, salt, and pepper; cook, stirring, 1 minute longer. Yield: 12 servings.

Mushroom Rice

1   cup uncooked regular rice
2   (4-ounce) cans sliced mushrooms, undrained
1   (10½-ounce) can beef broth
2   tablespoons sherry
¼   teaspoon salt
⅛   teaspoon garlic powder
⅛   teaspoon seasoned pepper
½   cup melted butter or margarine

Combine all ingredients in a 1½-quart casserole. Bake, uncovered, at 350° for 1 hour. Yield: 6 servings.

Pilaf

1   cup chopped green onion
1   green pepper, chopped
1   (4-ounce) can sliced mushrooms, drained
¼   cup melted butter or margarine
1   cup uncooked long grain rice
2   cups chicken broth
1   small bay leaf
½   teaspoon salt

Sauté onion, pepper, and mushrooms in butter just until tender; add rice and cook, stirring, 5 minutes. Stir in broth, bay leaf, and salt. Pour mixture into a greased 1½-quart casserole; cover and bake at 350° for 25 to 30 minutes or until rice is tender. Yield: 6 servings.

Rice Supreme

2   cups turkey or chicken broth
1   teaspoon salt
1   tablespoon lemon juice
½   teaspoon tarragon
1   cup uncooked regular rice
¼   cup finely chopped mushrooms
¼   cup melted butter or margarine
Pepper to taste
¼   cup dry sherry
2   tablespoons chopped parsley
½   cup coarsely chopped toasted almonds or filberts

Bring broth to a boil in a small saucepan; remove from heat. Stir in salt, lemon juice, tarragon, and rice; return to a boil. Cover and simmer over very low heat until liquid is absorbed and rice is tender (about 20 minutes).

Sauté mushrooms in butter; add pepper, sherry, and parsley. Add mushroom mixture to rice and toss with a fork. Spoon into a serving dish; top with almonds. Yield: 6 servings.

Rice 'n Cheese Croquettes

3 cups cold cooked rice
1 egg, beaten
1 egg, separated
1 cup shredded Cheddar cheese
1 teaspoon Worcestershire sauce
1 tablespoon water
Fine breadcrumbs
Hot salad oil

Combine rice, beaten egg, egg yolk, Cheddar cheese, and Worcestershire sauce, blending well. Chill at least 1 hour. Shape mixture into croquettes. Combine egg white and water; beat well. Coat croquettes with egg white, then with breadcrumbs; chill well.

Heat oil to 375°; deep fry croquettes until golden brown. Yield: about 1 dozen croquettes.

Risotto Parmigiana

½ pound chicken livers, quartered
½ cup chopped onion
½ cup melted butter or margarine, divided
3 cups uncooked regular rice
3½ to 4 cups hot chicken broth
   Salt and pepper to taste
1½ cups grated Parmesan cheese

Sauté chicken livers and onion in ¼ cup butter; add rice and cook 5 minutes, stirring constantly. Add chicken broth, salt, and pepper; simmer about 20 minutes or until rice is tender and all liquid is absorbed. Stir in remaining butter and Parmesan cheese. Yield: 6 servings.

Saffron Rice

3 (5-ounce) packages saffron rice
2 (6-ounce) cans button mushrooms, drained, divided
4 tablespoons chopped pimiento, divided

Prepare rice according to package directions. Set aside several mushrooms for garnish. Stir remaining mushrooms and 3 tablespoons pimiento into rice; heat thoroughly. Garnish with reserved mushrooms and 1 tablespoon pimiento. Yield: about 12 servings.

Shrimp Fried Rice

4 green onions, sliced
2 tablespoons melted margarine
3 slices bacon
2 eggs, beaten
1 cup cooked regular rice
1 (4-ounce) can sliced mushrooms, drained
1 (4½-ounce) can small shrimp, drained
1 (8-ounce) can water chestnuts, drained and sliced
1 tablespoon soy sauce

Sauté onion in margarine; set aside. Cook bacon until crisp; remove from pan, and drain well. Crumble bacon and set aside.

Scramble eggs in bacon drippings over low heat. Stir in rice, mushrooms, shrimp, water chestnuts, soy sauce, and sautéed onion. Sprinkle with bacon. Yield: 4 servings.

Spanish Rice

½ pound ground beef
¼ cup chopped onion
1 tablespoon salad oil
¼ cup chopped green pepper
6 tablespoons uncooked long grain rice
1 (6-ounce) can tomato paste
1 teaspoon salt
   Dash of pepper
2 cups hot water

Brown beef and onion in oil; drain on paper towels. Return to skillet, and add remaining ingredients. Cover, and cook over low heat 20 minutes or until rice is cooked. Stir mixture occasionally. Yield: 2 servings.

Cheesy Grits with Bacon

1½ cups uncooked regular grits
5   cups boiling water
1   teaspoon salt
¾   cup butter or margarine
1   (8-ounce) jar process cheese spread
1   cup milk
5   eggs, beaten
8   to 10 slices bacon, cooked and crumbled
1   cup shredded Cheddar cheese

Stir grits into boiling water; reduce heat, and stir in salt. Cover and cook, stirring occasionally, until grits are done, about 10 minutes. Add butter and cheese spread; stir until melted.

Combine milk and eggs; add a small amount of hot grits, stirring well. Stir milk and egg mixture into remaining grits, stirring constantly until well blended. Stir in bacon.

Spoon mixture into a greased 13- x 9- x 2-inch baking dish. Sprinkle with Cheddar cheese, and bake at 375° for 40 minutes. Yield: 10 to 12 servings.

Baked Grits with Caviar

2   cups quick-cooking grits
1   cup milk
4   eggs, beaten
1   (3-ounce) package cream cheese, softened
6   tablespoons butter or margarine
1   pound bacon, cooked and crumbled
1   (8-ounce) can mushroom pieces, drained
1   (8-ounce) can water chestnuts, drained and chopped
½   to ¾ cup chopped pecans
3   (4-ounce) cans red caviar

Cook grits according to package directions. Add milk, eggs, cream cheese, and butter; blend well. Stir in bacon, mushrooms, water chestnuts, and pecans, blending well.

Spoon into a greased shallow 2-quart casserole; bake at 350° for 20 to 30 minutes. Spread caviar on top, and serve hot. Yield: 12 servings.

Easy Cheesy Grits

6   cups boiling water
2   teaspoons salt
1½ cups uncooked regular grits
3   eggs, beaten
¾   cup melted butter or margarine
2   cups shredded Cheddar cheese
Dash of hot sauce
1   tablespoon seasoned salt
⅛   teaspoon paprika

Combine water and salt; bring to a boil. Stir in grits; cover and cook over low heat 20 to 30 minutes or until done.

Combine remaining ingredients. Add a small amount of hot grits to egg mixture, stirring well; stir egg mixture into remaining grits. Spoon mixture into well-greased 3-quart casserole. Bake at 250° for 1 hour. Yield: 10 servings.

Creamy Grits

1   cup uncooked regular grits
3¼ cups milk
¼   cup water
1   teaspoon salt
Butter or gravy

Combine grits, milk, water, and salt in top of a double boiler. Cook over low heat 1½ hours, stirring occasionally. Serve with butter or gravy. Yield: 6 to 8 servings.

Baked Cheese Grits

6   cups water
2½ teaspoons salt
1½ cups uncooked regular grits
½   cup butter
3   eggs, beaten
1   pound sharp cheese, shredded and divided

Bring water to a boil in a saucepan; add salt and grits. Cook until done, following package directions. Remove from heat. Stir in remaining ingredients except ¼ cup of cheese.

Pour into a buttered 2-quart baking dish. Top with remaining cheese. Bake at 350° for 1 hour and 15 minutes. Yield: 6 to 8 servings.

Homemade Granola

5 cups regular oats, uncooked
1 cup sunflower seeds
1 cup flaked coconut
1 cup chopped pecans
1 cup sesame seeds
1 cup soy flour
1 cup nonfat dry milk powder
1 cup wheat germ
1 cup honey
1 cup milk
1 cup salad oil

Combine first 8 ingredients, and mix well. Combine honey, milk, and salad oil; pour over dry mixture, and stir until well blended. Spread mixture on cookie sheets; bake at 300° for 1 hour, stirring often. Cool and store granola in an airtight container until serving time. Yield: about 3 quarts.

All Natural Granola

½ cup safflower oil
½ cup honey
½ teaspoon vanilla extract
4 cups old-fashioned oats
1 cup wheat germ
1 cup sliced almonds
1 cup sunflower seeds
½ cup sesame seeds
½ cup 100% bran cereal
1 cup ground roasted soybeans (optional)
1 cup raisins (optional)

Combine oil, honey, and vanilla; blend well, and set aside. Combine remaining ingredients except raisins in a large bowl; add liquid mixture, mixing well.

Spread granola on a large baking sheet; bake at 250° for 45 minutes, stirring every 15 minutes. Stir in raisins, if desired. Store in airtight containers. Yield: about 12 cups.

Hominy with Tomato Gravy

1 (14½-ounce) can hominy
2 pork chops
Tomato Gravy

Drain hominy, reserving ⅓ cup liquid; set aside.

Cut pork chops into bite-size pieces; sauté until lightly browned. Drain, reserving 1 tablespoon drippings. Add reserved drippings to pork along with hominy and reserved hominy liquid. Cover tightly and cook until liquid evaporates. Serve with Tomato Gravy. Yield: 2 servings.

Tomato Gravy:

1 canned tomato, chopped
¼ cup tomato juice
1 tablespoon all-purpose flour
3 tablespoons water
2 teaspoons butter or margarine

Heat tomato and juice in a small saucepan. Combine flour and water; stir into hot tomato mixture. Add butter; cook, stirring constantly, until thickened. Yield: about ¾ cup.

Hominy au Gratin

2 tablespoons butter or margarine
2 tablespoons all-purpose flour
2 cups milk
1 teaspoon salt
¼ teaspoon pepper
¾ cup shredded Cheddar cheese
1 (29-ounce) can hominy, drained
½ cup buttered breadcrumbs

Melt butter, and blend in flour. Gradually add milk; cook, stirring constantly, until thickened. Season with salt and pepper; add cheese, stirring until cheese melts.

Alternate layers of hominy and sauce in a lightly greased 2-quart casserole; top with breadcrumbs. Bake at 375° for 25 to 30 minutes or until breadcrumbs are lightly browned. Yield: 6 servings.

Cookies, Candies, and Confections

Home-baked cookies are good anytime—for snacks, for desserts, or as gifts. They are so easy to make, and the necessary ingredients are usually on hand. Everyone has a favorite that he or she grew up with—probably chocolate chip, peanut butter, or sugar cookies—but the variety goes on and on. Recipes for delicious brownies (frosted or minted, with marshmallows or nuts), fruit bars, and nut bars are included. There are also shaped, rolled, and dropped cookies—filled with fruit, laced with nuts, or rolled in sugar.

Candies and confections, like fudge and divinity, are particular favorites during the holiday season. But watch the kids' eyes light up when you surprise them with some unexpected peanut brittle, pralines, or toffee! Little surprises make treasured memories long after the candy is gone.

Lemon Crumble Squares

⅔ cup butter or margarine, softened
1 cup firmly packed brown sugar
1 cup old-fashioned oats
1 teaspoon baking powder
½ teaspoon salt
1½ cups all-purpose flour
1 (15-ounce) can sweetened condensed milk
½ cup lemon juice
2 egg yolks
1 teaspoon grated lemon rind

Cream butter and brown sugar; stir in oats and dry ingredients. Mix until crumbly. Spread half of mixture in greased 13- x 9- x 2-inch pan, packing firmly.

Combine condensed milk, lemon juice, egg yolks, and lemon rind; let stand 1 minute to thicken. Spread over crumb crust; sprinkle with remaining crumb mixture. Bake at 350° for 25 minutes. Cool 15 minutes in pan. Chill in refrigerator until firm. Cut into 1¾-inch squares. Yield: 2 dozen squares.

Prune Bars

1 cup diced prunes
1 cup chopped walnuts
1 cup firmly packed brown sugar
¾ cup all-purpose flour
1½ teaspoons baking powder
¼ teaspoon salt
3 eggs, slightly beaten
Powdered sugar

Combine prunes, walnuts, brown sugar, flour, baking powder, and salt; mix thoroughly. Add eggs, blending well. Spread dough evenly in a greased 9-inch square pan. Bake at 325° about 30 minutes or until done. Cool 10 to 15 minutes. Cut into bars; roll each in powdered sugar. Yield: 1½ to 2 dozen bars.

Sugar Cookies (page 99), cut in the shape of favorite animals, and Oatmeal-Coconut Crispies (page 96) are sure to please the youngsters.

Apple-Nut Squares

  2   *cups sugar*
  ¾ *cup salad oil*
  3   *eggs*
  1   *teaspoon soda*
  3   *cups all-purpose flour*
  3   *cups peeled, chopped apple*
  2   *teaspoons vanilla extract*
  1   *cup chopped pecans*
     Topping

Combine sugar, salad oil, eggs, soda, flour, apple, vanilla, and pecans; mix well. Spread evenly in a greased 13- x 9- x 2-inch pan. Bake at 325° for 1 hour. Spread Topping evenly over top. Cool and cut into squares. Yield: about 3 dozen squares.

   Topping:

  ½ *cup butter or margarine*
  1   *cup firmly packed light brown sugar*
  ¼ *cup evaporated milk*

Combine all ingredients in a small saucepan. Place over low heat, and bring to a boil; cook 2 minutes. Yield: about 1¾ cups.

Bran Apricot Bars

  ½ *cup diced dried apricots*
  1   *cup boiling water*
  ½ *cup butter or margarine, softened*
  ¼ *cup sugar*
  1   *cup all-purpose flour, divided*
  ¾ *cup 100% bran cereal*
  2   *eggs*
  1   *cup firmly packed brown sugar*
  ½ *teaspoon vanilla extract*
  ½ *teaspoon baking powder*
  ½ *teaspoon salt*
  ½ *cup chopped walnuts*

Combine apricots and water in a small saucepan, and simmer 10 minutes; drain and set aside.

    Cream butter and sugar until fluffy. Stir in ½ cup flour and cereal. Press into bottom of a 9-inch square pan. Bake at 350° for 15 minutes.

Beat eggs until thick and lemon colored. Stir in brown sugar, vanilla, remaining flour, baking powder, and salt. Add walnuts and apricots, mixing well. Pour over baked crust. Bake at 350° for 25 to 30 minutes. Cool, and cut into 2- x 1-inch bars. Yield: about 2 dozen bars.

Wine Fruit Bars

  1½ *cups currants*
  1½ *cups raisins*
  1½ *cups candied cherries, halved*
  1½ *cups chopped candied pineapple*
  1½ *cups sweet wine*
  ½ *cup butter or margarine, softened*
  1½ *cups firmly packed brown sugar*
  3   *eggs*
  2   *cups all-purpose flour*
  1   *teaspoon ground cinnamon*
  1   *teaspoon ground cloves*
  1   *teaspoon ground allspice*
  ¼ *teaspoon ground nutmeg*
  ½ *teaspoon soda*
  ½ *teaspoon salt*
     Lemon Glaze

Combine fruit and wine in a bowl; cover and let mixture stand 24 hours or longer; drain fruit, and discard wine.

    Cream butter and sugar; add eggs, beating until light and fluffy. Combine dry ingredients; stir into creamed mixture. Blend in fruits.

    Spread dough in a greased 13- x 9- x 2-inch pan. Bake at 325° about 35 minutes or until done. Cool; drizzle with Lemon Glaze. Cut into bars. Yield: about 35 bars.

   Lemon Glaze:

  1   *cup sifted powdered sugar*
  1   *tablespoon lemon juice*
  2   *tablespoons milk*

Combine all ingredients, blending until smooth. Add more milk if necessary to make proper consistency. Yield: about ½ cup.

Flaky Pineapple Squares

    2   *cups butter or margarine*
    4   *cups all-purpose flour*
    1   *(8-ounce) carton commercial sour cream*
    1   *teaspoon vanilla extract*
    1   *cup sugar*
    3   *tablespoons cornstarch*
    1   *(29½-ounce) and 1 (13¼-ounce) can*
        crushed pineapple, well drained
        Powdered sugar

Cut butter into flour with pastry blender; add sour cream and vanilla, mixing well. (Dough will be very stiff; use hands to mix, if necessary.) Refrigerate 2 hours.

Combine sugar and cornstarch in a saucepan; stir in pineapple. Cook until thickened and clear, stirring constantly. Set aside to cool.

Divide dough in half. Roll one portion into a 15½- x 10½-inch rectangle on a piece of floured waxed paper; place in a 15½- x 10½- x 1-inch pan. Spread pineapple mixture evenly over dough.

Roll remaining dough to same dimensions; place over pineapple. Bake at 325° for 55 minutes or until golden brown.

Sprinkle cookies with powdered sugar. Cut into squares. Store in refrigerator. Yield: about 54 squares.

Mincemeat Fudge Squares

    ½   *cup butter or margarine, melted*
    1   *cup sugar*
    2   *eggs*
    1   *cup mincemeat with brandy and rum*
    1   *teaspoon vanilla extract*
    ⅔   *cup chopped pecans*
    1½ *(1-ounce) squares unsweetened*
        chocolate, melted
    ¾   *cup all-purpose flour*
    ¼   *teaspoon salt*
        Powdered sugar

Combine butter and sugar, mixing well. Add eggs, one at a time, beating well after each addition. Combine mincemeat, vanilla, pecans, and chocolate; add to sugar mixture, and mix well. Blend in flour and salt.

Spoon batter into a greased and floured 12- x 8- x 2-inch pan. Sprinkle with powdered sugar, and bake at 350° for 35 minutes. Cool. Cut into squares. Yield: about 28 squares.

Kahlúa Classics

    ½   *cup raisins*
    ¼   *cup Kahlúa or other coffee-flavored*
        liqueur
    ½   *cup butter or margarine*
    1½ *(1-ounce) squares unsweetened*
        chocolate
    ¾   *cup sugar*
    ½   *teaspoon vanilla extract*
    1   *cup all-purpose flour*
    1   *teaspoon baking powder*
    ¼   *teaspoon salt*
    1½ *teaspoons instant coffee granules*
    2   *eggs*
    ½   *cup finely chopped pecans*
        Kahlúa Frosting

Combine raisins and Kahlúa in a small bowl; let stand 15 minutes.

Combine butter and chocolate in a saucepan; place over low heat until melted. Cool slightly; stir in sugar and vanilla, and set aside.

Combine dry ingredients; blend in chocolate mixture. Add eggs, beating well. Stir in raisin-Kahlúa mixture; blend well.

Spread dough in a greased 8-inch square baking dish; sprinkle with pecans. Bake at 350° for 30 minutes. Cool slightly; then spread with Kahlúa Frosting. Cut into 2-inch squares. Serve warm or cold. Yield: 16 (2-inch) squares.

    Kahlúa Frosting:

    1⅓ *cups powdered sugar*
        Dash of salt
        About 2 teaspoons warm water
    1   *teaspoon evaporated milk*
    ¼   *cup Kahlúa or other coffee-flavored*
        liqueur

Combine all ingredients, blending until smooth. Yield: about ⅔ cup.

Rocky Road Brownies

1   *cup all-purpose flour*
1   *cup sugar*
2   *teaspoons cocoa*
1   *cup melted butter or margarine*
2   *eggs*
1   *teaspoon vanilla extract*
1   *cup chopped nuts*
1   *(6¼-ounce) package miniature*
      marshmallows
Fudgy Frosting

Combine flour, sugar, and cocoa; stir in melted butter. Add eggs, one at a time, beating well after each addition. Stir in vanilla and nuts.

Pour batter into a greased and floured 13- x 9- x 2-inch baking pan. Bake at 275° for 35 to 40 minutes. Sprinkle marshmallows evenly over top of hot brownies. Spread with Fudgy Frosting; cool and cut into squares. Yield: about 30 brownies.

Fudgy Frosting:

1   *(1-pound) package powdered sugar*
⅓   *cup cocoa*
½   *cup melted butter or margarine*
⅓   *cup evaporated milk*
½   *teaspoon vanilla extract*

Combine powdered sugar and cocoa; add remaining ingredients, and beat well. Yield: about 2 cups.

★
Chocolate Dreams

1   *cup shortening*
4   *(1-ounce) squares unsweetened*
      chocolate
2   *cups sugar*
4   *eggs, well beaten*
1   *teaspoon vanilla extract*
1½   *cups all-purpose flour*
½   *teaspoon salt*
1   *cup chopped pecans*
Frosting

Melt shortening and chocolate in top of a double boiler; add sugar, mixing well. Add eggs and vanilla; mix well. Stir in flour and salt, and mix thoroughly. Remove from heat, and stir in pecans.

Spread batter in a well-greased 13- x 9- x 2-inch pan. Bake at 400° for 20 minutes. Cool; spread with Frosting. Yield: about 36 squares.

Frosting:

2   *(1-ounce) squares unsweetened*
      chocolate
3   *tablespoons hot water*
1   *tablespoon butter or margarine*
2   *to 2½ cups powdered sugar*
½   *teaspoon vanilla extract*
1   *egg*

Melt chocolate with water, and blend in butter. Stir in powdered sugar and vanilla; beat in egg. Yield: enough frosting for 36 squares.

Minted Brownies

2   *(1-ounce) squares unsweetened*
      chocolate
½   *cup butter or margarine*
1   *cup sugar*
2   *eggs, beaten*
1   *teaspoon peppermint extract, divided*
Dash of salt
½   *cup all-purpose flour*
½   *cup chopped pecans*
2   *tablespoons melted butter or margarine*
1   *cup powdered sugar*
1   *tablespoon milk or half-and-half*

Melt chocolate and ½ cup butter in a small saucepan over low heat; stir in sugar. Cool.

Combine eggs, ¼ teaspoon peppermint, and salt; stir in chocolate mixture. Add flour, mixing well; stir in pecans. Pour into a greased 9-inch square baking pan. Bake at 350° for 20 to 25 minutes. Cool.

Combine melted butter, powdered sugar, milk, and remaining ¾ teaspoon peppermint; mix well. Spread over brownies; chill. Cut into 1-inch squares. Yield: 3 dozen brownies.

Southern Pecan Bars

⅓ cup butter or margarine, softened
½ cup firmly packed brown sugar
1⅓ cups all-purpose flour
½ teaspoon baking powder
¼ cup finely chopped pecans
   Pecan Topping

Cream butter and sugar; add flour and baking powder, blending until mixture resembles coarse cornmeal. Stir in pecans.

Pat pecan mixture firmly into a well-greased 13- x 9- x 2-inch pan. Bake at 350° for 10 minutes. Cover with Pecan Topping, and bake 25 to 30 additional minutes. Let cool before cutting into bars. Yield: 30 bars.

Pecan Topping:
2 eggs, beaten
¾ cup dark corn syrup
¼ cup firmly packed brown sugar
3 tablespoons all-purpose flour
½ teaspoon salt
1 teaspoon vanilla extract
¾ cup chopped pecans

Combine all ingredients except pecans; pour over partially baked crust. Sprinkle with pecans. Yield: topping for 30 bars.

Pecan Bars

1 cup butter or margarine, softened
1 cup sugar
1 egg, separated
2 cups all-purpose flour
2 teaspoons ground cinnamon
1 tablespoon milk
1 cup chopped pecans

Cream butter and sugar; add egg yolk, beating well. Add flour, cinnamon, and milk; mix well. (Dough will be very stiff.)

Pat dough out evenly in a greased 13- x 9- x 2-inch pan. Beat egg white slightly, and brush over top of dough; sprinkle with pecans, and press lightly into dough. Bake at 350° about 35 to 45 minutes. Cut into bars while hot. Yield: 2½ dozen bars.

Maple Walnut Bars

1 egg, beaten
½ cup sugar
⅓ cup melted butter or margarine
½ cup self-rising flour
1 teaspoon maple flavoring
1 cup coarsely broken English walnuts
½ cup raisins

Combine egg and sugar, beating well. Add remaining ingredients; mix well. Spread evenly in a greased 8-inch square baking pan. Bake at 350° for 30 minutes. Cool in pan; cut into bars or squares. Yield: about 20 bars.

Carrot Bars

½   cup butter or margarine, softened
1½ cups firmly packed brown sugar
2   eggs
2   cups all-purpose flour
1   teaspoon baking powder
½   teaspoon salt
½   teaspoon ground cinnamon
⅛   teaspoon ground cloves
1   cup grated raw carrots
1   cup seedless raisins
    Lemon Frosting

Combine butter and sugar, beating until light and fluffy. Add eggs, one at time, beating well after each addition.

Combine flour, baking powder, salt, and spices; stir into creamed mixture. Fold carrots and raisins into batter. Spoon batter into a greased 13- x 9- x 2-inch pan, spreading evenly. Bake at 350° for 25 to 30 minutes or until cake tests done. Cool in pan.

Spread cake with a thin layer of Lemon Frosting. Cut into 1½- x 1¾-inch bars after frosting has set. Yield: 42 bars.

Lemon Frosting:
1½ cups sifted powdered sugar
1   teaspoon lemon juice
1   teaspoon melted butter or margarine
1   tablespoon warm water

Combine all ingredients, stirring until smooth. Yield: ½ cup.

Coconut Crunch Bars

½ cup butter or margarine, softened
1½ cups firmly packed brown sugar,
      divided
1¼ cups all-purpose flour, divided
¾ teaspoon salt
1 (3½-ounce) can flaked coconut
1 teaspoon vanilla extract
2 eggs, beaten
½ cup chopped pecans

Cream butter and ½ cup sugar; add 1 cup flour, blending well. Pat mixture into a greased 13- x 9- x 2-inch pan. Bake at 375° for 10 to 12 minutes or until lightly browned.

Combine remaining 1 cup brown sugar, ¼ cup flour, and remaining ingredients, stirring well. Spread mixture over pastry. Bake at 375° for 15 to 20 minutes; cut into bars while still warm. Yield: about 30 bars.

Coffee Bars

1 cup firmly packed brown sugar
½ cup shortening
1 egg
1½ cups all-purpose flour
½ teaspoon baking powder
½ teaspoon soda
¼ teaspoon salt
½ teaspoon ground cinnamon
1 teaspoon vanilla extract
½ cup strong coffee
½ cup chopped dates or pecans (optional)
   Frosting (optional)

Cream brown sugar and shortening until light and fluffy; add egg, beating well. Combine flour, baking powder, soda, salt, and cinnamon; add to creamed mixture. Add vanilla and coffee, mixing well. Stir in dates, if desired.

Pour batter into a greased 13- x 9- x 2-inch baking pan. Bake at 375° for 15 to 20 minutes or until done. Cool; frost with your favorite frosting, if desired. Cut into bars to serve. Yield: about 4 dozen bars.

Chewy Peanut Butter Bars

⅓ cup butter or margarine, softened
¼ cup firmly packed brown sugar
1 cup sugar
½ cup peanut butter
1 teaspoon vanilla extract
2 eggs
1 cup all-purpose flour
1 teaspoon baking powder
¼ teaspoon salt
1⅓ cups flaked coconut

Cream butter, sugar, and peanut butter until light and fluffy. Add vanilla and eggs, beating well. Combine flour, baking powder, and salt; stir into sugar mixture just until blended. Stir in coconut.

Spread dough evenly in a greased 13- x 9- 2-inch baking pan. Bake at 350° for 25 minutes. Cool and cut into bars. Yield: about 3 dozen bars.

Oatmeal Squares

½ cup butter or margarine, softened
1 cup sugar
2 eggs
¾ cup all-purpose flour
1 teaspoon ground cinnamon
¼ teaspoon baking powder
1 teaspoon vanilla extract
¾ cup uncooked old-fashioned oats

Cream butter and sugar until light and fluffy. Add eggs, one at a time, beating well after each addition.

Combine flour, cinnamon, and baking powder. Add to creamed mixture, blending well. Stir in vanilla and oats. Pour into a greased 9-inch square pan.

Bake at 350° for 25 minutes. Cut into squares; remove from pan while warm. Yield: 3 dozen squares.

★
Peanut Butter Fingers

      1   *cup all-purpose flour*
      ½   *cup sugar*
      ½   *cup firmly packed brown sugar*
      ½   *teaspoon soda*
      ¼   *teaspoon salt*
      ½   *cup butter or margarine, softened*
      ⅓   *cup crunchy peanut butter*
      1   *egg*
      1   *cup uncooked oats*
      1   *(12-ounce) package semisweet chocolate
              morsels*
      ½   *cup sifted powdered sugar*
      ¼   *cup crunchy peanut butter*
      2   *to 4 tablespoons milk*

Combine flour, sugar, soda, salt, butter, ⅓ cup peanut butter, egg, and oats in a large mixing bowl; mix well.

Press dough into a greased 13- x 9- x 2-inch pan. Bake at 350° for 20 minutes. Remove from oven, and sprinkle with chocolate morsels. Let stand 5 minutes or until melted; spread evenly.

Combine powdered sugar, ¼ cup peanut butter, and milk; beat well. Drizzle over cookies. Cut into 2½- x ¾-inch bars. Yield: about 32 bars.

Hoarder's Cookies

      1   *cup butter or margarine, softened*
      ½   *cup sugar*
      1   *cup firmly packed brown sugar, divided*
      2   *eggs, separated*
      1   *tablespoon water*
      1   *teaspoon vanilla extract*
      2   *cups all-purpose flour*
      1   *teaspoon soda*
      ¼   *teaspoon salt*
      1   *(12-ounce) package semisweet chocolate
              morsels*
      1   *cup skinless salted peanuts, chopped*

Cream butter, sugar, and ½ cup brown sugar until light and fluffy; add beaten egg yolks, mixing well. Stir in water and vanilla.

Combine flour, soda, and salt; add to creamed mixture, blending well. Spread

mixture in a greased 13- x 9- x 2-inch baking pan; sprinkle chocolate morsels evenly over top.

Beat egg whites until foamy; gradually add remaining ½ cup brown sugar, beating until stiff. Spread meringue over chocolate morsels; sprinkle with nuts. Bake at 350° for 35 minutes. Cool and cut into 2-inch squares. Yield: about 2 dozen cookies.

Chocolate Macaroons

      4   *egg whites*
    1½   *cups sugar*
      1   *cup chopped nuts*
      1   *(6-ounce) package chocolate morsels*

Beat egg whites until stiff but not dry. Gradually add sugar, beating until mixture will hold its shape. Fold in nuts and chocolate morsels. Drop from teaspoon onto well-greased cookie sheets. Bake at 350° for 20 minutes. Cool. Yield: 4 dozen cookies.

Oatmeal-Chocolate Chip Cookies

      1   *cup all-purpose flour*
      ¾   *teaspoon soda*
      ½   *teaspoon salt*
      1   *teaspoon ground cinnamon*
      1   *teaspoon ground nutmeg*
      ¾   *cup shortening*
    1⅓   *cups firmly packed brown sugar*
      2   *eggs*
      1   *teaspoon vanilla extract*
      1   *(6-ounce) package semisweet chocolate
              morsels*
      2   *cups regular oats, uncooked*

Combine flour, soda, salt, cinnamon, and nutmeg; set aside.

Cream shortening and sugar until light and fluffy; add eggs and beat well. Add vanilla. Stir in flour mixture until well blended; add chocolate morsels and oats, mixing well.

Drop mixture by teaspoonfuls onto greased cookie sheets. Bake at 350° for 12 to 15 minutes. Yield: about 4 dozen cookies.

Oatmeal-Coconut Crispies

    1 *cup butter or margarine, softened*
    1 *cup sugar*
    1 *cup firmly packed brown sugar*
    2 *eggs, beaten*
  2½ *cups all-purpose flour*
    1 *teaspoon soda*
    1 *teaspoon salt*
    1 *teaspoon vanilla extract*
    1 *cup flaked coconut*
    1 *cup uncooked regular oats*

Cream butter and sugar until light and fluffy; add eggs, blending well. Combine flour, soda, and salt; add to creamed mixture, mixing well. Stir in vanilla, coconut, and oats.

Drop dough by half teaspoonfuls on greased cookie sheets. Bake at 375° about 8 to 10 minutes or until lightly browned. Remove to wire rack immediately. Yield: 5 dozen cookies.

Christmas Fruit Cookies

    ½ *cup shortening*
    ½ *cup firmly packed brown sugar*
    2 *eggs*
    ½ *teaspoon vanilla extract*
    ½ *teaspoon soda*
  1½ *tablespoons buttermilk*
    1 *cup all-purpose flour*
    ¼ *teaspoon ground allspice*
    ¼ *teaspoon ground nutmeg*
    ¼ *teaspoon ground cinnamon*
    ¼ *cup bourbon*
    ½ *pound white raisins*
    ½ *pound chopped candied cherries*
    ½ *pound chopped candied pineapple*
    ½ *cup all-purpose flour*
    ½ *pound chopped pecans*

Cream shortening and sugar; beat in eggs, and add vanilla. Dissolve soda in buttermilk. Combine 1 cup flour and spices; add to creamed mixture alternately with buttermilk and bourbon. Beat well after each addition.

Coat fruit with ½ cup flour; stir fruit and nuts into batter. Drop dough by teaspoonfuls onto greased baking sheets; bake at 350° for 10 to 15 minutes. Yield: 6 dozen cookies.

Toasted Oatmeal Cookies

  1½ *cups regular oats, uncooked*
    2 *cups firmly packed brown sugar*
    ¾ *cup shortening*
    2 *eggs*
  2¼ *cups all-purpose flour*
    1 *teaspoon soda*
    1 *teaspoon baking powder*
    1 *teaspoon ground cinnamon*
    1 *teaspoon ground cloves*
    1 *teaspoon ground nutmeg*
    ⅓ *cup buttermilk or sour milk*
    1 *teaspoon vanilla extract*
    1 *cup chopped dates*
    1 *cup chopped nuts*
    1 *cup raisins*

Toast oats under broiler, stirring frequently to avoid scorching; set aside. Cream sugar, shortening, and eggs until light and fluffy.

Combine flour, soda, baking powder, cinnamon, cloves, and nutmeg; add to creamed mixture alternately with buttermilk. Stir in vanilla. Add oats, dates, nuts, and raisins; mix thoroughly.

Drop by teaspoonfuls onto greased cookie sheets. Bake at 375° for 10 to 12 minutes. Yield: about 7½ dozen cookies.

Sesame Seed Wafers

    ¾ *cup sesame seeds*
    ¾ *cup salad oil*
    2 *cups firmly packed brown sugar*
    1 *egg*
    1 *cup all-purpose flour*
    ½ *teaspoon baking powder*
    ¼ *teaspoon salt*
    1 *teaspoon vanilla extract*

Brown sesame seeds in a heavy skillet, stirring frequently, until lightly browned; set aside. Combine salad oil, brown sugar, and egg in a large bowl; beat until light and fluffy. Add flour, baking powder, and salt; mix well. Stir in vanilla and sesame seeds.

Drop dough by half-teaspoonfuls onto greased cookie sheets. Bake at 325° about 10 minutes or until golden. Remove from oven;

let stand about 1 minute before removing from pan. Cool. Store in a covered container. Yield: about 8 dozen wafers.

Golden Coconut Drops

⅔ cup butter or margarine, softened
⅔ cup sugar
1 egg
2 cups grated fresh coconut
1 cup all-purpose flour
1 teaspoon vanilla extract
1 teaspoon grated orange rind

Cream butter, sugar, and egg until light and fluffy. Stir in remaining ingredients, mixing well. Drop by teaspoonfuls onto lightly greased baking sheets. Bake at 350° about 8 minutes or until golden. Cool slightly; remove from pan. Yield: about 3 dozen cookies.

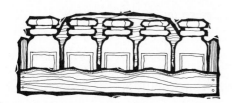

Cook-While-You-Sleep Cookies

2 egg whites
Pinch of salt
¼ teaspoon cream of tartar
⅔ cup sugar
¼ teaspoon vanilla extract
1 cup chopped nuts
1 cup chocolate morsels (optional)

Preheat oven to 350°. Beat egg whites until foamy; add salt and cream of tartar, and beat until stiff. Add sugar, 2 tablespoons at a time, beating well after each addition. Stir in vanilla and nuts. Add chocolate morsels, if desired.

Drop by teaspoonfuls onto cookie sheets lined with aluminum foil. Put in oven; turn off heat immediately. Do not open oven door for at least 8 hours. Carefully remove cookies from foil. Yield: about 4 dozen cookies.

Quick Butterscotch Cookies

1 teaspoon soda
2 teaspoons hot water
1 (1-pound) package light brown sugar
⅔ cup butter or margarine, softened
2 eggs, well beaten
2¼ cups all-purpose flour
1 cup chopped pecans

Dissolve soda in hot water. Cream sugar and butter thoroughly; add eggs and soda mixture, beating until smooth. Add flour and pecans; mix well.

Drop teaspoonfuls of dough 2 inches apart onto lightly greased baking sheets. Bake at 350° for 10 to 15 minutes. Yield: 6 dozen cookies.

Filled Christmas Cookies

½ cup shortening
1 cup sugar
1 egg, beaten
½ cup milk
1 teaspoon vanilla extract
3½ cups all-purpose flour
1 teaspoon soda
2 teaspoons cream of tartar
Preserves

Cream shortening and sugar until light and fluffy; stir in egg. Combine milk and vanilla; set aside. Combine flour, soda, and cream of tartar; add to creamed mixture alternately with milk mixture, beginning and ending with flour mixture and mixing well after each addition.

Roll half of dough on lightly floured board to ⅛-inch thickness; cut with 2-inch round cookie cutters. Place on lightly greased baking sheets; spread 1 teaspoon preserves over each.

Roll remaining dough to ⅛-inch thickness; cut with 2-inch round cookie cutters. Cut a 1-inch round center from each cookie round; place doughnut-shaped round over cookie rounds spread with preserves. Lightly press outer edges together.

Bake at 350° for 10 minutes or until lightly browned. Yield: about 4 dozen cookies.

Old-Fashioned Christmas Cookies

1   *cup butter or margarine, softened*
2   *cups sugar*
¼   *cup firmly packed brown sugar*
2   *eggs*
6   *tablespoons milk*
2   *teaspoons vanilla extract*
4   *cups all-purpose flour*
2   *teaspoons baking powder*
½   *teaspoon salt*
Decorator candies
Decorator icing

Cream butter and sugar until light and fluffy; add eggs, mixing well. Stir in milk and vanilla. Combine flour, baking powder, and salt; add to creamed mixture, mixing well. Chill.

Roll dough out on a lightly floured board to ⅛-inch thickness; cut with shaped cookie cutters. Place on lightly greased baking sheets; bake at 350° for 10 to 12 minutes.

Decorate as desired with decorator candies and icing. Yield: about 5 dozen cookies.

Gingerbread Men

½   *cup butter or margarine, softened*
¾   *cup sugar*
1   *egg, beaten*
¼   *cup molasses*
Juice of ½ orange
3½   *to 4 cups all-purpose flour*
½   *teaspoon salt*
1   *teaspoon soda*
1   *teaspoon ground cinnamon*
1   *teaspoon ground ginger*
Raisins
Decorator candies
Decorator icing

Cream butter and sugar; beat in egg. Add molasses and orange juice to creamed mixture. Combine dry ingredients, and blend into creamed mixture. Chill dough about 1 hour or until stiff enough to handle.

Work with half of dough at a time; store remainder in refrigerator. Roll dough ¼ to ⅛ inch thick between two pieces of waxed paper. Cut with a 4- or 7-inch gingerbread man cutter, and remove excess dough.

Place greased cookie sheet on top of gingerbread men; invert and remove waxed paper. Press raisins into dough for eyes and nose, and decorate as desired with decorator candies.

Bake at 350° for 10 minutes. Cool 1 minute; remove cookies to wire rack to finish cooling. Trim with decorator icing. Yield: 2 dozen (4-inch) or 1 dozen (7-inch) gingerbread men.

Swedish Molasses Cookies

½   *cup butter or margarine, softened*
¾   *cup sugar*
1   *egg*
¾   *cup molasses*
2   *teaspoons grated orange rind*
3½   *cups all-purpose flour*
1   *teaspoon soda*
1½   *teaspoons ground ginger*
1½   *teaspoons ground cinnamon*
1   *teaspoon ground cloves*
¼   *teaspoon ground cardamom*

Cream butter and sugar in a mixing bowl until light and fluffy. Add egg, molasses, and orange rind, mixing well. Combine dry ingredients; gradually add to creamed mixture, stirring well. Cover and refrigerate overnight.

Roll out on a lightly floured pastry cloth to ⅛-inch thickness; cut with 2-inch cookie cutter. Place on a well-greased cookie sheet; bake at 350° for 8 to 10 minutes. Yield: about 6 dozen cookies.

★ Church Windows

1   *(12-ounce) package chocolate morsels*
½   *cup butter or margarine*
1   *(10½-ounce) package multicolored miniature marshmallows*
1   *cup finely chopped pecans*

Melt chocolate and butter over low heat; cool. Add marshmallows and pecans to chocolate mixture. Shape into 2 rolls 1½ to 2 inches in diameter. Refrigerate.

When thoroughly chilled, slice rolls into ½-inch slices. Yield: about 3 dozen cookies.

Lunchbox Cookies

    1   *cup cane syrup*
    ½   *cup shortening*
    1   *teaspoon soda*
    2¼ *cups all-purpose flour*
    1¾ *teaspoons baking powder*
    1   *teaspoon salt*
    1   *teaspoon ground ginger*
    ½   *teaspoon ground cloves*
    ½   *teaspoon ground cinnamon*
    ½   *teaspoon ground nutmeg*

Heat syrup to boiling point in a saucepan large enough for mixing cookies. Remove from heat; stir in shortening and soda.

Combine flour, baking powder, salt, and spices; add to syrup mixture, mixing well. Chill 8 hours or overnight.

Roll dough out to 1/16-inch thickness on lightly floured board or pastry cloth. Cut with a 1½-inch cookie cutter. Place on lightly greased baking sheets and bake at 350° for 5 to 7 minutes. Yield: 6½ dozen cookies.

Date Swirls

    ½   *cup shortening*
    ½   *cup firmly packed brown sugar*
    ½   *cup sugar*
    1   *egg, beaten*
    2   *cups all-purpose flour*
    ½   *teaspoon soda*
    ¼   *teaspoon salt*
    Date Filling

Cream shortening and sugar; add egg, beating well. Combine flour, soda, and salt; add to creamed mixture, blending well. Chill.

Roll dough into a ¼-inch-thick rectangle on a lightly floured surface; spread evenly with Date Filling. Roll jellyroll fashion, and wrap in waxed paper; chill overnight.

Slice roll into ¼-inch-thick slices, and place on lightly greased cookie sheets. Bake at 375° for 8 to 10 minutes or until lightly browned. Yield: about 4 dozen cookies.

    Date Filling:

    1   *(8-ounce) package pitted dates, finely*
        chopped
    ¼   *cup sugar*
    ⅛   *teaspoon salt*
    ⅓   *cup water*
    ¼   *cup chopped pecans*

Combine dates, sugar, salt, and water; cook over low heat 5 minutes. Remove from heat; add pecans. Cool slightly. Yield: about 1½ cups.

Sugar Cookies

    ½   *cup butter or margarine, softened*
    ¾   *cup sugar*
    ¾   *teaspoon vanilla extract*
    1   *egg*
    2   *cups all-purpose flour*
    ½   *teaspoon soda*
    ½   *teaspoon salt*
    Sugar

Cream butter and ¾ cup sugar until light and fluffy; add vanilla and egg, mixing well. Combine flour, soda, and salt; add to creamed mixture, blending well (mixture will be very stiff).

Divide dough into 3 parts; roll each part on lightly floured waxed paper to ⅛-inch thickness.

Cut out cookies with a cutter, and place on lightly greased cookie sheets. Sprinkle cookies with sugar, and bake at 375° for 10 minutes or until lightly browned. Yield: about 5 dozen (2½-inch) cookies.

Cottage Cheese Crescents

1   (8-ounce) carton cottage cheese
2   cups all-purpose flour
1   cup butter or margarine
About ¾ cup apricot or other jam
1   egg, slightly beaten
Powdered sugar

Put cottage cheese through a food mill or strainer, or mash until smooth. Combine cottage cheese and flour; cut in butter with pastry blender or 2 knives until mixture resembles coarse crumbs.

Form dough into a ball; then knead lightly, adding more flour if necessary, until dough is smooth and no longer sticks to board or hands. Wrap in waxed paper, and refrigerate about 2 hours.

Work with a third of dough at a time; store remaining dough in refrigerator. Place dough on a lightly floured board; roll into an oblong less than ⅛ inch thick. Cut into 2½-inch strips; then cut each strip into 2½-inch squares. Roll each square again to make a 3½-inch square. (Dough is lightest when rolled thin.)

Place 1 teaspoon jam on each square. Roll up lightly, beginning at one corner and rolling to opposite corner. Bend into a crescent so that overlapping corner faces away from you; place on ungreased baking sheets.

Brush top of crescents with egg. Bake at 350° about 15 minutes or until golden brown.

Remove from baking sheets while hot. When completely cool, store in an airtight container.

Serve crescents cold or slightly warm. Dust with powdered sugar before serving. Yield: 30 to 40 crescents.

Butternut Balls

1   cup margarine, softened
½   cup sifted powdered sugar
½   teaspoon salt
2   teaspoons vanilla extract
2   cups all-purpose flour
1   cup finely chopped pecans
Powdered sugar

Cream margarine and sugar until light and fluffy. Add salt, vanilla, and flour, mixing well. Stir in pecans. Shape dough into 1-inch balls, and place on ungreased cookie sheets. Bake at 375° for 10 to 12 minutes or until lightly browned. Roll each in powdered sugar while warm. Yield: 3 dozen balls.

Almond Treats

3   eggs, well beaten
½   cup melted shortening
¾   cup sugar
3   cups all-purpose flour
¼   teaspoon salt
3   teaspoons baking powder
½   cup coarsely chopped almonds
1   teaspoon vanilla extract
1   teaspoon almond extract

Combine eggs and shortening, beating well; gradually add sugar, mixing well. Combine flour, salt, and baking powder; gradually add to creamed mixture, blending well. Stir in almonds and flavorings.

Lightly grease hands, and shape dough into six 4-inch-long loaves. Place on a lightly greased cookie sheet. Bake at 325° for 20 to 25 minutes; remove carefully.

Cut each loaf into ½-inch slices. Place cookies, cut side down, on cookie sheets; bake an additional 15 minutes or until lightly browned. Remove to wire racks to cool. Yield: about 3 dozen cookies.

★
Chocolate Buttersweets

½   cup butter or margarine, softened
½   cup powdered sugar
¼   teaspoon salt
 1   teaspoon vanilla extract
1¼ cups all-purpose flour
     Creamy Nut Filling
     Chocolate Frosting

Cream butter and sugar until light and fluffy; add salt and vanilla, beating well. Gradually stir in flour, mixing until well blended.

Shape dough into 1-inch balls, and place on ungreased cookie sheets. Using index finger or a thimble dipped in flour, press a hole in center of each ball. Bake at 350° for 12 to 15 minutes or until lightly browned.

While cookies are still warm, fill center of each with about 1 teaspoon Creamy Nut Filling. Cool completely, and spread with Chocolate Frosting. Yield: about 3 dozen cookies.

Creamy Nut Filling:

 1   (3-ounce) package cream cheese,
       softened
 1   cup sifted powdered sugar
 2   tablespoons all-purpose flour
 1   teaspoon vanilla extract
½   cup chopped walnuts
¼   cup flaked coconut

Combine cream cheese, powdered sugar, flour, and vanilla; beat until smooth. Stir in walnuts and coconut. Yield: about 1 cup.

Chocolate Frosting:

½   cup semisweet chocolate morsels
 2   tablespoons butter or margarine
 2   tablespoons water
½   cup sifted powdered sugar

Combine chocolate, butter, and water in a small saucepan; place over low heat, stirring until chocolate and butter are melted. Remove from heat, and stir in powdered sugar; beat until smooth.

If frosting gets too thick to spread smoothly, blend in a few more drops of water. Yield: about 1 cup.

Chocolate Crinkle Cookies

 4   (1-ounce) squares unsweetened
       chocolate, melted
½   cup salad oil
 2   cups sugar
 4   eggs
 2   cups all-purpose flour
 2   teaspoons baking powder
½   teaspoon salt
     About ¾ cup powdered sugar

Combine chocolate, oil, and sugar. Add eggs, one at a time, beating well after each addition. Combine flour, baking powder, and salt; add to chocolate mixture, mixing well. Chill several hours or overnight.

Roll dough into 1-inch balls; roll each in powdered sugar, and roll again between palms of hands. Place 2 inches apart on lightly greased cookie sheets. Bake at 350° for 10 to 12 minutes (centers will be somewhat soft). Remove to wire rack to cool. Yield: 6 dozen cookies.

Chocolate Crunch Cookies

 1   cup sugar
 1   cup firmly packed brown sugar
 1   cup salad oil
 2   eggs
 1   teaspoon vanilla extract
 4   cups all-purpose flour
 4   teaspoons cream of tartar
 2   teaspoons soda
 1   teaspoon salt
 1   cup crunchy nutlike cereal nuggets
 1   (12-ounce) package chocolate morsels

Combine sugar and salad oil; cream until smooth. Beat in eggs and vanilla. Combine flour, cream of tartar, soda, and salt; stir into creamed mixture. Add cereal and chocolate morsels, mixing well.

Shape dough into 1-inch balls. (Mixture will be crumbly.) Place on greased cookie sheets about 2 inches apart. Bake at 350° for 10 to 12 minutes. Yield: 4 dozen cookies.

★
Whole Wheat Peanut Butter Cookies

½ cup butter or margarine, softened
½ cup peanut butter
½ cup sugar
½ cup firmly packed brown sugar
1 egg
½ teaspoon vanilla extract
1¼ cups whole wheat flour
½ teaspoon baking powder
¾ teaspoon soda
¼ teaspoon salt

Cream butter, peanut butter, sugar, egg, and vanilla until light and fluffy. Combine flour, baking powder, soda, and salt, blending well; stir into creamed mixture.

Cover dough tightly, and refrigerate several hours or overnight.

Shape dough into balls about ¾ inch in diameter. Place balls 3 inches apart on a greased cookie sheet; flatten each cookie with the tines of a fork. Bake at 375° for 8 to 12 minutes or until set but not hard. Yield: about 4 dozen cookies.

Crunchy Peanut Butter-Oatmeal Cookies

½ cup shortening
1 cup sugar
½ cup crunchy peanut butter
1 egg, beaten
2 tablespoons milk
1¼ cups all-purpose flour
½ teaspoon soda
½ teaspoon salt
1 cup uncooked regular oats

Cream shortening and sugar until light and fluffy. Add peanut butter, egg, and milk; beat well. Combine dry ingredients; add to creamed mixture, mixing well. Chill 30 minutes.

Shape dough into walnut-size balls; place on lightly greased cookie sheets. Press flat with a fork. Bake at 375° about 10 minutes or until lightly browned. Yield: 4 dozen cookies.

Swedish Butter Cookies

1 cup butter, softened
¼ cup powdered sugar
2 cups all-purpose flour
¼ teaspoon baking powder
½ teaspoon vanilla extract
Frosting

Cream butter and sugar until fluffy. Add flour, baking powder, and vanilla; mix well. Shape into 2 rolls, and chill until firm. Cut each roll into ¼-inch slices; place on lightly greased cookie sheets. Bake at 375° for 10 minutes or until edges are lightly browned. Remove to wire racks to cool. Spread with Frosting. Yield: 4 dozen cookies.

Frosting:

3 tablespoons melted butter or margarine
1 cup powdered sugar
2 teaspoons vanilla extract
Boiling water

Cook butter until browned; add sugar, vanilla, and a small amount of boiling water. Beat until spreading consistency. Yield: frosting for 4 dozen cookies.

Pineapple Preserves Cookies

1 cup sugar
¾ cup margarine, softened
1 egg
2¼ cups all-purpose flour
1 teaspoon soda
½ teaspoon salt
¼ cup pineapple preserves
Additional pineapple preserves

Cream sugar and margarine until light and fluffy; add egg, beating well. Combine flour, soda, and salt; add to creamed mixture, mixing well. Stir in ¼ cup pineapple preserves.

Shape dough into walnut-size balls; place on greased cookie sheets. Make a slight indentation in each cookie. Spoon a small amount of pineapple preserves in each indentation. Bake at 375° for 10 minutes or until done. Yield: about 5 dozen cookies.

Merry Mincemeat Cookies

½ cup shortening
½ cup butter or margarine, softened
½ cup firmly packed brown sugar
¼ cup sugar
1 egg, well beaten
1½ teaspoons vanilla extract
1 (9-ounce) package condensed mincemeat
2½ cups all-purpose flour
1 teaspoon baking powder
½ teaspoon salt

Cream shortening, butter, and sugar until light and fluffy; add egg and vanilla, beating well. Break mincemeat into small pieces; stir into creamed mixture. Combine flour, baking powder, and salt; add to creamed mixture, blending well. Chill at least 2 hours.

Shape dough into walnut-size balls, and place on a lightly greased cookie sheet. Gently press each cookie flat with bottom of a glass. Bake at 400° for 5 to 8 minutes or until lightly browned. Remove from cookie sheet at once, and cool on a wire rack. Yield: about 6½ dozen cookies.

Sesame Cookies

6 eggs
2 cups sugar
2 cups margarine, softened
6 cups all-purpose flour
3 tablespoons baking powder
1 teaspoon salt
1 teaspoon ground cinnamon
Sesame seeds

Combine eggs and sugar; beat until light and lemon colored. Add margarine, and continue beating until mixture is fluffy. Combine flour, baking powder, salt, and cinnamon; add to egg mixture, and mix well. Mixture will be very stiff and may require mixing with hands.

Pinch off about a teaspoon of dough at a time, and shape into small balls or oblongs. Roll each in sesame seeds, and place about ½ inch apart on greased cookie sheets. Bake at 325° about 15 to 18 minutes. Yield: about 10 dozen cookies.

Turtle Cookies

2 (1-ounce) squares semisweet chocolate
⅓ cup butter or margarine
2 eggs, beaten
¾ cup sugar
1 teaspoon vanilla extract
1 cup all-purpose flour
Frosting
Pecan halves

Combine chocolate and butter in a heavy saucepan. Place over low heat, stirring constantly until melted; cool. Combine eggs, sugar, vanilla, and chocolate mixture, blending well. Add flour, mixing well.

Preheat waffle iron on medium heat. Drop batter by teaspoonfuls onto waffle iron, spacing about 2 inches apart. Close waffle iron, and bake about 1½ minutes or until cookies are done. Cool on wire racks and frost with your favorite frosting; top with pecan halves. Yield: about 2 dozen cookies.

Peanut Brittle

2 cups sugar
1 cup light corn syrup
½ cup water
2½ cups raw peanuts
1 tablespoon butter or margarine
1 teaspoon salt
1 teaspoon vanilla extract
2 teaspoons soda

Combine sugar, syrup, and water in a saucepan; cook over low heat until mixture comes to a boil. Add peanuts, and cook until candy thermometer registers 290°. Remove from heat; add butter, salt, vanilla, and soda, mixing well. Spread thinly onto 2 buttered cookie sheets. Cool and break into pieces. Yield: about 2 pounds peanut brittle.

Sesame Seed Brittle

1 *cup sesame seeds*
1 *cup sugar*
1 *cup dark corn syrup*
¼ *cup water*
2 *tablespoons butter or margarine*
1 *teaspoon soda*

Toast sesame seeds on a large baking sheet at 350° about 15 minutes, stirring frequently. Set aside.

Combine sugar, corn syrup, water, and butter in a 2-quart saucepan. Bring to a boil over medium heat, stirring constantly until sugar is dissolved. Reduce heat, and cook without stirring until mixture reaches the hard-crack stage (300° on the candy thermometer).

Remove from heat; stir in sesame seeds and soda. Pour onto a greased surface, and spread evenly to about ⅛-inch thickness. Cool. Break into pieces. Yield: about 1½ pounds.

★ Double Almond Toffee

2 *cups butter or margarine*
2½ *cups sugar*
1½ *cups whole unblanched almonds*
1½ *cups semisweet chocolate morsels, melted, divided*
1½ *cups chopped almonds, lightly toasted, divided*

Melt butter in a large, heavy skillet; add sugar. Cook, stirring constantly, over high heat until mixture foams vigorously (about 6 minutes). Reduce heat to low; cook and stir 5 minutes.

Add whole almonds to sugar mixture; increase heat to high. Cook, stirring constantly, until almonds begin to pop (about 5 minutes).

Reduce heat; cook, stirring constantly, 7 minutes. (If mixture begins to get too dark, remove from heat but continue to stir entire 7 minutes.) Pour into a 15- x 10- x 1-inch pan; cool until firm.

Spread half of melted chocolate over toffee layer. Sprinkle with half of chopped almonds; cool. (Refrigerate if necessary to firm chocolate.)

Turn candy out on waxed paper; spread remaining chocolate over other side. Sprinkle with remaining chopped almonds; cool. Break into pieces. Store in waxed paper-lined covered metal containers. Yield: about 3 pounds toffee.

Bourbon Pralines

2 *cups sugar*
1 *teaspoon soda*
1 *cup buttermilk*
Pinch of salt
2 *tablespoons butter or margarine*
2⅓ *cups broken pecans or walnuts*
5 *tablespoons bourbon*

Combine sugar, soda, buttermilk, and salt in a large saucepan. Cook, stirring frequently, until candy thermometer registers 210°. Add butter and pecans. Cook, stirring constantly, to the soft-ball stage (230°).

Remove from heat, and stir in bourbon; cool about 1 minute. Beat by hand until mixture begins to thicken (about 5 minutes). Drop by tablespoonfuls onto waxed paper; let stand until firm. Yield: about 2½ dozen pralines.

Pralines

2 *cups sugar*
1 *cup milk*
8 *large marshmallows*
2 *tablespoons butter or margarine*
½ *teaspoon vanilla extract*
1 *to 2 cups pecans*

Combine sugar, milk, and marshmallows in a heavy 4-quart saucepan; cook over medium heat to the soft-ball stage (230°), stirring constantly. Remove from heat; stir in butter and vanilla. Beat until creamy. Add pecans; beat just until mixture begins to thicken.

Working rapidly, drop mixture by tablespoonfuls onto lightly buttered waxed paper; cool. Store in an airtight container. Yield: about 15 (3-inch) pralines.

Divine Divinity

2½ cups sugar
½ cup light corn syrup
½ cup warm water
2 egg whites, stiffly beaten
1 cup chopped nuts
1 tablespoon vanilla extract

Combine sugar, corn syrup, and water in a saucepan. Place over low heat; boil until mixture forms threads when dropped from a spoon (230° on candy thermometer). Slowly pour half the syrup into the egg whites, beating while pouring.

Boil remaining syrup until a hard ball is formed when syrup is dropped from a spoon into cold water (262° on candy thermometer). Slowly pour syrup into egg white mixture, beating until thick. Stir in nuts and vanilla.

Drop candy by teaspoonfuls onto waxed paper or a lightly buttered cookie sheet. Cool; store in airtight container. Yield: about 2 dozen pieces.

★
Millionaires

1 (14-ounce) package caramels
3 to 4 tablespoons milk
2 cups pecan pieces
Butter or margarine
¼ (4-ounce) bar paraffin
1 (12-ounce) package semisweet chocolate morsels

Melt caramels in milk over low heat; add pecans. Drop by teaspoonfuls onto buttered waxed paper. Chill. Melt paraffin and chocolate morsels in a heavy saucepan over low heat. Dip candy into chocolate, and return to waxed paper. Chill. Yield: 3½ dozen.

Coconut Caramels

1 cup sugar
¾ cup light corn syrup
1½ cups half-and-half, divided
1 (3½-ounce) can coconut
2 tablespoons butter or margarine
1 tablespoon vanilla extract

Combine sugar, corn syrup, and ½ cup half-and-half in a heavy saucepan. Cook over low heat, stirring constantly, until mixture reaches soft-ball stage (230° on candy thermometer).

Add ½ cup half-and-half; cook, stirring constantly, until mixture reaches soft-ball stage again. Add remaining half-and-half; cook, stirring constantly, until mixture again reaches the soft-ball stage.

Remove mixture from heat; add coconut, butter, and vanilla. Stir until butter is melted. Pour into a greased 8- x 4- x 2⅝-inch loafpan; let stand until cool.

Turn candy out onto a marble slab or waxed paper. Cut into 1-inch squares. Let stand overnight. Wrap individually in plastic wrap. Yield: about 32 (1-inch) pieces.

Nutty Marshmallow Log

2 cups chopped pecans
About 1¼ cups sifted powdered sugar, divided
1 (16-ounce) package marshmallows
3 to 4 tablespoons peanut butter

Combine pecans and 1 cup powdered sugar; sprinkle evenly over a large sheet of waxed paper, and set aside.

Melt marshmallows in top of a double boiler; stir in peanut butter. Pour mixture over powdered sugar-pecan mixture. Mix with hands until pecans and sugar are blended into marshmallow mixture and mixture resembles soft dough.

Shape into 2 rolls, 1 inch in diameter. Let stand about 45 minutes. Roll candy in remaining powdered sugar. Let stand 30 minutes. Cut into ¼-inch slices. Store in a covered container, separating layers with waxed paper. Yield: about 100 slices.

Cream Cheese Mints

2½   cups powdered sugar
1   (3-ounce) package cream cheese, softened
½   teaspoon peppermint extract
7   drops red food coloring
7   drops green food coloring
Sugar

Cream powdered sugar and cream cheese together in a small bowl. Blend in peppermint. Divide mixture in half; add red food coloring to half of mixture and green food coloring to the other half. Knead each mixture until consistency of pie dough. Form dough into ½-inch balls; roll balls in sugar. Press into candy molds, and remove immediately. Yield: about 2 dozen mints.

Chocolate Balls

1   tablespoon cocoa
½   cup powdered sugar
¼   cup bourbon
1   tablespoon light corn syrup
½   cup finely ground pecans
1¼   cups finely crushed vanilla wafers
2   egg whites
12   ounces chocolate sprinkles

Sift cocoa and sugar together; set aside. Combine bourbon and corn syrup in a bowl; stir in cocoa mixture, pecans, and vanilla wafers.

Roll mixture into 1-inch balls. Dip each ball into egg white, and roll in chocolate sprinkles. Store in a covered container. These freeze well. Yield: about 20 chocolate balls.

★
Peanut Butter Balls

1½   cups crunchy peanut butter
2   cups margarine
1   teaspoon vanilla extract
2½   (16-ounce) packages powdered sugar
1   (12-ounce) package semisweet chocolate morsels
¼   (4-ounce) bar paraffin

Melt peanut butter and margarine in a saucepan over low heat; stir in vanilla, and remove from heat. Add powdered sugar; mix well, and shape into 1-inch balls.

Melt chocolate morsels and paraffin in a saucepan over very low heat. Dip each ball into chocolate, and cool on waxed paper. Reheat chocolate if it thickens. Yield: 9 dozen balls.

Creamy Peanut Butter Fudge

2   cups sugar
⅔   cup milk
¾   cup smooth peanut butter
¾   cup marshmallow cream
¼   cup butter or margarine

Combine sugar and milk in a saucepan; cook to soft-ball stage (230° on candy thermometer). Remove from heat; add remaining ingredients, mixing well. Pour into a buttered 8-inch square dish. Allow to cool before cutting into squares. Yield: 32 (2-inch) squares.

German Chocolate Fudge

1   (12-ounce) package semisweet chocolate morsels
3   (4-ounce) bars sweet chocolate, broken into pieces
1   (7-ounce) jar marshmallow cream
4½   cups sugar
2   tablespoons butter or margarine
1   (13-ounce) can evaporated milk, undiluted
Pinch of salt
2   cups chopped nuts

Combine chocolate morsels, sweet chocolate, and marshmallow cream in a large bowl; set aside. Combine sugar, butter, milk, and salt in a heavy skillet. Bring mixture to a boil; boil 6 minutes, stirring constantly.

Pour hot syrup over chocolate mixture; stir with a wooden spoon until smooth. Add nuts, and mix well. Spread fudge in a buttered 15½- x 10½- x 1-inch pan; when cool, cut into squares. Yield: about 5 pounds fudge.

Strawberry Candies

1 (15-ounce) can sweetened condensed
    milk
1 pound finely ground coconut
2 (3-ounce) packages strawberry-flavored
    gelatin, divided
1 cup finely ground almonds
1 tablespoon sugar
1 teaspoon vanilla extract
1 (4½-ounce) can green decorator icing

Combine milk, coconut, 1 package gelatin, almonds, sugar, and vanilla; mix well. Shape mixture into strawberries. Roll candies in remaining gelatin, coating thoroughly. Let candies dry until firm. Make leaves with icing on top of candies. Store in a covered container. Yield: about 48 pieces.

Citrus Bonbons

3 cups finely crushed vanilla wafers
2 tablespoons cocoa
1 cup powdered sugar
1 cup finely chopped pecans
¼ cup lemon juice
¼ cup orange juice
1 tablespoon grated orange rind
Granulated sugar

Combine all ingredients except granulated sugar in a large mixing bowl; mix well. Shape into ½-inch balls; roll each in granulated sugar. Place on waxed paper, and let stand 1 hour. Store in a tightly covered container. Yield: about 47 (½-inch) bonbons.

Candied Fresh Coconut

1 cup sugar
½ cup water
1 fresh coconut, sliced into ¼-inch strips

Combine sugar and water in a saucepan; cook, stirring constantly, until mixture spins a thread (230° on candy thermometer). Stir in coconut, and cook until syrup begins to sugar. Turn out on waxed paper, and separate pieces. Yield: about 3 cups.

Chocolate Covered Strawberries

1 pint fresh strawberries
3 tablespoons butter or margarine,
    softened
3 tablespoons light corn syrup
Dash of salt
2 cups sifted powdered sugar
2 (12-ounce) packages milk chocolate
    morsels

Wash strawberries; remove stems, if desired. Drain well; dry on paper towels. Combine butter, corn syrup, and salt, blending well; stir in powdered sugar. Knead sugar mixture until smooth; chill about 30 minutes.

Shape a small amount of sugar mixture around each strawberry. Place on waxed paper; chill until firm. Melt chocolate over low heat; dip each strawberry into chocolate. Place on waxed paper; chill. Store in a cool place. Yield: about 25 strawberries.

Stuffed Dates

1½ pounds pitted dates
¾ cup powdered sugar
¼ cup butter or margarine, softened
Dash of salt
½ teaspoon grated orange rind
⅓ cup finely chopped walnuts
Few drops of imitation brandy extract
    (optional)
Powdered sugar

Cut one side of dates with scissors or knife; spread apart. Cream sugar, butter, and salt until very light and fluffy; add orange rind, nuts, and brandy extract, if desired. Stuff each date generously; then press 2 whole dates together to make one, and roll each in powdered sugar. Let stand several hours before serving. Yield: about 4 dozen dates.

Crazy Crunch

2   quarts popped corn
1⅓ cups pecans
⅔   cup almonds
1⅓ cups sugar
1   cup butter or margarine
½   cup light corn syrup
1   teaspoon vanilla extract

Combine popped corn, pecans, and almonds on a cookie sheet. Combine sugar, butter, and corn syrup in a 1½-quart saucepan. Bring to a boil; cook over low heat 10 to 15 minutes or until mixture turns a light-caramel color. Remove from heat, and stir in vanilla.

Pour over popped corn mixture, and mix to coat well; spread thinly over sheet. Break apart when cool, and store in a tightly covered container. Yield: 2 pounds.

Fruit Balls

½   cup seedless raisins, ground
½   cup pitted dates, ground
½   cup dried figs, ground
½   cup medium-size dried apricots, ground
Juice and grated rind of 1 orange
Chopped walnuts or pecans

Combine raisins, dates, figs, and apricots; add orange rind and just enough juice to soften. Shape into walnut-size balls, and roll each in walnuts. Yield: about 1½ dozen.

Apricot-Coconut Balls

2   (6-ounce) packages dried apricots, ground
2   cups shredded coconut
⅔   cup sweetened condensed milk
Powdered sugar

Combine apricots and coconut; stir to mix. Add condensed milk and mix well. Shape into 1-inch balls and coat with powdered sugar. Yield: about 5 dozen.

Caramel Corn

2   cups firmly packed brown sugar
1   cup butter or margarine
½   cup white corn syrup
2   teaspoons salt
1   teaspoon soda
1   cup peanuts or pecans
7½ quarts popped corn

Combine brown sugar, butter, syrup, and salt in a saucepan. Bring to a boil; boil 5 minutes. Beat in soda vigorously. Stir in nuts. Place corn in a large shallow pan. Pour sugar mixture over corn; stir. Bake at 200° for 1 hour, stirring every 15 minutes. Yield: 7½ quarts.

Holiday Fruit Balls

¼   cup butter or margarine
½   pound miniature marshmallows
½   cup evaporated milk
½   pound graham cracker crumbs
½   pound candied pineapple, chopped
½   pound candied cherries, chopped
½   pound light raisins
1½ pounds chopped nuts
1   cup flaked coconut

Combine margarine, marshmallows, and milk in a saucepan. Cook over low heat until melted, stirring constantly.

Combine cracker crumbs, fruits, and nuts in a large mixing bowl. Add milk mixture, stirring until well mixed. Form into 1½-inch balls and roll in coconut. Yield: 5 dozen.

Clungoes

  1 *(12-ounce) box vanilla wafers*
 ¼ *to ½ cup melted butter or margarine*
  1 *cup powdered sugar*
  1 *cup chopped pecans*
  1 *(6-ounce) can frozen orange juice
      concentrate, thawed and undiluted*
     Powdered sugar

Crush vanilla wafers into fine crumbs; add butter, 1 cup powdered sugar, and pecans. Add orange juice concentrate; blend well. Chill.

Form mixture into 1-inch balls; roll each in powdered sugar. Refrigerate 24 hours before serving. These may be frozen. Yield: 2 to 2½ dozen.

Chocolate-Covered Easter Eggs

  ½ *cup light corn syrup*
 2½ *cups sugar*
  ¼ *teaspoon salt*
  ½ *cup water*
  2 *egg whites, beaten stiff*
  3 *cups chopped pecans*
 1½ *cups candied cherries, halved (optional)*
  1 *(12-ounce) package semisweet chocolate
      morsels*
  ¼ *bar paraffin wax*
     Decorator icing

Combine corn syrup, sugar, salt, and water, mixing well. Cook over medium heat, stirring constantly until sugar dissolves. Cook without stirring until mixture reaches firm-ball stage (248° on candy thermometer). Slowly pour half of sugar mixture over beaten egg whites, beating constantly with electric mixer.

Cook remaining half of sugar mixture over medium heat to hard-ball stage (260° on candy thermometer). Pour mixture slowly over egg white mixture; beat until mixture holds its shape and mixer cannot beat any more. Beat with wooden spoon until mixture is no longer glossy.

Stir in pecans and cherries. Shape mixture into 2-inch eggs or 2 large (1¼-to 1½-pound) eggs.

Melt chocolate morsels and paraffin in a saucepan over very low heat, stirring constantly. Dip each egg into chocolate; cool on waxed paper. Reheat chocolate if it thickens. Decorate as desired with decorator icing. Yield: about 30 (2-inch) eggs or 2 (1¼-to 1½-pound) eggs.

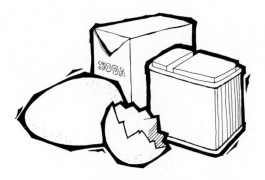

Nutty Popcorn Balls

  2 *cups sugar*
  ¾ *cup light corn syrup*
  ¾ *cup water*
 1½ *teaspoons salt*
  ½ *cup butter or margarine*
 1½ *teaspoons vanilla extract*
  3 *quarts popped corn*
  1 *cup coarsely chopped pecans*

Combine sugar, corn syrup, water, and salt in a saucepan; place over medium heat, stirring until sugar is dissolved. Cook, without stirring, until syrup forms a hard ball when dropped in cold water or until candy thermometer registers 250°. Remove from heat, and add butter and vanilla.

Combine popped corn and pecans in large pan; pour hot syrup over top, mixing well. Grease hands with butter, and shape mixture into balls; place on waxed paper to dry. Yield: about 1 dozen.

Desserts

In the South, no meal is complete without dessert. And it's no wonder when you discover what some of them are. Old traditions as simple as Ambrosia or as elaborate as Chocolate Cherry Cheesecake tempt everyone's sweet tooth.

To relieve the summer's heat, we reach for the ice cream freezer, choose a flavor, and invite friends over to enjoy homemade ice cream. Select from vanilla, or a new flavor like lemon, taffy apple, peach, chocolate mint, rhubarb, and a host of creamy sherbets.

Every family has its favorite desserts like puddings, custards, and apple dumplings. These join a delicious array of elegant sweets. A light soufflé sparked with coffee-flavored liqueur, a cream puff filled with strawberries (not as difficult as they look), and a rich chocolate mousse are only a few waiting to be tried.

Apricot Crêpes

    2   eggs, beaten
    1   cup milk
    1   cup club soda
    2   cups all-purpose flour
    ¼   teaspoon salt
    1   teaspoon vanilla extract
    ½   cup melted butter or margarine
    1   cup apricot jam
    1   cup ground walnuts
        Powdered sugar

Combine eggs, milk, and club soda quickly. Add flour and salt, stirring constantly; stir in vanilla. Brush the bottom of a 6- or 7-inch crêpe pan or heavy skillet lightly with melted butter, and place pan over medium heat until just hot, not smoking.

Pour 2 tablespoons batter in pan, and quickly tilt pan in all directions so batter covers pan in a thin film. Cook about 1 minute. Lift edge of crêpe to test for doneness.

The crêpe is ready for flipping when it can be shaken loose from pan. Flip the crêpe and cook about 30 seconds on the other side; this is rarely more than a spotty brown and is used as the side on which filling is placed.

Spread jam over each crêpe, and roll up; keep warm while making the remaining crêpes. Sprinkle with walnuts and powdered sugar before serving. Serve warm. Yield: 16 to 18 crêpes.

Note: Crêpes can be made in advance and stacked between layers of waxed paper or paper towels to prevent sticking. Crêpes can be frozen, filled or unfilled. Heat them in a covered dish at 300° to thaw.

Gingered Fruit Compote

    2   apples, cored and sliced
    2   oranges, peeled and sectioned
    2   bananas, sliced
    ½   cup orange juice
    1½ tablespoons grated fresh ginger

Combine all ingredients; cover and chill 2 hours. Yield: 4 servings.

Fresh Peach Ice Cream (page 129) is one of the many bonuses of the peach season.

Ambrosia

6 *oranges, peeled and sectioned*
½ *cup sugar or to taste*
1 *coconut, grated*

Place a layer of orange sections in a glass bowl; sprinkle with sugar, and layer with coconut. Repeat layers, ending with coconut. Chill. Yield: 6 to 8 servings.

Hawaiian Ambrosia

1 *fresh pineapple, peeled, cored, and cut into chunks*
3 *papayas, peeled, seeded, and cut into chunks*
4 *mangoes, peeled, seeded, and cut into chunks*
6 *bananas, sliced*
3 *cups melon balls*
½ *cup light honey*
¾ *cup kirsch*

Combine fruits with honey; mix gently. Chill. Just before serving, add kirsch, and mix lightly. Yield: 10 servings.

Sugar-Crusted Apples

6 *large cooking apples*
⅓ *cup all-purpose flour*
⅔ *cup sugar*
½ *teaspoon ground cinnamon*
⅓ *cup margarine, softened*
1 *egg, slightly beaten*
¾ *cup orange juice*
Whipped cream

Core and peel apples. Combine flour, sugar, and cinnamon; cut in margarine with 2 knives or a pastry blender until mixture resembles coarse cornmeal. Brush apples with egg, and roll each in flour mixture.

Arrange apples in a greased, shallow baking pan; fill cavities of apples with any remaining flour mixture. Pour orange juice into pan; bake, uncovered, at 350° for 1 hour or until apples are tender. Serve warm with pan liquid; top with whipped cream. Yield: 6 servings.

Baked Cinnamon Apples

1 *cup water*
1 *cup sugar*
1 *cup red cinnamon candies*
6 *medium-size baking apples, peeled, cored, and quartered*

Combine water and sugar in a saucepan; bring to a boil. Add candies, stirring constantly until melted.

Place apples in a 7½- x 11¾-inch baking dish; pour candy syrup over apples. Bake at 400° for 20 minutes. Turn apples over; bake 20 additional minutes, basting frequently with syrup. Yield: 6 servings.

Note: Whole baking apples may be substituted for wedges. Bake at 400° for 40 minutes, basting frequently.

Strawberries with Mint

1 *quart fresh strawberries*
2 *tablespoons chopped fresh mint*
½ *cup orange juice*
1 *teaspoon grated orange rind*
½ *cup powdered sugar*
Whipped cream (optional)

Cap strawberries; rinse and drain. Combine strawberries, mint, orange juice, and orange rind; toss gently. Sprinkle with sugar; chill at least 1 hour. Garnish with whipped cream, if desired. Yield: 6 to 8 servings.

Rhubarb-Strawberry Rolls

    1   *cup water*
    1¼ *cups sugar, divided*
    2   *cups (about 1 pound) diced rhubarb*
    1   *cup sliced strawberries*
    2   *cups all-purpose flour*
    ½   *teaspoon salt*
    4   *teaspoons baking powder*
    1   *tablespoon sugar*
    ⅓   *cup shortening*
    1   *egg, well beaten*
    ½   *cup milk*
    2   *tablespoons melted butter or margarine*
        Cream (optional)

Combine water and ¾ cup sugar in a small saucepan; bring to a boil, and cook 5 minutes. Pour syrup into a greased 8-inch square pan.

Combine rhubarb, strawberries, and ½ cup sugar; set aside.

Combine flour, salt, baking powder, and 1 tablespoon sugar; cut in shortening until mixture resembles coarse meal. Combine egg and milk; add to flour mixture, and stir just until moistened. Turn dough out onto a lightly floured surface, and roll to a ½-inch thickness; brush dough with butter.

Drain any excess juice from fruit and add juice to syrup in pan; arrange fruit on dough and roll up jellyroll fashion, pinching edges to seal. Slice roll into 8 pieces and place, cut side down, in hot syrup in pan. Bake at 425° for 30 to 35 minutes. Serve warm with cream, if desired. Yield: 8 servings.

★ Cherries Jubilee

    1   *(16-ounce) can dark pitted cherries*
    ½   *cup sugar*
        Dash of salt
    1   *tablespoon cornstarch*
    2   *to 4 tablespoons brandy*
        Vanilla ice cream

Drain cherries; reserve juice, and set cherries aside. Add enough water to juice to make 1 cup liquid.

Combine juice, sugar, salt, and cornstarch in a saucepan; cook over medium heat, blending until smooth. Add cherries; cook, stirring constantly, until slightly thickened. Heat brandy over medium heat. Do not boil. Ignite and pour over sauce. Spoon over ice cream. Yield: 6 to 8 servings.

Pears in Caramel Cream

    6   *firm pears, peeled, cored, and quartered*
    ¾   *cup sugar*
    2   *tablespoons butter or margarine*
    ½   *pint whipping cream*

Place pears in a buttered shallow baking pan; sprinkle with sugar, and dot with butter. Bake at 475° for 15 minutes or until sugar turns brown; baste several times. Pour cream over pears, stirring gently. Bake 2 additional minutes. Serve hot. Yield: 6 servings.

Blueberry Mystery Dessert

    2   *cups blueberries*
    1   *tablespoon lemon juice*
    ¾   *cup sugar*
    3   *tablespoons butter or margarine*
    1   *teaspoon baking powder*
    ¼   *teaspoon salt*
    1   *cup all-purpose flour*
    ½   *cup milk*
    ½   *cup sugar*
    ½   *teaspoon salt*
    1   *tablespoon cornstarch*
    1   *cup boiling water*
        Vanilla ice cream (optional)

Combine blueberries and lemon juice; spoon into a greased 8-inch square pan.

Combine ¾ cup sugar and butter, mixing well; stir in baking powder and ¼ teaspoon salt. Add flour to sugar mixture alternately with milk, beating well after each addition. Spoon batter over berries.

Combine ½ cup sugar, ½ teaspoon salt, and cornstarch; sprinkle over batter. Pour boiling water over all. Bake at 400° for 45 minutes. Serve warm with ice cream, if desired. Yield: about 6 servings.

Hot Fruit Compote

½   cup canned pears
½   cup canned peaches
½   cup pineapple chunks
½   cup canned plums
1½ cups applesauce
 1   teaspoon ground cinnamon
½   teaspoon ground ginger
½   teaspoon ground nutmeg
Juice and grated rind of ½ lemon
Whipping cream or half-and-half (optional)

Combine fruit in a 1½-quart casserole; add spices and lemon juice and rind. Mix well. Cover and bake at 250° for 1 hour. Serve hot. Top with whipping cream, if desired. Yield: 4 servings.

Macedoine Francaise

2   cups seedless green grapes
2   cups cubed pineapple
2   cups halved strawberries
2   cups melon balls
2   cups sliced bananas
2   oranges, peeled and sectioned
¾   cup sugar
½   cup Madeira
⅓   cup Cognac
Lemon sherbet

Combine fruit in a large bowl. Combine sugar, Madeira, and Cognac; pour over fruit. Chill until ready to serve. Top each serving with a scoop of lemon sherbet. Yield: about 15 servings.

Cranberry-Oatmeal Delight

 1   (16-ounce) can whole cranberry sauce
1½ cups chopped cooking apples
 1   cup regular oats, uncooked
½   cup firmly packed brown sugar
¼   cup all-purpose flour
¼   cup melted butter or margarine
½   teaspoon salt
½   cup chopped pecans

Combine cranberry sauce and apples; spoon into a buttered 10- x 6- x 1¾-inch baking dish.

Combine oats, sugar, flour, butter, and salt; spread over cranberry mixture. Sprinkle pecans over top. Bake at 350° for 50 minutes or until bubbly. Yield: 6 to 8 servings.

Apricot Dream Dessert

4   eggs, separated
1   teaspoon ice water
¼   teaspoon cream of tartar
1   cup sugar
6   tablespoons lemon juice
1   (14-ounce) can sweetened condensed
     milk
1   (17-ounce) can apricot halves, drained
     and mashed
1   teaspoon vanilla extract
½   pint whipping cream, whipped

Beat egg whites, ice water, and cream of tartar until foamy. Gradually add sugar; beat until stiff. Spread in a greased 13- x 9- x 2-inch pan. Bake at 275° for 1 hour; cool.

Beat egg yolks; stir in lemon juice. Add sweetened condensed milk, beating constantly. Stir in apricots and vanilla. Spread over meringue base. Chill several hours or until firm. Spread whipped cream over top. Yield: 12 to 15 servings.

Fresh Coconut Delight

2   envelopes unflavored gelatin
½   cup cold water
1   cup milk, scalded
1   cup sugar
2   cups grated fresh coconut
1   pint whipping cream, whipped

Dissolve gelatin in cold water. Combine gelatin, milk, and sugar; stir until gelatin and sugar are dissolved. Cool. Fold in coconut and whipped cream. Pour into 8 individual molds or a 2-quart dish. Refrigerate until firm. Yield: 8 servings.

★ Charlotte Russe

    4 eggs, separated
   10 tablespoons sugar, divided
    1 envelope unflavored gelatin
    ½ cup cold water
    1 pint whipping cream, whipped and
         divided
    1 teaspoon vanilla extract
   12 to 18 ladyfingers

Beat egg yolks and 4 tablespoons sugar until thick and lemon colored; set aside. Soften gelatin in cold water; place over hot water and stir until dissolved. Add gelatin to yolk mixture.

Beat egg whites in a large bowl; gradually add 6 tablespoons sugar and continue to beat until stiff peaks form. Reserve ½ cup whipped cream for garnish. Fold remaining whipped cream, yolk mixture, and vanilla into egg whites.

Split ladyfingers in half lengthwise. Line an 8-cup glass or crystal bowl with ladyfingers. Pour in filling; chill until set. Garnish with reserved ½ cup whipped cream. Yield: 8 to 10 servings.

Note: Individual compotes may be used. Quarter ladyfingers lengthwise. Line compotes, and fill as directed.

Kahlúa Soufflé

    ½ cup sugar, divided
    1 envelope unflavored gelatin
       Dash of salt
    1 cup cold water
    ½ cup Kahlúa or other coffee-flavored
         liqueur
    3 eggs, separated
    ½ pint whipping cream, whipped
    2 bananas, sliced
    ¼ cup chopped pecans
       Chocolate curls (optional)

Cut a piece of waxed paper or aluminum foil long enough to fit around a 1-quart soufflé dish, allowing a 1-inch overlap. Fold paper lengthwise into thirds. (Aluminum foil should be greased.) Wrap around dish, allowing paper to extend 2 inches above rim of dish to form a collar. Secure with cellophane tape.

Combine ¼ cup sugar, gelatin, salt, cold water, and Kahlúa in a saucepan. Cook over low heat until gelatin dissolves, stirring constantly. Stir a small amount of gelatin mixture into slightly beaten egg yolks; gradually add yolk mixture to gelatin mixture, stirring constantly. Cook over low heat, stirring constantly, until mixture coats a metal spoon (about 3 minutes). Chill until slightly thickened, stirring occasionally.

Fold whipped cream, bananas, and nuts into gelatin mixture. Beat egg whites until foamy; gradually add ¼ cup sugar, and continue beating until stiff peaks form. Fold egg whites into gelatin mixture. Pour into prepared soufflé dish. Chill until firm (about 6 hours). Garnish with chocolate curls, if desired. Remove collar before serving. Yield: 8 servings.

Chocolate Mint Squares

    1 cup finely crushed vanilla wafers
    ½ cup finely chopped walnuts
    ½ cup butter or margarine, softened
   1½ cups powdered sugar
    1 teaspoon vanilla extract
    3 (1-ounce) squares unsweetened
         chocolate, melted
    3 eggs
    ½ pint whipping cream, whipped
   1½ cups miniature marshmallows
    ½ cup crushed peppermint candy

Combine crushed vanilla wafers and walnuts; sprinkle half in the bottom of an 11¾- x 7½- x 1¾-inch pan.

Cream butter and sugar until light and fluffy; add vanilla and chocolate, mixing well. Add eggs, one at a time, beating well after each addition. Spread chocolate mixture carefully over crumbs.

Combine whipped cream, marshmallows, and candy; spread over chocolate layer. Sprinkle top with remaining crumbs. Refrigerate overnight. Yield: 10 to 12 servings.

Chocolate Delight

¾ cup butter or margarine, melted
1½ cups all-purpose flour
¾ cup finely chopped pecans
1 (8-ounce) package cream cheese, softened
1 cup powdered sugar
1 (13½-ounce) carton frozen whipped topping, thawed and divided
1 (3¾-ounce) package vanilla instant pudding mix
1 (4½-ounce) package chocolate instant pudding mix
3 cups milk
Chopped pecans
Grated chocolate

Combine butter, flour, and pecans, mixing well. Press into a 13- x 9- x 2-inch pan. Bake at 375° for 15 minutes; cool completely.

Combine cream cheese, powdered sugar, and 1½ cups whipped topping; blend thoroughly. Spread over crust; chill.

Combine pudding mixes and milk; beat 2 minutes with rotary mixer at medium speed. Spread over cream cheese layer. Spread remaining whipped topping over pudding layer. Garnish with pecans and chocolate. Refrigerate. Yield: about 15 servings.

Fancy Rice

1 (8-ounce) can crushed pineapple
⅔ cup instant rice
⅔ cup water
½ teaspoon salt
1½ cups miniature marshmallows
1 banana, diced
2 teaspoons lemon juice
½ pint whipping cream, whipped

Drain pineapple, reserving juice. Combine rice, water, pineapple juice, and salt in a saucepan. Bring to a boil; then reduce heat. Cover and simmer for 5 minutes; remove from heat, and let stand 5 minutes. Stir in pineapple, marshmallows, banana, and lemon juice; cool. Fold in whipped cream. Chill. Yield: 6 to 8 servings.

Coffee Charlotte

1 envelope unflavored gelatin
2 tablespoons cold water
2 egg yolks, slightly beaten
⅓ cup sugar
½ cup milk
½ cup strong coffee
¾ cup whipping cream, whipped
¼ cup rum
1 dozen ladyfingers, split

Soften gelatin in cold water. Combine egg yolks, sugar, milk, and coffee in top of a double boiler; add gelatin. Cook, stirring constantly, until mixture coats spoon; cool. When mixture begins to thicken, fold in whipped cream; chill.

Pour rum over ladyfingers. Alternate layers of ladyfingers and whipped cream mixture in an 8- x 4- x 2⅝-inch loafpan, ending with ladyfingers. Chill until firm; unmold to serve. Yield: 8 to 10 servings.

★ Crème de Menthe Parfait

1 quart vanilla ice cream, softened
1 pint lime sherbet, softened
1 (4½-ounce) container frozen whipped topping, thawed
¼ cup green crème de menthe

Combine all ingredients in container of electric blender; blend at medium speed until well mixed. Spoon into parfait glasses. Place parfaits in freezer 3 to 4 hours. Yield: 6 to 8 servings.

★ Chocolate Mousse

1 (6-ounce) package semisweet chocolate
    morsels
6 eggs, separated
2 teaspoons vanilla extract

Melt chocolate in top of a double boiler; re-move from heat. Beat yolks, and stir in a small amount of chocolate. Gradually add yolk mixture to remaining chocolate, stirring until blended well. Cool. Stir in vanilla.

Beat egg whites until stiff peaks form; fold into chocolate mixture. Spoon into individual serving dishes. Chill at least 4 hours before serving. Yield: 8 to 10 servings.

Pumpkin Dessert Squares

1¾ cups graham cracker crumbs
1⅓ cups sugar, divided
½ cup melted margarine
5 eggs, divided
1 (8-ounce) package cream cheese,
    softened
2 cups cooked, mashed pumpkin or 1
    (16-ounce) can pumpkin
½ cup firmly packed brown sugar
½ cup milk
½ teaspoon salt
2 teaspoons ground cinnamon
1 envelope unflavored gelatin
¼ cup water
    Whipped cream (optional)

Combine graham cracker crumbs and ⅓ cup sugar in a mixing bowl; stir in margarine, mixing well. Press evenly in bottom of a 13- x 9- x 2-inch baking pan.

Combine 2 beaten eggs, ¾ cup sugar, and cream cheese; beat until fluffy. Pour over crust. Bake at 350° for 20 minutes. Remove from oven.

Combine pumpkin, 3 egg yolks, brown sugar, milk, salt, and cinnamon in top of double boiler; cook over boiling water, stir-ring constantly, until thickened (about 5 to 10 minutes).

Sprinkle gelatin over ¼ cup water in a small mixing bowl; stir to dissolve gelatin. Stir into pumpkin mixture; cool.

Beat 3 egg whites until foamy; gradually add ¼ cup sugar, and beat until stiff. Fold into pumpkin mixture. Pour over baked mixture. Refrigerate. To serve, cut into squares; top with whipped cream, if desired. Yield: about 12 to 15 servings.

Pretty Rice Parfait

2 cups hot cooked rice
1 (3-ounce) package strawberry-flavored
    gelatin
2 cups miniature marshmallows
1 cup sugar
1 (2-ounce) bottle maraschino cherries,
    halved and undrained
1 (15½-ounce) can crushed pineapple,
    undrained
1 cup chopped pecans
1 pint whipping cream, whipped

Combine rice with dry gelatin, marshmal-lows, sugar, fruit, and pecans. Fold in whipped cream. Chill at least 4 hours before serving. Yield: 10 to 12 servings.

Prune Whip

8 ounces dried pitted prunes
1 cup water
1 teaspoon unflavored gelatin
1 tablespoon water
4 egg whites
2 teaspoons lemon juice
4 to 5 teaspoons sugar

Combine prunes and water in a saucepan; simmer about 8 minutes or until prunes are soft. Place in container of electric blender, and blend until smooth. Set aside.

Soften gelatin in water; add to warm prune mixture, stirring until gelatin is dissolved. Set aside to cool. Beat egg whites until foamy; gradually add lemon juice and sugar, beating until stiff. Fold in prune mixture. Chill sev-eral hours. Yield: about 6 servings.

Dream Cream

2   *cups sugar*
3   *eggs, well beaten*
1   *(13-ounce) can evaporated milk*
1   *(14-ounce) can sweetened condensed milk*
1   *(6-ounce) package strawberry-flavored gelatin*
1   *teaspoon vanilla extract*
2   *(10-ounce) packages frozen strawberries, thawed*
    About 1 gallon milk

Combine sugar, eggs, evaporated milk, sweetened condensed milk, gelatin, and vanilla; mix well. Stir in strawberries. Pour into freezer can of a 1½- to 2-gallon hand-turned or electric freezer.

Add enough milk to fill can about three-fourths full. Freeze according to manufacturer's instructions. Let ripen at least 2 hours. Yield: 1½ gallons.

Rich Homemade Ice Cream

2   *rennet tablets*
2   *tablespoons cold water*
6   *eggs, separated*
    Pinch of salt
2   *(3¾-ounce) packages chocolate or lemon pudding and pie filling mix*
5   *pints half-and-half, divided*
2   *cups sugar*
1   *teaspoon vanilla extract*

Dissolve rennet tablets in water; set aside. Beat egg whites until foamy. Add salt, and beat until stiff but not dry; set aside.

Combine pudding mix, egg yolks, and 3 cups half-and-half in a saucepan; cook over medium heat until slightly thickened, stirring constantly. Remove from heat and add sugar, stirring until sugar is dissolved. Add remaining half-and-half, vanilla, and dissolved rennet tablets; blend well. Fold in egg whites.

Pour mixture into freezer can of a 1-gallon hand-turned or electric freezer. Freeze according to manufacturer's instructions. Let ripen at least 2 hours. Yield: 1 gallon.

Chocolate Mint Ice Cream

2   *cups sugar*
4   *eggs, beaten*
¼   *teaspoon salt*
5   *(13-ounce) cans evaporated milk*
1   *(6-ounce) bar milk chocolate, grated*
1½ *teaspoons mint extract*
    Green food coloring

Gradually add sugar to eggs, beating until stiff. Stir in salt, evaporated milk, chocolate, and mint; add food coloring to desired shade of green.

Pour mixture into freezer can of a 1-gallon hand-turned or electric freezer. Freeze according to manufacturer's instructions. Let ripen at least 2 hours. Yield: 1 gallon.

Creamy Peach Ice Cream

1¼ *cups sugar, divided*
1½ *teaspoons unflavored gelatin*
4   *cups half-and-half, divided*
1   *egg, slightly beaten*
1   *teaspoon vanilla extract*
¼   *teaspoon almond extract*
    Dash of salt
3   *cups mashed ripe peaches*

Combine ½ cup sugar and gelatin in a saucepan; stir in 2 cups half-and-half. Cook over low heat until gelatin dissolves, stirring constantly. Gradually stir a small amount of hot mixture into egg; slowly stir egg mixture into remaining hot mixture. Cook about 1 minute, stirring constantly, or until mixture thickens slightly. Chill.

Add remaining 2 cups half-and-half, vanilla, almond, and salt to chilled custard. Combine peaches and remaining ¾ cup sugar; stir into custard. Pour into freezer can of a 1-gallon hand-turned or electric freezer. Freeze according to manufacturer's instructions. Let ripen about 4 hours. Yield: 2 quarts.

Lime Sherbet

    1   (3-ounce) package lime-flavored gelatin
    1   cup boiling water
   1¼ cups sugar
        Juice and grated rind of 2 lemons
    1   quart milk

Dissolve gelatin in boiling water; add sugar, and stir until dissolved. Add lemon juice, lemon rind, and milk; mix well. Freeze until slushy; remove from freezer, and beat well. Return to freezer, and freeze until firm. Yield: about 8 to 10 servings.

Lemon Ice Cream

    3   cups sugar
    4   cups milk
    1   cup half-and-half
    1   pint whipping cream
        Grated rind of 5 to 6 lemons
   ¾   cup fresh lemon juice
    2   egg whites, beaten
        Yellow food coloring (optional)

Combine sugar, milk, half-and-half, whipping cream, and lemon rind. Pour lemon juice over milk mixture, and beat well. Fold in egg whites. Add food coloring, if desired.

Pour mixture into freezer can of a 1-gallon hand-turned or electric freezer. Freeze according to manufacturer's instructions. Let ripen at least 2 hours. Yield: 1 gallon.

Rhubarb Ice Cream

    2   cups (about 1 pound) diced rhubarb
    1   cup water
    1   cup sugar
    1   tablespoon lemon juice
    3   drops red food coloring (optional)
    1   egg white, stiffly beaten
   ½   pint whipping cream, whipped

Combine rhubarb, water, and sugar in a saucepan. Bring to a boil and cook until thickened, about 10 minutes; cool. Add lemon juice; if desired, add food coloring. Pour into 2 freezer trays and freeze until slushy, about 1 to 2 hours.

Pour mixture into a bowl; add beaten egg white, and beat on low speed of electric mixer until well blended. Fold in whipped cream. Pour mixture back into freezer trays, and freeze 2 hours. Yield: about 8 servings.

Strawberry Ice Cream

    4   eggs
   2½ cups sugar
    1   pint half-and-half
    1   (13-ounce) can evaporated milk
    1   teaspoon vanilla extract
   ¼   teaspoon salt
    2   pints strawberries, mashed
        Red food coloring (optional)
        Milk

Beat eggs at high speed of electric mixer until very thick (about 10 minutes). Lower mixer speed to medium, and gradually beat in sugar. Stir in half-and-half, evaporated milk, vanilla, and salt; mix well. Add strawberries, and stir in food coloring, if desired.

Pour mixture into container of a 1-gallon hand-turned or electric freezer. Fill to within 3 inches of top with milk. Freeze according to manufacturer's instructions. Let ripen at least 2 hours. Yield: 1 gallon.

Southern Belle Dessert

   ¼   cup sugar
    1   egg, slightly beaten
    1   cup half-and-half, scalded
    1   (8-ounce) package chopped dates
   ¼   cup bourbon
   ½   pint whipping cream, whipped
   ¾   cup chopped almonds, toasted
    1   cup finely chopped pecans

Combine sugar and egg; gradually stir into half-and-half. Cook over low heat until slightly thickened, stirring constantly. Pour over dates; cool. Add bourbon, stirring until well blended.

Fold whipped cream into date mixture. Pour into an 8-inch square pan. Freeze until slushy; remove from freezer, and stir in nuts. Freeze until firm. Yield: 8 servings.

Butterscotch Squares

  1   *cup all-purpose flour*
  ¼   *cup quick-cooking oats*
  ¼   *cup firmly packed brown sugar*
  ½   *cup margarine, softened*
  ½   *cup chopped pecans*
  1   *(12-ounce) jar butterscotch ice cream*
      topping, divided
  1   *quart chocolate ice cream, softened*

Combine flour, oats, and sugar. Using 2 knives or a pastry cutter, cut in margarine until mixture resembles crumbs. Stir in pecans.

Pat mixture into a lightly greased 13- x 9- x 2-inch pan. Bake at 400° for 15 minutes. While dough is still warm, stir to crumble; cool.

Spread half the crumbs in a 9-inch square pan; drizzle half of butterscotch topping over crumbs. Spoon ice cream over topping; drizzle with remaining topping, and sprinkle with remaining crumbs. Freeze until firm. Yield: 12 servings.

Strawberry Surprise

  ½   *cup melted butter or margarine*
  ¼   *cup sugar*
  1   *cup all-purpose flour*
  ½   *cup chopped nuts*
  2   *(10-ounce) packages frozen*
      strawberries, thawed
  2   *eggs whites, stiffly beaten*
  2   *tablespoons lemon juice*
  1   *(9-ounce) carton frozen whipped*
      topping, thawed

Cream butter and sugar; add flour, mixing well. Stir in nuts, and press mixture into a 13- x 9- x 2-inch pan. Bake at 350° for 20 minutes. Cool and crumble. Sprinkle two-thirds of crumbs back into pan; set aside remaining crumbs.

Combine strawberries, egg whites, and lemon juice; fold in whipped topping. Pour mixture over crumbs in pan; top with remaining crumbs. Freeze. Remove from freezer shortly before serving; cut into squares. Yield: 12 servings.

Chocolate Velvet Dessert

  1½   *cups finely crushed chocolate wafers*
  ⅓   *cup butter or margarine, melted*
  1   *(8-ounce) package cream cheese,*
      softened
  ½   *cup sugar, divided*
  1   *teaspoon vanilla extract*
  2   *eggs, separated*
  1   *(6-ounce) package semisweet chocolate*
      morsels, melted
  ½   *cup whipping cream, whipped*
      Chopped pecans

Combine crushed wafers and butter; mix well, and press into a 9-inch piepan. Bake at 325° for 10 minutes; cool.

Combine cream cheese, ¼ cup sugar, and vanilla. Stir in egg yolks and chocolate; cool. Beat egg whites until soft peaks form. Add remaining ¼ cup sugar gradually, beating until stiff peaks form. Fold in whipped cream.

Gently fold egg white mixture into chocolate mixture; mix just enough to marble. Pour into crust, and sprinkle with pecans. Freeze. Yield: about 8 servings.

Taffy Apple Ice Cream

  1   *cup sugar*
  ½   *cup firmly packed brown sugar*
  ¼   *cup all-purpose flour*
  ¼   *teaspoon salt*
  2   *(13-ounce) cans evaporated milk*
  2   *tablespoons molasses*
  4   *eggs, beaten*
  1   *pint whipping cream*
  2   *cups peeled, finely chopped apples*
  2   *teaspoons vanilla extract*

Combine sugar, flour, and salt in a saucepan; gradually stir in evaporated milk and molasses. Cook over low heat, stirring constantly, until mixture thickens and bubbles. Gradually stir a small amount of hot mixture into eggs; slowly stir egg mixture into remaining hot mixture. Cook 1 minute, stirring constantly; cool.

Stir cream, apples, and vanilla into cooled custard. Pour into freezer can of a 1-gallon hand-turned or electric freezer. Freeze according to manufacturer's instructions. Let ripen at least 2 hours. Yield: 2½ quarts.

Frozen Rocky Road

 ¼ *cup sugar*
 ¾ *cup milk*
 1 *(1-ounce) square unsweetened chocolate, grated*
 1 *teaspoon unflavored gelatin*
 1 *tablespoon cold water*
 10 *large marshmallows, quartered*
 ½ *cup chopped nuts*
 3 *tablespoons Kahlúa or coffee-flavored liqueur*
 ½ *pint whipping cream, whipped*

Combine sugar, milk, and chocolate in a saucepan; bring to a boil, stirring constantly. Soften gelatin in water; stir into milk mixture. Remove from heat, and cool slightly.

Stir in marshmallows, nuts, Kahlúa, and whipped cream. Pour into a 9-inch square pan; freeze. Yield: about 6 servings.

Chocolate Ice Cream

 5 *eggs*
 2 *cups sugar*
 1 *teaspoon vanilla extract*
 3 *(13-ounce) cans evaporated milk*
 1 *(16-ounce) can chocolate syrup*
 Milk

Beat eggs until light and fluffy; stir in sugar, vanilla, evaporated milk, and chocolate syrup. Pour into freezer can of a 1-gallon hand-turned or electric freezer. Fill to within 3 inches of top of can with milk. Freeze according to manufacturer's instructions. Let ripen at least 2 hours. Yield: 1 gallon.

Pineapple Sherbet

 1 *pint half-and-half*
 6 *cups milk*
 3 *cups sugar*
 Juice of 4 lemons
 ½ *pint whipping cream*
 1 *(15½-ounce) can crushed pineapple, drained*

Combine half-and-half and milk; add sugar, stirring until dissolved. Stir in lemon juice. Whip cream slightly; add to mixture. Fold in pineapple. Pour into freezer can of a 1-gallon hand-turned or electric freezer. Freeze according to manufacturer's instructions. Let ripen at least 2 hours. Yield: 1 gallon.

★
Creamy Cheesecake

 1½ *cups graham cracker crumbs*
 ¼ *cup melted butter or margarine*
 2 *cups sugar, divided*
 3 *eggs*
 3 *(8-ounce) packages cream cheese, softened*
 6 *tablespoons half-and-half or milk*
 2 *(8-ounce) cartons commercial sour cream*
 1 *tablespoon vanilla extract*
 Fresh strawberries (optional)
 Mint sprigs (optional)

Combine crumbs, butter, and ½ cup sugar. Press into an 11¾- x 7½- x 1¾-inch baking dish; set aside.

Beat eggs and 1 cup sugar until thick. Blend in cream cheese. Add half-and-half, and beat until very smooth. Pour into crust. Bake at 350° for 45 minutes. Turn off oven; leave cake in oven 30 minutes. Remove and cool at least 30 minutes.

Combine sour cream, vanilla, and remaining ½ cup sugar; mix well. Spread over cheesecake. Bake at 450° for 10 minutes. Cool. Garnish each serving with a fresh strawberry and a sprig of mint, if desired. Yield: 12 to 15 servings.

★
Favorite Cheesecake

1   *cup graham cracker crumbs*
2   *(8-ounce) packages cream cheese,*
      softened
¾   *cup sugar*
4   *eggs, separated*
1   *tablespoon lemon juice*
2   *teaspoons vanilla extract*
Topping

Spread graham cracker crumbs in bottom of a 9-inch springform pan. Combine cream cheese and sugar, beating until smooth; add egg yolks, mixing thoroughly. Add lemon juice and vanilla, blending well.

Beat egg whites until stiff; add to cheese mixture, folding for a total of 8 minutes. Spread filling over crumbs. Bake at 350° for 30 minutes. Spread Topping over cheesecake; bake 5 minutes longer. Refrigerate overnight. Yield: 8 to 10 servings.

Topping:

1   *(8-ounce) carton commercial sour cream*
2   *tablespoons sugar*
1   *teaspoon vanilla extract*

Combine all ingredients, and blend well. Yield: 1 cup.

★
Chocolate-Cherry Cheesecake

44   *chocolate wafers, divided*
6   *tablespoons butter or margarine, melted*
1   *(22-ounce) can cherry pie filling*
2   *envelopes whipped topping mix*
½   *cup powdered sugar*
1   *(8-ounce) package cream cheese,*
       softened

Crush 32 chocolate wafers; set aside ¼ cup crumbs. Combine remaining crumbs and butter; mix well, and press onto bottom of a 9-inch springform pan. Stand remaining whole wafers around edge of pan, pressing into crumb crust.

Spread pie filling over crust. Prepare whipped topping mix according to package directions; set aside.

Combine powdered sugar and cream cheese; cream until smooth. Add to prepared topping mix, blending well; pour over pie filling. Sprinkle ¼ cup reserved crumbs over top. Refrigerate 4 hours or overnight. Remove sides of springform pan to serve. Yield: 10 to 12 servings.

Lemon Cheesecake

1½   *cups zwieback crumbs*
1   *cup sugar, divided*
¾   *teaspoon ground cinnamon*
6   *tablespoons melted butter or margarine*
¼   *cup all-purpose flour*
¼   *teaspoon salt*
2   *(8-ounce) packages cream cheese,*
       softened
1   *teaspoon vanilla extract*
2   *tablespoons lemon juice*
½   *teaspoon grated lemon rind*
4   *eggs, separated*
1   *cup evaporated milk or whipping cream*

Combine zwieback crumbs, ¼ cup sugar, cinnamon, and butter; mix well, and press onto bottom and sides of an 8-inch springform pan.

Combine ½ cup sugar, flour, and salt; add cream cheese, and beat until light and fluffy. Add vanilla, lemon juice, and lemon rind. Add egg yolks, one at a time, beating well after each addition; add evaporated milk, blending well.

Beat egg whites until foamy; gradually add remaining ¼ cup sugar, and beat until stiff. Fold egg whites into cream cheese mixture. Pour mixture into prepared crust, and bake at 325° for 1 hour and 15 minutes. Cool before removing from pan. Yield: 10 servings.

Tropical Cheesecake

  ½ cup graham cracker crumbs
  2 tablespoons melted butter or margarine
  1 (8-ounce) package cream cheese,
      softened
  ½ cup sifted powdered sugar
  1 (20-ounce) can crushed pineapple, well
      drained
  1 envelope whipped topping mix

Combine graham cracker crumbs and butter; mix well. Reserve 2 tablespoons crumbs; sprinkle remaining crumbs in bottom of an 8-inch round cakepan. Chill. Combine cream cheese and powdered sugar; beat until light and fluffy. Stir in pineapple.

Prepare whipped topping mix according to package directions; fold into cream cheese mixture. Spoon filling over crust, and sprinkle with reserved crumbs. Chill thoroughly. Yield: 6 to 8 servings.

Baked Custard

  3 eggs, slightly beaten
  ½ cup sugar
  ¼ teaspoon salt
  2 cups scalded milk
  1 teaspoon vanilla extract
    Ground nutmeg

Combine eggs, sugar, and salt. Slowly add milk and vanilla, blending well. Pour mixture into a 1-quart casserole or individual custard cups; sprinkle with nutmeg.

Place casserole or cups in a shallow pan with a small amount of water. Bake at 325° for 30 to 40 minutes or until knife inserted between center and edge comes out clean. Serve warm or chilled. Yield: 4 servings.

Boiled Custard

  1 cup sugar
  4 eggs
  1 quart milk, warmed
  5 to 6 large marshmallows, quartered
  1 teaspoon vanilla extract

Combine sugar and eggs in top of a double boiler, blending thoroughly. Gradually stir in milk.

Place over hot water, and stir constantly until mixture is hot; add marshmallows, and continue stirring until marshmallows are melted and mixture coats a metal spoon.

Remove from heat; strain through a sieve, if necessary. Stir in vanilla. Chill well.

Serve plain or as a sauce for cake or fruit. Yield: 6 to 8 servings.

Lemony Boiled Custard

  ¾ cup sugar
  2½ tablespoons all-purpose flour
    Dash of salt
  4 eggs, separated
  2 cups milk, warmed
  ½ teaspoon lemon extract

Combine sugar, flour, and salt in top of a double boiler; stir in egg yolks, blending well. Gradually add milk, stirring constantly until smooth. Place over hot water, and cook until mixture coats a metal spoon; stir constantly. Remove from heat.

Beat egg whites until stiff peaks form, and fold into hot mixture. Stir in lemon extract. Chill well. Serve plain or over pound cake. Yield: 6 servings.

Grated Sweet Potato Pudding

  4 cups grated raw sweet potatoes
  ½ cup sugar
  ½ cup light corn syrup
  1½ cups milk
  ⅓ cup melted butter or margarine
  3 eggs, beaten
  1 teaspoon ground nutmeg
  1 teaspoon ground cinnamon
  ½ teaspoon salt

Combine all ingredients, mixing well. Spoon mixture into a lightly greased 2-quart casserole. Bake at 325° for 1½ hours or until slightly firm. Yield: 6 to 8 servings.

Cherry Pudding

    1   (3⅛-ounce) package vanilla instant
        pudding and pie filling
    1½ cups milk
    1   teaspoon almond extract
    1   (8-ounce) carton commercial sour cream
    1   (7-ounce) angel food cake, broken into
        small pieces
    1   (22-ounce) can cherry pie filling
    ½   cup nuts (optional)

Prepare pudding according to package directions, using 1½ cups milk and adding almond extract. Chill until slightly set; fold in
sour cream.

Arrange half of cake pieces in bottom of an
8-inch square pan. Pour half of pudding
mixture over cake; spread half of pie filling
over pudding layer. Repeat layers. Top with
nuts, if desired. Chill before serving. Yield: 6
to 8 servings.

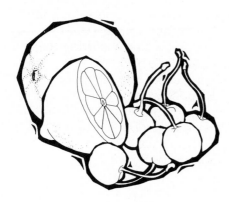

Rhubarb and Strawberry Pudding

    2   cups (about 1 pound) sliced fresh
        rhubarb
    1   cup sliced strawberries
    1½ cups sugar, divided
    1   cup plus 3 tablespoons all-purpose
        flour, divided
    1   egg, beaten
    3   tablespoons lemon juice
    ½   teaspoon grated lemon rind
    ¼   teaspoon ground nutmeg
    ½   cup butter or margarine
        Whipped cream or ice cream (optional)

Combine rhubarb and strawberries in a
greased 8-inch square pan. Combine 1 cup
sugar and 3 tablespoons flour; add egg,
lemon juice, and lemon rind, mixing well.
Spoon mixture over rhubarb and
strawberries.

Combine remaining ½ cup sugar, 1 cup
flour, and nutmeg; cut in butter until mixture
is crumbly. Sprinkle crumb mixture over fruit
in pan. Bake at 350° for 50 minutes or until
golden. Serve with whipped cream or ice
cream, if desired. Yield: 6 to 8 servings.

Rice Pudding with Marmalade Sauce

    6   cups milk
    1   cup short grain rice, uncooked
    ½   teaspoon salt
    1   cup sugar
    3   eggs, beaten
    ¼   cup butter or margarine
    1   teaspoon vanilla extract
        Marmalade Sauce

Bring milk to a boil in a 3-quart saucepan; add
rice and salt, stirring until milk returns to a
boil. Cover saucepan and reduce heat; simmer about 50 minutes. Stir in sugar.

Spoon a small amount of hot mixture into
beaten eggs, and mix well. Add egg mixture
to mixture in saucepan, stirring constantly;
cook and stir about 5 minutes longer, and
remove from heat. Stir in butter and vanilla,
blending well.

Spoon pudding into a buttered 1-quart
mold and refrigerate overnight, or spoon into
custard cups and serve warm or cold. Top
with Marmalade Sauce. Yield: 8 servings.

Marmalade Sauce:

    1   teaspoon cornstarch
    ⅓   cup cream sherry
    1   cup orange marmalade
    ¼   cup chopped nuts

Dissolve cornstarch in sherry in a small
saucepan; stir in marmalade and nuts. Cook
over low heat, stirring constantly, just until
hot. Yield: 1½ cups.

Yogurt Fruit Pudding

1 (3¾-ounce) package vanilla instant
   pudding and pie filling mix
1 cup milk
1 (8-ounce) carton strawberry or other
   fruit yogurt
Strawberries (optional)

Combine pudding mix and milk in small
bowl of electric mixer; mix until thickened
and smooth. Fold in yogurt. Chill at least 5
minutes before serving. Garnish with strawberries, if desired. Yield: 4 servings.

Raspberry Cream

1 (3¾-ounce) package vanilla instant
   pudding and pie filling mix
1 (16-ounce) carton commercial sour
   cream
1 (10-ounce) package frozen raspberries,
   thawed
Pastry shells

Combine pudding mix, sour cream, and
raspberries; beat at medium speed of electric
mixer until smooth. Serve in pastry shells.
Yield: about 4 cups.

★
Apple Dumplings

2 to 2½ cups all-purpose flour
2 teaspoons baking powder
1 teaspoon salt
¾ cup shortening
½ cup milk
4 to 6 cooking apples, peeled, cored, and
   cut into eighths
Sugar
Ground cinnamon
Ground nutmeg
Butter or margarine
2 cups sugar
¼ teaspoon ground cinnamon
¼ teaspoon ground nutmeg
2 cups hot water
¼ cup butter or margarine, melted
Cream (optional)

Combine flour, baking powder, and salt; cut
in shortening until mixture resembles coarse
meal. Gradually add milk, stirring to make a
soft dough. Roll dough into a ⅛-inch-thick
rectangle on a lightly floured surface; cut into
5-inch squares.

Place 3 to 4 pieces of apple on each square.
Sprinkle each with 2 teaspoons sugar and
cinnamon and nutmeg to taste; dot with butter. Moisten edges of each dumpling with
water; bring corners to center, pinching
edges to seal.

Place dumplings 1 inch apart in a lightly
greased shallow baking dish.

Combine 2 cups sugar, ¼ teaspoon cinnamon, ¼ teaspoon nutmeg, 2 cups hot water,
and ¼ cup butter; stir to dissolve sugar. Pour
syrup over dumplings. Bake at 375° for 35 to
45 minutes or until golden brown. Serve hot
with cream, if desired. Yield: about 1 dozen
dumplings.

Crusty Apple Delight

1½ cups sugar, divided
1 cup all-purpose flour
½ cup butter or margarine, softened
3 cups peeled, sliced apple
Ground cinnamon
Whipped cream or ice cream (optional)

Combine 1 cup sugar and flour. Using 2
knives or a pastry blender, cut butter into
flour mixture until crumbly; set aside.

Place a layer of apple slices in a buttered
8-inch square baking dish. Sprinkle with
some of remaining sugar; add cinnamon to
taste. Repeat this procedure until all apple
slices are used. Place crumb mixture on top of
apple slices, patting until apples are covered.
Bake at 350° for 30 minutes or until golden
brown. Top with whipped cream, if desired.
Yield: about 6 servings.

Bavarian Apple Torte

½ *cup butter or margarine, softened*
⅓ *cup sugar*
¼ *teaspoon vanilla extract*
1 *cup all-purpose flour*
1 *(8-ounce) package cream cheese, softened*
¼ *cup sugar*
1 *egg*
½ *teaspoon vanilla extract*
⅓ *cup sugar*
½ *teaspoon ground cinnamon*
4 *cups peeled, sliced apples*
¼ *cup sliced almonds*

Cream butter and ⅓ cup sugar until light and fluffy; stir in ¼ teaspoon vanilla, and blend in flour. Mixture will be slightly crumbly. Press pastry in bottom and 1½ inches up sides of a 9-inch springform pan.

Combine cream cheese and ¼ cup sugar; blend until smooth. Add egg and ½ teaspoon vanilla; mix well. Spread evenly over pastry. Combine ⅓ cup sugar, cinnamon, and apples, tossing lightly. Spoon over cream cheese mixture, and sprinkle with almonds.

Bake at 450° for 10 minutes. Reduce heat to 400°, and bake 25 additional minutes. Remove from oven; cool about 5 minutes, and loosen rim of pan. Allow torte to cool completely before removing rim. Yield: 8 to 10 servings.

Fresh Peach Crisp

1 *cup all-purpose flour*
½ *cup sugar*
½ *cup firmly packed light brown sugar*
¼ *teaspoon salt*
½ *teaspoon ground cinnamon*
½ *cup margarine*
4 *cups sliced fresh peaches*
1 *tablespoon lemon juice*
2 *tablespoons water*

Combine flour, sugar, salt, and cinnamon; cut in margarine with 2 knives or a pastry blender until mixture resembles coarse cornmeal.

Combine peaches, lemon juice, and water; spoon into a greased 9-inch square baking dish. Sprinkle flour mixture over peaches. Bake, covered, at 350° for 15 minutes; remove cover, and bake 35 to 45 minutes longer. Yield: 6 servings.

Strawberry Cream Puffs

¼ *cup butter or margarine*
½ *cup boiling water*
½ *cup all-purpose flour*
¼ *teaspoon salt*
2 *eggs*
About 3 cups sliced strawberries, sweetened to taste
Whipped cream
Whole strawberries

Melt butter with boiling water in a small saucepan. Stir in flour and salt; cook over low heat, stirring constantly, until mixture leaves sides of pan in a smooth ball. Remove from heat and cool. Add eggs, one at a time, beating well after each addition.

Drop mixture by heaping spoonfuls (about 2 inches apart) onto a greased cookie sheet. Bake at 400° for 40 minutes; cool.

Cut top off cream puffs and fill with sweetened strawberries; top with whipped cream. Replace tops, and garnish with whipped cream and whole strawberries. Yield: 6 servings.

★ Grand Marnier Puffs

 1 *cup water*
 ½ *cup butter or margarine*
 ¼ *teaspoon salt*
 1 *cup all-purpose flour*
 4 *eggs*
 Crème Pâtissière
 Powdered sugar
 Orange and lemon slices (optional)

Combine water, butter, and salt in a saucepan; heat to boiling point. Remove from heat; add flour all at once, stirring vigorously until mixture leaves sides of pan and forms a ball around spoon. (If a ball does not form almost immediately, place saucepan over low heat and beat briskly for a few minutes.) Cool 5 minutes.

Add eggs, one at a time, beating until mixture is smooth and glossy after each addition. Drop batter by rounded teaspoonfuls onto a greased baking sheet, spacing about 2 inches apart. Bake at 425° for 15 minutes. Reduce temperature to 350°, and bake an additional 8 minutes. (Inside should be dry and firm.) Cool.

Just before serving, cut top off each puff; fill bottom of each with Crème Pâtissière. Replace tops, and sprinkle with powdered sugar. Garnish with orange and lemon slices, if desired. Yield: about 3 dozen puffs.

Crème Pâtissière:

 ¾ *cup sugar*
 7 *egg yolks*
 ⅓ *cup all-purpose flour*
 Pinch of salt
 2 *cups milk, scalded*
 1½ *teaspoons vanilla extract*
 Grated rind of 3 oranges
 1 *to 2 tablespoons Grand Marnier or other orange-flavored liqueur*

Combine sugar and egg yolks, beating until pale yellow and fluffy. Combine flour and salt; gradually add to yolk mixture, beating well. Very gradually stir milk into yolk mixture; pour into a heavy saucepan. Cook over low heat until thickened, stirring constantly.

Remove custard from heat; stir in vanilla, orange rind, and Grand Marnier. Cover with plastic wrap, pressing onto surface to prevent formation of a crust. Chill well. Yield: about 3 cups.

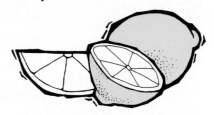

Orange-Lemon Torte

 7 *egg whites (at room temperature)*
 1 *tablespoon white vinegar*
 2 *cups sugar*
 Orange-Lemon Custard Filling
 ½ *pint whipping cream, whipped*
 Fresh orange sections (optional)

Grease three 9-inch cakepans, and line bottom of each with waxed paper; grease waxed paper. Set aside.

Combine egg whites and vinegar; beat until frothy. Gradually add sugar, 1 tablespoon at a time, beating until glossy and stiff peaks form. Spoon into cakepans, spreading evenly. Bake at 350° for 45 minutes.

Gently loosen meringues from sides of pan, if necessary. Turn out on wire racks to cool.

Spread half of Orange-Lemon Custard Filling on one meringue layer; top with second layer and spread with remaining Filling. Add third layer, and spread whipped cream over top. Chill in an airtight container at least 24 hours before serving. Garnish with orange sections, if desired. Yield: 12 to 14 servings.

Orange-Lemon Custard Filling:

 7 *egg yolks, beaten*
 Juice of 1 orange
 Juice of 1 lemon
 ⅔ *cup sugar*
 ¼ *teaspoon salt*

Combine all ingredients in top of a double boiler; cook over boiling water until thickened, stirring constantly. Yield: about 1 cup.

Chocolate Meringues

3 *egg whites (at room temperature)*
1 *teaspoon vanilla extract*
¼ *teaspoon cream of tartar*
1 *cup sugar, sifted*
Chocolate Fluff Filling

Combine egg whites, vanilla, and cream of tartar; beat until frothy. Gradually add sugar, 1 tablespoon at a time, beating until glossy and stiff peaks form. Do not underbeat.

Drop meringue by ⅓ cupfuls onto well-greased cookie sheets. Using back of spoon, shape meringue into circles about 3½ inches in diameter; then shape each circle into a shell (sides should be about 1 inch high).

Bake at 275° for 1 hour. Turn off oven; leave meringues in oven with door closed 1 hour for crisper meringue. Cool meringues away from drafts. Fill with Chocolate Fluff Filling. Yield: 8 servings.

Chocolate Fluff Filling:

¾ *cup butter or margarine, softened*
1 *cup sugar*
4 *eggs*
2 *teaspoons vanilla extract*
4 *(1-ounce) squares unsweetened
      chocolate, melted*

Cream butter and sugar until light and fluffy; add eggs, one at a time, beating well after each addition. Add vanilla and chocolate, blending well. Chill. Filling may be made ahead and frozen. Yield: 3 to 4 cups.

Bananas au Rhum

¼ *cup melted margarine*
6 *ripe bananas, peeled and halved*
¼ *cup firmly packed brown sugar, divided*
¼ *teaspoon ground cinnamon, divided*
½ *cup rum*

Combine margarine and bananas in a skillet. Sprinkle with half the sugar and cinnamon; cook until bananas are lightly browned. Turn and sprinkle with remaining sugar and cinnamon.

Heat rum in a small saucepan over medium heat. Do not boil. Ignite and pour over bananas. Serve immediately. Yield: 6 servings.

Apple Squares

2½ *cups all-purpose flour*
1 *tablespoon sugar*
1 *teaspoon salt*
1 *cup shortening*
1 *egg, separated*
Milk
⅔ *cup cornflake crumbs*
5 *cups peeled, sliced apples*
1½ *cups sugar*
1 *teaspoon ground cinnamon*
1 *cup powdered sugar*
2 *tablespoons lemon juice*

Combine flour, 1 tablespoon sugar, and salt; cut in shortening until mixture resembles coarse meal. Place egg yolk in a measuring cup, and beat well; add enough milk to make ⅔ cup, mixing well. Add milk mixture to flour mixture, and stir until a ball is formed.

Divide dough in half; on a lightly floured board, roll out each half to a 16- x 11-inch rectangle. Place 1 pastry rectangle in a lightly greased 15- x 10- x 1-inch jellyroll pan; sprinkle with cornflake crumbs.

Arrange the apple slices on the pastry; combine 1½ cups sugar with cinnamon, and sprinkle over apples.

Brush edges of pastry with milk, and top with remaining rectangle of pastry. Pinch edges together; trim, if necessary. Beat egg white until stiff peaks form; brush over top surface of pastry. Bake at 400° for 40 minutes.

Combine powdered sugar and lemon juice; blend until smooth. Drizzle glaze over hot pastry. Cool and cut into squares. Yield: 12 servings.

Fresh Peach Ice Cream

      5   *eggs*
   2½   *cups sugar, divided*
      1   *(14-ounce) can sweetened condensed
              milk*
      1   *(13-ounce) can evaporated milk*
      1   *tablespoon vanilla extract*
   Milk
      2   *cups mashed peaches*

Beat eggs until frothy; add 2 cups sugar, and beat well. Add condensed milk, evaporated milk, and vanilla; continue to beat until well blended. Pour mixture into a 1-gallon freezer container.

Add milk to fill freezer container 4 inches from top; freeze about 5 minutes or until custard is thick.

Combine peaches and ½ cup sugar; remove dasher, and add peaches to custard. Return dasher, and freeze until firm according to freezer instructions. Let ripen about 1 hour. Yield: 1 gallon.

Pumpkin Roll

      3   *eggs*
      1   *cup sugar*
   ⅔   *cup cooked, mashed pumpkin*
      1   *teaspoon lemon juice*
   ¾   *cup all-purpose flour*
      2   *teaspoons ground cinnamon*
      1   *teaspoon baking powder*
   ½   *teaspoon salt*
      1   *teaspoon ground ginger*
      1   *teaspoon ground nutmeg*
   1¼   *cups powdered sugar, divided*
      1   *(8-ounce) package cream cheese,
              softened*
   ¼   *cup butter or margarine, softened*
   ½   *teaspoon vanilla extract*

Beat eggs 5 minutes at high speed of electric mixer. Gradually add sugar, beating well. Stir in pumpkin and lemon juice.

Combine flour, cinnamon, baking powder, salt, ginger, and nutmeg; add to pumpkin mixture, and blend well. Spoon batter into a greased and floured 15- x 10- x 1-inch

jellyroll pan, spreading evenly to corners. Bake at 375° for 15 minutes.

Turn cake out onto a towel sprinkled with ¼ cup powdered sugar. Beginning at narrow end, roll up cake and towel together, jellyroll fashion; cool.

Combine 1 cup powdered sugar, cream cheese, butter, and vanilla; beat until smooth and creamy. Unroll cake, and spread with filling. Roll cake up again; chill, seam side down. Yield: about 10 servings.

Angel Dessert

      2   *eggs, separated*
   Dash of salt
   ⅔   *cup sugar*
      1   *teaspoon vanilla extract*
      2   *tablespoons all-purpose flour*
   1½   *cups milk*
      1   *envelope unflavored gelatin*
   ¼   *cup cold water*
      1   *cup frozen whipped topping, thawed,
              divided*
   ½   *(17¼-ounce) package bakery angel food
              cake or about 6 cups small pieces
              angel food cake*
   Frozen whipped topping, thawed
   Sliced, sweetened peaches

Combine egg yolks, salt, sugar, vanilla, flour, and milk in a medium saucepan. Cook over medium heat, stirring constantly, until slightly thickened.

Dissolve gelatin in ¼ cup cold water; stir into custard. Cool. Beat egg whites until stiff. Fold egg whites and 1 cup thawed, whipped topping into custard.

Break cake into small pieces, and place in an 8-inch square dish. Pour custard over cake pieces; chill. Serve with whipped topping and peaches. Yield: 8 to 10 servings.

Eggs and Cheese

Eggs are one of the most important ingredients in any cookbook. Their versatility takes them from a fluffy eggnog to a high-rise angel food cake. Yet they are at their finest when featured as themselves. They are a star at the breakfast table, whether scrambled, poached, as an omelet filled with a variety of ingredients, or as Eggs Benedict at a weekend brunch. Deviled eggs come easily to mind, and you'll love them stuffed with crab or shrimp. Egg salad, interesting egg casseroles, even Pickled Eggs emphasize the egg.

Almost as essential and every bit as popular an ingredient is cheese. Cheddar, Longhorn, cottage, cream cheese, Swiss, and blue add their creaminess and flavor to some delicious dishes.

Creole Eggs

    8   tablespoons butter or margarine,
          divided
    3   tablespoons all-purpose flour
    1   cup milk
    1   cup chopped celery
    1   cup chopped onion
    1   cup chopped green pepper
    1   (28-ounce) can tomatoes
    1   teaspoon salt
    ¼   teaspoon pepper
    6   hard-cooked eggs, sliced
    Buttered breadcrumbs

Melt 3 tablespoons butter in a saucepan; gradually add flour, stirring constantly. Gradually add milk; cook, stirring constantly, until thick.

Melt remaining 5 tablespoons butter in a skillet; sauté celery, onion, and green pepper until tender. Add tomatoes, salt, and pepper; cook over medium heat until thick. Add to white sauce, mixing well.

Place a layer of egg slices in a lightly greased 2-quart casserole; pour half of creamed mixture over eggs. Repeat layers. Sprinkle with breadcrumbs. Bake at 350° for 20 to 30 minutes. Yield: 6 to 8 servings.

Golden Egg Casserole

    12   hard-cooked eggs, finely chopped
    ¼   cup chopped pimiento
    ½   cup minced celery with leaves
    2   cups mayonnaise
    1   teaspoon salt
    1½   teaspoons garlic salt
    ¾   teaspoon pepper
    ½   cup milk
    2¾   cups fine saltine cracker crumbs,
           divided
    ¼   cup melted butter or margarine

Combine first 8 ingredients; blend well, and stir in 2 cups cracker crumbs. Spoon into a lightly greased 2-quart casserole.

Combine remaining cracker crumbs and butter; sprinkle over egg mixture. Bake at 400° for 25 minutes or until golden brown. Yield: 10 to 12 servings.

A Golden Filled Omelet (page 136) is an easy dish to prepare and is as appropriate to serve for lunch or supper as it is for breakfast.

Confetti Scrambled Eggs

12   *eggs*
1⅓   *cups milk*
1   *teaspoon salt*
⅛   *teaspoon pepper*
2   *tablespoons all-purpose flour*
2   *tablespoons chopped pimiento*
2   *tablespoons chopped parsley*
¼   *cup butter or margarine*

Combine eggs, milk, salt, pepper, and flour; beat well. Add pimiento and parsley. Melt butter in a skillet; add egg mixture, and cook over medium heat.

As eggs begin to set, lift cooked portion so that uncooked portion can flow to bottom. Cook until eggs are thickened but still moist (3 to 5 minutes). Yield: 6 servings.

Poached-Fried Egg

1   *teaspoon butter*
1   *egg*
1   *tablespoon water*

Melt butter in heavy skillet, and heat until hot enough to sizzle a drop of water. Break egg into a saucer; carefully slip egg into skillet. Cook egg over low heat until edges turn white. Add water; cover skillet tightly, and cook to desired doneness. Yield: 1 serving.

Cheese Eggs

1   *cup shredded American cheese*
6   *eggs*
½   *teaspoon salt*
¼   *teaspoon pepper*
1   *tablespoon melted margarine*
½   *cup milk*

Place equal amounts of cheese in 6 greased custard cups. Break an egg into each cup. Sprinkle with salt and pepper.

Pour a small amount of margarine and milk over each egg. Place in a pan of hot water, and bake at 350° for 20 to 30 minutes or until desired doneness. Yield: 6 servings.

Scrambled Eggs with Cheese

8   *eggs*
6   *tablespoons milk*
Salt and pepper to taste
½   *cup shredded sharp Cheddar cheese*
3   *tablespoons butter or margarine*

Beat eggs with a fork until well blended; stir in milk, salt, pepper, and cheese. Melt butter in a heavy skillet; add egg mixture. Cook and stir until eggs are set but still moist. Yield: 4 to 6 servings.

★ Cheesy Mexican Omelet

4   *eggs, well beaten*
2   *tablespoons milk*
½   *cup picante sauce, divided*
⅛   *teaspoon salt*
⅛   *teaspoon pepper*
1   *tablespoon butter or margarine*
1   *to 1½ cups shredded sharp Cheddar cheese*

Combine eggs, milk, 2 tablespoons picante sauce, salt, and pepper; mix well. Melt butter in an 8- or 10-inch omelet pan or skillet; heat until just hot enough to sizzle a drop of water. Pour in egg mixture all at once.

As mixture starts to cook, gently lift edges of omelet with a fork and tilt pan to allow uncooked egg mixture to run underneath.

When mixture is set and no longer runs, sprinkle cheese on half of omelet; cover pan. Remove pan from heat and let stand 1 to 2 minutes or until cheese melts and eggs are firm on top.

Fold omelet in half, and place on a warm platter. Top with remaining picante sauce. Yield: 2 to 3 servings.

★
Eggs Benedict

 2 *English muffins*
 Butter or margarine, softened
 4 *slices Canadian bacon, cooked*
 4 *poached eggs*
 Hollandaise Sauce
 Pitted ripe olives

Separate muffins into halves; spread cut sides with butter. Broil until lightly browned.

Place a slice of Canadian bacon on each muffin half; top with poached egg, and cover with Hollandaise Sauce. Top each with a ripe olive. Yield: 4 servings.

Hollandaise Sauce:

 4 *egg yolks*
 2 *tablespoons lemon juice*
 1 *cup melted butter*
 ¼ *teaspoon salt*
 ⅛ *teaspoon white pepper*

Beat egg yolks in top of double boiler; stir in lemon juice. Place over hot (not boiling) water. Add butter a little at a time, stirring constantly with a wooden spoon. Add salt and pepper. Continue cooking slowly until thickened. Yield: about 1½ cups.

★
Breakfast Soufflé

 1½ *pounds bulk pork sausage*
 9 *eggs, beaten*
 3 *cups milk*
 1½ *teaspoons dry mustard*
 1 *teaspoon salt*
 3 *slices bread, cut into ¼-inch cubes*
 1½ *cups shredded Cheddar cheese*

Cook sausage over medium heat until done, stirring to crumble. Drain well on paper towels; set aside.

Combine sausage and remaining ingredients, mixing well. Pour into a well-greased 13- x 9- x 2-inch baking pan. Refrigerate, covered, overnight. Bake at 350° for 1 hour. Yield: 8 to 10 servings.

Egg Casserole

 1½ *cups croutons*
 1 *cup shredded sharp Cheddar cheese*
 4 *eggs*
 2 *cups milk*
 1 *tablespoon prepared mustard*
 Salt and pepper to taste
 Onion salt to taste

Spread croutons in a buttered 10- x 6- x 1¾-inch baking dish; sprinkle with cheese.

Combine eggs, milk, and seasonings; beat well, and pour over cheese. Set aside 5 minutes. Bake at 325° for 50 minutes. Yield: 6 servings.

Egg Salad

 4 *hard-cooked eggs, chopped*
 2 *tablespoons prepared mustard*
 2 *tablespoons mayonnaise*
 ¼ *teaspoon salt*
 ¼ *cup diced celery*

Combine all ingredients, mixing well. Keep refrigerated until ready to use. Yield: about 1½ cups.

Sherried Eggs

 1 *(4-ounce) can sliced mushrooms, drained*
 1 *large onion, chopped*
 3 *tablespoons melted margarine*
 9 *hard-cooked eggs, coarsely chopped*
 1 *(10¾-ounce) can cream of mushroom soup, undiluted*
 ¼ *cup sherry*
 Salt and pepper to taste
 ½ *teaspoon Worcestershire sauce*
 ½ *teaspoon hot sauce*
 Buttered breadcrumbs

Sauté mushrooms and onion in margarine until onion is clear; stir in all remaining ingredients except breadcrumbs. Pour into a shallow casserole, and sprinkle with breadcrumbs. Bake at 350° about 20 minutes until bubbly. Yield: 4 to 5 servings.

Shrimp Stuffed Eggs

8   *hard-cooked eggs*
2   *tablespoons mayonnaise*
1   *cup cooked, shredded shrimp*
2   *tablespoons minced celery*
2   *tablespoons minced onion*
2   *tablespoons sweet pickle relish*
Salt and pepper
Lemon halves
Paprika

Slice eggs in half lengthwise, and carefully remove yolks. Mash yolks with mayonnaise; blend in next 5 ingredients. Spoon shrimp mixture into egg whites. Garnish with lemon and paprika. Yield: 6 to 8 servings.

Shrimp-Crab Stuffed Eggs

1½   *dozen hard-cooked eggs*
1   *(6-ounce) package frozen shrimp and*
      crabmeat, thawed and drained
⅔   *cup mayonnaise or salad dressing*
1   *tablespoon chili sauce*
1   *tablespoon grated onion*
1   *teaspoon finely chopped green pepper*
1   *teaspoon chopped pimiento*
Parsley
Pitted ripe olives, quartered

Cut eggs in half; remove yolks, and place in small mixing bowl. Mash egg yolks, and blend in next 6 ingredients; stuff egg whites with yolk mixture. Garnish with parsley and ripe olives. Yield: 3 dozen eggs.

Swiss Egg Bake

1   *cup chopped onion*
1   *tablespoon butter or margarine*
8   *hard-cooked eggs, sliced*
2   *cups shredded Swiss cheese*
1   *(10¾-ounce) can cream of mushroom*
      soup, undiluted
¾   *cup milk*
1   *teaspoon prepared mustard*
½   *teaspoon seasoned salt*
¼   *teaspoon pepper*
¼   *teaspoon dillweed*
6   *slices rye bread*

Sauté onion in butter until tender; sprinkle in an 11½- x 7½- x 1½-inch dish. Arrange egg slices over onion; sprinkle with cheese.

Combine soup and remaining ingredients except bread; blend well. Pour over cheese. Cut bread into triangles, and arrange on top of soup mixture. Bake at 350° for 40 minutes. Place under broiler 1 minute. Yield: about 6 servings.

Pickled Eggs

2   *teaspoons ground ginger*
2   *teaspoons pickling spice*
12   *peppercorns*
2   *cups malt vinegar*
12   *hard-cooked eggs, peeled*
2   *medium-size onions, sliced*
3   *cloves garlic*
½   *teaspoon dillweed*
Salt and pepper to taste

Combine ginger, pickling spice, peppercorns, and vinegar in a medium saucepan. Bring to a boil; reduce heat, and simmer 5 minutes.

Place eggs in a crock or glass jar. Pour hot liquid over eggs to cover; add water if necessary to cover. Add onion, garlic, and dillweed.

Cover, and refrigerate at least 4 days. Eggs may be kept in pickling liquid several months. Serve in wedges with salt and pepper. Yield: 12 to 24 servings.

Serving Cheese

One of the most popular ways to enjoy cheese today is in its own simple but natural form. It can be served as an appetizer with wine or with fresh fruit for dessert.

Good cheese is beautiful in itself, and no elaborate serving pieces are needed. It can be most attractive when it is served on plain wood or other natural materials or on a white plate.

These tips will enhance your expertise in serving cheese.

—Cheese should be served at room temperature to enjoy its true flavor. The full characteristic flavor develops if it is allowed to stand out of the refrigerator about an hour before serving. Soft-ripening cheese will come to room temperature in less than an hour.

—Cut and serve only the amount of cheese you expect to use. Cheese looks more attractive and does not dry out as quickly when left in a wedge or large piece rather than cut into small pieces.

—A well-shaped hardwood board makes a practical tray for serving cheese. When serving several cheeses, leave enough room around each cheese for easy handling and cutting.

—Provide plenty of knives and other cutters to avoid mixing the flavors of various cheeses. (Many cheese shops offer an assortment of knives, wire slicers, and planes for cutting cheese.)

—Avoid placing strong and mild cheeses next to each other. These should be placed apart or served on separate trays.

—Avoid overpowering delicate cheeses with strong flavored crackers, breads, or beverages. Whatever is served with cheese should complement rather than camouflage the taste of the cheese.

—Although wine is the classic accompaniment to cheese, there are no firm rules for matching cheese varieties with wine. Rich, tangy cheeses are generally preferred with full-bodied red wines, while more delicately flavored cheeses are best enjoyed with light white wines.

★
Cheese Crock

    1 *pound sharp Cheddar cheese, shredded*
    1 *(3-ounce) package cream cheese*
    2 *tablespoons olive oil*
 1½ *teaspoons dry mustard*
 1¼ *teaspoons minced garlic*
    3 *tablespoons brandy*
      Crackers, melba toast, or party rye bread

Let cheeses stand at room temperature until soft; blend together until very smooth. Add olive oil, mustard, garlic, and brandy, blending well. Pack into a stoneware cheese crock; cover and refrigerate at least 1 week before serving. To serve, allow cheese to soften at room temperature 1 hour; serve on crackers, melba toast, or party rye bread. Yield: about 3 cups.

Note: Cheese can be kept going as long as part of the original mixture is left. To add to crock, any firm cheese such as Cheddar, Swiss, or Monterey Jack may be used. Shred any cheese scraps and blend with a small amount of cream cheese and olive oil until smooth; add beer, sherry, kirsch, or brandy, keeping the original proportion the same. Let mixture age a few days before serving again.

Welsh Rarebit

    1 *tablespoon butter or margarine*
    1 *pound sharp Cheddar cheese, cut into ½-inch cubes*
 ¾ *to 1 cup milk or beer*
    1 *teaspoon Worcestershire sauce*
 ½ *teaspoon salt*
 ½ *teaspoon paprika*
 ½ *teaspoon dry mustard*
      Dash of red pepper
    1 *egg, beaten*
    6 *tomato slices*
    6 *slices bread, toasted*
    6 *slices bacon, cooked and halved*

Combine butter and cheese in top of a double boiler; stir until cheese is melted. Gradually stir in milk; add Worcestershire sauce, salt, paprika, mustard, and pepper. Stir in egg. Cook until slightly thickened, stirring constantly.

To serve, pour cheese sauce into a chafing dish. Place a tomato slice on each slice of bread; top each tomato with 2 bacon halves. Spoon cheese sauce over bacon, and serve immediately. Yield: 6 servings.

Homemade Cottage Cheese

1   *tablespoon commercial sour cream or* ¼
     rennet tablet
2   *tablespoons water*
2   *quarts skim milk or reconstituted*
     nonfat dry milk
¼   *cup buttermilk*
½   *teaspoon salt*
½   *cup half-and-half*

Combine sour cream and 2 tablespoons water. Heat skim milk to 72°; add sour cream mixture and buttermilk. Cover and let stand in a warm place (in oven or over a pan of warm water) until a slightly firm curd develops (12 to 24 hours). (Curd will form on bottom, and whey will rise to top.)

To determine if curd is firm enough, insert a knife at the side of container and gently pull curd away from side; if the curd breaks quickly and smoothly, it is ready. Break curd into chunks.

Set container in a pan of hot water and heat mixture to 110°, stirring occasionally. Hold at this temperature 20 to 30 minutes, stirring occasionally; curd will firm up at this point.

Line a colander with several layers of cheesecloth. Pour curd into colander, draining off whey; drain 5 minutes. Rinse curd with cold water, and drain 5 minutes longer.

Place curd in a bowl, and break into ¼- to ½-inch pieces. Add salt and mix well. Stir in half-and-half. Store in refrigerator. Yield: about 1 cup.

Baked Macaroni and Cheese

1   *cup uncooked macaroni*
3   *eggs, beaten*
3   *cups milk*
½   *pound Cheddar cheese, cut in cubes*
Salt and pepper to taste
Paprika (optional)
2   *tablespoons margarine*

Cook macaroni according to package directions; drain. Combine eggs and milk in a large bowl; stir in macaroni, cheese, and seasonings. Add paprika, if desired.

Spoon mixture into a 2-quart casserole; dot with margarine. Bake at 325° for 40 to 60 minutes or until set. Yield: 4 servings.

Golden Filled Omelet

2   *eggs*
¼   *teaspoon salt*
Dash of pepper
1   *tablespoon water*
About 1 tablespoon butter or margarine
2   *tablespoons sautéed mushroom slices*
2   *tablespoons shredded cheese*

Gently blend first 4 ingredients. Melt butter in an 8- or 10-inch omelet pan or skillet; heat until just hot enough to sizzle a drop of water. Pour egg mixture into pan.

Lift edge of omelet with a spatula and tilt pan to allow uncooked egg mixture to run underneath. When mixture is set, sprinkle mushroom and cheese on half of omelet. Fold omelet in half and place on a warm plate. Yield: 1 serving.

Cheese-a-Roni

3½   *cups cooked elbow macaroni, divided*
1   *(10½-ounce) can asparagus tips,*
      drained
2   *tablespoons chopped green pepper*
2   *tablespoons chopped onion*
2   *tablespoons melted butter or margarine*
2   *tablespoons all-purpose flour*
1   *cup cottage cheese*
½   *cup cream cheese*
½   *cup commercial sour cream*
2   *cups cubed cooked chicken*
1   *(4-ounce) can sliced mushrooms,*
      drained
1   *tablespoon blue cheese*
1   *cup shredded Cheddar cheese*
½   *teaspoon salt*
¼   *teaspoon pepper*
½   *cup half-and-half*

Place half of the macaroni in a lightly greased 4-quart casserole; cover with asparagus tips.

Sauté green pepper and onion in butter in a small skillet; add flour, stirring until vegetables are coated. Remove from heat; stir in cottage cheese, cream cheese, and sour cream. Spread over asparagus.

Spoon chicken over cheese mixture, and top with remaining macaroni and mushrooms. Sprinkle with blue cheese, Cheddar cheese, salt, and pepper. Pour half-and-half over all. Bake at 350° for 30 to 40 minutes. Yield: 10 servings.

Carbonara

> 1 *cup chopped green onions*
> ¾ *cup chopped cooked ham*
> 6 *tablespoons melted butter or margarine*
> 4 *tablespoons all-purpose flour*
> 1 *quart half-and-half*
> ¾ *cup grated Parmesan cheese*
> *Salt and pepper to taste*
> 1 *(12-ounce) package vermicelli or spaghetti*
> *Grated Parmesan cheese*

Sauté onion and ham in butter until tender; blend in flour, stirring until smooth. Gradually add half-and-half; cook, stirring constantly, until smooth and slightly thickened. Gradually stir in ¾ cup cheese. Keep sauce warm while preparing vermicelli.

Cook vermicelli according to package directions; drain and rinse. Return cooked vermicelli to pan and add sauce; toss lightly. Place in individual casseroles, and sprinkle with additional Parmesan cheese. Yield: 8 servings.

Note: Sauce may be prepared ahead of time and thinned slightly with milk or half-and-half. This is very good served with Lemon Veal (see Index).

Noodles Romanoff

> 1½ *tablespoons salt*
> 5 *quarts boiling water*
> 1 *(12-ounce) package ½-inch-wide noodles*
> 1 *(24-ounce) carton creamed cottage cheese*
> 2 *(8-ounce) cartons commercial sour cream*
> 6 *tablespoons melted butter or margarine, divided*
> 1½ *cups chopped green onions*
> 1 *clove garlic, crushed*
> ¼ *teaspoon pepper*
> ½ *cup fine breadcrumbs*

Add salt to rapidly boiling water; add noodles gradually so that water continues to boil. Cook, uncovered, for 7 minutes; stir occasionally. Drain; set aside.

Combine cottage cheese, sour cream, 4 tablespoons butter, onion, garlic, and pepper. Add noodles and toss lightly with a fork. Spoon into a lightly greased 4-quart casserole.

Combine breadcrumbs and remaining 2 tablespoons butter, stirring well; sprinkle over noodles. Bake at 350° for 25 to 30 minutes. Yield: 10 to 12 servings.

Sour Cream Noodles

> 1 *(8-ounce) package fine noodles*
> 1 *cup cottage cheese*
> 1 *(8-ounce) carton commercial sour cream*
> ⅛ *teaspoon garlic salt*
> 1 *onion, finely grated*
> 1 *tablespoon Worcestershire sauce*
> *Grated Parmesan cheese*

Cook noodles according to package directions; drain. Combine noodles and remaining ingredients except Parmesan cheese, mixing gently. Spoon mixture into a lightly greased 2-quart casserole; sprinkle with Parmesan cheese. Bake at 350° for 45 minutes. Yield: 6 to 8 servings.

Fish and Shellfish

From the vast expanse of coastline to the crystal-clear lakes and streams, we have a wide selection of fish and shellfish available. The Atlantic Ocean and the Gulf of Mexico keep us well supplied with treasures from the sea. Southerners will barbecue anything and find it delicious; oysters and shrimp are no exception. Crab and shrimp are stuffed with well-seasoned fillings or blended into rich creamy sauces.

Lakes and streams decorate the Southern landscape, and fishermen reel in many freshwater fish from them. What could be better than a fish fry with catfish, bass, or bream caught and cooked the same day? Although frying is the traditional method, you'll be delighted with the different ideas for preparing your catch that are presented in this chapter.

Easy Lobster Newburg

¼ cup melted butter or margarine
¼ cup all-purpose flour
½ teaspoon dry mustard
½ teaspoon paprika
¾ cup milk
½ cup whipping cream
1 pound cooked lobster, cut into chunks
½ cup sliced mushrooms
1 teaspoon salt
¼ cup sherry
   Hot cooked rice

Combine butter, flour, mustard, and paprika; cook over low heat about 2 minutes. Gradually add milk and cream; cook, stirring constantly, until smooth and thickened. Stir in lobster, mushrooms, salt, and sherry.

Transfer to a chafing dish set on low heat. Serve over rice. Yield: 4 to 5 servings.

Beer Batter Bream (page 155), hush puppies, and coleslaw are the makings of an old-fashioned Southern fish fry.

Broiled Lobster

2 (1-pound) live lobsters
1 tablespoon melted butter or margarine
¼ teaspoon salt
   Dash white pepper
   Dash paprika
¼ cup melted butter or margarine
1 tablespoon lemon juice

Kill each lobster by placing it on its back and inserting a sharp knife between body shell and tail segment, cutting down to sever the spinal cord. Cut in half lengthwise. Remove the stomach (located just back of the head) and the intestinal vein (runs from the stomach to the tip of the tail). Do not discard the green liver and coral roe; they are delicious. Crack claws.

Place lobster, opened flat, on a broiler pan. Brush lobster meat with 1 tablespoon melted butter. Sprinkle with salt, pepper, and paprika. Broil about 4 inches from heat for 12 to 15 minutes or until lightly browned. Combine ¼ cup melted butter and lemon juice; serve with lobster. Yield: 2 servings.

Boiled Lobster

2 *(1-pound) live lobsters*
3 *quarts boiling water*
3 *tablespoons salt*
Melted butter

Plunge lobsters headfirst into boiling salted water. Cover and return to boiling point. Simmer about 15 minutes; drain. Place lobster on its back; insert a sharp knife between body shell and tail segment, cutting down to sever the spinal cord. Cut in half lengthwise. Remove the stomach (located just back of the head) and the intestinal vein (runs from the stomach to the tip of the tail). Do not discard the green liver and coral roe; they are delicious. Crack claws. Serve lobster with melted butter. Yield: 2 servings.

★
Crab Quiche

Pastry for 9-inch quiche pan or piepan
½ *cup mayonnaise*
2 *tablespoons all-purpose flour*
2 *eggs, beaten*
½ *cup milk*
1 *(6-ounce) package frozen crabmeat, thawed and drained*
½ *pound Swiss cheese, cut into ¼-inch cubes*
⅓ *cup chopped green onion*
Parsley

Line a 9-inch quiche pan with pastry, and trim off excess around edge of pan. Place a piece of buttered aluminum foil, buttered side down, over pastry; gently press into pastry shell. This will keep the sides of the shell from collapsing.

Cover foil with a layer of dried peas or beans. Bake at 400° for 10 minutes; remove foil and peas. Prick shell, and bake 3 to 5 additional minutes or until lightly browned. Cool.

Combine mayonnaise, flour, eggs, and milk; mix thoroughly. Stir in crabmeat, cheese, and onion. Spoon into quiche shell, and bake at 350° for 30 to 40 minutes or until firm in center; garnish with parsley. Yield: one 9-inch quiche.

Crabmeat Casserole

1 *(6-ounce) package frozen crabmeat, thawed and drained*
1 *(10¾-ounce) can cream of mushroom soup, undiluted*
1 *cup milk*
1 *cup uncooked small seashell macaroni*
½ *cup shredded Cheddar cheese*
2 *tablespoons grated onion*

Combine all ingredients in a 1½-quart casserole; cover and refrigerate overnight.

Bake at 350° about 1 hour or until macaroni is tender. Yield: 4 servings.

Crab with Sweet-and-Sour Orange Sauce

2 *cloves garlic, mashed*
2 *onions, chopped*
¼ *cup melted butter or margarine*
2 *tomatoes, peeled, seeded, and chopped*
1 *apple, peeled and chopped*
½ *cup finely chopped celery*
¼ *cup shredded coconut*
½ *teaspoon ground ginger*
2 *cups hot chicken broth*
Juice of 1 lemon
1 *tablespoon water*
1½ *tablespoons curry powder*
1½ *tablespoons all-purpose flour*
½ *teaspoon dry mustard*
4 *(6-ounce) packages frozen king crabmeat, thawed and drained*
2 *cups uncooked regular rice*
Sweet-and-Sour Orange Sauce
Chopped peanuts
Shredded coconut
Chopped green pepper

Sauté garlic and onion in butter until golden. Stir in tomato, apple, celery, ¼ cup coconut, and ginger; simmer 2 to 3 minutes. Add broth, blending well.

Combine lemon juice, water, curry powder, flour, and mustard; blend to a smooth paste.

Add to broth mixture, stirring until smooth and thickened; simmer 30 to 40 minutes. Add crabmeat; simmer 5 minutes.

Cook rice according to package directions; drain. While hot, pack tightly into a buttered 6-cup ring mold. Let stand a few minutes; invert on a large serving platter. Fill center with crabmeat mixture.

Serve Sweet-and-Sour Orange Sauce, chopped peanuts, shredded coconut, and chopped green pepper as accompaniments. Yield: 8 servings.

Sweet-and-Sour Orange Sauce:

½ cup apple butter
Coarsely grated rind of 1 orange
¼ cup orange juice
½ cup golden seedless raisins
1 tablespoon Worcestershire sauce

Combine all ingredients, and blend well. Yield: 1¼ cups.

Stuffed Crab Shells

1 onion, chopped
1 green pepper, chopped
1 clove garlic, minced
½ cup melted butter or margarine
1 (12-ounce) package frozen crabmeat, thawed, drained, and flaked
1½ cups Italian breadcrumbs, divided
¼ cup water
Juice of 1 lemon
1 tablespoon chopped parsley
Dash of Worcestershire sauce
Dash of hot sauce
⅛ teaspoon cayenne pepper
Salt and pepper to taste
Crab shells

Sauté onion, green pepper, and garlic in butter 5 minutes. Add crabmeat, ¾ cup breadcrumbs, water, and lemon juice; simmer 20 minutes. Stir in parsley and remaining seasonings. Spoon into 12 crab shells. Butter remaining breadcrumbs, and sprinkle over crab mixture. Bake at 450° for 3 to 5 minutes. Yield: 12 servings.

Note: Stuffing may be baked at 400° for 15 minutes in a greased 1-quart casserole instead of crab shells.

Crabmeat Witchery

3 cups (about 1 pound) crabmeat
¼ cup melted butter or margarine
1 teaspoon salt
½ teaspoon ground mace
¼ teaspoon ground red pepper
1½ cups half-and-half
½ cup sherry
1 teaspoon lemon juice
1 teaspoon grated lemon rind
2 tablespoons all-purpose flour
Patty shells or toast

Combine first 9 ingredients in a saucepan; cook over low heat about 5 minutes, stirring constantly.

Blend together a small amount of crabmeat mixture and flour; blend mixture into remaining crabmeat. Cook over low heat, stirring constantly, until thickened and bubbly. Serve over patty shells or toast. Yield: 4 to 5 servings.

Note: Mixture may be frozen. Combine first 9 ingredients in a saucepan; cook over low heat about 5 minutes, stirring constantly. Spoon into a freezer proof casserole or container. Seal securely and freeze. To serve, thaw overnight in refrigerator. Proceed as directed.

Sweet-and-Sour Shrimp Skillet

1 medium-size green pepper, chopped
½ cup chopped green onion
1 tablespoon salad oil
1 (8-ounce) can tomato sauce
½ cup steak sauce
2 tablespoons vinegar
¼ cup firmly packed brown sugar
1 tablespoon soy sauce
2 pounds shrimp, cooked, peeled, and deveined
Hot cooked rice

Sauté pepper and onion in oil until tender. Add next 5 ingredients; stir well. Add shrimp; heat thoroughly, stirring often. Transfer to a chafing dish set on low heat. Serve over rice. Yield: 6 servings.

Tangy Crab Casseroles

2   *(6½-ounce) cans crabmeat*
1   *(8-ounce) carton commercial sour cream*
⅓   *cup grated Parmesan cheese*
1   *tablespoon lemon juice*
1   *tablespoon grated onion*
½   *teaspoon salt*
   Dash of hot sauce
¾   *cup breadcrumbs*
2   *tablespoons melted butter or margarine*
   Paprika
   Lemon slices or parsley

Remove any cartilage or shell from crabmeat. Combine sour cream, cheese, lemon juice, onion, salt, and hot sauce; mix thoroughly. Add crabmeat. Spoon into 6 well-greased individual shells or custard cups.

Combine breadcrumbs and butter; sprinkle over crabmeat mixture. Sprinkle with paprika. Bake at 350° for 30 minutes or until lightly browned. Garnish with lemon slices. Yield: 6 servings.

Skillet Shrimp Dinner

3   *tablespoons melted butter or margarine*
1   *medium-size onion, minced*
1   *green pepper, finely chopped*
1   *clove garlic, minced*
¼   *cup chopped pimiento*
1   *cup uncooked long grain regular rice*
½   *cup chopped mushrooms*
1¼   *pounds shrimp, peeled and deveined*
1   *teaspoon salt*
1   *bay leaf*
1   *(8-ounce) can tomato sauce*
1   *cup chicken broth or water*

Combine butter, onion, green pepper, garlic, pimiento, and rice in a skillet; mix well. Stir in mushrooms, shrimp, salt, bay leaf, tomato sauce, and broth. Cover and simmer 30 minutes or until rice is tender. Yield: 4 servings.

★
Shrimp Stuffed with Crabmeat

18   *jumbo shrimp, peeled and deveined*
   Salt to taste
1   *(6-ounce) package frozen crabmeat, thawed, drained, and flaked*
2   *hard-cooked eggs, finely chopped*
2   *sprigs parsley, chopped*
1   *tablespoon finely chopped pimiento*
3   *slices soft white bread, cubed*
2   *dashes Worcestershire sauce*
   Dash of salt
6   *tablespoons melted butter or margarine*
5   *tablespoons mayonnaise, divided*
4   *teaspoons milk*
   Paprika

Slit each shrimp down the back, slicing deeply to make shrimp lay flat. Salt each shrimp.

Combine crabmeat, eggs, parsley, pimiento, bread cubes, Worcestershire sauce, salt, butter, and 3 tablespoons mayonnaise. Stuff each shrimp with 1 tablespoon crabmeat mixture; place in a buttered baking dish.

Combine remaining 2 tablespoons mayonnaise and milk, stirring well. Pour ½ teaspoon milk mixture over each shrimp; sprinkle with paprika. Bake at 325° for 20 minutes or until stuffing is golden brown and shrimp are pink. Yield: 4 to 6 servings.

★
Shrimp Cocktail

1   *cup chili sauce*
1   *cup catsup*
2   *tablespoons horseradish*
2   *tablespoons vinegar*
1   *tablespoon Worcestershire sauce*
2   *teaspoons lemon juice*
   Dash of hot sauce
   Cooked shrimp, peeled and deveined
   Lemon wedges (optional)

Combine first 7 ingredients, mixing well. Chill sauce at least half an hour before serving. Serve with shrimp, and garnish with lemon wedges, if desired. Yield: about 2 cups.

Shrimp in Remoulade Sauce

3   quarts water
1   (3¼-ounce) package crab and shrimp
      boil mix
1   tablespoon salt
1   onion, quartered
1   clove garlic
1   lemon, sliced
3   pounds shrimp
6   tablespoons tarragon vinegar
3   tablespoons Creole mustard
4   green onions with tops, minced
1   stalk celery, minced
⅔   cup salad oil or olive oil
Lettuce
2   hard-cooked eggs, sliced
1   avocado, peeled and cut in wedges

Bring water to a boil; add crab and shrimp boil mix, salt, onion, garlic, lemon slices, and shrimp. Cover and simmer 5 minutes or until shrimp are pink and tender. Drain and chill. Peel and devein shrimp.

Combine vinegar, mustard, green onion, celery, and salad oil; mix well. Pour sauce over shrimp, coating shrimp thoroughly. Cover and refrigerate several hours. Toss shrimp; serve on lettuce. Garnish with egg slices and avocado wedges. Yield: 6 servings.

Shrimp Spaghetti

1   onion, chopped
½   cup chopped green onion tops
1   green pepper, chopped
¼   cup chopped celery
4   cloves garlic, minced
¼   cup salad oil
1   (8-ounce) can tomato sauce
½   (10-ounce) can tomatoes with hot
      peppers, undrained and chopped
¼   teaspoon oregano
Pinch of rosemary
Dash of thyme
Pinch of sugar
Salt and pepper to taste
¼   to ½ cup water
1   pound shrimp, peeled and deveined
Hot cooked spaghetti

Sauté onion, green pepper, celery, and garlic in salad oil until tender. Add tomato sauce, tomatoes with hot peppers, seasonings, and water; cover and simmer 30 minutes, stirring occasionally. Add shrimp and simmer, covered, about 10 more minutes. Serve sauce over cooked spaghetti. Yield: about 4 servings.

Shrimp Casserole

1   pound cooked, peeled, deveined shrimp,
      divided
1   tablespoon lemon juice
3   tablespoons salad oil
¾   cup uncooked regular rice
¼   cup finely chopped green pepper
¼   cup finely chopped onion
¼   cup melted butter or margarine, divided
1   teaspoon salt
⅛   teaspoon pepper
⅛   teaspoon ground mace
Dash of cayenne
1   (10¾-ounce) can tomato soup,
      undiluted
¼   cup water
½   pint whipping cream
¼   cup sherry
½   cup slivered blanched almonds, divided
1   cup corn flake crumbs

Set aside 8 shrimp for topping. Combine remaining shrimp, lemon juice, and salad oil in a lightly greased 2-quart casserole.

Cook rice according to package directions; set aside.

Sauté green pepper and onion in 2 tablespoons butter for 5 minutes; add to rice along with seasonings, tomato soup, water, whipping cream, sherry, and ¼ cup almonds. Add to shrimp mixture, stirring gently. Bake at 350° about 20 minutes.

Combine 2 tablespoons butter, corn flake crumbs, ¼ cup almonds, and reserved shrimp; sprinkle over casserole. Bake an additional 15 minutes or until the mixture is bubbly and crumbs lightly browned. Yield: 8 servings.

Shrimp Jambalaya

     4   large onions, chopped
     ¾   cup chopped green pepper
     3   cloves garlic, minced
    Salad oil
     2   pounds shrimp, peeled and deveined
     3   cups water
     2   cups uncooked regular rice
    Cayenne pepper to taste
    Black pepper to taste
     1   teaspoon salt

Sauté onion, green pepper, and garlic in enough oil to cover bottom of a heavy Dutch oven. When vegetables are tender, add shrimp and cook about 15 minutes. Add water and bring to a boil. Stir in rice and seasonings. Cook, covered, for 20 to 25 minutes over low heat or until rice is tender. Lightly stir; cover and set aside for 10 minutes. Yield: 8 to 10 servings.

Shrimp with Wild Rice

     ½   cup all-purpose flour
     1   cup melted butter or margarine, divided
     4   cups chicken broth
     ¼   teaspoon white pepper
     1   cup thinly sliced onion
     ½   cup thinly sliced green pepper
     1   cup thinly sliced mushrooms
     2   pounds cooked, peeled, deveined shrimp
     2   tablespoons Worcestershire sauce
    Few drops of hot sauce
     4   cups cooked wild rice

Gradually add flour to ½ cup melted butter; cook over low heat, stirring constantly, until bubbly. Gradually add broth; cook until smooth and thickened, stirring constantly. Add white pepper; simmer 2 to 3 minutes.

Sauté onion, green pepper, and mushrooms in remaining ½ cup butter; drain. Combine white sauce, sautéed vegetables, and remaining ingredients; spoon into 2 greased, shallow 2-quart casseroles. Bake at 300° for 45 to 50 minutes or until bubbly.

Before serving, transfer to a chafing dish set on low heat. Yield: 12 servings.

★ Biloxi Jambalaya

     1   pound shrimp, peeled and deveined, or 1 (10-ounce) package peeled, deveined frozen shrimp, thawed
     ¼   cup melted butter or margarine
     1   cup minced onion
     2   cloves garlic, minced
     2   green peppers, diced
    1½   cups cooked regular rice
     1   (28-ounce) can tomatoes, undrained and chopped
     2   cups water
     2   tablespoons salt
     ¼   teaspoon pepper
     1   bay leaf
     1   pound cooked ham, cut into ½-inch cubes

Sauté shrimp in butter 2 to 3 minutes or until pink; remove from pan and set aside.

Add onion, garlic, and green pepper to remaining butter in pan; cook 2 minutes, stirring occasionally. Add rice; mix well. Add tomatoes, water, salt, pepper, and bay leaf; bring to a boil. Cover and simmer 15 minutes.

Add ham and shrimp; cover and cook 10 minutes or until all liquid is absorbed. Yield: 8 servings.

★ Barbecued Shrimp

     5   pounds shrimp, unpeeled
     1   bunch celery with leaves, very coarsely chopped
     3   to 4 cloves garlic, chopped
     6   lemons, cut in half
     1   pound butter, cut into cubes
     ½   to 1 (2¼-ounce) jar cracked black pepper
    Worcestershire sauce to taste
     1   to 2 tablespoons salt
    Hot sauce to taste
    French bread

Wash shrimp thoroughly and place in a very large, shallow pan. Add celery and garlic. Squeeze lemons over top and reserve squeezed lemon halves. Dot shrimp with butter, and sprinkle with remaining seasonings. Arrange lemon halves on top.

Place shrimp under broiler until butter melts and shrimp start to turn pink (about 5 minutes), stirring several times. When all shrimp are slightly pink, reduce temperature to 350° and bake in oven 15 to 25 minutes or until done, stirring often. Do not overcook, or shrimp will become mushy. Taste for doneness. Serve hot with plenty of French bread to dip in the juice. Yield: 4 large servings.

Note: Flavor improves if shrimp is cooked ahead of time and then reheated, but do not overcook.

Okra Shrimp Creole

  ¾ *cup chopped green pepper*
  1 *cup diced celery*
  1 *large onion, chopped*
  ½ *cup melted butter or margarine*
  ½ *teaspoon sugar*
  2 *teaspoons salt*
  ¼ *teaspoon hot sauce*
  ¼ *teaspoon black pepper*
  ¼ *teaspoon cayenne pepper*
  2 *teaspoons Worcestershire sauce*
  2 *tablespoons all-purpose flour*
  1 *cup water*
  1 *cup tomato sauce*
  1 *(12-ounce) can cocktail vegetable juice*
  1 *(16-ounce) can okra and tomatoes*
  1 *(8-ounce) can tomatoes, pureed*
  2 *pounds shrimp, peeled and deveined*
  ½ *cup sliced water chestnuts*
Hot cooked rice
Parsley

Sauté green pepper, celery, and onion in butter. Add seasonings and flour, blending well. Stir in water, tomato sauce, vegetable juice, okra and tomatoes, and pureed tomatoes; simmer 20 minutes.

Stir in shrimp and water chestnuts, and simmer 10 to 15 minutes longer. Serve over rice, and garnish with parsley. Yield: 8 to 10 servings.

Shrimp and Mushroom Casserole

  1 *pound shrimp, peeled and deveined*
  ¼ *pound fresh mushrooms, sliced*
  ½ *cup melted butter or margarine, divided*
  1 *(10¾-ounce) can cream of shrimp soup, undiluted*
  1 *(10¾-ounce) can golden mushroom soup, undiluted*
  ¼ *cup white wine*
  2 *tablespoons grated Parmesan cheese*
  1 *cup breadcrumbs*
Hot cooked rice

Sauté shrimp and mushrooms in ¼ cup butter about 2 minutes. Add soup and wine; blend well. Spoon mixture into a shallow 2-quart casserole.

Combine remaining butter, Parmesan cheese, and breadcrumbs; sprinkle over shrimp mixture. Bake at 350° for 30 minutes. Serve over hot rice. Yield: 6 servings.

Shrimp Surprise

  2 *tablespoons melted butter or margarine*
  2 *tablespoons all-purpose flour*
  2 *cups milk*
Salt and pepper to taste
  2 *cups shredded Cheddar cheese, divided*
  1 *(14½-ounce) can asparagus spears, drained*
  1 *(4-ounce) can sliced mushrooms, drained*
  1 *pound shrimp, peeled and deveined*
  1 *(2-ounce) jar sliced pimiento, drained*
  1 *(5-ounce) package narrow noodles, cooked and drained*

Combine butter and flour in a saucepan; place over low heat, stirring until smooth. Gradually add milk; cook, stirring constantly, until smooth and thickened. Add salt, pepper, and 1 cup cheese; stir until cheese melts.

Layer asparagus, mushrooms, shrimp, pimiento, and noodles in a shallow 2-quart casserole. Spoon sauce over casserole, and sprinkle with remaining cheese. Bake at 300° for 1 hour. Yield: 6 servings.

Barbecued Oysters

     2   *dozen oysters*
     ⅓   *cup oyster liquid*
     ¼   *cup tomato paste*
     2   *tablespoons chili sauce*
     2   *tablespoons lemon juice*
     1   *teaspoon Worcestershire sauce*
     ½   *teaspoon horseradish*
     ¼   *teaspoon onion salt*
     ⅛   *teaspoon salt*
     ⅓   *cup bacon-flavored cracker crumbs*

Place oysters in a single layer in a shallow baking dish. Combine oyster liquid, tomato paste, chili sauce, lemon juice, Worcestershire sauce, horseradish, and salt in a saucepan; cook over medium heat 20 minutes.

Pour sauce over oysters; prick oysters with a fork to allow sauce to penetrate. Sprinkle with cracker crumbs. Bake at 350° for 25 minutes. Yield: 4 servings.

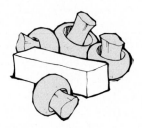

Easy Oyster Casserole

     1   *pint oysters*
     ¼   *pound mushrooms, sliced*
     2   *tablespoons melted butter or margarine*
     1   *(10¾-ounce) can cream of mushroom soup, undiluted*
     ¾   *cup oyster crackers*
     ¼   *cup grated Parmesan cheese*
     ¼   *cup cooking sherry*
         Cracker crumbs
         Butter or margarine

Drain oysters, and set aside.

Sauté mushrooms in butter; add mushroom soup, oyster crackers, cheese, cooking sherry, and oysters. Mix well. Spoon into a lightly greased 1½-quart casserole. Top with cracker crumbs, and dot with butter. Bake at 350° for about 20 minutes. Yield: 4 servings.

Minced Oysters

     1   *cup finely chopped celery*
     1   *tablespoon melted butter or margarine*
     1   *pint oysters, drained and chopped*
     1   *cup toasted breadcrumbs*
     2   *eggs, beaten*
     1   *tablespoon lemon juice*
     1   *teaspoon grated onion*
     ½   *teaspoon salt*
         Pepper to taste
         Additional breadcrumbs

Sauté celery in butter until tender; stir in oysters, 1 cup breadcrumbs, eggs, lemon juice, and seasonings. Cook until thoroughly heated.

Spoon mixture into 4 buttered 1-cup casseroles or shells. Sprinkle with additional breadcrumbs. Bake at 350° for 30 minutes. Yield: 4 servings.

Scalloped Oysters

     2   *cups cracker crumbs*
     1   *cup breadcrumbs*
     1   *cup melted butter or margarine*
     2   *pints oysters, divided*
         Salt to taste
         Coarsely ground pepper to taste
     ¼   *teaspoon celery salt, divided*
     ¼   *cup milk*
     3   *tablespoons evaporated milk*
     2   *teaspoons Worcestershire sauce*
     ¼   *teaspoon hot sauce*

Combine cracker crumbs and breadcrumbs; stir in melted butter. Drain oysters, reserving ½ cup liquid.

Place one-third of crumb mixture in a greased 11¾- x 7½- x 1¾-inch baking dish; cover with half of oysters. Sprinkle with salt, pepper, and half of celery salt. Combine reserved oyster liquid, milk, evaporated milk, Worcestershire sauce, and hot sauce; pour half over oysters. Repeat layers, and top with remaining crumb mixture.

Bake at 400° for 30 minutes or until a light crust forms. Yield: 8 servings.

Oyster Casserole

½ cup melted butter or margarine
⅔ cup chopped celery
¼ cup chopped green pepper
1 small onion, grated
2 tablespoons finely chopped parsley
Salt to taste
1 teaspoon Worcestershire sauce
1 pint raw oysters, drained
2 hard-cooked eggs, finely chopped
1½ cups cracker crumbs, divided
2 eggs, beaten
Butter or margarine

Combine ½ cup melted butter, celery, green pepper, onion, parsley, salt, and Worcestershire sauce; cook over low heat until vegetables are tender. Add oysters, and cook until edges curl; stir in hard-cooked eggs.

Combine oyster mixture, 1¼ cups cracker crumbs, and beaten eggs; mix well. Pour into a 1½-quart casserole; top with remaining cracker crumbs, and dot with butter. Bake at 325° for 15 minutes. Yield: 6 servings.

Oyster Patties

½ pound mushrooms, sliced
3 tablespoons melted butter or margarine
3 tablespoons all-purpose flour
1 cup milk
½ teaspoon salt
¼ teaspoon celery salt
Pepper to taste
1 teaspoon lemon juice
2 dozen (about 1 pint) small
     oysters, drained
Baked patty shells
Parsley (optional)

Sauté mushrooms in butter until tender; blend in flour, and cook until bubbly. Gradually add milk; cook until smooth and thickened, stirring constantly. Add salt, celery salt, pepper, lemon juice, and oysters.

Cook over medium-low heat until oysters start to curl up (about 5 minutes); stir occasionally. Serve in patty shells. Garnish with parsley, if desired. Yield: 6 to 8 servings.

★ Crusty Fried Oysters

1 egg, beaten
2 tablespoons cold water
1 (12-ounce) can fresh oysters, drained
1½ cups saltine cracker crumbs
Hot salad oil

Combine egg and water. Dip oysters in egg mixture, and roll each in cracker crumbs. Cook oysters in salad oil heated to 375° about 2 minutes or until golden brown. Yield: 3 to 4 servings.

★ Crisp Fried Catfish

6 small catfish, cleaned and dressed
1 teaspoon salt
¼ teaspoon pepper
1 (2-ounce) bottle hot sauce
2 cups self-rising cornmeal
Hot salad oil

Sprinkle catfish with salt and pepper. Marinate in hot sauce for 1 to 2 hours in refrigerator.

Place cornmeal in a paper bag; drop in catfish one at a time, and shake until coated completely. Fry in deep hot oil over high heat until fish float to the top and are golden brown. Drain well. Serve hot. Yield: 4 to 6 servings.

Baked Catfish

2 pounds catfish fillets, fresh or frozen
1 tablespoon lemon juice
1 tablespoon Worcestershire sauce
Salt and pepper to taste
1 (2-ounce) package seasoned coating mix
     for fish

Thaw frozen catfish. Score; rub with lemon juice, Worcestershire sauce, salt, and pepper. Coat completely with seasoned coating mix.

Place in a greased 13- x 9- x 2-inch pan. Bake at 450° for 10 minutes; reduce heat to 350° and bake for 10 to 15 minutes or until fish flakes. Yield: about 6 servings.

Salmon Loaf

    1   (15½-ounce) can salmon
    3   tablespoons salmon liquid
    1½ cups breadcrumbs
    1   egg
    2   teaspoons grated onion
    ⅓   cup evaporated milk
        Salt and pepper
        Butter Sauce

Combine first 7 ingredients. Pack into a greased and floured 8½- x 4½- x 2⅝-inch loafpan; bake at 350° for 35 minutes. Serve with Butter Sauce. Yield: about 4 to 6 servings.

Butter Sauce:

    3   tablespoons butter or margarine
    3   tablespoons all-purpose flour
        Salt and pepper
    1½ cups milk
    2   egg yolks, beaten
    1   teaspoon lemon juice

Melt butter in a small saucepan; stir in flour, salt, and pepper until smooth. Add milk slowly; cook until thickened, stirring constantly. Beat some of the hot mixture into egg yolks; stir into remaining hot mixture. Cook 1 minute. Stir in lemon juice. Yield: about 2 cups.

Salmon Puffs

    1   (7¾-ounce) can red salmon, drained
    1   egg, beaten
    ½   teaspoon salt
        Dash of pepper
    ⅔   cup all-purpose flour
    ⅓   cup plain cornmeal
    ½   teaspoon soda
    1½ teaspoons baking powder
    ⅓   cup buttermilk
        Salad oil

Combine all ingredients except salad oil. Drop batter by tablespoonfuls into deep oil heated to 370°; cook until golden brown, turning once. Yield: 6 to 8 servings.

★ Salmon Croquettes Supreme

    1   (15½-ounce) can red or pink salmon
    2   eggs, beaten
    1   cup toasted breadcrumbs
    ½   cup shredded Cheddar cheese
        Salt and pepper to taste
        Onion salt to taste
        All-purpose flour
        Hot salad oil

Drain salmon; remove skin and bones. Flake salmon with a fork. Add next 5 ingredients, blending well; shape mixture into croquettes. Coat with flour. Pan fry in hot oil until golden brown, turning only once. Yield: 6 servings.

Salmon Logs

    ½   cup finely chopped onion
    2   tablespoons melted butter or margarine
    1   (15½-ounce) can salmon, drained and
          flaked
    4   round buttery crackers, finely crushed
    2   egg yolks, well beaten
    1   tablespoon Worcestershire sauce
    1   teaspoon prepared mustard
    ¼   teaspoon salt
    ¼   teaspoon pepper
    ½   cup plain cornmeal
        Hot salad oil

Sauté onion in butter 5 minutes or until tender. Combine all ingredients except cornmeal and oil. Shape salmon mixture into logs 2 inches long; dredge in cornmeal. Cook in hot oil, browning evenly on all sides. Yield: about 4 to 6 servings.

Pirate's Treasure Casserole

  1 *(8-ounce) package macaroni twists*
  ¼ *cup minced onion*
  ¼ *cup minced celery*
  ½ *cup melted butter or margarine*
  ¼ *cup all-purpose flour*
  1 *teaspoon salt*
  ¼ *teaspoon lemon-pepper seasoning*
  1 *cup milk*
  1 *(8-ounce) package pasteurized process cheese spread*
  1 *(15½-ounce) can salmon*
  1 *(10-ounce) package frozen peas with pearl onions, thawed*

Cook macaroni twists according to package directions; drain and set aside.

Sauté onion and celery in butter about 5 minutes or until tender; blend in flour, salt, and lemon-pepper seasoning. Gradually add milk; cook, stirring constantly, until smooth and thickened. Add cheese spread, stirring until melted.

Drain and flake salmon, reserving ⅓ cup liquid. Add macaroni twists, salmon, reserved liquid, and peas to cheese sauce; toss lightly.

Spoon mixture into a lightly greased 2½-quart casserole. Bake at 350° for 35 minutes or until hot and bubbly. Yield: 6 to 8 servings.

Salmon Burgers

  2 *(15½-ounce) cans salmon, drained*
  2 *eggs, beaten*
  1 *cup dry breadcrumbs, divided*
Hot salad oil
  8 *hamburger buns*
  8 *tomato slices*
Lettuce

Combine salmon, eggs, and ½ cup breadcrumbs; mix well, and shape into 8 patties. Coat both sides of patties with remaining breadcrumbs; slowly cook in hot oil until golden brown. Serve on warm hamburger buns with tomato slices and lettuce. Yield: 8 servings.

Italian Stuffed Trout

  1 *medium-size onion, chopped*
  1 *medium-size green pepper, chopped*
  1 *medium-size potato, peeled and chopped*
Pinch of basil leaves
Pinch of oregano
Salt and pepper to taste
  2 *(1½-pound) trout, cleaned and dressed*

Combine onion, green pepper, potato, and seasonings. Stuff trout with mixture. Place on a sheet of lightly greased, heavy-duty aluminum foil. Seal tightly.

Bake at 350° for 1 hour or until fish flakes easily when tested with a fork. Yield: 6 servings.

Trout Marguery

  1 *pound frozen trout fillets, thawed*
  3 *tablespoons olive oil*
Salt and pepper to taste
  2 *egg yolks, beaten*
  ½ *cup melted butter, cooled*
  1 *tablespoon all-purpose flour*
  ¼ *cup dry white wine*
  1 *tablespoon lemon juice*
  1 *cup chopped cooked shrimp*
  1 *(6-ounce) package frozen crabmeat, thawed*
  1 *(4-ounce) can sliced mushrooms, drained*
Paprika
Additional salt and pepper

Place fillets in a shallow 2-quart baking dish, and drizzle with olive oil. Sprinkle with salt and pepper. Bake at 375° for 20 minutes or until fish flakes easily when tested with a fork.

Place egg yolks in top of a double boiler; add melted butter and blend well. Place over boiling water; cook, stirring constantly, until mixture thickens. Stir in flour, blending well. Add wine, lemon juice, shrimp, crabmeat, mushrooms, paprika, salt, and pepper. Cook, stirring constantly, 15 minutes.

Place fish on a platter and cover with sauce. Yield: 4 servings.

Beer-Baked Stuffed Trout

1½ *cups uncooked regular rice*
1 *cup melted butter or margarine*
1 *(10½-ounce) can consommé*
1 *soup can water*
1 *cup seedless raisins*
½ *cup blanched almonds*
1 *(4- to 6-pound) trout, cleaned and dressed*
1 *(12-ounce) bottle beer*

Brown rice in butter; add consommé, water, raisins, and almonds. Cook over low heat about 25 minutes or until rice is tender.

Stuff trout with part of rice mixture, and place in a shallow casserole; spoon remaining rice around trout. Pour beer over trout.

Bake at 350° for 45 minutes or until tender. Yield: 6 servings.

Tuna St. Jacques

3 *green onions, finely chopped*
¼ *cup melted butter or margarine, divided*
¼ *pound fresh mushrooms, chopped*
1 *(10¾-ounce) can cream of chicken soup, undiluted*
½ *cup dry vermouth*
2 *(7-ounce) cans tuna, drained and flaked*
1 *tablespoon finely chopped parsley*
White pepper to taste
2 *tablespoons grated Parmesan cheese*
1 *slice bread*

Sauté onion in 2 tablespoons butter until tender; set aside. Quickly sauté mushrooms in 1 tablespoon butter; set aside.

Combine soup and vermouth; bring to a boil. Remove from heat, and add onion, mushrooms, tuna, parsley, and pepper; mix well. Spoon into 6 lightly greased seashells or small casseroles.

Place cheese and bread in container of electric blender; blend into fine crumbs. Combine breadcrumbs and 1 tablespoon butter; sprinkle over tuna mixture.

Bake at 350° for 10 to 15 minutes or until lightly browned and thoroughly heated. Yield: 6 servings.

Tuna Croquettes

½ *cup finely chopped onion*
3 *tablespoons melted butter or margarine*
3 *tablespoons all-purpose flour*
½ *cup milk*
2 *teaspoons salt*
½ *teaspoon pepper*
1 *teaspoon dry mustard*
1 *(9¼-ounce) can tuna, drained and flaked*
2 *cups cooked regular rice*
2 *teaspoons lemon juice*
2 *tablespoons water*
1 *egg*
Fine breadcrumbs
Hot salad oil

Sauté onion in butter until tender; stir in flour, blending well. Gradually stir in milk; cook, stirring constantly, until thick. Add salt, pepper, and mustard, stirring well. Add tuna, rice, and lemon juice. Chill.

Shape into croquettes. Combine water and egg, beating well. Coat croquettes with egg, then with breadcrumbs. Chill at least 15 minutes. Heat oil to 375°; deep fry croquettes in oil. Yield: 6 to 8 servings.

Tuna Patties

1 *(6-ounce) package chicken-flavored stuffing mix*
½ *cup hot water*
1 *(10¾-ounce) can cream of chicken soup, undiluted and divided*
2 *eggs, beaten*
1 *(9¼-ounce) can tuna, drained and flaked*
3 *tablespoons melted butter or margarine*
¼ *cup milk*

Remove vegetable seasoning packet and stuffing crumbs from package. Combine vegetable seasoning and water; stir until well blended. Add stuffing crumbs, half of soup, eggs, and tuna; blend well. Form into 6 patties, and brown in butter.

Combine remaining soup and milk; heat thoroughly. Serve as a sauce with patties. Yield: 6 servings.

Quick Chop Suey

1   *cup finely chopped onion*
1   *cup finely chopped celery*
¼   *cup melted margarine*
1   *(10¾-ounce) can cream of chicken soup,*
      undiluted
1   *(3-ounce) package cashew nuts, halved*
1   *(9¼-ounce) can tuna, drained and*
      flaked
1   *(3-ounce) can Chinese noodles*

Sauté onion and celery in margarine until transparent. Add chicken soup, cashews, and tuna; mix well. Spoon into a lightly greased 1½-quart casserole. Top with Chinese noodles. Bake at 350° for 20 to 30 minutes. Yield: 6 servings.

White Clam Spaghetti Sauce

¼   *cup olive oil*
½   *cup butter or margarine*
4   *cloves garlic, crushed*
¼   *cup chopped parsley*
3   *tablespoons grated Parmesan cheese*
Dash of pepper
1   *(8-ounce) can minced clams, undrained*
Hot cooked spaghetti
Parmesan cheese

Combine olive oil, butter, garlic, parsley, 3 tablespoons cheese, and pepper in a saucepan; simmer over low heat 10 minutes. Add clams with juice, and simmer 10 minutes longer. Serve over spaghetti, and top with cheese. Yield 6 to 8 servings.

Seafood-Wild Rice Casserole

1   *(6-ounce) package wild and white rice*
      mix
1   *(12-ounce) package frozen crabmeat,*
      thawed and drained
1   *pound frozen peeled shrimp, thawed*
      and drained
3   *(10¾-ounce) cans cream of mushroom*
      soup, undiluted
⅓   *cup grated onion*
1   *cup chopped green pepper*
1   *cup chopped celery*
1   *(4-ounce) jar pimiento, drained*
2   *tablespoons lemon juice*

Prepare rice mix according to package directions; drain. Add remaining ingredients, stirring well. Spoon mixture into a lightly greased 4-quart casserole. Bake at 325° for 1 hour. Yield: 10 to 12 servings.

★
Chafing Dish Seafood

¾   *cup butter or margarine*
½   *to 1 cup chopped chives*
5½ *tablespoons all-purpose flour*
3   *cups milk*
¾   *teaspoon salt*
¼   *teaspoon cayenne pepper*
½   *cup dry white wine*
1   *pound crabmeat*
1   *cup cooked and cleaned small shrimp*
1   *egg yolk, beaten*
Timbale cases or patty shells

Melt butter in a saucepan; add chives, and sauté until wilted. Add flour, blending until smooth; cook until bubbly. Stir in milk. Cook 3 to 4 minutes, stirring constantly. Add salt, cayenne pepper, and wines; cook about 10 minutes or until thickened, stirring constantly.

Add crabmeat and shrimp to sauce, stirring gently; heat thoroughly. Combine egg yolk and a small amount of hot mixture; then stir into remaining hot mixture in saucepan. Cook 3 to 4 minutes more. Pour into a chafing dish. Serve in timbale cases. Yield: 5 to 6 cups.

Savory Fish Loaf

2 *cups flaked cooked fish*
1½ *cups soft breadcrumbs*
¾ *cup cooked or canned chopped tomatoes*
1 *egg, beaten*
2 *tablespoons salad oil*
1 *tablespoon minced onion*
¼ *teaspoon ground savory*
Salt and pepper to taste

Combine all ingredients; pack into a lightly greased loafpan. Bake at 350° for 45 minutes or until firm. Yield: 6 servings.

★ Provolone-Parmesan Stuffed Sole

6 *tablespoons butter or margarine,*
   divided
½ *cup chopped green onion*
1 *cup shredded provolone cheese, divided*
¾ *cup grated Parmesan cheese, divided*
½ *cup breadcrumbs*
1⅓ *cups whipping cream, divided*
2 *pounds frozen sole fillets, thawed*
⅔ *cup dry white wine*
¼ *cup all-purpose flour*
1 *tablespoon basil*
½ *teaspoon salt*
⅛ *teaspoon pepper*
¼ *teaspoon oregano*

Melt 2 tablespoons butter in a small saucepan; sauté onion 2 minutes, and set aside.

Combine ½ cup provolone cheese, ½ cup Parmesan cheese, breadcrumbs, and ⅓ cup whipping cream; spread on skin side of fillets. Roll up each fillet, and arrange in a shallow 2-quart baking dish. Pour wine over fish; sprinkle sautéed onion on top. Cover dish with brown paper, and bake at 350° for 25 minutes.

Pour off liquid from baking dish; simmer liquid in a medium saucepan until it is reduced to 1 cup. Melt 4 tablespoons butter in another medium saucepan. Blend in flour; place over low heat and stir until bubbly. Add fish liquid; cook, stirring constantly, until thickened.

Stir in 1 cup whipping cream, remaining ½ cup provolone cheese, and ¼ cup Parmesan cheese; cook, stirring, over medium heat until cheese melts. Do not boil.

Remove from heat; stir in basil, salt, pepper, and oregano. Pour sauce over fish. Yield: 8 servings.

★ Fish Puffs

1 *pound frozen fish fillets, thawed*
Salt and pepper to taste
1 *egg white*
¼ *cup mayonnaise*
1 *teaspoon minced onion*
½ *teaspoon Worcestershire sauce*
Dash of hot sauce

Separate fillets; arrange, skin side down, in a buttered 8-inch square dish. Season with salt and pepper. Beat egg white until stiff but not dry; fold in mayonnaise, onion, Worcestershire sauce, and hot sauce. Spread mixture on fish fillets. Bake at 425° for 18 to 20 minutes or until fish flakes easily and sauce is golden brown. Yield: 4 servings.

Bass Fillets in White Wine

4 *potatoes, parboiled, peeled, and sliced*
½ *teaspoon chervil*
½ *teaspoon tarragon leaves*
½ *teaspoon chopped chives*
Salt and pepper to taste
4 *large bass fillets*
1 *cup dry white wine*
1 *cup buttered breadcrumbs*

Arrange potato slices in a buttered, shallow 2-quart baking dish. Combine chervil, tarragon, and chives; sprinkle over potatoes. Season with salt and pepper. Arrange fish on top; add additional salt and pepper.

Pour wine over fish; cover with breadcrumbs. Bake at 400° for 30 minutes. Yield: 4 servings.

Broiled Grouper Fillets

4 (4-ounce) grouper fillets
Juice of ½ lime
Freshly ground pepper
1 medium-size onion, thinly sliced
4 slices bacon
Mayonnaise

Arrange fillets in a shallow pan; sprinkle with lime juice and pepper. Cover fish with onion slices, and place bacon slices on top.

Broil 3 inches from heat about 5 minutes; remove from oven and brush lightly with mayonnaise. Broil 2 to 3 minutes longer or until fish flakes easily when tested with a fork and bacon is browned. Yield: 4 servings.

Stuffed Flounder

2 (2-pound) flounders or 1 (4-pound)
    flounder, pan-dressed
Salt and pepper to taste
1 (12-ounce) container fresh oysters
1½ cups soft breadcrumbs
¼ cup sliced green onions
¼ cup chopped parsley
¼ cup melted butter or margarine
1½ tablespoons lemon juice
⅛ teaspoon salt
⅛ teaspoon hot sauce
4 slices bacon

Rinse and dry fish thoroughly. Lay each fish flat on a cutting board, light side down; slit lengthwise down center of fish to tail. Cut flesh along both sides of backbone to the tail, allowing the knife to run along the rib bones to form a pocket for the stuffing. Sprinkle both sides of pocket with salt and pepper.

Drain oysters, reserving liquid; cut each oyster in half. Combine oysters, oyster liquid, and remaining ingredients except bacon, mixing lightly and thoroughly. Stuff fish loosely with oyster mixture; place bacon strips over top of fish.

Bake at 350° for 40 to 60 minutes (depending on size of fish) or until fish flakes easily when tested with a fork. Yield: 6 servings.

Fish Fillets Marinara

¼ cup chopped onion
1 clove garlic, minced
2 tablespoons olive oil
1 (16-ounce) can tomatoes, undrained
1 bay leaf, crushed
¾ teaspoon oregano
⅛ teaspoon basil
¾ teaspoon salt
⅛ teaspoon pepper
1 pound frozen fish fillets, thawed
½ cup grated Parmesan cheese
Lemon slices (optional)

Sauté onion and garlic in olive oil until tender. Add tomatoes and seasonings; simmer for 15 minutes.

Place fish fillets in a greased 8-inch square baking dish; pour sauce over fish. Bake at 375° for 25 minutes or until fish flakes easily when tested with a fork; baste often with sauce. Sprinkle fish with cheese; garnish with lemon, if desired. Yield: 4 servings.

★ Crunchy Fried Fillets

Salt
1 pound frozen perch fillets, thawed
All-purpose flour
1 egg, beaten
3 tablespoons water
25 to 30 saltine crackers, crushed
Hot salad oil

Lightly salt fillets; dredge each in flour. Beat egg and water; dip floured fillets in egg mixture. Coat well with cracker crumbs, pressing crumbs into fish. Fry fillets in hot oil over medium heat until browned. Drain on paper towels. Yield: about 4 servings.

Fish Fillets au Gratin

  6 *tablespoons butter or margarine*
  1 *cup chopped onion*
 ½ *cup chopped celery*
 ½ *cup chopped green pepper*
  6 *tablespoons all-purpose flour*
1½ *cups milk*
1½ *teaspoons salt*
  1 *teaspoon pepper*
 ¼ *teaspoon thyme*
    Dash of hot sauce
  1 *pound frozen fish fillets, thawed*
  1 *cup breadcrumbs*
 ½ *cup shredded Cheddar cheese*

Melt butter over low heat in a saucepan; sauté onion, celery, and green pepper until tender. Blend in flour, stirring well. Gradually add milk, stirring constantly. Cook over medium heat, stirring constantly, until smooth and thickened. Add salt, pepper, thyme, and hot sauce, blending well.

Place fish fillets in a buttered 8-inch square baking dish; cover with sauce. Combine breadcrumbs and cheese; sprinkle over sauce. Bake at 450° for 20 to 25 minutes or until fish is done. Yield: 6 servings.

Beer Batter Bream

    6 to 8 bream, cleaned and dressed
    Lemon juice
  2 *cups all-purpose flour, divided*
    Salt
  1 *tablespoon paprika*
  1 *(12-ounce) can beer*
    Salad oil
    Watercress or parsley sprigs
    Lemon wedges

Dry fish thoroughly, and sprinkle lemon juice over both sides; let stand 15 minutes.

Combine 1 cup flour and 1 teaspoon salt; set aside.

Combine 1 cup flour, paprika, and 1 tablespoon salt; add beer, stirring until well blended.

Dredge fish in flour mixture; dip into beer batter. Fry fish until golden brown on both sides in ½ inch oil heated to 370°. Drain on paper towels. Garnish with watercress and lemon wedges. Yield: 6 to 8 servings.

Note: Batter may be stored in refrigerator 3 to 4 days.

Shrimp-Stuffed Bass

   1 *(3- to 4-pound) bass, cleaned and*
      dressed
    Salt and pepper
 ⅓ *cup chopped green pepper*
 ½ *cup chopped onion*
 ¼ *cup chopped celery*
  6 *tablespoons melted butter or margarine*
1¾ *cups soft breadcrumbs*
 12 *medium-size shrimp, cooked, shelled,*
      and deveined
 ½ *cup chopped parsley*
 ½ *cup water*
    About 1 tablespoon butter or margarine
    Lemon juice
    Lemon wedges
    Celery leaves (optional)

Dry fish thoroughly. Lay fish flat on a cutting board; slit lengthwise down center of fish to tail. Cut flesh along both sides of backbone to the tail, allowing the knife to run along the rib bones to form a pocket for the stuffing. Sprinkle both sides of pocket with salt and pepper to taste.

Sauté green pepper, onion, and celery in melted butter 5 minutes. Add breadcrumbs, shrimp, parsley, water, ½ teaspoon salt, and pepper to taste; mix lightly, but thoroughly. Stuff fish with shrimp mixture.

Place stuffed fish on a lightly buttered sheet of heavy-duty aluminum foil; loosely crush foil around edge of fish. Dot fish with butter, and sprinkle with lemon juice.

Bake at 400° about 30 minutes or until fish flakes easily when tested with a fork. Serve with lemon wedges; garnish with celery leaves, if desired. Yield: 4 to 6 servings.

Note: A dozen oysters may be substituted for shrimp; cut oysters in half. Reserve oyster liquid; add water to equal ½ cup, and substitute for ½ cup water.

Meats

The meat—and what variety goes on Southern tables! When served as Beef Wellington or Beef en Gelee, beef tenderloin makes special meals even more memorable. Summertime features casual cookouts with beef kabobs, flank steak, briskets, and hamburgers taking on a luscious charcoal flavor. Who said that family suppers are routine? Not when you offer spaghetti sauce, meat loaf, round steak, and enchiladas.

From thinly sliced country ham, sausage soufflé, and ham quiche for breakfast or brunch to roasts, chops, frankfurters, and ribs, pork is always welcome.

With a little luck, hunting season provides our tables with wild game. You'll find some delicious and unusual recipes for venison, dove, and quail in these pages.

Barbecued Roast

1 (3- to 4-pound) boneless pot roast (bottom round, chuck, rump, or sirloin tip)
1 (16-ounce) can tomatoes
1 large onion, chopped
1 medium-size green pepper, chopped
1 cup catsup
1 cup water
¼ cup Worcestershire sauce
2 tablespoons vinegar
2 tablespoons salad oil
Juice of 1 lemon
Salt and pepper to taste

Place roast in a Dutch oven. Combine remaining ingredients; pour over roast. Cover and bake at 300° for 2½ to 3 hours. Yield: 6 to 8 servings.

A juicy Standing Rib Roast (page 201) is the ultimate in elegant dining. This one is surrounded with mushrooms stuffed with a savory filling.

Peppered Rib Eye

½ cup coarsely ground black pepper
1 (3- to 4-pound) rib eye roast
¾ cup vinegar
½ cup soy sauce
1 teaspoon paprika
½ teaspoon garlic powder
½ teaspoon tomato paste
1 cup water

Rub pepper over roast, pressing well into meat. Place roast in a shallow dish. Combine remaining ingredients except water; pour over roast. Cover and chill at least 8 hours, turning occasionally. Remove roast from marinade; discard marinade. Let roast stand at room temperature 1 hour.

Place roast in center of large piece of heavy-duty aluminum foil. Bring up sides of foil, and seal loosely at top and ends with double folds. Bake at 300° for 2 hours for medium or about 2½ hours for well done.

Carefully open foil; remove roast, and strain juice. For gravy, combine 1 cup juice and 1 cup water in a saucepan; heat thoroughly. Yield: 6 to 8 servings.

★
Beef Wellington

Pastry
1 *(5- to 5½-pound) beef tenderloin*
2 *(4¾-ounce) cans liver pâté*
1 *egg, beaten*
1 *teaspoon cold water*

Prepare Pastry; chill at least 1 hour.

Trim fat from tenderloin; reserve. Tuck small end of meat underneath tenderloin; tie securely with string at 2-inch intervals. Place meat on rack in an open pan. Lay pieces of fat on top of meat. (Do not add water, and do not cover.) Roast at 425° for 20 to 25 minutes for rare and 25 to 30 minutes for medium.

Remove meat from oven, and discard fat. Let stand 30 minutes to cool. Remove string; keep small end of meat tucked underneath.

Roll Pastry into an 18- x 14-inch rectangle on a lightly floured board or pastry cloth. Spread pâté over Pastry to within 1 inch of edge.

Place tenderloin lengthwise, top side down, in middle of Pastry. Bring long sides of Pastry up to overlap on underside of tenderloin. Combine egg and water; brush seam with egg mixture to seal. Trim ends of Pastry and fold over; brush with egg mixture to seal.

Place meat, seam side down, on a lightly greased baking sheet. Brush with egg mixture.

Roll Pastry trimmings; cut into decorative shapes and arrange on top of tenderloin. Brush with remaining egg mixture. Bake at 425° for 30 minutes or until Pastry is golden. Let stand 10 minutes before slicing. Garnish as desired. Yield: 12 to 14 servings.

Pastry:

3 *cups all-purpose flour*
½ *teaspoon salt*
¾ *cup shortening*
½ *to ¾ cup cold water*

Combine flour and salt; cut in shortening with pastry blender until mixture resembles coarse cornmeal. Add water, 1 tablespoon at a time, stirring with a fork until dough holds together. Shape into a ball. Wrap in waxed paper and chill until ready to use.

Roast on the Rocks

1 *(4- to 6-pound) top or bottom round*
    roast, untrimmed
Freshly ground pepper
Garlic cloves, sliced
8 *cups all-purpose flour*
8 *cups rock salt*
About 4½ cups water

Rub roast with pepper. Make slits in roast, and insert 1 slice garlic in each slit; set aside.

Combine flour and rock salt in a large bowl; add water to make a very stiff dough. Place dough in a large baking dish. Push roast down into dough, bringing dough up around meat to cover completely. (Dough should be about ½ inch thick.)

Make a paste of a small amount of flour and water; rub over surface of dough to seal. Bake at 500° for 8 minutes; lower heat to 325°, and bake 1½ hours for medium rare.

Remove from oven; leave encased in crust until ready to slice. Crack crust with a large spoon; pull away crust and discard. Trim fat and discard. Yield: 10 to 12 servings.

Sauerbraten

4 *pounds boneless chuck roast*
Salt and pepper
1½ *cups red wine vinegar*
2 *cups water*
4 *cloves garlic, pressed*
1 *cup sliced onion*
3 *bay leaves*
10 *peppercorns*
¼ *cup sugar*
8 *whole cloves*
1 *to 2 tablespoons salad oil*
3 *tablespoons all-purpose flour, divided*
1½ *cups commercial sour cream*

Sprinkle roast with salt and pepper; place in a large, deep glass or ceramic bowl. Combine vinegar and water in a saucepan; bring to a boil. Add garlic, onion, bay leaves, peppercorns, sugar, and cloves. Pour over meat; cover with plastic wrap. Marinate overnight or up to 2 days.

Remove meat from liquid, reserving marinade; dry meat with paper towels. Brown meat on all sides in salad oil in a large pot; sprinkle with about 1 tablespoon flour. Add 2 cups marinade; simmer 3 to 3½ hours. Remove meat to a heatproof platter; keep warm.

Make a paste of 2 tablespoons flour and 2 to 3 tablespoons cooking liquid. Gradually stir into remaining liquid; cook over low heat, stirring constantly, until smooth and thickened. Stir in sour cream. Serve sauce with meat. Yield: 8 to 10 servings.

★
Marinated Rump Roast

    1   (3-pound) rump roast
    4   cups beef broth
    ¾   cup claret or dry red wine
    1   large onion, chopped
    2   sprigs parsley
    1   bay leaf
        Juice of ½ lemon
    2   to 3 cloves
    ¼   cup butter or margarine
   10   pearl onions, peeled
    3   tablespoons all-purpose flour
    2   carrots, sliced
        Salt and pepper to taste
        Hot cooked rice (optional)

Place roast in a shallow dish. Combine broth, claret, chopped onion, parsley, bay leaf, lemon juice, and cloves; pour over roast. Marinate 2 hours, turning occasionally. Remove roast from marinade; drain well on paper towels. Strain marinade, and set aside; discard chopped onions, herbs, and spices.

Melt butter in a Dutch oven. Add roast and pearl onions; brown roast on all sides. Remove roast and onions from pan, and set aside. Stir flour into pan drippings; cook over medium heat until browned, stirring constantly. Add marinade; cook, stirring constantly, until mixture boils.

Add roast, pearl onions, carrots, salt, and pepper to Dutch oven. Cover tightly; cook over low heat 2½ hours or until tender. Serve with rice, if desired. Yield: 6 to 8 servings.

Saucy Pot Roast

    1   (3- to 3½-pound) boneless round roast
    ½   teaspoon salt
    ⅛   teaspoon pepper
    1   (8-ounce) can tomato sauce with onions
    1   slice bacon, cooked and crumbled
    1   teaspoon prepared mustard
    1   teaspoon brown sugar
    ½   teaspoon horseradish
    1   tablespoon cornstarch
    ¼   cup cold water

Place roast in center of large piece of heavy-duty aluminum foil; sprinkle with salt and pepper.

Combine tomato sauce, bacon, mustard, sugar, and horseradish; spoon over meat. Bring up sides of foil, and seal loosely at top with double fold; place in shallow baking pan. Bake at 325° for 2½ to 3 hours.

Carefully open foil; pour drippings into a saucepan. Dissolve cornstarch in water; stir into drippings. Bring to a boil; cook, stirring constantly, until smooth and thickened. Serve with meat. Yield: 6 servings.

Smoky Brisket

    1   teaspoon garlic salt
    1   teaspoon onion salt
    1   teaspoon celery salt
    2   tablespoons Worcestershire sauce
   1½   to 2 tablespoons liquid smoke
    1   (2- to 3-pound) beef brisket

Combine seasonings, and pour over brisket; marinate overnight. Place brisket in a roaster. Cover with aluminum foil; then place lid on roaster. Bake at 250° for 5 hours. Do not remove lid during baking. Let stand 15 minutes before slicing. Yield: 8 to 10 servings.

Sirloin Tip Roast Marinara

1   *(1-1/16-ounce) envelope instant meat marinade*
½   *cup dry red wine*
1   *(3- to 4-pound) sirloin tip roast*
1   *cup commercial marinara sauce*
1   *teaspoon sugar*
1   *medium-size onion, sliced*
1   *cup chopped celery*
1   *cup sliced fresh mushrooms*
½   *cup commercial sour cream*
¼   *cup water*
¼   *cup all-purpose flour*

Combine marinade and wine; add roast, and marinate according to directions on marinade package. Place marinade and roast in a Dutch oven; add marinara sauce and sugar. Cover and simmer 1½ hours.

Add vegetables to meat; cover and simmer 1 hour or until meat is tender. Remove roast and vegetables. Skim fat from sauce; measure 2 cups sauce, and return to pan. Combine sour cream, water, and flour; blend until smooth, and stir into sauce. Cook, stirring constantly, until thick and bubbly. Serve with roast. Yield: 6 to 8 servings.

★
Beef en Gelee

1   *(5- to 7-pound) whole beef tenderloin, trimmed*
Salt and pepper
2   *envelopes unflavored gelatin*
3   *(10½-ounce) cans consommé*
½   *cup dry white wine*
2   *carrots, sliced and slightly cooked*
¼   *pound sliced fresh mushrooms*
¼   *head cauliflower, halved and slightly cooked*
¼   *pound green beans, slightly cooked*
8   *to 10 cherry tomatoes*
Commercial Italian salad dressing
Parsley sprigs

Sprinkle beef with salt and pepper; bake at 425° until meat thermometer registers 140° (rare) or 160° (medium rare). Do not over-

cook. Cool; refrigerate overnight. Slice tenderloin into ¼-inch slices; set aside.

Soften gelatin in consommé; bring to a quick boil, stirring constantly. Remove from heat, and stir in wine. Pour a thin layer of consommé mixture into serving tray or platter; chill until set. Arrange carrot and mushroom slices on gelatin, and cover with another thin layer of consommé mixture; chill until set.

Arrange sliced beef in center of gelatin, forming into original tenderloin shape. Spoon remaining consommé mixture over top of beef to form a light glaze. Chill thoroughly.

Marinate cauliflower, green beans, and cherry tomatoes in Italian dressing for several hours. Arrange on the serving tray beside beef, and garnish with parsley. Yield: 8 to 10 servings.

Skewered Steak and Mushrooms

2   *pounds sirloin steak*
12 *large mushroom caps*
Rosemary Marinade

Cut steak into 1½-inch cubes. Marinate steak and mushrooms in Rosemary Marinade for 2 hours. Alternate steak and mushrooms on skewers. Broil 3 to 5 minutes on each side, basting frequently with Marinade. Yield: about 4 servings.

Rosemary Marinade:

½   *cup dry red wine*
1   *teaspoon Worcestershire sauce*
½   *teaspoon rosemary, crushed*
½   *teaspoon monosodium glutamate*
2   *tablespoons catsup*
1   *clove garlic*
½   *teaspoon salt*
½   *cup salad oil*
1   *teaspoon sugar*
1   *tablespoon vinegar*
½   *teaspoon marjoram*

Combine all ingredients, mixing well. Yield: about 1¼ cups.

★ Kabobs Italiano

2 *pounds sirloin steak, cut into 1½-inch cubes*
2 *large onions, quartered*
1 *pound fresh mushroom caps*
2 *green peppers, cut into 1-inch squares*
1 *pound yellow squash, cut into 2-inch-thick slices*
1 *cup commercial Italian salad dressing*

Combine meat cubes and vegetables; add salad dressing, and marinate in refrigerator 3 hours, turning occasionally. Drain, reserving marinade.

Alternate meat and vegetables on skewers. Grill over medium heat 10 to 15 minutes or until desired doneness, basting meat and vegetables with marinade and turning occasionally. Yield: 6 servings.

Burgundy Beef

2 *tablespoons shortening*
5 *medium-size onions, sliced*
½ *pound fresh mushrooms, sliced*
2 *pounds round steak, cut into 1-inch cubes*
1 *teaspoon salt*
¼ *teaspoon marjoram*
¼ *teaspoon thyme*
⅛ *teaspoon pepper*
2 *to 3 tablespoons all-purpose flour*
¾ *cup beef broth*
1½ *cups Burgundy*

Melt shortening in an electric skillet; heat to 300°. Add onion and mushrooms to skillet, and sauté until onion is tender; remove vegetables and set aside. Reserve drippings.

Brown steak in reserved drippings; sprinkle with seasonings. Combine flour and beef broth, blending well; pour over meat. Bring to boil, and boil 1 minute. Add wine; cover and simmer 1½ to 2 hours at 250° or until meat is tender.

Add onion and mushroom mixture to skillet, and cook 15 minutes or until thoroughly heated. Yield: 4 to 6 servings.

★ Steak Parmigiana

½ *cup all-purpose flour*
½ *cup shredded Cheddar cheese*
1 *(1½-pound) round steak, cut into 6 serving-size pieces*
1 *egg, beaten*
½ *cup salad oil*
1 *large onion, chopped*
1 *(6-ounce) can tomato paste*
1 *clove garlic, minced*
Salt and pepper to taste
2 *cups hot water*
1 *(8-ounce) package mozzarella cheese, sliced*
Hot cooked noodles

Combine flour and cheese. Dip steak into egg, and coat with flour mixture; brown in hot oil. Place in a shallow baking dish.

Sauté onion in oil; stir in tomato paste, garlic, salt, pepper, and water. Simmer 10 minutes. Pour sauce over steak and top with cheese slices. Bake, covered, at 350° for 1 hour. Serve over noodles. Yield: 6 servings.

Elegant Steak

2 *pounds (¾-inch-thick) New York strip, tenderloin, rib eye, club, boned T-bone, or porterhouse steak*
1 *clove garlic*
Freshly ground pepper to taste
2 *tablespoons butter or margarine*
½ *cup dry vermouth or dry sherry*
½ *teaspoon Worcestershire sauce*
¼ *cup chopped chives or green onion tops*
Salt to taste

Rub steak with garlic, and season with pepper. Melt butter in a large, heavy skillet; add vermouth, Worcestershire sauce, and chives. Simmer mixture 5 minutes.

Add steak to skillet; cook over high heat 3 to 5 minutes on each side for rare, 5 to 7 minutes for medium, or 7 to 10 minutes for well done. Sprinkle with salt, and serve immediately. Yield: 4 servings.

Polynesian Steak Kabobs

¾   *cup pineapple juice*
¼   *cup salad oil*
3   *tablespoons soy sauce*
2   *teaspoons brown sugar*
¾   *teaspoon ground ginger*
1   *clove garlic, minced*
1½   *to 2 pounds (1-inch-thick) round steak,
      cut into 1½-inch cubes*
1   *large green pepper, cut into 1-inch
      squares*
12   *cherry tomatoes*
12   *medium-size mushroom caps*
12   *pearl onions, cooked and drained*

Combine pineapple juice, salad oil, soy
sauce, brown sugar, ginger, and garlic. Add
meat; cover and marinate overnight in refrigerator.

Remove meat from marinade. Alternate
meat and vegetables on skewers. Grill 10 to
15 minutes over medium heat, basting with
marinade and turning occasionally. Yield: 4
to 6 servings.

London Broil

1   *(2-pound) flank steak*
Unseasoned meat tenderizer
2   *tablespoons salad oil*
2   *teaspoons lemon juice*
2   *teaspoons Ac'cent*
2   *teaspoons seasoned salt*
¼   *teaspoon seasoned pepper*
2   *cloves garlic, minced*
4   *teaspoons chopped parsley*

Trim excess fat from steak; score top in 1½-
inch squares. Wipe steak with damp paper
towels. Sprinkle with meat tenderizer, and
pierce with a fork. Let stand at room temperature 4 hours.

Combine remaining ingredients. Brush top
of steak with half of oil mixture. Place on a
lightly greased rack in a broiler pan. Broil 4
inches from heat for 5 minutes. Turn; brush
bottom of steak with remaining oil mixture.
Broil 5 minutes. To serve, slice across grain in
thin slices. Yield: 4 to 6 servings.

Swiss Bliss

1   *(2-pound) boneless chuck steak, cut into
      1-inch cubes*
¼   *teaspoon salt*
1   *(1⅜-ounce) package onion soup mix*
1½   *teaspoons melted butter or margarine*
1   *(16-ounce) can tomatoes*
½   *pound mushrooms, sliced*
1   *green pepper, cut into strips*
1   *tablespoon steak sauce*
1   *tablespoon cornstarch*
1   *tablespoon chopped parsley*

Place meat in center of a 20-inch sheet of
heavy-duty aluminum foil; sprinkle with
salt, onion soup mix, and butter.

Drain and chop tomatoes, reserving ½ cup
juice. Add tomatoes, mushrooms, and green
pepper to meat.

Combine steak sauce and cornstarch,
blending well; stir in reserved tomato juice.
Pour over meat and vegetables. Seal foil and
bake at 350° for 2 hours or until meat is
tender. Sprinkle with parsley before serving.
Yield: 4 to 6 servings.

Beef Rolls Piquant

2   *pounds top round steak*
Salt and pepper
1   *pound mild bulk sausage*
6   *tablespoons chopped parsley*
1   *medium-size onion, finely chopped*
All-purpose flour
Bacon drippings
1   *cup dry red wine*

Pound steak to ¼-inch thickness; cut into 4- x
6-inch strips. Sprinkle each strip with salt
and pepper; spread with thin layer of sausage. Sprinkle each slice with parsley and
onion. Roll each slice up jellyroll fashion; tie
securely with string at each end.

Dredge beef rolls in flour; brown in bacon
drippings in a large skillet.

Place rolls in a shallow baking dish; pour in
wine. Cover and bake at 325° for 1 hour or
until tender. Yield: about 6 servings.

Baked Swiss Steak

½ to ¾ pound boneless round steak, about
    ¾-inch thick
½ teaspoon salt
2 tablespoons all-purpose flour
2 tablespoons salad oil
1 (8-ounce) can stewed tomatoes
¼ cup chopped carrot
¼ cup chopped celery
1 tablespoon chopped onion
¼ teaspoon Worcestershire sauce
2 tablespoons shredded sharp process
    American cheese

Cut meat into 2 portions; pound ¼-inch thick. Combine salt and flour, and coat meat well with flour mixture. Set aside remaining flour mixture. Brown meat in oil; remove meat from skillet, and place in a small shallow baking dish.

Blend remaining flour with drippings in skillet. Add remaining ingredients except cheese; cook, stirring constantly, until mixture boils. Pour over meat; cover and bake at 350° about 2 hours or until meat and vegetables are tender.

Sprinkle cheese over meat, and return to the oven a few minutes. Yield: 2 servings.

★
Grilled Flank Steak

Garlic powder
3 pounds flank steak
½ cup soy sauce
¼ cup Worcestershire sauce
¼ cup salad oil

Sprinkle garlic powder lightly on both sides of steak. Prick both sides of steak with fork.

Combine soy sauce, Worcestershire sauce, and oil; pour over steak. Marinate 6 to 8 hours at room temperature, turning frequently.

Remove steak from marinade. Grill over medium heat about 7 minutes for medium rare. Slice across grain in thin slices. Yield: about 8 servings.

Note: Marinade may be refrigerated and used again.

Smothered Swiss Steak

¼ cup all-purpose flour
1 to 1½ teaspoons seasoned salt
¼ teaspoon pepper
2 pounds round steak
2 tablespoons shortening or salad oil
1 (16-ounce) can whole tomatoes,
    undrained
2 medium-size onions, sliced
1 (8-ounce) can tomato sauce
1 large green pepper, cut into rings
2 cloves garlic, crushed
6 carrots, peeled and sliced lengthwise
Hot cooked rice (optional)

Combine flour, seasoned salt, and pepper. Sprinkle half of flour mixture on steak; pound into steak. Turn steak and repeat process.

Cut steak into 6 serving-size pieces. Heat shortening in a 10-inch skillet; brown meat on both sides. Pour tomatoes over meat. Combine onion, tomato sauce, green pepper, and garlic; pour over steak.

Cover; simmer 30 minutes. Add carrots; cover and continue cooking 1 hour. Serve with hot rice, if desired. Yield: 6 servings.

Flank Steak Supreme

⅓ cup white wine vinegar
⅓ cup water
2 tablespoons soy sauce
1 medium-size onion, sliced
1 clove garlic, diced
Freshly ground pepper
2 pounds flank steak, scored
¼ cup crumbled blue cheese

Combine vinegar, water, soy sauce, onion, garlic, and pepper, mixing well. Pour mixture over steak; marinate about 5 hours, turning meat often.

Broil steak 4 to 5 inches from heat for 5 to 7 minutes. Turn steak, and sprinkle with blue cheese; continue to broil to desired doneness. To serve, slice steak across grain in thin slices. Yield: about 6 servings.

Stuffed Flank Steak

     3 *slices bacon, chopped*
  1½ *cups soft bread cubes*
  1½ *cups mashed potatoes*
     3 *tablespoons instant minced onion*
     1 *tablespoon parsley flakes*
     ¾ *teaspoon salt*
     ¾ *teaspoon poultry seasoning*
     ¼ *teaspoon pepper*
     ¼ *cup hot water*
     1 *(1½-pound) flank steak*
     ¾ *cup water*

Sauté bacon until crisp; remove skillet from heat. Add bread cubes, potatoes, onion, parsley, salt, poultry seasoning, and pepper; mix well. Gradually add ¼ cup hot water; set aside.

Score steak lightly on both sides in 1½-inch squares; pound both sides with a meat mallet. Spread stuffing to within ½ inch of edge. Roll steak up jellyroll fashion, and tie securely. Place seam side down on a rack in a 13- x 9- x 2-inch baking pan.

Pour ¾ cup water into pan, and cover with foil. Bake at 325° for 1 hour and 15 minutes or until meat is tender. To serve, slice crosswise. Yield: 6 servings.

Steak Rolls

     ⅓ *cup chopped onion*
     ⅓ *cup chopped green pepper*
     3 *tablespoons melted butter or margarine*
     3 *cups soft breadcrumbs*
     2 *tablespoons minced parsley*
     1 *teaspoon salt*
     ¼ *teaspoon pepper*
     ½ *teaspoon paprika*
     2 *(1-pound) round steaks*
     3 *tablespoons shortening*
     2 *cups water*
     ½ *cup commercial sour cream*
     1 *teaspoon curry powder*

Sauté onion and green pepper in butter until tender; stir in breadcrumbs, parsley, salt, pepper, and paprika.

If meat is more than ¼ inch thick, flatten with a meat mallet. Spread a thin layer of breadcrumb mixture over meat. Roll up tightly, and secure with toothpicks.

Cut roll into 10 pieces, and brown in hot shortening. Add water; simmer, covered, about 50 minutes or until meat is tender. Remove to a hot platter.

Combine sour cream, curry powder, and 1 cup pan liquid; heat thoroughly, stirring constantly. Serve with Steak Rolls. Yield: 5 to 6 servings.

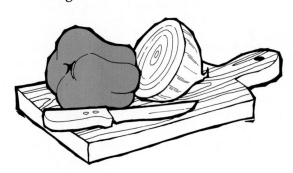

Creole Steak

     ¼ *cup all-purpose flour*
     2 *teaspoons salt*
     2 *teaspoons paprika*
     ½ *teaspoon pepper*
     1 *(1-pound) round steak, cut into*
          bite-size pieces
     2 *onions, chopped*
     ½ *green pepper, chopped*
     3 *tablespoons salad oil*
     ½ *cup uncooked regular rice*
     2 *(16-ounce) cans stewed tomatoes*

Combine flour, salt, paprika, and pepper; dredge steak in flour mixture. Sauté onion and green pepper in hot oil; remove from skillet. Brown meat in remaining oil in skillet; cover with onion mixture, and sprinkle with rice.

Drain tomatoes, reserving liquid. Add enough water to tomato liquid to make 2 cups. Spoon tomatoes over rice; sprinkle with any remaining flour mixture.

Pour liquid over meat mixture; cover and simmer 1 hour or until meat is tender. Yield: 4 to 6 servings.

Southern Steak and Grits

1 (2½-pound) round steak, cubed
2½ teaspoons salt
½ cup butter or margarine, divided
2 large onions, finely chopped
1½ cups water, divided
2 teaspoons all-purpose flour
½ cup finely chopped parsley
Hot cooked grits

Sprinkle steak with salt. Brown on both sides in ¼ cup butter. Remove from skillet, and set aside.

Melt remaining butter in skillet; add onion, and sauté until soft. Return steak to skillet, and add ½ cup water. Cover and cook 15 minutes over medium heat. Add ½ cup water; cover and cook over low heat 1 to 1½ hours or until tender.

Combine flour and remaining ½ cup water, stirring until smooth; add to steak mixture along with parsley. Cook until smooth and thickened, stirring constantly. Serve over hot grits. Yield: 4 to 6 servings.

★
Beef Burgundy

1 large onion, thinly sliced
1 tablespoon melted butter or margarine
1 pound boneless lean beef, cubed
1 tablespoon all-purpose flour
Salt and pepper to taste
Dash of marjoram
Dash of thyme
½ cup beef bouillon
1 cup Burgundy or dry red wine
1 (4-ounce) can whole mushrooms, drained
Hot cooked noodles

Sauté onion in butter until tender; remove from skillet, and set aside. Add beef to skillet, and sauté until brown. Stir in flour, salt, pepper, marjoram, thyme, bouillon, and wine.

Cover and cook over low heat 3 hours. Stir in mushrooms and sautéed onion. Serve over noodles. Yield: 3 to 4 servings.

Spanish Beef Ragout

2 slices bacon, chopped
2 pounds lean beef, cut into 1-inch cubes
2 medium-size onions, chopped
1 clove garlic, crushed
1 medium-size tomato, peeled and chopped
2 slices very stale bread
⅓ cup dry red wine
2 tablespoons brandy
1 bay leaf
Salt and pepper to taste

Cook bacon in a heavy skillet until crisp; add beef, and brown on all sides. Stir in onion, garlic, and tomato; cover and simmer 30 minutes.

Soften bread in wine; stir into meat mixture, breaking bread into pieces. Stir in brandy, bay leaf, salt, and pepper. Cover and simmer 2 hours or until meat is tender. Yield: 4 to 6 servings.

Pepper Steak

1 pound round steak
2 tablespoons bacon drippings
2 medium-size green peppers, cut into strips
1 medium-size onion, sliced into rings
2 to 3 medium-size tomatoes, pureed
1 (4-ounce) can mushrooms, drained
1 teaspoon salt
¼ teaspoon pepper
½ teaspoon ground ginger
2 tablespoons soy sauce
½ teaspoon sugar
½ cup water
2 tablespoons all-purpose flour
Hot cooked rice

Cut steak into ¼-inch strips; brown in bacon drippings. Add the vegetables, seasonings, sugar, and water. Cover and simmer over low heat 30 minutes.

Blend flour into a small amount of cooking liquid to make a paste, and add to meat; cook until thickened, stirring constantly. Serve over rice. Yield: about 6 servings.

Chinese Beef Skillet

1   (1-pound) round steak, cut into 2- to
      2½-inch strips
2   tablespoons salad oil
1¾   cups water, divided
¼   cup chopped onion
1   clove garlic, minced
1   beef bouillon cube
1   medium-size head cauliflower, broken
      into flowerets
Salt and pepper to taste
1   (6-ounce) package frozen pea pods,
      partially thawed
2   tablespoons cornstarch
2   tablespoons soy sauce

Brown steak quickly in hot oil. Add 1 cup water, onion, garlic, and bouillon cube; stir until bouillon is dissolved. Add cauliflower, salt, and pepper; cover and simmer 5 minutes.

Stir in pea pods; cover and continue cooking 5 to 8 minutes or until cauliflower is just tender. Using a slotted spoon, transfer meat and vegetables to a warm serving dish.

Combine cornstarch, ¾ cup water, and soy sauce; stir until smooth. Stir cornstarch mixture into liquid in skillet; cook, stirring constantly, until mixture thickens and bubbles. Pour over meat and vegetables. Yield: 5 to 6 servings.

Italian Steak

2   (¾-inch-thick) round steaks
Salt and pepper to taste
2   eggs, beaten
Breadcrumbs
2   tablespoons olive oil
Tomato Sauce

Cut steak into 6 serving-size pieces; pound to ¼-inch thickness. Season with salt and pepper. Dip steak in egg, then into breadcrumbs; brown quickly in olive oil in a large skillet.

Remove steak from skillet; transfer to a shallow baking dish. Top with Tomato Sauce, and bake at 300° for 45 minutes or until meat is tender. Yield: 6 servings.

Tomato Sauce:

1   onion, finely chopped
2   cloves garlic, minced
6   sprigs parsley, minced
2   tablespoons butter or margarine
2   whole cloves
1   bay leaf
Salt, pepper, and paprika to taste
1   (16-ounce) can tomatoes

Sauté onion, garlic, and parsley in butter; add seasonings and tomatoes. Cook over medium heat about 5 minutes. Yield: about 2 cups.

Beefy Supper Pot

1   to 1½ pounds round steak, cut into
      1-inch cubes
1   whole chicken breast
2   tablespoons butter or margarine
1   cup onion rings
8   small carrots, peeled
2   (10½-ounce) cans beef broth
1⅓   cups water
1   teaspoon salt
¼   teaspoon pepper
1   clove garlic, minced
4   medium-size potatoes, peeled and cubed
1   (10-ounce) can refrigerated biscuits
Grated Parmesan cheese (optional)

Brown steak and chicken in butter in a Dutch oven or electric skillet. Remove chicken from bone; cut into 1-inch pieces and return to pan. Add onion rings; sauté briefly. Add carrots, broth, water, salt, pepper, and garlic. Bring to a boil; cover and simmer 2 hours or until beef is tender.

Add potatoes; cook 30 minutes. Lay biscuits on top of meat mixture; cover and cook 20 minutes. Biscuits will resemble dumplings. Sprinkle with Parmesan cheese, if desired. Yield: 6 to 8 servings.

Piquant Round Steak

½ cup all-purpose flour
1 teaspoon salt
½ teaspoon pepper
1 (1½-pound) round steak, cut into
    bite-size pieces
¼ cup salad oil
3 cups water, divided
2 tablespoons dry onion soup mix
1 (6-ounce) can tomato paste
2 tablespoons brown sugar
½ cup shredded sharp Cheddar cheese
1 (6-ounce) can sliced mushrooms,
    drained
   Hot cooked rice

Combine flour, salt, and pepper in a bag; add steak, and shake well to coat. Brown steak in hot salad oil. Add 2½ cups water and onion soup mix; simmer 30 minutes.

Combine tomato paste, remaining ½ cup water, and brown sugar; add to steak, and simmer 15 to 20 minutes or until tender. Add cheese and mushrooms; simmer 10 minutes. Serve over rice. Yield: 4 to 6 servings.

Chinese Beef and Rice

1 tablespoon salad oil
⅓ cup long grain rice, uncooked
¾ cup boiling water
½ teaspoon instant beef bouillon granules
1½ teaspoons soy sauce
¾ teaspoon salt
   Dash of pepper
1 small onion, chopped
1 rib celery, chopped
1 small green pepper, chopped
¾ cup cooked, diced beef

Heat oil over medium heat; add rice, and cook until golden brown, stirring occasionally. Combine water, bouillon, soy sauce, salt, and pepper; stir into rice. Cover; lower heat, and simmer 20 minutes.

Add remaining ingredients. Cover, and simmer 10 minutes or until liquid has been absorbed. Yield: 2 servings.

American Chop Suey

1 pound ground round steak
2 tablespoons shortening
1 large onion, chopped
1 green pepper, chopped
¾ cup uncooked regular rice
1 cup chopped celery
1 (16-ounce) can tomatoes, undrained
1 (4-ounce) can mushrooms, undrained
1 teaspoon salt

Brown steak in shortening over high heat; add remaining ingredients. Cover tightly; cook over high heat about 5 minutes. Turn off heat; cover tightly, and let stand 1 hour. Yield: about 6 to 8 servings.

Home-Style Short Ribs

3 to 4 pounds lean beef short ribs
   Hot oil
4 potatoes, quartered
4 carrots, quartered
1 onion, sliced
2 tablespoons vinegar
2 teaspoons sugar
1 tablespoon horseradish
1 tablespoon prepared mustard
2 tablespoons catsup
1 cup beef broth
1 teaspoon salt
¼ teaspoon pepper
¼ cup all-purpose flour

Brown ribs in small amount of hot oil in a skillet; drain. Place potatoes, carrots, and onion in a 3-quart electric slow cooker. Arrange ribs over vegetables.

Combine vinegar, sugar, horseradish, mustard, catsup, broth, salt, and pepper; blend well. Pour over meat. Cover and cook on low setting 6 to 8 hours or until meat is tender.

Remove short ribs and vegetables. Dissolve flour in a small amount of water; stir into sauce. Cook, uncovered, on high setting 10 to 15 minutes or until thickened. Serve sauce with meat and vegetables. Yield: 6 servings.

Sweet-and-Sour Beef Short Ribs

6   pounds lean beef short ribs
1   teaspoon salt
½   teaspoon pepper
½   cup vinegar
3   tablespoons cornstarch
1   teaspoon paprika
1   cup firmly packed brown sugar
¼   teaspoon ground ginger
1   (8¼-ounce) can crushed pineapple,
      undrained
2   tablespoons soy sauce
¾   cup water

Sprinkle ribs with salt and pepper; place on a rack in a roasting pan. Bake, uncovered, at 400° for 1 hour; drain well. Place ribs in a clean roaster without the rack.

Combine vinegar and cornstarch, blending until smooth; stir in paprika, brown sugar, ginger, pineapple, soy sauce, and water. Pour over ribs.

Cover and bake at 300° for 1 to 1½ hours or until meat is tender. Turn ribs, basting with sauce, every half hour. Yield: 6 to 8 servings.

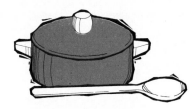

Spiced Rice and Beef

1   cup uncooked regular rice
1   pound ground beef
1   small green pepper, diced
1   (16-ounce) can tomatoes
1   teaspoon salt
½   teaspoon pepper
½   teaspoon dry mustard
1   teaspoon oregano
½   teaspoon chili powder
½   cup shredded Cheddar cheese

Cook rice according to package directions. Brown ground beef in a small skillet. Combine all ingredients except cheese in a 2-quart casserole. Sprinkle cheese over top. Bake at 350° for 30 minutes. Yield: 4 to 6 servings.

Cabbage and Beef Rollups

1   pound ground beef
1½   cups corn flake crumbs
⅓   cup chopped onion
1   teaspoon Worcestershire sauce
1   teaspoon salt
¼   teaspoon pepper
1   teaspoon paprika
1   (8-ounce) can tomato sauce, divided
8   cabbage leaves
¼   cup water

Combine ground beef, corn flake crumbs, onion, Worcestershire sauce, salt, pepper, paprika, and ½ cup tomato sauce; mix well.

Blanch cabbage leaves in boiling water for 3 to 4 minutes; drain. Place equal portions of meat mixture in center of each cabbage leaf; fold ends over, roll up, and fasten with toothpick.

Combine remaining ½ cup tomato sauce and ¼ cup water; pour over the cabbage rolls. Simmer, covered, 30 minutes. Yield: 4 servings.

Sweet Stuffed Cabbage Rolls

1   medium-size head cabbage, cored
¾   pound ground beef
⅓   pound bulk pork sausage
¼   cup chopped onion
⅓   cup instant rice, uncooked
1   egg, beaten
1   teaspoon ground cinnamon
½   teaspoon salt
⅛   teaspoon pepper
1   small onion, sliced
1   (15-ounce) can tomato sauce
1   tablespoon lemon juice
3   tablespoons brown sugar
1   (8-ounce) can sauerkraut, drained

Place cabbage, core end down, in a pan of boiling water to cover. Cook just until leaves are loosened; drain well, and cool. Separate leaves.

Combine beef, sausage, chopped onion, rice, egg, cinnamon, salt, and pepper; mix well.

Place equal portions of meat mixture in center of 6 outer cabbage leaves. Fold ends over and roll up; fasten with a toothpick. Arrange remaining leaves in a 10- x 6- x 2-inch baking dish. Place cabbage rolls, seam side down, over cabbage leaves. Place onion slices on top of each cabbage roll.

Combine tomato sauce, lemon juice, and brown sugar. Pour half of the tomato mixture over cabbage rolls.

Spread sauerkraut evenly over cabbage rolls. Pour remaining tomato mixture over sauerkraut. Cover baking dish tightly with aluminum foil, and bake at 375° for 1 hour. Yield: 6 servings.

Hamburger Pizza Popover

1   *pound ground beef*
1   *medium-size onion, chopped*
1   *(1½-ounce) package spaghetti sauce mix*
1   *(15½-ounce) can tomato sauce*
½   *cup water*
1   *(6-ounce) package sliced mozzarella cheese*
   Popover Batter
½   *cup grated Parmesan cheese*

Brown ground beef and onion in a skillet. Add spaghetti sauce mix, tomato sauce, and water; simmer 12 minutes. Spoon into a greased 13- x 9- x 2-inch baking pan, and top with mozzarella cheese. Bake at 400° for 10 minutes.

Remove meat mixture from oven; pour Popover Batter over top, and sprinkle with Parmesan cheese. Bake at 400° for an additional 30 minutes. Yield: 6 to 8 servings.

Popover Batter:

2   *eggs, beaten*
1   *cup milk*
1   *tablespoon salad oil*
1   *cup all-purpose flour*
½   *teaspoon salt*

Combine eggs, milk, and oil in a small mixing bowl; add flour and salt, mixing well. Yield: about 2 cups.

Sicily Steak

¾   *to 1 pound ground round*
2   *slices bread, finely torn*
1   *egg, beaten*
2   *tablespoons red wine*
½   *cup half-and-half*
1   *tablespoon chopped parsley*
¾   *teaspoon salt*
½   *teaspoon pepper*
2   *tablespoons melted margarine*
1   *(4-ounce) can sliced mushrooms, drained*
1   *cup beef gravy*

Combine beef, bread, egg, wine, half-and-half, parsley, salt, and pepper; mix lightly, and shape into 4 oval patties. Brown patties on both sides in melted margarine.

Add mushrooms to patties, and cook about 3 minutes. Add gravy and bring to a boil; cover and simmer over low heat about 10 minutes or until meat is thoroughly cooked. Yield: 2 to 4 servings.

Cottage Beef Bake

1   *(5-ounce) package medium noodles*
1   *pound ground beef*
1   *(8-ounce) can tomato sauce*
1   *teaspoon salt*
¼   *teaspoon garlic salt*
⅛   *teaspoon pepper*
1   *cup cottage cheese*
1   *(8-ounce) carton commercial sour cream*
½   *cup chopped onion*
¾   *cup shredded Cheddar cheese*

Cook noodles according to package directions; drain and rinse.

Sauté ground beef until lightly browned; drain. Add tomato sauce, salt, garlic salt, and pepper; simmer 5 minutes. Combine cottage cheese, sour cream, onion, and noodles.

Spread half of noodle mixture in a lightly greased 2-quart casserole; top with half of meat sauce. Repeat layers; top with cheese. Bake at 350° for 25 to 30 minutes or until bubbly and cheese is melted. Yield: 6 to 8 servings.

Make-Ahead Mexican Casserole

  1 *pound ground beef*
  1 *large onion, chopped*
  1 *(10-ounce) can tomatoes with green*
      chiles
  1 *(10¾-ounce) can cream of mushroom*
      soup, undiluted
  1 *(10¾-ounce) can cream of chicken soup,*
      undiluted
  1 *(10-ounce) can enchilada sauce*
  2 *dozen corn tortillas, cut into eighths*
  2 *cups shredded Cheddar cheese*

Sauté ground beef and onion until lightly browned, stirring to crumble meat. Stir in remaining ingredients except tortillas and cheese. Alternately layer meat mixture and tortillas, beginning and ending with meat mixture, in a greased 13- x 9- x 2-inch pan. Sprinkle with cheese. Cover with aluminum foil; seal securely, label, and freeze.

    To serve, thaw in refrigerator. Remove foil and bake at 350° for 35 minutes or until bubbly. Yield: 8 servings.

★
Best-Ever Enchiladas

   1 *large onion, chopped*
   2 *tablespoons hot salad oil*
   1 *pound ground beef*
   1 *tablespoon chili powder*
   1 *teaspoon garlic powder*
 1½ *tablespoons all-purpose flour*
   1 *teaspoon salt*
   1 *(16-ounce) can stewed tomatoes*
  ½ *teaspoon cumin seeds*
  ¼ *teaspoon sage*
 12 *corn tortillas*
   1 *medium-size onion, finely chopped*
  ½ *cup sliced black olives*
     Red Sauce
     Grated Parmesan cheese

Sauté large onion in salad oil. Combine beef, chili powder, garlic powder, and flour; add to onion. Cook 15 minutes, stirring occasionally. Stir in salt, tomatoes, cumin seeds, and sage. Keep warm.

Wrap tortillas in foil and heat at 325° about 10 minutes to soften. Combine chopped onion and olives; sprinkle over tortillas. Spoon about 2 tablespoons meat filling on each tortilla; roll tightly and place in a 13- x 9- x 2-inch baking pan. Pour Red Sauce over enchiladas; sprinkle with cheese. Bake at 350° about 20 minutes. Broil about 2 minutes to melt cheese. Yield: 12 enchiladas.

   Red Sauce:

  ½ *cup melted butter or margarine*
  ½ *cup all-purpose flour*
  8 *cloves garlic, pressed*
  2 *(8-ounce) cans tomato sauce*
  2 *cups beef broth*
  2 *teaspoons sage*
  2 *tablespoons chili powder*
  2 *teaspoons cumin seeds*
  ½ *teaspoon salt*

Combine all ingredients in a medium saucepan. Cook, stirring constantly, until smooth and heated through. Yield: about 4 cups.

Meaty Spaghetti Sauce

  2 *pounds ground beef*
  1 *pound ground pork*
  2 *cups chopped celery*
  2 *onions, chopped*
  1 *green pepper, chopped*
  4 *cloves garlic, minced*
  2 *(6-ounce) cans tomato paste*
  2 *(15-ounce) cans tomato sauce*
  ½ *cup hot water*
  2 *(4-ounce) cans sliced mushrooms,*
     undrained
  1 *tablespoon salt*
  1 *teaspoon pepper*
  1 *tablespoon oregano*
    Hot cooked spaghetti

Brown ground beef and pork over medium heat in a Dutch oven or electric skillet. Add celery, onion, green pepper, and garlic; cook, stirring, 5 minutes. Add remaining ingredients except spaghetti, and simmer over low heat 3 to 4 hours. Serve over spaghetti. Yield: 10 to 12 servings.

Spicy Spaghetti Sauce

 1 *pound ground beef*
 1 *pound ground veal*
 ½ *pound ground pork*
 ½ *cup olive oil*
 2 *large onions, chopped*
 ½ *pound mushrooms, sliced*
 2 *cloves garlic, minced*
 1 *(16-ounce) can tomatoes, chopped*
 1 *(10½-ounce) can tomato puree*
 2 *cups beef broth*
 ½ *cup red wine*
 ½ *teaspoon oregano*
 ½ *teaspoon basil*
 ¼ *teaspoon ground nutmeg*
 ⅛ *teaspoon rosemary*
 2 *to 3 teaspoons pepper*
 1 *teaspoon paprika*
 Salt to taste
 Hot cooked spaghetti

Brown meat in a Dutch oven; drain and remove from pan. Heat olive oil in Dutch oven. Add onion, mushrooms, and garlic; sauté 5 minutes. Add tomatoes, tomato puree, beef broth, and wine; cook 10 minutes, stirring occasionally. Add meat and seasonings, blending well. Simmer over low heat 1½ hours, stirring occasionally. Let stand at least 30 minutes; skim fat off top. Serve over hot spaghetti. Yield: 8 to 10 servings.

Creamy Cheesy Noodle Bake

 1 *(8-ounce) package narrow noodles*
 1 *pound ground beef*
 1 *tablespoon melted butter or margarine*
 1 *teaspoon salt*
 ⅛ *teaspoon pepper*
 ¼ *teaspoon garlic salt*
 1 *(8-ounce) can tomato sauce*
 1 *cup cream-style cottage cheese*
 1 *(8-ounce) carton commercial sour cream*
 1 *cup chopped green onions*
 1 *cup shredded sharp Cheddar cheese*

Cook noodles according to package directions; drain. Sauté beef in butter. Add salt, pepper, garlic salt, and tomato sauce to meat; simmer over low heat 5 minutes.

Combine cottage cheese, sour cream, onion, and noodles. Place a layer of noodle mixture in a shallow 2-quart casserole; top with a layer of meat mixture. Repeat procedure until all ingredients are used. Sprinkle with Cheddar cheese. Bake at 350° for 30 minutes. Yield: 8 servings.

Creole Stuffed Peppers

 6 *medium-size green peppers*
 1¼ *pounds ground beef*
 1 *tablespoon chopped onion*
 ⅓ *cup finely chopped celery*
 1 *cup cooked rice*
 1¼ *teaspoon salt*
 ⅛ *teaspoon pepper*
 Creole Sauce

Wash peppers; remove tops and seeds. Set aside.

Brown beef slightly, stirring to keep meat in small particles. Add onion and celery; cook 5 minutes or until vegetables are tender. Stir in rice, salt, pepper, and 1 cup Creole Sauce.

Fill peppers with beef and rice mixture; place in a shallow baking dish. Add water to barely cover bottom of baking dish, and tightly cover with aluminum foil. Bake at 375° for 25 to 30 minutes. Spoon remaining Creole Sauce over peppers before serving. Yield: 6 servings.

Creole Sauce:

 3 *tablespoons salad oil*
 ½ *cup finely chopped green pepper*
 ½ *cup finely chopped onion*
 1 *(28-ounce) can tomatoes, coarsely chopped*
 1 *tablespoon sugar*
 ⅛ *teaspoon ground cloves*
 1 *teaspoon salt*
 ¼ *teaspoon pepper*

Heat salad oil in a large saucepan. Add green pepper and onion; sauté 5 minutes or until soft but not brown. Add tomatoes with juice and remaining ingredients to sautéed vegetables. Cook over low heat 40 to 50 minutes. Yield: about 2 cups.

Beef Roll Mozzarella

1½ *pounds ground chuck*
 1 *teaspoon salt*
 ½ *teaspoon pepper*
 1 *tablespoon instant minced onion*
 1 *egg, beaten*
 ½ *cup breadcrumbs*
 1 *(4-ounce) can mushroom stems and*
      pieces
1½ *cups shredded mozzarella cheese*
 1 *(15-ounce) can tomato sauce with*
      tomato bits
 2 *tablespoons vermouth*

Combine ground chuck, salt, pepper, onion, egg, and breadcrumbs. Drain mushrooms, reserving liquid. Add enough water to mushroom liquid to make ½ cup; add to beef mixture, blending well.

Shape beef mixture into a 14- x 10-inch rectangle on a piece of waxed paper. Sprinkle with mozzarella, leaving a ½-inch border on each side. Roll up jellyroll fashion.

Place roll, seam side down, in a 13- x 9- x 2-inch baking dish. Combine tomato sauce and vermouth; pour half over roll. Bake at 375° for 45 minutes.

Combine remaining tomato sauce and mushrooms; pour over beef roll. Bake 10 additional minutes. Yield: 6 servings.

Simple Beef Stroganoff

 1 *onion, chopped*
1½ *tablespoons melted butter or margarine*
 1 *tablespoon all-purpose flour*
 ½ *cup beef broth*
 1 *tablespoon catsup*
 ½ *teaspoon Worcestershire sauce*
 ¼ *teaspoon salt*
 ⅛ *teaspoon pepper*
 ½ *pound ground round steak*
 1 *(4-ounce) can sliced mushrooms,*
      drained
 ½ *cup commercial sour cream*
    Hot cooked rice

Sauté onion in butter until tender. Add flour, stirring until smooth. Gradually add broth; cook, stirring constantly, until smooth and thickened. Add catsup, Worcestershire sauce, salt, and pepper; mix well.

Sauté meat until lightly browned; add to sauce.

Add mushrooms to pan drippings, and cook until tender; add to the meat mixture.

When ready to serve, stir in sour cream. Serve over rice. Yield: 4 servings.

Favorite Grilled Hamburgers

 1 *cup catsup*
 2 *teaspoons Worcestershire sauce*
 ½ *teaspoon celery salt*
 ⅛ *teaspoon hot sauce*
1½ *pounds ground beef*
 2 *tablespoons finely chopped onion*
    Salt and pepper to taste
 6 *hamburger buns, split, toasted, and*
      buttered

Combine catsup, Worcestershire sauce, celery salt, and hot sauce in a saucepan; bring to a boil, and set aside.

Combine beef, onion, salt, and pepper. Shape into 6 patties ½ inch thick. Place on grill 3 to 5 inches from coals; cook 3 to 5 minutes on each side or to desired degree of doneness. Baste occasionally with sauce.

Serve on buns with remaining sauce. Yield: 6 servings.

Potato Burgers

 1½ cups diced cooked potatoes
 1 teaspoon salt
 ¼ teaspoon pepper
 1 tablespoon chopped onion
 1 tablespoon chopped parsley
 1 (8-ounce) can tomato sauce, divided
 1 pound ground beef
 Hot salad oil

Combine potatoes, salt, pepper, onion, parsley, and ¼ cup tomato sauce; set aside. Shape beef into 8 thin patties. Spoon potato mixture equally over 4 patties. Place remaining patties over filling; seal edges together well. Brown in a small amount of hot salad oil in a large skillet. Turn patties; spoon remaining tomato sauce over patties. Cover and simmer 10 to 15 minutes. Yield: 4 servings.

Danish Cheeseburgers

 ¼ pound mushrooms, sliced
 ¼ cup chopped onion
 1 tomato, chopped
 ¼ cup chopped green pepper
 Melted butter or margarine
 1½ pounds ground beef
 1 egg, slightly beaten
 ¼ cup thinly sliced green onion
 1 teaspoon salt
 ¼ teaspoon pepper
 6 (¼-inch-thick) slices Havarti or Gouda cheese
 3 hamburger buns, warmed

Sauté mushrooms, onion, tomato, and green pepper in butter until tender; set aside, keeping mixture warm.

Combine ground beef, egg, green onion, salt, and pepper; mix well. Shape into 6 patties. Broil 3 to 6 minutes on each side, depending on desired degree of doneness.

Place 1 slice of cheese on each patty; return patties to broiler until cheese is slightly melted. Place each patty on a bun half, and top with sautéed vegetables. Yield: 6 servings.

★ Pizza-in-a-Burger

 1½ pounds ground beef
 ⅓ cup grated Parmesan cheese
 ¼ cup finely chopped onion
 ¼ cup chopped ripe olives
 1 teaspoon oregano
 1 teaspoon salt
 ¼ teaspoon pepper
 1 (6-ounce) can tomato paste
 8 slices mozzarella cheese, about the size of patties
 8 slices tomato
 8 slices French bread, toasted

Combine ground beef, Parmesan cheese, onion, olives, oregano, salt, pepper, and tomato paste. Shape mixture into 8 oval patties. Broil on one side 3 to 6 minutes. Turn patties over; top each with cheese and tomato. Broil 3 to 6 minutes, depending on desired degree of doneness. Serve each patty on a slice of bread. Yield: 8 servings.

Sweet 'n Sour Burgers

 1 (8-ounce) can tomato sauce, divided
 ⅓ cup finely chopped onion
 ⅓ cup crushed gingersnaps
 1 egg, slightly beaten
 ¼ cup seedless raisins
 ¾ teaspoon salt
 1½ pounds ground beef
 Hot salad oil
 2 tablespoons brown sugar
 1 teaspoon prepared mustard
 1 tablespoon vinegar
 Dash of pepper

Combine ¼ cup tomato sauce, onion, gingersnaps, egg, raisins, and salt, blending well. Add meat, mixing well. Shape mixture into 6 patties. Brown on both sides in a small amount of hot salad oil; drain.

Combine remaining tomato sauce, brown sugar, mustard, vinegar, and pepper. Spoon sauce over patties. Cover and simmer 20 minutes, basting patties occasionally with the sauce. Yield: 6 servings.

Marinated Hamburgers

1   *pound ground beef*
1   *(2¼-ounce) can deviled ham*
Dash of pepper
1   *(4-ounce) package blue cheese, quartered*
1½   *cups dry red wine*
1   *tablespoon melted butter or margarine*

Combine ground beef, deviled ham, and pepper; mix well. Divide mixture into 4 portions; mold each portion completely around a piece of cheese and gently shape into a patty.

Place patties in a glass container; pour wine over each. Tightly cover; refrigerate 3 hours, turning meat after 1½ hours. Remove patties from marinade, reserving marinade.

Brown patties in butter over medium-high heat 6 to 10 minutes, depending on desired degree of doneness. Place on a warm platter, and keep warm. Drain drippings from skillet. Pour marinade into skillet. Bring to a boil; let boil 5 minutes. Pour over hamburgers. Yield: 4 servings.

Sour Cream Beefburgers

1   *pound ground beef*
1   *cup coarse breadcrumbs*
4   *green onions, finely chopped*
5   *tablespoons commercial sour cream*
1   *tablespoon Worcestershire sauce*
½   *teaspoon salt*
½   *teaspoon pepper*

Combine all ingredients, mixing thoroughly. Shape mixture into 4 patties. Place waxed paper between patties; place in a plastic bag, and refrigerate several hours.

Broil patties 3 to 6 minutes on each side, depending on desired degree of doneness. Yield: 4 servings.

★ Hamburger Hawaiian

1½   *pounds ground beef*
⅔   *cup cracker crumbs*
½   *cup chopped onion*
⅔   *cup evaporated milk*
1   *teaspoon seasoned salt*
Hot salad oil
Hawaiian Sauce
3   *hamburger buns, warmed (optional)*

Combine ground beef, cracker crumbs, onion, evaporated milk, and seasoned salt, blending well. Shape mixture into 6 patties; brown on both sides in a small amount of hot salad oil. Spoon Hawaiian Sauce over patties; cover and simmer 15 minutes. Serve each patty on a bun, if desired. Yield: 6 servings.

Hawaiian Sauce:

1   *(13½-ounce) can pineapple chunks*
¼   *cup firmly packed brown sugar*
2   *tablespoons cornstarch*
¼   *cup vinegar*
2   *tablespoons soy sauce*
1   *cup coarsely chopped green pepper*

Drain pineapple, reserving juice; add enough water to juice to equal 1 cup liquid. Combine juice, brown sugar, cornstarch, vinegar, and soy sauce in a saucepan. Cook over low heat, stirring constantly, until thickened. Add pineapple and green pepper; stir until blended. Yield: about 2 cups.

Gardenburgers

1½   *pounds ground beef*
2   *eggs, slightly beaten*
¼   *cup finely chopped onion*
¼   *cup catsup*
1½   *teaspoons salt*
¼   *teaspoon pepper*
1   *(4-ounce) can sliced mushrooms, drained*
Melted butter or margarine
6   *thin slices onion*
6   *thin slices tomato*
6   *slices process Amercian cheese*

Combine beef, eggs, chopped onion, catsup, salt, and pepper; mix well. Shape into 12 thin patties. Place mushrooms on 6 patties; top with remaining patties, sealing edges well. Broil 3 to 6 minutes on each side, depending on desired doneness. Brush with melted butter. Place onion slices, tomato, and cheese on each patty; return patties to broiler until cheese begins to melt. Yield: 6 servings.

Stuffing Burgers

      1 *cup herb-seasoned stuffing mix*
      ¾ *cup milk*
      1 *teaspoon instant minced onion*
      1 *pound ground beef*
      1 *teaspoon salt*
      ¼ *teaspoon pepper*
      4 *hamburger buns, split and toasted*
      4 *thin slices onion*
      4 *thin slices tomato*

Combine stuffing mix, milk, and minced onion. Set aside until milk is absorbed; stir in beef, salt, and pepper. Shape into 4 patties.

Broil patties 3 to 4 inches from hot coals 5 to 10 minutes on each side, depending on desired doneness. Place patties on bottom of buns. Top each with onion and tomato slices; close with bun tops. Yield: 4 servings.

Meatballs in Beer Sauce

      2 *pounds ground beef*
      1 *(1⅜-ounce) package onion soup mix*
      Salt and pepper to taste
      Hot salad oil
      1 *(14-ounce) bottle catsup*
      1 *cup beer*

Combine beef, onion soup mix, salt, and pepper; shape mixture into 1-inch balls. Brown well in oil; drain.

Combine catsup and beer, blending well. Pour mixture over meatballs; cover and simmer 20 to 25 minutes. Yield: 6 servings.

Favorite Meatballs

      1½ *pounds ground beef*
      1   *egg*
      1   *cup breadcrumbs*
      ½   *cup milk*
      ½   *cup chopped onion*
      1½ *teaspoons salt*
          Pepper to taste
      4   *tablespoons all-purpose flour, divided*
          Hot salad oil
      1   *beef bouillon cube, crushed*
      ½   *cup commercial sour cream*
      1   *tablespoon lemon juice*
      ½   *cup grated Parmesan cheese*
          Hot cooked rice (optional)

Combine beef, egg, breadcrumbs, milk, onion, salt, and pepper; mix well, and shape into 2-inch balls. Roll balls in 2 tablespoons flour. Brown well in hot oil.

Combine remaining 2 tablespoons flour, bouillon, sour cream, lemon juice, and cheese; blend well. Spoon mixture over meatballs. Heat thoroughly. Serve over rice, if desired. Yield: about 6 to 8 servings.

Apple-Beef Balls

      1½ *pounds ground beef*
      1½ *cups fine, dry breadcrumbs*
      2   *eggs, well beaten*
          Dash of cayenne
      2   *apples, peeled and grated*
      ½   *cup apple-grape jelly, divided*
      1½ *teaspoons salt*
      ¼   *cup salad oil*
      1   *(10¾-ounce) can tomato soup, undiluted*
      1   *small onion, chopped*
          Hot cooked rice or noodles

Combine beef, breadcrumbs, eggs, cayenne, apple, ¼ cup jelly, and salt; shape mixture into 1½-inch balls. Brown well in oil; drain.

Combine remaining jelly, tomato soup, and onion; pour over meatballs. Cover and simmer 20 to 30 minutes, stirring occasionally. Serve over rice or noodles. Yield: 6 servings.

Oriental Meatballs

2 *pounds ground beef*
2½ *teaspoons salt, divided*
⅛ *teaspoon pepper*
2 *eggs, slightly beaten*
2 *tablespoons water*
¼ *cup all-purpose flour*
½ *cup hot salad oil*
1 *(14-ounce) can chicken broth, undiluted and divided*
3 *tablespoons cornstarch*
½ *cup vinegar*
½ *cup light corn syrup*
2 *teaspoons soy sauce*
3 *large green peppers, cut into strips*
1 *(8¼-ounce) can pineapple chunks, drained*
12 *maraschino cherries*
Hot cooked rice

Combine beef, 2 teaspoons salt, and pepper, blending well; shape into 30 (1-inch) balls.

Combine eggs, water, flour, and ½ teaspoon salt; beat until smooth. Dip meatballs in batter; brown well in oil. Remove meatballs from skillet; pour off all but 2 tablespoons drippings from skillet.

Combine ½ cup broth and cornstarch; set aside.

Combine remaining broth, vinegar, corn syrup, and soy sauce; add to drippings in skillet. Cook over medium heat about 1 minute. Gradually add cornstarch mixture; cook, stirring constantly, until thick and transparent. Add meatballs, green pepper, and fruit. Lower heat; cook 5 to 10 minutes. Serve over rice. Yield: 6 servings.

Sweet-and-Sour Meatballs

1½ *pounds ground round steak*
¾ *cup breadcrumbs*
1 *egg, beaten*
1 *small onion, grated*
Salt and pepper
1 *(8-ounce) can tomato sauce*
¾ *cup catsup*
½ *cup sugar*
Hot cooked noodles

Combine steak, breadcrumbs, egg, and onion; season with salt and pepper. Mix well, and shape into 1-inch balls.

Combine meatballs, tomato sauce, catsup, sugar, and ½ teaspoon salt in a 4-quart saucepan. Add enough water to cover meatballs; simmer 1½ to 2 hours, stirring occasionally. Refrigerate overnight. Heat thoroughly, and serve over noodles. Yield: 6 servings.

Easy Meatballs and Spaghetti

1 *large onion, chopped*
½ *cup chopped green pepper*
¼ *cup olive oil*
1 *(28-ounce) can tomatoes, undrained and chopped*
1 *(6-ounce) can tomato paste*
1 *(8-ounce) can tomato sauce*
1 *bay leaf*
1 *teaspoon oregano*
Garlic salt to taste
Black pepper to taste
¼ *teaspoon cayenne pepper*
2 *tablespoons bottled brown bouquet sauce*
1 *teaspoon sugar*
1 *(4-ounce) can sliced mushrooms, drained*
½ *cup water*
1 *pound ground beef*
½ *cup seasoned breadcrumbs*
1 *egg, beaten*
½ *cup chopped onion*
Hot cooked spaghetti

Sauté onion and green pepper in olive oil; add tomatoes, tomato paste, tomato sauce, bay leaf, oregano, garlic salt, black pepper, cayenne pepper, bouquet sauce, sugar, mushrooms, and water; simmer 35 to 40 minutes.

While sauce is cooking, combine ground beef, breadcrumbs, egg, and ½ cup onion; mix well. Shape into small meatballs, no larger than 1½ inches in diameter. Drop meatballs into sauce, and simmer about 1 hour.

Serve sauce and meatballs over spaghetti. Yield: 6 servings.

German-Style Meatballs

- 1½ *pounds ground beef*
- 2 *eggs, beaten*
- 2 *tablespoons breadcrumbs*
- 2 *tablespoons instant minced onion*
- 2 *tablespoons parsley flakes*
- 1½ *teaspoons salt*
- ¼ *teaspoon pepper*
- 1 *tablespoon lemon juice*
- 3 *tablespoons instant beef broth granules*
- 3 *cups boiling water*
- 3 *tablespoons all-purpose flour*
- ¼ *cup cold water*
- 1 *tablespoon Worcestershire sauce*
- 3 *tablespoons hamburger relish*
- *Hot cooked noodles*

Combine first 8 ingredients; shape into 2-inch balls.

Combine beef broth granules and boiling water. Add meatballs; heat to boiling. Lower heat; turn meatballs. Cover and simmer 30 minutes. Remove meatballs, and keep warm. Skim fat from broth; keep broth simmering.

Combine flour and cold water; gradually stir into broth. Add Worcestershire sauce and hamburger relish. Cook over medium heat, stirring constantly, until sauce thickens and bubbles. Pour sauce over meatballs. Serve over noodles. Yield: 4 to 6 servings.

Yorkshire Meatballs

- 1½ *pounds ground beef*
- ¼ *cup catsup*
- 1 *(1⅜-ounce) package onion soup mix*
- 1 *tablespoon instant minced parsley*
- ¼ *teaspoon pepper*
- 1 *egg, beaten*
- 1 *tablespoon water*
- 1½ *cups all-purpose flour*
- 1½ *teaspoons baking powder*
- 1 *teaspoon salt*
- 4 *eggs, beaten*
- 3 *tablespoons melted butter or margarine*
- ¾ *cup milk*
- *Cheese Sauce*

Combine ground beef, catsup, soup mix, parsley, pepper, 1 egg, and water. Shape into

24 meatballs. Place meatballs in a greased 13- x 9- x 2-inch baking dish; set aside.

Combine flour, baking powder, and salt. Combine 4 eggs, butter, and milk; stir in dry ingredients all at once, mixing just until smooth. Pour over meatballs. Bake at 350° for 30 to 40 minutes. Serve with Cheese Sauce. Yield: about 8 servings.

Cheese Sauce:

- ¾ *pound process American cheese, cubed*
- ⅓ *cup milk*
- ¼ *teaspoon Worcestershire sauce*

Combine all ingredients in a saucepan. Cook over medium heat, stirring constantly, until cheese is melted. Yield: 1½ cups.

★ Country-Style Meatballs

- 3 *slices white bread*
- ½ *cup milk*
- 1 *pound ground beef*
- 2 *cups cooked rice*
- 1 *teaspoon salt*
- ¼ *teaspoon ground thyme*
- ¼ *teaspoon garlic salt*
- *Corn flake crumbs*
- *Hot salad oil*
- 1 *(10¾-ounce) can cream of mushroom soup, undiluted*
- 1¼ *cups buttermilk*

Soak bread in ½ cup milk until soft. Add beef, rice, and seasonings. Shape mixture into 12 (1½-inch) balls; coat each with corn flake crumbs. Brown well in hot oil; transfer to a shallow baking dish.

Combine soup and buttermilk; pour over meatballs. Bake, uncovered, at 350° for 30 minutes. Yield: 6 servings.

Meatballs with Lemon Sauce

    1   *pound ground beef*
    ½   *cup Italian breadcrumbs*
    1   *egg, beaten*
    1   *teaspoon grated lemon rind*
    2   *beef bouillon cubes*
    1   *cup boiling water*
    1   *tablespoon lemon juice*
    1   *teaspoon cornstarch*
    2   *tablespoons cold water*
    1   *egg yolk, beaten*

Combine beef, breadcrumbs, egg, and lemon rind. Shape into 12 (1½-inch) balls.

Dissolve bouillon cubes in boiling water; lower heat. Add meatballs to bouillon. Cover and simmer 10 minutes. Remove meatballs, and keep warm.

Add lemon juice to bouillon. Dissolve cornstarch in cold water; gradually stir into bouillon. Cook, stirring constantly, until slightly thickened. Remove from heat. Stir a small amount of bouillon mixture into egg yolk. Gradually add yolk mixture to bouillon, stirring constantly. Pour sauce over meatballs. Yield: 4 servings.

Million Dollar Meatballs

    1   *pound ground beef*
    2   *eggs, slightly beaten*
    ½   *cup soft breadcrumbs*
    ¼   *cup grated Parmesan cheese*
    1   *(10-ounce) package frozen chopped*
         spinach, thawed and drained
    1   *teaspoon salt*
    3   *tablespoons hot salad oil*
    1¼   *cups cold water*
    2   *tablespoons lemon juice*
    1   *(¾-ounce) package brown gravy mix*
         Hot cooked noodles (optional)

Combine beef, eggs, breadcrumbs, cheese, spinach, and salt; mix well, and shape into 1½-inch balls. Brown well in hot oil; drain excess fat. Stir in water, lemon juice, and gravy mix, blending well. Simmer, uncovered, 15 minutes. Serve over noodles, if desired. Yield: 4 servings.

★ Hot Spiced Meatballs

    ¾   *pound ground beef*
    ¾   *cup fine, dry breadcrumbs*
    1½   *tablespoons minced onion*
    ¼   *teaspoon hot sauce*
    2   *eggs, beaten*
    ¾   *teaspoon salt*
    ½   *teaspoon pepper*
         Hot salad oil
    ¾   *cup catsup*
    ½   *cup water*
    ¼   *cup vinegar*
    1   *tablespoon minced onion*
    2   *tablespoons brown sugar*
    2   *teaspoons Worcestershire sauce*
    1   *teaspoon mustard*
    ¼   *teaspoon pepper*
    1½   *teaspoons salt*
    ¼   *teaspoon hot sauce*

Combine beef, breadcrumbs, 1½ tablespoons onion, ¼ teaspoon hot sauce, eggs, ¾ teaspoon salt, and ½ teaspoon pepper; blend well. Shape into ¾-inch balls. Brown well in oil; drain.

Combine remaining ingredients, blending well; pour over meatballs. Cover and simmer 10 minutes. Yield: 4 servings.

Meat Loaf Wellington

    2   *eggs, beaten*
    ¼   *cup milk*
    ¼   *cup catsup*
    1   *(1⅜-ounce) package dry onion soup*
         mix
    1   *tablespoon chopped parsley*
    2   *slices bread, torn into pieces*
    2   *pounds meat loaf mixture (ground beef,*
         pork, and veal)
         Pastry
    1   *(⅞-ounce) package mushroom gravy*
         mix

Combine eggs, milk, catsup, soup mix, parsley, and bread in a large bowl; mix well. Add meat, mixing thoroughly. Place mixture in a 13- x 9- x 2-inch baking pan, and shape into loaf.

Center Pastry over loaf, tucking Pastry around bottom of loaf to seal in juices. Prick top of Pastry with fork. Bake at 350° for 1 hour and 15 minutes. Prepare gravy according to package directions. Serve over meat loaf. Yield: 6 to 8 servings.

Pastry:

½ cup plus 2 tablespoons all-purpose flour
Dash of salt
1 tablespoon shortening
2 tablespoons butter or margarine, cut into pieces
1½ to 2 tablespoons cold water

Combine flour and salt in a mixing bowl. Cut in shortening with a pastry blender; then cut in butter until mixture resembles coarse meal. Stir in water with a fork. Wrap dough in waxed paper, and chill 30 minutes. Roll to about ⅛-inch thickness on a floured surface. Yield: enough for one meat loaf.

Gold Crowned Meat Loaf

1½ cups soft breadcrumbs
1½ pounds ground beef
4 eggs, separated
1½ teaspoons salt
2 tablespoons minced onion
½ cup catsup
6 tablespoons prepared mustard, divided
1½ teaspoons prepared horseradish
3 tablespoons finely chopped green pepper
¼ teaspoon cream of tartar

Combine breadcrumbs and beef; set aside. Combine egg yolks, salt, onion, catsup, 2 tablespoons mustard, horseradish, and green pepper; blend into meat mixture. Lightly pack into a 9-inch square baking dish. Bake at 325° for 30 minutes.

Beat egg whites until foamy. Add cream of tartar, and beat until very stiff. Gently fold in remaining 4 tablespoons mustard. Spoon over meat loaf. Bake 20 to 25 minutes or until lightly browned. Yield: 6 to 8 servings.

Tasty Meat Loaf

1 pound ground beef
½ pound bulk sausage
½ cup cracker crumbs
½ cup wheat germ
1 egg, beaten
½ cup milk
½ cup chopped onion
1 teaspoon salt
Dash of pepper
1 teaspoon basil
1 tablespoon grated Romano cheese
⅔ cup catsup
1 tablespoon Worcestershire sauce
1 teaspoon dried green pepper

Combine all ingredients. Spoon into a 9- x 5- x 3-inch pan. Bake at 350° about 50 to 55 minutes. Let stand in pan 5 minutes before removing. Yield: 6 to 8 servings.

Cheese-Stuffed Meat Loaf

2 pounds ground chuck
2 eggs, beaten
½ cup seasoned breadcrumbs
½ teaspoon salt
Dash of pepper
1 teaspoon oregano
1 cup tomato juice
2 small onions, finely chopped
2 tablespoons salad oil
8 thin slices boiled ham
1 (8-ounce) package mozzarella cheese, shredded

Combine ground chuck, eggs, breadcrumbs, salt, pepper, oregano, and tomato juice; mix well. Sauté onion in salad oil until golden; stir into meat mixture. Place on aluminum foil, and shape into a rectangle 1 inch thick.

Place ham slices on meat, keeping them about 1 inch from edge; sprinkle with cheese. Fold meat mixture over ham and cheese, using foil to help shape into a loaf; seal all openings.

Place loaf in a lightly greased 8- x 5- x 3-inch loafpan. Bake at 325° for 1 hour and 15 minutes. Yield: 8 to 10 servings.

Gourmet Meat Loaf

1½   *pounds ground beef*
¾   *cup uncooked regular oats*
2   *eggs, slightly beaten*
2   *teaspoons salt*
¼   *teaspoon pepper*
1   *teaspoon Worcestershire sauce*
⅔   *cup milk*
     Mushroom Filling

Combine all ingredients except Mushroom Filling. Place half of meat mixture in a lightly greased 10- x 6- x 2-inch baking dish; form into a loaf shape.

Make a shallow well lengthwise in meat. Spoon Mushroom Filling into well. Spoon remaining meat mixture over Filling, covering all of Filling and shaping into a loaf. Bake at 350° about 1 hour. Let stand 5 minutes before cutting. Yield: 6 to 8 servings.

Mushroom Filling:

1   *cup sliced mushrooms*
½   *cup chopped onion*
2   *tablespoons butter or margarine*
⅓   *cup commercial sour cream*

Sauté mushrooms and onion in butter until soft. Remove from heat, and stir in sour cream. Yield: about 1 cup.

Chili Meat Loaf

2   *pounds ground beef*
1   *(15-ounce) can chili con carne without*
     beans
2   *cups mashed potatoes or cooked rice*
1   *medium-size onion, grated*
½   *cup minced celery*
1   *small green pepper, minced*
1¼   *teaspoons salt*
¼   *teaspoon pepper*

Combine all ingredients; mix well. Pack into a lightly greased 2-quart loafpan. Bake at 350° about 1 hour or until done. Yield: 8 to 10 servings.

Barbecue Meat Loaf

1½   *pounds ground beef*
1   *cup breadcrumbs*
1   *medium-size onion, finely chopped*
1   *egg, beaten*
1½   *teaspoons salt*
¼   *teaspoon pepper*
1   *(8-ounce) can tomato sauce, divided*
½   *cup water*
3   *tablespoons brown sugar*
3   *tablespoons vinegar*
     Dash of hot sauce
2   *tablespoons prepared mustard*
2   *teaspoons Worcestershire sauce*

Combine beef, breadcrumbs, onion, egg, salt, pepper, and ½ cup tomato sauce. Spoon into a 10- x 6- x 2-inch baking dish, and shape into a loaf. Combine remaining ½ cup tomato sauce and remaining ingredients; pour over meat loaf. Bake at 350° for 1 hour and 15 minutes, basting occasionally with sauce. Yield: 6 to 8 servings.

Teriyaki Pork Chops

1   *cup soy sauce*
¾   *cup water*
½   *cup sweet vermouth*
½   *cup honey*
4   *cloves garlic, pressed*
1   *inch fresh gingerroot, grated*
8   *pork chops*

Combine first 6 ingredients. Pour marinade over chops; marinate overnight in refrigerator.

Grill chops 5 inches from heat 15 to 20 minutes; baste with marinade. Turn and grill an additional 20 minutes or until done, basting occasionally. Yield: 8 servings.

Mandarin Pork Chops

    6   *tablespoons soy sauce, divided*
    1   *clove garlic, crushed*
 1½   *teaspoons dry mustard*
    ⅛   *teaspoon monosodium glutamate*
    ½   *cup apple juice*
    ¼   *cup honey*
    1   *tablespoon ground ginger*
    ¼   *teaspoon Worcestershire sauce*
    ¼   *cup rum*
    6   *loin pork chops*
    ¾   *cup crabapple jelly*
    1   *tablespoon lemon juice*

Combine 4 tablespoons soy sauce, garlic, mustard, monosodium glutamate, apple juice, honey, ginger, Worcestershire sauce, and rum; blend well. Arrange pork chops in a single layer in a dish. Pour marinade over chops; cover and refrigerate overnight.

Drain marinade into a medium saucepan; add jelly and remaining 2 tablespoons soy sauce. Bring to a boil, and simmer 15 minutes over medium heat; stir in lemon juice.

Broil chops about 6 to 8 minutes on each side, basting frequently with marinade. Yield: 6 servings.

Fruited Smoked Pork Chops

    4   *smoked pork chops*
    ½   *teaspoon ground sage*
    ¼   *teaspoon salt*
    ¼   *teaspoon pepper*
    ¼   *cup seedless raisins*
    1   *small tart apple, cored and sliced*
    1   *tablespoon all-purpose flour*
    ¼   *cup water or fruit juice*
 1½   *teaspoons cider vinegar*
    2   *tablespoons brown sugar*

Grill chops over hot coals 10 minutes. Place on heavy-duty aluminum foil; sprinkle with sage, salt, and pepper. Top with raisins and apple; set aside.

Combine flour and water; cook over low heat, stirring constantly, until slightly thickened. Stir in vinegar and brown sugar; pour over chops. Seal securely. Return to grill for 30 minutes or until tender. Yield: 4 servings.

Glazed Pork Chops with Fruit

    ½   *cup honey*
    ½   *cup lime or lemon juice*
    ¼   *cup dark corn syrup or 2 tablespoons brown sugar*
    2   *tablespoons soy sauce*
    ½   *teaspoon ground cloves*
    ½   *teaspoon grated lime or lemon rind (optional)*
    ½   *teaspoon salt*
    6   *(1- to 1¼-inch-thick) loin pork chops*
    2   *large oranges, peeled and sliced*
    ½   *medium-size cantaloupe, peeled and cut into chunks*
    ½   *medium-size honeydew melon, peeled and cut into chunks*

Combine first 7 ingredients in saucepan; heat thoroughly.

Grill chops 5 inches from heat 15 to 20 minutes. Baste with glaze; turn and grill an additional 20 minutes or until done, basting occasionally.

Alternate fruit on skewers; brush with glaze. Grill 3 to 5 minutes. Yield: 6 servings.

Pork Chops in Wine

    1   *large onion, sliced*
    3   *tablespoons hot salad oil*
    ¼   *cup butter or margarine, softened*
    ½   *teaspoon dry mustard*
 1½   *teaspoons salt*
    ⅛   *teaspoon pepper*
    6   *(½- to ¾-inch-thick) loin pork chops*
    1   *cup dry white wine*
    3   *tablespoons chopped parsley*

Sauté onion in oil in a large skillet; drain on paper towels, and set aside. Reserve drippings.

Combine butter, mustard, salt, and pepper; stir to make a paste and spread on both sides of chops. Brown chops on both sides in reserved drippings; pour off drippings. Return onions to skillet; add wine. Cover and simmer 1 hour or until chops are done. Sprinkle with chopped parsley before serving. Yield: 6 servings.

Stuffed Pork Chops

  1 *cup chopped celery*
  2 *tablespoons chopped onion*
  ½ *teaspoon poultry seasoning*
  3 *tablespoons melted butter or margarine*
  2 *cups soft breadcrumbs*
  4 *(1-inch-thick) pork loin chops, cut with pockets*
Salt and pepper to taste
  2 *tablespoons melted shortening*
1½ *cups water, divided*
  1 *green pepper, cut in ½-inch strips*
  6 *carrots, cut in ½-inch slices*

Combine celery, onion, and poultry seasoning; sauté in butter 5 minutes or until vegetables are tender. Stir in breadcrumbs.

Season pockets of pork chops with salt and pepper; stuff with breadcrumb mixture, and secure with toothpicks. Brown chops on both sides in shortening. Pour ½ cup water over chops; cover and simmer 30 minutes. Add green pepper, carrots, and remaining 1 cup water; cover and simmer 15 minutes or until vegetables are crisp-tender. Yield: 4 servings.

★
Pork Chops and Cream Gravy

  4 *(½- to ¾-inch-thick) loin pork chops*
Salt and pepper to taste
  ¼ *cup hot salad oil*
  2 *tablespoons all-purpose flour*
1½ *cups milk*

Season chops with salt and pepper; brown on both sides in oil. Drain on paper towels, and set aside. Reserve pan drippings.

Add flour to drippings; cook over medium heat until bubbly, stirring constantly. Add milk; cook until thickened, stirring constantly. Season to taste with salt. Add chops to gravy; cover and simmer 45 minutes. Yield: 4 servings.

Pork Chops in Mushroom Gravy

  2 *loin pork chops*
  2 *tablespoons all-purpose flour*
  1 *teaspoon paprika*
Salt and pepper
  1 *tablespoon salad oil*
  1 *small onion, minced*
  ½ *green pepper, minced*
  6 *to 8 mushrooms, chopped*
  1 *cup milk*
Juice of ½ lemon

Remove excess fat from edge of chops. Combine flour, paprika, salt, and pepper, and dredge chops in mixture. Set aside remaining flour mixture. Brown chops in oil, and remove to a shallow casserole.

Add onion, pepper, and mushrooms to skillet, and sauté until soft. Add reserved flour mixture; cook, stirring, 3 minutes. Blend in milk, and cook until thick; stir in lemon juice. Pour sauce over chops; cover and bake at 350° for 1 hour. Remove cover, and bake 10 more minutes. Yield: 2 servings.

Pork Chops Mexicana

  6 *(½- to ¾-inch-thick) loin pork chops*
Salt to taste
Salad oil
  ¾ *cup uncooked regular rice*
1½ *cups water*
  1 *(8-ounce) can tomato sauce*
  1 *(1¼-ounce) package taco seasoning mix*
  1 *teaspoon salt*
  ½ *cup shredded Cheddar cheese*
  1 *medium-size green pepper, sliced into rings*

Sprinkle chops with salt; brown on both sides in a small amount of hot oil. Drain well on paper towels. Place chops in a 13- x 9- x 2-inch baking dish; sprinkle rice around chops.

Combine water, tomato sauce, taco seasoning, and 1 teaspoon salt; pour over chops and rice. Cover tightly, and bake at 350° for 1 hour. Remove cover; sprinkle with cheese, and top with green pepper. Cover and bake 15 minutes or until chops are done and rice is tender. Yield: 6 servings.

Batter-Fried Pork Chops

1   *cup all-purpose flour*
½   *cup breadcrumbs*
1   *cup milk*
1   *egg, beaten*
1   *teaspoon salt*
½   *teaspoon paprika*
¼   *teaspoon oregano*
6   *(½- to ¾-inch-thick) loin pork chops*
Hot salad oil

Combine flour, breadcrumbs, milk, egg, salt, paprika, and oregano. Dip each chop into batter; brown chops on both sides in oil heated to 350°. Drain well on paper towels. Yield: 6 servings.

★
Luau Pork Roast

1   *(5-pound) pork loin roast*
4   *(4¾-ounce) jars strained apricot baby*
    food
⅓   *cup honey*
½   *cup lemon juice*
½   *cup soy sauce*
½   *clove garlic, minced*
1   *small onion, finely chopped*
1   *cup ginger ale*
⅛   *teaspoon pepper*
1   *tablespoon coarsely grated lemon rind*
1   *(17-ounce) can whole apricots, drained*
Watercress

Have the butcher saw across the rib bones at the base of the backbone, separating ribs from backbone.

Combine 2 jars strained apricots, honey, lemon juice, soy sauce, garlic, onion, ginger ale, and pepper. Pour over roast; marinate overnight or at least 4 to 5 hours, turning occasionally.

Place roast in broiler pan. Bake at 350° about 3½ hours, basting frequently with marinade. Spread 1 jar strained apricots on top of roast during last 5 minutes of baking.

Combine remaining jar of strained apricots and lemon rind in a saucepan. Heat well; serve as sauce with roast.

For easy carving, remove backbone; allow roast to stand 15 to 20 minutes. Place roast on a serving platter; garnish with whole apricots and watercress. Yield: about 8 servings.

Stuffed Pork Loin Roast

1   *(6- to 8-pound) pork loin roast*
Salt
Sausage-Apple Dressing

Have the butcher saw across the rib bones at the base of the backbone, separating ribs from backbone.

Make 8 to 10 deep slits about 3 to 4 inches long on fat side of roast to serve as pockets for stuffing. Season with salt. Stuff pockets with Sausage-Apple Dressing. Bake at 350° about 3½ hours. For easy carving, remove backbone and allow roast to stand 15 to 20 minutes. Yield: 8 to 10 servings.

Sausage-Apple Dressing:

6   *slices white bread, crusts removed*
1   *cup milk*
2   *medium-size apples, peeled and diced*
⅓   *cup golden seedless raisins*
3   *tablespoons water*
¼   *pound bulk pork sausage*
1   *small onion, chopped*
1   *stalk celery, chopped*
½   *teaspoon sage*
1   *tablespoon chopped parsley*
Salt and pepper to taste

Soak bread in milk. Combine apple, raisins, and water in a small saucepan. Cover and simmer until soft.

Sauté sausage until brown; add onion and celery, and cook until tender. Combine all ingredients, mixing well. Yield: 3 cups.

Gingered Pork Roast

1 (3½-pound) pork loin roast, boned,
    rolled, and tied
About 2 tablespoons soy sauce
1 teaspoon dried orange peel
1 teaspoon ground ginger
1 teaspoon dry mustard
½ teaspoon seasoned salt
½ teaspoon garlic powder
¼ teaspoon curry powder
2 tablespoons honey
2 tablespoons catsup
1 tablespoon wine vinegar

Brush roast with soy sauce. Combine orange peel and seasonings; rub on roast. Insert spit through center of roast so that meat is well balanced. Slide holding forks into each end of roast, and tighten securely. Insert meat thermometer at an angle into thickest part of roast; be sure end of thermometer does not touch fat or spit. Cook on rotisserie 4 inches above heat 1 hour.

Combine honey, catsup, and wine vinegar. Brush meat with sauce every 15 minutes for an additional 1½ hours of cooking or until thermometer registers 185° (about 2½ hours total cooking time). Yield: 8 to 10 servings.

Barbecued Pork Roast

1 (5-pound) pork shoulder roast
½ cup catsup
1 (10¾-ounce) can tomato soup,
    undiluted
1⅓ cups water
⅓ cup vinegar
½ cup sugar
10 bay leaves
10 whole cloves or 1 tablespoon ground
    cloves
Salt and pepper to taste

Place pork roast in a broiler pan lined with foil; bake at 325° about 3½ hours.

Combine remaining ingredients to make a sauce. Baste roast frequently with sauce during last 30 minutes of baking. Leftover sauce can be used over ribs or hamburgers. Yield: about 8 servings.

Barbecued Ham

1 (1-inch) fully cooked center-cut ham
    slice
½ cup ginger ale
½ cup orange juice
¼ cup firmly packed brown sugar
1 tablespoon salad oil
1½ teaspoons wine vinegar
1 teaspoon dry mustard
¼ teaspoon ground ginger
⅛ teaspoon ground cloves

Slash edges of ham to prevent curling; pierce both sides of ham with fork. Place in a shallow pan. Combine remaining ingredients, and pour over ham. Refrigerate overnight. Grill over hot coals about 15 minutes on each side, basting often with marinade. Yield: 4 to 5 servings.

Asparagus Ham Bake

½ cup herb-seasoned stuffing mix, divided
1 tablespoon melted butter or margarine
2 cups diced cooked ham
2 cups cut cooked asparagus
Cheese Sauce

Sprinkle 3 tablespoons stuffing mix in a 2-quart casserole. Combine remaining stuffing and butter; set aside.

Layer half of ham, half of asparagus, and half of Cheese Sauce over stuffing. Repeat layers. Sprinkle reserved stuffing on top. Bake at 350° for 30 minutes. Yield: about 6 servings.

Cheese Sauce:

1 (10¾-ounce) can cream of celery soup,
    undiluted
1⅓ cups milk
¼ cup chopped onion
¼ teaspoon rosemary
¼ teaspoon marjoram
½ cup shredded Cheddar cheese

Combine all ingredients except cheese in a saucepan; heat to boiling. Blend in cheese, stirring until melted. Yield: about 3 cups.

Ginger Ale Ham

1 (3½-to 4-pound) fully cooked boneless
   ham
2 cups ginger ale
1 (8¼-ounce) can pineapple slices,
   drained

Place ham on a large sheet of aluminum foil; place in an open roasting pan. Pour ginger ale over ham. Wrap foil tightly around ham.

Bake at 375° about 45 minutes. Unwrap; arrange pineapple on top of ham. Bake 15 minutes longer. Yield: 6 to 8 servings.

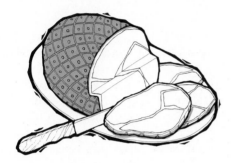

Country Ham

1 (10- to 15-pound) country ham
4 quarts ginger ale

Put ham in a clean can or very large pot filled with hot water (just below the boiling point). Let boil 10 or 15 minutes. This step gives the ham a good cleaning and removes excess salt from the outside. Remove ham, and discard water.

Place ham in can, and fill half full with hot water. Add ginger ale, and put top loosely on can. Bring to a full rolling boil; boil 30 minutes. (The ginger ale helps to bring out the flavor of the ham.)

Place about 4 thicknesses of newspaper on the floor, and set ham (still in can) on papers. Press can lid on tightly; pull papers around sides and top of can, and tie with string. Cover with quilts or blankets. Let sit for 10 to 14 hours according to size of ham. (A 12- to 13-pound ham requires about 10 hours.) Remove skin, and cut fat from ham.

Slices of country ham can be fried or baked. Yield: 24 to 30 servings.

Country Ham and Grits with Red-Eye Gravy

Grits
Country ham
Strong black coffee

Prepare grits according to package directions. Slice boiled country ham about ¼ to ½ inch thick. Cut gashes in fat to keep ham from curling. Place slices in a heavy skillet and cook slowly, turning several times; cook until ham is brown. Add a small amount of water to the skillet; let ham simmer a few minutes.

Remove ham from pan, and keep warm. For each pound of ham, add ¼ cup strong black coffee to pan drippings; bring to a boil, stirring well. Serve gravy over grits and ham.

Ham Quiche

Pastry for 9-inch quiche pan or piepan
Dried peas or beans
4 eggs, beaten
½ to ¾ cup milk
¼ teaspoon pepper
¼ teaspoon baking powder
1½ cups ground cooked ham
1 cup shredded Swiss or Cheddar cheese
¼ cup chopped green pepper (optional)
¼ cup chopped onion (optional)

Line a 9-inch quiche pan with pastry, and trim off excess around edge of pan. Place a piece of buttered aluminum foil, buttered side down, over pastry; gently press into pastry shell. This will keep the sides of the shell from collapsing.

Cover foil with a layer of dried peas or beans. Bake at 400° for 10 minutes; remove foil and peas. Prick shell, and bake 3 to 5 additional minutes or until lightly browned. Cool.

Combine eggs, milk, pepper, and baking powder; beat well. Stir in ham and cheese; add green pepper and onion, if desired. Spoon custard into shell, and bake at 425° for 25 to 30 minutes or until firm in center. Yield: one 9-inch quiche.

Ham on the Grill

1   *(1¾-inch-thick) slice fully cooked
    center-cut ham (about 3½ pounds)*
    Whole cloves (optional)
½   *cup dry sherry*
¼   *cup melted butter or margarine*

Score ham in a diamond pattern at ½-inch intervals; stud with whole cloves, if desired. Place ham in a heavy-duty plastic bag in a shallow pan; add sherry, and fasten bag securely. Refrigerate overnight, turning once. Drain, reserving sherry for basting during grilling.

Brush ham with melted butter, and place on grill 4 to 6 inches from coals. Grill 15 to 20 minutes on each side, basting frequently with butter and reserved sherry. Yield: 8 servings.

Fruit-Stuffed Fresh Ham

1   *(10- to 12-pound) bone-in fresh ham*
½   *to 1 cup pitted dried prunes*
½   *to 1 cup dried apricots*
2   *teaspoons salt*
⅛   *teaspoon pepper*
    Fresh Ham Gravy.

Wipe ham with damp paper towels. Trim fat, leaving ¼-inch thickness; score fat into 1-inch diamonds. Make deep slits all the way through to the bone, spacing slits 2 to 3 inches apart.

Using fingers, pack prunes and apricots alternately into slits in ham. Rub ham with salt and pepper. Insert meat thermometer, being careful to avoid slits; end should not touch fruit, fat, or bone.

Place ham, fat side up, on rack in a shallow roasting pan. Bake, uncovered, at 325° for 2 hours. Drain off fat, and discard. Pour 1 cup water over ham; return to oven. Continue baking until meat thermometer registers 170° (4½ to 5 hours); pour 1 cup water over ham every 30 minutes. Reserve pan drippings for Fresh Ham Gravy. Yield: 10 to 12 servings.

Fresh Ham Gravy:

2   *cups pan drippings*
½   *cup all-purpose flour*
2   *(13¾-ounce) cans clear chicken broth,
    undiluted and divided*
    Salt to taste

Skim fat from drippings, and discard. Combine flour and 1 cup chicken broth; stir until smooth, and set aside. Combine remaining broth and pan drippings in a saucepan; bring to a boil. Gradually add flour mixture; cook, stirring constantly, until mixture returns to a boil and thickens. Simmer 5 minutes, stirring occasionally. Add salt. Yield: about 4½ cups.

★ Golden Glazed Ham

1   *(6- to 7-pound) uncooked ham*
1   *(6-ounce) can frozen orange juice
     concentrate, undiluted*
1¼   *cups firmly packed brown sugar*
½   *cup steak sauce*
     Pineapple slices (optional)

Place ham fat side up, on a large piece of aluminum foil in a shallow roasting pan. Combine remaining ingredients except pineapple slices. Pour half of glaze mixture over ham. Wrap foil loosely around ham. Bake at 325° for 3 to 3½ hours (about 30 minutes per pound).

Remove ham from oven about 30 minutes before cooking time is up. Score ham in a diamond pattern, making cuts ¼ inch deep in ham fat. Spoon remaining glaze mixture over ham, and return ham to oven. Bake, uncovered, at 400° for 30 minutes, basting frequently. Garnish with pineapple slices, if desired. Yield: 12 to 14 servings.

Pineapple Upside-Down Ham Loaf

- ¼ cup firmly packed brown sugar
- 1 teaspoon dry mustard
- 3 tablespoons vinegar
- 3 slices canned pineapple, drained
- 3 maraschino cherries
- 2 cups ground ham
- 1 cup ground lean pork
- 2 eggs, slightly beaten
- 1 cup milk
- 1 cup cracker crumbs
- ¼ teaspoon salt
- ⅛ teaspoon pepper
- 1 tablespoon minced onion

Combine brown sugar, mustard, and vinegar; blend until smooth. Pour into a 9- x 5- x 3-inch loafpan. Place pineapple slices in a row in brown sugar mixture. Put a cherry in center of each.

Combine remaining ingredients, and spoon on top of pineapple slices. Bake at 350° for 1½ hours. Let stand 5 minutes; drain off excess drippings. Invert onto serving platter. Yield: about 8 servings.

Caribbean Ham Steak

- 1 (2-inch) fully cooked center-cut ham slice
- ¾ cup grenadine
- 2 tablespoons cider vinegar
- 2 teaspoons dry mustard
- 1 large orange
- 3 limes, cut into wedges

Place ham slice in a shallow baking dish or pan. Combine grenadine, vinegar, and mustard; pour over ham. Bake at 325° for 1 hour, basting frequently. Remove ham to warm serving dish.

Peel orange and slice diagonally; place in sauce. Cook over low heat about 1 minute. Spoon sauce and orange slices over ham. Garnish with lime wedges. Yield: 6 servings.

Ham Croquettes

- 2 cups ground cooked ham
- ¾ to 1 cup mashed potatoes
- 1 tablespoon chopped onion
- 1 tablespoon chopped parsley
- Salt and pepper to taste
- 1 tablespoon water
- 1 egg
- Fine breadcrumbs
- Hot salad oil

Combine ham, potatoes, onion, parsley, salt, and pepper. Shape into 8 croquettes. Combine water and egg; beat well. Coat croquettes with egg, then with breadcrumbs. Deep fry in hot salad oil until golden brown. Yield: 8 servings.

Polish Sausage and Cabbage

- ½ medium-size head cabbage, coarsely shredded
- ½ cup chopped green pepper
- Salt and pepper to taste
- ¼ cup water
- 1 pound Polish sausage, cut in 1-inch slices

Combine cabbage and green pepper in a large skillet; season with salt and pepper. Add water, and heat until water begins to boil. Reduce heat, and place sausage on top of cabbage mixture. Cover and simmer about 15 minutes. Yield: 4 servings.

Sausage-Oyster Surprise

- 1 pint oysters, chopped
- 2 cups biscuit mix
- 1 pound mild bulk sausage, uncooked and crumbled

Drain oysters, reserving liquid. Add enough water to oyster liquid to make ½ cup; stir into biscuit mix. Add oysters, stirring gently. Spread in a well-greased 10-inch piepan. Sprinkle sausage over top. Bake at 350° for 20 to 25 minutes. Yield: 8 servings.

★
Sausage Breakfast Casserole

    1   *pound bulk sausage*
    6   *slices white bread, crusts removed*
    Softened butter or margarine
    1½ *cups shredded Longhorn cheese*
    5   *eggs*
    2   *cups half-and-half*
    1   *teaspoon salt*
    1   *teaspoon dry mustard*

Cook sausage over medium heat until done, stirring to crumble well. Drain sausage on paper towels; set aside.

Spread each slice of bread with butter; cut into cubes. Place bread cubes in a 13- x 9- x 2-inch baking pan; sprinkle with sausage, and top with cheese.

Combine remaining ingredients; beat well, and pour over mixture in baking pan. Chill at least 8 hours; remove from refrigerator. Bake at 350° for 40 to 50 minutes. Yield: 6 servings.

Sausage Strata

    1   *pound hot bulk sausage*
    6   *slices white bread, crusts removed*
    6   *slices Swiss cheese*
    1   *cup milk*
    1   *cup half-and-half*
    4   *eggs, beaten*
    ½   *teaspoon salt*
    ½   *teaspoon pepper*
    ¼   *teaspoon rosemary*
    ¼   *teaspoon thyme*
    ¼   *teaspoon sage*
    Pinch of nutmeg
    1   *teaspoon Worcestershire sauce*
    1   *teaspoon prepared mustard*
    Chopped parsley or chives

Crumble sausage in a skillet, and cook until done. Drain on paper towels. Place bread slices in a buttered 13- x 9- x 2-inch baking dish, and cover with cheese. Top with sausage.

Combine remaining ingredients except parsley in a mixing bowl; pour over sausage. Sprinkle with parsley. Bake at 350° for 50 minutes. Yield: 6 servings.

Smokies with Caraway Kraut

    3   *cups coarsely chopped onion*
    1   *clove garlic, minced*
    2   *tablespoons melted shortening*
    1   *(16-ounce) can sauerkraut*
    1   *tablespoon paprika*
    2   *teaspoons sugar*
    1   *teaspoon caraway seeds*
    1   *teaspoon salt*
    ⅛   *teaspoon pepper*
    1   *pound smoked sausage links, cut
        diagonally into thirds*

Sauté onions and garlic in shortening. Add remaining ingredients except sausage; cover and simmer over low heat 20 minutes. Add sausage; cover and simmer 10 minutes. Yield: about 4 to 6 servings.

Deep-Dish Pizza

    1   *package dry yeast*
    1½ *cups warm water (105° to 115°),
        divided*
    1   *teaspoon salt*
    About 4 cups all-purpose flour
    1   *(15-ounce) can tomato sauce*
    Chopped onion
    Grated Parmesan cheese
    Ground oregano
    1   *pound Italian sausage, cooked and cut
        into ¼-inch slices*
    1   *pound shredded mozzarella cheese*

Dissolve yeast in 1 cup water; add salt and enough flour to make a doughlike consistency. Add remaining ½ cup water; add more flour until dough is no longer sticky.

Turn dough out on a floured surface, and knead gently 6 to 8 times; let dough rest 5 minutes. Press evenly into a 15- x 10- x 1-inch pan or into 2 (9-inch) cakepans.

Spread tomato sauce over dough; sprinkle with onion, Parmesan cheese, and oregano. Arrange sausage on top; sprinkle mozzarella cheese over all. Bake at 425° for 30 minutes. Let stand 10 minutes before cutting. Yield: 1 (15- x 10- x 1-inch) or 2 (9-inch) thick-crust pizzas.

Note: Crust may be made ahead. Bake at 350° for 5 minutes, and set aside until needed. Fill as desired; alternate garnishes might be ground beef, pepperoni, mushrooms, bacon, or any combination. Bake at 425° for 20 to 25 minutes.

Barbecued Franks

¼   cup chopped onion
    Salad oil
1   cup catsup
½   cup water
2   tablespoons brown sugar
½   teaspoon salt
    Dash of pepper
2   tablespoons vinegar
¼   cup lemon juice
3   tablespoons Worcestershire sauce
½   teaspoon prepared mustard
½   cup chopped celery
1   pound frankfurters, cut in half

Brown onion in oil; add remaining ingredients except franks. Cover and simmer 20 minutes. Add franks, and simmer 15 minutes. Yield: 4 servings.

Franks in Buns

2   cups thinly sliced frankfurters
¼   cup shredded Cheddar cheese
1½   teaspoons prepared mustard
2   hard-cooked eggs, chopped
1   teaspoon Worcestershire sauce
2   tablespoons pickle relish
¼   teaspoon garlic salt
2   tablespoons mayonnaise
¼   cup chili sauce
8   to 10 hot dog buns

Place frankfurters in a saucepan; cover with water, and simmer 10 minutes. Drain. Combine frankfurters and next 8 ingredients; spoon into buns. Place under broiler and broil 5 to 8 minutes, or wrap tightly in aluminum foil and grill about 15 minutes. Yield: 4 to 5 servings.

Kentucky Franks

1   (20-ounce) bottle catsup
5   tablespoons lemon juice
⅓   cup bourbon
3   tablespoons vinegar
2   tablespoons Worcestershire sauce
2   tablespoons instant minced onion
1   clove garlic, pressed
5   drops liquid smoke
2   teaspoons salt
½   teaspoon pepper
1   teaspoon dry mustard
1   cup firmly packed brown sugar
4   (12-ounce) packages frankfurters, cut in
     thirds

Combine all ingredients except frankfurters in a large skillet; stir until sugar is dissolved. Add frankfurters; simmer about 1 hour. Yield: about 10 servings.

Frank and Bean Bake

1   pound frankfurters
2   (16-ounce) cans pork and beans
1   cup shredded Cheddar cheese
2   tablespoons brown sugar
2   teaspoons parsley flakes
½   teaspoon onion salt
1   (3-ounce) can French-fried onions,
     divided

Combine all ingredients except half of onion rings. Spoon mixture into a lightly greased 1½-quart casserole. Bake at 350° for 25 minutes. Top with remaining onions, and bake an additional 5 minutes. Yield: 6 servings.

Kraut-Pork Pinwheel

 1 *pound bulk sausage*
 ½ *cup fine dry breadcrumbs*
 1 *egg, slightly beaten*
 1 *teaspoon salt*
 Dash of pepper
 ¼ *teaspoon Worcestershire sauce*
 1 *(16-ounce) can chopped sauerkraut,*
     drained
 ¼ *cup chopped onion*
 5 *slices bacon, halved*

Combine sausage, breadcrumbs, egg, salt, pepper, and Worcestershire sauce. Pat meat mixture into a 10- x 7-inch rectangle on waxed paper.

Combine sauerkraut and onion; spread evenly over meat. Roll up jellyroll fashion, starting at narrow side. Place loaf in a shallow baking dish. Arrange bacon slices across top. Bake at 350° for 40 to 45 minutes. Yield: 8 servings.

Sweet-and-Sour Pork

 2 *pounds boneless pork*
 1 *egg, beaten*
 2 *tablespoons all-purpose flour*
 1 *teaspoon salt*
 ¼ *teaspoon pepper*
 ¾ *cup salad oil*
 1 *clove garlic, crushed*
 3 *green peppers, cut into 1-inch pieces*
 1 *(20-ounce) can pineapple chunks,*
     undrained
 3 *tablespoons cornstarch*
 ½ *cup sugar*
 ½ *cup chicken broth*
 ½ *cup vinegar*
 2 *teaspoons soy sauce*
 Hot cooked rice

Trim fat from pork, and cut meat into 1-inch cubes. Combine egg, flour, salt, and pepper; mix well. Pour batter over pork cubes, coating well.

Heat salad oil and garlic in a heavy skillet over medium heat; add pork, one piece at a time, and cook until golden brown on all sides. Drain off pan drippings, reserving 1 tablespoon.

Add 1 tablespoon pan drippings, green pepper, and undrained pineapple to pork in skillet. Simmer over low heat 5 minutes. Combine cornstarch and sugar, and stir in chicken broth, vinegar, and soy sauce; add to skillet. Cook over low heat, stirring constantly, until sauce is smooth and thickened. Serve over rice. Yield: 6 to 8 servings.

★
Korean Pork Platter

 2 *pounds boneless lean pork, cut into*
     1-inch cubes
 2 *tablespoons all-purpose flour*
 Salt to taste
 ¼ *cup salad oil, divided*
 1 *tablespoon curry powder*
 ⅓ *cup soy sauce*
 ½ *cup water*
 2 *large onions, sliced*
 2 *cups sliced celery*
 1 *(9-ounce) package frozen cut green*
     beans, partially thawed
 2 *medium-size yellow squash, sliced*
 1 *teaspoon celery salt*
 ¼ *cup water*

Dredge pork in flour, and season with salt; brown in 2 tablespoons hot oil, and stir in curry powder. Add soy sauce and ½ cup water to pork; cover and simmer over low heat 1 hour and 15 minutes or until pork is tender.

Sauté onion in remaining oil 3 minutes, stirring constantly; push to one side. Add celery and cook 3 minutes, stirring constantly; push to one side. Add green beans and squash; sprinkle with celery salt. Add ¼ cup water; cover and steam 10 minutes or until vegetables are tender but crisp. Spoon vegetables onto a large platter, and top with pork. Yield: 6 servings.

Peachtree Ribs

    4   pounds spareribs
    1   (7¾-ounce) jar strained junior peaches
    ⅓   cup catsup
    ⅓   cup vinegar
    2   tablespoons soy sauce
    ½   cup firmly packed brown sugar
    2   cloves garlic, finely minced
    1   teaspoon ground ginger

Cut ribs into serving-size pieces, and place in a large pot. Cover with water, and bring to a boil; reduce heat, and simmer until tender (40 to 50 minutes). Drain; place meat in a shallow baking pan.

Combine remaining ingredients, and pour over meat. Let marinate in refrigerator overnight. Drain well, reserving marinade.

Grill ribs over hot coals for 40 to 50 minutes, depending upon thickness. Baste with marinade frequently during cooking. Yield: 4 servings.

Stuffed Pork Rolls

    8   slices lean pork, about ⅜-inch thick
    Salt and pepper to taste
    8   pitted prunes
    8   thin apple wedges
    2   tablespoons melted butter or margarine
    1   cup boiling water
    1   cup beef or chicken broth
    ½   cup milk
    2   tablespoons all-purpose flour

Sprinkle pork slices with salt and pepper. Place 1 prune and 1 apple wedge on each slice; roll up, and secure with toothpick. Brown rolls in butter in a large skillet. Add boiling water; cover and simmer 45 minutes. Remove rolls to serving dish; remove toothpicks and discard. Keep rolls warm.

Add broth and milk to drippings in skillet, and bring to a boil. Blend flour with a small amount of broth mixture to make a smooth paste. Add to skillet; bring to a boil, stirring until thickened and smooth. Simmer about 5 minutes. Serve gravy over pork rolls. Yield: 4 servings.

Sweet-and-Sour Spareribs

    2   pounds spareribs
    1⅔ cups water, divided
    Salad oil
    ¼   cup chopped onion
    1   cup drained pineapple chunks
    ¾   cup sugar
    ¼   cup soy sauce
    ⅓   cup vinegar
    3   tablespoons cornstarch

Simmer ribs in 1 cup water 20 minutes or until ribs are tender; drain. Deep fry in oil until crisp and brown; drain.

Sauté onion and pineapple 1 minute in 2 tablespoons oil; drain. Combine sugar, soy sauce, vinegar, and ⅔ cup water. Blend in cornstarch; cook over low heat, stirring constantly, until smooth and thickened. Stir in onion and pineapple; add spareribs, and heat thoroughly. Yield: 4 servings.

Cantonese Pork

    2   pounds boneless pork shoulder, cut in ½-inch cubes
    1   tablespoon shortening or bacon drippings
    1½ cups water
    2   tablespoons soy sauce
    1   (1⅜-ounce) package dry onion soup mix
    2   tablespoons cornstarch
    ¼   cup water
    1   cup sliced mushrooms
    1   (8-ounce) can water chestnuts, drained and sliced
    1   (9-ounce) package frozen Italian green beans

Brown pork cubes in shortening in a large skillet. Combine 1½ cups water, soy sauce, and soup mix; stir into pork. Cover and cook over low heat about 30 minutes or until pork is tender.

Blend cornstarch and ¼ cup water until smooth. Add to meat mixture; cook until thickened, stirring constantly. Stir in mushrooms, water chestnuts, and green beans. Cover and cook 7 minutes. Yield: about 6 to 8 servings.

★ Pork Loaf

2 *pounds ground pork*
1 *pound ground cooked ham*
1 *egg, beaten*
1 *cup breadcrumbs*
½ *cup milk*
3 *tablespoons tomato soup*
½ *teaspoon paprika*
¼ *teaspoon salt*
1 *medium-size onion, sliced*
Mustard Sauce

Combine all ingredients except onion and Mustard Sauce. Shape into a loaf in a 10- x 6- x 2-inch baking dish; arrange onion slices over top. Bake at 350° for 1½ hours. Baste occasionally with a few tablespoons of hot water. Serve with Mustard Sauce. Yield: about 8 servings.

Mustard Sauce:

1 *(10¾-ounce) can minus 3 tablespoons tomato soup, undiluted*
½ *cup prepared mustard*
½ *cup butter or margarine*
½ *cup vinegar*
½ *cup sugar*
3 *egg yolks, beaten*

Combine all ingredients. Cook over low heat, stirring occasionally, until thickened. Serve hot. May be kept in refrigerator indefinitely. Yield: about 2½ cups.

Stuffed Peppers Paprika

5 *to 6 medium-size green peppers*
1 *pound lean ground pork*
½ *cup chopped onion*
1 *clove garlic, minced*
2 *teaspoons salt*
2 *teaspoons paprika*
¼ *teaspoon black pepper*
1½ *cups cooked rice*
1 *egg, beaten*
1 *(6-ounce) can tomato paste*
1½ *cups water*
Parsley (optional)

Cut off top of each green pepper; remove seeds. Cook peppers in boiling salted water to cover 5 minutes; drain.

Combine pork, onion, and garlic in a skillet; cook until pork is browned. Drain and cool. Add salt, paprika, black pepper, rice, and egg to pork mixture; mix well.

Combine tomato paste and water; add 1 cup to pork mixture. Stuff peppers with pork mixture, and place in a shallow baking dish. Spoon remaining tomato mixture over peppers. Bake at 375° for 25 to 30 minutes. Garnish with parsley, if desired. Yield: about 5 to 6 servings.

Smokey Sticks

1 *pound lean ground beef*
1 *tablespoon brown sugar*
1 *teaspoon instant minced onion*
1 *tablespoon lemon juice*
¾ *teaspoon salt*
¼ *teaspoon pepper*
Dash of garlic powder
1 *(12-ounce) package smoked sausage links*
Onion salt

Combine hamburger and next 6 ingredients, mixing well. Shape hamburger mixture around sausage links, and sprinkle with onion salt. Grill over medium heat about 20 minutes or until done, turning often. Yield: 8 servings.

Curry Kabobs

Canadian bacon, cut into 1½-inch cubes
Pineapple cubes
Maraschino cherries
Cherry tomatoes
Green pepper, cut into 1-inch squares
Zucchini, cut into ½-inch slices
Curry Sauce

Alternate meat, fruits, and vegetables on skewers. Brush with Curry Sauce. Grill 5 to 10 minutes over medium heat, basting with Sauce and turning occasionally.

Curry Sauce:

¼ *cup honey*
2 *tablespoons butter or margarine*
1 *tablespoon soy sauce*
¾ *teaspoon curry powder*
½ *teaspoon Dijon mustard*

Combine ingredients in a saucepan; cook over medium heat until butter melts, stirring to blend. Yield: about ⅓ cup.

Other Variations: Kabobs may be made of a variety of other ingredients such as unpeeled orange wedges, Vienna sausage, frankfurters, fresh mushroom caps, and water chestnuts.

★
Mexicali Liver and Onions

1 *cup all-purpose flour*
1½ *teaspoons salt*
¼ *teaspoon pepper*
½ *teaspoon paprika*
1½ *pounds beef liver, cut into 2-inch pieces*
3 *to 4 cloves garlic, crushed*
1 *jalapeño pepper, thinly sliced*
3 *to 4 tablespoons salad oil*
2 *medium-size onions, sliced*
2 *to 3 cups water*

Combine flour, salt, pepper, and paprika in a plastic bag; add liver and shake until well coated with flour. Set aside.

Sauté garlic and jalapeño pepper in salad oil until tender. Add liver, and brown slowly on both sides. Place onion slices on top of liver. Add water; cover and simmer over low heat 30 to 40 minutes, stirring occasionally. Yield: 6 servings.

Liver Patties

1½ *pounds beef liver*
½ *cup minced onion*
2 *eggs, well beaten*
¾ *teaspoon salt*
⅛ *teaspoon pepper*
2 *tablespoons all-purpose flour*
8 *slices bacon, partially cooked*

Cover liver with boiling water in a large skillet; simmer 5 minutes. Remove from skillet, and grind liver. Combine with remaining ingredients except bacon. Shape into 8 patties; wrap each with a slice of bacon, and fasten with a toothpick. Cook in a skillet over low heat about 5 minutes on each side or until browned. Yield: 8 servings.

Liver Tyrolian

1 *to 1½ pounds chicken livers or calves liver*
Salt and pepper to taste
All-purpose flour
Hot salad oil
½ *cup chopped onion*
2 *tablespoons tarragon vinegar*
½ *cup chicken broth*
1 *tablespoon all-purpose flour*
½ *cup commercial sour cream*

Sprinkle livers with salt and pepper; dredge with flour. Brown in ¼ inch of hot oil; remove from skillet, and drain well. Reserve 2 tablespoons pan drippings. Keep livers warm in oven while preparing sauce.

Sauté onion in reserved drippings; add vinegar, and cook until evaporated. Add broth, stirring to loosen pan particles; simmer 2 to 3 minutes.

Combine 1 tablespoon flour and sour cream; add to broth. Heat thoroughly, stirring constantly; do not boil. Pour over livers. Yield: 4 to 5 servings.

Creamy Liver

¼   to ½ cup all-purpose flour
1   teaspoon salt
¼   teaspoon pepper
1   pound sliced calves liver
3   tablespoons melted butter or margarine
1   small onion, thinly sliced and separated
      into rings
2   cloves garlic, minced
½   to 1 cup sliced mushrooms
1   (10¾-ounce) can cream of mushroom
      soup, undiluted
3   tablespoons chopped parsley
1   teaspoon basil
Milk (optional)
Cooked noodles

Combine flour, salt, and pepper. Dredge liver in seasoned flour. Brown on both sides in butter in a skillet over medium heat; remove from skillet, and set aside.

Add onion, garlic, and mushrooms to skillet; cook about 1 minute. Stir in soup, parsley, and basil, scraping up browned bits from pan. Add milk if a thinner sauce is desired.

Return liver to skillet; cover and simmer 2 to 3 minutes or until thoroughly heated. Serve over cooked noodles. Yield: 4 to 6 servings.

Liver Loaf

1   pound beef liver
½   pound bulk sausage
1   cup breadcrumbs
2   eggs, beaten
1   teaspoon Worcestershire sauce
1   teaspoon lemon juice
1   teaspoon salt
2   to 3 slices bacon

Cover liver with boiling water, and simmer 5 minutes. Drain, reserving ½ cup liquid; cool. Chop liver; add sausage, breadcrumbs, eggs, Worcestershire sauce, lemon juice, salt, and reserved stock, mixing thoroughly.

Press into an 8- x 4- x 2½-inch loafpan. Top with bacon, and bake at 350° for 45 minutes. Broil 2 to 3 minutes to crisp bacon slices. Yield: 4 to 6 servings.

Liver and Rice Casserole

½   cup uncooked regular rice
2¾ cups boiling water, divided
1   medium-size onion, chopped
3   tablespoons melted butter
1   pound beef liver, cubed
2   tablespoons salad oil
1   (16-ounce) can stewed tomatoes
Salt and pepper to taste

Cook rice in 2 cups boiling water 5 minutes; drain and rinse with cold water. Brown onion in butter, and place in a 2-quart casserole.

Brown liver in oil; drain and add to casserole. Cover with rice, tomatoes, and remaining ¾ cup water. Season with salt and pepper. Bake at 400° for 1 hour. Yield: 6 servings.

Easy Veal Parmigiana

1   (10¾-ounce) can tomato soup,
      undiluted
1   (8-ounce) can tomato sauce
1   (6-ounce) can tomato paste
½   cup black coffee
¼   teaspoon basil leaves, crushed
Pepper to taste
1   (16-ounce) package frozen breaded veal
      cutlets
6   tablespoons hot salad oil
1   medium-size onion, chopped
2   cloves garlic, minced
2   cups shredded mozzarella cheese
Grated Parmesan cheese to taste
Hot cooked spaghetti (optional)

Combine soup, tomato sauce, tomato paste, coffee, basil, and pepper in a saucepan; simmer 30 minutes.

Brown cutlets on both sides in oil, and drain well on paper towels; reserve drippings. Sauté onion and garlic in reserved drippings until crisp-tender.

Place cutlets in a lightly greased 13- x 9- x 2-inch baking pan. Pour two-thirds of sauce over cutlets; sprinkle with mozzarella cheese. Pour remaining sauce over cheese, and sprinkle with Parmesan. Bake at 375° for 30 minutes. Serve over spaghetti, if desired. Yield: 10 servings.

Liver and Lima Casserole

1 *pound beef liver, cut in 1-inch pieces*
2 *tablespoons salad oil*
1 *chopped onion*
1 *cup chopped celery*
1 *(10¾-ounce) can cream of mushroom soup, undiluted*
1 *cup shredded Cheddar cheese*
2 *cups cooked lima beans*
¼ *cup milk*

Brown liver in oil. Add onion and celery; simmer 10 minutes. Remove from heat, and stir in remaining ingredients. Spoon mixture into a 1½-quart casserole. Bake at 300° for 30 minutes. Yield: about 4 servings.

Veal with Mushrooms and Peppers

¼ *cup salad oil*
¼ *cup lemon juice*
1 *teaspoon salt*
1 *teaspoon paprika*
1 *teaspoon prepared mustard*
¼ *teaspoon ground nutmeg*
1 *clove garlic, minced*
1½ *pounds veal sirloin steak or shoulder, cut into serving-size pieces*
¼ *cup all-purpose flour*
3 *tablespoons melted butter or margarine*
1⅓ *cups chicken broth*
1 *medium-size green pepper, seeded and cut into rings*
1 *cup sliced fresh mushrooms*
1 *medium-size onion, sliced and separated into rings*

Combine oil, lemon juice, salt, paprika, mustard, nutmeg, and garlic. Pour marinade over veal; marinate 15 minutes. Remove veal from marinade, reserving marinade.

Dredge veal in flour; brown on both sides in butter. Place veal in a 2-quart casserole. Combine marinade, broth, green pepper, and mushrooms; pour over veal. Cover and bake at 350° for 30 minutes. Remove cover; top with onion rings. Bake, uncovered, 15 minutes. Yield: 4 servings.

★ Lemon Veal

16 *veal scallops*
Salt and pepper to taste
All-purpose flour
2 *tablespoons olive oil*
2 *tablespoons melted butter or margarine*
1 *cup beef stock*
Juice of 2 lemons
2 *lemons, thinly sliced*

Sprinkle veal with salt and pepper; dredge in flour. Heat olive oil and butter in a skillet; brown veal slowly on both sides.

Remove veal from skillet; drain off excess fat. Add beef stock and lemon juice; heat thoroughly. Add veal and top with lemon slices; cover. Simmer slowly until beef stock is reduced by two-thirds, about 20 to 30 minutes. Yield: 8 servings.

Veal Cordon Bleu

3 *(⅓-inch-thick) boneless veal cutlets*
Salt and pepper to taste
6 *thin slices boiled ham*
6 *slices mozzarella or American cheese*
½ *cup butter or margarine*
6 *lemon wedges*
6 *sprigs parsley*

Cut each cutlet in half. Place cutlets on a sheet of waxed paper; flatten to ¼-inch thickness, using a meat mallet or rolling pin. Season with salt and pepper.

Place 1 slice ham and 1 slice cheese on each cutlet. Fold ends toward center, and overlap slightly; secure with toothpicks. Melt butter in a large skillet over medium heat; add veal. Brown on all sides, turning gently. Garnish with lemon wedges and parsley. Yield: 6 servings.

Veal Scallopini

  2 *to 3 large green peppers, cut into strips*
  ¼ *cup salad oil*
  2 *pounds veal cutlets or steaks*
     Salt and pepper to taste
  1 *(28-ounce) can whole tomatoes*
  1 *(4-ounce) can whole mushrooms,*
     undrained
  ½ *cup dry red wine*
  1 *clove garlic, crushed*
     Hot cooked spaghetti (optional)

Sauté green pepper in hot salad oil until tender; remove from skillet, and set aside.

Season veal with salt and pepper; brown on both sides in salad oil. Add tomatoes, mushrooms, wine, garlic, and green pepper.

Simmer, uncovered, 1 hour or until meat is tender. Season with salt and pepper. Serve over spaghetti, if desired. Yield: 6 servings.

★
Wiener Schnitzel

  2 *to 3 pounds (⅓-inch-thick) boneless*
     veal cutlets
     Salt and pepper to taste
  ½ *to 1 cup all-purpose flour*
  3 *eggs, beaten*
 1½ *cups breadcrumbs*
     Salad oil
     Lemon slices
     Parsley sprigs

Place cutlets on a sheet of waxed paper; using a meat mallet or rolling pin, flatten to ¼-inch thickness. If cutlets are too large for individual servings, cut into 2 or 3 pieces.

Season cutlets with salt and pepper. Dredge in flour, and dip in egg; then coat in breadcrumbs.

Deep fry cutlets in oil heated to 360° until breading turns dark gold and has broad ripples. Garnish with lemon and parsley; serve immediately. Yield: 6 to 8 servings.

Savory Lamb

  1 *(3-pound) boneless leg of lamb, cut into*
     1½-inch cubes
     Salt and pepper to taste
  ¼ *cup olive oil*
 1½ *cups minced onion*
  2 *cloves garlic, crushed*
  ½ *cup dry red wine*
  1 *(6-ounce) can tomato paste*
  2 *tablespoons wine vinegar*
  1 *teaspoon ground thyme*
     Hot cooked rice

Place lamb in a mixing bowl, and sprinkle with salt and pepper; add oil, and stir to coat meat cubes. Place lamb, onion, and garlic in a Dutch oven.

Combine wine, tomato paste, vinegar, and thyme; blend well, and spoon over meat. Cover and bake at 325° for 1½ to 2 hours, stirring occasionally. Serve over rice. Yield: 6 servings.

Lamb Shanks in Fruit-Wine Sauce

  4 *lamb shanks*
     All-purpose flour
  1 *cup red wine*
  1 *(8-ounce) package dried apricots, cooked*
     and drained
  1 *cup pitted prunes, cooked and drained*
  ¼ *cup golden seedless raisins*
  ¼ *cup sugar*
  2 *tablespoons vinegar*
  2 *tablespoons lemon juice*
  2 *tablespoons honey*
  2 *tablespoons salt*
  2 *tablespoons pepper*
  ½ *teaspoon ground cinnamon*
  ½ *teaspoon ground allspice*

Dredge lamb with flour, and place in a lightly greased 2-quart casserole. Cover and bake at 350° for 1½ hours.

Combine remaining ingredients in a saucepan; bring to a boil. Simmer fruit mixture about 4 to 6 minutes. Drain drippings from lamb; cover with fruit sauce. Cover and bake at 400° for 30 minutes. Yield: 4 servings.

Lamb à la King

½ cup sliced mushrooms
1 green pepper, chopped
3 tablespoons melted butter or margarine,
    divided
3 tablespoons all-purpose flour
1½ cups milk
1 egg yolk, well beaten
Salt and pepper to taste
2 cups chopped cooked lamb
2 tablespoons chopped pimiento
Toast or hot cooked rice

Sauté mushrooms and green pepper in 1 tablespoon butter; drain and set aside.

Combine remaining 2 tablespoons butter and flour in a saucepan; place over low heat, blending well. Gradually stir in milk; cook until smooth and thickened, stirring constantly.

Add a small amount of hot mixture to egg yolk, stirring well. Add egg yolk mixture to remaining hot mixture; cook over low heat 1 minute, stirring constantly. Season with salt and pepper.

Add mushrooms, green pepper, lamb, and pimiento to sauce. Heat thoroughly, and serve over toast. Yield: 4 to 6 servings.

★
Orange Lamb Chops

6 (½-inch-thick) loin lamb chops
3 tablespoons hot salad oil
½ cup orange juice
¼ cup soy sauce
1½ teaspoons ground ginger
½ teaspoon garlic salt
¼ teaspoon pepper
½ teaspoon sugar
2 small oranges, peeled and sectioned

Trim excess fat from chops. Lightly brown chops in salad oil, and drain on paper towels. Place chops in a shallow baking dish.

Combine orange juice, soy sauce, ginger, garlic salt, pepper, and sugar; pour marinade over chops. Cover and refrigerate 2 hours, turning once. Remove from refrigerator, but do not uncover.

Bake at 350° for 45 to 55 minutes or until chops are tender. Place orange sections on chops. Replace cover; bake 10 minutes. Spoon sauce over chops before serving. Yield: 6 servings.

★
Shish Kabobs Italiano

½ cup commercial Italian salad dressing
¼ cup lemon juice
1 teaspoon crushed oregano
¼ teaspoon salt
⅛ teaspoon pepper
2 pounds boneless lamb, cut into 2-inch
    cubes
Salt to taste
Hot cooked rice

Combine salad dressing, lemon juice, oregano, ¼ teaspoon salt, and pepper; add meat. Cover; marinate 2 hours at room temperature or overnight in refrigerator, turning meat several times.

Remove meat from marinade; place on skewers. Add salt. Grill 20 to 25 minutes over medium heat, baste with marinade and turn occasionally. Serve on rice. Yield: 4 servings.

Spicy Lamb Pizza

1 pound ground lamb
¼ cup chopped green pepper
½ teaspoon chili powder
½ teaspoon salt
¼ teaspoon black pepper
1 (8½-ounce) package corn muffin mix
1 (10½-ounce) can pizza sauce with
    cheese
2 cups shredded mozzarella cheese

Combine lamb, green pepper, chili powder, salt, and black pepper; sauté until meat is brown and green pepper is tender. Drain.

Prepare corn muffin mix according to package directions. Spread batter evenly in a greased 12-inch pizza pan; sprinkle with meat mixture. Pour pizza sauce over meat, and top with mozzarella cheese.

Bake at 400° for 20 minutes. Let stand 5 minutes before cutting. Yield: 6 to 8 servings.

Venison Pot Roast

1   *(3- to 4-pound) venison roast*
1   *(8-ounce) can tomato herb sauce*
1   *cup water*
1   *(1⅜-ounce) package onion soup mix*
2   *teaspoons caraway seeds*
2   *bay leaves*

Trim fat from roast. Brown roast in an electric skillet. Combine remaining ingredients, and pour over roast. Cover and cook slowly (225°) for 2½ to 3 hours or until tender. Yield: 6 to 8 servings.

★ Venison Curry

1   *leg venison*
3   *(½-inch-thick) ham slices*
2   *large onions, chopped*
1   *cup raisins or currants*
6   *tablespoons curry powder*
2   *cups beef broth*
Cooked rice
¾   *cup diced celery*
4   *lemons or limes, halved*
Paprika
Chopped parsley

Place vension, fat side up, on rack in roasting pan. Do not season or add water. Roast, uncovered, at 325° for 20 to 25 minutes per pound. Allow to cool; cut into cubes. Fry ham, and reserve drippings; cut ham into cubes.

Sauté onion in reserved ham drippings until transparent. Add venison and ham; sauté an additional 5 minutes. Add raisins, curry powder, and beef broth; simmer, uncovered, 30 minutes. Add additional curry powder or broth if needed.

Spoon rice onto a large serving platter, shaping into a ring; add curry, and sprinkle with celery. Dip lemon halves in paprika, and sprinkle with parsley; use to garnish curry.

Serve curry with several of the following condiments: flaked coconut, almonds, pineapple chunks, chutney, bacon chips, banana slices, and chopped hard-cooked egg. Yield: about 10 to 12 servings.

Venison Schnitzel

6   *(¼-inch-thick) venison loin cutlets*
½   *cup all-purpose flour*
2   *teaspoons salt*
½   *teaspoon pepper*
2   *eggs, beaten*
¼   *cup milk*
1½   *cups breadcrumbs*
2   *teaspoons paprika*
Salad oil

To tenderize cutlets, pound with a meat mallet; set aside. Combine flour, salt, and pepper; combine eggs and milk. Combine breadcrumbs and paprika. Dredge cutlets in flour mixture, and dip into egg mixture; coat with breadcrumb mixture. Sauté in hot oil 2½ to 3 minutes on each side. Yield: about 6 servings.

Baked Doves with Apple Dressing

2   *cups water*
1   *teaspoon salt*
12   *doves*
Apple Dressing

Combine water and salt in a saucepan; add doves. Cover and simmer about 15 minutes or until tender. Drain, and set aside. Spoon Apple Dressing into a lightly greased baking dish; arrange doves, breast side down, on dressing. Bake at 375° for ½ hour or until birds are well browned. Yield: 12 servings.

Apple Dressing:

- 3 cups crumbled cornbread or breadcrumbs
- 2 cups peeled and chopped cooking apples
- ½ cup chopped celery
- 1 small onion, chopped
- ¼ cup melted butter or margarine
- ½ teaspoon salt
- ½ teaspoon poultry seasoning
- ½ cup milk

Combine all ingredients in a large mixing bowl. Yield: about 5 cups.

Doves with Wild Rice

- 12 medium-size doves, cleaned
- ½ teaspoon seasoned salt
- ½ teaspoon salt
- ¼ teaspoon freshly ground black pepper
- 1 cup water, divided
- ½ cup melted butter or margarine
- 2 tablespoons lemon juice
- 1 tablespoon all-purpose flour
- Cooked wild rice

Do not wash doves unless necessary, and then very quickly. Wipe with a clean, damp cloth or paper towels. Place doves in a large iron skillet. Combine salt and pepper; sprinkle over doves.

Pour ½ cup water into skillet; cover tightly, and steam over medium heat 20 minutes. Remove lid, and continue cooking until all water is gone.

Add butter and lemon juice to skillet. Continue cooking until doves are brown on all sides, turning occasionally; remove doves from skillet, and place in a casserole.

Add flour to drippings in skillet, stirring until smooth; cook over low heat until lightly browned. Add remaining ½ cup water; cook until thickened, stirring constantly. Pour gravy over doves; serve with wild rice. Yield: 6 servings.

★ Saucy Dove

- About 1 cup all-purpose flour
- 1¼ teaspoons salt
- ¼ teaspoon pepper
- ½ teaspoon poultry seasoning
- 12 to 15 medium-size doves, cleaned
- ½ cup melted butter or margarine
- 1 (8-ounce) can tomato sauce
- 1 (4-ounce) can mushroom stems and pieces, drained
- 1 large onion, diced
- About ⅓ cup milk

Combine flour, salt, pepper, and poultry seasoning in a bag; add doves and shake to coat birds well. Brown doves in butter in a large skillet. Add tomato sauce, mushrooms, and onion. Cover and cook over low heat until tender, about 20 minutes. Remove doves, and keep warm.

Add milk to pan drippings, scraping sides and bottom of skillet. Heat, stirring constantly, to make a sauce; spoon over doves. Yield: about 6 servings.

Note: Quail may be used instead of dove.

Doves with Orange Glaze

- 12 doves, cleaned
- Juice of 2 lemons
- ¾ cup Worcestershire sauce
- 1 teaspoon salt
- Dash of pepper
- 6 slices bacon, halved
- 1 (12-ounce) can frozen orange juice concentrate, thawed and undiluted

Place doves in a large bowl. Pour lemon juice over each bird; add Worcestershire sauce, salt, and pepper. Cover tightly, and marinate several hours, turning to marinate all sides.

Remove from marinade. Wrap each bird with bacon, securing with a toothpick. Place in a shallow roasting pan, and pour orange juice concentrate over birds. Bake at 350° for 1 hour, turning and basting birds frequently. Yield: 6 to 12 servings.

Stuffed Quail

    3 *cups breadcrumbs*
 1½ *cups crumbled cornbread*
    1 *tablespoon chopped parsley*
    2 *teaspoons salt*
    1 *teaspoon poultry seasoning*
  ⅛ *teaspoon pepper*
    2 *tablespoons melted butter or margarine*
  ¼ *cup finely chopped onion*
  ¼ *cup finely chopped celery*
    2 *eggs, beaten*
  ¼ *cup milk*
    1 *chicken bouillon cube*
    1 *cup boiling water*
    8 *quail, cleaned*
 Salt and pepper
    8 *oysters*
    8 *strips bacon*

Combine breadcrumbs, cornbread, parsley, salt, poultry seasoning, pepper, butter, onion, celery, eggs, and milk; blend well. Dissolve bouillon cube in boiling water; add to stuffing mixture, and set aside.

Sprinkle outside of quail with salt and pepper. Place an oyster in each quail; lightly stuff birds with stuffing mixture. Wrap each bird with a strip of bacon.

Spoon any leftover stuffing into a 10- x 6- x 2-inch baking dish; arrange quail over mixture. Cover and bake at 350° for 45 minutes; uncover, and bake 15 to 20 minutes or until done. Yield: 8 servings.

Southern Fried Quail

    6 *whole quail, cleaned and split down*
         back
 Salt and pepper
 All-purpose flour
 Salad oil
 Lemon slices
 Parsley

Spread quail open, and wipe dry with paper towels. Sprinkle with salt and pepper, and dredge in flour. Fill a deep, heavy skillet half full of salad oil; heat to 350°.

Cook quail in hot oil 5 minutes; cover and continue cooking until golden brown, turning once. Drain well. Serve birds on a hot platter, and garnish with lemon slices and parsley. Yield: 6 servings.

★ Country-Style Quail

    6 *quail, cleaned and split down back*
  ¼ *cup all-purpose flour*
    1 *teaspoon salt*
  ½ *teaspoon pepper*
 Salad oil
    3 *tablespoons all-purpose flour*
    1 *cup water*
  ½ *teaspoon salt*
 Hot cooked rice

Spread quail open; pat dry with paper towels. Combine ¼ cup flour, 1 teaspoon salt, and pepper; dredge quail in flour mixture. Heat ¼ inch of oil in skillet; place quail in skillet, and brown on both sides, turning once. Remove from skillet.

Combine 3 tablespoons flour, 1 cup water, and ½ teaspoon salt; stir until smooth. Blend into drippings in skillet. Place quail in gravy, and add enough water to half cover birds. Cover; reduce heat to low, and simmer 30 minutes or until tender. Serve birds, breast side up, over hot cooked rice. Yield: 6 servings.

Quail in Red Wine

6 quail, cleaned
Brandy
All-purpose flour
6 tablespoons butter or margarine
2 cups sliced mushrooms
¼ cup melted butter or margarine
1 cup consommé
1 cup dry red wine
1 stalk celery, quartered
Salt and pepper
Juice of 2 oranges, strained
Cooked wild rice (optional)

Rub quail with a cloth soaked in brandy, and dust with flour. Melt 6 tablespoons butter in a heavy skillet; add quail, and sauté 10 minutes.

Sauté mushrooms in ¼ cup butter; pour over quail. Add consommé, wine, celery, salt, and pepper. Cover and simmer 20 to 30 minutes or until quail is tender. Discard celery, if desired; stir in orange juice. Heat thoroughly. Serve with wild rice. Yield: 6 servings.

Standing Rib Roast

1 (6½-pound) standing rib roast
Salt and pepper to taste
12 large mushrooms
About 2 tablespoons salad oil
¼ cup sliced green onion
3 tablespoons melted butter or margarine
⅓ cup breadcrumbs
½ teaspoon dried dillweed
¼ teaspoon salt
Dash of Worcestershire sauce
Parsley (optional)
Cherry tomatoes (optional)

Sprinkle roast with salt and pepper. Place roast, fat side up, on rack in a shallow roasting pan. Insert meat thermometer, making certain end of thermometer does not touch fat or bone.

Bake at 325° as follows, depending on desired degree of doneness: rare, 27 minutes per pound or 140° on meat thermometer; medium, 30 minutes per pound or 160°; well done, 36 minutes per pound or 170°.

Let roast stand at room temperature about 15 minutes before carving

Cut off and discard about ¼ inch of mushroom stems. Gently rinse mushrooms, and pat dry. Remove and chop stems. Brush outside of caps with salad oil, and place in a buttered baking dish.

Sauté chopped mushrooms and onion in butter until tender; stir in breadcrumbs, dillweed, ¼ teaspoon salt, and Worcestershire. Stuff mushroom caps with breadcrumb mixture. Bake at 325° for 15 minutes; arrange around roast. Garnish roast with parsley and cherry tomatoes, if desired. Yield: 12 servings.

Creole Jambalaya

1 pound boneless pork, cut into ½-inch squares
2 medium-size onions, chopped
1 tablespoon butter or margarine
1 (about 1 pound) slice ham, chopped
2 cloves garlic, minced
2 teaspoons thyme
2 bay leaves
2 sprigs parsley, chopped
Pinch of ground cloves
1 pound smoked sausage links, cut into ¼-inch slices
2 quarts beef broth
1½ cups uncooked regular rice
½ teaspoon chili powder or red pepper flakes
½ teaspoon salt
Black pepper to taste

Sauté pork and onions in butter in a Dutch oven until lightly browned; stir frequently. Add ham, garlic, thyme, bay leaves, parsley, and cloves; cook 5 minutes. Add sausage, and cook 5 minutes.

Add broth to sausage mixture and bring to a boil. Stir in rice, chili powder, salt, and pepper. Cook 30 minutes or until rice is done. Yield: 6 to 8 servings.

Pies and Pastry

How do you choose a filling for a homemade pie? The decision is a hard one, for each has its own appeal. A slice of pecan pie or a bowl of spicy deep-dish apple pie can warm even the coldest winter night. Summertime roadside markets and backyard gardens offer any number of fresh fruits to make delicious mouth-watering pies. Top them with a lattice crust, or a second pastry—or, of course, a scoop of ice cream or a dollop of whipped cream. Cool, creamy pies in banana, coconut, lemon, coffee, and cantaloupe flavors are refreshing on a hot day.

The base of all pies is a shell of flaky pastry or buttery crumbs. For a different flavor and texture, try making the pastry from whole wheat flour.

Sweet Potato Cobbler

    2 cups peeled, sliced sweet potatoes
       Pastry for double-crust pie
  1½   cups sugar
    ¼ cup plus 1 tablespoon melted butter,
         divided
       Dash of ground nutmeg
    1 teaspoon grated orange rind

Put potatoes in just enough water to cover; cook about 10 minutes or until tender.

Roll pastry to ⅛-inch thickness. Line a greased 10- x 6-inch pan with half of pastry. Spoon in potatoes and liquid; add sugar, ¼ cup melted butter, nutmeg, and orange rind. Top with remaining pastry, pressing edges to seal. Make several slits in top to allow steam to escape; brush with remaining melted butter. Bake at 350° for 30 minutes or until done. Yield: 6 to 8 servings.

Some pies—like Mississippi Lemon Chess Pie (page 217), Coconut Supreme Cream Pie (page 212), and Pecan Party Tarts (page 217)—have a way of making guests feel right at home.

★ Peach Cobbler Supreme

       About 8 cups sliced fresh peaches
    2 cups sugar
    2 to 4 tablespoons all-purpose flour
    ½ teaspoon ground nutmeg
    1 teaspoon almond extract
    ⅓ cup melted butter or margarine
       Pastry for double-crust 8-inch pie

Combine peaches, sugar, flour, and nutmeg; set aside until syrup forms. Bring peaches to a boil; reduce heat to low, and cook 10 minutes or until tender. Remove from heat, and blend in almond extract and butter.

Roll out half of pastry to ⅛-inch thickness on a lightly floured board; cut to fit a 2-quart shallow casserole. Spoon half of peaches into lightly buttered casserole, and top with cut pastry. Bake at 475° for 12 minutes or until golden brown. Spoon remaining peaches over baked pastry.

Roll out remaining pastry, and cut into ½-inch strips; arrange in lattice design over the peaches. Return to oven for 10 to 15 minutes or until lightly browned. Yield: 8 to 10 servings.

★
Southern Blackberry Cobbler

    4 *cups fresh blackberries or 2 (16-ounce)*
       packages frozen blackberries, thawed
    ¾ *cup sugar*
    3 *tablespoons all-purpose flour*
    1½ *cups water*
    1 *tablespoon lemon juice*
       Pastry
    2 *tablespoons melted butter or margarine*
       Cream and sugar (optional)

Place berries in a lightly greased 2-quart baking dish. Combine sugar and flour; add water and lemon juice, mixing well. Pour syrup over berries; bake at 350° about 15 minutes while preparing Pastry.

Place Pastry over hot berries; brush with butter. Bake at 425° for 20 to 30 minutes or until Pastry is golden brown. Serve warm with cream and sugar, if desired. Yield: 8 servings.

Pastry:

    1¾ *cups all-purpose flour*
    2 *to 3 tablespoons sugar*
    2 *teaspoons baking powder*
    1 *teaspoon salt*
    ¼ *cup shortening*
    6 *tablespoons whipping cream*
    6 *tablespoons buttermilk or sour milk*

Combine flour, sugar, baking powder, and salt. Cut in shortening until mixture resembles coarse crumbs; stir in whipping cream and buttermilk. Knead dough 4 or 5 times; roll to about ¼-inch thickness on a lightly floured surface. Cut dough to fit baking dish. Yield: pastry for 1 cobbler.

Apple-Cheese Cobbler

    2 *(17-ounce) cans apple pie filling*
    1 *cup shredded Cheddar cheese*
    2 *tablespoons ground cinnamon*
    2 *tablespoons sugar*
    1 *(9.5-ounce) can refrigerated flaky*
       biscuits
    ¼ *cup melted margarine*

Spoon pie filling into a lightly greased 1½-quart casserole or an 8-inch pan. Sprinkle with cheese.

Combine cinnamon and sugar; sprinkle 1 teaspoon of mixture over pie filling.

Dip both sides of biscuits in margarine, then in remaining cinnamon mixture. Place biscuits on top of cheese. Bake at 425° for 15 to 20 minutes or until brown. Yield: 6 to 8 servings.

Apple Cobbler

    5 *large apples, peeled, cored, and sliced*
    1¼ *cups sugar, divided*
    1 *teaspoon ground cinnamon*
    ½ *cup butter or margarine, divided*
    1 *tablespoon all-purpose flour*
    ¾ *cup water*
       Pastry

Place apple slices in an 8-inch square baking dish. Combine ½ cup sugar with cinnamon, and sprinkle over apples. Dot with 2 tablespoons butter.

Combine remaining ¾ cup sugar and flour in a small saucepan; add ¼ cup butter and water. Place over medium heat until syrup boils, stirring constantly. Pour half of syrup over apples.

Prepare Pastry, and place over apples. Dot with remaining 2 tablespoons butter. Bake at 375° for 20 minutes. Pour remaining half of syrup over top of Pastry, and bake 20 more minutes or until Pastry is golden brown. Yield: 6 to 8 servings.

Pastry:

    1½ *cups all-purpose flour*
       Pinch of salt
    ½ *cup shortening*
    3 *tablespoons cold water*

Combine flour and salt; cut in shortening until mixture resembles coarse crumbs. Add water, and mix well. Roll dough to about ¼-inch thickness on a lightly floured surface; cut to fit baking dish. Yield: pastry for 8-inch cobbler.

Cherry Cobbler

   2   *(16-ounce) cans red tart pitted cherries*
1½   *cups sugar*
1⅓   *cups all-purpose flour, divided*
      Butter or margarine
   1   *teaspoon baking powder*
   ¼   *teaspoon salt*
   3   *tablespoons shortening*
   ⅓   *cup milk*

Drain cherries, reserving juice. Combine sugar and ⅓ cup flour in a saucepan; add cherry juice, blending until smooth. Cook over low heat until thickened, stirring constantly; add cherries, and pour into a shallow 2-quart baking dish. Dot with butter.

Combine remaining 1 cup flour with baking powder and salt; cut in shortening until mixture resembles coarse meal. Stir in milk. Turn pastry out onto a floured surface, and knead 4 or 5 times; then roll out to ¼-inch thickness.

Place pastry on top of cherries; trim edges, if necessary. Make several slits in top to allow steam to escape. Bake at 400° for 20 to 30 minutes or until pastry is golden brown. Yield: about 8 servings.

Baked Alaska Mincemeat Pie

   1   *(9-ounce) package dry mincemeat or 1½ cups prepared mincemeat*
   ½   *cup water*
   1   *quart vanilla ice cream, softened*
   1   *baked 9-inch pastry shell*
   3   *egg whites*
   6   *tablespoons sugar*

Boil dry mincemeat in water 3 minutes; cool. If prepared mincemeat is used, heat thoroughly and then cool.

Combine mincemeat and ice cream; spoon into pastry shell. Freeze until firm.

Beat egg whites until stiff. Gradually add sugar, beating well after each addition. The meringue should be light and dry. Spread over frozen pie, and bake at 450° for 3 to 4 minutes or until lightly browned. Serve immediately. Yield: one 9-inch pie.

Makes-Its-Own-Crust Cherry Cobbler

   2   *cups sugar, divided*
   1   *egg, beaten*
   ½   *cup milk*
   ¾   *cup self-rising flour*
   1   *tablespoon melted butter or margarine*
   1   *(16-ounce) can tart red pitted cherries, undrained*

Combine ½ cup sugar, egg, milk, flour, and butter; beat well. Pour into a greased 1½-quart, deep baking dish. Combine remaining 1½ cups sugar and cherries in a saucepan; bring to a boil, and pour over batter. Bake at 425° for 15 to 20 minutes or until top is brown and crusty. Yield: 6 servings.

Apricot Soufflé Pie

   1   *(6-ounce) package dried apricots*
   3   *eggs*
1¼   *to 1½ cups sugar*
   ¼   *cup water*
   1   *(8-ounce) carton commercial sour cream*
1½   *teaspoons vanilla extract*
   1   *unbaked 9-inch pastry shell*

Cover apricots with water, and soak 1 hour; drain and set aside. Place eggs in blender container; process on medium speed 10 seconds. Add sugar and blend 30 seconds longer. Add apricots, ¼ cup water, sour cream, and vanilla; process 20 seconds. Pour mixture into pastry shell, and bake at 375° for 45 minutes or until center of pie is firm. Yield: one 9-inch pie.

★ Crunch-Top Apple Pie

Pastry for double-crust 9-inch pie
¾ cup sugar
1 tablespoon all-purpose flour
½ teaspoon ground cinnamon
Dash of salt
3½ cups peeled, chopped cooking apples
1 (16-ounce) can applesauce
1 tablespoon lemon juice
1 to 2 tablespoons butter or margarine
Crunch Topping

Roll half of pastry ⅛ inch thick; fit into a 9-inch piepan. Combine sugar, flour, cinnamon, and salt; stir in apples, applesauce, and lemon juice. Spoon apple mixture into piepan, and dot with butter.

Roll out remaining pastry to ⅛-inch thickness, and cut into strips; arrange in lattice design over apples. Prepare Crunch Topping, and sprinkle over top crust.

Bake at 425° for 10 minutes; reduce heat to 350°, and bake about 45 minutes or until crust is golden brown. Yield: one 9-inch pie.

Crunch Topping:

3 tablespoons all-purpose flour
1 tablespoon sugar
Dash of salt
1 tablespoon butter or margarine

Combine flour, sugar, and salt; cut in butter until mixture resembles crumbs. Yield: about ¼ cup.

★ Deep-Dish Apple Pie

8 cooking apples, peeled and thinly sliced
1¼ cups sugar
3 tablespoons all-purpose flour
1½ teaspoons ground cinnamon
¼ teaspoon ground nutmeg
⅛ teaspoon salt
3 tablespoons butter or margarine
Pastry

Arrange apple slices in a lightly greased 9-inch square baking dish. Combine sugar,

flour, cinnamon, nutmeg, and salt; sprinkle over apples, and dot with butter. Top with Pastry, and bake at 400° for 40 minutes or until golden brown. Yield: 6 to 8 servings.

Pastry:

1¼ cups all-purpose flour
¼ teaspoon salt
2 tablespoons shortening
4 tablespoons cold butter or margarine
3 to 4 tablespoons cold water

Combine flour and salt; cut in shortening. Cut butter into small pieces, and add to flour mixture; cut in until mixture resembles coarse cornmeal. Stir in only enough water to moisten flour; form dough into a ball. Wrap in plastic wrap, and chill 30 minutes.

Roll dough to ¼-inch thickness on a lightly floured surface, and cut into 1-inch-wide strips. Arrange lattice fashion over filling. Yield: pastry for one 9-inch pie.

★ Summer Peach Pie

1 envelope plus 1 teaspoon unflavored gelatin
½ cup plus 2 tablespoons cold water, divided
¼ cup sugar
1 (12-ounce) can peach nectar
1 tablespoon lemon juice
4 large fresh peaches, peeled and sliced
1 baked 9-inch pastry shell
1 pint whipping cream, whipped
Additional peach slices

Dissolve gelatin in ½ cup cold water; bring to a boil, stirring constantly. Remove from heat; stir in sugar and peach nectar. Chill until thickened.

Combine lemon juice and remaining 2 tablespoons water; stir in peaches until well coated with liquid. Drain peach slices; arrange in pastry shell. Cover with gelatin mixture; chill until firm.

Just before serving, top with whipped cream and garnish with additional peach slices. Yield: one 9-inch pie.

Cherry-Peach Pie

    1 (16-ounce) can red tart pitted cherries,
         undrained
    2 cups sliced peaches
    ¾ cup sugar
    ¼ cup cornstarch
    1 tablespoon lemon juice
    2 tablespoons butter or margarine
       Pastry for double-crust 9-inch pie

Combine cherries, peaches, and sugar in a bowl; let stand at room temperature 1 hour. Drain fruit thoroughly, reserving syrup. Add enough water to syrup to make 1 cup liquid.

Combine liquid and cornstarch in a saucepan, blending until smooth. Cook over low heat until thickened, stirring constantly. Add lemon juice, drained fruit, and butter.

Pour filling into a 9-inch piepan lined with pastry. Cut remaining pastry into strips, and arrange in lattice design over filling. Trim edges; then seal and flute. Bake at 400° for 35 minutes or until golden brown. Yield: one 9-inch pie.

Rhubarb Pie Supreme

       Pastry for double-crust 9-inch pie
    2 pounds rhubarb, sliced
    2 cups sugar
    ¼ cup all-purpose flour
    2 tablespoons butter or margarine
       Pinch of ground cinnamon
    1 teaspoon sugar
       Ice cream (optional)

Line a 9-inch piepan with half of pastry.

Combine rhubarb, 2 cups sugar, and flour; mix lightly, and spoon into pastry shell. Dot with butter. Cover with top crust; slit in several places to allow steam to escape. Seal and flute edges.

Combine cinnamon and 1 teaspoon sugar; sprinkle over pastry. Bake at 425° for 15 minutes; reduce heat to 350°, and bake an additional 30 to 40 minutes. Serve warm with ice cream, if desired. Yield: one 9-inch pie.

Rhubarb Pie

    3 to 4 cups sliced rhubarb
    ¼ cup applesauce
    1½ to 2 cups sugar
    1 unbaked 9-inch pastry shell
    2 tablespoons butter or margarine

Place rhubarb in a large bowl; cover with boiling water, and let stand 5 minutes. Drain. Combine rhubarb, applesauce, and sugar; spoon into pastry shell, and dot with butter. Bake at 400° for 30 to 40 minutes. (Filling will be quite thin when pie is removed from oven, but it firms up as pie cools.) Cool pie completely before serving. Yield: one 9-inch pie.

Cranberry Mincemeat Pie

    1 (1-pound) can whole cranberry sauce
    2 cups prepared mincemeat
    1 unbaked 9-inch pastry shell
    1 cup finely chopped pecans
    2 tablespoons sugar
    2 tablespoons melted butter or margarine
    3 tablespoons brandy

Combine cranberry sauce and mincemeat; pour into pastry shell. Combine pecans, sugar, and butter; sprinkle over filling. Bake at 425° for 30 minutes or until crust is brown and filling is bubbly. Cool on wire rack at least 1 hour before slicing.

Just before serving, heat brandy in a small saucepan over low heat. Ignite with match, and pour flaming brandy over pie; serve at once. Yield: one 9-inch pie.

Mincemeat Crunch Pie

1   (28-ounce) jar prepared mincemeat
1   unbaked 9-inch pastry shell
1   tablespoon instant orange peel
¼   cup all-purpose flour
¼   cup firmly packed brown sugar
2   tablespoons margarine, softened
¼   cup chopped pecans or walnuts

Spoon mincemeat into pastry shell; sprinkle with orange peel.

Combine flour and sugar in a bowl. Using a pastry blender or two knives, cut in margarine until mixture resembles cornmeal. Stir in pecans. Sprinkle mixture over pie. Bake at 425° for 25 to 30 minutes. Yield: one 9-inch pie.

Unusual Blueberry Pie

1   (2-ounce) package whipped topping mix
¾   cup cold milk
1   teaspoon vanilla extract
1   cup sugar
1   (8-ounce) package cream cheese, softened
1   large banana, sliced
1   baked 10-inch pastry shell
1   (22-ounce) can blueberry pie filling

Combine whipped topping mix, milk, and vanilla; blend well. Add sugar and cream cheese; beat until stiff.

Arrange banana slices in bottom of pastry shell; spread cream cheese mixture over banana slices. Spread blueberry pie filling over cream cheese mixture. Chill at least 4 hours or overnight. Yield: 8 to 10 servings.

Blueberry Pie

1   teaspoon vinegar
1   cup sugar
2   tablespoons all-purpose flour
⅛   teaspoon ground nutmeg
1   quart fresh blueberries
Pastry for double-crust 9-inch pie
2   tablespoons butter

Combine vinegar, sugar, flour, and nutmeg. Mix with berries. Put in pastry-lined piepan and dot with butter. Cover with top crust. Bake at 425° for 10 minutes; reduce heat to 375° and bake an additional 25 minutes or until brown. Yield: one 9-inch pie.

★
Rum Pecan Pie

½   cup butter or margarine, softened
½   cup sugar
¾   cup light corn syrup
¼   cup maple-flavored syrup
3   eggs, lightly beaten
2   tablespoons rum
¾   cup coarsely chopped pecans
Brandied Butter Pastry
¾   cup pecan halves

Cream butter and sugar until light and fluffy. Add corn syrup, maple syrup, eggs, and rum; beat well. Stir in chopped pecans.

Line a 9-inch piepan with Brandied Butter Pastry. Pour filling into Pastry, and top with pecan halves. Bake at 350° for 55 minutes. Yield: one 9-inch pie.

Brandied Butter Pastry:

1   cup all-purpose flour
¼   teaspoon salt
6   tablespoons cold butter or margarine
2   to 3 tablespoons cold brandy

Combine flour and salt; cut in butter until mixture resembles coarse meal. Sprinkle brandy over mixture, and stir until particles cling together when pressed gently.

Shape dough into a ball, and chill 10 minutes before rolling out.

Yield: pastry for single crust (9-inch) pie.

★ Pecan Tarts

- ¾ cup firmly packed light brown sugar
- 1 teaspoon butter or margarine, softened
- 1 egg
- ¼ teaspoon salt
- 1 teaspoon vanilla extract
- ⅔ cup chopped pecans
- Pastry shells

Combine first 6 ingredients, mixing well; spoon 1 teaspoonful filling into each pastry shell. Bake at 350° for 17 minutes. Yield: 2 dozen tarts.

Pastry Shells:

- 1 (3-ounce) package cream cheese, softened
- ½ cup butter or margarine, softened
- 1 cup all-purpose flour

Combine cream cheese and butter; blend until smooth. Add flour, mixing well. Refrigerate dough 1 hour; then shape into 24 balls.

Put each ball in a greased miniature muffin tin, shaping into a shell. Bake at 350° for 15 minutes before filling. Yield: 2 dozen.

Old-Fashioned Egg Custard Pie

- 3 eggs, beaten
- ¾ cup sugar
- ¼ teaspoon salt
- 1 teaspoon vanilla extract
- ½ teaspoon ground nutmeg
- 2 cups milk, scalded
- 1 unbaked 9-inch pastry shell
- Additional ground nutmeg

Combine eggs and sugar, beating well; add salt, vanilla, and ½ teaspoon nutmeg. Gradually add scalded milk, stirring constantly. Pour mixture into pastry shell, and sprinkle with additional nutmeg.

Bake at 400° for 10 minutes. Reduce oven temperature to 325°, and bake an additional 25 minutes or until a knife inserted halfway between center and edge comes out clean. Cool thoroughly before serving. Yield: one 9-inch pie.

Pecan Pie

- ⅔ cup sugar
- 3 eggs, well beaten
- Dash of salt
- 1 cup dark corn syrup
- ⅓ cup melted butter or margarine
- 1 cup pecan halves
- 1 unbaked 9-inch pastry shell

Combine sugar and eggs, beating until creamy; blend in salt, corn syrup, and butter. Stir in pecans. Pour into pastry shell; bake at 350° for 50 minutes. Yield: one 9-inch pie.

Old-Fashioned Potato Pie

- 1 unbaked 9-inch pastry shell
- 3 eggs, beaten
- 1 cup sugar
- ¾ cup half-and-half
- 1 cup riced cooked potatoes
- 1 tablespoon vanilla extract
- Ground nutmeg to taste (optional)

Bake pastry shell at 450° for 10 minutes; set aside.

Combine eggs, sugar, and half-and-half; beat well. Stir in potatoes and vanilla. Pour mixture into pastry shell; sprinkle with nutmeg, if desired. Bake at 350° for 30 minutes or until set. Yield: one 9-inch pie.

Oatmeal Pie

- ⅔ cup regular oats, uncooked
- ⅔ cup light corn syrup
- 2 eggs, beaten
- ⅔ cup sugar
- 1 teaspoon vanilla extract
- ¼ teaspoon salt
- ⅔ cup melted butter or margarine, cooled
- 1 unbaked 8-inch pastry shell

Combine oats, corn syrup, eggs, sugar, vanilla, and salt; add butter and mix thoroughly. Pour into pastry shell and bake at 350° for 1 hour. Let cool before serving. Yield: one 8-inch pie.

Chocolate Oatmeal Pie

  2 *eggs, beaten*
  ½ *cup butter or margarine, melted*
  1 *cup sugar*
  ⅔ *cup uncooked oats*
  ¼ *teaspoon salt*
  1 *teaspoon vanilla extract*
  2 *tablespoons cocoa*
  1 *unbaked 8-inch pastry shell*

Combine first 7 ingredients in the order listed; blend well. Pour into pastry shell. Bake at 300° for 45 minutes. Cool before serving. Yield: one 8-inch pie.

Fudge Pie

  2 *(1-ounce) squares unsweetened chocolate*
  ½ *cup butter or margarine*
  2 *eggs, well beaten*
  1 *cup sugar*
  ¼ *cup all-purpose flour*
     Vanilla ice cream (optional)

Melt chocolate and butter over medium heat. Combine eggs, sugar, and flour; stir into chocolate mixture. Pour into an 8-inch pie-pan. Bake at 350° for 20 to 25 minutes. (Center of pie will be soft.) Serve hot with vanilla ice cream, if desired. Yield: one 8-inch pie.

Southern Peanut Pie

  1 *cup sugar*
  ¾ *cup light corn syrup*
  ½ *cup melted margarine*
  3 *eggs*
  ½ *teaspoon vanilla extract*
 1½ *cups roasted peanuts or commercial dry-roasted peanuts*
  1 *unbaked 9-inch pastry shell*

Combine sugar, corn syrup, margarine, eggs and vanilla; beat until thoroughly blended. Stir in peanuts. Pour filling into pastry shell; bake at 375° for 45 minutes. Serve warm or cold. Yield: one 9-inch pie.

Golden Carrot Pie

  2 *cups sliced cooked carrots, pureed*
  3 *eggs, slightly beaten*
  ½ *teaspoon salt*
  ½ *teaspoon ground nutmeg*
  ½ *teaspoon ground ginger*
  1 *teaspoon ground cinnamon*
  ⅛ *teaspoon ground cloves*
  ¾ *cup evaporated milk*
  1 *cup honey*
  1 *unbaked 9-inch pastry shell*
     Whipped cream

Combine carrots, eggs, salt, and spices; mix well. Add milk and honey, blending until smooth. Pour filling into pastry shell. Bake at 400° for 40 to 45 minutes; allow pie to cool. Garnish with whipped cream before serving. Yield: one 9-inch pie.

Cherry Custard Pie

  1 *(22-ounce) can cherry pie filling*
  1 *unbaked 9-inch pastry shell*
  4 *(3-ounce) packages cream cheese, softened*
  2 *eggs*
  ½ *cup sugar*
  ½ *teaspoon vanilla extract*
  1 *(8-ounce) carton commercial sour cream*
     Ground nutmeg

Spread pie filling in bottom of pastry shell; bake at 425° for 15 minutes.

    Combine cream cheese, eggs, sugar, and vanilla; beat until smooth. Spread cheese mixture over cherries, and bake at 350° for 30 minutes; cool. Spread sour cream over top, and sprinkle with nutmeg. Chill. Yield: one 9-inch pie.

Sour Cream Chess Pie

¼   cup butter or margarine, softened
¾   cup sugar
1   tablespoon cornmeal
¼   teaspoon ground mace
3   eggs, beaten
1   (8-ounce) carton commercial sour cream
1   unbaked 9-inch pastry shell

Cream butter and sugar until light and fluffy; add cornmeal and mace. Combine eggs and sour cream; add to creamed mixture, stirring until well mixed.

Pour filling into pastry shell. Bake at 400° for 10 minutes; reduce heat to 350°. Bake 20 to 25 minutes or until set. Yield: one 9-inch pie.

Old-Fashioned Lemon Pie

¼   cup margarine, softened
2   cups sugar
4   eggs
Juice and rind of 2 lemons
1   unbaked 9-inch pastry shell

Cream margarine and sugar; add eggs, one at a time, beating well after each addition. Stir in lemon juice and rind; mix well. Pour into pastry shell, and bake at 350° for 40 minutes or until set and lightly browned. Yield: one 9-inch pie.

Osgood Pie

3   eggs, beaten
1   cup sugar
1   teaspoon ground cinnamon
½   teaspoon ground cloves
1½   teaspoons vinegar
1   cup raisins
⅔   cup chopped pecans
1   unbaked 9-inch pastry shell

Combine eggs and sugar; beat well. Add spices, vinegar, raisins, and pecans; pour into pastry shell. Bake at 350° for 45 minutes. Yield: one 9-inch pie.

Pumpkin-Ice Cream Pie

1   cup canned pumpkin
½   cup firmly packed brown sugar
½   teaspoon salt
½   teaspoon ground cinnamon
½   teaspoon ground ginger
¼   teaspoon ground nutmeg
1   quart vanilla ice cream, softened
1   baked 9-inch pastry shell

Combine pumpkin, brown sugar, salt, and spices; mix well. Fold in ice cream. Pour into pastry shell; freeze until firm. Yield: one 9-inch pie.

Crunch Top Sweet Potato Pie

1¾   cups cooked, mashed sweet potatoes
1   cup frozen whipped topping, thawed
½   cup powdered sugar
½   (8-ounce) package cream cheese, softened
1   teaspoon vanilla extract
Coconut Crust
¼   cup chopped pecans
¼   cup all-purpose flour
¼   cup firmly packed brown sugar
2   tablespoons butter or margarine, melted
½   teaspoon ground cinnamon
Dash of ground nutmeg

Combine sweet potatoes, whipped topping, powdered sugar, cream cheese, and vanilla in a mixing bowl; beat with electric mixer until smooth. Pour mixture into Coconut Crust.

Combine remaining ingredients, stirring well; sprinkle over pie. Bake at 325° about 10 minutes or until topping begins to brown. Chill thoroughly before serving. Yield: one 8-inch pie.

Coconut Crust:

1   (3½-ounce) can flaked coconut
2   tablespoons butter or margarine, melted

Combine coconut and butter; press into an 8-inch piepan. Bake at 325° for 8 to 10 minutes or until lightly browned. Cool. Yield: one 8-inch pie crust.

Pumpkin Pie

1½ cups sugar
2½ tablespoons margarine, softened
2 eggs, separated
1 cup cooked or canned pumpkin
2 tablespoons all-purpose flour
2 teaspoons ground cinnamon
½ teaspoon ground nutmeg
1 teaspoon vanilla extract
1 pint whipping cream or half-and-half
1 unbaked 9-inch pastry shell

Combine sugar, margarine, egg yolks, pumpkin, flour, spices, vanilla, and whipping cream; beat until well blended. Beat egg whites until stiff, and fold into pumpkin mixture. Pour into unbaked pastry shell. Bake at 425° for 10 to 15 minutes; reduce heat to 325° and bake 40 to 45 minutes or until set. Yield: one 9-inch pie.

★ Sweet Potato Pie

2 cups cooked, mashed sweet potatoes
½ cup butter or margarine, softened
2 eggs, separated
1 cup firmly packed brown sugar
¼ teaspoon salt
½ teaspoon ground ginger
½ teaspoon ground cinnamon
½ teaspoon ground nutmeg
½ cup milk
¼ cup sugar
1 unbaked 9-inch pastry shell
Additional spices (optional)
Whipped cream
Orange rind

Combine sweet potatoes, butter, egg yolks, brown sugar, salt, and spices; mix well. Add milk, blending until smooth.

Beat egg whites until foamy; gradually add ¼ cup sugar, beating until stiff. Fold into sweet potato mixture. Pour filling into pastry shell; sprinkle with additional spices if desired. Bake at 400° for 10 minutes. Reduce heat to 350°, and bake 30 additional minutes. When cool, garnish with whipped cream and orange rind. Yield: one 9-inch pie.

Banana Cream Pie

2 ripe bananas
1 baked 9-inch pastry shell, cooled
1 (8-ounce) carton commercial sour cream
1 cup milk
1 (3¾-ounce) package instant vanilla pudding and pie filling

Slice bananas into bottom of completely cooled pastry shell. Combine sour cream and milk, blending well. Add pudding, and beat until thickened. Pour over bananas, and chill thoroughly. Yield: one 9-inch pie.

Coconut Supreme Cream Pie

¼ cup cornstarch
⅔ cup sugar
½ teaspoon salt
3 cups milk
3 eggs, separated
1 teaspoon vanilla extract
¾ cup flaked coconut
1 baked 9-inch pastry shell
6 tablespoons sugar
¼ cup flaked coconut

Combine cornstarch, ⅔ cup sugar, and salt in top of a double boiler. Gradually add milk, stirring until smooth. Cook over boiling water, stirring constantly until thickened. Cover; cook 10 minutes longer, stirring occasionally.

Beat egg yolks. Blend a small amount of hot mixture into egg yolks, mixing well; stir egg yolks into remaining hot mixture. Cook over boiling water 2 minutes, stirring constantly. Remove from water; stir in vanilla and ¾ cup coconut. Cool; pour into pastry shell.

Beat egg whites until foamy. Gradually add 6 tablespoons sugar; continue beating until stiff peaks form. Spread meringue over pie; sprinkle ¼ cup coconut over top. Bake at 425° for 5 minutes. Yield: one 9-inch pie.

★
Southern Coconut Cream Pie

  1 *large coconut*
  About 1 cup milk
  1 *(5.33-ounce) can evaporated milk*
  2¼ *cups sugar, divided*
  6 *eggs, separated*
  4 *teaspoons cornstarch*
  ½ *cup water*
  2 *teaspoons vanilla extract*
  2 *baked 9-inch pastry shells*

Crack coconut, reserving milk. Remove meat from coconut and grate; set aside.

Add enough milk to coconut milk to make 1½ cups. Combine milk, evaporated milk, 1½ cups sugar, and egg yolks in a saucepan. Cook, stirring constantly, over low heat until mixture comes to a boil. Dissolve cornstarch in water; add to milk mixture. Cook, stirring frequently, until thickened. Remove from heat; stir in vanilla and reserved grated coconut. Pour into pastry shells.

Beat egg whites, gradually adding remaining ¾ cup sugar; beat until stiff peaks form. Spread meringue over each pie, being careful to seal edges. Bake at 350° about 10 minutes or until golden. Yield: two 9-inch pies.

Coffee Cream Pie

  1 *egg, separated*
  ¼ *teaspoon salt*
  ¼ *cup sugar*
  1½ *cups finely chopped pecans*
  1 *tablespoon instant coffee granules*
  ¼ *cup boiling water*
  2¼ *cups miniature marshmallows*
  ½ *teaspoon almond extract*
  1 *pint whipping cream, divided*
  Grated chocolate

Combine egg white and salt; beat until stiff but not dry. Gradually beat in sugar; then fold in pecans. Spread into a well-greased 8-inch piepan. Prick with fork. Bake at 400° for 12 minutes; cool.

Dissolve coffee in boiling water, and add marshmallows; place over medium heat until marshmallows melt. Beat egg yolk. Slowly add marshmallow mixture, beating constantly; beat until mixture begins to set. Stir in almond extract.

Whip ½ pint whipping cream; fold into filling. Spoon into crust; chill. Whip remaining cream, and spread over top. Garnish with grated chocolate. Yield: one 8-inch pie.

Peanut Butter Cream Pie

  3 *egg yolks*
  3 *cups milk*
  1 *cup sugar*
  ½ *cup cornstarch*
  ¼ *teaspoon salt*
  ⅓ *cup chunky peanut butter*
  2 *teaspoons vanilla extract*
  1 *baked 9-inch pastry shell*
  ½ *cup whipping cream, whipped*
  Chopped peanuts

Combine egg yolks and milk in a medium saucepan, blending well. Combine sugar, cornstarch, and salt; stir into egg mixture. Cook, stirring constantly, until thick. Pour hot filling into bowl; cover with waxed paper, and chill.

Whip chilled mixture with electric mixer until creamy. Add peanut butter and vanilla, beating until smooth. Pour filling into pastry shell; spoon whipped cream around edges. Sprinkle chopped peanuts over top. Yield: one 9-inch pie.

Strawberry Cream Pie

  1 *(14-ounce) can sweetened condensed
      milk*
  ¼ *cup lemon juice*
  ½ *pint whipping cream, whipped*
  2 *cups sliced strawberries, divided*
  1 *(9-inch) graham cracker crust, baked*

Combine condensed milk and lemon juice; beat until thick. Fold in whipped cream; chill 10 minutes. Add 1½ cups strawberries; spoon into crust. Garnish with remaining strawberries. Chill 1 hour. Yield: one 9-inch pie.

Cantaloupe Pie

    1 *small cantaloupe, peeled and diced*
    Milk
    ¾ *cup sugar*
    6 *tablespoons all-purpose flour*
    ¼ *teaspoon salt*
    2 *eggs, separated*
    1 *tablespoon butter*
    ½ *teaspoon vanilla extract*
    1 *baked 9-inch pastry shell*
    ¼ *teaspoon cream of tartar*

Combine cantaloupe and about 3 table-spoons milk in a saucepan; simmer until cantaloupe is soft. Mash melon; add additional milk to make 2 cups.

Heat 1½ cups cantaloupe mixture in a saucepan. Combine sugar, flour, salt, egg yolks, and remaining ½ cup cantaloupe mixture; stir into hot mixture. Cook until thick, stirring constantly. Remove from heat; stir in butter and vanilla. Pour into pastry shell.

Beat egg whites until foamy. Add cream of tartar, and continue beating until stiff peaks form. Spread meringue over pie. Bake at 400° about 10 minutes or until brown. Yield: one 9-inch pie.

Chocolate Pie

    4 *tablespoons cocoa*
    1½ *cups sugar*
    6 *heaping teaspoons all-purpose flour*
    4 *eggs, separated*
    2 *cups milk*
    1 *tablespoon butter or margarine*
    1 *teaspoon vanilla extract*
    1 *baked 9-inch pastry shell*
    ½ *cup sugar*
    ¼ *teaspoon cream of tartar*

Combine cocoa, 1½ cups sugar, and flour in a medium saucepan; set aside. Beat egg yolks. Gradually stir yolks and milk into cocoa mixture; add butter. Cook over medium heat until thick, stirring constantly. Remove from heat, and stir in vanilla. Pour filling into pastry shell.

Beat egg whites until foamy; gradually add ½ cup sugar and cream of tartar. Continue beating until stiff peaks form. Spread meringue over pie, being careful to seal edges. Bake at 400° about 10 minutes or until lightly browned. Cool to room temperature; then chill until serving time. Yield: one 9-inch pie.

Butterscotch Cream Pie

    2 *cups firmly packed light brown sugar*
    ¾ *cup all-purpose flour*
    4 *egg yolks*
    2½ *cups half-and-half*
    1 *tablespoon butter or margarine*
    1 *teaspoon vanilla extract*
    1 *baked 9-inch pastry shell*
    Whipped cream

Combine sugar, flour, and egg yolks in a large saucepan. Gradually add half-and-half, stirring well. Add butter; cook over medium heat, stirring constantly, until thickened. Stir in vanilla; cool. Pour into pastry shell; chill several hours or until set. Garnish with whipped cream. Yield: one 9-inch pie.

★
Luscious Lemon Pie

    1 *cup sugar*
    3 *tablespoons cornstarch*
    1 *tablespoon grated lemon rind*
    ¼ *cup butter or margarine*
    ¼ *cup lemon juice*
    1 *cup milk*
    3 *egg yolks, slightly beaten*
    1 *(8-ounce) carton commercial sour cream*
    1 *baked 9-inch pastry shell*
    Whipped cream
    Additional grated lemon rind (optional)

Combine sugar, cornstarch, 1 tablespoon lemon rind, butter, lemon juice, milk, and egg yolks in a heavy saucepan. Cook over medium heat until smooth and thickened, stirring constantly; cover and cool.

Fold sour cream into filling, and pour into pastry shell; chill at least 2 hours before serving. Top with whipped cream; garnish with grated lemon rind, if desired. Yield: one 9-inch pie.

Cherry Cheese Pie

4 *(3-ounce) packages cream cheese,*
   softened
2 *tablespoons milk*
1 *cup powdered sugar*
1 *(9-inch) graham cracker crust*
½ *cup chopped pecans*
1 *(22-ounce) can cherry pie filling*
1 *teaspoon almond extract*
1 *envelope whipped topping mix*

Combine cream cheese, milk, and powdered sugar; beat until smooth. Spread in bottom of crust, and sprinkle with pecans. Combine pie filling and almond extract; spread over cheese layer.

Prepare whipped topping according to package directions; spoon over cherries around outer edge of crust. Chill thoroughly. Yield: one 9-inch pie.

Marble-Top Chocolate Rum Pie

¾ *cup sugar, divided*
1 *envelope unflavored gelatin*
Dash of salt
1 *cup milk*
2 *eggs, separated*
1 *(6-ounce) package semisweet chocolate*
   morsels
⅓ *cup rum*
1 *teaspoon vanilla extract*
½ *pint whipping cream, whipped*
1 *baked 10-inch pastry shell*

Combine ½ cup sugar, gelatin, and salt in a saucepan; stir in milk and egg yolks. Cook over low heat until slightly thickened, stirring constantly; remove from heat. Add chocolate morsels, stirring until melted. Stir in rum. Chill until partially set.

Beat egg whites until soft peaks form. Gradually add ¼ cup sugar, beating until stiff peaks form. Fold into chocolate mixture. Fold vanilla into whipped cream.

Spoon half of chocolate mixture into pastry shell; top with half of whipped cream. Repeat layers. Swirl top to marble. Chill several hours until firm. Yield: one 10-inch pie.

Lime Parfait Pie

1 *(3-ounce) package lime-flavored gelatin*
1 *cup boiling water*
1 *cup cold water*
3 *tablespoons lime juice*
1 *pint vanilla ice cream*
Chocolate Crumb Crust
Lime slices (optional)

Combine gelatin and boiling water, stirring until gelatin is dissolved. Add cold water, lime juice, and ice cream; stir until ice cream melts. Chill until thickened.

Pour filling into Chocolate Crumb Crust, and chill until firm. Garnish with lime slices, if desired. Yield: one 9-inch pie.

Chocolate Crumb Crust:

1 *(8½-ounce) package chocolate wafers*
½ *cup melted butter or margarine*

Crush chocolate wafers, and combine with butter; press firmly and evenly into a 9-inch piepan. Yield: one 9-inch pastry shell.

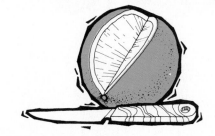

Quick Lime Pie

½ *pint whipping cream, whipped*
1 *(14-ounce) can sweetened condensed*
   milk
½ *cup lime juice*
⅛ *teaspoon grated lime rind*
1 *(9-inch) graham cracker crust*
Lime twists

Fold whipped cream into sweetened condensed milk. Add lime juice and rind; stir until smooth and thickened. Spoon into crust. Freeze pie until almost firm, or freeze until firm and let stand at room temperature until slightly thawed. Garnish with lime twists. Yield: one 9-inch pie.

★
Mile High Pie

 1   *(10-ounce) package frozen strawberries,*
       thawed
 1   *cup sugar*
 1   *tablespoon lemon juice*
 2   *egg whites, unbeaten*
 1   *pint whipping cream, whipped*
 1   *teaspoon vanilla extract*
 1   *baked 10-inch pastry shell*

Combine strawberries, sugar, lemon juice, and egg whites in a large mixing bowl; beat 15 minutes or until very stiff. Fold in whipped cream and vanilla. Spoon into pastry shell. Freeze until firm. Yield: one 10-inch pie.

Note: For a higher pie, add more berries and beat 25 to 30 minutes.

Easy Strawberry Pie

 3   *tablespoons cornstarch*
 ½   *cup water*
 1   *tablespoon lemon juice*
 ⅛   *teaspoon salt*
 1   *cup sugar*
 2   *cups crushed strawberries*
 2   *cups sliced strawberries*
 1   *baked 9-inch pastry shell*
     Whipped cream
     Strawberry halves

Combine cornstarch and water; blend until smooth. Add lemon juice, salt, sugar, and crushed strawberries. Cook, stirring constantly, over low heat until mixture thickens (about 5 minutes); cool. Add sliced strawberries, and pour mixture into pastry shell. Chill thoroughly. Spread top with whipped cream, and garnish with strawberry halves. Yield: one 9-inch pie.

Basic Pastry

 1   *cup all-purpose flour*
 ½   *teaspoon salt*
 ⅓   *cup plus 1 tablespoon shortening*
 2   *to 3 tablespoons cold water*

Combine flour and salt in bowl; cut in shortening with pastry blender until mixture resembles coarse cornmeal. Sprinkle cold water evenly over surface; stir with a fork until all dry ingredients are moistened. Shape into a ball; chill. Roll to fit a 9-inch quiche pan or piepan. Yield: one 9-inch pastry shell.

Hot Water Pastry

 2   *cups all-purpose flour*
 ½   *teaspoon baking powder*
 1   *teaspoon salt*
 ⅓   *cup boiling water*
 ⅔   *cup shortening*

Combine flour, baking powder, and salt. Pour boiling water over shortening, and beat until creamy. Add flour mixture, stirring until well mixed. Chill slightly. Roll dough to ⅛-inch thickness on a lightly floured surface. Yield: pastry for 2 single-crust pies or 1 double-crust pie.

Whole Wheat Pastry

 1   *cup plus 2 tablespoons whole wheat*
       flour
 1   *tablespoon sugar*
 ⅛   *teaspoon salt*
 7   *tablespoons salad oil*
 2   *tablespoons cold water*

Combine all ingredients in a 9-inch piepan, blending well. Press onto bottom and sides of piepan. Yield: one 9-inch piecrust.

Note: To use for quiche, omit sugar.

Oatmeal Pie Crust

1 *cup all-purpose flour*
1 *teaspoon salt*
¼ *cup sugar*
½ *cup shortening*
½ *cup uncooked oats*
3 to 4 *tablespoons water*

Combine flour, salt, and sugar in mixing bowl; cut in shortening until mixture resembles coarse cornmeal. Stir in oats. Sprinkle water evenly over surface; stir with a fork until all dry ingredients are moistened.

Shape into a ball; chill. Roll to fit a 9-inch piepan. Yield: one 9-inch pastry shell.

Deluxe Pie Crust

2½ *cups graham cracker crumbs*
2 *tablespoons brown sugar*
¼ *cup ground pecans*
½ *cup melted butter or margarine*

Combine graham cracker crumbs, sugar, and pecans; add butter. Press firmly and evenly into a 9-inch pieplate. Bake at 350° for 12 to 15 minutes. Yield: one 9-inch pastry shell.

Pecan Party Tarts

1 *cup sugar*
½ *cup dark corn syrup*
¼ *cup light corn syrup*
1 *tablespoon lemon juice*
1 *teaspoon vanilla extract*
6 *tablespoons melted butter or margarine*
3 *eggs, beaten*
10 *unbaked 3-inch tart shells*
1 *cup pecan halves*

Combine first 7 ingredients, mixing well. Spoon into tart shells, filling two-thirds full; cover with pecan halves. Bake at 325° for 30 minutes. Yield: 10 tarts.

Note: Tart shells can be made by shaping pastry circles around the back of muffin tins or custard cups.

Mississippi Lemon Chess Pie

2 *cups sugar*
1 *tablespoon all-purpose flour*
1 *tablespoon cornmeal*
¼ *teaspoon salt*
¼ *cup melted butter or margarine*
¼ *cup lemon juice*
Grated rind of 2 lemons
¼ *cup milk*
4 *eggs*
1 *unbaked 9-inch pastry shell*

Combine sugar, flour, cornmeal, and salt. Add butter, lemon juice, lemon rind, and milk; mix well. Add eggs, one at a time, beating well after each addition. Pour into pastry shell. Bake at 350° for 50 minutes. Yield: one 9-inch pie.

Coconut Cream Pie

2 *eggs, separated*
½ *cup sugar*
5 *tablespoons all-purpose flour*
1 *cup evaporated milk*
1 *cup water*
1 *cup flaked coconut*
Pinch of salt
1 *teaspoon vanilla extract*
4 *tablespoons butter or margarine*
1 *baked 9-inch pastry shell*
¼ *cup sugar*
¼ *teaspoon cream of tartar*

Beat egg yolks. Combine yolks, ½ cup sugar, flour, milk, water, coconut, and salt in a medium saucepan; blend thoroughly. Cook over medium heat, stirring frequently, until thickened. Remove from heat; stir in vanilla and butter. Spoon mixture into pastry shell.

Beat egg whites until foamy. Gradually add ¼ cup sugar and cream of tartar; continue beating until stiff peaks form. Spread meringue over pie, being careful to seal edges. Bake at 400° about 10 minutes or until lightly browned. Cool. Refrigerate until serving time. Yield: one 9-inch pie.

Poultry and Dressings

A good deal can be said in favor of the all-time Southern favorite—chicken. In fact, chicken fried to perfection is still a tradition for many Sunday lunches all across the South. But whether chicken is fried, baked, grilled, or braised, it's one dish that you can count on to be a favorite with family and guests.

Its popularity is quite understandable since chicken can come to the table in an endless variety of dishes: as a dinner entree, luncheon dish, or even as a tempting appetizer. Chicken is also a popular choice for picnics, cookouts, and barbecues.

A golden, roasted turkey stuffed with dressing is synonymous with Thanksgiving Day in almost every Southern home. Turkey is not just a holiday dish but a year-round treat for the family. Tradition and family tastes demand a variety in typical Southern dressings. Some of these favorite dressings are made of cornbread, rice, bread, and crackers.

Golden Crisp Chicken

- 1 (2- to 3-pound) broiler-fryer chicken, cut up
- 1 tablespoon salt
- 4 cups cold water
- 1¼ cups all-purpose flour
- 1 tablespoon paprika
- 2 teaspoons salt
- 1 teaspoon white pepper
- 1 cup buttermilk
- Salad oil

Rinse chicken pieces in a mixture of 1 tablespoon salt and 4 cups water; drain chicken, and chill 1 hour. Combine flour, paprika, 2 teaspoons salt, and pepper. Dip chicken in buttermilk; then dredge in flour mixture.

Heat 1 inch of oil to 375°. Cook chicken 5 minutes on each side or until browned; drain well on paper towels.

Place chicken in shallow baking dish; cover and bake at 350° for 30 minutes. Drain chicken again if necessary. Yield: 4 servings.

Cornish Hens Véronique (page 237), served with wild rice and broiled tomatoes, will add an extra measure of elegance to your party table.

★ Marinated Fried Chicken

- 2 (2- to 3-pound) broiler-fryer chickens, cut up
- 2 cups salad oil
- 2 eggs, beaten
- 1 teaspoon oregano
- 1 teaspoon rosemary
- 1 teaspoon tarragon or poultry seasoning
- 1 teaspoon paprika
- 2 cloves garlic, crushed
- 2 cups all-purpose flour
- Salt and pepper
- Hot salad oil

Place chicken in a 13- x 9- x 2-inch pan. Combine 2 cups salad oil, eggs, oregano, rosemary, tarragon, paprika, and garlic; pour over chicken, turning to coat both sides. Refrigerate 2 hours; remove chicken from marinade.

Season flour with salt and pepper. Lightly salt chicken pieces, and dredge in seasoned flour. Heat 1 inch of salad oil in a skillet over medium heat. Place chicken in skillet; fry over medium heat 30 minutes, turning occasionally. Drain on paper towels. Yield: 10 to 12 servings.

Dixie Fried Chicken

  1 *(2- to 3-pound) broiler-fryer chicken,*
     cut up
Salt and pepper
  2 *cups all-purpose flour*
  1 *teaspoon red pepper*
  1 *egg, slightly beaten*
  ½ *cup milk*
Hot salad oil

Season chicken with salt and pepper. Combine flour and red pepper; set aside. Combine egg and milk. Dip chicken in egg mixture; then dredge in flour mixture, coating well.

    Heat 1 inch of salad oil in a skillet; place chicken in skillet. Cover and cook over medium heat about 30 minutes or until golden brown; turn occasionally. Drain on paper towels. Yield: 4 servings.

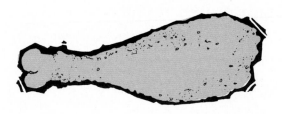

Golden Chicken Nuggets

  3 *whole chicken breasts, skinned and*
     boned
  ½ *cup all-purpose flour*
  ¾ *teaspoon salt*
  2 *teaspoons sesame seeds*
  1 *egg, slightly beaten*
  ½ *cup water*
Hot salad oil

Cut chicken into 1- x 1½-inch pieces; set aside. Combine remaining ingredients except salad oil. Dip chicken into batter, and sauté in hot oil until golden brown (about 7 to 10 minutes). Yield: about 6 servings.

    Note: Batter is also good for fish.

Smothered Fried Chicken

  1½ *cups all-purpose flour*
  1½ *teaspoons salt*
  1½ *teaspoons garlic salt*
  ½ *teaspoon pepper*
  1 *(2- to 3-pound) broiler-fryer chicken,*
     cut up
  1 *cup buttermilk*
  1 *cup hot salad oil*

Combine flour and seasonings. Dip chicken in buttermilk; then dredge in flour mixture. Brown chicken on both sides in hot salad oil over high heat. Cover and reduce heat to low, and cook 45 minutes or until chicken is tender. Drain on paper towels. Yield: 4 servings.

Sour Cream Marinated Chicken Breasts

  1 *(8-ounce) carton commercial sour cream*
  ¼ *cup lemon juice*
  2 *teaspoons Worcestershire sauce*
  2 *teaspoons celery salt*
  1 *teaspoon paprika*
  2 *cloves garlic, minced*
  2 *teaspoons pepper*
  5 *whole chicken breasts, split*
Salt
Breadcrumbs
  ½ *cup melted butter or margarine*
  ¼ *cup melted shortening*

Combine sour cream, lemon juice, Worcestershire sauce, celery salt, paprika, garlic, and pepper; blend well. Sprinkle chicken with salt, and coat with sour cream mixture. Cover and refrigerate at least 12 hours.

    Remove chicken from refrigerator, and coat with breadcrumbs. Place in a single layer in a lightly greased 13- x 9- x 2-inch baking dish. Combine butter and shortening; pour half of mixture over chicken. Bake at 350° for 45 minutes. Pour remainder of butter mixture over chicken, and continue to bake 15 minutes. Yield: 10 servings.

★
Chicken Beer Bake

    3 *whole chicken breasts, split*
    4 *or 5 tablespoons all-purpose flour*
Salt and pepper to taste
Hot salad oil
    2 *(10¾-ounce) cans cream of chicken*
        soup, undiluted
    1 *tablespoon soy sauce*
  ¼ *cup toasted slivered almonds, divided*
  ½ *cup beer*
    1 *(3-ounce) can sliced mushrooms,*
        drained, or ⅓ cup cooked sliced
        mushrooms

Remove skin from chicken; wash chicken, and dry well with paper towels. Combine flour, salt, and pepper. Dredge chicken in flour mixture, and brown in heated oil.

Place chicken in a shallow pan. Combine soup, soy sauce, 2 tablespoons almonds, beer, and mushrooms; pour over chicken. Bake, uncovered, at 350° for 1 hour, basting occasionally. Sprinkle with remaining almonds. Yield: 6 servings.

Crab Stuffed Chicken Rolls

    4 *whole chicken breasts, split, boned, and*
        skinned
    3 *slices bread, toasted*
  ⅓ *cup mayonnaise*
    1 *tablespoon lemon juice*
  ½ *cup chicken bouillon*
Dash of hot sauce
  ⅔ *cup finely chopped celery*
  ⅔ *cup finely chopped green onion*
  ¾ *cup melted butter or margarine, divided*
  ¼ *teaspoon basil*
  ¼ *teaspoon marjoram*
  ¼ *teaspoon thyme*
    1 *teaspoon sage*
  ¼ *teaspoon pepper*
  ½ *teaspoon seasoned salt*
    1 *cup fresh, flaked crabmeat*
  ⅓ *cup shredded Swiss cheese*
    2 *tablespoons minced parsley*
  ⅓ *cup all-purpose flour*
Paprika
Parsley

Place each half of chicken breast on a sheet of waxed paper. Flatten to ¼-inch thickness, using a meat mallet or rolling pin; set aside.

Tear bread into small pieces. Combine mayonnaise, lemon juice, bouillon, and hot sauce; pour over bread. Sauté celery and onion in ½ cup butter; add to bread mixture. Stir in seasonings, crabmeat, cheese, and 2 tablespoons minced parsley; mix well.

Place an equal amount of stuffing mixture on each chicken breast. Fold long sides of chicken over stuffing; roll up, and secure with toothpick. Dredge each roll in flour, and dip in remaining ¼ cup butter. Place in a 10- x 6- x 1¾-inch baking dish, and sprinkle with paprika. Bake at 350° for 45 minutes to 1 hour. Garnish with parsley. Yield: 8 servings.

Spanish Chicken

    1 *(2½- to 3-pound) chicken, cut up*
Salt and pepper to taste
Melted shortening
    1 *cup chopped onion*
  ½ *cup chopped celery*
  ½ *cup chopped green pepper*
    2 *cloves garlic, minced*
    2 *tablespoons melted butter or margarine*
 1½ *teaspoons salt*
    1 *teaspoon black pepper*
    1 *tablespoon all-purpose flour*
    4 *cups tomato sauce*
 1½ *teaspoons sugar*
    1 *teaspoon ground marjoram*
  ½ *teaspoon grated lemon rind*
  ½ *teaspoon ground thyme*
     Hot cooked rice (optional)

Sprinkle chicken with salt and pepper, and brown in hot shortening in a skillet. Remove chicken from skillet; place in a 13- x 9- x 2-inch baking dish.

Sauté onion, celery, green pepper, and garlic in butter; spoon over chicken. Combine remaining ingredients, except rice, in a saucepan; simmer over low heat 10 to 12 minutes. Pour over chicken. Bake, uncovered, at 350° for 1 hour. Serve over rice, if desired. Yield: 4 to 6 servings.

Chicken Paprikash

1   *(2½- to 3-pound) chicken, cut up*
¼   *cup melted butter or margarine*
½   *cup chopped onion*
¼   *cup all-purpose flour*
2   *teaspoons salt*
2   *tablespoons paprika*
¼   *teaspoon pepper*
1   *(10½-ounce) can chicken broth*
2   *(8-ounce) cartons commercial sour*
      cream
½   *teaspoon Worcestershire sauce*
1   *(8-ounce) package medium noodles*

Lightly brown chicken in butter in a skillet; remove and set aside.

Sauté onion in pan drippings until tender; blend in flour, salt, paprika, and pepper. Cook over low heat until bubbly. Gradually add chicken broth; cook, stirring constantly, until smooth and thickened. Remove from heat; stir in sour cream and Worcestershire sauce.

Cook noodles according to package directions; drain. Combine noodles and half of sour cream sauce; spoon into a shallow 2-quart casserole. Top with chicken; pour remaining sauce over chicken. Bake at 325° for 1 hour. Yield: 6 servings.

★ Monterey Chicken

4   *whole chicken breasts, split, boned, and*
      skinned
1   *(8-ounce) package Monterey Jack cheese*
2   *eggs, beaten*
1½ *cups dry breadcrumbs*
⅔   *cup butter or margarine, divided*
1   *chicken bouillon cube*
1   *cup boiling water*
½   *cup chopped onion*
½   *cup chopped green pepper*
2   *teaspoons all-purpose flour*
1   *teaspoon salt*
¼   *teaspoon pepper*
3   *cups cooked rice*
1   *(4-ounce) can sliced mushrooms,*
      drained
2   *tablespoons chopped pimiento*

Place each half of chicken breast on waxed paper; carefully flatten to ¼-inch thickness, using a meat mallet or rolling pin.

Cut cheese into 8 equal portions; place one portion in center of each half of chicken breast. Fold long sides of chicken over cheese; fold ends over, and secure with toothpicks. Dip each chicken breast in egg; then coat with breadcrumbs. Brown meat on all sides in ⅓ cup butter; set aside.

Dissolve bouillon in boiling water. Sauté onion and green pepper in ⅓ cup butter until tender. Stir in bouillon, flour, salt, and pepper; cook until thickened. Stir in rice, mushrooms, and pimiento.

Spoon rice mixture into an 11¾- x 7½- x 1¾-inch baking dish. Arrange browned chicken over rice mixture. Bake at 400° for 20 to 30 minutes. Yield: 8 servings.

Dressed-Up Chicken Breasts

2½ *cups unseasoned croutons*
2   *teaspoons sage*
1½ *tablespoons chopped onion*
1   *egg, slightly beaten*
1¼ *cups chicken bouillon*
6   *whole chicken breasts, boned and*
      skinned
1   *(2½-ounce) package sliced dried beef*
12 *slices bacon*
1   *(10¾-ounce) can cream of mushroom*
      soup, undiluted
1   *(8-ounce) carton commercial sour cream*

Combine croutons, sage, onion, egg, and bouillon. Place about 3 tablespoons stuffing in center of each chicken breast; place 2 slices dried beef on top of each mound of dressing. Roll up each breast tightly, and secure with toothpicks.

Cook bacon briefly on both sides until partly done but still pliable. Wrap 2 slices bacon around each roll. Place rolls in a greased baking dish.

Combine soup and sour cream; spoon over chicken rolls. Cover and bake at 325° for 90 minutes. Uncover and bake 30 more minutes or until tender. Yield: 6 servings.

Herbed Chicken

  1 *(2- to 3-pound) broiler-fryer, quartered*
Salt and pepper
All-purpose flour
Hot salad oil
  ½ *teaspoon rosemary, crushed*
  ½ *teaspoon basil*
  ½ *teaspoon finely chopped parsley*
  ½ *cup orange juice*
1½ *cups commercial sour cream*
  4 *(½-inch) strips orange rind*

Season chicken with salt and pepper; dredge in flour. Brown chicken on both sides in oil.

Arrange chicken in a shallow baking dish, and sprinkle with herbs. Combine orange juice and sour cream; pour over chicken, covering completely. Place a strip of orange rind on each piece of chicken.

Cover and bake at 325° for 45 minutes or until tender. Remove orange rind. Bake, uncovered, 5 minutes or until lightly browned. Yield: 4 servings.

Orange Glazed Chicken with Wild Rice Stuffing

  1 *(5-pound) chicken*
Salt and pepper to taste
  ½ *teaspoon ground ginger*
  1 *small onion, finely chopped*
  2 *tablespoons melted butter or margarine*
  1 *(6-ounce) package long grain and wild rice mix*
  1 *(14-ounce) can chicken broth*
  1 *(3-ounce) can sliced mushrooms*
Orange Glaze

Season cavity of chicken with salt, pepper, and ginger; refrigerate overnight. Sauté onion in butter until tender; add rice mix and broth. Drain mushrooms, reserving liquid. Add mushroom liquid to rice; cook according to package directions. Stir in mushrooms.

Place chicken, breast side up, on a rack in a shallow roasting pan; stuff lightly with rice mixture. Bake at 350° for 2 to 2½ hours or until done. Baste during last 15 minutes with Orange Glaze. Yield: 6 to 8 servings.

Orange Glaze:

  3 *tablespoons grated orange rind*
  ⅓ *cup orange juice*
  ⅓ *cup honey*
  ¼ *teaspoon ground ginger*

Combine all ingredients in a saucepan; bring to a boil. Yield: about ⅔ cup.

Elegant Chicken

  8 *chicken breasts, skinned and boned*
Seasoned salt
  ¼ *cup melted butter or margarine*
  2 *(9-ounce) packages frozen artichoke hearts, thawed and halved*
  ½ *pound mushrooms, sliced*
  ¼ *cup melted butter or margarine*
  3 *tablespoons all-purpose flour*
1½ *cups chicken broth*
  ⅓ *cup sherry*

Sprinkle chicken with salt, and brown in ¼ cup butter. Arrange chicken in a shallow baking dish. Add artichokes, and set aside.

Sauté mushrooms in ¼ cup butter until tender. Sprinkle flour over mushrooms, stirring until blended. Gradually add chicken broth and sherry, stirring constantly; simmer for 5 minutes, and pour over chicken. Bake, covered, at 375° for 45 minutes. Yield: 8 servings.

★ Chicken Kiev

1 cup butter, softened
2 tablespoons chopped parsley
1 teaspoon rosemary
¾ teaspoon salt
⅛ teaspoon pepper
6 whole chicken breasts, split, boned, and skinned
¾ cup all-purpose flour
3 eggs, well beaten
1½ to 2 cups breadcrumbs
Salad Oil

Combine butter and seasonings in a small bowl; blend thoroughly. Shape butter mixture into 2 sticks; cover and put in freezer about 45 minutes or until firm.

Place each half of chicken breast on a sheet of waxed paper; flatten to ¼-inch thickness, using a meat mallet or rolling pin.

Cut each stick of butter mixture into 6 pats; place a pat in center of each half of chicken breast. Fold long sides of chicken over butter; fold ends over and secure with toothpick. Dredge each piece of chicken in flour, dip in egg, and coat with breadcrumbs. Cover and refrigerate about 1 hour.

Cook chicken in salad oil heated to 350°. Cook 5 minutes on each side or until browned, turning with tongs. Place in warm oven until all chicken is cooked. Yield: 12 servings.

★ Sesame Seed Chicken

1 teaspoon salt
½ teaspoon pepper
¾ cup all-purpose flour, divided
4 whole chicken breasts, split and boned
4 eggs, beaten
4 tablespoons milk
6 tablespoons sesame seeds
Hot salad oil
Supreme Sauce

Combine salt, pepper, and ¼ cup flour in a bag. Add chicken, and shake to coat. Combine eggs and milk in a small bowl; set aside.

Combine remaining flour and sesame seeds in a small bowl.

Dip each chicken breast in egg mixture; then coat with sesame seed mixture. Heat salad oil to 350°; add chicken, and sauté about 15 minutes or until golden brown. Serve with Supreme Sauce. Yield: 8 servings.

Supreme Sauce:

6 tablespoons butter or margarine
4 tablespoons all-purpose flour
3 cups chicken broth
2 egg yolks, beaten

Melt butter in a small saucepan over low heat; add flour, blending until smooth. Gradually add chicken broth; cook, stirring constantly, until slightly thickened. Gradually add about ½ cup hot mixture to egg yolks; then beat yolk mixture into remaining hot mixture. Cook over low heat, stirring constantly, until sauce is thickened and smooth. Yield: about 2 cups.

Cozy Chicken

1 (4-ounce) can whole mushrooms, drained
½ cup commercial Italian salad dressing
2 tablespoons all-purpose flour
Salt and pepper
2 whole chicken breasts, halved
2 tablespoons salad oil
1 (10¾-ounce) can cream of mushroom soup, undiluted
½ cup water
1 cup dry white wine
Hot cooked noodles

Marinate mushrooms in salad dressing overnight; drain. Combine flour, salt, and pepper; dredge chicken in flour mixture. Brown in hot oil in an electric skillet. Add remaining flour mixture to skillet, and stir until smooth. Add soup, water, and mushrooms; cover and cook over low heat 30 minutes. Stir in wine. Cook 15 to 30 minutes or until tender. Serve over cooked noodles. Yield: 2 servings.

Easy Chicken Tetrazzini

1 cup chopped onion
1 cup chopped celery
2 tablespoons butter or margarine
1 (10¾-ounce) can cream of mushroom soup, undiluted
1 (10¾-ounce) can cream of chicken soup, undiluted
1 cup shredded Cheddar cheese
1 (2-ounce) jar chopped pimientos, drained
1 (2½- to 3-pound) chicken, cooked, boned, and chopped
Salt and pepper to taste
Garlic salt
Hot cooked rice

Sauté onion and celery in butter. Add soup, cheese, pimiento, chicken, salt, and pepper; blend well. Sprinkle with garlic salt; simmer 30 minutes. Serve over rice. Yield: 6 to 8 servings.

Chicken Dijon

4 chicken breasts, split, boned, and skinned
3 tablespoons melted butter or margarine
2 tablespoons all-purpose flour
1 cup chicken broth
½ cup half-and-half
2 tablespoons Dijon mustard

Sauté chicken in butter over low heat about 20 minutes or until tender. Remove chicken to a warm platter.

Blend flour into pan drippings; cook over low heat, stirring constantly, until bubbly. Gradually stir in broth and half-and-half; cook until smooth and thickened, stirring constantly. Stir in mustard. Add chicken; cover and simmer for 10 minutes. Yield: 4 servings.

★ Chicken Marengo

1 cup sliced fresh mushrooms
2 tablespoons butter or margarine
3 pounds chicken thighs, legs, and breasts or 1 (3-pound) broiler-fryer, cut in serving-size pieces
Salt and pepper to taste
2 to 3 tablespoons olive oil or salad oil
4 green onions with tops removed, sliced
1 clove garlic, minced
½ cup dry white wine or consommé
2 tomatoes, cut in wedges and seeded
¼ teaspoon thyme
1 tablespoon minced parsley
Parsley sprigs

Sauté mushrooms in butter 2 minutes; set aside.

Sprinkle chicken with salt and pepper; sauté in hot oil until brown. Remove chicken from skillet, and set aside; reserve drippings. Sauté onion and garlic in drippings until onion is soft. Stir in wine, tomatoes, thyme, salt, and pepper, scraping bottom of skillet well.

Add chicken to skillet; cover and simmer 30 minutes or until chicken is tender. Add sautéed mushrooms; sprinkle with minced parsley, and garnish with sprigs of parsley. Yield: 6 servings.

Chicken Nicoise

2 (3-pound) chickens, cut in serving-size pieces
About 2 tablespoons olive oil
1 clove garlic, chopped
2 tablespoons freeze-dried chopped shallots
1 onion, diced
1 cup white wine
1 small eggplant, peeled and diced
3 zucchini, sliced
3 ripe tomatoes, quartered

Sauté chicken in olive oil. Add garlic, shallots, onion, and wine; cover and simmer 20 minutes. Add eggplant, zucchini, and tomatoes; simmer about 25 minutes or until chicken and vegetables are tender. Yield: 6 servings.

Tropical Chicken Delight

1   *broiler-fryer chicken, cut up*
½   *cup vinegar*
1   *clove garlic, minced*
⅔   *cup soy sauce*
1   *bay leaf*
¼   *teaspoon pepper*
1   *cup pineapple chunks*
1   *large tomato, diced*
¼   *cup melted butter or margarine*
     Hot cooked rice

Combine chicken, vinegar, garlic, soy sauce, bay leaf, and pepper in a Dutch oven. Cover and simmer over low heat 25 to 30 minutes or until chicken is tender. Remove chicken and bay leaf from Dutch oven; reserve cooking liquid.

Remove chicken from bone, and cut into bite-size pieces. Add chicken, pineapple, tomato, and butter to cooking liquid; cover and cook until heated through. Serve over hot rice. Yield: 6 servings.

★
Lemon-Barbecue Chicken

3   *(2- to 2½-pound) broiler-fryer chickens*
1   *cup salad oil*
½   *cup lemon juice*
1   *tablespoon salt*
1   *teaspoon paprika*
2   *teaspoons crushed basil*
2   *teaspoons onion powder*
½   *teaspoon crushed thyme*
1   *clove garlic, crushed*
1   *lemon, sliced*

Split chickens in halves or quarters; place in shallow baking pans. Combine remaining ingredients in a jar, and shake well to blend. Pour sauce over chicken; cover tightly and marinate in refrigerator 6 to 8 hours or overnight, turning chicken occasionally.

Remove chicken from refrigerator about an hour before grilling. Place chicken on grill, skin side up, and cook 20 to 25 minutes, brushing often with marinade. Turn chicken, and cook an additional 20 minutes. Yield: 6 to 12 servings.

Cantonese Dinner

½   *barbecued chicken, cut up*
1   *onion, sliced*
1   *(6-ounce) can tomato paste*
½   *cup chopped green pepper*
1   *(8-ounce) can water chestnuts, sliced*
3   *tablespoons brown sugar*
1½   *tablespoons cider vinegar*
1½   *teaspoons salt*
2   *teaspoons Worcestershire sauce*
1   *(16-ounce) can Chinese vegetables, drained*
1   *cup frozen peas, thawed*
     Hot cooked rice
     Toasted slivered almonds

Combine all ingredients except rice and almonds in an electric slow cooker. Cover and cook on low setting 6 to 8 hours. Serve on a bed of rice and sprinkle with almonds. Yield: 6 servings.

Skewered Chicken

4   *whole chicken breasts, skinned, boned, and cut into 1½-inch pieces*
2   *green peppers, cut into 1-inch pieces*
2   *(16-ounce) cans whole boiled onions, drained*
     Salt and pepper to taste
½   *cup melted butter or margarine*
1   *tablespoon tarragon*
1   *tablespoon lemon juice*

Alternate pieces of chicken, green pepper, and onion on skewers; sprinkle with salt and pepper.

Combine remaining ingredients; baste kabobs with sauce. Grill kabobs 20 to 25 minutes over medium heat, basting with sauce and turning occasionally. Yield: 6 servings.

Fruit and Chicken Kabobs

¼ cup corn oil
2 tablespoons lemon juice
2 whole chicken breasts, skinned, boned,
    and cut into 1½-inch pieces
½ teaspoon salt
⅛ teaspoon pepper
1 teaspoon Ac'cent
1 large green pepper, cut into 1-inch
    squares
1 (8-ounce) can pineapple chunks,
    drained
1 orange, cut into eighths
¼ cup commercial barbecue sauce
1 (12-ounce) jar pineapple preserves

Combine oil and lemon juice; add chicken and marinate at least 1 hour in refrigerator. Drain chicken, reserving marinade; sprinkle meat with salt, pepper, and Ac'cent. Alternate pieces of chicken, green pepper, pineapple chunks, and orange wedges on skewers.

Combine reserved marinade, barbecue sauce, and pineapple preserves in saucepan; heat thoroughly, stirring constantly. Baste kabobs with sauce. Grill kabobs 20 to 25 minutes over medium heat, basting with sauce and turning occasionally. Yield: 4 servings.

Honey-Barbecued Chicken

¾ cup melted butter or margarine
⅓ cup vinegar
¼ cup honey
2 cloves garlic, minced
2 teaspoons salt
½ teaspoon dry mustard
Dash of pepper
1 (2- to 3-pound) broiler-fryer, halved

To prepare sauce, combine first 7 ingredients.

Hook chicken wing tips behind shoulder joint into back. Place chicken on grill, skin side up, about 5 inches above hot coals. Cook slowly for 30 to 35 minutes or until tender, turning frequently and basting with sauce each time. Watch chicken closely so that it does not burn. Yield: 6 servings.

Chicken-Sour Cream Casserole

¼ cup melted butter or margarine
1 cup cracker crumbs
3 whole chicken breasts, cooked and cut
    into bite-size pieces
1 (8-ounce) carton commercial sour cream
1 (10¾-ounce) can cream of chicken soup,
    undiluted
¼ cup chicken broth
Salt and pepper to taste

Combine butter and cracker crumbs; blend well. Spoon half the crumbs into a shallow 2-quart casserole, and cover with chicken.

Combine sour cream, soup, broth, salt, and pepper; blend well. Pour over chicken, and top with remaining cracker crumbs. Bake at 350° for 20 to 25 minutes. Yield: 6 servings.

Chicken and Noodle Casserole

1 (2½- to 3-pound) chicken
1 (5-ounce) package egg noodles, cooked
    and drained
½ cup chopped celery
⅓ cup chopped green pepper
⅓ cup chopped onion
½ teaspoon salt
1 tablespoon chopped pimiento
1 cup mayonnaise
1 (10¾-ounce) can cream of mushroom or
    cream of celery soup, undiluted
½ cup milk
1 cup shredded mild Cheddar cheese
½ cup sliced almonds

Cook chicken until tender in salted water. Remove from water; cool. Bone chicken, and cut meat into small pieces.

Combine chicken, noodles, celery, green pepper, onion, salt, pimiento, and mayonnaise; set aside. Combine soup and milk; heat thoroughly, stirring constantly. Add cheese, stirring until cheese melts.

Combine chicken mixture and soup mixture; spoon into a greased 2-quart shallow casserole. Bake at 425° for 15 minutes. Remove from oven; top with almonds. Bake 5 additional minutes. Yield: 6 to 8 servings.

Chicken-Wild Rice Casserole

1	(6-ounce) package long grain and wild rice mix
¼	cup butter or margarine
¼	cup all-purpose flour
1	(13-ounce) can evaporated milk, undiluted
1½	cups chicken broth
2½	cups diced cooked chicken
1	(3-ounce) can sliced mushrooms, drained
⅓	cup chopped green pepper
¼	cup chopped pimiento
	Salt to taste
¼	cup slivered almonds, toasted

Prepare rice mix according to package directions, using the seasoning packet; set aside. Melt butter in a heavy saucepan; stir in flour until well blended. Gradually stir in milk and broth; cook, stirring constantly, over medium heat until mixture is smooth and thickened.

Add sauce to cooked rice; mix in chicken, mushrooms, green pepper, pimiento, and salt. Spoon into a greased 2-quart casserole; sprinkle top with toasted almonds, and bake at 350° for 30 to 40 minutes. Yield: about 8 servings.

★ Chicken Divan

2	whole chicken breasts
	Pinch of rosemary
	Salt and pepper to taste
1	cup water
2	tablespoons melted butter or margarine
2	tablespoons all-purpose flour
1	cup milk
1	egg yolk, beaten
	Juice of ½ lemon
½	teaspoon grated lemon rind
½	cup mayonnaise
2	(10-ounce) packages frozen spinach, asparagus, or broccoli, cooked and drained
	Grated Parmesan cheese

Place chicken breasts, rosemary, salt, pepper, and water in a saucepan; bring to a boil. Cover and cook over low heat 10 to 15 minutes or until chicken is tender. Drain, reserving chicken broth. Bone and chop chicken; set aside.

Combine butter and flour; cook over low heat, stirring constantly, until smooth. Combine milk and ½ cup reserved chicken broth; gradually add to flour mixture. Cook, stirring constantly, until smooth and thickened. Season with salt and pepper. Blend in egg yolk, lemon juice, and lemon rind; cook 1 minute, stirring constantly. Add mayonnaise, mixing well.

Layer half of spinach, chicken, and sauce in a lightly greased 2-quart casserole. Repeat layers; sprinkle with cheese. Bake at 350° for 30 minutes. Yield: 6 to 8 servings.

Crunchy Chicken Casserole

3	cups chopped cooked chicken
½	cup slivered almonds
1	(8½-ounce) can water chestnuts, drained and thinly sliced
¼	cup chopped pimiento
¼	teaspoon celery salt
⅛	teaspoon pepper
⅛	teaspoon paprika
1	tablespoon chopped parsley
1	(10¾-ounce) can cream of mushroom soup, undiluted
½	cup French-fried onion rings, crumbled
½	cup shredded sharp Cheddar cheese

Combine all ingredients except onion rings and cheese; pour into a greased 1½-quart casserole. Sprinkle onion rings and cheese over top. Bake at 350° for 30 minutes. Yield: 6 servings.

Chipper Chicken Casserole

1 (2½- to 3-pound) broiler-fryer chicken,
    cooked, boned, and diced
1½ cups cooked rice
1 cup sliced celery
⅓ cup finely chopped onion
½ cup toasted slivered almonds
¾ cup mayonnaise
¼ cup water
1 (10¾-ounce) can cream of chicken soup,
    undiluted
1 (4-ounce) can sliced mushrooms,
    drained
1 tablespoon lemon juice
½ teaspoon salt
¼ teaspoon pepper
3 hard-cooked eggs, sliced
2 cups crushed potato chips

Combine all ingredients except eggs and potato chips; stir until well blended. Gently stir
egg slices into chicken mixture. Spoon mixture into a lightly greased 2-quart casserole.
Top with potato chips. Bake at 350° for 1 hour
and 15 minutes or until bubbly. Yield: 6
servings.

Note: Casserole may be made ahead and
frozen. Spoon mixture into a lightly greased
2-quart freezer-to-oven casserole; cover with
aluminum foil, sealing well. Freeze.

When ready to serve, thaw in refrigerator.
Top with potato chips. Bake as directed
above.

Cheesy Chicken

1 slice bacon, diced
¼ cup minced onion
¼ cup minced green pepper
1 cup diced cooked chicken
1 cup shredded Cheddar cheese
2 tablespoons chopped pimiento
1 cup cooked cut green beans
½ teaspoon salt
¼ teaspoon pepper
  Garlic powder to taste
1 tablespoon chopped parsley
1 cup cooked macaroni
¼ cup buttered breadcrumbs

Cook bacon until crisp. Add onion and green
pepper; cook until tender. Combine all ingredients except breadcrumbs. Spoon mixture into a buttered 1-quart casserole; sprinkle with breadcrumbs. Bake at 350° for 15 to
20 minutes. Yield: 4 servings.

Fresh Mushrooms and Chicken Livers

1 pound mushrooms
1 pound chicken livers
¼ cup melted butter or margarine
4 tablespoons all-purpose flour
2 cups chicken broth
½ teaspoon salt
¼ teaspoon pepper
¼ cup sherry
  Hot cooked wild rice

Sauté mushrooms and chicken livers in butter over low heat. Sprinkle livers with flour,
stirring to mix well. Add chicken broth, salt,
and pepper; cook until thickened, stirring
constantly. Stir in sherry. Serve over hot
cooked wild rice. Yield: 6 to 8 servings.

Sautéed Chicken Livers

2 tablespoons all-purpose flour
¼ teaspoon salt
¼ teaspoon pepper
1 pound chicken livers
2 tablespoons salad oil
6 tablespoons melted butter or margarine
2 medium-size onions, chopped
1 cup sliced mushrooms
¼ cup dry sherry
¼ cup chopped parsley

Combine flour, salt, and pepper; dredge
livers in flour mixture. Heat oil and butter in a
skillet; brown chicken livers. Remove from
skillet and set aside. Sauté onion in pan
drippings until tender; add mushrooms and
cook until tender. Return livers to pan; add
sherry and simmer 6 to 7 minutes. Sprinkle
with parsley. Yield: 4 servings.

Chicken Livers Stroganoff

    2   *cups thinly sliced onion*
    ¼   *cup melted butter or margarine*
    ½   *pound chicken livers, halved*
    1   *tablespoon paprika*
    ½   *teaspoon salt*
        Dash of pepper
    1   *(8-ounce) carton commercial sour cream*
        Hot cooked rice
        Parsley

Sauté onion in butter until tender. Add
livers; sprinkle with paprika, salt, and pepper. Cook livers over low heat until lightly
browned; cover and simmer 5 minutes or
until tender. Stir in sour cream; heat through.
Serve over hot cooked rice; garnish with
parsley. Yield: 4 servings.

Polynesian Turkey

    1   *(20-ounce) can pineapple chunks*
        Pineapple juice
    ½   *cup rosé*
    2   *tablespoons soy sauce*
    ½   *teaspoon salt*
    ⅛   *teaspoon ground ginger*
    1   *clove garlic, crushed*
    3   *cups diced cooked turkey*
    3   *tablespoons cornstarch*
    1   *(6-ounce) can pitted ripe olives, drained
          and cut in half*
    1   *green pepper, chopped*
    1   *pimiento, chopped*
        Hot cooked rice

Drain pineapple, reserving syrup. Add
enough pineapple juice to reserved syrup to
make 1 cup. Add rosé, soy sauce, salt, ginger, and garlic to 1 cup pineapple juice; pour
over turkey and marinate 1 hour.

Drain marinade into a skillet; add cornstarch, mixing well. Bring mixture to a boil;
cook, stirring constantly, until thickened,
about 5 minutes. Add turkey, olives, green
pepper, pimiento, and pineapple. Cover and
simmer 5 to 10 minutes. Serve over rice.
Yield: 6 to 8 servings.

★ Chicken Livers in Wine

    12 *slices bacon*
    4   *small green onions, finely chopped*
    ¼   *cup chopped green pepper*
    1   *pound chicken livers*
        About ⅓ cup all-purpose flour
    1   *cup white wine*
    1   *tablespoon parsley flakes*
    ⅛   *teaspoon thyme*
    ¼   *teaspoon salt*
    ⅛   *teaspoon freshly ground pepper*
        English muffins, halved and toasted

Cook bacon until crisp; drain and crumble.
Set aside.

Sauté onion and green pepper in bacon
drippings until tender. Dredge livers in flour;
add to sautéed vegetables, and cook about 5
minutes. Add wine and seasonings; cover
and simmer 5 minutes or until livers are
done. Serve on English muffins; sprinkle
with bacon. Yield: 6 servings.

Old-Fashioned Roast Turkey

Select a 12- to 14- pound turkey. Remove
giblets, and rinse turkey thoroughly with
cold water; pat dry. Sprinkle inside cavity
with salt. Tie ends of legs to tail with cord or
string, or tuck them under flap of skin
around tail. Lift wingtips up and over back so
they are tucked under bird.

Brush entire bird with melted butter or
margarine; place on a roasting rack, breast
side up. Insert meat thermometer in breast or
meaty part of thigh, making sure it does not
touch bone. Bake at 325° until meat thermometer reaches 190° (about 5 to 6 hours). If turkey starts to get too brown, cover lightly with
aluminum foil.

When turkey is two-thirds done, cut the
cord or band of skin holding the drumstick
ends to the tail; this will ensure that the inside of the thighs is cooked. Turkey is done
when drumsticks are easy to move up and
down. Garnish with spiced crabapples and
parsley. Yield: 20 to 24 servings.

★ Cornish Hens Teriyaki

½ cup melted butter or margarine
4 cups seasoned croutons
½ cup diced mandarin orange sections
8 Cornish hens
½ cup soy sauce
2 cloves garlic, crushed

Combine butter, croutons, and mandarin orange sections; mix well. Place hens, breast side up, in a shallow roasting pan; stuff with crouton mixture.

Combine soy sauce and garlic; brush on hens. Bake at 350° about 1 hour, basting every 15 minutes with pan drippings. Yield: 8 servings.

Cornish Hens Italiano

2 (0.6-ounce) packages Italian dressing mix
½ cup butter or margarine
½ cup lime juice
¼ cup salad oil
4 (¾- to 1-pound) Cornish hens

Combine first 4 ingredients; simmer 5 minutes or until butter melts. Truss hens, and thread on spit. Secure with holding forks. Cook on rotisserie 1 hour and 15 minutes or until done, basting often with sauce. Yield: 4 to 8 servings.

Turkey Patties with Cheese Sauce

⅓ cup melted butter or margarine
½ cup all-purpose flour
1¾ cups milk
2 cups ground cooked turkey
¼ teaspoon garlic salt
Dash of pepper
1 egg, beaten
1 cup fine cracker crumbs
Hot salad oil
½ cup milk
1 (8-ounce) jar pasteurized process cheese spread

Combine butter and flour in a saucepan; cook over low heat until bubbly. Gradually stir in 1¾ cups milk; cook, stirring constantly, until smooth and thickened. (This will make a heavy white sauce.)

Combine turkey, garlic salt, pepper, egg, and 1 cup white sauce, reserving remaining white sauce. Chill turkey mixture. Shape into patties and roll each in cracker crumbs. Sauté patties in hot oil until golden brown.

Combine ½ cup milk with remaining white sauce; heat, stirring well. Add cheese, stirring until melted. Serve over patties. Yield: 6 to 8 servings.

Creamed Turkey on French Toast

5 to 7 tablespoons melted butter or margarine, divided
1 tablespoon all-purpose flour
2 cups half-and-half, divided
½ cup turkey broth
2 cups diced cooked turkey
2 eggs, slightly beaten
½ teaspoon salt
1 tablespoon sherry
6 (1-inch-thick) slices bread
¼ cup toasted almonds or pine nuts

Combine 1 tablespoon butter and flour in a saucepan. Gradually stir in 1 cup half-and-half and broth. Cook, stirring constantly, until smooth and thickened. Stir in turkey. Keep warm over very low heat.

Combine eggs, salt, sherry, and remaining 1 cup half-and-half in a shallow dish. Dip both sides of bread slices in mixture. Sauté in 4 to 6 tablespoons butter until golden brown; turn and sauté on other side.

Spoon turkey mixture over toast. Sprinkle each serving with almonds. Serve at once. Yield: 6 servings.

Turkey-Ham Casserole

1 *(8-ounce) package spaghetti*
¼ *cup finely chopped onions*
1 *(4-ounce) can sliced mushrooms,*
    drained
¼ *cup butter or margarine*
1½ *cups diced cooked turkey*
1 *cup diced cooked ham*
½ *teaspoon salt*
⅛ *teaspoon pepper*
½ *teaspoon celery salt*
1 *(8-ounce) carton commercial sour cream*
1 *cup creamed cottage cheese*
1 *cup shredded sharp Cheddar cheese*

Break spaghetti into 1½-inch pieces, and cook according to package directions; drain and set aside.

Sauté onion and mushrooms in butter; stir in turkey, ham, and seasonings. Heat thoroughly. Combine sour cream, cottage cheese, and spaghetti; add meat mixture, mixing lightly.

Spoon mixture into a buttered 1½-quart casserole; top with Cheddar cheese. Bake at 350° for 20 to 30 minutes or until bubbly and browned. Yield: 6 to 8 servings.

Chicken Loaf

1 *(4- to 5-pound) hen*
Boiling, salted water
1 *cup cooked regular rice*
2 *cups toasted breadcrumbs*
1 *cup milk*
1 *(2-ounce) jar chopped pimiento, drained*
4 *eggs, beaten*
1 *(8-ounce) can green peas, drained*

Cook hen in boiling salted water until tender; remove chicken from broth, reserving 2 cups broth. Cool hen; remove chicken from bones, and grind meat.

Combine chicken, reserved broth, and remaining ingredients. Spoon into a greased 9¼- x 5¼- x 2¾-inch loafpan and bake at 375° for 60 to 75 minutes or until firm. Yield: 8 to 10 servings.

Chicken Croquettes

¼ *cup melted butter or margarine*
3 *tablespoons all-purpose flour*
1 *cup chicken broth*
½ *teaspoon salt*
¼ *teaspoon pepper*
2 *cups ground cooked chicken*
2 *tablespoons chopped pimiento*
1 *egg*
1 *tablespoon water*
½ *cup fine breadcrumbs*
Hot salad oil

Combine butter and flour in a saucepan; blend well, and cook over low heat until bubbly. Gradually stir in broth; cook 5 to 10 minutes, stirring constantly, until smooth and thickened (mixture will be very thick). Stir in salt, pepper, chicken, and pimiento. Chill until stiff.

Shape into croquettes. Combine egg and water; beat well. Roll croquettes in breadcrumbs; dip in egg, and roll again in breadcrumbs. Deep fry in hot oil until golden brown. Yield: about 6 to 8 servings.

Chicken Spaghetti

1 *(3- to 5-pound) hen*
1 *(8-ounce) package spaghetti*
1 *(10¾-ounce) can cream of mushroom*
    soup, undiluted
1 *(10¾-ounce) can cream of celery soup,*
    undiluted
1 *(4-ounce) can sliced mushrooms,*
    undrained
1 *(2-ounce) jar pimientos, drained and*
    chopped
1 *tablespoon basil (optional)*
1 *teaspoon curry powder (optional)*
Salt and pepper to taste

Cook hen in boiling salted water until tender; drain, reserving broth. Remove meat from bones, and cut into bite-size pieces.

Cook spaghetti in reserved broth until tender; drain, reserving 1 cup broth. Combine chicken, spaghetti, soup, mushrooms, pimiento, reserved 1 cup broth, and seasonings. Heat through before serving. Yield: about 8 servings

★ Elegant Chicken Crêpes

Crêpes
Chicken Filling
Velouté Sauce
½ *cup shredded Swiss cheese*
¼ *cup grated Parmesan cheese*

Spread the center of each crêpe with 3 tablespoons Chicken Filling; roll up, and place seam side down in a buttered baking dish. Pour 3 cups Velouté Sauce over crêpes (remaining 3 cups of sauce is used in Chicken Filling); sprinkle Swiss and Parmesan cheese over sauce. Bake at 350° for 20 minutes or until golden brown. Yield: 32 crêpes.

Crêpes:

3 *eggs*
1½ *cups milk*
½ *cup butter or margarine, melted*
1½ *cups all-purpose flour*
½ *teaspoon salt*
Salad oil

Combine eggs, milk, butter, flour, and salt in container of an electric blender; blend 30 seconds. Scrape flour adhering to sides of container with a rubber spatula; blend 5 more seconds.

Refrigerate batter at least 1 hour. Batter should be the consistency of half-and-half. If too thick, add milk by tablespoons to batter; if too thin, add 1 to 2 tablespoons flour.

Brush the bottom of 6- or 7-inch crêpe pan or heavy skillet with salad oil; place over medium heat until just hot, not smoking.

Pour 2 tablespoons batter in pan; quickly tilt pan in all directions so batter covers the pan in a thin film. Cook about 1 minute.

Lift edge of crêpe to test for doneness. The crêpe is ready for flipping when it can be shaken loose from pan. Flip the crêpe, and cook about 30 seconds on the other side; this is rarely more than a spotty brown and is used as the side on which filling is placed.

Place hot crêpe on a towel to cool; stack crêpes between layers of waxed paper to prevent sticking. Yield: 32 crêpes.

Chicken Filling:

5 *pounds chicken breasts*
7 *cups water*
1 *tablespoon salt*
2 *ribs celery, sliced*
2 *carrots, sliced*
¼ *teaspoon ground thyme*
½ *teaspoon white pepper*
1¼ *cups half-and-half*
2½ *tablespoons chopped fresh parsley*
2¼ *teaspoons grated onion*
3 *cups Velouté Sauce*
3 *egg yolks, slightly beaten*
⅛ *teaspoon sage*
7 *slices cooked bacon, crumbled*
¼ *cup shredded Swiss cheese*
¼ *cup grated Parmesan cheese*

Place chicken, water, salt, celery, carrots, thyme, and pepper in a Dutch oven. Bring to a boil; cover and simmer 45 minutes or until done. Remove chicken; set aside to cool. Strain broth, and set aside.

Remove bones and cartilage from chicken; finely chop meat but do not grind. Combine chicken, half-and-half, parsley, and onion in a large saucepan; simmer 10 minutes.

Gradually stir ¼ cup Velouté Sauce into egg yolks. Gradually add yolk mixture to 2¾ cups Velouté Sauce; stir in sage. Combine sauce with chicken mixture; cook over low heat until slightly thickened. Add bacon, Swiss cheese, and Parmesan cheese; stir until thoroughly blended. Yield: 6 cups.

Velouté Sauce:

¾ *cup butter or margarine*
¾ *cup all-purpose flour*
6 *cups strained chicken broth*
1½ *teaspoons salt*
½ *teaspoon white pepper*

Melt butter in a saucepan; gradually add flour, stirring constantly. Cook over low heat, stirring constantly, until roux is foaming. Gradually add broth. Cook, stirring constantly, until thick and smooth. Add salt and pepper, and simmer 5 minutes. Yield: 6 cups.

Paella

20 *chicken thighs*
   Salt and pepper
½ *cup olive oil*
½ *cup butter*
1 *pound lean round beef, cut into ¼-inch cubes*
1 *pound ham, cut into ¼-inch cubes*
1 *pound lean pork, cut into ¼-inch cubes*
1 *(16-ounce) package smoked pork sausage links*
1½ *pounds codfish sticks*
1 *pound fresh green beans, sliced*
   Pinch of ground nutmeg
6 *drops lemon juice*
3 *tomatoes*
2 *green peppers, sliced lengthwise into eighths*
3 *medium-size carrots, sliced*
1 *large onion, finely chopped*
4 *large cloves garlic, diced*
1 *(4-ounce) jar pimientos, coarsely chopped and divided*
1 *teaspoon freshly ground black pepper*
3 *cups uncooked regular rice*
2 *tablespoons chicken-seasoned stock base*
6 *cups boiling water*
1 *(10-ounce) package frozen peas, cooked*
1 *(10-ounce) package frozen limas, cooked*
1 *(7-ounce) can crabmeat, drained and cartilage removed*
1 *pound medium-size shrimp, peeled and deveined*
6 *to 6½ cups boiling chicken broth*

Season chicken with salt and pepper; cook, skin side down, in hot olive oil and butter until golden brown. Remove from skillet. Add beef, ham, and pork to skillet, and cook until brown; remove meat, and reserve drippings in skillet.

Place sausage links in a small skillet; add water to a depth of 1 inch. Simmer 10 minutes, piercing sausage to drain juices; pour off water, and cut sausage into ⅛-inch slices. Brown sausage in reserved drippings; remove from skillet. Add codfish sticks to skillet, and cook until tender; remove fish, and reserve drippings in skillet. Set aside.

Cook green beans in water seasoned with salt, nutmeg, and lemon juice. Place tomatoes in saucepan with beans for 2 to 3 minutes or long enough for skins to loosen. Core, peel, and chop tomatoes. Cook beans an additional 12 minutes or until partially tender. Drain beans and set aside.

Sauté green pepper in reserved drippings long enough for skin to loosen. Remove green pepper from skillet. Remove skin from green peppers. Strain drippings. Sauté carrots in drippings until tender; add onion and cook until transparent. Add garlic and tomatoes; simmer briskly for 15 minutes or until mixture becomes stiff. Add half of green pepper, half of pimiento, and freshly ground black pepper.

Wash rice several times. Add chicken-seasoned stock base to boiling water, stirring until dissolved. Add rice and cook over low heat 20 minutes or until partially tender.

Spoon rice into a large casserole (14 to 16 inches in diameter and 3½ to 4 inches deep). Add tomato mixture, peas, limas, green beans, beef, ham, pork, sausage, crabmeat, and shrimp. Break codfish into small pieces and add to mixture. Mix until all ingredients are evenly blended. Arrange chicken thighs on top, and garnish with remaining green pepper and pimiento.

Pour boiling chicken broth over paella mixture. Bake at 400° for 45 to 50 minutes or until rice is tender and juices have cooked down. Remove from oven; cover with a heavy towel, and let sit for 5 to 10 minutes before serving. Yield: 12 to 15 servings.

Christmas Roast Duckling

1   (5- to 6-pound) dressed duckling
1   teaspoon salt
10   slices white bread, diced
1½   cups peeled, chopped apple
1   cup chopped walnuts
½   cup chopped celery
1   cup orange juice
¾   to 1 cup firmly packed light brown
     sugar
1   egg, slightly beaten
2   teaspoons grated orange rind
1   teaspoon salt
¼   teaspoon pepper
Green grapes (optional)
Fresh parsley (optional)

Rub cavity of duckling with 1 teaspoon salt. Combine remaining ingredients except grapes and parsley, and stir until well moistened. Stuff dressing into cavity of duckling. Spoon remaining dressing into a shallow casserole; set aside. Close cavity of duckling with skewers.

Place duckling, breast side up, on rack in a shallow roasting pan. Bake, uncovered, at 425° for 20 minutes. Lower heat to 325°, and bake 2 hours or until drumsticks and thighs move easily. Bake extra stuffing at 325° for 30 minutes.

Serve duckling on platter garnished with grapes and parsley, if desired. Yield: 6 to 8 servings.

Texas Cornbread Dressing

10   (2-inch) cornbread muffins, crumbled
6   slices white bread, crumbled
5   cups chicken or turkey broth
2   medium-size onions, chopped
4   stalks celery, chopped
½   cup melted butter or margarine
½   pound mild sausage
2   eggs, beaten
Salt and pepper to taste

Soak cornbread and bread slices in chicken broth; stir until liquid is absorbed. Sauté onion and celery in butter until vegetables are tender; add sausage and cook over low heat until sausage changes color.

Combine bread mixture, sausage mixture, eggs, salt, and pepper; mix until thoroughly blended.

Stuff turkey lightly with dressing, or spoon dressing into a buttered 13- x 9- x 2-inch baking pan. Bake at 350° for 45 minutes or until lightly browned. Yield: 10 to 12 servings.

Cornbread Dressing

4   cups crumbled cornbread
1   cup cracker crumbs
1   cup crumbled lightbread
1   teaspoon poultry seasoning
½   teaspoon salt
½   teaspoon sage
½   teaspoon pepper
½   teaspoon celery salt
½   cup chopped onion
3   hard-cooked eggs, chopped
2   to 2½ cups chicken or turkey broth

Combine all ingredients in a mixing bowl; mix well. Stuff turkey lightly or place in a greased 3-quart casserole; bake at 350° for 30 minutes or until done. Yield: 8 to 10 servings or enough to stuff a 10- to 12-pound turkey.

Cornbread-Sage Dressing

2   cups dried breadcrumbs
2   cups dried cornbread crumbs
2   cups chicken broth
½   cup chopped celery
1   small onion, chopped
2   eggs, beaten
2   tablespoons melted butter or margarine
1   teaspoon sage
Salt and pepper to taste

Combine all ingredients in a mixing bowl; mix well. Stuff turkey lightly, or place in a greased 13- x 9- x 2-inch baking pan and bake at 350° for 30 minutes or until done. Yield: 6 to 8 servings or enough dressing to stuff a 10- to 12-pound turkey.

Southwest Cornbread Dressing

    2   (6-ounce) packages cornbread mix
    1   cup chopped celery
    1   cup chopped green onion
    ½   cup chopped green pepper
    1   clove garlic, minced
    ½   cup melted butter or margarine
        Turkey giblets
    2   slices bread
    1   (10¾-ounce) can chicken broth
    3   eggs, slightly beaten
    6   tamales, mashed
    ½   teaspoon salt
        Crushed red pepper to taste

Prepare cornbread mix according to package directions; cool. Crumble cornbread into a large bowl, and set aside. Sauté celery, onion, green pepper, and garlic in butter until soft. Stir into cornbread, and set aside.

Put giblets in a saucepan; cover with water, and bring to a boil. Reduce heat; cover and simmer until tender. Chop liver; add to cornbread mixture along with ⅓ cup stock. Reserve remaining giblets for gravy.

Soak bread in chicken broth, and stir into cornbread mixture. Add remaining ingredients, mixing thoroughly. Spoon into a greased 2-quart casserole. Bake at 350° for 30 to 35 minutes. Yield: about 8 servings.

Oyster Dressing

    4   cups cubed white bread
    4   cups chicken or turkey broth
    1   (12-ounce) can fresh oysters, well
          drained
    6   cups crumbled cornbread
    1½ cups chopped onion
    1   cup chopped celery
    4   eggs, well beaten
    2   teaspoons salt
    1   teaspoon pepper
        Pinch of sage

Combine white bread and broth; set aside 5 minutes. Cut each oyster into quarters. Combine all ingredients; spoon into a lightly greased 13- x 9- x 2-inch pan. Bake at 325° for 1 hour. Yield: 12 servings.

★ Cornbread-Oyster Dressing Supreme

    3   slices toasted white bread
    2   slices toasted wheat bread
    2   slices toasted rye bread
    6   cups crumbled cornbread
    2   tablespoons parsley flakes
    1   teaspoon sage
    1   cup finely chopped celery
    1   cup chopped onion
    ¼   cup melted butter or margarine
    2   eggs, beaten
    4   to 5 cups chicken or turkey broth (at
          room temperature)
    1   (12-ounce) jar oysters, undrained and
          chopped
    1   teaspoon salt
    1   teaspoon pepper

Cut bread slices into ½-inch cubes; combine with cornbread, parsley, and sage in a large mixing bowl. Sauté celery and onion in butter until tender; cool. Combine bread mixture, sautéed vegetables, eggs, and enough broth to moisten bread; add oysters, salt, and pepper.

Stuff bird with mixture, or bake as follows. Generously grease a 13- x 9- x 2-inch baking pan; heat until a drop of water sizzles in pan. Spoon dressing into hot pan and bake at 350° for 35 to 40 minutes. Yield: 10 to 12 servings.

Rice and Oyster Dressing

    3   pounds picnic or Boston butt roast
    1   pound pork liver
    1   cup chopped onion
    ½   cup chopped celery
    ½   cup chopped green pepper
        Salt
    1   cup water
    2   cups uncooked regular rice
    1   pint oysters, drained
    1½ cups chopped green onion
    1   cup chopped parsley
        Salt and pepper to taste

Cook pork roast, liver, onion, celery, green pepper, and salt to taste in 1 cup water for 30 minutes; cool. Remove pork and liver from cooking liquid, and put through food chopper on coarse blade. Return ground meat to cooking liquid. (Meat may be refrigerated until next day or frozen at this stage.)

Cook rice according to package directions. Combine rice, meat mixture, oysters, green onion, parsley, salt, and pepper; mix well. Spoon into a greased 13- x 9- x 2-inch pan. Cover and bake at 350° about 30 minutes, stirring occasionally. Yield: 12 to 14 servings.

Note: About 7 cups crumbled cornbread may be substituted for rice.

Nut Dressing

½ cup butter or margarine
½ large onion, chopped
2 cups chopped pecans or Brazil nuts
3 tablespoons chopped parsley
1 cup chopped celery
2 teaspoons salt
¼ teaspoon pepper
1 teaspoon poultry seasoning
2 eggs, beaten
8 cups soft breadcrumbs
1 cup chicken or turkey stock

Melt butter in a large skillet; sauté onion in melted butter until tender. Remove from heat; stir in pecans, parsley, celery, salt, pepper, poultry seasoning, and eggs. Stir in breadcrumbs. Add stock, and toss lightly.

Spoon into a greased 3-quart casserole. Bake at 350° for 30 minutes. Yield: 10 to 12 servings.

Note: Dressing may be used to stuff a 12-pound turkey.

Cornish Hens Véronique

4 (1-pound) Cornish hens
Salt
¼ cup melted butter or margarine
1 (8-ounce) can light seedless grapes
3 tablespoons sugar
¼ cup sauterne
2 tablespoons lemon juice
1 tablespoon cornstarch
¼ teaspoon salt
¼ teaspoon grated orange rind
¼ teaspoon grated lemon rind
Fresh seedless grape clusters (optional)

Sprinkle inside of hens with salt; truss hens and place breast side up in a shallow roasting pan. Cover loosely with aluminum foil; bake at 375° for 30 minutes.

Remove aluminum foil. Bake at 375° for an additional 15 minutes, basting frequently with butter.

Drain grapes, reserving liquid; set grapes aside. Melt sugar in a heavy saucepan over medium heat until sugar is a deep golden brown. Remove from heat; set aside. Bring reserved grape liquid to a boil in a small saucepan; gradually stir into caramelized sugar. Cook over medium heat, stirring constantly, until caramel dissolves. Combine sauterne, lemon juice, cornstarch, ¼ teaspoon salt, and orange and lemon rind; stir into syrup mixture. Cook, stirring constantly, until mixture thickens and bubbles; stir in reserved grapes.

Bake hens at 375° an additional 15 minutes, basting frequently with syrup mixture. Garnish with fresh grape clusters, if desired. Yield: 4 servings.

Salads and Salad Dressings

There's a salad to please every taste and suit every occasion. With such variety in salad ingredients available, it's no wonder there are salads suitable for the beginning of the meal or for the main dish itself. The varieties of fruits, vegetables, and salad greens are so numerous that the only limitation on what goes into a salad lies in the imagination of the preparer.

Of all salads, clearly the most popular is the accompaniment salad. Whether served as a first course appetizer or along with the entree, these salads stimulate the appetite and add color to any meal.

A hearty main-dish salad gives a change of pace to your normal menu. Containing meat, seafood, cheese, or eggs, main-dish salads brighten a winter day or provide a refreshing summertime meal.

The finishing touch to a salad is the dressing selected. The natural flavor of homemade salad dressing gives zest and sparkle to any salad.

Orange Fruit Bowls

    4   oranges
    3   bananas, sliced
    1   cup halved strawberries
    1   cup seedless grapes
    ½   cup commercial sour cream
    1   tablespoon honey
    1   tablespoon orange juice

Cut oranges in half. Remove orange sections from peel, leaving peel intact; reserve shells for salad bowls. Separate orange sections, and remove seeds and membrane. Combine orange sections with remaining fruit.

Combine sour cream, honey, and orange juice; pour over fruit. Toss to coat evenly with dressing. To serve, spoon fruit into orange shells. Yield: 8 servings.

Warm temperatures and these cool salads are a fine combination: Zesty Vegetable Tray (page 275), Chicken Salad in Aspic Ring (page 274), and Fresh Spinach Salad (page 262).

★ Exquisite Avocado Salad

    2   grapefruits
    2   avocados
    1   cup mayonnaise
    ½   cup commercial sour cream
    ¼   cup powdered sugar
    2   mint leaves
    ½   cup halved strawberries
        Toasted slivered almonds

Section grapefruits, reserving juice. Cut avocado into halves lengthwise; twist gently to separate, and remove seed. Scoop out avocado using a melon ball scoop, leaving shells intact; set aside shells. Place avocado balls in grapefruit juice to keep from darkening.

Combine mayonnaise, sour cream, sugar, mint, and strawberries in container of electric blender; blend dressing until smooth.

Drain fruit, and spoon into avocado shells; sprinkle with almonds. Serve with dressing. Yield: 4 servings.

Tangy Cottage Cheese Salad

1   *envelope unflavored gelatin*
¼   *cup cold water*
½   *teaspoon salt*
2   *cups small-curd cottage cheese*
1   *(4-ounce) package blue cheese, crumbled*
2   *tablespoons chopped chives*
½   *cup whipping cream, whipped*
Peach halves
Pear halves
Avocado slices
Pineapple slices
Apple wedges
Lemon-Honey Dressing

Soften gelatin in cold water; add salt, and stir over low heat until gelatin is dissolved. Combine cottage cheese and blue cheese, blending well; stir in gelatin and chives. Fold in whipped cream. Chill several hours.

Arrange fruit on a serving platter; serve with cottage cheese mixture and Lemon-Honey Dressing. Yield: about 6 servings.

Lemon-Honey Dressing:

1   *(8-ounce) carton commercial sour cream*
3   *tablespoons honey*
3   *tablespoons lemon juice*
½   *teaspoon grated lemon rind*
½   *teaspoon salt*

Combine all ingredients, blending well. Chill thoroughly. Yield: about 1¼ cups.

Heavenly Cream Grapefruit

2   *large grapefruits, halved*
½   *pint whipping cream, whipped*
½   *cup commercial sour cream*
2   *cups orange sections*
1   *cup flaked coconut*
1   *cup miniature marshmallows*

Remove sections and membrane from grapefruit shells. Place shells in ice water to keep firm. Combine grapefruit sections and remaining ingredients; chill several hours. Drain grapefruit shells, and fill with fruit mixture. Yield: 4 servings.

Great Grapefruit Salad

4   *cups grapefruit sections*
Lettuce leaves
Special Fruit Dressing

Arrange grapefruit sections on lettuce leaves. Serve with Special Fruit Dressing. Yield: 8 to 10 servings.

Special Fruit Dressing:

½   *cup sugar*
1   *teaspoon salt*
1   *teaspoon dry mustard*
1   *teaspoon celery salt*
1   *teaspoon paprika*
1   *teaspoon grated onion*
¼   *cup vinegar*
1   *cup salad oil*

Combine dry ingredients; add onion and vinegar. Add oil slowly, beating with a fork. Store in refrigerator. Let stand at room temperature before serving; blend well. Yield: 1½ cups.

★
Pineapple Surprise Salad

2   *teaspoons melted butter or margarine*
2   *teaspoons all-purpose flour*
½   *cup milk*
1   *egg, beaten*
¼   *cup vinegar*
½   *teaspoon prepared mustard*
1   *(8¼-ounce) can pineapple chunks, drained*
2   *cups miniature marshmallows*
½   *pint whipping cream, whipped*
½   *cup chopped pecans*

Combine butter and flour in a saucepan. Gradually stir in milk; cook over medium heat, stirring constantly, until smooth and thickened. Add egg, vinegar, and mustard; beat well. Cook 3 minutes over medium heat, stirring constantly.

Remove dressing from heat, and stir in pineapple and marshmallows; chill overnight. Fold in whipped cream and pecans before serving. Yield: 6 servings.

Ambrosia Pineapple Boats

2 *fresh pineapples*
2 *(11-ounce) cans mandarin oranges,*
   drained
1 *cup diced apple*
½ *cup chopped dates*
½ *cup raisins*
½ *cup chopped walnuts*
1 *cup shredded coconut*
3 *(8-ounce) cartons pineapple-flavored*
   yogurt
½ *cup commercial sour cream*
1 *tablespoon honey*

Cut pineapples in half lengthwise. Scoop out pulp, leaving shells intact; set aside shells. Cut pineapple pulp into chunks, and reserve 1 cup. (Use remaining pineapple chunks as desired.)

Combine 1 cup pineapple chunks with fruits, nuts, and coconut. Combine yogurt, sour cream, and honey; pour over fruit mixture and toss. Chill well; spoon into reserved pineapple shells. Yield: 4 large servings.

Papaya Boats

2 *medium-size papayas*
1 *(8¼-ounce) can pineapple chunks,*
   undrained
2 *bananas, sliced*
2 *oranges, peeled and sectioned*
1 *cup sugar*

Cut papayas in half; scoop out seeds with a spoon. Remove pulp; use a melon ball scoop and leave shells intact. Set aside shells.

Combine papaya balls and remaining ingredients. Fill papaya shells with fruit mixture; chill well. Yield: about 4 servings.

Tropical Waldorf Salad

3 *cups diced unpeeled apple*
2 *bananas, sliced*
2 *tablespoons orange juice*
1 *cup chopped celery*
½ *cup flaked coconut*
½ *cup raisins*
½ *cup chopped walnuts*
   Mayonnaise or salad dressing
   Lettuce

Combine apple and banana; sprinkle with orange juice, and toss lightly. Add celery, coconut, raisins, and walnuts; stir in enough mayonnaise to moisten. Serve on lettuce. Yield: 6 servings.

Citrus Salad

2 *large oranges, peeled*
1 *large grapefruit, peeled*
1 *(15-ounce) can kidney beans, rinsed*
   and drained
½ *cup chopped celery*
½ *pound mushrooms, sliced*
1 *small onion, separated into rings*
¼ *cup chopped parsley*
   Dressing
¼ *cup sesame seeds, toasted*

Section oranges and grapefruit; set aside ⅓ cup fruit juice for Dressing. Combine fruits, beans, celery, mushrooms, onion, and parsley in a large bowl. Chill until ready to serve. Pour Dressing over salad. Top with sesame seeds. Yield: 6 to 8 servings.

Dressing:

⅓ *cup reserved fruit juice*
¼ *teaspoon sugar*
¼ *cup salad oil*
1 *tablespoon white vinegar*
¼ *teaspoon salt*
¼ *teaspoon oregano*

Combine all ingredients in a jar with a lid; shake well to blend. Yield: about ¾ cup.

Spiced Peach Salad

1 (29-ounce) can peach halves
1 teaspoon ground cinnamon
½ teaspoon ground cloves
1 teaspoon ground allspice
¾ cup firmly packed brown sugar
½ cup cider vinegar
1 (3-ounce) package cream cheese,
     softened
1 tablespoon half-and-half

Drain peaches, and reserve ¾ cup juice. Combine spices, brown sugar, vinegar, and reserved juice. Bring to a boil; reduce heat, and simmer 5 minutes. Pour over peach halves while hot. Chill several hours or overnight.

Before serving, combine cream cheese and half-and-half; blend well. Place a teaspoon of this mixture in center of each peach half. Yield: 7 to 8 servings.

Peachy Fruit Salad

1 (29-ounce) can peach halves
½ cup water
1 cup sugar
½ cup vinegar
1 cinnamon stick
1 tablespoon pickling spices
¼ teaspoon red food coloring (optional)
2 teaspoons prepared horseradish
¼ teaspoon salt
½ cup commercial sour cream
   Lettuce or watercress
   Seedless green grapes

Drain peaches, reserving syrup. Combine peach syrup, water, sugar, vinegar, and spices in a saucepan; stir in food coloring, if desired. Bring to a boil, and boil 5 minutes; add peaches. Lower heat, and simmer mixture 5 minutes; refrigerate peaches in syrup overnight.

Combine horseradish, salt, and sour cream; blend well. Arrange peaches on lettuce. Place a few grapes in center of each peach half; spoon sour cream dressing over each. Garnish with additional grapes. Yield: 6 to 8 servings.

Fresh Pear Salad

¼ cup sugar
2 tablespoons cornstarch
⅛ teaspoon salt
1 cup pear juice or nectar
½ cup orange juice
2 tablespoons lemon juice
6 to 8 medium-size pears, peeled, halved,
     and cored
   Lettuce
   Cottage cheese

Combine sugar, cornstarch, and salt in a saucepan; stir in juices. Cook over medium heat until thickened, stirring constantly. Refrigerate at least 2 hours.

Arrange pear halves on lettuce leaves; spoon a small amount of cottage cheese into center of each. Spoon fruit dressing over each pear. Yield: 6 to 8 servings.

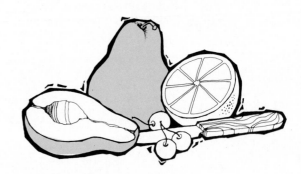

Glazed Fruit Salad

1 (15-ounce) can fruit cocktail, drained
1 (11-ounce) can mandarin orange
     sections, drained
1 (15¼-ounce) can pineapple chunks,
     drained
2 bananas, sliced
1 cup flaked coconut
1 cup miniature marshmallows
1 (21-ounce) can peach pie filling

Combine all ingredients, stirring gently to mix. Chill at least 2 hours before serving. Yield: 8 servings.

Yogurt Fruit Salad

1½   *cups orange yogurt*
⅓   *cup mayonnaise*
1   *(11-ounce) can mandarin orange*
    sections, drained
1   *(20-ounce) can pineapple chunks,*
    drained
1   *(17-ounce) can light, sweet cherries,*
    drained and pitted
1   *cup miniature marshmallows*

Combine yogurt and mayonnaise; stir in remaining ingredients. Chill at least 1 hour. Yield: 10 to 12 servings.

Happy Day Fruit Salad

1   *(3¾-ounce) package instant vanilla*
    pudding
½   *pint whipping cream, whipped*
1   *(30-ounce) can fruit cocktail, drained*
1   *(11-ounce) can mandarin orange*
    sections, drained
1   *(4-ounce) jar maraschino cherries,*
    drained and halved
4   *bananas, diced*
1   *cup miniature marshmallows*

Prepare pudding according to package directions; fold in whipped cream. Fold in remaining ingredients, and chill well. Yield: 8 to 10 servings.

Pistachio Salad

1   *(3½-ounce) package instant pistachio*
    pudding mix
1   *(13½-ounce) carton frozen whipped*
    topping, thawed
1   *(8¼-ounce) can crushed pineapple,*
    drained
1   *(11-ounce) can mandarin orange*
    sections, drained
1   *cup miniature marshmallows*
1   *(12-ounce) carton cottage cheese*

Fold pudding mix into whipped topping; fold in remaining ingredients. Chill thoroughly. Yield: 10 to 12 servings.

Tropical Fruit Salad

2   *mangoes*
3   *bananas, sliced*
Lemon juice
3   *apples, chopped*
1   *orange, sectioned and seeded*
1   *kiwi, peeled and sliced*
3   *to 4 tablespoons sugar*
Whipped cream

Cut mangoes in half; remove seeds with a spoon. Scoop out pulp with a melon ball scoop, leaving shells intact; set aside shells.

Dip banana slices in lemon juice to prevent darkening.

Combine mango, bananas, apples, orange, kiwi, and sugar; chill several hours. Spoon chilled mixture into mango shells, and serve with whipped cream. Yield: 4 servings.

Paradise Fruit Salad

½   *pint whipping cream*
¼   *cup powdered sugar*
Juice and grated rind of 1 lime
1   *banana, sliced*
1   *(15¼-ounce) can crushed pineapple,*
    drained
½   *cup maraschino cherries, chopped*
1   *cup miniature marshmallows*
1   *teaspoon light rum or rum extract*
½   *cup plain yogurt*
Lettuce leaves

Beat whipping cream until thick, gradually adding sugar. Sprinkle lime juice over banana; stir in pineapple, cherries, marshmallows, lime rind, rum, and yogurt. Fold fruit mixture into whipped cream. Spoon into an 8-inch square pan, and freeze until firm. Cut into squares, and serve on lettuce leaves. Yield: 6 to 8 servings.

24-Hour Salad

2 *eggs, beaten*
¼ *cup vinegar*
¼ *cup sugar*
2 *tablespoons butter or margarine*
2 *cups halved light sweet cherries*
2 *cups pineapple tidbits*
2 *cups mandarin orange sections*
2 *cups halved seedless grapes*
2 *cups miniature marshmallows*
½ *pint whipping cream, whipped*

Combine eggs, vinegar, and sugar in the top of a double boiler; cook over low heat, beating constantly, until smooth and thickened. Remove from heat, and add butter; cool.

Fold in fruit, marshmallows, and whipped cream. Cover and refrigerate 24 hours. Yield: 12 to 14 servings.

★ Cranberry Salad

1 *pound fresh cranberries*
1 *(6-ounce) package strawberry-flavored gelatin*
1 *cup sugar*
1 *cup boiling water*
1 *(8-ounce) can crushed pineapple, undrained*
Juice of 1 orange
1 *cup pecans, chopped*

Carefully sort and wash cranberries; grind finely, and set aside.

Dissolve gelatin and sugar in water. Add cranberries and remaining ingredients; stir well. Chill, stirring occasionally, until consistency of unbeaten egg white.

Spoon mixture into a 5-cup mold; chill until set. Yield: 6 to 8 servings.

★ Overnight Dessert Salad

2 *eggs, slightly beaten*
2 *tablespoons sugar*
3 *tablespoons lemon juice*
1 *tablespoon butter or margarine, melted*
1 *(8¼-ounce) can crushed pineapple*
1 *envelope whipped topping mix or ½ pint whipping cream plus 4 tablespoons sugar*
½ *cup commercial sour cream*
1 *cup miniature marshmallows*
2 *(11-ounce) cans mandarin oranges, drained*
1 *cup sliced strawberries*
1 *large banana, sliced*
Whole strawberries and mandarin orange sections

Combine eggs, 2 tablespoons sugar, lemon juice, and butter in top of a double boiler; beat well. Drain pineapple, and reserve juice. Add 1 tablespoon reserved pineapple juice to egg mixture.

Cook over boiling water about 7 minutes or until very thick, stirring constantly; cool. Add pineapple.

Prepare whipped topping according to package directions, or whip cream with 4 tablespoons sugar until stiff. Fold into cooked mixture along with sour cream, marshmallows, 2 cans mandarin oranges, and sliced fruit. Chill thoroughly. To serve, garnish with whole strawberries and orange sections. Yield: 6 to 8 servings.

Burgundy Cran-Apple Salad

1 *(6-ounce) package strawberry-flavored gelatin*
1½ *cups boiling water*
1 *(16-ounce) can whole cranberry sauce*
1 *cup apple cider*
½ *cup burgundy*
2 *cups chopped apples*

Dissolve gelatin in boiling water. Stir in cranberry sauce. Add apple cider and burgundy, mixing well. Chill until partially congealed; fold in apples. Pour into a 6-cup mold, and chill until firm. Yield: 10 to 12 servings.

Frozen Cranberry Salad

1 (16-ounce) can jellied cranberry sauce
2 tablespoons lemon juice
1 (8-ounce) package cream cheese, softened
¼ cup milk
¼ cup mayonnaise
¼ cup powdered sugar
½ cup chopped walnuts

Crush cranberry sauce with a fork; stir in lemon juice. Spread evenly in a 9- x 5- x 3-inch pan; set aside.

Combine cream cheese, milk, and mayonnaise in a small bowl; beat until smooth. Stir in powdered sugar and walnuts. Spread mixture over cranberry sauce. Freeze until firm. Yield: about 8 servings.

Christmas Layer Salad

1 (3-ounce) package lime-flavored gelatin
1 cup boiling water
½ cup cold water
1 (8¼-ounce) can crushed pineapple, drained
2 (3-ounce) packages cream cheese, softened
1 (3-ounce) package lemon-flavored gelatin
1 cup boiling water
1 cup cold water
1 (3-ounce) package strawberry-flavored gelatin
1 cup boiling water
1 (17-ounce) can apricots, drained and pureed

Dissolve lime gelatin in 1 cup boiling water; stir in ½ cup cold water and pineapple. Pour into an 11¾- x 7½- x 1¾-inch pan. Chill until firm.

Combine cream cheese and lemon gelatin; mix thoroughly. Add 1 cup boiling water; stir until well blended. Add 1 cup cold water. Cool; pour over first layer. Chill until firm.

Dissolve strawberry gelatin in 1 cup boiling water; stir in apricots. Cool; then pour over lemon layer. Chill until firm. Yield: 12 to 15 servings.

Yummy Cherry Salad

1 (3-ounce) package raspberry-flavored gelatin
2 cups boiling water, divided
1 (22-ounce) can cherry pie filling
1 (3-ounce) package lemon-flavored gelatin
1 (3-ounce) package cream cheese, softened
⅓ cup mayonnaise
1 (8¼-ounce) can crushed pineapple, undrained
1 cup miniature marshmallows
½ pint whipping cream, whipped
¼ cup chopped pecans

Dissolve raspberry-flavored gelatin in 1 cup boiling water; stir in pie filling. Pour into a 9-inch square pan; chill until partially set.

Dissolve lemon-flavored gelatin in 1 cup boiling water. Combine cream cheese and mayonnaise, mixing well; stir in lemon-flavored gelatin, pineapple, and marshmallows. Fold in whipped cream. Spread lemon mixture over cherry layer; sprinkle with pecans. Chill until firm. Cut into squares to serve. Yield: 10 to 12 servings.

Cinnamon Applesauce Swirl Salad

⅓ cup red cinnamon candies
1 (6-ounce) package lemon-flavored gelatin
2 cups boiling water
1 (16-ounce) can applesauce
2 (3-ounce) packages cream cheese, softened
¼ cup half-and-half
2 tablespoons mayonnaise or salad dressing

Dissolve candies and gelatin in water; stir in applesauce. Chill until partially set. Pour into an 8-inch square pan. Combine cheese, half-and-half, and mayonnaise in a small mixing bowl; mix until smooth. Stir into applesauce mixture for swirl effect. Chill until firm. Yield: 8 to 10 servings.

★
Pineapple Cheddar Salad

 1 *(3-ounce) package lemon-flavored gelatin*
 1 *cup boiling water*
 1 *(8¼-ounce) can crushed pineapple, undrained*
 ¾ *cup sugar*
 ½ *pint whipping cream, whipped*
 1 *cup shredded mild Cheddar cheese*
 ½ *cup chopped pecans (optional)*

Dissolve gelatin in boiling water. Stir in pineapple and sugar; cool. Fold in remaining ingredients; add pecans, if desired. Spoon into a 9-inch square pan; chill until firm. Cut into squares to serve. Yield: 9 servings.

Ginger Ale Salad

 1 *(3-ounce) package lemon-flavored gelatin*
 ½ *cup boiling water*
 1½ *cups ginger ale*
 ¼ *cup finely chopped pecans*
 ¼ *cup finely chopped celery*
 1 *(8¾-ounce) can fruit cocktail, drained*
 1 *tablespoon finely chopped crystallized ginger*

Dissolve gelatin in boiling water, and stir in ginger ale. Chill mixture until slightly thickened; then fold in remaining ingredients. Pour mixture into a 1½-quart mold, and chill until firm. Yield: 6 to 8 servings.

Frozen Pineapple Salad

 1 *(8-ounce) package cream cheese, softened*
 ½ *cup orange juice*
 ½ *cup powdered sugar*
 1 *(20-ounce) can crushed pineapple, drained*
 ½ *cup chopped pecans*

Combine cream cheese and orange juice; beat until smooth. Gradually add powdered sugar, mixing well. Stir in pineapple and

pecans. Pour into a 10- x 6- x 1¾-inch pan. Freeze until firm. Let stand at room temperature briefly before serving. Yield: about 10 servings.

Frozen Waldorf Salad

 1 *(8¼-ounce) can crushed pineapple*
 2 *eggs, slightly beaten*
 ½ *cup sugar*
 ¼ *cup lemon juice*
 ⅛ *teaspoon salt*
 ½ *cup whipping cream, whipped*
 2½ *cups diced unpeeled apple*
 ½ *cup sliced celery*
 ½ *cup coarsely chopped walnuts*

Drain pineapple, reserving juice. Combine pineapple juice, eggs, sugar, lemon juice, and salt; cook over low heat, stirring constantly, until slightly thickened. Cool.

Fold remaining ingredients into cooked mixture. Spoon into an 8-inch pan and freeze. Cut into squares to serve. Yield: 8 to 10 servings.

Frozen Fruit Cup

 1 *(17-ounce) can apricot halves, drained and cubed*
 1 *(16-ounce) can peach slices, drained and cubed*
 2 *bananas, cubed*
 ½ *(10-ounce) package frozen strawberries, thawed*
 ¾ *cup sugar*
 1 *cup pineapple juice*
 1 *(6-ounce) can frozen orange juice concentrate, thawed and undiluted*
 ¼ *cup lemon juice*

Combine all ingredients. Spoon into a 13- x 9- x 2-inch baking pan or into 5-ounce paper cups, filling two-thirds full; freeze. Remove from freezer 15 minutes before serving. Yield: 15 servings.

Layered Eggnog Ring

    1 (3-ounce) package lemon-flavored
         gelatin
    2 cups boiling water, divided
    ¼ cup cold water
    ¼ teaspoon rum extract or rum
    ¾ cup commercial eggnog
    1 (11-ounce) can mandarin orange
         sections
    1 (8½-ounce) can pear halves
    1 (3-ounce) package raspberry-flavored
         gelatin
 1½ cups chopped pecans
       Additional mandarin orange sections
         (optional)

Dissolve lemon-flavored gelatin in 1 cup boiling water; stir in cold water and rum extract. Add eggnog to ¾ cup lemon-flavored gelatin mixture; set remaining gelatin aside. Pour into a 6-cup mold; chill until set but not firm.

Drain mandarin orange sections and pears, reserving juices. Dice pears, and set aside.

Dissolve raspberry-flavored gelatin in 1 cup boiling water; add ¾ cup reserved fruit juice and remaining lemon-flavored gelatin. Chill until consistency of egg white. Fold in mandarin orange sections, pears, and pecans; spoon over eggnog layer. Chill until firm.

Unmold and garnish with additional mandarin orange sections, if desired. Yield: 8 servings.

Rhubarb Salad

    1 (6-ounce) package strawberry-flavored
         gelatin
 1½ cups boiling water
 1½ cups cold water
    1 (16-ounce) package frozen rhubarb
    1 (10-ounce) package frozen strawberries,
         thawed
    1 (13¼-ounce) can pineapple chunks,
         undrained

Dissolve gelatin in boiling water; stir in cold water. Refrigerate until slightly thickened.

Cook rhubarb in a small amount of water until soft. Drain and chop. Stir rhubarb, strawberries, and pineapple into gelatin. Refrigerate until firm. Yield: 8 to 10 servings.

Strawberry-Rhubarb Salad Mold

    1 (10-ounce) package frozen rhubarb,
         thawed
    ¼ cup sugar
 1¼ cups boiling water, divided
    1 envelope unflavored gelatin
    ¼ cup cold water
    1 (3-ounce) package strawberry-flavored
         gelatin
    1 (10-ounce) package frozen strawberries,
         thawed
       Lettuce
       Whole fresh strawberries

Combine rhubarb, sugar, and ¼ cup boiling water in a small saucepan; cook until rhubarb is tender, about 5 minutes. Soften unflavored gelatin in ¼ cup cold water; set aside. Dissolve strawberry gelatin in remaining 1 cup boiling water; add softened unflavored gelatin, and stir until dissolved. Stir in cooked rhubarb and thawed strawberries.

Pour into a 4-cup mold, and chill until firm. Unmold on a bed of lettuce, and garnish with fresh strawberries. Yield: 6 to 8 servings.

★
Apricot Congealed Salad

    1 (17-ounce) can apricots
    1 (3-ounce) package lemon-flavored
         gelatin
    ½ cup finely chopped celery
    ½ cup chopped pecans
    ½ cup miniature marshmallows
    1 cup frozen whipped topping, thawed
    ⅓ cup mayonnaise

Drain apricots, reserving syrup. Add water to syrup to make 1 cup liquid. Heat to boiling; add gelatin, stirring to dissolve. Cool.

Chop apricots, and combine with remaining ingredients. Stir into gelatin. Pour into a 4-cup mold, and chill until firm. Yield: 6 servings.

Blackberry Salad

2   (3-ounce) packages black
      raspberry-flavored gelatin
2   cups boiling water
1   cup cold water
1   cup fresh blackberries
½   cup chopped pecans
1   (2-ounce) envelope whipped topping
      mix
1   (8-ounce) package cream cheese,
      softened
½   cup sugar

Dissolve gelatin in boiling water, and stir in cold water. Chill until consistency of unbeaten egg white.

Fold blackberries and pecans into thickened gelatin. Pour into a 9-inch square dish, and chill until set.

Prepare whipped topping mix according to package directions; add cream cheese and sugar, blending until smooth. Spread over gelatin layer, and chill several hours. Yield: 9 servings.

White Congealed Salad

1   (16-ounce) can pears
1   (15½-ounce) can sliced pineapple
1   (17-ounce) can pitted light sweet
      cherries
Juice of 1 lemon
10 large marshmallows
2   envelopes unflavored gelatin
½   cup cold water
½   cup mayonnaise
½   pint whipping cream, whipped
1   cup chopped pecans

Drain fruits, reserving liquid; chop fruit. Combine liquid and lemon juice; bring to a boil. Add marshmallows, stirring until melted. Soften gelatin in cold water; add to marshmallow mixture, and stir until dissolved. Chill until consistency of unbeaten egg white.

Fold in mayonnaise, whipped cream, pecans, and fruits. Spoon into a 13- x 9- x 2-inch pan, and chill until firm. Yield: 8 to 10 servings.

Congealed Ambrosia Salad

1   (3-ounce) package orange-flavored
      gelatin
½   cup sugar
1   cup boiling water
3   oranges, peeled and cut into 1-inch
      pieces
1   (8¼-ounce) can crushed pineapple,
      undrained
1   cup flaked coconut
1   cup chopped pecans
1   (8-ounce) carton commercial sour cream

Dissolve gelatin and sugar in boiling water; chill until mixture starts to thicken. Fold in remaining ingredients, and blend well. Pour into a 13- x 9- x 2-inch pan; chill until firm. Yield: 10 to 12 servings.

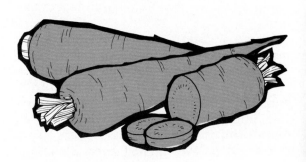

Sangría Fruit Salad

3   envelopes unflavored gelatin
1   cup orange juice
½   cup sugar
¼   cup lemon juice
2½ cups red wine
¾   cup club soda
2   oranges, peeled and sliced crosswise
1   banana, peeled and sliced
2   peaches, peeled and chopped
1   cup halved strawberries

Soften gelatin in orange juice; place over low heat, stirring until gelatin dissolves. Add sugar, stirring until dissolved. Remove from heat, and add lemon juice, wine, and club soda. Chill until consistency of unbeaten egg white.

Fold fruit into thickened gelatin, and spoon into an 8-cup mold. Chill until firm. Yield: 12 to 15 servings.

★
Red Raspberry Ring

1 (10-ounce) package frozen raspberries, thawed
2 (3-ounce) packages raspberry-flavored gelatin
2 cups boiling water
1 pint vanilla ice cream, softened
1 (6-ounce) can frozen pink lemonade concentrate, thawed and undiluted
¼ cup chopped pecans

Drain raspberries, reserving juice. Dissolve gelatin in boiling water; add ice cream by spoonfuls, stirring until melted. Stir in lemonade and reserved juice. Chill until partially set.

Fold in raspberries and pecans. Spoon into a 6-cup mold, and chill until firm. Yield: 8 servings.

Crème de Menthe Salad

1 (8½-ounce) can pears
1 (8¼-ounce) can pineapple chunks
1 (3-ounce) package lime-flavored gelatin
¼ cup crème de menthe
½ cup mayonnaise
1 envelope whipped topping mix

Drain pears and pineapple, reserving juice; bring juice to a boil in a saucepan. Remove from heat; add gelatin, stirring until dissolved. Blend in crème de menthe and mayonnaise. Chill until consistency of unbeaten egg white.

Chop pears, and fold into thickened gelatin along with pineapple. Prepare whipped topping mix according to package directions, and fold into gelatin mixture. Pour into a 4-cup mold, and chill until firm. Yield: 6 servings.

Carrot Ambrosia

4 cups shredded carrots
¼ cup lemon juice
1 cup chopped orange sections
1 (3½-ounce) can flaked coconut
1½ cups miniature marshmallows
3 tablespoons honey
½ cup commercial sour cream
¼ cup mayonnaise
Lettuce leaves (optional)

Combine carrot, lemon juice, oranges, coconut, and marshmallows. Combine honey, sour cream, and mayonnaise; mix well, and pour over carrot mixture. Toss lightly. Serve on lettuce, if desired. Yield: 6 to 8 servings.

Carrot Salad

1 pound carrots, peeled and grated
2 tablespoons honey
2 tablespoons lemon juice
2 tablespoons commercial sour cream
½ cup miniature marshmallows
½ cup flaked coconut
1 (8-ounce) can crushed pineapple, undrained

Combine all ingredients, mixing well. Refrigerate overnight. Yield: 6 servings.

Refrigerator Cucumber Salad

7 cups thinly sliced cucumber
1 cup chopped onion
1 medium-size green pepper, chopped
1 tablespoon salt
1 tablespoon celery seeds
2 cups sugar
1 cup vinegar

Combine cucumber, onion, and green pepper in a large bowl. Combine remaining ingredients, mixing until smooth; pour over vegetable mixture. Cover and refrigerate at least 3 hours; stir several times. May be stored in refrigerator several days. Yield: about 12 servings.

★
Marinated Carrot Salad

2   pounds carrots, peeled and sliced
1   head cauliflower, sliced
1   large onion, sliced
1   green pepper, chopped
1   (10¾-ounce) can tomato soup,
       undiluted
1   cup sugar
1   teaspoon dry mustard
1   cup vinegar
1   teaspoon salt
¾   cup salad oil

Cook carrots until crisp-tender in a small amount of boiling water; drain. Combine carrots, cauliflower, onion, and green pepper; set aside. Combine remaining ingredients, stirring until well mixed.

Pour over vegetables; toss lightly. Refrigerate several hours or overnight. Yield: 8 to 10 servings.

Hot Celery Salad

1   bunch celery
4   slices bacon, diced
¾   cup minced onion
5   teaspoons sugar
2   teaspoons all-purpose flour
1¼ teaspoons salt
¼   teaspoon black pepper
¼   cup water
¼   cup white vinegar
½   cup sliced radishes
¼   cup chopped parsley
    Celery leaves (optional)

Separate celery into stalks; wash, trim ends, and remove leaves. Cut each stalk into ½-inch slices; set aside.

In a large saucepan, cook bacon until crisp; add onion and sauté 2 minutes. Add celery and sauté 5 minutes.

Combine sugar, flour, salt, pepper, water, and vinegar; add to celery mixture. Cook 2 to 3 minutes, stirring constantly, or until mixture boils and thickens.

Remove from heat; stir in radishes and parsley. Garnish with celery leaves, if desired. Serve hot. Yield: 4 to 6 servings.

Cauliflower-Bacon Salad

1   medium-size head cauliflower
1   small head iceberg lettuce, shredded
1   pound bacon, cooked and crumbled
2   to 4 tablespoons sugar
¼   cup grated Parmesan cheese
1   cup mayonnaise or salad dressing

Wash cauliflower; remove green leaves, and break into flowerets. In a large bowl, layer all ingredients in order given; chill. Toss lightly before serving. Yield: 10 to 12 servings.

Easy Coleslaw

1   small head cabbage, shredded
½   cup diced green pepper
½   cup mayonnaise
¼   cup commercial sour cream
2   teaspoons lemon juice
½   teaspoon salt
¼   teaspoon dry mustard

Combine cabbage and green pepper in a medium bowl; set aside.

Combine mayonnaise, sour cream, lemon juice, salt, and mustard; mix well. Spoon over cabbage and green pepper; toss well. Yield: 4 to 6 servings.

★
Crispy Slaw

1   medium-size head cabbage, shredded
1   small onion, chopped
1   green pepper, chopped
1   cup sugar
1   cup vinegar
1   teaspoon salt
1   teaspoon mustard seeds
1   teaspoon celery seeds
¼   teaspoon ground turmeric

Combine cabbage, onion, and green pepper in a large bowl; set aside.

Combine remaining ingredients in a saucepan; bring to a boil. Pour over vegetables and toss well. Chill several hours or overnight. Yield: about 6 to 8 servings.

Barbecued Coleslaw

  1   *small head cabbage, shredded*
  2   *stalks celery, finely chopped*
  1   *green pepper, finely chopped*
  1   *medium-size onion, finely chopped*
  ¾   *cup catsup*
  ¼   *cup vinegar*
  2   *tablespoons sugar*
  1   *tablespoon Worcestershire sauce*
  1   *tablespoon prepared mustard*
  1   *teaspoon salt*
      Dash of cayenne pepper

Combine vegetables. Combine remaining
ingredients, and pour over vegetables; mix
well. Chill several hours before serving.
Yield: 6 to 8 servings.

Fruity Coleslaw

  3   *tablespoons salad oil*
  3   *tablespoons honey*
  2   *tablespoons mayonnaise*
  ½   *cup frozen whipped topping, thawed*
        (optional)
  2   *cups shredded cabbage*
  1   *apple, cored and chopped*
  1   *(11-ounce) can mandarin orange*
        sections, drained
  ½   *cup seedless raisins*
  ¼   *cup chopped pecans*

Combine oil, honey, and mayonnaise; mix
well. Combine remaining ingredients. Add
oil mixture; toss well. Yield: 4 to 5 servings.

Corn Salad

  1   *(12-ounce) can whole kernel corn,*
        drained
  1   *cup finely chopped celery*
  1   *cup chopped green pepper*
  1   *cup chopped green onion*
  2   *teaspoons prepared mustard*
  ¼   *cup chopped pimiento*
  3   *tablespoons salad oil*
  ¼   *cup vinegar*

Combine all ingredients. Chill until serving
time. Yield: 4 to 6 servings.

Waldorf Coleslaw

  1   *cup seedless raisins*
  3   *cups shredded cabbage*
  1½   *cups chopped apple*
  2   *tablespoons minced onion*
  1   *cup mayonnaise or salad dressing*
  1   *teaspoon salt*
  1   *tablespoon sugar*
  1   *tablespoon dry mustard*
  3   *tablespoons lemon juice*

Plump raisins by soaking in boiling water
several minutes. Combine raisins, cabbage,
apple, and onion; set aside.
  Combine mayonnaise, salt, sugar, mustard, and lemon juice; blend well. Add
dressing to cabbage mixture; stir to coat.
Chill. Yield: 6 to 8 servings.

Green Vegetable Salad

  1   *(16-ounce) can French-style green*
        beans, drained
  1   *(16-ounce) can small peas, drained*
  1   *(8-ounce) can lima beans, drained*
  1   *small onion, cut into rings*
  ½   *cup chopped green pepper*
  ½   *cup salad oil*
  ¾   *cup sugar*
  1   *teaspoon salt*
  ½   *cup vinegar*
  ½   *teaspoon pepper*

Combine vegetables; set aside. Combine remaining ingredients, blending well; stir into
vegetable mixture. Cover; refrigerate several
hours or overnight, stirring occasionally.
Yield: 8 to 10 servings.

★
Avocado-Tomato Salad

1   *(0.6-ounce) package old-fashioned French dressing mix*
2   *avocados, sliced*
1   *(14½-ounce) can sliced baby tomatoes*
1   *medium-size red onion, sliced*
    Lettuce

Prepare dressing mix according to package directions. Combine avocados, tomatoes, and onion; add dressing, and marinate at least 2 hours in refrigerator. Drain, and serve on lettuce. Yield: 6 servings.

Three-Green Salad

2   *(10-ounce) packages frozen French-style green beans or cut green beans*
1   *(10-ounce) package frozen chopped broccoli or baby broccoli spears*
1   *(8½-ounce) can artichoke hearts, drained and quartered*
½   *cup chopped onion*
1   *cup buttermilk-style salad dressing*
2   *tablespoons anchovy paste or chopped anchovies*

Cook vegetables according to package directions; drain well.

Combine vegetables and remaining ingredients, tossing lightly to mix. Refrigerate until ready to serve. Yield: 6 servings.

Fresh Mushroom Salad

¼   *cup wine vinegar*
¼   *cup olive oil*
1   *egg yolk*
¼   *teaspoon thyme leaves, crushed*
¼   *teaspoon tarragon leaves, crushed*
¼   *teaspoon dry mustard*
    Salt and pepper to taste
1   *pound fresh mushrooms, cleaned and sliced*
    Lettuce leaves

Combine vinegar, oil, egg yolk, and seasonings; beat until well mixed. Pour over mushrooms, and serve on lettuce leaves. Yield: 4 servings.

★
Favorite Three-Bean Salad

1   *(16-ounce) can green beans, drained*
1   *(16-ounce) can wax beans, drained*
1   *(15-ounce) can kidney beans, rinsed and drained*
1   *medium-size green pepper, sliced*
1   *medium-size onion, sliced*
½   *cup salad oil*
½   *cup cider vinegar*
¾   *cup sugar*
1½ *teaspoons salt*
½   *teaspoon pepper*

Combine vegetables, stirring gently. Combine remaining ingredients; pour over vegetables, stirring gently to blend well. Cover and chill overnight. Yield: 6 to 8 servings.

Lima Bean Salad

2   *(10-ounce) packages frozen baby lima beans*
½   *cup mayonnaise*
3   *tablespoons tarragon vinegar*
1   *teaspoon salt*
    Pepper to taste
2   *cups chopped onion*
1   *(2-ounce) jar chopped pimiento, drained*
3   *medium-size cucumbers, sliced*
    Tomato wedges (optional)
    Parsley (optional)

Cook beans according to package directions; drain and cool.

Combine mayonnaise, vinegar, salt, and pepper; stir in beans, onion, pimiento, and cucumber. Chill at least 2 hours. Garnish with tomato and parsley, if desired. Yield: 8 to 10 servings.

Piquant Lima Bean Salad

2 (10-ounce) packages frozen lima beans
1 cup diced celery
1 dill pickle, diced
4 green onions, chopped
½ cup commercial sour cream
¼ cup mayonnaise
2 tablespoons lemon juice
3 tablespoons prepared horseradish
    mustard

Cook lima beans according to package directions; drain. Combine remaining ingredients; toss with lima beans. Refrigerate at least 8 hours. Yield: 4 to 6 servings.

Crisp Winter Salad

1 (15-ounce) can kidney beans, drained
    and divided
4 cups shredded cabbage
2 tablespoons chopped onion
½ teaspoon celery seeds
½ teaspoon salt
3 tablespoons vinegar
½ cup mayonnaise
1 hard-cooked egg, sliced

Set aside ¼ cup beans. Combine remaining beans, cabbage, and onion; add celery seeds, salt, vinegar, and mayonnaise. Toss thoroughly. Chill. Garnish with reserved beans and egg. Yield: 4 to 6 servings.

Fresh Okra Salad

6 slices bacon
1½ pounds fresh okra
1 cup plain cornmeal
1 tablespoon all-purpose flour
½ teaspoon salt
1 large tomato, chopped
1 medium-size onion, chopped
1 teaspoon salt
  Pepper to taste

Cook bacon until crisp, and drain well on paper towels; reserve bacon drippings. Crumble bacon, and set aside.

Wash okra well; drain. Cut off tip and stem ends; cut okra crosswise into ½-inch slices.

Combine cornmeal, flour, and ½ teaspoon salt. Roll okra in cornmeal mixture, and sauté in reserved bacon drippings until golden brown. Drain on paper towels.

Combine okra, tomato, and onion. Add bacon, 1 teaspoon salt, and pepper; toss lightly. Yield: about 4 to 6 servings.

★ Marinated Vegetable Tray

½ cup white wine vinegar
¾ cup salad oil
½ teaspoon dry mustard
½ teaspoon garlic salt
½ teaspoon basil
⅛ teaspoon pepper
1 tablespoon instant minced onion
1 cup sliced squash
1 cup sliced mushrooms
1 (16-ounce) can carrots, drained
1 (15-ounce) can asparagus spears,
    drained
1 (14-ounce) can artichoke hearts, drained

Combine vinegar, oil, and seasonings in a jar; shake well. Pour marinade over vegetables; refrigerate 2 hours before serving. Drain marinade from vegetables and arrange on tray. Yield: 6 to 8 servings.

★ Marinated Tomatoes

8 ripe tomatoes, cut into 1-inch cubes
¾ cup salad oil
⅓ cup tarragon vinegar
⅓ cup chopped chives or chopped green
    onion tops
⅓ cup minced parsley
¾ teaspoon thyme leaves
1¼ teaspoons salt
¼ teaspoon pepper
  Chopped parsley (optional)

Combine all ingredients except chopped parsley, stirring gently. Cover and chill 12 hours; stir occasionally. Sprinkle with chopped parsley before serving, if desired. Yield: 8 to 10 servings.

Favorite Potato Salad

    6 medium-size baking potatoes
    1 pound bacon, cooked and crumbled
    6 hard-cooked eggs, chopped
    ¾ cup chopped green onions with tops
    ⅓ cup vinegar
    2 teaspoons salt
    ¼ teaspoon white pepper
    ¼ teaspoon celery salt
    About 1 cup mayonnaise
    3 green pepper rings

Cook potatoes in jackets. Peel while warm; dice. Combine potatoes, bacon, eggs, and onion; set aside. Combine vinegar, salt, pepper, celery salt, and mayonnaise; add to potato mixture. Stir gently to mix well. Garnish with green pepper. Yield: 6 to 8 servings.

Saucy Potato Salad

    9 medium-size potatoes, cooked, peeled,
         and sliced
    ⅓ cup commercial Italian salad dressing
    ¾ cup sliced celery
    ⅓ cup sliced green onion
    3 hard-cooked eggs
    1 cup mayonnaise
    ¼ cup chopped pimiento
    ½ cup commercial sour cream
    Salt to taste
    Ground celery seeds to taste

While potatoes are still warm, combine them with dressing; chill 2 hours. Add celery, onion, and chopped egg whites. Sieve egg yolks. Combine egg yolks and remaining ingredients; add to potato mixture, tossing gently to mix. Chill. Yield: 8 servings.

★ Potato Salad

    1 medium-size onion, divided
    3 cups boiling water
    1¾ teaspoons salt, divided
    6 medium-size potatoes, peeled and sliced
    6 hard-cooked eggs, halved
    1 cup sweet pickle cubes or relish
    1 cup finely chopped celery
    ¾ cup mayonnaise
    2 tablespoons sweet pickle juice

Cut 2 slices from onion; place in boiling water. Finely chop remaining onion; set aside. Add 1 teaspoon salt and potatoes to water; cover and simmer 10 minutes or until done. Drain and cool.

Separate yolks and whites of eggs. Finely chop whites; combine with pickles, celery, and chopped onion.

Mash yolks; blend in mayonnaise, pickle juice, and remaining ¾ teaspoon salt, blending well. Combine yolk mixture with egg white mixture. Cube potatoes; blend into egg mixture. Cover and refrigerate several hours. Yield: 10 to 12 servings.

Irish Potato Salad

    3 tablespoons vinegar, divided
    1 teaspoon celery seeds
    1 teaspoon sugar
    1½ teaspoons salt, divided
    3 cups sliced cooked potatoes
    1 (12-ounce) can corn beef, chilled and
         cubed
    1½ cups finely shredded cabbage
    ¼ cup minced dill pickle
    2 tablespoons minced onion
    ¾ cup mayonnaise
    2 tablespoons milk

Combine 2 tablespoons vinegar, celery seeds, sugar, and ½ teaspoon salt; sprinkle over potatoes. Set aside for 1 hour; then add corn beef, cabbage, pickle, and onion. Chill thoroughly.

Combine mayonnaise, milk, 1 tablespoon vinegar, and 1 teaspoon salt; add to potato mixture, tossing gently. Chill several hours. Yield: 8 to 10 servings.

Crisp Pea Salad

    3   cups shredded lettuce
    ¾   cup minced green pepper
    ⅔   cup minced green onion
    1   cup mayonnaise
    1   tablespoon curry powder
   Juice of ½ lemon
    1   (15-ounce) can black-eyed peas, drained
        and rinsed
    ¾   cup grated Parmesan cheese
    4   slices bacon, cooked and crumbled

Spread lettuce over bottom of an 8-inch casserole. Layer green pepper and onion over lettuce. Combine mayonnaise, curry powder, and lemon juice; spread over onion and pepper.

Spoon black-eyed peas over mayonnaise mixture; sprinkle with cheese, and top with bacon. Chill several hours. Salad can be made a day in advance. Yield: 6 servings.

Stuffed Cherry Tomatoes

   About 4½ to 5 dozen cherry tomatoes
    2   (8-ounce) packages cream cheese,
        softened
    ¼   cup mayonnaise
    2   tablespoons half-and-half
    2   tablespoons finely chopped onion
    2   tablespoons finely chopped green pepper
    ½   teaspoon hot sauce
    ⅛   teaspoon garlic salt
    ¼   teaspoon salt
    ½   teaspoon Worcestershire sauce
    2   teaspoons seasoned salt
   Capers
   Lettuce

Cut a slice from top of each tomato; scoop out pulp, leaving shells intact. Invert tomatoes to drain. Reserve pulp for soups or sauces.

Combine cream cheese, mayonnaise, and half-and-half; mix until smooth. Stir in remaining ingredients except capers and lettuce.

Spoon mixture into tomato shells; chill. Garnish with capers. Arrange on a bed of lettuce. Yield: about 4½ to 5 dozen tomatoes.

Stuffed Tomato Salad

    4   tomatoes
    ½   cup cottage cheese
    1   teaspoon Worcestershire sauce
    ½   teaspoon chopped chives
    4   slices bacon, cooked and crumbled
    ½   teaspoon horseradish
   Salt to taste
   Lettuce leaves

Slice off top and scoop out pulp from each tomato; reserve pulp for use in other recipes. Sprinkle inside of shells with salt, and invert on paper towels.

Combine remaining ingredients, except lettuce leaves; fill tomatoes with mixture. Serve on lettuce leaves. Yield: 4 servings.

★
Zucchini-Tomato Salad

    6   small raw zucchini, thinly sliced
    4   tomatoes, cut into wedges
    1   green pepper, thinly sliced into rings
    ¼   cup chopped green onion
    ¼   cup vinegar
    ½   teaspoon salt
    ½   teaspoon garlic salt
    ½   teaspoon pepper
    ¾   cup salad oil
   Lettuce (optional)

Combine zucchini, tomatoes, green pepper, and green onion; toss lightly. Combine vinegar, salt, garlic salt, pepper, and salad oil; mix well, and pour over vegetables. Chill several hours, stirring occasionally. Serve on lettuce, if desired. Yield: 6 to 8 servings.

Make-Ahead Oriental Salad

1 *(17-ounce) can tiny peas, drained*
1 *(16-ounce) can bean sprouts, drained*
1 *(12-ounce) can whole kernel white corn, drained*
2 *(5-ounce) cans water chestnuts, drained and sliced*
1 *(6-ounce) can sliced mushrooms, drained*
1 *(4-ounce) jar pimiento, drained and sliced*
1 *large green pepper, thinly sliced*
1 *large onion, thinly sliced*
1 *cup sliced celery*
1 *cup salad oil*
1 *cup water*
1 *cup sugar*
½ *cup vinegar*
   Seasoned salt and pepper to taste

Combine vegetables in a large bowl, stirring gently. Combine remaining ingredients, and pour over vegetables. Cover and chill 24 hours. Drain before serving. Yield: 10 to 12 servings.

Salad à la Italiano

1 *clove garlic*
1 *hard-cooked egg, finely chopped*
2 *or 3 small yellow squash, finely chopped*
4 *scallions with tops, thinly sliced*
5 *mushrooms, sliced*
   About ½ cup commercial Italian salad dressing
1 *small head iceberg lettuce*
1 *cup croutons*
½ *cup crumbled blue cheese*

Rub a wooden salad bowl with cut end of garlic clove. Combine egg, squash, scallions, mushrooms, and about ½ cup Italian dressing in bowl. Refrigerate several hours, stirring mixture occasionally.

Tear lettuce into bite-size pieces; toss with vegetable mixture. Add more Italian dressing, if needed. Add croutons and blue cheese; toss lightly and serve at once. Yield: 4 to 6 servings.

Raw Turnip Salad

½ *cup commercial sour cream*
1 *tablespoon cider vinegar*
2 *tablespoons finely chopped onion*
2 *tablespoons finely chopped parsley*
1 *teaspoon sugar*
1 *teaspoon salt*
⅛ *teaspoon pepper*
4 *cups peeled, shredded white turnip*
1 *unpeeled apple, cored and diced*

Combine sour cream, vinegar, onion, parsley, sugar, salt, and pepper, stirring well. Add turnip, mixing well. Cover and chill several hours. Stir in apple before serving. Yield: 6 to 8 servings.

Saturday Supper Salad

2 *cups cooked black-eyed peas*
⅓ *cup chopped roasted peanuts (optional)*
1 *tablespoon minced onion*
½ *cup diced celery*
¼ *cup diced green pepper*
2 *cups shredded cabbage*
2 *cups shredded carrots*
½ *cup mayonnaise*
½ *cup commercial French dressing*
   Salt to taste
   Lettuce leaves
   Hard-cooked eggs, sliced
   Paprika

Combine first 7 ingredients. Blend mayonnaise and French dressing; add to vegetables, and toss lightly. Add salt. Serve salad on lettuce leaves. Garnish with eggs; sprinkle with paprika. Yield: 6 to 8 servings.

Garden Salad

6 *to 8 fresh mushrooms, sliced*
1 *medium-size green pepper, thinly sliced*
2 *to 3 stalks celery, sliced*
1 *small head cauliflower, broken into flowerets*
   Dressing
10 *to 12 cherry tomatoes*

Combine first four ingredients. Chill several hours. Add Dressing and tomatoes just before serving. Yield: about 4 servings.

Dressing:

    1   *cup salad oil*
    ⅓   *cup wine vinegar*
    1   *teaspoon sugar*
    ¼   *teaspoon dry mustard*
    2   *tablespoons finely chopped onion*
    1½ *teaspoons salt*
    ½   *teaspoon pepper*

Combine all ingredients in container of electric blender. Blend until creamy. Yield: about 1½ cups.

Emerald Salad Ring

    1   *cup shredded, unpeeled cucumbers*
    2   *tablespoons grated onion*
    1   *(3-ounce) package lime-flavored gelatin*
    ¾   *cup boiling water*
    1   *cup cream-style cottage cheese*
    1   *cup mayonnaise*
    ⅓   *cup slivered blanched almonds*

Combine cucumbers and onion; drain well. Dissolve gelatin in boiling water; chill until slightly thickened.

Fold cucumbers, onion, cottage cheese, mayonnaise, and almonds into gelatin. Spoon into a 5-cup ring mold; chill until set. Unmold and garnish as desired. Yield: 8 servings.

Avocado Ribbon Aspic

Avocado Layer:

    1   *envelope unflavored gelatin*
    ¼   *cup cold water*
    ½   *cup boiling water*
    1   *teaspoon salt*
    3   *tablespoons lemon juice*
    ¼   *teaspoon hot sauce*
    1½ *cups mashed ripe avocado*
        Green food coloring (optional)

Soften gelatin in cold water; add boiling water, stirring until gelatin dissolves. Add salt, lemon juice, and hot sauce; chill until slightly thickened. Stir in avocado. Add food coloring, if desired. Pour mixture into a 9¼- x 5¼- x 2¾-inch loafpan; chill until set but not firm.

Cream Cheese Layer:

    2   *teaspoons unflavored gelatin*
    ¼   *cup cold water*
    4   *(3-ounce) packages cream cheese, softened*
    ½   *cup milk*
    1   *teaspoon salt*
    ⅔   *cup mayonnaise*
    ¼   *teaspoon Worcestershire sauce*

Soften gelatin in cold water; place over boiling water, stirring until gelatin dissolves. Set aside. Beat cream cheese until smooth, gradually adding milk. Add salt, mayonnaise, and Worcestershire sauce; mix well. Stir in softened gelatin, and spread over Avocado Layer. Chill.

Tomato Layer:

    3   *cups tomato juice*
    1   *small bay leaf*
    2   *whole cloves*
    2   *or 3 parsley sprigs*
    2   *stalks celery, cut into pieces*
    ¾   *teaspoon salt*
        Dash of cayenne
    2   *envelopes unflavored gelatin*
    ⅓   *cup cold water*
    1½ *tablespoons vinegar*
    1½ *teaspoons grated onion*
        Lettuce (optional)
        Tomato wedges (optional)

Combine tomato juice, bay leaf, cloves, parsley, celery, salt, and cayenne in a saucepan; simmer over low heat 10 minutes. Strain, discarding residue.

Soften gelatin in cold water; stir in hot tomato juice mixture, vinegar, and onion. Cool; then pour over Cream Cheese Layer. Chill until firm.

Unmold salad on bed of lettuce and garnish with tomato wedges, if desired. To serve, cut into slices. Yield: 8 to 10 servings.

Molded Avocado Salad

    1 (3-ounce) package lemon-flavored
         gelatin
 1¾ cups boiling water
    ¼ teaspoon salt
    2 tablespoons plus 1 teaspoon lemon juice
    1 tablespoon prepared horseradish
    1 teaspoon grated onion
    2 medium-size avocados, peeled and diced
    ½ cup finely chopped celery
        Lettuce
        Herb Mayonnaise

Dissolve gelatin in boiling water; stir in salt, lemon juice, horseradish, and onion. Chill until partially set.

Beat gelatin with electric mixer until smooth; fold in avocados and celery. Pour into an oiled 4-cup mold; refrigerate until firm. Unmold on lettuce, and serve with Herb Mayonnaise. Yield: about 6 servings.

Herb Mayonnaise:

    1 cup mayonnaise
    ½ teaspoon lemon juice
    ¼ teaspoon salt
    ¼ teaspoon paprika
    ¼ cup finely chopped parsley
    1 tablespoon grated onion
    1 tablespoon chopped chives
        Dash of Worcestershire sauce
    1 clove garlic, minced
    1 tablespoon capers (optional)
    ½ cup commercial sour cream

Combine all ingredients except sour cream; stir until well blended. Fold in sour cream. Serve over any congealed vegetable salad or with shrimp. Yield: about 1½ cups.

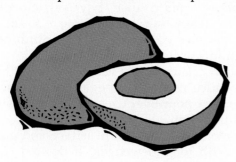

Favorite Tomato Aspic

    2 envelopes unflavored gelatin
    ¼ cup cold water
    ½ cup boiling water
    4 cups tomato juice
    1 tablespoon minced onion
    1 teaspoon sugar
    ½ teaspoon celery seeds or several minced
         celery tops
    1 teaspoon seasoned salt
    2 bay leaves
    1 teaspoon Worcestershire sauce
    2 whole cloves
    1 teaspoon salt
        Juice of 1 lemon

Soak gelatin in cold water 5 minutes; dissolve in boiling water, and set aside.

Combine remaining ingredients except lemon juice in a large saucepan; simmer 15 minutes. Strain; add lemon juice and gelatin.

Pour into a 10-inch ring mold or 6 individual molds; chill until set. Yield: 6 servings.

Note: For a delicious variation, add chopped vegetables or seafood when aspic is partially set.

Layered Tomato Aspic

    3 cups tomato juice
    ½ cup coarsely chopped celery tops
    6 whole cloves
    2 tablespoons sugar
    2 tablespoons vinegar
    2 tablespoons lemon juice
    2 teaspoons coarsely chopped onion
         (optional)
 1½ teaspoons salt, divided
        Cayenne pepper to taste
    2 envelopes unflavored gelatin
    ½ cup cold water, divided
    2 (3-ounce) packages cream cheese
    ¼ cup milk
    ½ teaspoon grated onion
 1½ teaspoons unflavored gelatin
    ½ cup finely chopped celery
    8 stuffed olives, chopped
        Lettuce
        Mayonnaise or salad dressing

Combine tomato juice, celery tops, cloves, sugar, vinegar, lemon juice, chopped onion (if desired), 1 teaspoon salt, and cayenne in a medium saucepan. Bring to a boil, and simmer 10 minutes.

Soften 2 envelopes gelatin in ¼ cup cold water; let stand 5 minutes. Strain tomato juice mixture, discarding vegetables and spices. Add softened gelatin, stirring until dissolved. Set aside to cool.

Combine cream cheese, milk, grated onion, and ½ teaspoon salt; beat until smooth. Soften 1½ teaspoons gelatin in ¼ cup cold water; place over hot water, stirring until dissolved. Add dissolved gelatin to cream cheese mixture, mixing well; stir in finely chopped celery and olives.

Pour half of tomato mixture into a lightly oiled 5-cup mold; chill until set. Spoon cream cheese mixture over tomato layer, spreading evenly; chill until firm.

Pour remaining tomato juice mixture over cream cheese layer, and chill until firm. Unmold on bed of lettuce, and top with mayonnaise. Yield: 8 to 10 servings.

Limey Spring Salad

    1   (3-ounce) package lime-flavored gelatin
    ½   cup boiling water
    1   (10¾-ounce) can cream of celery soup,
          undiluted
    ½   cup mayonnaise
    1   tablespoon apple cider vinegar
    1   teaspoon minced onion
    1   or 2 drops green food coloring
    ½   cup shredded unpeeled cucumber
    ¼   cup chopped celery
    1   tablespoon minced parsley

Dissolve gelatin in water, stirring well; add soup, stirring until smooth and well blended. Add mayonnaise, vinegar, onion, and food coloring; blend well, and chill until consistency of unbeaten egg whites. Beat mixture until light and fluffy. Fold in remaining ingredients, and pour into a 3-cup mold. Chill until firm. Yield: 6 servings.

Beet-Relish Salad

    2   (16-ounce) cans whole beets
    2   envelopes unflavored gelatin
    ½   cup sugar
    1   teaspoon salt
    ⅔   cup vinegar
    5   tablespoons prepared horseradish
    ¼   cup chopped onion
    1   cup finely chopped celery
    ½   cup finely chopped green pepper

Drain and chop beets, reserving juice. Sprinkle gelatin over 1½ cups beet juice. Place mixture over low heat; cook, stirring constantly, about 3 minutes or until gelatin dissolves. Stir in remaining ingredients.

Pour mixture into a 1½-quart mold, and chill until firm. Yield: 8 to 10 servings.

Luncheon Salad

    1½ tablespoons unflavored gelatin
    ⅓   cup cold water
    2   (3-ounce) packages cream cheese,
          softened
    ¾   cup mayonnaise
    1   (10¾-ounce) can tomato soup,
          undiluted
    1   cup chopped celery
    2   tablespoons chopped green pepper
    1   teaspoon minced onion (optional)
    ½   cup chopped pecans
    2   tablespoons chopped stuffed olives

Soften gelatin in cold water. Combine cream cheese and mayonnaise, and blend until smooth; add tomato soup and gelatin, mixing well. Stir in remaining ingredients, and pour into a 4-cup mold. Chill until firm. Yield: 8 servings.

Vegetable Aspic Ring

    3   envelopes unflavored gelatin
    1   (12-ounce) can tomato juice
    1   (28-ounce) can stewed tomatoes,
          undrained
    ¼   cup lemon juice
    4   teaspoons Worcestershire sauce
    1   teaspoon salt
 Dash of hot sauce
    2   (15-ounce) cans three bean salad,
          drained
    ¾   cup finely chopped green onion
 Bibb lettuce
 Mayonnaise

Soften gelatin in tomato juice. Bring tomatoes to a boil in a saucepan; stir in gelatin mixture, and heat until gelatin is dissolved. Stir in lemon juice, Worcestershire sauce, salt, hot sauce, three bean salad, and onion.

Pour the mixture into an oiled 8-cup mold. Chill until firm. Unmold aspic on Bibb lettuce, and serve with mayonnaise. Yield: about 10 servings.

Mixed Green Salad

    1   small head romaine, torn
    1   small head Boston lettuce, torn
    1   small head endive, torn
 1½   cups sliced fresh mushrooms
 Croutons
 Tart and Tangy Dressing

Combine all ingredients except Tart and Tangy Dressing. Pour Dressing over salad; toss. Serve at once. Yield: about 10 servings.

Tart and Tangy Dressing:

    1   tablespoon grated onion
    2   tablespoons white wine vinegar
    2   teaspoons Dijon mustard
    ⅛   teaspoon freshly ground pepper
 1½   teaspoons salt
    ½   cup olive oil
 4½   teaspoons lemon juice

Combine all ingredients in a jar. Cover and shake until well blended. Yield: about ¾ cup.

Confetti Relish Mold

    2   beef bouillon cubes
    1   (3-ounce) package lemon-flavored
          gelatin
    1   cup boiling water
    2   tablespoons tarragon vinegar
    ½   teaspoon salt
    1   (8-ounce) carton commercial sour cream
    ½   cup chopped cucumber
    ¼   cup finely chopped green pepper
    ¼   cup sliced radishes
    2   tablespoons sliced green onion

Dissolve bouillon cubes and gelatin in boiling water; add vinegar and salt. Chill until mixture is partially set.

Stir sour cream into thickened gelatin, beating until smooth; fold in remaining ingredients. Pour into a 3-cup mold, and chill until firm. Yield: 6 to 8 servings.

Avocado, Artichoke, Tomato Salad

    8   cups torn salad greens
    2   ripe avocados, sliced
    1   (6-ounce) jar marinated artichoke
          hearts, drained
    1   small onion, sliced
    2   large tomatoes, cut in wedges
 Caesar Salad Dressing

Combine vegetables in a large salad bowl. Toss with Caesar Salad Dressing just before serving. Yield: about 8 servings.

Caesar Salad Dressing:

    1   egg
    1   tablespoon anchovy paste or 2 to 3
          anchovies, mashed
    1   tablespoon lemon juice
    ¼   cup red wine vinegar
    ½   cup salad oil
    ½   teaspoon Worcestershire sauce
    1   clove garlic, crushed
    2   tablespoons seasoned Italian
          breadcrumbs
    4   tablespoons grated Parmesan cheese
    1   teaspoon salt

Run hot water over egg in shell until shell feels warm to touch. Combine egg and remaining ingredients; mix well. Let mixture stand at room temperature 1 hour. If Dressing becomes too thick, add a small amount of water, mixing well. Yield: about 1 cup.

Savory Salad Oriental

1   (16-ounce) can bean sprouts, drained
1   cup sliced fresh mushrooms
1   (8-ounce) package natural brick cheese slices, cut into julienne strips
¼   cup sliced water chestnuts
2   tablespoons toasted sesame seeds
Mayonnaise Dressing
2   cups bite-size pieces lettuce

Combine bean sprouts, mushrooms, cheese, water chestnuts, and sesame seeds. Pour Mayonnaise Dressing over mixture; chill at least 30 minutes. Toss with lettuce just before serving. Yield: 6 servings.

Mayonnaise Dressing:

1   egg
¼   teaspoon salt
2   tablespoons lemon juice
1   cup salad oil, divided
1   teaspoon seasoned salt
1   teaspoon soy sauce
¼   teaspoon garlic powder

Combine egg, salt, lemon juice, and ¼ cup salad oil in container of electric blender; process until mixture begins to thicken. Without turning off blender, immediately pour in remaining oil in a slow, steady stream. Blend in remaining ingredients. Yield: about 1 cup.

Gourmet Salad Supreme

1   large head romaine, torn
1   medium-size onion, thinly sliced
1   (11-ounce) can mandarin orange sections, drained
⅓   cup black walnuts, toasted
Blue Cheese Dressing

Combine romaine, onion, orange sections, and walnuts in a large bowl. Toss with as much Blue Cheese Dressing as desired. Serve at once. Yield: about 8 servings.

Blue Cheese Dressing:

½   cup commercial sour cream or yogurt
½   cup mayonnaise
¼   clove garlic, minced
2   teaspoons grated onion
Tarragon vinegar to taste
1   (4-ounce) package blue cheese, crumbled
Salt and pepper to taste

Combine all ingredients, blending well. Yield: 1½ cups.

Syrian Salad

10   mint leaves, chopped
2   cloves garlic, crushed
1   teaspoon salt
Juice of 2 lemons
½   cup salad oil
1   head lettuce, torn
2   tomatoes, chopped
2   green peppers, chopped
1   small red onion, thinly sliced and separated into rings
1   cucumber, sliced
1   avocado, peeled and sliced
1   (8½-ounce) can artichoke hearts, drained and halved

Combine mint leaves, garlic, salt, lemon juice, and salad oil; mix well, and let stand at least 2 hours.

Combine remaining ingredients, and toss lightly. Serve with salad dressing. Yield: 6 to 8 servings.

Tossed Spinach-Orange Salad

1½ cups torn lettuce
1½ cups torn fresh spinach
3 medium-size oranges, peeled and sliced
1 tablespoon sugar
Salt to taste
¼ cup Tomato Salad Dressing
½ onion, sliced into rings
Additional orange slices

Combine lettuce, spinach, orange slices, sugar, and salt in a large bowl. Add ¼ cup Tomato Salad Dressing (more, if desired); toss. Garnish with onion rings and additional orange slices. Yield: 6 to 8 servings.

Tomato Salad Dressing:

1 (10¾-ounce) can tomato soup, undiluted
¾ cup vinegar
½ cup salad oil
¼ cup sugar
1 tablespoon Worcestershire sauce
3 tablespoons grated onion
1 teaspoon salt
1 tablespoon dry mustard
1 teaspoon paprika
2 cloves garlic

Combine all ingredients except garlic in a quart jar; shake well. Add garlic; let stand about 1 hour for flavor to develop. Chill. Remove garlic before serving. Yield: 1 quart.

Fresh Spinach Salad

1 pound fresh spinach
½ pound fresh mushrooms
6 to 8 green onions, chopped
8 slices bacon, cooked and crumbled
1 cup salad oil
⅔ cup sugar
½ teaspoon dry mustard
½ teaspoon onion juice
½ teaspoon salt
⅓ cup cider vinegar
Salt and pepper to taste

Remove stems from spinach; wash leaves thoroughly, and pat dry. Tear into bite-size

pieces. Quickly rinse mushrooms in cold water; drain well, and slice thin. Combine spinach, mushrooms, onion, and bacon in a large bowl; set aside.

Combine salad oil, sugar, mustard, onion juice, and salt in container of electric blender; blend well. Remove lid of container; slowly add vinegar while blender is running.

Toss spinach mixture with dressing until well coated. Season with salt and pepper. Yield: about 8 servings.

Ham-Avocado Salad

3 cups cubed cooked ham
4 hard-cooked eggs, chopped
2 sweet pickles, chopped
2 green onions, chopped
1½ cups chopped celery
½ cup mayonnaise
1 tablespoon sweet pickle juice
2 avocados, sliced
½ cup cashew nuts
16 cherry tomatoes

Combine first 7 ingredients, mixing well. Spoon ham mixture on avocado slices, and garnish with nuts and tomatoes. Yield: 4 servings.

Exotic Green Salad

¼ cup salad oil
2 tablespoons vinegar
1 tablespoon minced parsley
1 teaspoon Worcestershire sauce
½ teaspoon salt
⅛ teaspoon pepper
2 (8½-ounce) cans artichoke hearts, drained and cut into quarters
6 cups torn mixed salad greens
2 pink grapefruit, peeled and sectioned

Combine oil, vinegar, parsley, Worcestershire sauce, salt, and pepper. Pour marinade over artichokes; cover and chill 4 hours or overnight.

Add salad greens and grapefruit sections to artichokes and toss lightly. Yield: 6 to 8 servings.

Spinach Avocado Salad

      2 *pounds fresh spinach, torn*
      1 *large head Boston lettuce, torn*
      3 *ripe avocados, peeled and sliced*
         Lemon juice
         Honey-Lime Dressing

Combine salad greens in a large bowl. Brush avocado with lemon juice; add to salad. Toss with Honey-Lime Dressing. Yield: about 8 servings.

   Honey-Lime Dressing:

      ¼ *cup lemon juice*
      3 *tablespoons lime juice*
      ¼ *cup salad oil*
      ¼ *cup honey*
      ½ *teaspoon salt*
      ¼ *teaspoon dry mustard*

Combine all ingredients; blend well. Chill. Yield: about 1 cup.

★
Spinach Salad

      ½ *small onion, thinly sliced*
      ¼ *cup red wine vinegar*
      2 *pounds fresh spinach, torn*
      4 *hard-cooked eggs, chopped*
      1 *(5-ounce) can water chestnuts, drained*
         and sliced
      ½ *pound fresh mushrooms, sliced*
      6 *slices cooked, crumbled bacon or ½ cup*
         imitation bacon
      ⅔ *cup salad oil or olive oil*
         Salt to taste

Soak onion slices in vinegar 20 to 30 minutes; drain, reserving vinegar. Combine onion, spinach, eggs, water chestnuts, mushrooms, and bacon; toss lightly. Combine reserved vinegar and salad oil; pour over spinach and toss again. Season with salt. Yield: 6 to 8 servings.

Fruited Ham and Cheese Salad

      ¼ *cup mayonnaise*
      3 *tablespoons commercial sour cream*
      1 *tablespoon catsup*
      1 *tablespoon brandy (optional)*
      1 *tablespoon chopped parsley*
      ½ *teaspoon paprika*
      ⅛ *teaspoon salt*
      ⅛ *teaspoon white pepper*
      ⅛ *teaspoon sugar*
      1 *small cantaloupe or honeydew, peeled*
         and cut in 1-inch cubes
      8 *ounces cooked ham, cut in ¼-inch*
         cubes
      8 *ounces Swiss cheese, cut into ½-inch*
         cubes
      1 *medium-size apple, peeled and diced*
      2 *hard-cooked eggs, chopped*
      ⅓ *cup coarsely chopped walnuts*
         Boston lettuce

Combine first 9 ingredients in a large bowl, mixing well. Stir in remaining ingredients except lettuce. Cover and refrigerate at least 30 minutes. Serve on lettuce. Yield: about 6 servings.

Dilly Beef Salad

      3 *cups cubed cooked beef*
      ¾ *cup chopped green pepper*
      5 *large stuffed olives, sliced*
     10 *pickled onions, chopped*
      ⅛ *teaspoon pepper*
      ½ *teaspoon salt*
      ¼ *teaspoon dry mustard*
      1 *teaspoon dillweed*
      ½ *cup mayonnaise*
      ¼ *cup beer*
      1 *tablespoon lemon juice*
         Pickled onions and stuffed olives

Combine beef, green pepper, sliced olives, and chopped pickled onion; chill. Combine pepper, salt, mustard, dillweed, mayonnaise, beer, and lemon juice; mix well, and add to meat mixture. Toss lightly. Chill at least 1 hour. Garnish with pickled onions and olives. Yield: 6 servings.

Corn Beef Salad

1   envelope unflavored gelatin
1½   cups hot water
2   tablespoons lemon juice
1   (12-ounce) can corn beef, flaked
1   (4-ounce) can sliced mushrooms,
        drained
2   cups diced celery
4   hard-cooked eggs, sliced
2   tablespoons minced onion
2   tablespoons finely chopped green pepper
1   cup mayonnaise

Soften gelatin in hot water, and add lemon juice; cool. Combine corn beef, mushrooms, celery, eggs, onion, green pepper, and mayonnaise; add gelatin mixture, mixing well. Pour into a 6-cup mold, and chill until firm. Yield: 6 to 8 servings.

Taco Salad

1½   pounds ground beef
1½   cups chopped onion
1   cup chopped celery
1   cup chopped green pepper
1   tablespoon chili powder
3   cloves garlic, minced
Pinch of cumin seeds
Salt and pepper to taste
½   cup water
2   pounds pasteurized process cheese
        spread
1   (10-ounce) can tomatoes with hot
        peppers, undrained and chopped
1   head lettuce, torn into bite-size pieces
2   to 3 large tomatoes, chopped
1   (6-ounce) package corn chips, crushed

Sauté ground beef, onion, celery, and green pepper until meat is lightly browned. Stir in seasonings and water; cover and simmer 25 to 30 minutes.

Combine cheese and tomatoes with hot peppers in top of a double boiler, and place over boiling water; cook until cheese melts, stirring constantly. Toss together meat mixture, cheese mixture, lettuce, tomatoes, and corn chips. Serve immediately. Yield: 8 to 10 servings.

Ham and Orange Salad

1   clove garlic
2   cups cubed cooked ham
1½   cups drained orange sections
1   cup diced celery
½   cup chopped walnuts
½   cup minced onion
⅓   cup mayonnaise
2   tablespoons whipping cream
1   to 2 teaspoons vinegar
½   teaspoon salt
Dash of pepper

Rub garlic in salad bowl; discard garlic. Put ham, orange sections, celery, walnuts, and onion in salad bowl.

Combine remaining ingredients, and add to ham mixture; toss gently to coat. Serve cold. Yield: 8 servings.

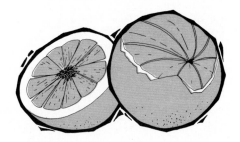

Sausage-Potato Salad

1   (12-ounce) package smoked sausage
        links, cut into 1-inch pieces
½   cup hot water
1   (8-ounce) carton commercial sour cream
2   tablespoons prepared mustard
1   teaspoon salt
1   teaspoon sugar
¼   cup chopped green onion
4   cups hot cooked cubed potatoes

Place sausage in hot water in a skillet; cover and cook over low heat 10 minutes. Drain. Combine sour cream, mustard, salt, sugar, and green onion in a small saucepan; cook over low heat 5 minutes. (Do not let boil.)

Combine sausage and potatoes; add sour cream mixture, and toss well. Serve warm. Yield: 6 to 8 servings.

Meat and Black-Eyed Pea Salad

1   cup cubed cooked lean beef
1   cup cubed cooked ham
5   cups cooked, drained black-eyed peas
1   cup chopped celery
1   green pepper, chopped
1   onion, chopped
2   teaspoons prepared mustard
1   cup mayonnaise or salad dressing
Salt and pepper to taste

Combine all ingredients; chill thoroughly before serving. Yield: 12 servings.

★ Chicken-Fruit Salad

1   (16-ounce) can pineapple chunks
1   apple, cored and sliced
1   cup seedless grapes
3   cups diced cooked chicken
Whipped Cream Fruit Dressing
Lettuce
⅓   cup toasted slivered almonds

Drain pineapple chunks, reserving juice. Dip apple slices in pineapple juice. Combine fruit and chicken; chill. Add Whipped Cream Fruit Dressing, and toss lightly. Serve on lettuce, and top with almonds. Yield: 6 to 8 servings.

Whipped Cream Fruit Dressing:

3   tablespoons butter or margarine
3   tablespoons all-purpose flour
¼   cup sugar
1   teaspoon salt
⅓   cup lemon juice
⅓   cup pineapple juice
2   egg yolks, slightly beaten
½   cup whipping cream, whipped

Melt butter in a small saucepan over low heat; blend in flour. Add sugar, salt, lemon juice, and pineapple juice; cook until thickened, stirring constantly.

Stir a small amount of hot mixture into egg yolks; stir into remaining hot mixture. Cook about 2 minutes, stirring constantly. Chill. Fold in whipped cream. Yield: about 1 cup.

★ Hot Chicken Salad

1   cup all-purpose flour
1   teaspoon salt, divided
⅓   cup plus 1 tablespoon shortening
1   cup shredded sharp Cheddar cheese, divided
2   tablespoons water
2   cups cubed cooked chicken
1   cup chopped celery
1   cup chopped green pepper
2   teaspoons grated onion
1   tablespoon lemon juice
1   (4-ounce) jar pimiento, drained and chopped
1   cup mayonnaise
1   cup crushed potato chips

Combine flour and ½ teaspoon salt; cut in shortening with 2 knives or a pastry blender until mixture resembles coarse cornmeal. Add ½ cup cheese and water; stir until mixture forms a ball.

Roll dough to ⅛-inch thickness on a lightly floured board. Fit into a 9-inch piepan, and crimp edges to seal. Prick bottom and sides of pastry with a fork. Bake at 475° for 8 to 10 minutes.

Combine chicken, celery, green pepper, onion, lemon juice, ½ teaspoon salt, pimiento, and mayonnaise; mix well. Pour into pastry shell, and sprinkle with remaining ½ cup cheese and potato chips. Bake at 350° for 20 minutes. Yield: 6 to 8 servings.

Cucumber-Tuna Salad

½   cup mayonnaise
¼   cup commercial sour cream
1   tablespoon lemon juice
½   teaspoon horseradish
1   teaspoon dried dillweed
3   tablespoons capers
⅛   teaspoon salt
1   cucumber, peeled and diced
2   (7-ounce) cans tuna, drained and flaked

Combine mayonnaise and sour cream; add remaining ingredients, mixing well. Chill thoroughly. Yield: 4 to 6 servings.

Almond Chicken Salad

4 *cups diced cooked chicken*
1 *cup thinly sliced celery*
1 *medium-size green pepper, chopped*
⅔ *cup sliced stuffed olives (optional)*
1 *teaspoon salt*
¼ *teaspoon pepper*
2 *teaspoons grated onion*
⅔ *cup mayonnaise*
¼ *cup commercial mustard-mayonnaise sandwich sauce*
⅔ *cup toasted slivered almonds*
Lettuce leaves or tomato cups

Combine first 7 ingredients. Combine mayonnaise and sandwich sauce; add to chicken mixture, and toss lightly. Chill.

When ready to serve, add almonds. Serve on lettuce, or stuff in tomato cups. Yield: 6 servings.

Carolina Plantation Salad

1 *cup deveined, diced, cooked shrimp*
1 *tablespoon lemon juice*
3 *cups diced cooked chicken*
1 *cup diced celery*
⅔ *cup mayonnaise*
Salt and pepper to taste
Lettuce
3 *hard-cooked eggs, sliced*
Parsley

Sprinkle shrimp with lemon juice; set aside. Combine chicken, celery, mayonnaise, salt, and pepper; stir in shrimp. Serve on lettuce. Garnish with egg slices and parsley. Yield: 8 servings.

★ Smoked Turkey Salad

7 *hard-cooked eggs, divided*
5 *cups coarsely chopped smoked turkey*
1 *tablespoon pepper*
¾ *cup chopped green olives*
1 *cup chopped sweet pickles*
1 *(1.5-ounce) package buttermilk-mayonnaise salad dressing mix*

Mash egg yolks and set aside. Chop egg whites; add turkey, pepper, olives, and pickles. Prepare salad dressing according to package directions. Combine egg yolks and 3 cups dressing (store remaining dressing for other use). Pour dressing over salad and mix well. Chill about 12 hours before serving. Yield: 10 servings.

Southwestern Chicken Salad

3 *tablespoons bottled creamy French dressing*
3 *cups diced cooked chicken*
2 *medium-size oranges, peeled and sectioned*
½ *cup mayonnaise*
6 *pimiento-stuffed olives, sliced*
2 *medium-size avocados, peeled and sliced*
2 *tablespoons lemon juice*
Lettuce

Combine French dressing and chicken; refrigerate at least 2 hours. Combine chicken mixture, orange sections, mayonnaise, and olives; mix well, and set aside.

Brush avocado slices with lemon juice. Arrange lettuce leaves on 6 salad plates. Arrange avocado slices on lettuce, and spoon chicken salad onto avocado. Yield: 6 servings.

Special Shrimp Salad

1 *tablespoon lemon juice*
2 *cups diced, cooked shrimp*
1 *cup diced cantaloupe or honeydew*
1 *cup cold cooked rice*
½ *teaspoon salt*
¼ *teaspoon white pepper*
½ *cup mayonnaise*
Parsley

Sprinkle lemon juice over shrimp; add cantaloupe, rice, salt, and pepper. Toss lightly, and stir in mayonnaise. Chill. Garnish with parsley. Yield: about 6 servings.

Cauliflower-Shrimp Salad

     2   cups cooked, peeled, and deveined
           shrimp
    1½   cups cooked rice
     1   cup raw cauliflowerets
     ⅓   cup chopped green pepper
     2   tablespoons finely chopped onion
    12   pimiento-stuffed olives, sliced
     ½   cup mayonnaise
         Juice of ½ lemon
     ¼   teaspoon paprika
         Dash of hot sauce
         Salt and pepper to taste
         Lettuce leaves

Combine all ingredients except lettuce leaves, mixing well. Chill. Serve on lettuce leaves. Yield: 6 servings.

Dill-Shrimp Salad

     3   pounds uncooked shrimp
     ½   onion, peeled and sliced
     1   tablespoon salt
     1   tablespoon seafood seasoning
     1   (5-ounce) can water chestnuts, drained
           and sliced
     5   tablespoons bottled Italian dressing
     2   teaspoons chopped dillweed
     ½   teaspoon salt
     1   small head romaine lettuce
         Parsley
         Celery
         Tomato wedges
         Lemon wedges
         Carrot curls

Combine shrimp, onion, 1 tablespoon salt, and seafood seasoning in a large saucepan; add boiling water to cover. Bring to a boil, and simmer 4 to 5 minutes or until shrimp are pink. Drain and peel shrimp.

Combine shrimp, water chestnuts, Italian dressing, dillweed, and ½ teaspoon salt; chill thoroughly. Serve on lettuce; garnish with parsley, celery, tomato wedges, lemon wedges, and carrot curls. Sprinkle with additional Italian dressing, if desired. Yield: 6 to 8 servings.

Shrimp and Rice Salad

     1   pound shrimp, cooked, peeled, and
           deveined
     2   cups cooked rice
     ¼   cup thinly sliced celery
     ¼   cup sliced stuffed olives
     ¼   cup chopped green pepper
     ¼   cup chopped pimiento
     ¼   cup minced onion
     ½   teaspoon salt
     ¼   teaspoon pepper
     3   tablespoons mayonnaise or salad
           dressing
         Lettuce
     2   tomatoes, cut in wedges
         Celery leaves
         Commercial French dressing

Combine first 10 ingredients, and toss lightly. Chill thoroughly. Serve on lettuce and garnish with tomato wedges and celery leaves. Serve with French dressing. Yield: 4 servings.

Shrimp Luncheon Mold

     1   envelope unflavored gelatin
     ⅔   cup cold water
     1   (8-ounce) carton commercial sour cream
     ¼   cup chili sauce
     ½   teaspoon salt
     ⅓   cup frozen lemonade concentrate,
           thawed and undiluted
     1   cup cooked, peeled shrimp
     ½   cup diced celery
     ¼   cup diced green pepper

Soften gelatin in cold water; place over low heat, and stir until gelatin is dissolved. Blend in sour cream, chili sauce, salt, and lemonade concentrate; chill until thickened.

Fold shrimp, celery, and green pepper into gelatin mixture. Pour into 5 or 6 individual molds or a 3½-cup mold; chill until firm. Yield: 5 to 6 servings.

★ Crab Louis Salad

½   *cup mayonnaise*
½   *cup chili sauce*
2   *tablespoons chopped green pepper*
2   *tablespoons chopped sweet pickle*
1   *tablespoon chopped onion*
1   *tablespoon lemon juice*
1½   *cups lump crabmeat or 1 (12-ounce)
    package frozen lump crabmeat, thawed
    and drained*
    Lettuce
2   *tomatoes, quartered*
2   *green peppers, sliced*
2   *hard-cooked eggs, sliced*
    Pimiento strips

Combine mayonnaise, chili sauce, chopped green pepper, sweet pickle, onion, and lemon juice; blend well. Add crabmeat, tossing lightly. Chill thoroughly.

At serving time, spoon salad on lettuce. Garnish with tomatoes, green pepper slices, eggs, and pimiento. Yield: 4 servings.

★ Crab-Stuffed Avocados

2   *tablespoons minced green onion*
3   *tablespoons melted butter or margarine*
3   *tablespoons all-purpose flour*
½   *cup milk*
1   *(12-ounce) package frozen crabmeat,
    thawed, drained, and flaked*
1   *tablespoon lemon juice*
1   *teaspoon salt*
2   *avocados*

Sauté onion in butter until tender. Blend in flour; cook over low heat until bubbly, stirring constantly. Add milk; cook, stirring constantly, until thickened. Stir in crabmeat, lemon juice, and salt; set aside.

Cut avocados in half; carefully remove pulp to within ¼ inch of edges, reserving shells. Chop pulp, and stir into crabmeat mixture. Spoon crabmeat mixture into shells. Bake at 325° for 20 minutes. Yield: 4 servings.

Tuna Salad Oriental

2   *(7-ounce) cans tuna, drained and flaked*
1   *(8½-ounce) can water chestnuts,
    drained and sliced*
1   *cup bean sprouts*
1   *(3¼-ounce) can pitted ripe olives,
    drained and sliced*
1   *cup purple or green grapes, halved and
    seeded*
2   *tablespoons chopped dill pickle*
1   *avocado, peeled and sliced*
    Tangy Dressing
    Tomato wedges
    Egg slices

Combine tuna, water chestnuts, bean sprouts, olives, grapes, and dill pickle; toss lightly. Top with avocado slices. Serve with Tangy Dressing, and garnish with tomato wedges and egg slices. Yield: 6 servings.

Tangy Dressing:

½   *cup commercial sour cream*
½   *cup mayonnaise*
¼   *teaspoon seasoned salt*
¼   *teaspoon garlic salt*

Combine all ingredients, mixing until well blended. Yield: 1 cup.

Salmon Salad Piquant

1   *envelope unflavored gelatin*
½   *cup cold water*
2   *egg yolks, slightly beaten*
¾   *cup milk*
½   *teaspoon salt*
1½   *teaspoons prepared mustard*
    Dash of cayenne pepper
1½   *tablespoons butter or margarine*
½   *cup lemon juice*
1   *(7¾-ounce) can salmon, drained and
    flaked*
    Lettuce
    Lemon slices
    Cucumber Cream Dressing

Soften gelatin in cold water; set aside. Combine egg yolks, milk, salt, mustard, and cayenne in top of a double boiler. Place over simmering water; cook until thickened (about 8 minutes), stirring constantly. Blend in butter and lemon juice. Add softened gelatin, stirring until dissolved. Remove from heat, and stir in salmon. Cool.

Pour salmon mixture into an oiled 1-quart mold, and chill until firm. Unmold on bed of lettuce, and garnish with lemon slices. Serve with Cucumber Cream Dressing. Yield: 6 servings.

Cucumber Cream Dressing:

 1 *medium-size cucumber, peeled*
 2 *tablespoons sugar*
 2 *tablespoons vinegar*
 ½ *pint whipping cream, whipped*

Cut cucumber in half lengthwise; remove seeds and discard. Cut cucumber into ¼-inch cubes; combine with sugar and vinegar, and fold in whipped cream. Chill. Yield: about 3 cups.

Congealed Salmon Salad

 1 *(15½-ounce) can salmon*
 2 *envelopes unflavored gelatin*
 1 *cup chopped celery*
 ¼ *cup chopped green pepper*
 1 *teaspoon finely chopped onion*
 ¾ *cup salad dressing*
 3 *tablespoons lemon juice*
 ½ *teaspoon salt*
 2 *hard-cooked eggs, sliced*
    Lettuce

Drain salmon, reserving liquid; add enough hot water to salmon liquid to measure 1 cup. Bring liquid to a boil; pour over gelatin, stirring well. Chill until slightly thickened.

Flake salmon; add gelatin mixture, vegetables, salad dressing, lemon juice, and salt. Stir until blended well. Arrange egg slices in bottom of a 4-cup mold. Spoon salmon mixture over egg, and chill until firm. Unmold on lettuce. Yield: 6 to 8 servings.

Note: Mayonnaise should not be substituted for salad dressing.

Hot Macaroni Salad

 1 *(8-ounce) package uncooked elbow macaroni*
 ½ *cup vinegar*
 ½ *cup water*
 1 *tablespoon sugar*
 1½ *teaspoons salt*
 ½ *teaspoon pepper*
 6 *slices bacon, cut into 1-inch pieces*
 1 *tablespoon all-purpose flour*
 1 *medium-size onion, sliced*
 6 *to 8 radishes, thinly sliced*
 2 *tablespoons chopped fresh parsley*

Cook macaroni according to package directions; drain. Rinse with hot water; drain. Cover with a hot damp cloth, and set aside.

Combine vinegar, water, sugar, salt, and pepper; mix well, and set aside.

Sauté bacon until crisp; drain on paper towels, reserving 1 tablespoon bacon drippings. Stir flour into reserved drippings; cook over low heat, stirring constantly, until bubbly. Add vinegar mixture; cook, stirring constantly, until slightly thickened.

Combine macaroni, bacon, onion, radishes, and parsley. Pour vinegar mixture over salad, and toss lightly. Serve hot. Yield: 6 to 8 servings.

Artichoke-Rice Salad

 1 *(6-ounce) package chicken-flavored vermicelli-rice mix*
 2 *(7-ounce) jars marinated artichoke hearts*
 ⅓ *cup mayonnaise*
 ¼ *teaspoon curry powder*
 12 *green olives, sliced*
 ½ *green pepper, chopped*
 1 *green onion, sliced*

Cook rice mix according to package directions, omitting butter; cool. Drain artichokes, reserving liquid.

Combine reserved artichoke liquid, mayonnaise, and curry powder; blend well. Combine all ingredients, mixing thoroughly; chill. Yield: 6 servings.

Hot or Cold Macaroni Salad

1 *cup uncooked elbow macaroni*
4 *slices bacon, cooked and crumbled*
½ *cup chopped celery*
¼ *cup chopped green pepper*
¾ *cup chopped dill pickle*
¼ *cup chopped onion*
2 *tablespoons chili sauce*
½ *teaspoon Worcestershire sauce*
1 *teaspoon salt*
⅛ *teaspoon pepper*
1 *teaspoon sugar*
¼ *cup mayonnaise*

Cook macaroni according to package directions; drain. Combine macaroni, bacon, celery, green pepper, pickle, and onion; set aside. Combine remaining ingredients; pour over macaroni mixture, and toss gently.

To serve hot, place over low heat and warm. Chill overnight to serve cold. Yield: 8 to 10 servings.

Marinated Macaroni Salad

1 *(8-ounce) package uncooked elbow macaroni*
¾ *cup commercial Italian salad dressing*
1 *cup chopped celery*
¾ *cup shredded carrots*
¾ *cup chopped green pepper*
¼ *cup chopped onion*
½ *cup diced pasteurized process American cheese*
1 *(8-ounce) carton commercial sour cream*
Imitation bacon bits

Cook macaroni according to package directions; drain. Rinse with cold water; drain.

Combine macaroni and salad dressing; cover, and chill overnight. Add vegetables and cheese; mix well. Add sour cream, and stir gently. Sprinkle with bacon bits. Yield: 6 to 8 servings.

Polynesian Rice Salad

1 *cup long grain rice, uncooked*
½ *cup salad oil*
¼ *cup cider vinegar*
2 *tablespoons soy sauce*
½ *teaspoon salt*
1 *cup thinly sliced celery*
¼ *cup thinly sliced green onion tops*
1 *(8½-ounce) can water chestnuts, drained and sliced*
1 *cup sliced fresh mushrooms*
1 *(11-ounce) can mandarin oranges, drained*
Lettuce (optional)

Cook rice according to package directions; let cool to room temperature. Combine salad oil, vinegar, soy sauce, salt, celery, and onion; stir in rice. Fold in water chestnuts, mushrooms, and oranges just until blended. Chill thoroughly; serve in a lettuce-lined bowl, if desired. Yield: 6 servings.

Macaroni-Ham Salad

2 *cups uncooked elbow macaroni*
3 *hard-cooked eggs, chopped*
1 *cup minced boiled ham*
2 *tablespoons diced pimiento*
⅔ *cup commercial sour cream*
⅓ *cup mayonnaise*
1 *teaspoon salt*
½ *teaspoon dry mustard*
Chopped parsley (optional)
Sliced green olives (optional)

Cook macaroni according to package directions; drain. Rinse with cold water; drain.

Combine macaroni, eggs, ham, and pimiento; toss gently.

Combine sour cream, mayonnaise, salt, and mustard; mix well. Pour dressing over salad, and toss gently. Chill. Garnish with parsley or olives, if desired. Yield: 8 to 10 servings.

Macaroni Harlequin Salad

1   (8-ounce) package uncooked elbow
      macaroni
4   hard-cooked eggs, chopped
1   small onion, chopped
¼   cup finely chopped celery
¼   cup finely chopped sweet pickles
¼   cup chopped green pepper
1   (2-ounce) jar chopped pimiento
1   (12½-ounce) can tuna, drained and
      flaked
½   cup mayonnaise
1   tablespoon prepared mustard

Cook macaroni according to package directions; drain. Rinse with cold water; drain. Combine macaroni and remaining ingredients; stir well. Chill overnight. Yield: 10 to 12 servings.

Zesty Rice Salad

2   cups uncooked regular rice
1   (17-ounce) can green peas, drained
½   cup minced onion
1   (4-ounce) can mushrooms, drained and
      sliced
1½ cups chopped celery
¾   cup mayonnaise
2   teaspoons salt
1   teaspoon pepper
2   tablespoons lemon juice
¼   teaspoon rosemary

Cook rice according to package directions, omitting salt. Chill. Add peas, onion, mushrooms, and celery to rice; toss until well mixed.

Combine mayonnaise, salt, pepper, lemon juice, and rosemary; add to rice mixture, mixing well. Chill well before serving. Yield: 8 to 10 servings.

Orange Rice Salad

1   (20-ounce) can crushed pineapple
2   (3-ounce) packages orange-flavored
      gelatin
2   cups boiling water
1   cup cooked regular rice, chilled
1   (3-ounce) package whipped topping
      mix, whipped
Salad greens
Orange slices

Drain pineapple, reserving juice. Add enough water to juice to make 2 cups liquid; set aside.

Dissolve gelatin in 2 cups boiling water; stir in pineapple juice. Chill until consistency of unbeaten egg white.

Fold pineapple, rice, and whipped topping into thickened gelatin. Spoon into an 8-cup mold, and chill until firm. Unmold and garnish with salad greens and orange slices. Yield: 8 servings.

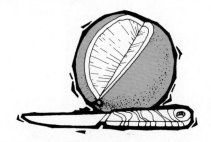

Rice Salad Ceylon

1   cup mayonnaise or salad dressing
1   teaspoon curry powder
3   cups cold cooked rice
1   cup cooked chicken, cut in thin strips
½   cup thinly sliced green pepper
1   cup sliced celery
Salt and pepper to taste
¼   cup seedless raisins
1   (11-ounce) can mandarin oranges,
      drained
Pimiento

Combine mayonnaise and curry powder; stir in rice, chicken, green pepper, and celery. Add salt and pepper. Fold in raisins and oranges, and chill thoroughly. Garnish with pimiento before serving. Yield: 6 servings.

★ Super Rice Salad

1½ cups water
1½ cups instant rice
½ cup chopped celery
¼ cup chopped dill pickle
1 tablespoon chopped onion
1 tablespoon chopped parsley
½ teaspoon dry mustard
1 cup mayonnaise
Salt and pepper to taste
Hard-cooked egg slices or stuffed olive
    slices

Bring water to a boil, and stir in rice. Cover; remove from heat, and let stand 5 minutes. Add celery, dill pickle, onion, parsley, mustard, and mayonnaise; chill at least 1 hour. Add salt and pepper, and garnish with egg or olive slices. Yield: 6 servings.

Honey Dressing

⅔ cup sugar
1 teaspoon dry mustard
1 teaspoon celery seeds
½ teaspoon salt
½ teaspoon paprika
¼ teaspoon pepper
1 cup salad oil
⅓ cup honey
7 tablespoons lemon juice
1 tablespoon vinegar
1 teaspoon grated onion

Combine all ingredients in a small bowl; mix thoroughly. Refrigerate 8 hours before serving. Yield: 2 cups.

Blue Cheese Salad Dressing

2 cups mayonnaise
1 teaspoon lemon juice
1 teaspoon white vinegar
¼ cup buttermilk
½ cup commercial sour cream
½ teaspoon salt
¼ teaspoon pepper
¼ teaspoon garlic powder
1 (4-ounce) package blue cheese, crumbled

Combine all ingredients except blue cheese; blend well. Gently stir in blue cheese. Refrigerate until needed. Yield: about 3 cups.

Cheese and Garlic Salad Dressing

1 (5-ounce) package Romano cheese,
    grated
4 cloves garlic, crushed
2 teaspoons salt
½ teaspoon pepper
4 teaspoons lemon juice
Salad oil

Combine cheese, garlic, salt, pepper, and lemon juice; add enough salad oil to make 3 cups dressing, and blend well. Yield: 3 cups.

★ Avocado Salad Dressing

1 medium-size avocado, peeled and
    chopped
1 small onion, quartered
2 teaspoons sugar
1 tablespoon lemon juice
Dash of hot sauce
⅛ teaspoon Ac'cent
1 teaspoon Worcestershire sauce
⅛ teaspoon garlic powder
1 cup mayonnaise
1 drop green food coloring (optional)

Combine all ingredients except mayonnaise and food coloring in container of electric blender. Blend well. Add mayonnaise; add food coloring, if desired. Blend until smooth. Store in refrigerator. Yield: about 2 cups.

★
Roquefort Dressing

¾ cup mayonnaise
⅓ cup commercial sour cream
1 (1½-ounce) package Roquefort cheese, crumbled
1 teaspoon Worcestershire sauce
Dash of garlic powder
Salt and pepper to taste

Combine all ingredients; chill thoroughly in a covered container. Stir well before serving on tossed salad. Yield: about 1 cup.

French Dressing

1 cup salad oil
¾ cup distilled vinegar
½ cup tarragon vinegar or red wine vinegar
½ cup catsup
½ cup chili sauce
¼ cup sugar
1 tablespoon prepared mustard
1 tablespoon Worcestershire sauce
1 tablespoon prepared horseradish
1 large onion, finely chopped
Salt to taste

Combine all ingredients; stir well. Chill. Store, covered, in refrigerator. Serve over fruit or salad greens. Stir well before serving. Yield: 4½ cups.

Herb Salad Dressing

1 cup mayonnaise
1½ tablespoons lemon juice
¼ teaspoon salt
¼ teaspoon paprika
1 teaspoon mixed salad herbs
1 tablespoon grated onion
1 clove garlic, grated
⅛ teaspoon curry powder
½ teaspoon Worcestershire sauce
1 (8-ounce) carton commercial sour cream

Combine all ingredients, mixing well. Refrigerate several hours or overnight. Serve over crisp salad greens. Yield: 1 pint.

★
Fluffy Fruit Salad Dressing

1 tablespoon all-purpose flour
1 tablespoon sugar
1 cup pineapple juice
1 egg, slightly beaten
12 large marshmallows
½ pint whipping cream, whipped

Combine flour and sugar in a small saucepan; gradually add pineapple juice, mixing thoroughly. Add egg, stirring well. Place over low heat; cook, stirring constantly, until thickened. Add marshmallows, and stir until melted.

Remove mixture from heat, and cool completely. Fold in whipped cream. Serve over fresh fruit. Yield: about 3 cups.

Tangy Louis Dressing

2 cups mayonnaise
1½ cups chili sauce
⅓ cup minced celery
⅓ cup minced sour pickles
2 tablespoons lemon juice
1 tablespoon Worcestershire sauce
1 teaspoon prepared horseradish

Combine all ingredients, stirring well; chill. Store, covered, in refrigerator. Serve over seafood, ham, or salad greens. Yield: 4 cups.
Note: This recipe may be halved.

Tomato Soup Dressing

1 (10¾-ounce) can tomato soup, undiluted
1½ cups salad oil
¾ cup vinegar
¾ cup sugar
1 tablespoon Worcestershire sauce
1 tablespoon onion juice
1 teaspoon paprika
1 teaspoon prepared mustard
1 teaspoon salt
1 teaspoon pepper

Combine all ingredients; stir until well blended. Chill. Store, covered, in refrigerator. Stir well before using. Yield: 4 cups.

Paprika Salad Dressing

1   *cup mayonnaise*
3   *cloves garlic*
2   *tablespoons chili sauce*
2   *tablespoons catsup*
1   *teaspoon paprika*
1   *teaspoon pepper*
1   *teaspoon dry or prepared mustard*
1   *teaspoon onion juice*
1   *teaspoon Worcestershire sauce*
1   *teaspoon water*
¼   *teaspoon salt*
    Juice of 1 lemon
    Dash of hot sauce
½   *cup salad oil*

Combine all ingredients except salad oil in container of electric blender; blend 5 seconds. Add salad oil slowly, continuing blending; blend 5 seconds after adding oil. Yield: 2 cups.

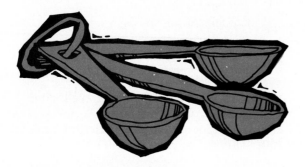

Poppy Seed Dressing

1   *cup sugar*
⅔   *cup vinegar*
3   *tablespoons onion juice*
2   *teaspoons dry mustard*
2   *teaspoons salt*
2   *cups salad oil*
2   *tablespoons poppy seeds*

Combine sugar, vinegar, onion juice, mustard, and salt in container of electric blender; blend well. Slowly add oil, continuing to blend; blend until thick. Add poppy seeds; blend 2 minutes. Chill. Store, covered, in refrigerator. Serve over fresh fruit. Yield: 3½ cups.

Thousand Island Dressing

½   *cup catsup*
¼   *cup relish sandwich spread*
¼   *cup mayonnaise*
1   *teaspoon salad oil*

Combine all ingredients, stirring well; chill. Store, covered, in refrigerator. Yield: 1 cup.

Chicken Salad in Aspic Ring

1   *(3-ounce) package lemon-flavored gelatin*
1   *cup boiling water*
1   *(8-ounce) can tomato sauce*
¼   *cup cold water*
    Salt to taste
½   *cup stuffed olives, sliced*
¼   *cup finely chopped celery*
    Lettuce leaves
    Deluxe Chicken Salad

Combine gelatin and boiling water, stirring until gelatin dissolves; cool. Stir in tomato sauce, cold water, and salt. Chill until slightly thickened; then stir in olives and celery.

Spoon gelatin mixture into a 6-cup ring mold, and chill until firm. Unmold on lettuce leaves; line center with lettuce leaves, and fill with Deluxe Chicken Salad. Yield: 6 to 8 servings.

Deluxe Chicken Salad:

2   *cups diced cooked chicken*
¾   *cup diced celery*
¾   *teaspoon salt*
⅛   *teaspoon pepper*
¼   *cup mayonnaise*
2   *tablespoons commercial sour cream*
1   *tablespoon lemon juice*
1   *teaspoon minced onion*

Combine chicken, celery, salt, and pepper; stir well. Combine remaining ingredients; add to chicken mixture, and toss lightly. Spoon into center of aspic. Yield: 2 cups.

Zesty Vegetable Tray

2 *new potatoes, cooked and sliced*
3 *medium-size yellow squash, sliced*
3 *hard-cooked eggs, sliced*
1 *medium-size cucumber, sliced*
3 *medium-size tomatoes, sliced*
Salt and freshly ground pepper to taste
1 *to 2 cloves garlic, minced*
Chopped parsley
⅓ *cup vinegar*
⅔ *cup peanut oil*
Parsley

Arrange vegetables in alternate rows on a tray; season with salt and pepper. Sprinkle with garlic and chopped parsley. Combine vinegar and oil in a jar; tighten lid securely, and shake well. Pour over vegetables. Garnish with parsley. Yield: 8 servings.

Lemon-Poppy Seed Dressing

2 *tablespoons poppy seeds*
¼ *cup honey*
½ *cup salad oil*
½ *teaspoon ground cinnamon*
¼ *teaspoon ground coriander*
¾ *teaspoon salt*
⅓ *cup lemon juice*

Put poppy seeds in blender; blend on high speed for 1 minute or until seeds are crushed. Add honey, salad oil, cinnamon, coriander, and salt. Blend until well mixed. Add lemon juice and blend until creamy. Store in a tightly covered jar in refrigerator until ready to use. Yield: 1 cup.

Honey French Dressing

¼ *cup cider vinegar*
¾ *cup salad oil*
¼ *teaspoon paprika*
½ *teaspoon salt*
1 *teaspoon sugar*
½ *cup honey*

Combine all ingredients in a jar with a tight-fitting lid. Shake well and chill. Shake again before serving. Serve on fruit or vegetable salads. Yield: 1¼ cups.

Celery Seed Dressing

1 *teaspoon salt*
1 *teaspoon dry mustard*
1 *teaspoon paprika*
1 *teaspoon celery seeds*
½ *cup light corn syrup*
¼ *to ⅓ cup vinegar*
1 *cup corn oil*
1 *tablespoon grated onion*

Combine all ingredients. Beat with rotary beater until well blended and thick. Place in a covered container in the refrigerator and chill for several hours. Shake thoroughly before serving. Yield: about 1¾ cups.
Note: For variety, substitute poppy seeds or sesame seeds for celery seeds.

Horseradish-Cream Salad Dressing

½ *cup whipping cream, whipped*
¼ *cup drained bottled horseradish*
¾ *teaspoon salt*
2 *teaspoons sugar*
Dash cayenne pepper
4 *drops hot pepper sauce*
3 *drops Worcestershire sauce*
1 *cup mayonnaise*

Fold first seven ingredients into the mayonnaise. Chill before serving. Serve on fruit or vegetable salads. Yield: 2 cups.

Shrimp Salad Dressing

1 *cup mayonnaise*
½ *cup chili sauce*
⅓ *cup drained pickle relish*
Dash of salt
2 *hard-cooked eggs, chopped*
¼ *cup finely chopped celery*
1 *tablespoon finely chopped onion*
1 *cup chopped cooked shrimp*

Combine all ingredients except shrimp; mix well. Chill thoroughly. Add shrimp just before serving. Serve over lettuce wedges. Yield: about 2½ cups.

Sauces and Marinades

A sauce is the delight of many a dish, but it should never be used to mask the natural flavors of meats or vegetables. But sauces do more than flavor; they add variety to the familiar and enhance the appeal and appearance of every-day food.

One of the simplest and most versatile sauces is white sauce. This smooth, creamy sauce is the basis for many creamed dishes as well as other sauces. Barbecue sauce, one of the South's most popular sauces, greatly improves the flavor and aroma of meats cooked on an outdoor grill.

A dessert sauce can transform an ordinary dessert into something special. A plain pound cake can be perked up with a rich lemon sauce. Ice cream can be dressed up with a chocolate fudge sauce.

Marinades, like sauces, enhance the flavor of meat while tenderizing the meat at the same time. This is especially true of less-expensive cuts of meat.

Smoky Barbecue Sauce

    2   medium-size onions, finely chopped
    2   cloves garlic, finely chopped
    ¾   cup butter or margarine
    3   cups tomato juice
    1   tablespoon salt
    1   tablespoon sugar
    3   tablespoons catsup
    ¼   cup Worcestershire sauce
    Red pepper to taste
    Black pepper to taste
    1   tablespoon chili powder
    1   teaspoon Dijon mustard
    ¼   cup vinegar
    1   teaspoon brown sugar
    2   teaspoons paprika
    ½   cup liquid smoke
    3   cups water

Sauté onion and garlic in butter. Stir in remaining ingredients, and simmer 30 minutes. May be prepared ahead and stored in refrigerator. Yield: about 6½ cups.

The pleasingly tart flavor of Tangy Barbecue Sauce (page 282) makes grilled pork, beef, or chicken even better.

Buttery Barbecue Sauce

    1½ cups melted butter or margarine
    3   tablespoons hot sauce
    1   tablespoon Worcestershire sauce
    1   teaspoon garlic powder
    Juice of 2 lemons

Combine all ingredients, mixing well. Use to baste chicken. Yield: about 2 cups or enough for 3 chickens.

Quick-and-Easy Barbecue Sauce

    1   cup beer
    1½ cups chili sauce
    2   tablespoons grated onion
    2   tablespoons vinegar
    2   teaspoons sugar
    2   tablespoons Worcestershire sauce
    2   teaspoons chili powder

Combine all ingredients in a saucepan, and bring to a boil. Lower heat, and simmer 2 minutes. Use on chicken, ribs, or frankfurters. Yield: about 2½ cups.

Beer Barbecue Sauce

  1 *cup beer*
  ½ *teaspoon salt*
  1 *cup catsup*
  ⅓ *cup vinegar*
  ⅓ *cup firmly packed brown sugar*
  3 *tablespoons Worcestershire sauce*
  1 *teaspoon dry mustard*
  1 *teaspoon paprika*
  ½ *teaspoon chili powder*
  1 *medium-size onion, sliced*
  1 *small lemon, sliced*

Combine all ingredients except onion and lemon in a saucepan; bring mixture to a boil. Lower heat, and simmer about 5 minutes. Add onion and lemon; simmer about 2 minutes. Use on ribs, hamburgers, frankfurters, and chicken. Yield: 2½ cups.

Bourbon Barbecue Sauce

  1 *medium-size onion, minced*
  1 *cup melted butter or margarine*
  1 *teaspoon garlic salt*
  ½ *cup firmly packed brown sugar*
  3 *tablespoons vinegar*
  ¾ *cup prepared mustard*
  1 *tablespoon salt*
  1 *tablespoon pepper*
  ¼ *cup bourbon*

Sauté onion in butter until tender; stir in remaining ingredients except bourbon. Cook over medium heat 5 minutes. Remove from heat, and add bourbon. Use on chicken, pork chops, ribs, or hamburgers. Yield: about 2 cups.

Zippy Basting Sauce

  ½ *cup melted butter or margarine*
  ¼ *cup lemon juice*
  1 *tablespoon Worcestershire sauce*
  1 *teaspoon Dijon mustard*
  ½ *teaspoon salt*
  3 *tablespoons finely chopped onion*
  1 *teaspoon sugar*
     Dash of pepper

Heat butter until amber in color; stir in remaining ingredients. Cover and simmer 5 minutes. Use on chicken, pork chops, ribs, or kabobs. Yield: about 1 cup.

Best-Ever Barbecue Sauce

  ⅓ *cup salad oil*
  ⅓ *cup melted margarine*
  ½ *cup vinegar*
  1 *cup orange juice*
  ¼ *cup catsup*
  ¼ *cup finely chopped onion*
  ¼ *cup Worcestershire sauce*
  2 *teaspoons hot sauce*
  2 *teaspoons salt*
  1 *teaspoon cayenne or red pepper*
  ¼ *teaspoon ground oregano*
  ⅛ *teaspoon chili powder (optional)*

Combine all ingredients in a saucepan; bring mixture to a boil. Lower heat, and simmer 10 minutes. Use on chicken, pork chops, or ribs. Yield: 2½ cups.

Fiery Barbecue Sauce

  ½ *cup water*
  ¼ *cup plus 2 tablespoons catsup*
  ¼ *cup vinegar*
  ¼ *cup Worcestershire sauce*
  ¼ *cup plus 2 tablespoons firmly packed brown sugar*
  4 *tablespoons butter or margarine*
  2 *tablespoons lemon juice*
  2 *teaspoons salt*
  2 *teaspoons dry mustard*
  2 *teaspoons chili powder*
  2 *teaspoons ground paprika*
  1 *teaspoon ground red pepper*

Combine all ingredients in a saucepan; cook over medium heat until sugar dissolves, stirring occasionally. Use on pork chops or chicken. May be prepared ahead and stored in refrigerator. Yield: about 2 cups.

Mustard Sauce

2 hard-cooked egg yolks
1 uncooked egg yolk
¼ cup salad oil
1 tablespoon sugar
¼ teaspoon salt
Dash of pepper
1½ tablespoons lemon juice
Pulp from ½ lemon
1 tablespoon prepared brown mustard
1 tablespoon whipping cream

Press hard-cooked egg yolks through a fine sieve; blend in uncooked yolk to make a smooth paste. Add oil, a few drops at a time, beating well after each addition. Add remaining ingredients in order listed, beating thoroughly after each addition. Yield: about 1 cup.

★ Sweet and Spicy Mustard

5 tablespoons dry mustard
½ cup sugar
1 tablespoon all-purpose flour
½ teaspoon salt
Dash of red pepper
2 eggs, beaten
½ cup vinegar
1 tablespoon butter or margarine

Combine mustard, sugar, flour, salt, and red pepper in top of a double boiler. Add eggs and vinegar, blending thoroughly. Place over boiling water; cook, stirring constantly, until thickened. Add butter; stir until melted. Cool mixture; then store in a jar in the refrigerator. Yield: 1⅓ cups.

Sauce Supreme

1 (16-ounce) jar applesauce
2 tablespoons prepared horseradish
1 teaspoon slivered lemon peel
⅛ teaspoon salt

Combine all ingredients; blend well. Chill overnight. Serve cold with ham. Yield: about 2½ cups.

★ Raisin Sauce

½ cup sugar
¼ cup water
½ cup raisins
1 tablespoon butter or margarine
1 tablespoon vinegar
Dash of Worcestershire sauce
¼ teaspoon salt
⅛ teaspoon ground cloves
1 teaspoon cornstarch

Combine all ingredients except cornstarch; bring to a boil. Cook until raisins are plump. Dissolve cornstarch in a small amount of cold water; gradually add to hot mixture. Cook until clear, stirring constantly. Yield: about 1 cup.

Hollandaise Sauce

4 egg yolks
2 tablespoons lemon juice
1 cup butter, melted
¼ teaspoon salt
Dash pepper

Beat egg yolks in top of a double boiler. Stir in lemon juice. Cook very slowly over low heat, never letting water in bottom of pan come to a boil. Add butter, a small amount at a time, stirring constantly with a wooden spoon. Add salt and pepper; continue cooking until mixture has thickened. This sauce is excellent on vegetables. Yield: 1 cup.

Blender Hollandaise Sauce

3 egg yolks
Juice of 1 lemon
Dash of hot sauce
Salt to taste
½ cup melted butter

Combine egg yolks, lemon juice, hot sauce, and salt in blender; process on high speed until well blended. Gradually add melted butter and continue to blend. Yield: about ½ cup.

Cheese Sauce

    2 tablespoons butter or margarine
    2 tablespoons all-purpose flour
    1 cup milk
    ¼ teaspoon salt
    ½ cup shredded Cheddar cheese

Combine butter and flour in top of double boiler. Mix well. Gradually add milk, stirring constantly until mixture thickens. Add salt and cheese, stirring until cheese is melted. Serve on eggs or vegetables. Yield: 1½ cups.

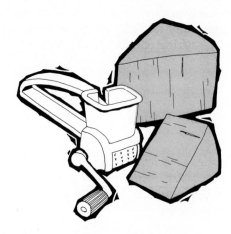

Medium White Sauce

    2 tablespoons butter or margarine
    2 tablespoons all-purpose or
         instant-blending flour
    1 cup warm milk
    Salt and pepper to taste

Melt butter in a heavy saucepan over low heat, and blend in flour. Cook 3 or 4 minutes, stirring constantly.

Gradually add milk to roux, stirring constantly with a whisk or wooden spoon. (Lumping will be less likely to occur if you remove roux from heat before adding milk.) Cook over low heat, stirring constantly, about 6 to 8 minutes or until thickened. Add salt and pepper. Yield: about 1 cup.

Variations: To make 1 cup Light White Sauce, decrease butter and flour to 1 tablespoon. For 1 cup Heavy White Sauce, increase butter and flour to 3 tablespoons.

Giblet Gravy

    Giblets from 1 turkey
    Turkey neck
    2 cups chicken broth
    1 medium-size onion, chopped
    1 cup chopped celery
    ½ teaspoon poultry seasoning
    ½ cup cornbread dressing
    Salt and pepper to taste
    2 hard-cooked eggs, sliced

Cook giblets and turkey neck in chicken broth until tender (about 2 hours). Remove meat from broth, and discard neck; chop giblets, and return to broth.

Add onion, celery, poultry seasoning, and dressing to broth mixture; cook until vegetables are tender. Stir in salt, pepper, and egg slices. If thicker gravy is desired, add more dressing. Yield: about 2 cups.

Note: Flour may be used instead of dressing to thicken gravy. Dissolve 2 tablespoons flour in a small amount of water, and stir into broth.

★
Relish Hot Sauce

    1 cup minced onion
    ½ cup chopped green pepper
    1 clove garlic, minced
    1 tablespoon salad oil
    1 (7-ounce) can whole kernel corn,
         drained
    1 (16-ounce) can tomatoes, drained and
         chopped
    1 (4-ounce) can green chiles, undrained
         and chopped fine
    4 tablespoons hot chili sauce
    1 tablespoon chili powder
    1 teaspoon salt
    2 teaspoons pepper

Sauté onion, green pepper, and garlic in oil until wilted; stir frequently. Add remaining ingredients; heat well, stirring occasionally. Serve hot or cold. Store in refrigerator. This sauce may be served on chalupas, tacos, hamburgers, hot dogs, or as a dip. Yield: about 1½ pints.

Cream Gravy

    4 tablespoons drippings
    4 tablespoons all-purpose flour
 2½ to 3 cups hot milk
    Salt and pepper to taste

Pour off all except 4 tablespoons drippings in which chicken was fried. Place skillet over medium heat; add flour and stir until browned. Gradually add hot milk; cook, stirring constantly, until thickened. Add salt and pepper. Serve hot. Yield: about 2 cups.

★ Chicken Liver Sauce

   10 slices bacon
    1 cup chopped chicken livers
   ¼ cup chopped onion
    Dash of garlic salt
    1 (10¾-ounce) can cream of chicken soup, undiluted
   ¾ cup water
   ½ teaspoon salt
   ⅛ teaspoon pepper
    Hot mashed potatoes

Cook bacon until crisp; crumble and set aside, reserving drippings. Cook livers, onion, and garlic salt in reserved bacon drippings over low heat until lightly browned. Add soup, water, salt, pepper, and bacon; simmer 45 minutes, adding more water if necessary. Serve over hot mashed potatoes. Yield: 4 to 6 servings.

Ginger Glaze

   ¼ cup commercial Russian dressing
   ½ cup orange juice
   ¼ cup firmly packed light brown sugar
 1½ teaspoons ground ginger
 1½ teaspoons grated orange peel

Combine all ingredients in small saucepan; cook over low heat until smooth. Spoon over ham during last 30 minutes of baking time. Yield: about 1 cup.

★ Orange Glaze

    1 (6-ounce) can frozen orange juice concentrate, thawed and undiluted
   ½ teaspoon ground ginger
    4 tablespoons prepared mustard
   ¼ cup sugar

Combine all ingredients, and stir until smooth. Spoon over ham during last 30 minutes of baking time. Yield: about 1 cup.

★ Mushroom Sauce

   ½ pound fresh mushrooms, sliced
    3 tablespoons melted margarine, divided
    1 tablespoon all-purpose flour
   ¾ cup half-and-half
    1 teaspoon soy sauce

Sauté mushrooms in 2 tablespoons margarine; set aside.

Combine flour and remaining margarine; place over low heat, stirring until smooth. Gradually add half-and-half; cook, stirring constantly, until smooth and thickened. Stir in soy sauce and mushrooms. Serve hot with roast or steak. Yield: about 1½ cups.

Remoulade Sauce for Seafood

    1 cup mayonnaise
    1 tablespoon chopped onion
    1 tablespoon chopped parsley
    1 tablespoon chopped celery
    2 tablespoons Dijon mustard
    1 tablespoon prepared horseradish
    1 teaspoon paprika
   ½ teaspoon salt
    Dash of hot sauce
   ¼ cup salad oil
    1 tablespoon vinegar
   ½ teaspoon Worcestershire sauce

Combine all ingredients in a small bowl; mix until well blended. Refrigerate several hours or overnight. Yield: 1½ cups.

Mayonnaise Basting Sauce

6 tablespoons mayonnaise
3 tablespoons lemon juice
3 tablespoons vinegar
2 tablespoons sugar
1 teaspoon salt
1 teaspoon pepper

Combine all ingredients, and mix well. Use as a basting sauce for chicken. Yield: about 1 cup.

Chili Marinade

½ cup vinegar
½ cup catsup
2 tablespoons salad oil
2 tablespoons finely chopped onion
2 teaspoons chili powder
1 teaspoon salt
⅛ teaspoon pepper

Combine all ingredients. Use to marinate chuck steak or other beef before grilling; use also to baste during cooking. Yield: 1¼ cups.

Sweet 'n Easy Marinade

2 tablespoons soy sauce
2 tablespoons sherry
4 tablespoons honey
1 clove garlic, sliced

Combine all ingredients. Use to marinate flank steak or sirloin steak. Yield: about ⅓ cup.

Tangy Marinade

1 cup pineapple juice
⅓ cup soy sauce
1 teaspoon ground ginger
1 teaspoon sugar
1 clove garlic, crushed
⅓ cup salad oil

Combine all ingredients. Use to marinate flank steak or pork chops before grilling; use also to baste during cooking. Yield: 1⅔ cups.

Tart Garlic Marinade

¾ cup vinegar
¾ cup salad oil
¾ cup soy sauce
¼ cup hot sauce
½ cup Worcestershire sauce
½ cup vermouth
¼ cup honey
¼ cup wine vinegar
5 cloves garlic, crushed
1½ teaspoons dry mustard
2 tablespoons salt
1½ teaspoons pepper

Combine all ingredients in a saucepan, and simmer 10 minutes. Store in refrigerator until needed. Yield: about 4 cups.

Teriyaki Marinade

⅓ cup soy sauce
2 tablespoons honey
1 clove garlic, crushed
¼ teaspoon ginger

Combine all ingredients, and mix well. Use as a marinade for beef or chicken. Yield: ⅓ cup.

Tangy Barbecue Sauce

1 small onion, minced
1 clove garlic, minced
2 tablespoons melted butter or margarine
1 (8-ounce) can tomato sauce
¾ cup vinegar
¾ cup water
¾ cup catsup
¼ cup lemon juice
3 tablespoons Worcestershire sauce
¾ teaspoon chili powder
3 bay leaves
1 tablespoon dry mustard
¼ cup tarragon vinegar
¼ cup steak sauce
1 teaspoon barbecue spice

Sauté onion and garlic in butter until tender. Stir in remaining ingredients. Bring to a boil;

reduce heat and simmer 30 minutes, stirring occasionally. Use on grilled chicken, pork or beef. Yield: about 1 quart.

Lemon Butter

Grated rind and juice of 2 lemons
2   eggs
2   cups sugar
¼   cup butter or margarine, melted
½   cup water

Combine all ingredients in a saucepan; cook, stirring constantly, over low heat until mixture thickens. Serve with cake or bread. Yield: about 2 cups.

Magic Eggnog Sauce

1   egg
1⅓   cups sweetened condensed milk
½   teaspoon rum flavoring
¼   teaspoon ground nutmeg
½   pint whipping cream, whipped

Beat egg until foamy in the top of a double boiler; stir in condensed milk. Cook over hot, not boiling, water 10 minutes. Stir in rum flavoring and nutmeg; fold in whipped cream. Serve hot or cold over fruitcake or ice cream. Yield: about 2 cups.

Pistachio Sauce

1   (3⅝-ounce) package instant pistachio
      pudding mix
⅔   cup light corn syrup
¾   cup evaporated milk, undiluted

Combine all ingredients, and mix thoroughly. Chill and serve over ice cream or cake. Yield: 1½ cups.

★
Cinnamon Cream Syrup

1   cup sugar
½   cup light corn syrup
¼   cup water
½   to ¾ teaspoon ground cinnamon
½   cup evaporated milk

Combine sugar, syrup, water, and cinnamon in a saucepan; bring to a boil over medium heat. Boil 2 minutes, stirring constantly. Cool 5 minutes; stir in milk. Serve warm. Yield: 1⅔ cups.

Brandied Pear Sauce

5   ripe pears, peeled, cored, and quartered
1   orange, peeled and sliced
1   cup sugar
1   teaspoon ground cloves
½   cup fruit-flavored brandy (apricot,
        cherry, or orange)

Combine fruit and sugar in a Dutch oven, mixing well. Cover and cook until fruit is very soft (about 30 minutes). Process fruit mixture in electric blender until smooth, or put through food grinder or sieve.

Pour fruit mixture back into Dutch oven, and add cloves and brandy; cook until mixture is as thick as applesauce (about 1 hour). Pour into hot, sterilized jars; seal. Yield: about 2 pints.

★
Chocolate Fudge Sauce

½   cup cocoa
1   cup light corn syrup
1   cup sugar
½   cup half-and-half
3   tablespoons butter or margarine
¼   teaspoon salt
1   teaspoon vanilla extract
Ice cream

Combine first 6 ingredients in a saucepan; bring to a boil, and boil 5 minutes. Remove from heat, and stir in vanilla. Serve over ice cream. Yield: 2 cups.

Soups, Stews, and Chowders

Savory and mouth-watering soups, stews, and chowders are popular throughout the South. Each has its own special combination of meats, seafood, vegetables, and seasonings. The specialty food of a region usually tells you the favorite soup, stew, or chowder of an area.

Nutritious and satisfying soups and chowders can be whatever you want them to be—first course or main dish, fancy or plain. They can be made with almost anything you have on hand and need not simmer for hours to be good.

A robust stew is a meal in itself for lunch or supper. Nothing tempts appetites more on a wintry day than a hearty pot of bubbling stew, rich with meat, vegetables, and seasonings. Most stews can be made the day before serving and have an even better flavor after standing.

Creamy Broccoli Soup

      2   tablespoons minced onion
      3   tablespoons butter or margarine
      3   tablespoons all-purpose flour
    1½   teaspoons salt
      3   cups milk
      3   cups chicken broth
      1   (10-ounce) package frozen chopped
            broccoli, slightly thawed, or 2 cups
            chopped fresh broccoli
      2   cups thinly sliced carrots
          Salt and pepper to taste

Sauté onion in butter until tender; stir in flour and 1½ teaspoons salt. Gradually add milk, stirring constantly; bring to a boil. Add broth, broccoli, and carrots. Cook over low heat about 25 minutes or until carrots are tender; stir occasionally. Do not boil. Add salt and pepper. Yield: 2 quarts.

On a hot day, the sight of these chilled soups is quite refreshing: Gazpacho (page 287), Cold Cream of Spinach Soup (page 303), and Cucumber Soup (page 286).

Cream of Jerusalem Artichoke Soup

      1   large onion, diced
      2   tablespoons butter or margarine,
            divided
      2   cups peeled, cubed Jerusalem artichokes
      1   tablespoon all-purpose flour
     ½   teaspoon salt
     ⅛   teaspoon ground nutmeg
          Pinch of sugar
      2   cups water
      1   cup evaporated milk
      1   egg yolk, slightly beaten

Sauté onion in 1 tablespoon butter 5 minutes in a Dutch oven; add artichoke, and sauté 3 minutes. Stir in flour, salt, nutmeg, and sugar; gradually add water, stirring constantly. Cook over medium heat until artichoke is tender.

Mash artichoke in liquid; add milk, and simmer 5 to 10 minutes. Add 1 tablespoon butter. Stir a small amount of hot mixture into egg yolk; gradually add to remaining hot mixture, stirring well. Yield: 6 to 8 servings.

Cream of Avocado Soup

 2 *large avocados, peeled*
 2 *cups half-and-half*
1¾ *cups chicken broth*
 1 *tablespoon lemon juice*
 ½ *teaspoon salt*
 ⅛ *teaspoon pepper*
 Dillweed (optional)

Combine all ingredients except dillweed in container of electric blender; blend until smooth. Chill 6 hours or overnight. Serve cold; garnish with dillweed, if desired. Yield: 6 to 8 servings.

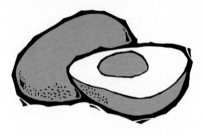

★
Avocado Cream Soup

 3 *large ripe avocados, peeled and diced*
1½ *cups whipping cream, divided*
 6 *cups chicken broth*
 1 *teaspoon salt*
 ½ *teaspoon ground white pepper*
 ¼ *cup dry sherry (optional)*
 Lemon slices (optional)
 Tortilla chips (optional)

Combine 1 avocado and ½ cup whipping cream in container of electric blender; process until smooth. Remove mixture from blender container, and repeat procedure with remaining avocados and whipping cream.

 Bring broth to a boil; reduce heat to low, and stir in avocado puree. Add salt and pepper, mixing well; add sherry, if desired. Chill thoroughly. Garnish with lemon slices or tortilla chips, if desired. Yield: 8 to 10 servings.

Frosted Asparagus Soup

 1 *(9-ounce) package frozen asparagus tips*
 1 *(8-ounce) carton commercial sour cream, divided*
 1 *(2¾-ounce) package leek soup mix*
2½ *cups milk*
 1 *teaspoon lemon juice*
 Chopped chives

Cook asparagus according to package directions; drain. Combine asparagus, ¾ cup sour cream, soup mix, milk, and lemon juice in blender container; process until smooth. Chill thoroughly. Garnish with remaining sour cream, and sprinkle with chives. Yield: 1 quart.

Cold Quick Borscht

 1 *(16-ounce) can whole beets, undrained*
 1 *(10¾-ounce) can chicken broth*
 1 *(8-ounce) carton commercial sour cream*
 ¾ *teaspoon salt*
 ⅛ *teaspoon white pepper*
1½ *teaspoons lemon juice*
 2 *tablespoons chopped chives*

Drain beets, reserving liquid. Put beets through a sieve, or puree in electric blender. Combine all ingredients except chives with beet liquid; mix well. Chill. When ready to serve, sprinkle with chives. Yield: 4 servings.

Cucumber Soup

 1 *to 1½ cups grated cucumber*
 1 *quart buttermilk*
 2 *tablespoons chopped green onion*
 1 *teaspoon salt*
 Cucumber slices
 Chives

Combine grated cucumber, buttermilk, onion, and salt; mix well. Cover and chill at least 2 or 3 hours. Mix again before serving in chilled cups. Garnish with cucumber slices and chives. Yield: 6 to 8 servings.

 Note: Scoop out and discard seeds before grating cucumber.

Gazpacho

½ cup diced celery
½ cup diced green pepper
½ cup diced onion
½ cup thinly sliced cucumber
1 cup diced tomatoes
1 (10¾-ounce) can tomato soup, undiluted
1 soup can water
1½ cups cocktail vegetable juice
1 tablespoon wine vinegar
1 tablespoon commercial Italian dressing
Garlic salt to taste
¼ teaspoon salt
⅛ teaspoon pepper
4 dashes of hot sauce
Dash of Worcestershire sauce

Combine all ingredients in a large bowl. Cover and refrigerate at least 4 hours. Stir gently. Serve in chilled bowls or mugs. Yield: 6 to 8 servings.

Fresh Mushroom Bisque

2 tablespoons melted butter or margarine
3 tablespoons all-purpose flour
¾ teaspoon salt
Dash of white pepper
1⅓ cups half-and-half, scalded
⅓ cup chicken broth, heated
1½ cups milk, scalded and divided
½ cup sliced mushrooms
½ cup chopped mushrooms
½ teaspoon minced onion
2 teaspoons melted butter or margarine

Combine 2 tablespoons melted butter, flour, salt, and pepper in a heavy saucepan; blend well. Simmer 2 minutes. Combine half-and-half, broth, and 1¼ cups milk; gradually add to flour mixture, stirring constantly, until smooth. Cook over medium heat until thickened. Remove from heat, and set aside.

Sauté mushrooms and onion in 2 teaspoons melted butter 6 to 8 minutes, stirring frequently. Add remaining ¼ cup milk; heat to simmering. Stir into milk mixture; heat thoroughly. Serve immediately. Yield: about 4 servings.

Peanut Soup

1 medium-size onion, minced
1 cup sliced celery
½ cup butter or margarine
2 tablespoons all-purpose flour
2 quarts chicken broth
1 cup creamy peanut butter
1 cup half-and-half
¼ cup chopped parsley
¼ cup chopped salted peanuts

Sauté onion and celery in butter until tender. Stir in flour, blending well. Stir in chicken broth; cook, stirring frequently, until mixture comes to a boil. Reduce heat to simmer; stir in peanut butter and half-and-half. Simmer 5 to 10 minutes. Top with parsley and peanuts before serving. Yield: about 10 servings.

Onion Soup

3 pounds red onions, sliced
½ cup melted butter or margarine
6 beef bouillon cubes
10 cups water, divided
1 (8-ounce) loaf French bread, cubed
2 tablespoons salt
Grated Parmesan cheese

Sauté onion in butter about 15 minutes or until tender. Dissolve bouillon cubes in 1 cup boiling water.

Combine onion, beef bouillon, and remaining water in a large saucepan; add bread cubes, and bring to a boil. Cook over low heat 5 to 6 hours. Add salt during last hour of cooking time.

Ladle soup into individual casseroles; sprinkle generously with Parmesan cheese. Place under broiler until cheese melts. Yield: 10 to 12 servings.

★
French Onion Soup au Gratin

    2   *medium-size onions, very thinly sliced*
    2   *tablespoons melted butter or margarine*
    4   *cups beef broth*
    ½   *cup water*
        Salt and pepper to taste
    ½   *cup Madeira wine (optional)*
        Parmesan Croutons
    ½   *cup shredded Swiss cheese*

Cook onions in butter in a large skillet, covered, until onions are tender (about 5 minutes). Uncover skillet, and continue cooking onions until well browned; stir occasionally. Stir in broth and water; cover and simmer 30 minutes. Add salt and pepper; stir in wine, if desired.

Ladle soup into individual ovenproof dishes; place a Parmesan Crouton on each serving, and sprinkle with Swiss cheese. Bake at 400° for 15 minutes or until cheese is melted and golden brown. Yield: 4 to 6 servings.

    Parmesan Croutons:

    2   *to 3 (1-inch-thick) slices French bread, cut in half*
    ¼   *cup melted butter or margarine*
    ¼   *cup grated Parmesan cheese*

Brush both sides of bread with butter; sprinkle with Parmesan cheese. Place on a cookie sheet, and bake at 350° for 20 minutes or until crisp and brown. Yield: 4 to 6 large croutons.

Black-Eyed Pea Soup

    2   *cups dried black-eyed peas*
    3   *or 4 (about 1 pound) ham hocks*
    ½   *cup chopped onion*
    3   *cups chopped celery with leaves*
    3   *cups sliced carrots*
    2   *to 4 tablespoons chili powder*
        Salt to taste
        Freshly ground black pepper
    1   *pound Polish or German smoked sausage, sliced*
    1   *cup half-and-half*

Combine peas, ham hocks, onion, celery, carrots, chili powder, salt, and pepper in a large saucepan; add water to cover. Cook over low heat 2 to 3 hours or until peas are tender. Remove ham hocks; cut meat from bones, and chop finely. Drain vegetables, reserving 2 cups liquid. Puree vegetables in electric blender or food mill.

Combine vegetable puree, reserved liquid, ham, and sausage; simmer over low heat 30 minutes. Stir in half-and-half, and heat thoroughly. Yield: 12 servings.

Instant Vichyssoise

    3   *cups chicken broth*
    1   *cup milk*
    1½ *teaspoons onion powder*
    ½   *teaspoon salt*
    ⅛   *teaspoon pepper*
    1   *(2-ounce) package instant mashed potato flakes*
    1   *cup half-and-half*

Combine broth, milk, onion powder, salt, and pepper in a medium saucepan; bring to a boil. Remove from heat; stir in potato flakes. Cool. Add half-and-half, and chill several hours or overnight. Serve cold. Yield: about 4 servings.

Zucchini Soup

    1   *pound zucchini, sliced*
    ¼   *cup chopped onion*
    1   *(10¾-ounce) can cream of chicken soup, undiluted*
    1⅓ *cups water*
        Salt and pepper to taste
    ¼   *to ½ cup white wine*

Combine all ingredients except wine; cook over medium heat 10 to 12 minutes or until squash is tender. Cool slightly. Pour into container of electric blender; blend until smooth. Stir in wine. Chill thoroughly. Yield: 4 to 6 servings.

Minestrone

¼ pound lean salt pork, finely diced
2 quarts hot water
1½ cups tomato juice
2 (15-ounce) cans kidney beans
1 (11½-ounce) can bean with bacon soup, undiluted
6 beef bouillon cubes
1 cup diced carrot
1 cup chopped celery
1 cup shredded cabbage
1 cup chopped green onions
1 cup chopped spinach or ½ (10-ounce) package frozen chopped spinach
1 teaspoon sweet basil
1 teaspoon monosodium glutamate
½ teaspoon salt
½ teaspoon freshly ground pepper
¾ cup uncooked regular rice
Grated Parmesan cheese

Sauté salt pork in a deep saucepan until crisp and brown. Add remaining ingredients except rice and cheese; bring to a boil. Cover and simmer over low heat 1 hour, stirring occasionally. Add rice, and simmer an additional 30 minutes. Ladle into soup bowls, and sprinkle with cheese. Yield: 10 servings.

Prince and Pauper Vegetable Soup

1 pound meaty beef bones
Salt and pepper to taste
¼ teaspoon chili powder
¼ teaspoon Worcestershire sauce
⅛ teaspoon hot sauce
1 (16-ounce) can stewed tomatoes
1 large onion, chopped
3 stalks celery, chopped
3 carrots, chopped
2 cups shredded cabbage
1 small turnip, chopped
1 (8-ounce) can whole kernel corn, drained
½ (10-ounce) package frozen okra
¼ cup red wine

Combine beef bones, salt, pepper, chili powder, Worcestershire sauce, and hot sauce in a large saucepan; add water to cover. Place over heat; cover and simmer for 1 hour.

Add tomatoes, onion, and celery; cook for 1 hour. Add carrots, cabbage, and turnip; continue to cook over low heat for 1 hour. Add remaining ingredients and cook for 30 minutes. Yield: 10 servings.

Salad Soup

1 (46-ounce) can tomato juice
1 tablespoon lemon juice
1 teaspoon Worcestershire sauce
1 tablespoon olive oil
1 teaspoon onion salt
½ teaspoon celery salt
½ cup finely chopped green onion
½ cup finely chopped cucumber
½ cup finely chopped green pepper
½ cup finely chopped celery
½ cup finely chopped carrot

Combine all ingredients, mixing well. Refrigerate, covered, at least 24 hours. Serve cold. Yield: 6 to 8 servings.

Corned Beef-Vegetable Soup

1 (46-ounce) can tomato juice
1 (17-ounce) can green peas, undrained
1 (17-ounce) can cream-style corn
1 (12-ounce) can corned beef, chopped
1 cup water
Salt and pepper to taste
½ to 1 cup uncooked elbow macaroni

Combine all ingredients except macaroni in a Dutch oven; bring to a boil, and simmer 20 minutes. Add macaroni; simmer 8 to 10 minutes or until macaroni is just tender, stirring occasionally. Yield: 8 to 10 servings.

Beef-Vegetable Soup

    1 (2½- to 3-pound) chuck roast, cut into
          cubes
    4 quarts water
    1 tablespoon salt
    ½ head cabbage, chopped
   1½ cups chopped onion
    6 carrots, cut into 1-inch pieces
    ¾ cup chopped celery
    ¼ cup chopped green pepper
    1 (28-ounce) can tomatoes, chopped and
          undrained
    1 cup lima beans
    1 cup cut green beans
    1 cup green peas
    1 (12-ounce) can whole kernel corn,
          drained
    3 to 4 potatoes, cubed
    2 tablespoons chopped parsley
    1 (6-ounce) can tomato paste or ¾ cup
          catsup

Combine roast, water, and salt in a large saucepan or Dutch oven; cover and bring to a boil. Add cabbage, onion, carrots, celery, green pepper, and tomatoes; return to a boil. Lower heat; cover and simmer 30 minutes. Add remaining ingredients; cover and simmer 3½ hours. Yield: 12 to 15 servings.

Country Soup

    2 pounds boneless chuck roast, cut into
          cubes
   1½ teaspoons salt
    2 cups diced potatoes
    2 cups diced carrots
    1 cup diced turnips
    1 cup chopped onion
    ½ cup cut green beans
    ½ cup English peas
    ½ cup chopped kale
    1 cup chopped cabbage
    1 cup chopped tomatoes

Cover beef with water in a Dutch oven; add salt, and simmer until meat is tender. Add next 7 ingredients; simmer 1 hour. Add cabbage and tomatoes; cook 10 minutes. Yield: 6 to 8 servings.

Crab Bisque

   1½ tablespoons butter or margarine
   1½ tablespoons all-purpose flour
    3 cups half-and-half
    ½ cup whipping cream
    2 tablespoons diced celery
    1 (6½-ounce) can crab, drained and
          flaked
    ½ teaspoon salt
       Pepper to taste
    2 tablespoons sherry
       Paprika

Melt butter in a heavy saucepan; blend in flour, and cook until bubbly. Gradually stir in half-and-half; cook over low heat, stirring constantly, until slightly thickened. Add whipping cream, celery, crab, salt, pepper, and sherry. Heat thoroughly, stirring frequently. Garnish with paprika. Yield: about 4 servings.

Chicken and Vermicelli Soup

    1 (1- to 1½-pound) chicken, cut in
          serving-size pieces
    9 cups boiling water
   1½ teaspoons freshly ground black pepper
    1 teaspoon salt
    ½ teaspoon crushed thyme
    1 bay leaf
    1 teaspoon chopped parsley
    1 medium-size onion, chopped
    ⅓ pound fresh mushrooms, sliced
    2 tablespoons white wine
    1 teaspoon lemon juice
    2 teaspoons butter or margarine
       Salt and pepper to taste
    1 (7-ounce) package vermicelli

Add chicken to boiling water; stir in next 6 ingredients, and cook until meat pulls away from bones. Remove chicken from broth; cool, and cut meat into bite-size pieces.

Combine mushrooms, wine, lemon juice, and butter; cook until mushrooms are tender. Season with salt and pepper. Add mushroom mixture to broth along with meat and vermicelli; cook until vermicelli is tender. Yield: 8 to 10 servings.

Chicken Bisque

2 *tablespoons butter or margarine*
2 *tablespoons all-purpose flour*
1 *cup ground cooked chicken*
3 *cups chicken broth*
1 *cup half-and-half, scalded*
Salt and pepper to taste
Chopped parsley (optional)

Melt butter in a heavy saucepan; blend in flour, and cook until bubbly. Add chicken and broth; cook, stirring constantly, until mixture boils. Reduce heat; stir in half-and-half. Season with salt and pepper. Serve immediately. Garnish with parsley, if desired. Yield: about 4 servings.

★
Portuguese Soup

1½ *pounds Portuguese or Polish sausage, sliced*
5 *cups water, divided*
2 *(15-ounce) cans kidney beans, drained*
2 *carrots, diced*
½ *head cabbage, coarsely chopped*
1 *medium-size onion, chopped*
2 *medium-size potatoes, diced*
½ *green pepper, chopped*
1 *clove garlic, finely chopped*
1 *(8-ounce) can tomato sauce*

Simmer sausage in 2 cups water 30 to 45 minutes. Add remaining ingredients, and simmer 1 to 1½ hours. Yield: 10 servings.

Pork and Parsnip Stew

2 *pounds pork shank or pork ribs, cut into serving-size pieces*
1 *quart water*
1 *tablespoon salt*
4 *cups diced parsnips*
2½ *cups diced potatoes*
¼ *teaspoon black pepper*
¼ *teaspoon celery salt*
¼ *cup snipped parsley*

Place meat, water, and salt in a Dutch oven. Cover and simmer 1 to 1½ hours or until meat is tender. Add parsnips, and cook over low heat 20 minutes. Add remaining ingredients; continue cooking 20 minutes or until vegetables are tender. Yield: 6 to 8 servings.

Ham and Vegetable Soup

1½ *pounds meaty ham hock*
2 *(28-ounce) cans whole tomatoes, undrained*
1 *(8-ounce) can tomato sauce*
4 *potatoes, diced*
1 *cup uncooked elbow macaroni*
1 *cup chopped celery*
4 *carrots, sliced*
½ *cup chopped green pepper*
1 *teaspoon celery seeds*
1 *tablespoon salt*
3 *bay leaves*
1 *teaspoon pepper*
1 *dried chili pepper, crumbled*
Garlic salt to taste
2 *cups yellow whole kernel corn*
2 *cups baby lima beans*
2 *cups cut green beans*
2 *cups English peas*

Cover ham hock with water in a large saucepan or Dutch oven. Add tomatoes and tomato sauce; bring to boil. Add next 11 ingredients; cover and simmer about 1 hour. Add remaining ingredients and simmer about 45 minutes.

Remove ham hock and bay leaves from soup. Remove meat from ham hock, then chop meat and return to soup. Yield: 10 to 12 servings.

Turkey Soup

1½   *cups turkey broth*
2½   *cups water*
2   *cups chopped turkey*
1   *large onion, chopped*
1   *cup sliced okra*
1   *tablespoon salt*
Pepper to taste
⅓   *cup uncooked regular rice*
1   *(10½-ounce) can chicken gravy*

Combine broth and water in a large saucepan; bring to a boil. Add turkey, onion, okra, salt, and pepper; return to a boil. Stir in rice. Simmer for 30 minutes or until rice is tender. Stir in gravy, blending well. Yield: 6 to 8 servings.

★
Shrimp Bisque

2   *pounds raw shrimp, peeled and chopped*
¼   *cup chopped mushrooms*
2   *tablespoons chopped onion*
2   *tablespoons chopped celery*
1   *tablespoon chopped carrot*
3   *tablespoons melted butter or margarine*
Salt to taste
Cayenne pepper to taste
2   *cups chicken broth*
1½   *cups half-and-half*
½   *cup dry white wine*

Sauté shrimp and vegetables in butter over low heat about 2 minutes. Stir in salt, cayenne, and chicken broth; bring to a boil, and cook 20 minutes.

Pour shrimp mixture into container of electric blender; blend until smooth. Combine shrimp puree, half-and half, and wine in a saucepan; heat thoroughly. Serve immediately. Yield: about 6 servings.

Salmon Bisque

1   *tablespoon minced onion*
6   *tablespoons melted butter or margarine*
5   *tablespoons all-purpose flour*
1   *bay leaf*
1¾   *cups chicken broth*
½   *cup dry white wine*
1   *tablespoon tomato paste*
1   *(7¾-ounce) can pink salmon, undrained*
1   *cup half-and-half*
Croutons (optional)

Sauté onion in butter in a saucepan about 5 minutes or until onion is transparent. Blend in flour; cook until bubbly, stirring constantly. Add bay leaf. Gradually stir in broth; cook, stirring constantly, until smooth and thick.

Stir wine into sauce; cook over low heat 10 minutes, stirring occasionally. Discard bay leaf; stir in tomato paste and salmon liquid. Mash salmon, and stir into sauce.

Pour mixture into container of electric blender; blend until smooth. Return to saucepan; add half-and-half, and heat thoroughly. Serve immediately; garnish with croutons, if desired. Yield: about 4 servings.

Cheese Soup

¾   *cup finely chopped carrot*
⅔   *cup finely chopped celery*
⅓   *cup finely chopped green onion*
¼   *cup melted butter or margarine*
⅓   *cup all-purpose flour*
2   *cups chicken broth*
2   *cups half-and-half*
¼   *teaspoon salt*
1½   *cups shredded sharp Cheddar cheese*
1   *tablespoon brandy*
Chopped fresh parsley

Sauté vegetables in butter until soft but not brown; blend in flour. Gradually stir in broth, then half-and-half; cook, stirring constantly, until mixture thickens and boils. Stir in salt, cheese, and brandy; heat just until cheese melts. Sprinkle with parsley. Yield: 6 to 8 servings.

Beer-Cheese Soup

½ cup diced celery
½ cup diced carrots
½ cup diced onion
¾ cup melted butter or margarine
½ cup all-purpose flour
½ teaspoon dry mustard
¼ teaspoon Ac'cent
5 cups chicken broth
1½ cups shredded Cheddar cheese
2 tablespoons grated Parmesan cheese
¾ to 1¼ cups beer

Sauté vegetables in butter until tender. Blend in flour, mustard, Ac'cent, and chicken broth; cook 5 minutes. Add cheese and beer; simmer 10 minutes. Yield: 8 servings.

★ Calico Cheese Soup

½ clove garlic
¼ cup salad oil
½ cup finely chopped carrots
½ cup finely chopped celery
   Boiling water
2 tablespoons minced onion
4 tablespoons butter or margarine
3 tablespoons all-purpose flour
2 cups milk, scalded
2 cups chicken broth
2 cups shredded Cheddar cheese
2 cups medium bread cubes
¼ cup grated Parmesan cheese

Soak garlic in salad oil 2 to 3 hours; set aside. Place carrots and celery in boiling, salted water to cover; cover and cook just until crisp-tender. Drain and set aside.

Sauté onion in butter until tender. Stir in flour, milk, and chicken broth, blending well. Cook, stirring constantly, until slightly thickened. Add cheese; stir until melted. Add vegetable mixture; cook 10 minutes.

Toast bread cubes until golden brown. Remove garlic from oil. Combine oil and Parmesan cheese; toss with croutons. Serve on top of hot soup. Yield: 4 to 6 servings.

Pimiento Cheese Soup

2½ cups milk, scalded
2 tablespoons butter or margarine
1 teaspoon cornstarch
⅛ teaspoon paprika
¼ teaspoon salt
¼ teaspoon celery salt
   Dash of cayenne pepper
¼ cup chopped pimiento
8 ounces American cheese, shredded

Combine milk and butter in a saucepan; heat until butter melts. Stir in cornstarch and seasonings; add pimiento and cheese. Cook over low heat, stirring constantly, until cheese melts. Yield: about 4 servings.

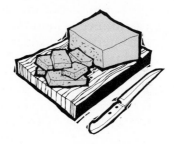

Old English Cheese Soup

¾ cup butter or margarine, divided
½ cup finely chopped celery
½ cup finely chopped carrot
½ cup finely chopped onion
½ cup finely chopped green pepper
6 tablespoons all-purpose flour
4 cups milk
1 teaspoon salt
2 cups shredded sharp pasteurized process
      American cheese
2 cups clear chicken broth

Melt ¼ cup butter in a skillet; add vegetables, and sauté until crisp-tender. Set aside.

Melt ½ cup butter in a Dutch oven over low heat. Gradually stir in flour; cook, stirring constantly, until bubbly. Gradually stir in milk; cook, stirring constantly, until mixture is smooth and thickened. Add sautéed vegetables, salt, cheese, and broth; cook, stirring frequently, until cheese melts and mixture is well heated. Yield: 6 servings.

Cantaloupe Soup

       4 *medium-size cantaloupes or honeydew*
          melons
          Light rum
       2 *tablespoons butter or margarine, melted*
       ¼ *teaspoon ground nutmeg*
    1½ *cups grapefruit juice*
          Juice of 2 limes
       2 *tablespoons honey*
          Salt and pepper to taste
       ¼ *cup half-and-half*
       2 *tablespoons orange-flavored liqueur*

Using a melon ball scoop, scoop out 18 cantaloupe balls. Place in a small bowl, and cover with rum; chill at least 1 hour.

Dice enough remaining melon to yield 4 cups; sauté in butter 2 to 3 minutes, and sprinkle with nutmeg. Combine sautéed cantaloupe, grapefruit juice, lime juice, honey, salt, and pepper in container of electric blender; process until smooth. Stir in half-and-half and liqueur; chill thoroughly.

Just before serving, drain melon balls; place 3 in each serving dish, and add soup. Yield: 6 servings.

Scandinavian Fruit Soup

       1 *(6-ounce) package dried apricots,*
          coarsely chopped
       ½ *cup coarsely chopped prunes*
       1 *cup seedless raisins*
       1 *orange, sliced and seeded*
       1 *lemon, sliced and seeded*
       3 *to 4 tablespoons tapioca*
       1 *cup sugar*
       1 *stick cinnamon*
       3 *cooking apples, pared, cored, and diced*
       1 *(16-ounce) can pitted sour cherries,*
          undrained

Combine apricots, prunes, raisins, orange and lemon slices, tapioca, sugar, and cinnamon; cover with water, and let stand overnight. In the morning, add 2 cups water and apples; cook over medium heat, stirring, until fruit is soft. Stir in cherries. Serve hot or cold. Yield: 6 to 8 servings.

Strawberry Soup

       1 *cup fresh strawberries, washed and*
          capped
       1 *cup orange juice*
       ¼ *cup honey*
       ¼ *cup commercial sour cream*
       ½ *cup sweet white wine (optional)*

Combine all ingredients in container of electric blender; process until strawberries are pureed. Remove from blender container, and chill thoroughly. Stir before serving. Yield: 6 servings.

Spiced Plum Soup

       3 *tablespoons whole cloves*
       1 *stick cinnamon, broken into 3 pieces*
       1 *(16-ounce) jar purple plums, undrained*
          and pitted
       2 *cups cold water*
       ½ *cup dry red wine*
       1 *teaspoon lemon juice*
       2 *teaspoons grated lemon rind*
       3 *tablespoons honey*
       ¼ *teaspoon salt*
       2 *teaspoons cornstarch*
       ½ *cup plain yogurt*
       2 *teaspoons dark brown sugar*

Place cloves and cinnamon in a piece of cheesecloth; tie securely. Combine spice bag, plums, water, wine, lemon juice, lemon rind, honey, and salt in a saucepan; cook over medium heat 12 minutes. Remove and discard spice bag.

Remove plums from cooking liquid; put through a sieve, or puree in electric blender. Return pureed plums to cooking liquid.

Combine cornstarch and 2 tablespoons plum mixture, blending to a smooth paste; gradually stir into remaining plum mixture. Cook over medium heat until slightly thickened, stirring constantly. Chill thoroughly.

Combine yogurt and brown sugar, mixing well. Top each serving of soup with a heaping teaspoonful of yogurt mixture. Yield: 4 to 6 servings.

Swedish Fruit Soup

1   (8-ounce) package mixed dried fruits,
      cut into bite-size pieces
2½ cups water
½   teaspoon ground cinnamon
1   (3-ounce) package cherry-flavored
      gelatin
3   cups orange juice
    Commercial sour cream

Combine dried fruit, water, and cinnamon in
a large saucepan; bring to a boil. Cover; reduce heat, and simmer 20 minutes.

Remove from heat, and stir in gelatin until
dissolved; add orange juice. Chill.

Serve soup cold, topped with sour cream.
Yield: about 8 servings.

Strawberry Cooler

4   cups strawberries, divided
1   cup orange juice
1½ tablespoons cornstarch
½   cup sugar
1   tablespoon lemon juice
1   cup buttermilk

Combine 3¼ cups strawberries and orange
juice in container of an electric blender; blend
until smooth. Pour into medium saucepan.

Combine a small amount of blended mixture and cornstarch, blending until smooth;
add to remaining strawberry mixture. Cook
over medium heat until mixture comes to a
boil, stirring constantly. Cook 1 minute; remove from heat.

Stir in sugar, lemon juice, and buttermilk.
Chill at least 3 hours or until thoroughly cold.
Garnish with remaining ¾ cup strawberries.
Yield: 4 to 6 servings.

★ Salmon Stew

1   quart milk
½ cup butter or margarine
1   (16-ounce) can salmon, drained, bones
      removed, and flaked
½ cup milk
¼ cup all-purpose flour
    Salt and pepper to taste

Combine 1 quart milk and butter in a Dutch
oven; place over medium heat until butter
melts. Stir in salmon.

Combine ½ cup milk and flour, blending
until smooth; add to salmon mixture, stirring
well. Bring to a boil; then lower heat. Add salt
and pepper; simmer 5 minutes. Yield: 4 to 6
servings.

Chili Con Carne

1   pound dried pinto beans
3   pounds boneless beef, trimmed and cut
      into ½-inch cubes
¼   cup olive oil
1   quart water
⅓   cup chili powder
1   tablespoon salt
10 cloves garlic, minced
1   teaspoon ground cumin
1   teaspoon ground marjoram
1   teaspoon ground red pepper
1   tablespoon sugar
3   tablespoons paprika
3   tablespoons all-purpose flour
⅓   cup cornmeal
1   cup water

Cook beans according to package directions;
drain and set aside.

Brown beef in oil over high heat in a heavy
6-quart saucepan. Add 1 quart water; cover
and simmer over low heat 1 to 1½ hours. Add
beans and seasonings; simmer an additional
30 minutes.

Combine flour, cornmeal, and 1 cup water;
blend well. Add flour mixture to meat mixture; cook over low heat, stirring constantly,
until smooth and thickened. Yield: 6 to 8
servings.

Special Chili

       3   *tablespoons shortening*
    1½   *tablespoons all-purpose flour*
       1   *pound lean beef, cut into cubes*
       1   *or 2 cloves garlic, crushed*
       ½   *green pepper, chopped*
       1   *to 3 tablespoons chili powder*
       ½   *teaspoon ground cumin*
       1   *(16-ounce) can tomatoes, undrained*
            and chopped
    1½   *cups hot water*
           Salt and pepper to taste

Melt shortening; blend in flour, and allow to brown slightly. Add meat, and sauté until brown. Stir in garlic, green pepper, chili powder, and cumin; simmer 15 minutes.

Add tomatoes and hot water to meat mixture; simmer 1 hour or until meat is tender. Add more water, if necessary. Season with salt and pepper. Yield: 4 servings.

Brunswick Stew

       1   *(1½- to 2-pound) broiler-fryer chicken,*
            cut into serving-size pieces
       1   *tablespoon salt, divided*
           Paprika to taste
       ¼   *cup butter*
       2   *medium-size onions, sliced*
       1   *medium-size green pepper, diced*
       3   *cups water*
       2   *cups canned tomatoes, undrained*
       2   *tablespoons chopped parsley*
       ½   *teaspoon hot sauce*
       1   *teaspoon Worcestershire sauce*
       2   *cups whole kernel corn*
       1   *(10-ounce) package frozen lima beans,*
            thawed
       3   *tablespoons all-purpose flour*

Sprinkle chicken with 1 teaspoon salt and paprika. Heat butter in a large saucepan or Dutch oven; add chicken, and brown on all sides.

Add onion and green pepper to chicken; cook until onion is transparent. Add water, tomatoes, parsley, remaining salt, hot sauce, and Worcestershire sauce; bring to a boil. Cover; reduce heat, and simmer 30 minutes.

Add corn and lima beans; cook 20 minutes longer. Blend flour with a little cold water; gradually stir into stew. Cook 10 minutes longer, stirring constantly. Yield: 4 to 6 servings.

Kentucky Burgoo

       1   *(4- to 5-pound) hen*
       1   *pound beef stew meat*
       1   *pound veal stew meat*
    1½   *to 2 pounds beef or knuckle bones*
       1   *stalk celery*
       1   *carrot, peeled*
       1   *small onion, peeled*
       5   *to 6 sprigs parsley*
       1   *(10½-ounce) can tomato puree*
       4   *quarts water*
       1   *red pepper pod*
       2   *tablespoons salt*
       1   *tablespoon lemon juice*
       1   *tablespoon Worcestershire sauce*
       1   *tablespoon sugar*
    1½   *teaspoons black pepper*
       ½   *teaspoon cayenne*
       6   *onions, finely chopped*
       8   *to 10 tomatoes, peeled and chopped*
       1   *turnip, peeled and finely chopped*
       2   *green peppers, finely chopped*
       2   *cups fresh butterbeans*
       2   *cups thinly sliced celery*
       2   *cups finely chopped cabbage*
       2   *cups sliced fresh okra*
       2   *cups (3 to 4 ears) fresh corn*
       ½   *unpeeled lemon, seeded*

Combine first 17 ingredients in a large pot; bring to a boil. Cover and simmer 4 hours; cool. Strain meat mixture, reserving meat and stock; discard vegetables. Remove bone, skin, and gristle from meat; finely chop meat. Return meat to stock and refrigerate overnight.

The next day, remove fat layer on stock. Add remaining ingredients; cover and simmer 1 hour. Uncover and simmer about 2 hours longer, stirring frequently to prevent sticking. Burgoo is ready when it reaches the consistency of a thick stew. Yield: about 1 gallon.

Italian Beef Stew

    3 to 4 pounds lean beef for stewing
    1 large onion, chopped
    2 tablespoons melted shortening
    3 (8-ounce) cans tomato sauce
    1 (6-ounce) can tomato paste
    ⅔ cup water
    ½ teaspoon ground allspice
    ½ teaspoon poultry seasoning
    ½ teaspoon ground thyme
    6 cloves garlic, minced or mashed
    ¼ cup chopped parsley
    1 (6-ounce) can sliced mushrooms,
         drained
       Salt and pepper to taste
       Hot cooked spaghetti

Slowly brown meat and onion in shortening. Add remaining ingredients except spaghetti. Cover and simmer 1½ hours. Serve over spaghetti.

To freeze sauce, line a 1½-quart casserole with heavy-duty aluminum foil. Pour in sauce; cool. Seal and label; freeze.

To serve, thaw overnight in refrigerator and bake at 300° about 45 minutes or until warm. Serve over spaghetti. Yield: 6 to 8 servings.

Irish Lamb Stew

    8 medium-size potatoes, thinly sliced
    4 large onions, thinly sliced
    1 (3-pound) boneless shoulder of lamb,
         cubed, or 3 pounds neck slices, cut
         crosswise
    1½ teaspoons salt
    ½ teaspoon pepper
    ½ teaspoon ground thyme
    2 cups water
       Chopped parsley

Layer half of potatoes and onions in a large Dutch oven; add meat, and top with remaining vegetables. Sprinkle with salt, pepper, and thyme; add water. Cover and bake at 350° for 2 to 2½ hours or until meat is tender. Sprinkle with parsley before serving. Yield: 6 servings.

★ Southern Catfish Stew

    4 medium-size catfish, cleaned and
         dressed
    4 cups boiling water
    4 cups diced potatoes
    2 cups diced onion
    2 cups frozen corn
    2 tablespoons butter or margarine
    2 cups milk
       Salt and pepper to taste

Simmer catfish in water until fish will flake from bone. Remove fish from liquid, reserving broth. Remove bones from fish; set meat aside.

Add potatoes and onion to fish broth; cook until tender, about 10 to 15 minutes. Add corn and cook until tender, about 10 minutes. Stir in butter, milk, salt and pepper, and reserved fish. Heat thoroughly. Yield: about 8 servings.

Venison Stew

    2 pounds boneless venison, cubed
       All-purpose flour
       Bacon drippings
    1 tablespoon catsup
    1 tablespoon Worcestershire sauce
    2 teaspoons salt
    ¼ teaspoon pepper
    1 large onion, thinly sliced
    2 large carrots, peeled and cut into large
         pieces
    3 medium-size potatoes, peeled and cubed
    1 (15-ounce) can garbanzo beans,
         undrained
    1 (2-ounce) jar chopped pimiento, drained

Coat venison with flour; brown in bacon drippings in a large Dutch oven. Cover meat with water; add catsup, Worcestershire sauce, salt, and pepper. Cover and simmer until meat is tender, about 20 minutes.

Add onion, carrots, and potatoes; simmer about 45 minutes. Add garbanzo beans and pimiento; cook 15 minutes or until vegetables are tender. Yield: 6 to 8 servings.

★
Oyster Stew

  1 *quart half-and-half or milk*
  2 *tablespoons butter or margarine*
  2 *green onions, chopped*
  1 *pint oysters, undrained*
Salt to taste
Red pepper to taste

Heat half-and-half in top of a double boiler until hot but not boiling. Melt butter in a saucepan over medium heat; add onion, and sauté lightly. Add oysters; cook until edges begin to curl. Combine oyster mixture with half-and-half; stir in salt and red pepper. Serve with crackers. Yield: 6 to 8 servings.

Chicken Gumbo

  1 *(3- to 3½-pound) chicken, cut up*
Salt and pepper to taste
  4 *cups water*
  ¼ *cup all-purpose flour*
  2 *tablespoons salad oil*
 2½ *cups chopped onion*
  3 *stalks celery and tops, chopped*
 1½ *cups chopped green pepper, divided*
  1 *clove garlic, minced*
  1 *(12-ounce) package little smoked*
     sausage links, sliced
  1 *bunch green onions with tops, chopped*
Hot cooked rice

Simmer chicken, salt, and pepper in water until tender. Remove chicken from broth; reserve broth. Remove meat from bones, and cut into small pieces.

    Brown flour in oil over medium heat 25 to 30 minutes, stirring constantly. Add 2½ cups onion, celery, 1 cup green pepper, garlic, and 2 cups chicken broth; season with salt and pepper. Bring mixture to a boil; lower heat and simmer 1 hour.

    Add chicken and 2 cups chicken broth; simmer 40 minutes. Add sausage, green onion, and remaining ½ cup green pepper; simmer 15 to 20 minutes. Serve over rice. Yield: 8 to 10 servings.

★
Chicken-Oyster Gumbo

  1 *(2½- to 3-pound) chicken, cut up*
Salt
Red and black pepper
  ½ *cup salad oil*
  ½ *cup all-purpose flour*
  1 *large or 2 medium-size onions, chopped*
  2 *quarts hot water*
  1 *to 2 pints oysters, undrained*
  2 *stalks celery, chopped*
  ½ *green pepper, chopped*
  ½ *cup chopped parsley*
  ½ *cup chopped green onion tops*
Hot cooked rice
Gumbo filé (optional)

Season chicken with salt and pepper. Heat salad oil in a heavy iron pot; add chicken, and cook until browned. Remove chicken from pot, and stir flour into oil; cook over medium heat until a dark roux is formed, stirring constantly.

    Add onion to roux, and cook until tender; add chicken. Gradually stir in hot water, blending well. Bring to a boil, and simmer until chicken is tender (about 1 hour). Remove chicken bones, if desired. Season with salt and pepper.

    Add oysters, celery, green pepper, parsley, and green onion to gumbo; simmer 20 minutes longer. Serve over rice. Thicken with gumbo filé, if desired. Yield: 8 to 10 servings.

Chicken and Okra Gumbo

  1 *large onion, chopped*
  2 *cups sliced okra, fresh or frozen*
Salad oil or bacon drippings
  1 *(2½- to 3-pound) chicken, cut up*
Salt
Red and black pepper
  2 *quarts warm water*
Hot cooked rice
Gumbo filé

Sauté onion and okra in ¼ cup salad oil over low heat about 30 minutes, stirring often. Season chicken with salt and pepper; brown chicken in additional salad oil in a heavy skillet. Pour off excess oil; add okra and onion mixture, and gradually stir in water.

Season gumbo to taste with salt and pepper. Cook over medium heat until chicken is tender (about 45 minutes). Remove bones from chicken, if desired. Serve gumbo over hot cooked rice, and thicken with gumbo filé. Yield: 8 to 10 servings.

Ham, Sausage, Beef, and Chicken Gumbo

Salad oil
1 pound ham, cut into ½-inch cubes
1 pound smoked sausage, cut into ½-inch slices
1 pound beef stew meat, cut into 1-inch pieces
6 chicken thighs
1 large onion, chopped
4 cloves garlic, minced
½ green pepper, chopped
¼ cup all-purpose flour
2 quarts water
½ teaspoon crushed red pepper
½ teaspoon thyme
Salt and black pepper to taste
¼ cup chopped parsley
½ cup chopped green onion tops
Hot cooked rice
Gumbo filé (optional)

Heat oil in a large iron pot over medium heat; brown each meat, one at a time, and remove from pot. Add onion, garlic, and green pepper to drippings, and sauté until tender; remove from pot. Pour off all but ¼ cup drip-

pings, and blend in flour; cook over medium heat, stirring constantly, until a medium roux is formed.

Gradually add water to roux, blending well. Stir in meats, sautéed vegetables, red pepper, thyme, salt, and black pepper; bring to a boil. Reduce heat; simmer, uncovered, 1½ to 2 hours. Cool; skim grease off top. Remove bones from chicken, if desired.

Bring gumbo to a boil; add parsley and green onion tops. Cook about 10 minutes longer. Serve over rice. Thicken with gumbo filé, if desired. Yield: 8 to 10 servings.

Turkey and Sausage Gumbo

1 turkey carcass
½ cup salad oil
½ cup all-purpose flour
1½ large onions, chopped
½ green pepper, chopped
1 stalk celery, chopped
1½ pounds smoked sausage, cut into 2½-inch pieces
Salt
Red and black pepper
¼ cup chopped parsley
¼ cup chopped green onion tops
Hot cooked rice
Gumbo filé (optional)

Use a turkey carcass with a little meat left on it; a smoked turkey is best. Cover carcass with water, and boil until meat leaves bones (about 1 hour). Reserve broth, and remove meat from carcass; discard bones.

Combine salad oil and flour in a large iron pot; cook over medium heat, stirring constantly, until a medium roux is formed. Add onion, green pepper, and celery; cook about 5 minutes or until tender, stirring constantly. Add sausage, turkey, and 2 to 3 quarts broth (add water to make 2 quarts, if necessary); simmer 1 hour.

Season gumbo to taste with salt and pepper. Stir in parsley and green onion; cook 10 minutes longer. Serve over rice. Thicken with gumbo filé, if desired. Yield: 8 to 10 servings.

★
Seafood Gumbo

    1 *cup salad oil or bacon drippings*
    1 *cup all-purpose flour*
    2 *large onions, chopped*
    2 *stalks celery, chopped*
    1 *large green pepper, chopped*
    6 *cloves garlic, minced*
    1 *gallon warm water*
    4 *cups sliced okra*
    3 *tomatoes, peeled and chopped*
    2 *tablespoons salt*
       Red and black pepper to taste
    1 *pint oysters, undrained*
    1 *dozen cleaned fresh crabs* with claws or*
         1 pound fresh or frozen crabmeat
 1½ *to 2 pounds fresh or frozen medium*
         shrimp, peeled and deveined
    ½ *cup chopped parsley*
    ½ *cup chopped green onion tops*
       Hot cooked rice
       Gumbo filé (optional)

Combine oil and flour in a heavy pot over medium heat; cook, stirring constantly, until roux is the color of a copper penny (about 10 to 15 minutes). Add onion, celery, green pepper, and garlic to roux; cook, stirring constantly, until vegetables are tender. *Do not let roux burn* as it will ruin gumbo; reduce heat, if necessary.

Gradually add 1 gallon warm water to roux, in small amounts at first, blending well after each addition; add okra and tomatoes. Bring mixture to a boil. Reduce heat; simmer, stirring occasionally, at least 20 minutes (1 to 1½ hours is better as the roux develops more flavor at this point). Stir in salt, pepper, and seafood.

Bring gumbo to a boil, and simmer 10 minutes. Add parsley and green onion; simmer 5 minutes longer. Remove from heat, and serve the gumbo over hot rice.

Gumbo can be further thickened, if desired, by adding a small amount of filé to each serving. Yield: 12 to 14 servings.

*To clean fresh crabs: Pour scalding water over crabs to kill them; remove large claws, and wash thoroughly. Turn crab upside down and lift the long, tapered point (the apron); pull off shell and remove the soft, spongy mass. Remove and discard legs. Wash crab thoroughly, and break body in half lengthwise; add to gumbo along with claws.

Note: Almost any kind of meat, poultry, or game can be substituted for the seafood in this recipe. Just cut it into pieces and brown it before adding to the roux.

Easy Okra Gumbo

 2½ *cups sliced okra*
    3 *tablespoons bacon drippings*
    1 *large onion, chopped*
    1 *medium-size green pepper, chopped*
    1 *(8-ounce) can tomato sauce*
    1 *(6-ounce) package crabmeat, drained*
         and flaked
    1 *teaspoon ground thyme*
    2 *tablespoons all-purpose flour*
    1 *(12-ounce) can oysters, undrained*
    4 *cups water*
    ¼ *cup diced ham*
    2 *medium-size bay leaves*
    1 *teaspoon chopped fresh parsley*
    1 *teaspoon salt*
       Dash of black pepper
    ½ *teaspoon cayenne pepper*

Brown okra lightly in bacon drippings. Add remaining ingredients; simmer 1½ hours. Remove bay leaves before serving. Yield: 6 to 8 servings.

Spinach Chowder

2   *cups chopped spinach*
1   *cup water*
3   *medium-size potatoes, sliced*
3   *slices bacon*
½   *cup sliced onion*
3   *tablespoons all-purpose flour*
1   *cup evaporated milk*
2   *teaspoons salt*

Add spinach to 1 cup boiling water. Cover; lower heat, and simmer 3 to 5 minutes. Drain, reserving liquid.

Cook potatoes in salted water to cover until tender. Drain, reserving liquid.

Fry bacon in a Dutch oven until brown; remove bacon, and reserve drippings. Drain bacon thoroughly on a paper towel; crumble, and set aside.

Sauté onion in bacon drippings until lightly browned. Blend in flour; gradually add milk, spinach liquid, and potato water. Cook, stirring constantly, until mixture boils and thickens. Add salt, spinach, and potatoes. Bring to a boil; lower heat, and simmer 5 minutes. Garnish each serving with crumbled bacon. Yield: 6 to 8 servings.

Vegetable Chowder

2   *cups diced carrots*
3   *cups diced potatoes*
1   *cup diced celery*
1   *cup diced onion*
12 *slices bacon, cooked and crumbled*
1   *(8¾-ounce) can whole kernel corn,*
        undrained
1   *(10¾-ounce) can tomato soup,*
        undiluted
1   *cup half-and-half*
1   *cup milk*
1   *teaspoon salt*
½   *teaspoon pepper*

Combine carrots, potatoes, celery, and onion; cook in water to cover until tender. Drain. Combine cooked vegetables and remaining ingredients. Simmer until well heated. Yield: 8 to 10 servings.

Ham and Corn Chowder

3   *slices bacon, chopped*
2   *medium-size onions, chopped*
1   *cup diced celery*
2   *tablespoons all-purpose flour*
2   *(13¾-ounce) cans chicken broth*
4   *medium-size potatoes, diced*
1   *(10-ounce) package frozen whole kernel*
        corn
3   *cups milk*
2   *cups cubed cooked smoked ham*
1   *teaspoon salt*
⅛   *teaspoon pepper*

Fry bacon until crisp. Add onion and celery, and sauté until golden brown. Sprinkle with flour, blending well; gradually stir in chicken broth. Add potatoes; cover and simmer until potatoes are done. Stir in remaining ingredients. Heat thoroughly, but do not boil. Yield: 8 to 10 servings.

Lima Bean-Ham Chowder

1½ *cups large dried lima beans*
1   *quart water*
1   *(1-pound) meaty ham hock*
1   *teaspoon salt*
1   *cup chopped onion*
½   *cup chopped green pepper*
2   *tablespoons melted butter or margarine*
1   *(8¾-ounce) can cream-style corn*
2   *cups milk*
Salt and pepper to taste

Combine beans and water; bring to a boil, and simmer 2 minutes. Remove from heat, and let stand 1 hour. Add ham hock; cover and simmer 1 hour or until meat is tender. Add 1 teaspoon salt, and simmer 30 minutes.

Remove ham hock, and slightly mash beans with potato masher. Remove meat from ham hock; shred.

Sauté onion and green pepper in butter until tender; add to limas along with ham, corn, and milk; heat thoroughly, but do not boil. Season with salt and pepper. Yield: 4 to 6 servings.

Manhattan Seafood Chowder

    2 *tablespoons crab boil*
    2 *cups water*
    4 *ribs celery, chopped*
    1 *large onion, chopped*
    1 *small green pepper, chopped*
    1 *clove garlic, minced*
    ½ *cup melted butter or margarine*
    2 *(8-ounce) cans minced clams, drained*
    1 *(6-ounce) package frozen crabmeat,*
       thawed
    1 *cup chopped raw shrimp*
    1 *cup flaked raw haddock or flounder*
    1 *(28-ounce) can tomatoes*
    1 *tablespoon basil*
    1½ *teaspoons sugar*
       Juice of 1 lemon
       Salt and pepper to taste

Combine crab boil and water; bring to a boil. Cover and set aside to steep 10 minutes. Strain into a Dutch oven.

Sauté celery, onion, green pepper, and garlic in butter until tender. Add all ingredients to crab boil stock, stirring well; simmer 1 hour. Yield: 12 to 15 servings.

New England Clam Chowder

    1 *large onion, chopped*
    2 *cloves garlic, minced*
    6 *tablespoons butter or margarine,*
       divided
    3 *(8-ounce) cans minced clams, drained*
    2 *cups clam juice*
    ¾ *cups diced salt pork*
    2 *medium-size potatoes, cubed*
    2 *cups half-and-half*
       Salt and white pepper to taste
       Chopped parsley
       Chopped chives

Sauté onion and garlic in 2 tablespoons butter 5 minutes. Add clams and clam juice; cover, and cook over low heat 10 to 15 minutes.

Fry salt pork until golden brown; then drain well on paper towel. Cook potatoes in boiling salted water until barely done; drain.

Add salt pork and potatoes to clams. Gradually stir in half-and-half; heat thoroughly,

but do not boil. Add salt and pepper. Thinly slice 4 tablespoons butter, and float on top of chowder. Sprinkle each serving with parsley and chives. Yield: about 6 to 8 servings.

Golden Cheese Chowder

    3 *cups water*
    4 *medium-size potatoes, cubed*
    1 *cup sliced celery*
    1 *cup sliced carrots*
    ½ *cup diced onion*
    2 *teaspoons salt*
    ¼ *teaspoon pepper*
    ½ *cup butter or margarine*
    ½ *cup all-purpose flour*
    4 *cups milk*
    1 *pound sharp Cheddar cheese, shredded*
    2 *cups cubed cooked ham*
       Hot sauce to taste

Bring water to a boil in a Dutch oven, and add vegetables, salt, and pepper. Cover; lower heat, and simmer 10 minutes or until vegetables are done.

Melt butter in a large saucepan. Blend in flour, and gradually stir in milk. Cook over medium heat, stirring constantly, until mixture comes to a boil; boil for 1 minute. Add cheese, and stir until melted.

Stir cheese mixture into vegetables. Add ham and hot sauce, stirring well. Heat thoroughly; do not boil. Yield 12 servings.

Cold Cream of Spinach Soup

1 (10-ounce) package frozen chopped
   spinach
2 teaspoons finely chopped onion
2 tablespoons melted butter or margarine
¼ cup all-purpose flour
1 teaspoon salt
⅛ teaspoon white pepper
1 quart milk, divided
3 tablespoons lemon juice

Cook spinach according to package directions; drain well and set aside.

Sauté onion in butter; stir in flour, salt, and pepper. Cook over low heat, stirring constantly, until smooth and bubbly. Gradually stir in 2 cups milk; heat until mixture is thick.

Blend cream sauce and spinach; add remaining milk and lemon juice, and blend well. Cover and refrigerate at least 4 hours. Stir gently. Serve in chilled bowls or mugs. Yield: 6 to 8 servings.

Haddock Chowder

2 pounds haddock
2 cups water
2 tablespoons diced salt pork
2 medium-size onions, chopped
2 tablespoons salad oil
3 medium-size potatoes, thinly sliced
1 cup chopped celery
1 bay leaf
1 teaspoon salt
½ teaspoon white pepper
4 cups milk
2 tablespoons butter or margarine

Simmer fish in 2 cups water in a large saucepan 15 minutes. Drain, reserving broth. Remove bones, and cut fish into 1-inch squares.

Sauté salt pork and onion in salad oil 5 minutes in a Dutch oven. Add fish, potatoes, celery, bay leaf, salt, and pepper. Add enough boiling water to reserved broth to make 3 cups liquid, and pour over fish mixture. Simmer, uncovered, 30 minutes.

Gradually stir in milk and butter. Simmer, uncovered, 5 minutes; do not boil. Remove bay leaf before serving. Yield: 6 to 8 servings.

Corn Chowder

4 slices bacon
1 medium-size onion, chopped
2 (17-ounce) cans cream-style corn
2 cups milk
1 teaspoon salt
¼ teaspoon pepper
¼ cup butter or margarine

Fry bacon until crisp; remove from drippings and crumble.

Add onion to bacon drippings, and cook over medium heat until transparent. Stir in corn, milk, bacon, and seasonings. Cook over medium heat until hot, stirring constantly; add butter, stirring until melted. Yield: 6 servings.

Fish Chowder

3 tablespoons all-purpose flour
½ cup melted butter or margarine
1½ cups water
1 (10¾-ounce) can tomato soup,
   undiluted
2 large potatoes, cubed
1 large onion, chopped
1 cup shredded cabbage
1 teaspoon celery seeds
Salt and pepper to taste
1 to 2 pounds fish fillets, cut into 1-inch
   cubes

Stir flour into butter; cook over low heat until bubbly, stirring constantly. Add water and tomato soup, stirring until smooth. Add remaining ingredients except fish; mix well.

Bring mixture to a boil; lower heat immediately, and simmer 45 minutes or until potatoes are tender. Add fish; simmer 10 minutes or until fish flakes when tested with a fork. Yield: 6 to 8 servings.

Vegetables and Side Dishes

Consider the bright, bold colors and interesting textures of fresh vegetables, and you'll agree that this food group boasts some of the most beautiful foods we eat. Whether freshly picked from your own garden or selected from the supermarket counter, fresh vegetables are unmatched for flavor and nutrients.

With the bright colors and distinctive flavors that Southern vegetables add to the menu, your meals will never be ordinary. Choose the vivid red of tomatoes, the green of okra and beans, and the golden yellow of squash, sweet potatoes, and corn.

Most fresh vegetables maintain their food value, color, and flavor when quickly cooked in a minimum amount of water. Boiling and frying are the most common methods of vegetable cookery, but steaming and stir-frying are fast becoming popular.

Elegant Asparagus Vinaigrette

- ½   cup olive or peanut oil
- ½   teaspoon salt
- ½   teaspoon pepper
- 1   tablespoon prepared mustard
- ⅓   cup tarragon vinegar
- 1   tablespoon chopped chives
- 2   tablespoons pickle relish
- 2   hard-cooked eggs, finely sieved
- 2   pounds fresh asparagus spears, cooked and drained
- Lettuce leaves
- Pimiento strips

Combine first 8 ingredients in a jar; shake well. Arrange asparagus spears on lettuce leaves, and garnish with pimiento. Shake dressing well; pour over asparagus. Yield: 6 servings.

Zucchini, pattypan, and yellow squash can brighten your table in countless ways. Spinach-Stuffed Zucchini (page 340) and Tangy Yellow Squash (page 339) are only two of them.

Marinated Artichoke Hearts

- 2   teaspoons dillweed
- ¾   cup Tart and Tangy Dressing
- 2   (8½-ounce) cans artichoke hearts, drained
- Pimiento strips

Combine dillweed and Tart and Tangy Dressing; pour over artichoke hearts, and marinate several hours. Garnish with pimiento. Yield: about 8 servings.

Tart and Tangy Dressing:

- 1   tablespoon grated onion
- 2   tablespoons white wine vinegar
- 2   teaspoons Dijon mustard
- ⅛   teaspoon freshly ground pepper
- 1½   teaspoons salt
- ½   cup olive oil
- 4½   teaspoons lemon juice

Combine all ingredients in a jar. Cover and shake until well blended. Yield: about ¾ cup.

Artichoke Bottoms Stuffed with Spinach

    1   (10-ounce) package frozen chopped
          spinach
    ¼   cup minced onion
    3   tablespoons butter or margarine, melted
    ¼   cup commercial sour cream
    2   tablespoons grated Parmesan cheese
    ¾   teaspoon salt
    ¼   teaspoon black pepper
        Dash of red pepper
    1   (14-ounce) can artichoke bottoms or 2
          (8½-ounce) cans artichoke hearts,
          drained
        Grated Parmesan cheese

Cook spinach according to package directions; drain thoroughly. Sauté onion in butter 5 minutes or until tender. Stir in cooked spinach, sour cream, 2 tablespoons Parmesan cheese, salt, and pepper.

Spoon mixture onto artichoke bottoms (if using artichoke hearts, spread center leaves and stuff with spinach mixture); place in a shallow baking dish, and sprinkle Parmesan cheese over top. Add water to barely cover bottom of baking dish.

Bake at 350° for 15 to 20 minutes. Yield: 6 to 8 servings.

Cheesy Asparagus Casserole

    ¼   cup melted butter or margarine
    2   tablespoons all-purpose flour
    2   cups milk
    ½   cup shredded Cheddar cheese
    ¼   teaspoon salt
    3   cups cut cooked asparagus
    ¾   cup buttered breadcrumbs

Combine butter and flour in a small saucepan over low heat; blend until smooth.

Gradually stir milk into flour mixture; cook, stirring constantly, until smooth and thickened. Add cheese and salt, stirring until cheese melts.

Place asparagus in a lightly greased 2-quart casserole. Add cheese sauce; sprinkle with breadcrumbs. Bake at 325° for 30 minutes. Yield: 4 to 5 servings.

★ Marinated Asparagus

    ¼   cup lemon juice
    ⅓   cup olive oil
    ½   cup salad oil
    ½   teaspoon salt
        Dash of pepper
    ½   teaspoon dry mustard
    1   hard-cooked egg, chopped
    1   tablespoon chopped pimiento
    1   tablespoon capers
    1   tablespoon chopped green onion
    1   tablespoon chopped parsley
    1   pound fresh asparagus, cooked
        Salad greens

Combine lemon juice, oil, salt, pepper, and mustard, stirring until well blended; add egg, pimiento, capers, green onion, and parsley.

Place cooked asparagus in a shallow 1½-quart casserole and pour marinade over all; cover and chill 2 hours. Serve mixture over salad greens. Yield: about 4 servings.

Note: Hearts of palm, broccoli, or artichoke hearts may be used instead of fresh asparagus.

Asparagus Supreme

    2   tablespoons butter or margarine
    2   tablespoons all-purpose flour
    1   cup milk
    2   (10-ounce) packages frozen cut
          asparagus, cooked and drained
    2   hard-cooked eggs, sliced
    1   (2-ounce) jar sliced pimientos, drained
          and divided
    1   cup breadcrumbs
    1   cup shredded sharp Cheddar cheese

Melt butter in a small saucepan over low heat; blend in flour, stirring until smooth. Gradually blend in milk; cook until smooth and thickened, stirring constantly.

Place half of asparagus in a greased 1½-quart casserole. Top with slices from 1 egg, half of pimiento, and half of white sauce. Repeat layers. Top with breadcrumbs and cheese. Bake at 350° for 30 minutes or until thoroughly heated. Yield: 6 to 8 servings.

French-Fried Asparagus Tips

Fine dry breadcrumbs
Salt to taste
1 (15-ounce) can asparagus tips, well
   drained
1 egg, well beaten
Salad oil

Combine breadcrumbs and salt, blending
well. Dip asparagus in egg, then in breadcrumb mixture. Heat salad oil to 375°; fry
coated asparagus in oil until golden brown.
Drain on paper towels. Yield: 4 servings.

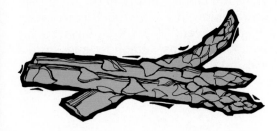

Asparagus with Egg Sauce

2 to 2½ pounds fresh asparagus
3 tablespoons butter or margarine
3 tablespoons all-purpose flour
1 teaspoon salt
2 cups milk
Dash of Worcestershire sauce
1 teaspoon lemon juice
¼ teaspoon onion juice
4 hard-cooked eggs, chopped
Lemon
Pimiento strips
Parsley

Cook asparagus in a small amount of boiling
salted water 12 to 15 minutes or until crisp-
tender; drain.
  Melt butter in a saucepan; blend in flour
and salt. Gradually stir in milk; cook over
medium heat, stirring constantly, until sauce
thickens. Add Worcestershire sauce, lemon
juice, and onion juice. Just before serving,
fold in chopped eggs.
  Serve sauce over asparagus. Garnish with
lemon, pimiento strips, and parsley. Yield: 6
to 8 servings.

Lima Bean Pot

1 pound dried lima beans
1 pound bulk sausage
1 onion, chopped
½ green pepper, chopped
½ cup chopped celery
1 (15-ounce) can tomato sauce
2 tablespoons brown sugar
1½ teaspoons salt
1 teaspoon chili powder
⅛ teaspoon cayenne pepper

Sort and wash beans. Cover with water, and
bring to a boil; boil 2 minutes. Remove from
heat, and let stand 1 hour. Return to a boil;
cover, reduce heat, and simmer until almost
tender (about 1 hour).
  Brown sausage in a skillet; add onion,
green pepper, and celery. Sauté until vegetables are tender. Add meat mixture and remaining ingredients. Continue cooking until
beans are tender, adding water if necessary.
Yield: 8 to 10 servings.

Baked Lima Beans

¼ cup chopped onion
¼ cup chopped celery
¼ cup butter or margarine
1 tablespoon all-purpose flour
1 cup milk
1 cup evaporated milk
1½ cups shredded sharp Cheddar cheese,
   divided
3 tablespoons pimiento
½ teaspoon salt
¼ teaspoon ground thyme
2 (10-ounce) packages frozen lima beans,
   thawed
Ground paprika

Sauté onion and celery in butter until wilted;
stir in flour, blending well. Stir in milk; cook,
stirring constantly, until thick. Stir in 1 cup
cheese, pimiento, salt, and thyme.
  Place half of lima beans in a 1½-quart casserole. Top with half of cheese sauce; repeat
layers. Sprinkle with remaining ½ cup
cheese and paprika. Bake at 350° for 1 hour.
Yield: 6 to 8 servings.

Lima Bean Casserole

    1   *teaspoon prepared mustard*
    1   *teaspoon Worcestershire sauce*
    ½   *teaspoon lemon juice*
    1½ *cups mayonnaise*
    1   *(5-ounce) can water chestnuts, drained*
        and sliced
    1   *small onion, chopped*
    1   *(10-ounce) package frozen lima beans,*
        cooked and drained
    1   *(10-ounce) package frozen French-cut*
        green beans, cooked and drained
    1   *(17-ounce) can green peas, drained*
    ½   *cup round buttery cracker crumbs*

Combine mustard, Worcestershire sauce, lemon juice, and mayonnaise. Stir in water chestnuts and vegetables. Spoon into an ungreased 2-quart casserole; sprinkle cracker crumbs on top. Bake at 350° for 45 minutes. Yield: 6 to 8 servings.

Swiss Green Beans

    2   *(10-ounce) packages frozen French-cut*
        green beans
    ¼   *cup melted margarine*
    2   *tablespoons all-purpose flour*
    1   *teaspoon salt*
    ¼   *teaspoon pepper*
    ¼   *teaspoon instant minced onion*
    1   *tablespoon sugar*
    1   *(8-ounce) carton commercial sour cream*
    1½ *cups shredded Swiss cheese*
    ¼   *cup buttery cracker crumbs*

Cook beans according to package directions; drain. Combine remaining ingredients except cheese and cracker crumbs, mixing well; stir in green beans. Pour mixture into a greased shallow 2-quart casserole. Top with cheese and cracker crumbs. Bake at 350° for 25 to 30 minutes. Yield: about 6 to 8 servings.

Green Bean Casserole

    2   *(16-ounce) cans French-cut green*
        beans, drained
    2   *(10¾-ounce) cans cream of mushroom*
        soup, undiluted
    1   *cup diced celery*
    1   *cup diced green pepper*
    1   *cup diced onion*
    5   *to 6 ripe olives, sliced*
    ¾   *cup crushed potato chips*
    ¼   *cup slivered almonds*
    5   *to 6 pimiento-stuffed olives, sliced*

Layer half of beans, soup, celery, green pepper, and onion in a buttered 2-quart casserole; repeat layers. Top with a layer of ripe olives, potato chips, almonds, and stuffed olives. Bake at 325° for 35 to 40 minutes. Yield: about 8 servings.

Baked Beans with Beef

    ½   *pound dried Great Northern beans*
    1   *(about 1-pound) ham hock*
    2   *medium-size onions, chopped*
    1   *tablespoon melted butter or margarine*
    1   *pound ground beef*
    1   *(28-ounce) can pear-shaped tomatoes*
    2   *tablespoons brown sugar*
    1   *tablespoon dry mustard*
    1   *tablespoon mustard seeds*
    1   *tablespoon chili powder*
    1   *teaspoon Worcestershire sauce*
    Salt and pepper to taste

Sort and wash beans; place in a heavy saucepan or Dutch oven. Cover with water, and bring to a boil; boil 2 minutes. Remove from heat, and soak 1 hour.

Add ham hock; cover and cook gently about 1 hour or until tender, adding more water if necessary.

Sauté onion in butter; add to beans. Brown ground beef, stirring to crumble; add remaining ingredients, and simmer 10 minutes. Add to beans.

Spoon bean mixture into a 2½-quart casserole. Bake at 400° for 30 minutes or until thickened. Yield: 6 servings.

Saucy Green Bean Delight

½ cup finely chopped celery
¼ cup butter or margarine, melted
3 tablespoons all-purpose flour
½ teaspoon salt
   Dash of pepper
1½ cups milk
¼ cup blue cheese, crumbled
4 cups cooked green beans, drained
2 tablespoons chopped pimiento

Sauté celery in butter until tender; blend in flour and seasonings. Gradually blend in milk; cook over low heat, stirring constantly, until thickened.

Add cheese; stir until melted. Stir in green beans and pimiento; heat thoroughly over low heat. Yield: 4 to 6 servings.

Stove-Top Baked Beans

2 (16-ounce) cans pork and beans
1 small onion, finely chopped
⅓ cup catsup
2 tablespoons prepared mustard
2 tablespoons dark corn syrup

Combine all ingredients in a medium saucepan. Cover and simmer about 45 minutes or until onion is tender, stirring frequently. Yield: about 6 servings.

Chili Beans

1 pound pinto beans
2 tablespoons chili powder
½ medium-size onion, chopped
1 clove garlic, pressed
   Dash of pepper
1 tablespoon salt

Wash beans well; cover with cold water, and soak overnight. The next day add chili powder, onion, garlic, and pepper.

Cook over low heat about 2 hours or until beans are tender. Add salt, and cook about 30 additional minutes. Yield: about 8 servings.

Creole Red Beans and Rice

1 pound dried red beans
1 pound smoked link sausage, cut into
      1-inch pieces
½ to 1 pound smoked ham, cubed
1 large onion, chopped
1 (1-pound) can tomatoes, undrained
1 clove garlic, crushed
1 tablespoon salt
   Pepper to taste
   Hot cooked rice

Sort and wash beans. Cover with water, and bring to a boil; cover and cook 2 minutes. Remove from heat, and let stand 1 hour. Bring to a boil; reduce heat, and simmer until beans are almost tender (1½ to 2 hours).

Add remaining ingredients except rice to beans; continue cooking, stirring occasionally, until beans are tender and a thick gravy is formed. If necessary, add more water to keep beans from sticking. Serve over rice. Yield: 8 to 10 servings.

Southern Baked Beans

2 cups dried Great Northern or navy
      beans
1 teaspoon salt
½ cup salt pork
½ cup chopped onion
½ cup dark molasses
2 tablespoons catsup
½ teaspoon prepared mustard
¼ teaspoon pepper
2 cups hot water
¼ cup butter or margarine

Wash beans; cover with cold water and soak overnight. Drain. Place beans in a large pot; cover with boiling water. Add salt, and cook over low heat 2 hours and 30 minutes; drain. Place beans in a 2½-quart greased baking dish; add salt pork and onion. Combine molasses, catsup, mustard, pepper, and 2 cups hot water; pour over beans. Dot with butter. Cover and bake at 350° for 3 hours, stirring each hour. Yield: about 8 servings.

Baked Beans with Smoked Sausage

1	pound Great Northern beans
1	cup catsup
½	cup firmly packed brown sugar
1½	teaspoons salt
1	teaspoon pepper
1	tablespoon dry mustard
¼	teaspoon ground cinnamon
⅛	teaspoon ground ginger
⅛	teaspoon ground nutmeg
1	tablespoon Worcestershire sauce
1	unpeeled tart apple, cored
1½	pounds smoked sausage

Sort beans, and wash thoroughly; cover with water, and soak overnight. Drain beans, and place in a heavy saucepan; cover with water, and bring to a boil. Reduce heat; cover and simmer 1 to 1½ hours or until skins begin to split. Drain, reserving 2 cups liquid.

Place beans in a 4½-quart casserole; stir in catsup, brown sugar, and seasonings. Slice apple, and arrange on top of beans. Cut sausage diagonally into 1-inch slices, and place on top of apple.

Cover and bake at 350° for 1 hour. Remove cover, and add enough reserved liquid to barely cover beans. Bake, uncovered, 30 minutes or until sausage is browned. Yield: 8 to 10 servings.

Beets in Orange Sauce

16	to 20 small beets, cooked and peeled, or 2 (16-ounce) cans small whole beets
2	tablespoons cornstarch
1¼	cups firmly packed light brown sugar
1	(6-ounce) can frozen orange juice concentrate, undiluted
¾	cup cider vinegar
1	tablespoon butter or margarine

Drain beets, reserving ¾ cup juice; set beets aside. Combine cornstarch, brown sugar, orange juice, vinegar, and reserved beet liquid. Cook until thick and clear, stirring constantly; stir in butter. Add beets, and heat thoroughly. Yield: 8 servings.

Gussied-Up Baked Beans

½	stalk celery, chopped
2	green peppers, chopped
2	large onions, chopped
1	clove garlic, minced
2	tablespoons bacon or ham drippings
2	(1-pound) cans pork and beans
½	cup dark corn syrup
¼	cup chopped salt meat
1	cup catsup
2½	tablespoons prepared mustard
2	tablespoons steak sauce
2	tablespoons Worcestershire sauce
½	teaspoon salt
½	teaspoon ground red pepper (optional)

Sauté celery, green pepper, onion, and garlic in bacon drippings. Add remaining ingredients, and bring to a boil. Spoon into a 3-quart beanpot or casserole; bake at 275° for 3 hours. Yield: 10 servings.

Stuffed Beets

6	medium-size beets
1	cup vinegar
½	teaspoon salt
¼	teaspoon pepper
¼	cup diced cooked potatoes
½	cup diced celery
1	hard-cooked egg, chopped
1	small green pepper, chopped
¼	cup mayonnaise
	Lettuce leaves

Leave rootlet and 1 inch of stem on beets; scrub with a brush. Place beets in a saucepan; add water to cover. Bring to a boil; cover and cook 35 to 40 minutes or until tender. Drain; pour cold water over beets, and drain.

Trim off beet stems and rootlets, and rub off skins; hollow out center of beets, using a melon-ball scoop or sharp paring knife. Set shells aside; pulp may be reserved for use in other dishes.

Combine vinegar, salt, pepper, potatoes, celery, egg, green pepper, and mayonnaise. Fill beet shells with vegetable mixture; serve on lettuce leaves. Yield: 6 servings.

Harvard Beets

12 *medium-size beets, cooked and drained*
¼ *cup sugar*
1 *tablespoon cornstarch*
¼ *teaspoon salt*
½ *cup vinegar*
¼ *cup grape jelly*
2 *tablespoons butter or margarine*
1 *teaspoon grated orange rind*

Remove skins from beets; slice, and set aside. Combine sugar, cornstarch, and salt in a saucepan. Blend in vinegar and jelly. Cook over medium heat, stirring constantly, until thickened and smooth. Add beets and butter; heat well, stirring occasionally. Garnish with orange rind. Yield: 6 servings.

Pickled Beets

3 *(16-ounce) cans whole or sliced beets*
1 *cup sugar*
2 *tablespoons cornstarch*
1 *cup vinegar*
24 *whole cloves*
3 *tablespoons catsup*
3 *tablespoons salad oil*
Dash of salt
1 *teaspoon vanilla extract*

Drain beets, reserving 1½ cups juice. Combine sugar and cornstarch in a large saucepan; add vinegar, cloves, catsup, oil, salt, and vanilla. Stir in reserved beet juice. Cook over medium heat 3 minutes, stirring until mixture thickens. Stir in beets; refrigerate overnight. Yield: about 10 servings.

Nippy Beets

2 *tablespoons butter or margarine*
1 *tablespoon cornstarch*
1 *tablespoon sugar*
¼ *teaspoon salt*
2 *tablespoons lemon juice*
⅔ *cup water*
2 *teaspoons horseradish*
8 *to 10 small beets, cooked and peeled, or 1 (16-ounce) can whole beets, drained*

Melt butter in a medium saucepan. Combine cornstarch, sugar, and salt; blend into butter. Stir in lemon juice and water; cook until thickened. Stir in horseradish. Pour over hot beets. Yield: 4 servings.

Ivy League Beets

1 *pound fresh beets*
1 *tablespoon cornstarch*
⅓ *cup water*
¼ *cup strawberry jelly*
2 *tablespoons lemon juice*
¼ *teaspoon salt*
¼ *teaspoon pumpkin pie spice*
2 *tablespoons butter or margarine*

Cook beets, covered, in a small amount of boiling salted water until tender (about 35 minutes). Drain, peel, and slice beets; set aside.

Combine cornstarch, ⅓ cup water, jelly, lemon juice, salt, and pumpkin pie spice. Cook, stirring constantly, over medium heat until mixture thickens and bubbles; stir in beets and butter. Heat thoroughly. Yield: 4 servings.

Beets with Pineapple

2 *tablespoons brown sugar*
1 *tablespoon cornstarch*
¼ *teaspoon salt*
1 *(8¼-ounce) can pineapple chunks*
1 *tablespoon butter or margarine*
1 *tablespoon lemon juice*
8 *to 10 small beets, cooked, peeled, and sliced, or 1 (16-ounce) can sliced beets, drained*

Combine brown sugar, cornstarch, and salt in a medium saucepan. Drain pineapple, reserving juice.

Stir pineapple juice into brown sugar mixture. Cook over medium heat, stirring constantly, until mixture thickens and bubbles. Stir in butter and lemon juice. Add beets and pineapple. Cook about 5 minutes or until thoroughly heated. Yield: about 4 servings.

Shredded Beets

1   *(1-pound) bunch beets, tops removed*
¼   *cup melted butter or margarine*
½   *teaspoon salt*
Dash of pepper
2   *tablespoons minced parsley*
1   *tablespoon lemon juice*

Wash, peel, and finely shred beets. Combine beets, butter, salt, and pepper in a skillet. Cover and cook over medium heat about 15 minutes or until beets are tender, stirring frequently. Sprinkle with parsley and lemon juice just before serving. Yield: 2 servings.

Broccoli and Egg Casserole

1   *(10-ounce) package frozen chopped broccoli or 2 cups chopped fresh broccoli*
½   *cup chopped onion*
1   *tablespoon butter or margarine*
1   *(10¾-ounce) can cream of mushroom soup, undiluted*
½   *teaspoon dry mustard*
½   *teaspoon salt*
4   *hard-cooked eggs, chopped*
1   *cup shredded Cheddar cheese*
1   *(3-ounce) can French-fried onions*

Cook broccoli in a small amount of boiling water just until tender; drain and set aside.

Sauté onion in butter until tender; stir in soup, mustard, and salt. Heat until bubbly.

Arrange half of broccoli in a 1-quart casserole; top with half of chopped egg, half of cheese, and half of mushroom sauce. Repeat layers. Bake at 350° for 20 minutes. Sprinkle onions over top; bake 5 more minutes. Yield: 6 servings.

Broccoli Soufflé

1   *pound fresh broccoli or 1 (10-ounce) package frozen chopped broccoli*
2   *tablespoons butter or margarine*
2   *tablespoons all-purpose flour*
½   *teaspoon salt*
½   *cup milk*
¼   *cup grated Parmesan cheese*
4   *eggs, separated*
Mushroom Sauce

Cook broccoli in a small amount of boiling water just until tender; drain and chop fine. Add butter to broccoli; cook and stir until butter is melted and moisture is evaporated. Set aside 2 tablespoons broccoli.

Blend flour and salt into remaining broccoli; stir in milk. Cook over medium heat, stirring constantly, until mixture thickens and bubbles. Remove from heat, and stir in Parmesan cheese.

Beat egg yolks until thick and lemon colored; stir in broccoli mixture. Pour Sauce over stiffly beaten egg whites; use a folding motion to mix thoroughly.

Pour mixture into an ungreased 1-quart soufflé dish. Bake at 350° for 20 minutes. Top with reserved broccoli; bake 15 minutes longer or until a knife inserted in center comes out clean. Serve with Mushroom Sauce. Yield: 4 to 6 servings.

Mushroom Sauce:

1   *(6-ounce) can sliced mushrooms, drained*
¼   *cup melted butter or margarine*
2   *tablespoons all-purpose flour*
Dash of salt and pepper
1   *cup water*
1   *chicken bouillon cube*
1   *tablespoon chopped pimiento*

Sauté mushrooms in butter until lightly browned; blend in flour, salt, and pepper. Add water and bouillon cube; cook until sauce is boiling, stirring constantly. Stir in pimiento; cook 1 to 2 minutes longer. Yield: about 2 cups.

Marinated Broccoli Supreme

1   teaspoon onion salt
1   teaspoon oregano
½   teaspoon thyme
1   teaspoon garlic salt
½   teaspoon pepper
½   teaspoon dry mustard
3   tablespoons white vinegar
⅔   cup salad oil
1   bunch fresh broccoli or 2 (10-ounce)
      packages frozen broccoli spears, cooked
      and drained
2   hard-cooked eggs, chopped
Lemon slices
Parsley

Combine first 8 ingredients in a mixing bowl; beat 1 minute at medium speed of electric mixer or process in a blender. Place broccoli in an 8-inch square dish; add marinade. Cover and refrigerate overnight.

Before serving, drain off marinade. Place broccoli in serving dish, and sprinkle with chopped eggs. Garnish with lemon slices and parsley. Yield: 6 servings.

Savory Broccoli Casserole

1   bunch fresh broccoli or 2 (10-ounce)
      packages frozen chopped broccoli
2   eggs, beaten
½   cup milk
1   (10¾-ounce) can cream of celery soup,
      undiluted
1   cup mayonnaise or salad dressing
1   cup shredded sharp Cheddar cheese
Buttered cracker crumbs

Cut broccoli into 1-inch pieces. Cook in a small amount of boiling salted water just until tender; drain. Combine eggs, milk, soup, mayonnaise, and cheese; stir in cooked broccoli.

Pour mixture into a greased 2-quart casserole, and sprinkle with cracker crumbs. Bake at 350° for 30 to 40 minutes or until golden brown. Let cool 15 minutes before serving. Yield: 6 to 8 servings.

Lemony Broccoli

2   (10-ounce) packages frozen broccoli
      spears
Salt and pepper to taste
Juice of 1 lemon
2   tablespoons butter or margarine

Place broccoli on a large piece of heavy-duty aluminum foil. Season with salt and pepper. Sprinkle with lemon juice, and dot with butter. Seal foil tightly, leaving a small amount of space for steam to escape.

Cook on grill about 10 minutes or to desired doneness, turning several times. Yield: 6 to 8 servings.

Broccoli Supreme

1   (10-ounce) package frozen chopped
      broccoli or 2 cups chopped fresh
      broccoli
3   carrots, sliced
1   (14-ounce) can artichoke hearts, drained
      and quartered
¾   (10¾-ounce) can cream of mushroom
      soup, undiluted
½   cup mayonnaise
2   eggs, slightly beaten
1   teaspoon lemon juice
1   teaspoon Worcestershire sauce
1   cup shredded sharp Cheddar cheese
Breadcrumbs
¼   cup melted butter or margarine
Garlic salt

Cook broccoli in a small amount of boiling water just until tender; drain and set aside. Cook carrots until tender in a small amount of boiling water; drain and set aside. Place artichokes in a buttered 9-inch shallow casserole.

Combine soup, mayonnaise, eggs, lemon juice, and Worcestershire sauce; mix well. Combine soup mixture, broccoli, and carrots; pour over artichokes. Sprinkle with cheese and breadcrumbs, and pour melted butter over top. Sprinkle with garlic salt. Bake at 350° for 25 minutes. Yield: 4 to 6 servings.

Sesame Broccoli

    2 *tablespoons salad oil*
    2 *tablespoons vinegar*
    2 *tablespoons soy sauce*
    8 *teaspoons sugar*
    2 *tablespoons sesame seeds, toasted*
    1 *large bunch broccoli, cooked and
       drained*

Combine first 5 ingredients in a small saucepan; bring to a boil. Remove from heat, and pour over broccoli. Yield: 6 to 8 servings.

Tangy Broccoli and Cauliflower

    2 *bunches broccoli*
    2 *heads cauliflower*
    1 *(4-ounce) jar whole pimientos, sliced*
    Lemon Sauce

Trim off large leaves of broccoli. Remove tough ends of lower stalks, and wash broccoli thoroughly. If stalks are more than 1 inch in diameter, make lengthwise slits in stalks. Cook broccoli, covered, in a small amount of boiling salted water 12 to 15 minutes or until crisp-tender. Drain.

Wash cauliflower, and remove green leaves. Separate cauliflower into flowerets. Cook, covered, in a small amount of boiling water about 10 minutes or just until tender. Drain.

Place vegetables on a serving platter; garnish with pimiento strips. Pour Lemon Sauce over vegetables. Yield: 16 servings.

Lemon Sauce:

    2 *tablespoons butter or margarine*
    2 *tablespoons all-purpose flour*
    ½ *cup water*
    ½ *cup lemon juice*
    5 *tablespoons sugar*
    Grated rind of 1 lemon
    ⅛ *teaspoon salt*

Melt butter in a saucepan; add flour, and stir over medium heat until smooth. Gradually add water and lemon juice; cook, stirring

constantly, until thick and smooth. Stir in sugar, lemon rind, and salt. Yield: about 1 cup.

Brussels Sprouts Medley

    ½ *cup chopped onion*
    2 *tablespoons melted margarine*
    2 *cups pared, sliced carrots*
    ¼ *teaspoon salt*
    ¼ *teaspoon hot sauce*
    1 *cup water*
    1 *chicken bouillon cube*
    ¼ *teaspoon marjoram leaves*
    ½ *pound fresh brussels sprouts or 1
       (10-ounce) package frozen brussels
       sprouts*

Sauté onion in margarine until tender. Add carrots, salt, hot sauce, water, and bouillon cube; cover and simmer 10 minutes. Add marjoram and brussels sprouts; cover and simmer 15 minutes. Yield: 4 to 5 servings.

★
Brussels Sprouts-Egg Bake

    1 *pound fresh or 2 (10-ounce) packages
       frozen brussels sprouts*
    1 *cup boiling water*
    3 *hard-cooked eggs, sliced*
    1 *cup shredded sharp pasteurized process
       American cheese*
    ¼ *cup milk*
    1 *(10¾-ounce) can cream of mushroom
       soup, undiluted*
    ½ *cup cornflake crumbs*
    2 *tablespoons melted butter or margarine*

Drop brussels sprouts in boiling water; return to a boil. Cover and cook 5 to 10 minutes or until tender; drain and cut sprouts in half. Place in a greased 10- x 6- x 1¾-inch baking dish. Arrange eggs over brussels sprouts; sprinkle with cheese.

Combine milk and soup; spoon over cheese. Combine cornflake crumbs and butter; sprinkle over top. Bake at 350° for 25 to 30 minutes. Yield: 6 to 8 servings.

Brussels Sprouts with Celery

2 *cups thinly sliced celery*
1 *medium-size onion, chopped*
3 *tablespoons melted butter or margarine*
3 *tablespoons all-purpose flour*
1 *teaspoon celery salt*
1 *(10¾-ounce) can chicken broth*
1 *pound fresh brussels sprouts or 2 (10-ounce) packages frozen brussels sprouts, cooked and drained*

Sauté celery and onion in butter in a small skillet; add flour and celery salt, blending until smooth. Gradually add chicken broth; cook over low heat, stirring constantly, until smooth and thickened. Add brussels sprouts; heat thoroughly, but do not boil. Yield: 6 to 8 servings.

Orange-Glazed Carrots

¼ *cup melted butter or margarine*
1 *teaspoon sugar*
1 *cup orange juice*
1 *pound carrots, peeled and sliced*

Combine all ingredients in a saucepan. Cover and simmer 15 to 20 minutes or until carrots are tender. Uncover and cook until liquid is absorbed. Yield: 4 to 6 servings.

Heavenly Carrots

4 *cups cooked sliced carrots*
1½ *cups croutons*
1¼ *cups shredded sharp Cheddar cheese*
2 *eggs, beaten*
¼ *cup half-and-half*
¼ *cup margarine, melted*
1 *teaspoon Worcestershire sauce*
1 *teaspoon salt*

Place carrots in a buttered 1½-quart casserole. Stir in croutons and cheese. Combine remaining ingredients, and pour over carrot mixture. Bake, uncovered, at 400° for 20 minutes or until brown. Yield: 6 servings.

★ Marinated Carrots

2 *pounds carrots, sliced*
1 *medium-size onion, sliced*
½ *green pepper, sliced*
1 *(10¾-ounce) can tomato soup, undiluted*
½ *cup vinegar*
½ *cup salad oil*
¾ *cup sugar*
1 *tablespoon prepared mustard*

Cook carrots until tender in a small amount of boiling salted water; drain. Combine carrots, onion, and green pepper; set aside.

Combine soup, vinegar, salad oil, sugar, and mustard; stir until well mixed. Pour over vegetables; toss lightly with a fork. Refrigerate overnight. Yield: 8 servings.

Sunday Carrots

2 *pounds carrots, peeled and sliced*
1 *large onion, finely chopped*
3 *tablespoons melted butter or margarine*
3 *tablespoons all-purpose flour*
2 *cups milk*
½ *teaspoon salt*
⅛ *teaspoon pepper*
1 *cup shredded Monterey Jack or Gruyère cheese*

Cook carrots and onion until tender in enough salted water to cover; drain.

Combine butter and flour; place over low heat, blending until smooth. Gradually add milk; cook, stirring constantly, until smooth and thickened. Add salt, pepper, and cheese, stirring until cheese melts.

Spoon cheese sauce over carrots and onion. Yield: 6 to 8 servings.

★
Lemony Carrots

    2   *tablespoons lemon juice*
    2   *tablespoons honey*
    ½   *cup water*
    2   *cups sliced carrots*
    2   *tablespoons melted margarine*
    2   *tablespoons minced fresh mint*

Combine lemon juice, honey, and water in a saucepan. Add carrots and bring to a boil; cover and simmer until tender. Drain carrots; dot with margarine, and sprinkle with mint. Yield: 4 servings.

Hawaiian Carrots

    6   *carrots, peeled and sliced*
    ½   *cup water*
    ⅛   *teaspoon salt*
    2   *tablespoons brown sugar*
    ½   *cup drained crushed pineapple*
    1   *tablespoon butter or margarine*
    2   *teaspoons cornstarch*

Combine carrots, water, and salt; cook until carrots are tender. Stir in brown sugar, pineapple, and butter.
   Make a smooth paste with cornstarch and a small amount of water; add to carrots. Cook over low heat, stirring constantly, until clear and thick. Yield: 4 servings.

Creole-Style Cabbage

    1   *small head cabbage*
    ½   *pound bulk sausage*
    1   *small onion, chopped*
    1   *clove garlic, minced*
    1   *(8-ounce) can tomato sauce*
    ¼   *teaspoon ground thyme*
    ½   *teaspoon salt*
    ¼   *teaspoon pepper*
    ¼   *teaspoon basil leaves*

Cut cabbage into 8 wedges. Sauté sausage, onion, and garlic in a skillet over low heat; drain. Add tomato sauce and seasonings; simmer 10 minutes.

Add cabbage wedges to sauce; cover and cook about 15 to 20 minutes. Add a small amount of water if sauce thickens too much. Yield: 6 servings.

Scalloped Cabbage

    1   *medium-size head cabbage, chopped*
    6   *slices bacon*
    2   *tablespoons chopped green pepper*
    1   *cup shredded Cheddar cheese, divided*
    2   *tablespoons chopped pimiento*
    White Sauce
    ½   *cup buttered breadcrumbs*

Cook cabbage, covered, 10 minutes in a small amount of boiling salted water; drain. Fry bacon until crisp, and drain on paper towels; crumble and set aside. Sauté green pepper in bacon drippings; drain.
   Place half of cabbage in a shallow 2½-quart casserole, and sprinkle with half of cheese; add bacon, pimiento, and green pepper. Top with remaining cabbage and cheese. Pour White Sauce over top, and sprinkle with breadcrumbs. Bake at 375° for 15 to 20 minutes. Yield: 6 to 8 servings.

White Sauce:

    3   *tablespoons melted butter or margarine*
    3   *tablespoons all-purpose flour*
    1½ *cups milk*
    ¾   *teaspoon salt*
    Dash of pepper
    Dash of paprika

Combine butter and flour in a small saucepan, blending until smooth. Cook over low heat until bubbly. Gradually add milk; cook, stirring constantly, until smooth and thickened. Stir in salt, pepper, and paprika. Yield: 1½ cups.

★ Layered Cabbage Casserole

  1 *medium-size head cabbage*
 ¼ *cup butter or margarine*
 ¼ *cup all-purpose flour*
 ½ *teaspoon salt*
 ¼ *teaspoon pepper*
  2 *cups evaporated milk*
 ¼ *cup chopped green pepper*
 ¼ *cup chopped sweet red pepper*
 ¼ *cup chopped onion*
 ⅔ *cup shredded Cheddar cheese*
 ½ *cup mayonnaise*
  3 *tablespoons chili sauce*

Cut cabbage into small wedges; cook in boiling salted water until tender. Drain.

Place wedges in a 13- x 9- x 2-inch baking dish. Set aside.

Melt butter in a small saucepan; stir in flour, ½ teaspoon salt, and pepper. Gradually stir in milk; cook over medium heat until thickened, stirring constantly. Pour sauce over cabbage wedges. Bake at 350° for 20 minutes.

Combine remaining ingredients, mixing well. Spoon over cabbage. Return to oven, and bake 20 minutes. Yield: about 8 servings.

★ Stuffed Cabbage

  1 *cup water*
  8 *to 10 cabbage leaves*
1½ *pounds ground beef*
 ½ *green pepper, chopped*
  1 *large onion, chopped*
1½ *teaspoons salt*
 ½ *teaspoon garlic salt*
 ½ *teaspoon pepper*
  3 *eggs, beaten*
 ¾ *cup uncooked regular rice*
  2 *tablespoons grated Romano cheese*
     (optional)
    Sauce

Bring 1 cup water to a boil in a Dutch oven; add cabbage leaves, and steam 5 minutes. Drain, reserving liquid for Sauce. Combine ground beef, green pepper, onion, seasonings, eggs, rice, and cheese; mix well.

Place about ¼ cup meat mixture on each cabbage leaf; roll up, turning edges in, and secure with toothpicks. Place rolls in a Dutch oven, and cover with Sauce. Cover and simmer 45 minutes. Yield: 8 to 10 rolls.

    Sauce:

  2 *cloves garlic, minced*
 ¼ *cup salad oil*
  2 *tablespoons all-purpose flour*
    Reserved cabbage liquid
  2 *(15-ounce) cans tomato sauce or 2*
     (1-pound) cans stewed tomatoes
  2 *teaspoons sugar*
  1 *teaspoon paprika*
 ½ *teaspoon pepper*
 ⅛ *teaspoon basil*
    Salt to taste

Sauté garlic in salad oil; remove from heat, and blend in flour. Gradually add reserved cabbage liquid, stirring until smooth. Add remaining ingredients, mixing well. Yield: about 5 cups.

Cauliflower Fritters

  1 *head cauliflower*
  1 *egg, beaten*
 ⅓ *cup milk*
  2 *teaspoons salad oil*
 ½ *teaspoon lemon juice*
  1 *cup all-purpose flour*
 ¼ *cup sugar*
  2 *teaspoons baking powder*
    Shortening

Wash cauliflower, and break into flowerets. Cook, covered, 8 minutes in a small amount of boiling salted water; drain well. Let cool.

Combine egg, milk, salad oil, and lemon juice in a small mixing bowl. Combine flour, sugar, and baking powder; gradually add to egg mixture, mixing well. (Batter will be thick.) Dip each floweret into batter, and deep fry in hot shortening over medium heat until golden brown. Yield: 4 servings.

Cauliflower au Gratin

1   *medium-size head cauliflower*
2   *tablespoons melted butter or margarine*
2   *tablespoons all-purpose flour*
1½ *cups milk*
½   *teaspoon salt*
¼   *teaspoon white pepper*
1   *cup grated Parmesan cheese*
1   *cup shredded Swiss cheese*
½   *cup chopped cooked ham*
½   *cup breadcrumbs*
¼   *cup melted butter or margarine*

Wash cauliflower, and break into flowerets. Cook, covered, in a small amount of boiling salted water about 10 minutes or until done; drain. Place in a 2-quart casserole; keep warm.

Combine 2 tablespoons butter and flour; cook over low heat until bubbly. Gradually add milk; cook, stirring constantly, until smooth and thickened. Season with salt and pepper. Add cheese, stirring until melted; add ham. Spoon sauce over cauliflower.

Sauté breadcrumbs in ¼ cup butter until golden; spoon over sauce. Yield: 4 servings.

Cauliflower with Peas and Mushrooms

1   *large head cauliflower*
2   *(10-ounce) packages frozen green peas*
¼   *cup melted margarine*
1   *(4-ounce) can mushroom slices, drained*
6   *tablespoons melted butter*
¼   *cup water*
¼   *teaspoon salt*
4   *egg yolks, beaten*
3   *tablespoons lemon juice*
Dash of cayenne

Wash cauliflower, and remove large outer leaves. Cook, covered, in a small amount of boiling salted water until just tender (about 20 minutes); drain. Place in a serving bowl.

Cook peas according to package directions; drain. Add ¼ cup margarine and mushrooms. Spoon around cauliflower. Set aside, and keep warm.

Combine 6 tablespoons butter, water, salt, and egg yolks in top of a double boiler. Cook over boiling water, stirring constantly, until smooth and thickened. Stir in lemon juice and cayenne. Serve as a sauce for cauliflower and peas. Yield: 6 to 8 servings.

★ Fried Cauliflower

1   *medium-size cauliflower*
1   *cup seasoned breadcrumbs*
¼   *cup all-purpose flour*
Salt and pepper to taste
Hot cooking oil

Break cauliflower into flowerets. Cook in a small amount of boiling salted water about 10 minutes; drain. Combine breadcrumbs, flour, salt, and pepper. Coat cauliflower with flour mixture. Fry in hot oil until golden brown. Yield: 4 servings.

Cauliflower Delight

1   *medium-size head cauliflower, sliced*
2   *stalks celery, chopped*
1   *medium-size green pepper, chopped*
1   *(2-ounce) jar pimientos, drained*
¾   *cup sliced stuffed olives*
½   *pound Cheddar cheese, cubed*
1   *(8-ounce) bottle Caesar salad dressing*
1   *(8-ounce) carton commercial sour cream*
3   *tablespoons olive juice*

Combine all ingredients, mixing well. Refrigerate several hours or overnight. Yield: 6 to 8 servings.

Far East Celery

      4 *cups 1-inch celery slices*
      1 *(8-ounce) can water chestnuts, drained*
          and sliced
      1 *(10¾-ounce) can cream of chicken soup,*
          undiluted
      ¼ *cup chopped pimiento*
      ¼ *teaspoon salt*
      ½ *cup chow mein noodles*
      ¼ *cup slivered almonds*
      2 *tablespoons melted butter or margarine*

Cook celery in a small amount of boiling salted water just until tender (about 6 to 8 minutes); drain. Combine celery with water chestnuts, soup, pimiento, and salt; mix well, and pour the mixture into a lightly greased 1½-quart casserole.

Combine chow mein noodles, almonds, and butter; toss lightly, and sprinkle over celery mixture. Bake at 350° for 35 minutes. Yield: 6 servings.

Celery Parmigiana

      2 *large bunches celery*
      2 *tablespoons melted butter or margarine*
      ⅓ *cup boiling water*
      2 *chicken bouillon cubes*
      ½ *cup chopped ham or 1 (2½-ounce) can*
          deviled ham
      1 *(8-ounce) can tomato sauce, divided*
          Salt and pepper to taste
      ½ *cup grated Parmesan cheese*

Wash and trim celery; slice ribs diagonally into ½-inch slices. Sauté celery slices in butter in a large skillet over medium heat about 10 minutes, stirring occasionally.

Combine boiling water and bouillon cubes, stirring until dissolved. Add ham, half of tomato sauce, and bouillon to celery; mix well, and cook 5 minutes longer. Remove from heat, and season with salt and pepper.

Spoon mixture into a greased 2-quart shallow casserole; sprinkle with cheese and remaining tomato sauce. Bake at 300° for 30 minutes. Yield: 8 servings.

Celery Amandine

      ⅓ *cup slivered almonds*
      2 *tablespoons butter or margarine*
      2 *tablespoons dry white wine*
      1 *tablespoon instant minced onion*
      1 *chicken bouillon cube, crushed*
      1 *teaspoon monosodium glutamate*
      ½ *teaspoon sugar*
      ⅛ *teaspoon garlic powder*
      ⅛ *teaspoon ground ginger*
      6 *cups diagonally sliced celery*

Sauté almonds in butter until lightly browned; stir in remaining ingredients. Cover; cook 5 to 8 minutes or until celery is crisp-tender, stirring several times. Do not overcook. Serve immediately. Yield: 6 servings.

Creamy Celery Bake

      4 *cups thinly sliced celery*
      6 *tablespoons melted butter or margarine,*
          divided
      3 *tablespoons all-purpose flour*
      1 *teaspoon salt*
      1 *cup milk*
      1 *(4-ounce) can chopped mushrooms,*
          drained
      2 *tablespoons chopped green pepper*
      2 *tablespoons chopped pimiento*
      1 *cup shredded sharp Cheddar cheese*
      1 *cup breadcrumbs*

Sauté celery in 4 tablespoons butter about 5 minutes or until tender. Remove celery, and set aside.

Add flour and salt to butter in skillet, blending until smooth. Gradually add milk; cook over low heat, stirring constantly, until smooth and thickened. Add mushrooms, green pepper, pimiento, and cheese, stirring until cheese is melted. Stir in celery.

Spoon into a lightly greased 10- x 6- x 1½-inch baking dish. Combine breadcrumbs and remaining 2 tablespoons butter; sprinkle over celery mixture. Bake at 350° for 20 minutes. Yield: 6 to 8 servings.

Fried Corn

About 2½ to 3 cups fresh corn cut from
   cob
3 tablespoons melted butter or margarine
3 tablespoons bacon drippings
½ cup boiling water
½ teaspoon salt
Dash of pepper

Combine corn, butter, bacon drippings, and
boiling water; cook over high heat 5 minutes,
stirring constantly. Reduce heat; cover and
cook an additional 15 minutes, stirring occasionally. Stir in salt and pepper. Yield: about
4 servings.

Grilled Corn on the Cob

6 ears fresh corn
Melted butter
Salt and pepper

Husk corn right before cooking. Brush with
melted butter, and sprinkle with salt and
pepper. Wrap each ear tightly in aluminum
foil. Roast on grill 10 to 20 minutes, turning
frequently. Yield: 6 servings.

Corn Relish

About 18 ears of corn
4 cups chopped cabbage
1 cup chopped sweet red pepper
1 cup chopped green pepper
1 cup chopped onion
1 tablespoon celery seeds
1 tablespoon salt
1 tablespoon turmeric
3 tablespoons mustard seeds
1 cup water
4 cups vinegar
2 cups sugar

Cook corn in boiling water 5 minutes; cut
from cob, and measure 8 cups. Combine corn
with remaining ingredients, and simmer 10
to 15 minutes. Bring to a boil; pack in hot,
sterilized jars. Seal. Process 15 minutes in
boiling-water bath. Yield: about 6 pints.

Corn Sauté

8 ears of corn
¼ cup butter or margarine
1 medium-size onion, thinly sliced
1 small green pepper, cut into ¼-inch
   strips
1½ teaspoons salt
¼ teaspoon oregano
2 tomatoes, cut in wedges
2 tablespoons half-and-half

Cut corn from cob. Melt butter in a skillet
over medium heat. Add corn, onion, green
pepper, salt, and oregano; cover and cook 7
minutes, stirring occasionally. Add tomatoes
and half-and-half. Simmer, uncovered, 2
more minutes or until tomatoes are hot but
still firm. Yield: 6 to 8 servings.

Maque Choux

12 ears corn
2 tablespoons butter or margarine, melted
1 medium-size onion, finely chopped
2 tablespoons canned tomatoes and green
   chiles
½ medium-size green pepper, finely
   chopped
¼ to ½ teaspoon sugar
Salt and pepper to taste

Cut corn from cob, scraping cob to remove
pulp. Combine corn and remaining ingredients in a heavy saucepan. Cook over low
heat 20 to 30 minutes or until corn is tender,
stirring frequently. Yield: 6 to 8 servings.

Corn Fritters

3 cups fresh corn cut from cob
2 eggs, beaten
¼ cup milk
6 tablespoons all-purpose flour
1½ teaspoons baking powder
½ teaspoon salt
3 tablespoons melted butter
Salad oil

Cook corn in a small amount of water until tender; drain. Combine eggs, milk, flour, baking powder, and salt; mix well. Stir in corn and butter.

For each fritter, pour about ¼ cup batter onto a hot, lightly greased griddle. Cook until golden brown on one side; turn and brown other side. Drain on paper towels. Yield: 6 servings.

Corn Pudding

    2   cups fresh corn cut from cob
    3   eggs, beaten
    About 1 cup milk
    2   to 4 tablespoons sugar
    3   tablespoons melted butter
    ¼   teaspoon salt

Combine all ingredients, mixing well. Pour into a lightly greased 1½-quart baking dish. Bake at 350° about 45 minutes or until knife inserted in center comes out clean. Yield: about 4 servings.

Note: The amount of milk will vary with the maturity of the corn. Very tender corn will need less milk; mature corn will need more.

★
Corn and Cheese Soufflé

    1   cup hot milk
    1½ cups soft breadcrumbs
    1½ cups shredded Cheddar cheese
    1   (17-ounce) can cream-style corn
    2   tablespoons melted butter or margarine
    ¾   teaspoon salt
    ¼   teaspoon pepper
    3   eggs, separated

Combine all ingredients except eggs, mixing well. Beat egg yolks until thick, and stir into corn mixture. Beat egg whites until stiff but not dry, and fold into mixture. Pour into a greased 2-quart casserole or soufflé dish.

Bake at 400° for 45 minutes or until a knife inserted in center comes out clean. Yield: 8 servings.

Fresh Corn Soufflé

    1   tablespoon melted butter or margarine
    1   tablespoon all-purpose flour
    ½   cup milk
    1   teaspoon salt
    ¼   teaspoon paprika
    ½   teaspoon pepper
    ¼   cup chopped pimiento
    2   cups fresh corn cut from cob
    2   eggs, separated

Combine butter and flour, blending well; cook over low heat about 1 minute. Gradually stir in milk; cook until smooth and thickened, stirring constantly. Cool. Add remaining ingredients except egg whites; mix well. Fold in stiffly beaten egg whites.

Pour into a lightly greased 1-quart casserole or soufflé dish; set in a pan of water. Bake at 375° for 30 to 35 minutes or until firm. Yield: 6 servings.

Cucumber in Sour Cream

    ½   cup commercial sour cream
    1   tablespoon minced onion
    ¼   teaspoon salt
    Pepper to taste
    1   medium-size cucumber, peeled and
            thinly sliced

Combine all the ingredients. Chill. Yield: 2 servings.

Cucumbers and Tomatoes in Yogurt

    2   (8-ounce) cartons plain yogurt
    3   medium-size cucumbers, peeled, seeded,
            and finely chopped
    3   medium-size tomatoes, finely chopped
    1   medium-size onion, finely chopped
    Salt and pepper to taste

Combine all ingredients, tossing lightly; cover and refrigerate several hours. Yield: 6 to 8 servings.

Cucumber Casserole

6 *large cucumbers, peeled and diced*
2 *cups water*
6 *slices bacon*
1 *medium-size onion, chopped*
2 *medium-size green peppers, chopped*
6 *medium-size tomatoes, peeled and*
chopped
1 *cup breadcrumbs*
1 *teaspoon salt*
⅛ *teaspoon pepper*
1 *cup shredded pasteurized process*
American or Cheddar cheese
Hot cooked rice (optional)

Combine cucumber and water in a saucepan; bring to a boil. Cover and simmer 15 minutes or until tender. Drain well.

Cook bacon until crisp, and drain well on paper towels; reserve 3 tablespoons bacon drippings. Crumble bacon, and set aside.

Sauté onion and green pepper in reserved bacon drippings 5 minutes; drain well on paper towels.

Combine vegetables, bacon, breadcrumbs, salt, and pepper; spoon into a 2-quart casserole. Sprinkle with cheese. Bake at 350° for 30 minutes. Serve over rice, if desired. Yield: 6 servings.

Eggplant Soufflé

1 *eggplant, peeled, cooked, and mashed*
½ *(10¾-ounce) can cream of mushroom*
soup, undiluted
¾ *cup soft breadcrumbs*
½ *cup shredded sharp Cheddar cheese*
2 *teaspoons grated onion*
1 *tablespoon catsup*
1 *teaspoon salt*
2 *eggs, separated*

Combine eggplant, soup, breadcrumbs, cheese, onion, catsup, salt, and egg yolks; mix well. Beat egg whites until stiff but not dry; fold into eggplant mixture. Pour into a greased 2-quart casserole or soufflé dish.

Bake at 375° for 45 minutes or until a knife inserted in center comes out clean. Yield: 6 to 8 servings.

Fried Eggplant Strips

1 *medium-size eggplant*
1½ *teaspoons salt, divided*
1 *cup all-purpose flour*
1 *egg, slightly beaten*
1 *cup milk*
1 *tablespoon salad oil*
Hot salad oil

Peel eggplant, and cut into finger-size strips. Sprinkle with 1 teaspoon salt; cover with water, and soak 1 hour. Drain and pat dry with paper towels.

Combine flour and ½ teaspoon salt in a mixing bowl. Add egg, milk, and 1 tablespoon salad oil; beat until smooth. Dip eggplant strips in batter, and fry in hot oil until golden brown; drain well. Yield: 6 servings.

Creole Eggplant

1 *medium-size eggplant, peeled and cubed*
1 *medium-size green pepper, chopped*
1 *medium-size onion, chopped*
1 *(8-ounce) can tomato sauce*
Salt and pepper to taste

Combine all ingredients in a skillet; cover and cook over low heat 15 to 20 minutes or until vegetables are tender. Yield: 6 servings.

Ratatouille

2½ *cups thinly sliced onion*
2 *teaspoons minced garlic*
¼ *cup salad oil*
2 *pounds eggplant, peeled and cubed*
2 *pounds zucchini, sliced*
3 *pounds tomatoes, quartered*
½ *cup chopped parsley*
2 *teaspoons basil*
Salt and pepper to taste

Sauté onion and garlic in oil until crisp-tender. Add eggplant, and cook 10 minutes; add zucchini, and cook 5 minutes. Add remaining ingredients. Cover and cook over low heat 30 minutes, stirring frequently. Serve hot or cold. Yield: 8 to 10 servings.

Eggplant Appetizer la Roma

1   *medium-size eggplant*
1   *large firm-ripe tomato, chopped*
1   *medium-size onion, sliced and separated*
      into rings
1   *medium-size green pepper, chopped*
¼   *cup olive oil*
1   *to 1½ teaspoons salt*

Trim stem end from eggplant. Place whole, unpeeled eggplant in skillet; cook over low heat, turning frequently, until skin breaks and outside feels soft to touch. Allow eggplant to cool; then peel and chop.

Combine all ingredients in an airtight container, and store at room temperature for several hours. Yield: about 6 servings.

★ Eggplant Parmigiana

2   *(1-pound) eggplants*
2   *tablespoons salad oil*
1   *pound ground beef*
1   *large onion, finely chopped*
1   *green pepper, finely chopped*
1   *(16-ounce) can tomatoes, drained and*
      chopped
1   *(8-ounce) can tomato sauce*
1   *tablespoon chopped fresh parsley*
1   *teaspoon salt*
¼   *teaspoon pepper*
½   *teaspoon oregano*
1   *teaspoon Worcestershire sauce*
1½ *cups breadcrumbs*
⅓   *cup grated Parmesan cheese*
1   *(6-ounce) package sliced mozzarella*
      cheese

Wash eggplant, and cut in half lengthwise. Remove pulp, leaving a ¼-inch shell; set shells aside. Chop pulp, and sauté in salad oil 5 minutes or until tender; drain on paper towels.

Combine ground beef, onion, and green pepper in skillet; cook until beef is brown and vegetables are tender. Drain pan drippings from skillet. Add pulp, tomatoes, tomato sauce, and seasonings; simmer 10 minutes. Stir in breadcrumbs and Parmesan cheese.

Stuff shells with eggplant mixture, and top with mozzarella cheese. Bake at 350° for 20 minutes. Yield: 4 servings.

★ Eggplant Moussaka

1½ *pounds ground beef*
3   *tablespoons chopped onion*
1   *cup tomato sauce*
2   *tablespoons minced parsley*
1   *cup water*
⅛   *teaspoon ground cinnamon*
Salt and pepper to taste
3   *medium-size eggplants*
Hot olive oil
2   *cups shredded mozzarella cheese,*
      divided
½   *cup plus 2 tablespoons all-purpose flour*
½   *cup melted butter or margarine*
1   *(13-ounce) can evaporated milk*
1   *cup water*
1   *teaspoon ground nutmeg*
2   *eggs, well beaten*

Combine ground beef and onion; sauté until beef is no longer red in color. Pour off drippings. Add tomato sauce, parsley, 1 cup water, cinnamon, salt, and pepper to ground beef mixture; cover and simmer 45 minutes.

Peel eggplants, and slice into ¼-inch slices. Sauté eggplant in olive oil until slightly tender; drain and cool. Arrange slices in a lightly greased 13- x 9- x 2-inch pan; top with meat mixture, and sprinkle with 1 cup mozzarella cheese.

Combine flour and butter in a medium saucepan, blending until smooth; cook over low heat 1 minute. Gradually add milk and 1 cup water; cook, stirring constantly, until smooth and thickened. Add salt to taste. Remove from heat; stir in nutmeg, eggs, and remaining cheese. Pour over meat mixture. Bake at 350° for 45 to 50 minutes or until golden brown. Cool slightly before cutting into squares. Yield: 6 to 8 servings.

Eggplant-Cheese Casserole

1   medium-size eggplant
1   cup onion and garlic croutons
1   cup shredded Cheddar cheese, divided
½   cup milk
1   tablespoon all-purpose flour
½   teaspoon salt
¼   teaspoon pepper
¼   teaspoon oregano
1   teaspoon butter or margarine

Peel eggplant, and cut into ¾-inch cubes. Cook, covered, in boiling salted water 3 minutes; drain. Combine eggplant, croutons, and ½ cup cheese; spoon mixture into a lightly greased 1-quart casserole.

Combine milk, flour, salt, pepper, and oregano; pour over eggplant mixture. Top with remaining cheese, and dot with butter. Cover and bake at 350° for 20 minutes; remove cover, and continue baking 5 to 10 additional minutes or until lightly browned. Yield: 4 servings.

Sautéed Mushrooms

2   tablespoons minced onion
¼   cup melted butter or margarine
1   pound fresh mushrooms, cleaned and
       thickly sliced
1   teaspoon lemon juice
½   teaspoon salt or seasoned salt
⅛   teaspoon pepper

Sauté onion in butter until tender. Add mushrooms; sauté over medium heat, stirring occasionally, 10 minutes. Sprinkle with lemon juice, salt, and pepper; stir lightly. Yield: 4 servings.

Mushroom Newberg

1   pound fresh mushrooms, cleaned and
       halved
1   to 2 tablespoons all-purpose flour
¼   cup melted butter or margarine
1¼ cups half-and-half
¼   cup dry sherry
¼   teaspoon salt
⅛   teaspoon ground nutmeg
3   egg yolks, beaten
4   frozen patty shells

Dredge mushrooms in flour. Sauté mushrooms in butter 5 minutes; add half-and-half, sherry, salt, and nutmeg. Simmer 2 minutes. Add 3 to 4 tablespoons hot mixture to egg yolks. Stir egg yolk mixture into mushroom mixture; cook, stirring constantly, 2 minutes or until mixture bubbles.

Prepare patty shells according to package directions. Spoon mushroom mixture into shells. Yield: 4 servings.

Mushroom-Cheese Bake

½   cup chopped celery
¼   cup chopped onion
3   tablespoons melted butter or margarine
½   pound fresh mushrooms, cleaned and
       sliced
4   cups cubed day-old whole wheat bread,
       divided
2   cups shredded Cheddar cheese, divided
2   eggs, beaten
2   cups milk
2   teaspoons dry mustard
1   teaspoon salt
½   teaspoon pepper

Sauté celery and onion in butter until crisp-tender; stir in mushrooms, and cook 5 minutes. Layer 2 cups bread cubes, half the mushroom mixture, and 1 cup cheese in a lightly greased 2-quart casserole; repeat layers.

Combine eggs, milk, and seasonings; beat until well mixed. Pour evenly over bread-mushroom mixture. Bake at 325° for 45 minutes. Let casserole stand 5 minutes before serving. Yield: 6 to 8 servings.

Mushroom Delight

1   *pound fresh mushrooms, cleaned and halved*
1   *cup sukiyaki sauce or soy sauce*
½   *cup water*
3   *to 4 tablespoons butter or margarine*

Place mushrooms in a shallow casserole. Combine sukiyaki sauce and water. Pour over mushrooms; dot with butter. Bake at 350° for 20 minutes. Yield: 4 to 6 servings.

★ Crab-Stuffed Mushrooms

12   *large or 18 medium-size mushrooms*
2   *tablespoons salad oil*
1   *(6-ounce) package frozen crabmeat, thawed and drained*
1   *egg, lightly beaten*
2   *tablespoons mayonnaise*
2   *tablespoons chopped onion*
1   *teaspoon lemon juice*
½   *cup soft breadcrumbs, divided*
2   *tablespoons butter or margarine, melted*

Gently rinse mushrooms, and pat dry. Remove stems. Brush caps with salad oil, and place in a buttered baking dish.

Combine crabmeat, egg, mayonnaise, onion, lemon juice, and ¼ cup breadcrumbs. Stuff caps with crabmeat mixture. Combine remaining ¼ cup breadcrumbs with butter; sprinkle over crab mixture. Bake at 375° for 15 minutes. Yield: 6 servings.

Note: Mushroom stems may be frozen for use in soups and sauces.

Baked Okra and Cheese

2   *(10-ounce) packages frozen whole okra, partially thawed*
Salt and pepper to taste
1½   *teaspoons butter or margarine*
4   *slices bacon, cut into 2-inch pieces*
1½   *cups shredded sharp Cheddar cheese*

Place okra in a single layer in a greased 9-inch square baking dish. Sprinkle with salt and pepper; dot with butter. Arrange bacon over okra, and cover tightly with aluminum foil.

Bake at 375° for 1 hour; remove foil. Place under broiler until bacon is brown and crisp. Sprinkle with cheese. Cover with foil, and bake at 375° for 10 minutes. Yield: 6 servings.

Okra-Onion Casserole

2   *cups sliced okra*
1   *small onion, chopped*
1   *cup buttered breadcrumbs, divided*
½   *cup shredded Cheddar cheese*
2   *tablespoons melted butter or margarine*
1   *egg, beaten*
½   *teaspoon salt*
½   *teaspoon pepper*

Combine all ingredients except ¼ cup breadcrumbs. Spoon into a lightly greased 1½-quart casserole. Bake at 350° for 30 minutes. Sprinkle with reserved breadcrumbs, and bake 5 additional minutes. Yield: 4 servings.

Fried Okra

4   *cups okra*
All-purpose flour
4   *slices bacon, coarsely chopped*
Bacon drippings
2   *cups peeled and chopped fresh tomatoes*
Salt and pepper to taste

Wash okra well; drain. Cut off tip and stem ends; cut okra crosswise into ½-inch slices, and dredge in flour.

Cook bacon until crisp; remove from skillet, and set aside. Fry okra in bacon drippings, turning often until browned; add bacon drippings as needed.

Add tomatoes to okra; stir in bacon, salt, and pepper. Simmer until tomatoes are tender, stirring often. Yield: 6 to 8 servings.

Okra with Cheese

1 *pound okra*
2 *eggs, beaten*
All-purpose flour
2 *teaspoons paprika*
Salad oil
1 *cup shredded Cheddar cheese*
Salt and pepper to taste

Wash okra well; drain. Cut off tip and stem ends; cut okra crosswise into ½-inch slices. Dip okra in egg, then in flour seasoned with paprika. Fry in hot oil until brown and crisp; drain slightly.

Add cheese, salt, and pepper to okra; stir gently to coat. Serve immediately. Yield: 4 to 5 servings.

Baked Onions and Cheese

6 *medium-size onions, peeled*
Salt to taste
Lemon-pepper seasoning to taste
Butter or margarine
½ *to ¾ cup shredded Cheddar cheese*
Paprika

Cook onions until tender in enough water to cover; drain well. Arrange in a shallow baking dish.

Sprinkle onions with salt and lemon-pepper seasoning. Place a pat of butter and a small amount of cheese in center of each onion. Sprinkle with paprika. Bake at 375° for 5 to 7 minutes or until cheese melts. Yield: 6 servings.

Pickled Onion Rings

1 *cup water*
1 *cup white or tarragon vinegar*
¼ *cup sugar*
½ *teaspoon salt*
2 *sticks cinnamon, broken into pieces*
6 *whole cloves*
2 *medium-size sweet Spanish or Bermuda onions, thinly sliced*
2 *medium-size red onions, thinly sliced*

Combine water, vinegar, sugar, salt, and spices; simmer 10 minutes. Strain and cool.

Separate onion slices into rings; place in a widemouthed jar. Pour vinegar mixture over onion rings. Cover and chill several hours or overnight. Yield: 8 to 10 servings.

★
French-Fried Onion Rings

3 *or 4 large Spanish or Bermuda onions*
2 *to 3 cups buttermilk or ice water*
1 *egg, beaten*
1 *teaspoon salt*
1½ *teaspoons baking powder*
⅔ *cup water*
1 *cup all-purpose flour*
1 *tablespoon salad oil*
1 *teaspoon lemon juice*
¼ *teaspoon cayenne pepper*
Salad oil

Peel onions and slice about ⅜ inch thick; separate into rings. Pour buttermilk into a shallow pan; add onion rings, and allow to soak 30 minutes.

Combine egg, salt, baking powder, water, flour, 1 tablespoon salad oil, lemon juice, and cayenne pepper; stir until smooth.

Heat salad oil to 375°. Remove onion rings from buttermilk, and dip into batter; fry in hot oil until golden brown. Drain on paper towels. Yield: 6 to 8 servings.

Peas and Mushrooms Elegant

Outer leaves of iceberg lettuce
1 *(16-ounce) package frozen green peas*
2 *tablespoons butter or margarine*
½ *teaspoon salt*
⅛ *teaspoon pepper*
Dash of ground nutmeg
6 *mushrooms, sliced*
1 *tablespoon melted butter or margarine*

Dip lettuce leaves in cold water; do not shake water from leaves. Make a nest of lettuce in a heavy saucepan; place peas in center of leaves. Add 2 tablespoons butter, salt, pepper, and nutmeg; cover peas with lettuce leaves. Cover tightly, and cook over low heat

15 minutes or to desired doneness. Discard lettuce leaves.

Sauté mushrooms in 1 tablespoon butter 5 minutes. Combine peas and mushrooms. Yield: 6 servings.

Baked Stuffed Onions

    8 *large Spanish onions*
    ½ *pound bulk pork sausage*
    ½ *cup chopped onion*
    1 *cup soft breadcrumbs*
    2 *tablespoons chopped parsley*
    1 *(7-ounce) can whole kernel corn,*
       drained
    2 *tablespoons melted butter or margarine*
    ½ *teaspoon paprika*

Peel onions, and cut a slice from top. Cook onions in boiling salted water about 12 minutes or until tender but not mushy. Cool; remove center of onions, leaving shells intact. Reserve onion centers for use in other recipes.

Cook sausage until browned, stirring to crumble; drain, reserving pan drippings. Sauté ½ cup chopped onion in sausage drippings until tender. Combine sausage, sautéed onion, breadcrumbs, parsley, and corn. Fill onion shells with sausage mixture; place in a greased shallow pan.

Combine butter and paprika; brush on onions. Cover and bake at 400° for 15 minutes. Remove cover, and bake an additional 5 minutes. Yield: 8 servings.

Peas and Cauliflowerets

    2   *tablespoons salad oil*
    1½ *cups small cauliflowerets*
    1   *(10-ounce) package frozen green peas*
    1   *pimiento, cut into ¼-inch strips*
        Salt and pepper to taste

Heat oil in a heavy skillet. Add cauliflowerets; cover and cook over low heat 10 minutes, shaking skillet occasionally to prevent sticking. Add peas; increase heat to medium.Cover and cook 5 to 8 minutes or until vegetables are crisp-tender. Stir in pimiento, salt, and pepper. Yield: 4 to 6 servings.

Dressed Up Peas

    2 *(10-ounce) packages frozen green peas*
    2 *tablespoons butter or margarine*
    1 *tablespoon grated orange rind*
    2 *tablespoons mint jelly*
    ¼ *teaspoon salt*
    1 *(5-ounce) can water chestnuts, drained*
       and sliced

Cook peas according to package directions. Melt butter in a small saucepan; add orange rind, jelly, and salt. Heat until jelly is melted, blending well. Stir water chestnuts into peas just before serving; heat. Pour jelly mixture over peas; stir and heat thoroughly. Yield: about 6 servings.

Barbecued Black-Eyes

    1   *cup dried black-eyed peas*
    1½ *cups boiling water*
    1   *teaspoon salt*
    ¼   *pound ground beef*
    ½   *medium-size onion, chopped*
    ½   *cup commercial barbecue sauce*
    1   *tablespoon prepared mustard*
    3   *tablespoons brown sugar*

Cook peas in boiling water with salt until peas are barely tender; add more water if necessary. Pour off half of liquid. Brown ground beef and onion; add to peas. Stir in barbecue sauce, mustard, and sugar. Bake at 200° for 1 to 1½ hours. Yield: 4 to 6 servings.

Southern Caviar

    2 *(15-ounce) cans black-eyed peas,*
       drained
    ⅓ *cup salad oil*
    ⅓ *cup wine vinegar*
    1 *clove garlic*
    ¼ *cup finely chopped onion*
    ½ *teaspoon salt*
       Cracked pepper to taste

Combine all ingredients; cover and chill 24 hours. Remove garlic. Chill 2 days to 2 weeks before serving. Yield: 6 to 8 servings.

Southern Black-Eyed Peas

1 *pound dried black-eyed peas*
3 *ham hocks*
2 *tablespoons bacon drippings*
1 *medium-size onion, minced*
1 *to 1½ teaspoons salt*
¼ *teaspoon pepper*

Sort and wash peas well. Place in a heavy saucepan or Dutch oven; cover with water. Bring to a boil, and boil 2 minutes. Cover and let soak 1 hour.

Add remaining ingredients to peas. Boil gently, not completely covered with lid, until tender (about 1 to 1½ hours).

Remove ham hocks from saucepan. Remove meat from bones, and return to peas. Yield: 8 servings.

Peas and Rice

1 *(10-ounce) package frozen green peas*
⅓ *cup finely chopped onion*
2 *tablespoons finely chopped parsley*
6 *tablespoons melted butter or margarine, divided*
1 *cup uncooked regular rice*
2 *cups water*
1 *teaspoon salt*
2 *tablespoons grated Parmesan cheese*

Cook peas according to package directions; drain and set aside.

Sauté onion and parsley in 4 tablespoons butter for 5 minutes. Add rice and sauté 5 minutes, stirring occasionally. Add water and salt; bring to a boil. Reduce heat; cover and simmer about 15 minutes or until liquid

is absorbed. Add peas and remaining butter. To serve, sprinkle with cheese. Yield: 6 servings.

Petits Pois and Asparagus

2 *(15-ounce) cans asparagus, drained*
2 *(17-ounce) cans small green peas, drained*
1 *(10¾-ounce) can cream of celery soup, undiluted*
1 *(4-ounce) can sliced mushrooms, drained*
¼ *cup shredded sharp Cheddar cheese*
1 *cup soft breadcrumbs*
2 *tablespoons melted margarine*

Arrange half the asparagus in a buttered 8-inch square baking dish. Combine peas, soup, mushrooms, and cheese, blending well; spoon half of mixture over asparagus. Repeat layers. Combine breadcrumbs and margarine; sprinkle over soup mixture. Bake at 350° about 30 minutes or until the breadcrumbs are lightly browned. Yield: 6 servings.

Green Peas Oriental

2 *(10-ounce) packages frozen green peas*
1 *pound mushrooms, sliced*
4 *tablespoons melted butter or margarine*
2 *(8-ounce) cans water chestnuts, drained and sliced*
1 *(16-ounce) can bean sprouts, rinsed and drained*
2 *(10¾-ounce) cans cream of mushroom soup, undiluted*
2 *(3-ounce) cans French-fried onion rings*

Cook peas according to package directions; drain.

Sauté mushrooms in butter 3 to 5 minutes. Combine all ingredients except onion rings; spoon into a greased 3-quart casserole. Bake, uncovered, at 350° for 30 minutes. Sprinkle onion rings on top of vegetables, and bake at 350° for 5 minutes. Yield: 12 servings.

Festive Green Peas

2 *(10-ounce) packages frozen green peas*
¾ *cup finely chopped onion*
¼ *cup finely chopped green pepper*
2 *tablespoons finely chopped pimiento*
1 *tablespoon chopped parsley*
½ *bay leaf*
3 *tablespoons melted butter or margarine*
½ *teaspoon salt*
⅛ *teaspoon ground nutmeg*
½ *teaspoon vinegar*
   Pinch of sugar

Cook peas according to package directions; drain.

Sauté onion, green pepper, pimiento, parsley, and bay leaf in butter 5 minutes or until vegetables are tender. Remove bay leaf. Stir in peas and other ingredients; heat thoroughly. Yield: 6 servings.

Peas with Bacon

4 *slices bacon*
1 *medium-size onion, chopped*
2 *tablespoons melted butter or margarine*
1 *tablespoon all-purpose flour*
1 *cup half-and-half*
2 *(10-ounce) packages frozen green peas,
   cooked and drained*
1 *(4-ounce) can sliced mushrooms,
   drained*

Cook bacon until crisp; drain, reserving drippings. Crumble and set aside.

Sauté onion in bacon drippings; pour off excess drippings. Add butter and flour to skillet, blending well. Gradually stir in half-and-half; cook over low heat until smooth and thickened, stirring constantly. Add peas and mushrooms; sprinkle with bacon. Yield: 6 servings.

Baked Sweet Potatoes

4 *medium-size sweet potatoes*
  Butter
  Salt and pepper

Wash potatoes well; rub with butter. Cut a slit lengthwise down center of each; wrap each in aluminum foil. Bake at 350° for 1 hour or until tender. Serve with butter, salt, and pepper. Yield: 4 servings.

Orange Glazed Sweet Potatoes

8 *medium-size sweet potatoes*
1¼ *teaspoons salt, divided*
2 *tablespoons butter or margarine*
1 *tablespoon grated orange rind*
¾ *cup dark corn syrup*

Wash and scrub sweet potatoes. Add 1 teaspoon salt to boiling water; cook potatoes in water until tender, about 30 to 40 minutes. Peel and cut in half. Arrange potatoes in a shallow baking dish; set aside.

Combine remaining ¼ teaspoon salt, butter, orange rind, and corn syrup in a small saucepan. Bring to a boil; spoon over sweet potatoes. Bake at 350° for 30 minutes, basting potatoes occasionally with syrup. Yield: 8 to 10 servings.

Skillet Sweet Potatoes

3 *tablespoons butter or margarine*
1 *tablespoon bacon drippings*
4 *medium-size sweet potatoes, peeled and
   thinly sliced*
⅓ *cup water*
1½ *cups sugar*

Melt butter and bacon drippings in a large heavy skillet. Add sweet potatoes and water; sprinkle sugar over all. Cook uncovered over medium heat, stirring frequently, until potatoes are tender and a thick sauce forms, about 30 minutes. Yield: 4 to 6 servings.

Barbecued Creamed Potatoes

3 *tablespoons butter or margarine*
3 *tablespoons all-purpose flour*
1½ *teaspoons salt*
2 *cups milk*
½ *teaspoon hot sauce*
1 *tablespoon chopped parsley*
2 *tablespoons chopped pimiento*
4 *cups cooked, diced potatoes*
½ *cup soft breadcrumbs*
1 *tablespoon butter or margarine, melted*
½ *cup shredded pasteurized process American cheese*
¼ *teaspoon paprika*

Melt butter in a medium saucepan; add flour and salt, stirring until smooth. Add milk slowly; cook, stirring constantly, until mixture thickens and comes to a boil. Stir in hot sauce, parsley, and pimiento; add potatoes. Spoon into a greased 1½-quart casserole.

Combine breadcrumbs, butter, cheese, and paprika; sprinkle over casserole. Bake at 400° for 30 minutes. Yield: 6 servings.

Note: This casserole may be made ahead of time and refrigerated. Bake at 350° for 50 minutes or until heated through.

Stuffed Baked Potatoes

4 *baking potatoes*
Butter
4 *slices bacon, chopped*
¼ *cup chopped green onion*
3 *tablespoons vinegar*
1 *teaspoon sugar*
1 *teaspoon salt*

Wash potatoes and rub skins with butter. Bake at 425° for 1 hour or until done.

Allow to cool to touch. Slice skin away from top of each potato. Carefully scoop out pulp, leaving shells intact; mash pulp.

Cook bacon; drain, reserving drippings. Sauté onion in bacon drippings. Combine potato pulp, bacon, onion, bacon drippings, and remaining ingredients, stirring well. Stuff shells with potato mixture. Serve hot. Yield: 4 servings.

★ Baked Potatoes with Shrimp Sauce

2 *(4½-ounce) cans tiny shrimp*
2 *tablespoons butter or margarine*
2 *egg yolks, beaten*
½ *cup whipping cream*
½ *teaspoon salt*
½ *cup commercial sour cream*
⅛ *teaspoon ground ginger*
1 *tablespoon chili sauce*
2 *teaspoons parsley flakes*
4 *hot baked potatoes*

Drain shrimp, reserving liquid; set shrimp aside.

Combine ¼ cup reserved shrimp liquid and butter in a small saucepan; heat. Stir in egg yolks and cream; cook slowly, stirring constantly, until slightly thickened. Remove from heat, and stir in salt, sour cream, ginger, chili sauce, and parsley. Cook over low heat 5 minutes; stir in shrimp.

Split the potatoes lengthwise, forcing open. Spoon sauce over each potato. Yield: 4 servings.

Twice-Baked Potatoes

4 *medium-size baking potatoes*
Salad oil
1 *(6-ounce) package frozen crabmeat, thawed and drained*
½ *cup melted butter or margarine*
½ *cup half-and-half*
1 *teaspoon salt*
Dash of pepper
4 *teaspoons grated onion*
1 *cup shredded Cheddar cheese*
½ *teaspoon paprika*

Wash potatoes and rub skins with oil. Bake at 425° for 45 minutes or until done.

Allow potatoes to stand until cool to the touch. Slice skin away from top of each potato. Carefully scoop out pulp, leaving shells intact; mash pulp.

Combine potato pulp and remaining ingredients except paprika, stirring well. Stuff shells with potato mixture. Sprinkle with paprika.

Bake at 350° for 15 minutes or until thoroughly heated. Yield: 4 servings.

Note: Potatoes can be frozen after stuffing shells. Seal securely in aluminum foil, label, and freeze. To serve, thaw in refrigerator. Bake at 350° for 20 minutes or until thoroughly heated.

Potato-Broccoli Bake

    4 *medium-size potatoes, peeled and thinly*
       sliced
    4 *tablespoons melted butter or margarine*
    1 *teaspoon salt*
    ¼ *teaspoon paprika*
    ⅛ *teaspoon pepper*
    1 *(10-ounce) package frozen broccoli*
       spears, thawed
       Pimiento Cheese Sauce

Place potato slices in a greased 13- x 9- x 2-inch baking dish. Combine butter, salt, paprika, and pepper. Brush potatoes with butter mixture. Bake, uncovered, at 425° for 45 minutes or until tender.

Arrange broccoli over potatoes; pour Pimiento Cheese Sauce over vegetables. Cover and bake at 425° for 10 minutes or until broccoli is tender and sauce is bubbly. Yield: 4 to 6 servings.

Pimiento Cheese Sauce:

    2 *tablespoons butter or margarine*
    2 *tablespoons all-purpose flour*
  1¼ *cups milk*
    1 *cup shredded Cheddar cheese*
    ¼ *cup chopped pimiento*
    ½ *teaspoon salt*
    ¼ *teaspoon pepper*

Melt butter in a heavy saucepan over low heat, and blend in flour; cook until bubbly, stirring constantly. Gradually add milk; cook over low heat, stirring constantly, until smooth and thickened. Add cheese, pimiento, salt, and pepper; stir until cheese melts. Yield: about 1½ cups.

Shrimp-Stuffed Potatoes

    6 *medium-size baking potatoes*
    ½ *cup butter or margarine*
    ½ *cup half-and-half*
    4 *teaspoons grated onion*
    1 *cup shredded sharp Cheddar cheese*
    1 *teaspoon salt*
    ½ *teaspoon paprika*
    1 *(4½-ounce) can shrimp, drained*
       Paprika
       Parsley

Scrub potatoes thoroughly; bake at 425° for 40 to 60 minutes or until done. When cool to touch, cut potatoes in half lengthwise. Carefully scoop out pulp, leaving a firm shell about ¼ inch thick.

Combine potato pulp, butter, half-and-half, onion, cheese, salt, and ½ teaspoon paprika; whip until smooth. Stir in shrimp.

Stuff shells with potato mixture, and sprinkle with paprika. Bake at 425° for 15 minutes. Garnish with parsley and serve. Yield: 6 servings.

German Hash Browns

    4 *medium-size potatoes, unpeeled*
    2 *to 3 tablespoons bacon drippings*
    1 *onion, thinly sliced*
       Salt and pepper to taste

Wash potatoes thoroughly, and pat dry; shred or slice very thin. Heat bacon drippings in a large iron skillet. Add potatoes and onion; sprinkle with salt and pepper.

Cover skillet and cook over medium-low heat until potatoes are tender, stirring occasionally. Remove cover, and continue cooking until potatoes are browned on both sides. Yield: 4 to 6 servings.

Potatoes in a Skillet

> 6 *medium-size potatoes, peeled and cut*
>   *into ¼-inch slices*
> 1 *large onion, sliced*
> 1 *large green pepper, sliced*
> 2 *large tomatoes, sliced*
> 1 *cup water*
> 2 *slices bacon, cut in half*
> 1¼ *teaspoons salt*
> ⅛ *teaspoon pepper*

Layer vegetables in a skillet or large saucepan; add remaining ingredients. Cover and simmer 45 minutes or until potatoes are done. Yield: 6 to 8 servings.

Browned Paprika Potatoes

> 6 *medium-size potatoes, peeled*
> 1 *tablespoon melted bacon drippings or*
>   *margarine*
> ¼ *cup fine cornflake crumbs*
> 1 *teaspoon paprika*
> 1 *to 2 teaspoons salt*

Cook potatoes in boiling salted water about 15 to 20 minutes; drain well. Brush with bacon drippings.

Combine cornflake crumbs, paprika, and salt. Roll potatoes in mixture until well coated. Bake in a greased shallow baking pan at 425° for 45 minutes or until done. Yield: 6 servings.

Potatoes in Mustard Sauce

> 6 *medium-size potatoes, cooked and diced*
> 1 *medium-size onion, chopped*
> 6 *tablespoons butter or margarine*
> 3 *tablespoons all-purpose flour*
> 1 *chicken bouillon cube*
> 1½ *cups boiling water*
> 1 *teaspoon salt*
> 1 *teaspoon pepper*
> 2 *tablespoons prepared mustard*
> 2 *tablespoons breadcrumbs*
> 2 *tablespoons grated Parmesan cheese*

Place potatoes in a greased 1½-quart casserole, and set aside. Sauté onion in butter until limp; stir in flour until smooth. Dissolve bouillon cube in boiling water, and gradually stir into flour mixture. Cook over low heat, stirring constantly, until sauce bubbles. Stir in salt, pepper, and mustard; simmer 10 minutes.

Pour sauce over the potatoes. Combine breadcrumbs and cheese; sprinkle over casserole. Bake at 375° about 20 minutes. Yield: 8 servings.

Herb Fried Potatoes

> 3 *tablespoons butter or margarine*
> 3 *medium-size potatoes, pared and cut in*
>   *⅛-inch strips*
> ½ *teaspoon ground oregano*
> 2 *tablespoons chopped parsley*
> ½ *teaspoon instant minced onion*
> ½ *teaspoon salt*
> *Pepper to taste*

Melt butter in an 10-inch skillet; add potatoes. Cover and cook over medium heat 10 minutes. Turn potatoes carefully; cook, uncovered, 10 minutes more, turning occasionally to brown all sides. Sprinkle with remaining ingredients during last 5 minutes of cooking. Yield: 4 servings.

Sesame Potato Sticks

> 6 *to 8 medium-size baking potatoes,*
>   *peeled*
> ¾ *cup sesame seeds*
> ½ *cup melted butter or margarine*
> *Salt*
> *Paprika*

Cut potatoes into strips 1 inch thick. Sprinkle sesame seeds in a thin layer on waxed paper. Dip potato sticks in butter; coat one side of sticks with sesame seeds. Place sticks, seed side up, on a well-greased baking sheet. Sprinkle with salt and paprika. Bake at 400° about 40 minutes or until done. Yield: about 8 servings.

Potato Pancakes

4 *large potatoes, peeled and chopped*
1 *large onion, chopped*
2 *eggs, beaten*
1 *tablespoon salad herbs*
¼ *cup all-purpose flour*
Salt and pepper to taste
Salad oil

Combine potatoes, onion, eggs, and herbs in container of an electric blender; blend at low speed until potatoes are grated. Combine potato mixture with flour, salt, and pepper.

Heat ¼ inch salad oil in a large heavy skillet. Spoon ¼ cup batter into oil to form a medium-size pancake. Fry until brown on one side; turn and fry until crisp. Repeat until all batter is used.

Serve with sour cream, catsup, or other favorite topping. Yield: about 20 pancakes.

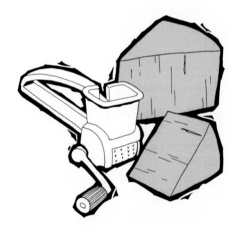

Cheesy Potato Casserole

4 *cups cubed cooked potatoes*
1 *(8-ounce) carton plain yogurt*
1 *cup cottage cheese*
½ *teaspoon salt*
¼ *teaspoon pepper*
¼ *teaspoon dillweed*
1 *cup shredded sharp Cheddar cheese*

Combine all ingredients except Cheddar cheese; spoon into a 9-inch square baking dish. Top with Cheddar cheese. Bake at 350° for 25 to 30 minutes. Yield: 4 to 6 servings.

Holiday Scalloped Potatoes

2 *tablespoons butter or margarine*
3 *tablespoons all-purpose flour*
2 *cups milk*
3 *cups diced cooked potatoes*
2 *tablespoons chopped parsley*
2 *tablespoons chopped pimiento*
1½ *teaspoons salt*
½ *cup shredded Cheddar cheese*
½ *cup buttered breadcrumbs*
¼ *teaspoon paprika*

Melt butter in a heavy saucepan over low heat; gradually add flour. Cook until bubbly, stirring constantly. Gradually add milk; cook, stirring constantly, until thickened. Stir in potatoes, parsley, pimiento, and salt. Spoon into a greased 1½-quart casserole.

Combine cheese, breadcrumbs, and paprika; sprinkle over potato mixture. Bake at 400° for 20 minutes. Yield: 4 to 6 servings.

Potato-Tomato Scallop

½ *cup cnopped onion*
2 *tablespoons melted butter or margarine*
2 *tablespoons all-purpose flour*
1 *teaspoon paprika*
½ *teaspoon salt*
⅛ *teaspoon pepper*
1 *cup water*
1 *(7½-ounce) can tomatoes*
2 *chicken bouillon cubes*
5 *cups peeled, thinly sliced potatoes*

Sauté onion in butter until barely tender; stir in flour, paprika, salt, and pepper. Cook over low heat, stirring constantly, until bubbly. Add water, tomatoes, and bouillon cubes. Cook over medium heat, stirring constantly, until bouillon cubes dissolve and mixture thickens.

Place potatoes in a greased 2-quart casserole; add tomato mixture. Cover and bake at 400° for 1 hour or until potatoes are tender. Yield: about 6 to 8 servings.

★
Potatoes Patrician

  3 *cups cream-style cottage cheese*
  ¾ *cup commercial sour cream*
  1½ *tablespoons finely grated onion*
  2½ *teaspoons salt*
  ⅛ *teaspoon white pepper*
  6 *medium-size potatoes, cooked and*
    mashed
  Melted butter or margarine
  ½ *cup chopped toasted almonds*

Puree cottage cheese in container of electric blender. Combine cottage cheese, sour cream, onion, salt, and pepper; stir in mashed potatoes. Spoon into a buttered 2-quart shallow casserole. Brush surface with butter.

Bake at 350° for 30 minutes. Place under broiler to brown; sprinkle with almonds. Yield: 8 to 10 servings.

Piquant Rutabagas

  3 *cups peeled and diced rutabaga*
  2 *tablespoons butter or margarine, melted*
  1 *tablespoon light brown sugar*
  2 *tablespoons soy sauce*
  1 *tablespoon lemon juice*
  1 *teaspoon Worcestershire sauce*

Cook rutabaga in a small amount of boiling water 20 minutes or until tender; drain. Combine butter, brown sugar, soy sauce, lemon juice, and Worcestershire sauce in a saucepan; heat thoroughly, but do not boil. Pour sauce over rutabaga; mix gently. Yield: 4 to 6 servings.

French-Fried Rutabagas

  1 *medium-size rutabaga, peeled*
  1 *teaspoon sugar*
  1 *to 1½ cups cornmeal*
  1 *to 2 teaspoons salt*
  1 *to 2 eggs, beaten*
  Salad oil

Slice rutabaga into ¼-inch-thick slices; cut slices into ¼-inch-thick strips. Parboil in a minimum amount of boiling water to which sugar has been added; drain and cool.

Combine cornmeal and salt, blending well. Dip rutabaga strips in egg and then in cornmeal. Fry in salad oil heated to 400° until golden brown. Drain on paper towels. Yield: 8 to 10 servings.

Note: To freeze, place French-fried strips on baking sheets (make sure strips do not touch each other); cover with aluminum foil, and freeze. Remove frozen strips from baking sheets, and store in plastic bags in freezer.

To serve, place on baking sheet and heat at 350° until hot.

Spinach au Gratin

  1 *pound fresh spinach*
  4 *to 5 slices bacon*
  2 *tablespoons all-purpose flour*
  1 *cup milk*
  ½ *cup shredded Cheddar cheese*
  ½ *cup breadcrumbs*

Wash spinach thoroughly and drain; chop coarsely. Cook in a covered saucepan, without adding water, until just tender.

Cook bacon until crisp, reserving ¼ cup drippings. Heat 2 tablespoons bacon drippings in a saucepan; blend in flour, stirring until smooth. Add milk gradually; cook, stirring constantly, until thickened. Add cheese, stirring until melted.

Combine cooked spinach and cheese sauce; spoon into a buttered 1-quart casserole. Crumble bacon over top. Combine breadcrumbs with remaining 2 tablespoons reserved bacon drippings; sprinkle over bacon. Bake at 350° for 20 minutes or until breadcrumbs are browned. Yield: 4 servings .

Spinach Soufflé

    1   tablespoon finely chopped onion
    1   tablespoon melted butter or margarine
    1½ tablespoons all-purpose flour
    1   cup milk
    2   cups chopped cooked spinach, drained
    ½   cup shredded Cheddar cheese
    ¾   teaspoon salt
    ½   teaspoon pepper
    4   eggs, separated

Sauté onion in butter until tender; stir in flour. Cook over low heat until bubbly, stirring constantly. Add milk; cook until thickened, stirring constantly. Stir in spinach, cheese, and seasonings; cook until cheese melts. Remove from heat; cool.

Beat egg yolks; stir into spinach mixture. Beat egg whites until stiff; fold into spinach mixture. Pour into a well-greased 2-quart casserole. Bake at 350° for 45 minutes or until firm. Yield: 8 servings.

Spinach Fluff

    2   (10-ounce) packages frozen chopped
          spinach, thawed and well drained
    2   cups milk, divided
    4   eggs
    1   (10¾-ounce) can cream of mushroom
          soup, undiluted
    ¼   cup melted butter or margarine
    1   teaspoon salt
    1   teaspoon Ac'cent
    1   teaspoon onion juice
    1   teaspoon garlic juice
    ½   cup grated Parmesan cheese

Combine 1 package spinach and 1 cup milk in container of electric blender; puree. Add remaining spinach; blend until smooth. Add remaining milk, eggs, soup, butter, salt, and Ac'cent; blend well. Stir in onion juice, garlic juice, and cheese.

Pour mixture into a well-greased, shallow 2-quart casserole. Bake at 325° for 1 hour or until inserted knife comes out clean. Yield: 6 to 8 servings.

★ Individual Spinach Quiches

    1   (10-ounce) package frozen chopped
          spinach
    2   tablespoons chopped onion
    3   tablespoons melted butter or margarine
    1   teaspoon salt
    1   teaspoon pepper, divided
    ½   teaspoon ground nutmeg
    3   eggs, beaten
    1½ cups half-and-half
    ¼   cup shredded Gruyère or Swiss cheese
    12 (2¾-inch) individual tart shells,
          unbaked
        Hard-cooked egg slices
        Parsley (optional)

Cook spinach according to package directions; drain well, and set aside. Sauté onion in butter until soft; add spinach. Cook and stir over medium heat about 3 minutes. Blend in salt, ½ teaspoon pepper, and nutmeg; set aside.

Combine eggs, half-and-half, and remaining ½ teaspoon pepper in a bowl; blend well. Stir in spinach and cheese. Spoon into tart shells. Bake at 375° about 20 minutes. Arrange on serving tray; garnish with egg slices and parsley, if desired. Yield: 12 individual quiches.

Herbed Spinach Casserole

    1   (10-ounce) package frozen chopped
          spinach, thawed
    1   (10¾-ounce) can cream of mushroom
          soup, undiluted
    ½   cup shredded sharp Cheddar cheese
    ¼   cup chopped onion
    1   cup herb-seasoned stuffing mix
    ¼   cup melted butter or margarine

Combine spinach, soup, cheese, and onion, blending well; spoon into a greased 1-quart baking dish. Combine stuffing mix and butter; sprinkle over spinach. Bake at 350° for 1 hour. Yield: 4 to 6 servings.

Spinach Lasagna

    2   cloves garlic, minced
    ¼   pound fresh mushrooms, sliced
    1   tablespoon olive oil
    2   tablespoons melted butter or margarine
    2   (15-ounce) cans tomato sauce
    1   tablespoon chopped onion
    2   tablespoons minced parsley
    ½   teaspoon salt
    ½   pound lasagna noodles, cooked and
          drained
    2   (10-ounce) packages frozen chopped
          spinach, partially thawed
    ½   cup ricotta or cottage cheese
    ½   pound mozzarella cheese, shredded
    2   tablespoons grated Parmesan cheese

Sauté garlic and mushrooms in oil and butter. Add tomato sauce, onion, parsley, and salt; simmer 10 minutes.

Layer half of noodles, spinach, ricotta, and mozzarella in a lightly greased 13- x 9- x 2-inch pan. Pour half of tomato sauce over layers. Repeat layers. Sprinkle with Parmesan cheese, and bake at 400° for 45 minutes. Yield: 8 to 10 servings.

Acorn Squash Surprise

    4   small acorn squash
    ½   cup boiling water
        Salt to taste
    ¾   cup firmly packed brown sugar, divided
    1   (20-ounce) can sliced apples, drained
        Ground nutmeg

Wash squash, and cut each in half lengthwise; remove seeds and membrane. Place cut side down in a shallow baking pan; add boiling water.

Bake at 350° for 45 minutes or until squash is tender. Remove from oven; turn cut side up, and sprinkle each with salt and 1 tablespoon brown sugar.

Combine apples and remaining brown sugar; spoon into squash cavities. Sprinkle with nutmeg. Bake at 425° for 10 minutes or until thoroughly heated. Yield: 8 servings.

Spinach Sauté

    1   pound fresh spinach
    1   large tomato, peeled and cut into thin
          wedges
    2   cloves garlic, crushed
    2   to 3 tablespoons salad oil
        Salt and pepper to taste

Wash spinach thoroughly and drain. Sauté tomato and garlic in salad oil in a large skillet. Add spinach; cover and cook over low heat 15 minutes, stirring once or twice. Add salt and pepper to taste. Cook, uncovered, 5 to 10 minutes longer, stirring occasionally. Yield: 4 servings.

★ Butternut Squash Soufflé

    2   cups cooked, mashed butternut squash
    1   teaspoon salt
    ¼   cup maple-flavored syrup
    2   tablespoons brown sugar
    3   tablespoons cornstarch
    3   eggs, separated
    1¼ cups whipping cream or evaporated
          milk
    ½   cup melted butter or margarine
        Slivered almonds

Combine squash, salt, syrup, brown sugar, and cornstarch; beat until fluffy. Add egg yolks, whipping cream, and butter; mix thoroughly.

Beat egg whites until stiff; fold into squash mixture. Pour into a buttered 1½-quart casserole. Sprinkle with slivered almonds. Bake at 350° for 1 hour. Serve at once. Yield: about 8 servings.

Fruited Acorn Squash

    3 *medium-size acorn squash*
    ½ *cup boiling water*
    Salt
    1 *(8¼-ounce) can crushed pineapple,*
       drained
    1 *medium-size apple, chopped*
    2 *tablespoons firmly packed brown sugar*
    2 *tablespoons butter or margarine*

Wash, halve, and remove seeds from squash. Place cut side down in a shallow baking dish. Add boiling water. Bake at 350° for 45 minutes. Turn cut side up, and sprinkle with salt; set aside.

Combine pineapple, apple, and brown sugar. Spoon filling into each squash half. Dot each with 1 teaspoon butter. Return to oven for 30 minutes or until squash is tender. Yield: 6 servings.

Acorn Squash Soufflé

    ¼   *cup butter or margarine*
    2   *tablespoons all-purpose flour*
    1   *cup milk*
    1   *teaspoon chopped onion*
    1½ *teaspoons salt*
    ⅛   *teaspoon pepper*
    2   *eggs, separated*
    2   *cups cooked acorn squash, well drained*
    ¾   *cup cracker crumbs*
    1   *cup shredded Cheddar cheese*

Melt butter in a heavy saucepan over low heat; blend in flour, and cook until bubbly. Gradually add milk; cook, stirring constantly, until smooth and thickened. Stir in onion, salt, and pepper; remove from heat, and cool slightly. Add egg yolks, beating well. Stir in squash, cracker crumbs, and cheese.

Beat egg whites until stiff but not dry; fold into squash mixture. Pour into a greased 1½-quart casserole or soufflé dish.

Bake at 350° for 45 minutes or until a knife inserted in center comes out clean. Yield: 6 to 8 servings.

Baked Butternut Squash

    1 *large butternut squash*
    1 *cup water*
    6 *tablespoons butter or margarine,*
       divided
    2 *tablespoons brown sugar*
    ½ *teaspoon salt*
    ½ *teaspoon ground ginger*
    1 *medium-size orange, halved*
    Additional ginger

Cut squash in half lengthwise; remove seeds. Place cut side down in a large baking dish. Add 1 cup water; bake at 350° for 30 minutes. Turn squash cut side up; add more water if necessary to cover bottom of pan.

Spread 1 tablespoon butter over neck of each squash half; place 1 tablespoon butter in cavity of each. Bake 30 to 45 minutes.

Scoop pulp from shell. Combine pulp, 2 tablespoons butter, brown sugar, salt, and ½ teaspoon ginger in a mixing bowl; beat with an electric mixer until smooth. Squeeze juice from half of orange; stir into squash mixture.

Spoon squash into a buttered 1½-quart casserole. Slice remaining orange half; place on squash. Sprinkle lightly with additional ginger. Bake at 350° about 15 minutes or until hot. Yield: about 6 to 8 servings.

Candied Squash

    2 *medium-size butternut or acorn squash*
    ½ *cup melted butter or margarine*
    ½ *cup firmly packed brown sugar*
    ½ *cup water*
    2 *tablespoons light corn syrup*
    ¼ *teaspoon ground cinnamon*

Parboil whole squash about 15 minutes or until tender; drain. Peel squash, and halve crosswise; remove seeds and membrane, and cut into ½-inch thick slices.

Combine remaining ingredients in a skillet; stir until well blended. Add squash; stir gently to coat well with butter mixture. Cover and cook over low heat for 10 minutes. Uncover and cook 5 additional minutes. Yield: 6 servings.

★ Stuffed Yellow Squash

    8 large yellow squash
    1 (10-ounce) package frozen peas,
         spinach, broccoli, or green beans
    ¼ cup melted butter or margarine
    ¼ cup half-and-half
    1 teaspoon salt
    ¼ teaspoon pepper
       Buttered breadcrumbs
       Grated Parmesan cheese

Wash squash thoroughly. Drop in boiling water; cover and simmer 10 to 15 minutes or until tender but still firm. Drain and cool slightly. Trim off stems. Cut squash in half lengthwise; remove pulp, leaving a firm shell. Set aside.

Cook peas according to package directions; drain. Combine peas, pulp, butter, half-and-half, salt, and pepper in container of an electric blender. Process until smooth.

Spoon pureed mixture into squash shells; sprinkle with breadcrumbs, then with cheese. Bake at 350° for 15 minutes; broil until golden brown. Yield: 8 servings.

Note: Any leftover puree can be spooned into a casserole dish and baked with the squash.

Summer Squash Special

    1 pound bulk pork sausage
    1 clove garlic, crushed
    4 cups sliced yellow squash
    ½ cup dry breadcrumbs
    ½ cup grated Parmesan cheese
    ½ cup milk
    1 tablespoon chopped parsley
    ½ teaspoon oregano
    ½ teaspoon salt
    2 eggs, beaten

Sauté sausage and garlic until sausage is lightly browned; drain. Cook squash in a small amount of boiling salted water until tender; drain.

Combine sausage, squash, and remaining ingredients; blend well. Spoon mixture into a lightly greased 10- x 6-x 1½-inch baking dish. Bake at 325° for 20 minutes. Yield: 6 servings.

★ Squash Fritters

    2 cups cooked, mashed yellow squash
    2 eggs, beaten
    1 small onion, chopped
       Salt and pepper to taste
    ½ cup cracker crumbs
       Hot salad oil

Combine squash, eggs, onion, seasonings, and cracker crumbs; mix well. Drop the mixture by tablespoonfuls into hot oil; cook until golden brown, turning once. Yield: 6 servings.

Squash Croquettes

    2 pounds yellow squash
    1 large onion, grated
    2 cups fine breadcrumbs
    2 eggs
    2 teaspoons salt
    1 teaspoon pepper
    1 cup cornmeal
       Hot salad oil

Cook squash in a small amount of water until tender; drain and mash. Add remaining ingredients except cornmeal and oil. Add more breadcrumbs if mixture is too soft to handle. Shape mixture into croquettes; roll each in cornmeal. Deep fry in hot oil until golden brown. Yield: 6 servings.

Yellow Squash Casserole

    2 to 3 pounds yellow squash, sliced
       Salt and pepper
    ½ cup butter or margarine, melted
    1 (8-ounce) carton commercial sour cream
    1 (10¾-ounce) can cream of chicken soup,
         undiluted
    2 onions, finely chopped
    1 (5-ounce) can water chestnuts, drained
         and sliced
    1 (2-ounce) jar pimientos, drained
    1 (8-ounce) package herb-seasoned
         stuffing mix, divided

Cook squash in boiling water until tender; drain, reserving 1½ cups liquid. Season to taste with salt and pepper; mash. Combine reserved liquid and remaining ingredients except ½ cup stuffing mix; stir in squash.

Pour mixture into a 2½-quart casserole. Top with reserved stuffing mix. Bake at 350° for 30 minutes. Yield: about 16 servings.

Tangy Yellow Squash

    5   medium-size yellow squash, thinly
            sliced
    ½   cup thinly sliced green onion
    ½   cup chopped green pepper
    ½   cup sliced celery
    2   tablespoons wine vinegar
    ¾   cup sugar
    1   teaspoon salt
    ½   teaspoon pepper
    ⅓   cup salad oil
    ⅔   cup cider vinegar
    1   clove garlic, crushed

Combine squash, green onion, green pepper, and celery in a large mixing bowl; toss lightly. Combine wine vinegar, sugar, salt, pepper, salad oil, cider vinegar, and garlic; stir well and spoon over vegetables. Chill about 12 hours, stirring occasionally. Drain and serve. Yield: 10 servings.

Squash Sauté

    ¾   pound zucchini, diced
    ¾   pound yellow squash, diced
    ½   cup chopped onion
    1   clove garlic, crushed
    3   tablespoons salad oil
    1   cup diced tomatoes
    1   tablespoon Worcestershire sauce
    2   tablespoons tomato paste
    1   tablespoon salt

Sauté squash, onion, and garlic in hot oil 3 minutes, stirring gently. Add remaining ingredients; simmer 8 to 10 minutes or until vegetables are crisp-tender, stirring occasionally. Yield: 6 servings.

Zucchini Provencale

    1   medium-size onion, chopped
    2   tablespoons olive oil
    1   clove garlic, minced
    1   teaspoon thyme
Dash of oregano
    1   (16-ounce) can tomatoes, undrained
    1   teaspoon salt
    ⅛   teaspoon pepper
    4   medium-size zucchini, cut into ½-inch
            slices
Chopped fresh parsley
Grated Romano cheese

Sauté onion in olive oil 5 minutes; stir in garlic, thyme, and oregano. Cut tomatoes into quarters; add tomatoes, tomato liquid, salt, and pepper to onion. Simmer 5 minutes; add zucchini, and simmer 10 minutes. Sprinkle with parsley and cheese. Yield: about 4 to 6 servings.

Zucchini Stuffed with Pork

    2   large zucchini
    2   tablespoons salad oil
    ¾   pound lean ground pork
    ¼   cup finely chopped onion
    ½   teaspoon garlic salt
    ⅛   teaspoon pepper
    ¼   teaspoon thyme
    2   eggs, beaten
    ⅓   cup grated Parmesan or Romano cheese
Buttered breadcrumbs

Wash zucchini thoroughly; cut in half lengthwise. Remove pulp, leaving a firm shell; chop pulp.

Heat salad oil in a skillet; add pork, and sauté until browned. Remove pork; drain on paper towels. Add onion to skillet, and sauté 5 minutes or until tender; drain pan drippings from skillet. Add pulp and pork; cover and simmer 10 minutes. Cool slightly, and stir in garlic salt, pepper, thyme, eggs, and cheese.

Stuff shells with zucchini mixture; sprinkle with breadcrumbs. Cover, and bake at 350° for 25 minutes. Yield: 4 servings.

Cheese-Topped Zucchini

    3 *medium-size zucchini*
    1 *onion, thinly sliced*
    1 *tablespoon salad oil*
    ¾ *teaspoon salt*
    ¼ *teaspoon pepper*
    ½ *teaspoon oregano*
    1 *(8-ounce) can tomato sauce*
    1 *(8-ounce) package sliced mozzarella
       cheese*

Wash zucchini and cut in half lengthwise. Sauté onion in salad oil until tender. Add zucchini halves, cut side up; add salt, pepper, oregano, and tomato sauce. Cover and simmer 15 minutes. Top with cheese. Place under broiler until cheese melts. Yield: 6 servings.

Indian-Style Stuffed Tomatoes

    6 *tomatoes*
    3 *tablespoons uncooked regular rice*
    ½ *cup boiling water*
    1 *teaspoon salt*
    1 *tablespoon melted margarine*
    2 *hard-cooked egg yolks, mashed*
    1 *teaspoon chopped celery*
    ⅛ *teaspoon pepper*
    ⅛ *teaspoon minced garlic*
    1 *teaspoon chopped parsley*
    ½ *teaspoon curry powder*
    1 *slice bread*
    2 *tablespoons milk*

Cut a slice from top of each tomato; scoop out pulp, leaving shells intact. Combine tomato pulp, rice, water, and salt; simmer about 15 minutes or until rice is tender. Stir in margarine, egg yolks, celery, and remaining seasonings.

Soak bread in milk until soft. Tear into small pieces, and add to rice mixture; mix well. Spoon into tomato shells, and place in a shallow baking dish. Bake at 350° about 20 minutes or until tomatoes are soft. Yield: 6 servings.

Spinach-Stuffed Zucchini

    3 *medium-size zucchini*
    Salt to taste
    1 *(10-ounce) package frozen chopped
       spinach*
    2 *tablespoons all-purpose flour*
    ½ *cup milk*
    4 *slices bacon, cooked, drained, and
       crumbled*
    ⅓ *cup shredded Cheddar cheese*
    Chopped pimiento (optional)

Wash zucchini thoroughly; cut off stem end. Drop zucchini into a small amount of boiling salted water; cover, lower heat, and cook 10 to 12 minutes. Drain, and allow to cool to touch.

Cut zucchini in half lengthwise; remove pulp, leaving a firm shell. Chop pulp. Sprinkle shells with salt to taste; set aside.

Cook spinach according to package directions; drain, and squeeze dry. Combine flour and milk; add zucchini pulp and spinach. Cook over low heat, stirring constantly, until thickened. Spoon spinach mixture into zucchini shells; sprinkle with bacon, then with cheese.

Place zucchini shells in a shallow baking pan, and bake at 350° for 15 to 20 minutes. Garnish with pimiento, if desired. Yield: 6 servings.

★
Crusty Broiled Tomatoes

    4 *medium-size tomatoes*
    Dijon-style mustard
    Salt
    Freshly ground pepper
    Cayenne pepper
    6 *tablespoons melted butter or margarine*
    ½ *cup seasoned breadcrumbs*
    ½ *cup grated Parmesan cheese*

Cut tomatoes in half. Spread cut side with mustard; sprinkle with salt, pepper, and cayenne pepper to taste.

Combine butter, breadcrumbs, and cheese. Spoon crumb mixture on top of each tomato half. Broil until crumbs are brown and tomatoes are tender. Yield: 8 servings.

Italian Tomatoes

2   *tablespoons basil*
1   *tablespoon parsley*
1   *clove garlic, chopped*
5   *tablespoons olive oil*
1½ *tablespoons red wine vinegar*
    Salt and pepper
4   *medium-size tomatoes, sliced*
1   *red onion, thinly sliced*

Combine first 6 ingredients in container of electric blender; blend well, and set aside. Arrange tomatoes in a shallow dish; pour dressing over tomatoes. Top with onion rings. Refrigerate until serving time. Yield: about 6 servings.

Zesty Broiled Tomatoes

2   *tablespoons commercial sour cream*
2   *tablespoons mayonnaise*
1   *tablespoon grated Parmesan cheese*
¼   *teaspoon garlic salt*
1½ *teaspoons lemon juice*
¼   *teaspoon chopped parsley*
1   *green onion, chopped*
2   *to 3 tomatoes, halved*

Combine sour cream, mayonnaise, Parmesan, and seasonings; mix well. Spoon a small amount of sour cream mixture on cut side of each tomato half. Broil until lightly browned and bubbly. Yield: 4 to 6 servings.

Tomato Strata

½   *cup chopped onion*
3   *tablespoons melted margarine*
2¼ *cups soft breadcrumbs*
2   *tablespoons chopped parsley*
3½ *teaspoons Worcestershire sauce, divided*
1½ *teaspoons salt*
1½ *pounds fresh tomatoes, peeled*
2   *tablespoons olive oil*

Sauté onion in margarine 5 minutes; stir in breadcrumbs, parsley, 1½ teaspoons Worcestershire sauce, and salt; set aside.

Slice tomatoes into ¼-inch-thick slices; arrange a layer in a lightly greased 1½-quart casserole.

Combine oil and remaining Worcestershire sauce; sprinkle a small amount over tomatoes. Sprinkle lightly with breadcrumb mixture. Repeat layers, ending with breadcrumbs.

Cover and bake at 375° for 30 minutes. Uncover; bake an additional 15 minutes or until breadcrumbs are lightly browned. Yield: 6 servings.

Stuffed Tomato Surprise

3   *slices bacon*
¼   *cup chopped onion*
½   *pound fresh spinach, chopped*
½   *cup commercial sour cream*
    Dash of hot sauce
4   *medium-size tomatoes*
    Salt
½   *cup shredded mozzarella cheese*

Cook bacon until crisp; drain, reserving 2 tablespoons drippings. Crumble bacon, and set aside.

Sauté onion in reserved bacon drippings until tender; stir in spinach. Cover and cook 3 to 5 minutes or until tender. Remove from heat; stir in sour cream, bacon, and hot sauce.

Cut tops from tomatoes; scoop out pulp, leaving shells intact. Chop pulp, and add to spinach mixture. Drain tomato shells, and sprinkle with salt; fill with vegetable mixture.

Place stuffed tomatoes in an 8-inch square baking dish; bake at 375° for 20 to 25 minutes. Top with cheese; bake an additional 3 minutes or until cheese melts. Yield: 4 servings.

Stir-Fried Bok Choy

⅓ cup water
1 tablespoon cider vinegar
1 tablespoon sugar
2 teaspoons soy sauce
2 teaspoons cornstarch
1 medium-size head bok choy
2 teaspoons peanut oil
1 teaspoon salt

Combine water, vinegar, sugar, soy sauce, and cornstarch; set aside.

Separate bok choy into stalks; wash well. Tear leaves into 1½-inch pieces; then slice stalks into ½-inch pieces.

Heat wok or skillet at 375° for 3 minutes; add oil and salt, and heat 1 minute. Add stalks; stir-fry 2 minutes. Add leaves and soy sauce mixture; cook, stirring constantly, about 10 seconds or until sauce thickens. Yield: 4 to 6 servings.

Stir-Fried Nappa

1 medium-size nappa
2 teaspoons peanut oil
1 teaspoon salt

Separate nappa leaves; wash each well. Tear leaves into 1½-inch pieces; slice white center into ½-inch pieces.

Heat wok or skillet at 375° for 3 minutes. Add oil and salt, and heat 1 minute; add nappa, and stir-fry 2 minutes. Yield: 4 to 6 servings.

Savory Succotash

3 (10-ounce) packages frozen succotash
3 tablespoons butter or margarine
Ground savory to taste
¾ teaspoon salt
Pepper to taste

Prepare succotash according to package directions; add remaining ingredients. Simmer about 2 minutes. Yield: 8 servings.

Stir-Fried Vegetables

1½ dozen fresh water chestnuts, peeled and sliced, or 1 (5-ounce) can water chestnuts, drained and sliced
½ pound bok choy
2 tablespoons salad oil or peanut oil
1 medium-size onion, diagonally sliced
½ pound sliced fresh mushrooms
2 medium-size yellow squash, diagonally sliced
Soy sauce to taste

Cover fresh water chestnuts with water; chill. Drain before using.

Separate bok choy into stalks; wash well. Tear leaves into 1½-inch pieces, and cut stalks diagonally into ½-inch slices; set aside.

Pour oil into wok or skillet; heat at 375° for 3 minutes. Add onion, and stir-fry 2 minutes; push onion up sides of wok. Continue same procedure for mushrooms, squash, bok choy stems, bok choy leaves, and water chestnuts; add more oil, if needed. Add soy sauce. Yield: 4 to 6 servings.

Vegetable Soufflé

3 tablespoons melted butter or margarine
3 tablespoons all-purpose flour
½ teaspoon salt
⅛ teaspoon pepper
1 cup milk
3 eggs, separated
1 cup vegetable puree (green peas, green beans, potatoes, etc.)
¼ teaspoon onion juice

Combine butter and flour in a heavy saucepan, blending well; cook over low heat until bubbly. Stir in salt and pepper. Gradually stir in milk; cook until smooth and thickened, stirring constantly. Remove from heat, and cool slightly. Stir in egg yolks. Add vegetable puree and onion juice, mixing well.

Beat egg whites until stiff but not dry; fold into vegetable mixture. Pour into a greased 1-quart casserole or soufflé dish. Bake at 350° for 30 minutes or until a knife inserted in center comes out clean. Yield: 6 servings.

Vegetable Casserole

1 (10-ounce) package frozen cauliflower, slightly cooked
2 cups sliced, cooked carrots
1 (17-ounce) can green peas with onions, drained
1 (5-ounce) can water chestnuts, drained and sliced
2 (10¾-ounce) cans cream of mushroom soup, undiluted
8 ounces Cheddar cheese, shredded

Combine vegetables and soup; toss well. Spoon mixture into a greased 2-quart freezer-to-oven casserole; sprinkle with cheese. Bake at 325° until bubbly, about 30 minutes. Yield: 8 servings.

Note: This casserole freezes well. Cover with aluminum foil, sealing well. Freeze. To serve, thaw in refrigerator. Bake at 325° until bubbly, about 30 minutes.

Vegetable Mélange

4 to 5 medium-size yellow squash
1 large green pepper, sliced
1 medium-size onion, sliced
¼ pound fresh mushrooms, sliced
2 tablespoons butter or margarine
2 tomatoes, quartered
1½ teaspoons salt
1 teaspoon ground ginger

Sauté squash, green pepper, onion, and mushrooms in butter until tender. Stir in tomato, salt, and ginger. Cover and simmer 5 to 10 minutes or until tomatoes are warm. Yield: 4 to 6 servings.

Belgian Endive with Ham Sauce

6 stalks Belgian endive, trimmed and washed
3 tablespoons lemon juice
¼ cup melted butter or margarine
1 carrot, finely chopped
1 onion, chopped
2 cloves garlic, minced
1 tablespoon melted butter or margarine
1 cup chopped cooked ham
1 small tomato, peeled and chopped
½ cup beef broth
½ cup Madeira or sherry

Arrange endive in a shallow baking dish; add water almost to cover. Add lemon juice and ¼ cup melted butter. Cover and bake at 350° for 20 minutes, turning once. Drain.

Sauté carrot, onion, and garlic in 1 tablespoon butter. Add ham, tomato, beef broth, and Madeira; simmer 15 minutes. Spoon ham mixture over endive. Yield: 6 servings.

Horseradish Relish

2 pounds fresh horseradish
2 teaspoons salt, divided
Distilled white vinegar

Scrub root, using a vegetable brush; peel and shred. Pack sterilized pint jars two-thirds full; add 1 teaspoon salt to each. Pour vinegar into jars, covering horseradish; seal tightly. Store in refrigerator. Yield: 2 pints.

Kohlrabi

4 medium-size kohlrabies
1 cup water
½ teaspoon salt
Salt and pepper
Butter or margarine

Remove and discard tops from kohlrabies; rinse bulbs in cold water. Peel and dice. Combine kohlrabi, water, and ½ teaspoon salt. Bring to a boil; cover and simmer 25 to 30 minutes. Drain; season to taste with salt, pepper, and butter. Yield: 4 to 6 servings.

Baked Apricots

2 *(17-ounce) cans apricot halves, drained and divided*
2 *cups firmly packed light brown sugar, divided*
2 *cups crushed round buttery crackers, divided*
Butter or margarine

Layer half of the apricots, brown sugar, and cracker crumbs in a greased 8-inch square baking dish. Dot with butter. Repeat layers. Bake at 300° for 1 hour. Yield: about 8 servings.

Glazed Whole Apricots

1 *(16-ounce) can whole apricots*
1 *cup firmly packed brown sugar*
¼ *cup butter*
Whole cloves

Drain apricots, reserving ½ cup juice. Combine apricots, reserved juice, brown sugar, and butter in a large skillet; cook slowly, turning apricots frequently until glazed. Drain. Stud with cloves, and use to garnish turkey. Yield: about 12 servings.

Baked Cranberry Pears

6 *to 8 firm pears, peeled, halved, and cored*
1 *(16-ounce) can whole cranberry sauce*
1 *lemon, thinly sliced*
Ground cinnamon

Arrange pears in a 13- x 9- x 2-inch baking dish. Spoon 1 tablespoon cranberry sauce into center of each pear half; reserve remaining sauce. Top each pear half with a lemon slice; sprinkle with cinnamon.

Cover and bake at 350° for 30 to 35 minutes or until tender. Chill several hours or overnight. Garnish with reserved cranberry sauce. Yield: 6 to 8 servings.

Curried Baked Fruit

1 *(29-ounce) can pear halves, drained*
1 *(29-ounce) can peach halves, drained*
2 *(16-ounce) cans apricot halves, drained*
1 *(20-ounce) can pineapple chunks, drained*
1 *(3½-ounce) package sliced almonds, toasted*
1 *(20-ounce) can sliced pineapple, drained*
1 *(4-ounce) jar maraschino cherries, drained*
1½ *cups firmly packed light brown sugar*
1 *to 2 tablespoons curry powder*
½ *cup butter or margarine, melted*

Alternate fruit halves, pineapple chunks, and almonds in layers in a 3-quart casserole. Arrange sliced pineapple on top of fruits, and place a maraschino cherry in the center of each slice.

Combine sugar, curry powder, and butter; sprinkle over fruit. Bake at 325° for 1 hour. Yield: 16 servings.

Note: This can be made ahead and reheated before serving.

Hot Gingered Fruit

1 *(20-ounce) can sliced pineapple*
1 *(29-ounce) can peach halves, drained*
2 *(16-ounce) cans apricot halves, drained*
1 *(29-ounce) can pear halves, drained*
10 *maraschino cherries*
¾ *cup firmly packed light brown sugar*
¼ *cup melted butter or margarine*
½ *teaspoon ground ginger*

Drain pineapple, reserving 2 tablespoons juice. Arrange pineapple, peaches, apricots, and pears in a 2-quart casserole; top with cherries.

Combine sugar, butter, 2 tablespoons reserved pineapple juice, and ginger in a saucepan. Cook over low heat until sugar melts; pour over fruits. Bake at 325° for 40 minutes. Yield: 12 servings.

Tropical Grilled Bananas

4 *slightly underripe bananas*
Toppings

Lay unpeeled bananas on flattest side. Carefully slit skin the length of banana, and loosen. Spoon in choice of Topping; carefully close skin. Cook on grill 15 minutes. Yield: 4 servings.

Toppings:

Choose from the following: honey combined with ginger and brandy to taste, orange marmalade, or brown sugar combined with curry powder to taste.

Baked Bananas

4 *firm bananas*
Grated rind and juice of 2 lemons
¼ *cup firmly packed brown sugar*
¼ *cup melted butter or margarine*

Cut bananas in half lengthwise; place cut side down in a buttered baking dish. Brush bananas with lemon juice; sprinkle with grated lemon rind and brown sugar. Drizzle with butter.

Bake at 350° for 15 to 20 minutes. Serve warm as a side dish with meat, or as a dessert, plain or with ice cream. Yield: 4 servings.

Pineapple Casserole

1 *(20-ounce) can pineapple chunks*
½ *cup sugar*
3 *tablespoons all-purpose flour*
1 *cup shredded Cheddar cheese*
¼ *cup melted butter or margarine*
½ *cup buttery cracker crumbs*

Drain pineapple, reserving 3 tablespoons juice. Combine sugar and flour, and stir in reserved pineapple juice; add cheese and pineapple chunks, mixing well. Spoon mixture into a greased 1-quart casserole.

Combine melted butter and cracker crumbs, stirring well; sprinkle over pineapple mixture. Bake at 350° for 20 to 30 minutes or until crumbs are lightly browned. Yield: 4 to 6 servings.

★ Cold Spiced Fruit

1 *to 2 unpeeled oranges, sliced and seeded*
1 *(20-ounce) can pineapple chunks*
1 *(16-ounce) can sliced peaches*
1 *(16-ounce) can apricot halves*
1 *(29-ounce) can pear halves*
1 *cup sugar*
½ *cup vinegar*
3 *sticks cinnamon*
5 *whole cloves*
1 *(3-ounce) package cherry-flavored gelatin*

Cut orange slices in half; place in a saucepan and cover with water. Simmer until rind is tender; drain well and set aside.

Drain canned fruits well, reserving all of the pineapple juice and half of the peach and apricot juice.

Combine reserved juice, sugar, vinegar, cinnamon, cloves, and gelatin; simmer 30 minutes. Combine fruits in a 9-cup container; pour hot juice mixture over fruit. Refrigerate at least 24 hours. Yield: about 15 servings.

APPENDICES

Handy Substitutions

Even the best of cooks occasionally runs out of an ingredient she needs and is unable to stop what she is doing to go to the store. At times like those, sometimes another ingredient or combination of ingredients can be used. Here is a list of substitutions and equivalents that yield satisfactory results in most cases.

Ingredient called for	Substitution
1 cup self-rising flour	1 cup all-purpose flour plus 1 teaspoon baking powder and ½ teaspoon salt
1 cup cake flour	1 cup sifted all-purpose flour minus 2 tablespoons
1 cup all-purpose flour	1 cup cake flour plus 2 tablespoons
1 teaspoon baking powder	½ teaspoon cream of tartar plus ¼ teaspoon soda
1 tablespoon cornstarch or arrowroot	2 tablespoons all-purpose flour
1 tablespoon tapioca	1½ tablespoons all-purpose flour
2 large eggs	3 small eggs
1 egg	2 egg yolks (for custard)
1 egg	2 egg yolks plus 1 tablespoon water (for cookies)
1 cup commercial sour cream	1 tablespoon lemon juice plus evaporated milk to equal 1 cup; or 3 tablespoons butter plus ⅞ cup sour milk
1 cup yogurt	1 cup buttermilk or sour milk
1 cup sour milk or buttermilk	1 tablespoon vinegar or lemon juice plus sweet milk to equal 1 cup
1 cup fresh milk	½ cup evaporated milk plus ½ cup water
1 cup fresh milk	3 to 5 tablespoons nonfat dry milk solids in 1 cup water
1 cup honey	1¼ cups sugar plus ¼ cup liquid
1 square (1 ounce) unsweetened chocolate	3 tablespoons cocoa plus 1 tablespoon butter or margarine
1 clove fresh garlic	1 teaspoon garlic salt or ⅛ teaspoon garlic powder
1 teaspoon onion powder	2 teaspoons minced onion
1 tablespoon fresh herbs	1 teaspoon ground or crushed dry herbs
¼ cup chopped fresh parsley	1 tablespoon dehydrated parsley
1 teaspoon dry mustard	1 tablespoon prepared mustard
1 pound fresh mushrooms	6 ounces canned mushrooms

Equivalent Weights and Measures

Food	Weight or Count	Measure
Apples	1 pound (3 medium)	3 cups, sliced
Bacon	8 slices cooked	½ cup, crumbled
Bananas	1 pound (3 medium)	2½ cups, sliced, or about 2 cups, mashed
Bread	1 pound	12 to 16 slices
Bread	About 1½ slices	1 cup soft crumbs
Butter or margarine	1 pound	2 cups
Butter or margarine	¼-pound stick	½ cup
Butter or margarine	Size of an egg	About ¼ cup
Candied fruit or peels	½ pound	1¼ cups, cut
Cheese, American	1 pound	4 to 5 cups, shredded
cottage	1 pound	2 cups
cream	3 ounces	6 tablespoons
Chocolate morsels	6-ounce package	1 cup
Cocoa	1 pound	4 cups
Coconut, flaked or shredded	1 pound	5 cups
Coffee	1 pound	80 tablespoons
Cornmeal	1 pound	3 cups
Cream, heavy or whipping	½ pint	2 cups, whipped
Dates, pitted	1 pound	2 to 3 cups, chopped
Dates, pitted	7¼-ounce package	1¼ cups, chopped
Eggs	5 large	About 1 cup
Eggs whites	8 large	About 1 cup
Egg yolks	12 large	About 1 cup
Flour		
all-purpose	1 pound	3½ cups
cake	1 pound	4¾ to 5 cups, sifted
whole wheat	1 pound	3½ cups, unsifted
Graham crackers	16 to 18 crackers	1⅓ cups crumbs
Lemon juice	1 medium	2 to 3 tablespoons
Lemon rind	1 medium	2 teaspoons, grated
Macaroni	4 ounces (1 cup)	2¼ cups, cooked
Milk		
evaporated	6-ounce can	¾ cup
evaporated	14½-ounce can	1⅔ cups
sweetened condensed	14-ounce can	1¼ cups
sweetened condensed	15-ounce can	1⅓ cups
Miniature marshmallows	½ pound	4½ cups
Nuts, in shell		
almonds	1 pound	1 to 1¾ cups nutmeats
peanuts	1 pound	2 cups nutmeats
pecans	1 pound	2¼ cups nutmeats
walnuts	1 pound	1⅔ cups nutmeats
Nuts, shelled		
almonds	1 pound, 2 ounces	4 cups
peanuts	1 pound	4 cups

Equivalent Weights and Measures (continued)

Food	Weight or Count	Measure
pecans	1 pound	4 cups
walnuts	1 pound	3 cups
Orange, juice	1 medium	⅓ cup
Orange, rind	1 medium	2 tablespoons, grated
Potatoes	2 pounds	6 medium
Potatoes	4 to 5 medium	4 cups, cooked and cubed
Raisins, seedless	1 pound	3 cups
Rice	1 cup	About 4 cups, cooked
Spaghetti	7 ounces	About 4 cups, cooked
Sugar		
brown	1 pound	2¼ cups, firmly packed
powdered	1 pound	3½ cups, unsifted
granulated	1 pound	2 cups
Whipping cream	1 cup	2 cups, whipped

Equivalent Measurements

Use standard measuring cups (both dry and liquid measure) and measuring spoons when measuring ingredients. All measurements given below are level.

3 teaspoons	1 tablespoon
4 tablespoons	¼ cup
5⅓ tablespoons	⅓ cup
8 tablespoons	½ cup
16 tablespoons	1 cup
2 tablespoons (liquid)	1 ounce
1 cup	8 fluid ounces
2 cups	1 pint (16 fluid ounces)
4 cups	1 quart
4 quarts	1 gallon
⅛ cup	2 tablespoons
⅓ cup	5 tablespoons plus 1 teaspoon
⅔ cup	10 tablespoons plus 2 teaspoons
¾ cup	12 tablespoons
Few grains (or dash)	Less than ⅛ teaspoon
Pinch	As much as can be taken between tip of finger and thumb

Metric Measures

Approximate Conversion to Metric Measures

When you know . . .	Multiply by . . .	To find . . .	Symbol
	Mass (weight)		
ounces	28	grams	g
pounds	0.45	kilograms	kg
	Volume		
teaspoons	5	milliliters	ml
tablespoons	15	milliliters	ml
fluid ounces	30	milliliters	ml
cups	0.24	liters	l
pints	0.47	liters	l
quarts	0.95	liters	l
gallons	3.8	liters	l

Cooking Measure Equivalents

Metric Cup	Volume (Liquid)	Liquid Solids (Butter)	Fine Powder (Flour)	Granular (Sugar)	Grain (Rice)
1	250 ml	200 g	140 g	190 g	150 g
¾	188 ml	150 g	105 g	143 g	113 g
⅔	167 ml	133 g	93 g	127 g	100 g
½	125 ml	100 g	70 g	95 g	75 g
⅓	83 ml	67 g	47 g	63 g	50 g
¼	63 ml	50 g	35 g	48 g	38 g
⅛	31 ml	25 g	18 g	24 g	19 g

HERB CHART

For:	Appetizers & Garnishes	Soups	Fish	Eggs or Cheese	Meats	Poultry & Game	Vegetables	Salads	Sauces
Use:									
Basil	Tomato Juice, Seafood Cocktail	Tomato, Chowders, Spinach, Minestrone	Shrimps, Broiled Fish	Scrambled Eggs, Cream Cheese, Welsh Rarebit	Liver, Lamb, Sausage	Venison, Duck	Eggplant, Squash, Tomatoes, Onions	Tomato, Seafood, Chicken	Tomato, Spaghetti, Orange (for Game), Butter (for Fish)
Bay Leaves	Tomato Juice, Aspic	Stock, Bean	Court Bouillon, Poached Halibut, Salmon		Stews, Pot Roast, Shish Kabob, Tripe	Chicken, Fricassee, Stews	Tomatoes	Aspic, Marinades for Beet, Onion	All, Marinades, Espagnole, Champagne
Dillweed	Cheese Dips, Seafood Spreads, Pickles	Borscht, Tomato, Chicken	Halibut, Shrimp, Sole	Omelet, Cottage Cheese	Beef, Sweetbreads, Veal, Lamb	Chicken Pie, Creamed Chicken	Cabbage, Beets, Beans, Celery	Coleslaw, Cucumber, Potato	White (for Fish), Tartare
Fines Herbs			Baked or Broiled Cod or Halibut, Dressings	Omelet, Scrambled Eggs, Cheese Sauce, Soufflés	Broiled Liver and Kidneys, Roast Pork, Pot Roast, Stews, Meat Loaf, Hamburgers	Dressings, Broiled Chicken	Peas, Mushrooms, Tomatoes		
Marjoram	Liver Pâté, Stuffed Mushrooms, Butters	Spinach, Clam, Mock Turtle, Onion	Crab, Tuna, Clams, Halibut, Salmon	Omelet, Scrambled Eggs	Pot Roast, Pork, Beef, Veal	Creamed Chicken, Dressings, Goose	Carrots, Zucchini, Peas	Chicken, Mixed Green	White, Brown, Sour Cream
Oregano	Guacamole, Tomato	Tomato, Bean, Minestrone	Shrimp, Clams, Lobster	Huevos Rancheros	Sausage, Lamb, Meat Loaf	Marinades, Dressings, Pheasant, Guinea Hen	Tomatoes, Cabbage, Lentils, Broccoli	Vegetable, Bean, Tomato	Spaghetti, Tomato

HERB CHART — Continued

For:	Appetizers & Garnishes	Soups	Fish	Eggs or Cheese	Meats	Poultry & Game	Vegetables	Salads	Sauces
Peppermint*	Fruit Cup Melon Balls Cranberry Juice	Pea	Garnish for Broiled Shrimps Prawns	Cream Cheese	Lamb Veal		Carrots New Potatoes Spinach Zucchini	Fruit Coleslaw Orange Pear	Mint
Rosemary	Fruit Cup	Turtle, Pea Spinach Chicken	Salmon Halibut	Omelet Scrambled Eggs	Lamb, Veal Beef Ham Loaf	Partridge Capon, Duck Rabbit	Peas Spinach Potatoes	Fruit	White Barbecue Tomato
Saffron		Bouillabaisse Chicken, Turkey	Halibut Sole	Cream Cheese Scrambled Eggs	Veal	Chicken Rabbit	Risotto Rice	Seafood Chicken	Fish Sauce
Sage	Sharp Cheese Spreads	Chicken Chowders	Halibut Salmon	Cheddar Cottage	Stews Pork Sausage	Goose Turkey Rabbit Dressings	Lima Beans Eggplant Onions Tomatoes		
Salad Herbs	Fruit Cup Vegetable and Tomato Juices Seafood Cocktail Sauce		All Fish		Meat Loaf			All Salads	
Savory	Vegetable Juice Cocktail	Lentil Bean Vegetable	Crab Salmon	Scrambled or Deviled Eggs	Pork Veal	Chicken Dressings	Beans, Rice Lentils Sauerkraut	Mixed Green String Bean Potato	Horseradish Fish Sauce
Tarragon	Tomato Juice Cheese Spreads Liver Pâtés	Chicken Mushroom Tomato Pea	All Fish	All Egg Dishes	Veal Sweetbreads Yorkshire Pudding	Chicken Squab Duck	Salsify Celery Root Mushrooms	Mixed Green Chicken Fruit Seafood	Bearnaise Tartare Verte Mustard
Thyme	Tomato Juice Fish Spreads Cocktails	Borscht Gumbo, Pea Clam Chowder Vegetable	Tuna Scallops Crab Sole	Shirred Eggs Cottage Cheese	Mutton Meat Loaf Veal Liver	Dressings Venison Fricassee Pheasant	Onions Carrots Beets	Beet Tomato Aspics	Creole Espagnole Herb Bouquets

*Use ½ teaspoon for 6 servings

Courtesy of Spice Islands

SPICE CHART

For:	Appetizers & Garnishes	Fish	Eggs or Cheese	Meats	Poultry & Game	Vegetables	Sauces	Desserts & Beverages
Use: **Allspice**	*Marinades			Pot Roast, Stew, Braised Veal, Pork, Lamb	*Marinades (for Game)	*Pickling liquids for all vegetables	Chili, Catsup, Barbecue, Spaghetti, Brown	Fruit and Spice Cakes, Mincemeat, Apple Pie, Pumpkin Pie
Beau Monde Seasoning	Dips, Spreads	Broiled, Baked	All Egg Dishes	Steaks, Chops, Roasts	Chicken, Duck, Turkey		White, Tomato, Barbecue	
Cardamom				Spareribs, Ham, Pork			Barbecue	Coffee Cakes, Breads, Fruitcake, Cookies, Hot Fruit Punches, *Mulled Wines
Chili Con Carne Seasoning	Cheese Dips, Spreads		Welsh Rarebit, Soufflés, Baked or Scrambled Eggs	Marinades for Pork, Lamb, Beef	Marinades for Chicken	Corn, Rice, Kidney, Pink or Lima Beans	Barbecue, Cheese	
Cinnamon	Cranberry Sauce, Pickled or Spiced Fruits, Broiled Grapefruit, *Pickles, *Chutney, Catsup	*Court Bouillon for all Fish and Shellfish		Ham, Lamb, Pork Chops, Beef Stews, *Stock for Pickled or Smoked Meats	Dressing for Goose			All Milk Drinks, Custard, Fruit or Rice Puddings, Pumpkin, Apple, Peach, Cream or Custard Pies, *Mulled Wine, *Hot Tea, *Coffee, *Chocolate, *Spiced and Pickled Fruits
Cloves		*Court Bouillon, Baked Fish	Scrambled or Creamed Eggs	*Marinades for Beef, Pork, Lamb, Veal, *Stock for Boiling Meat Loaf	*Marinades for Game, *Stock for Boiling Poultry	Harvard Beets, Sweet Potatoes, Tomatoes	Spaghetti, Chili, Wine, Barbecue	*Hot or Cold Fruit Punches, *Mulled Wines, All spice cakes, cookies, and puddings
Curry Powder	Dips	Broiled, Baked	Deviled Eggs, Egg Salad, Cheese Spreads	Lamb, Pork, Beef	Chicken	Cooked Vegetables	Curry, Marinades for Lamb, Beef, Chicken, Fish, Game, White Sauce	
Ginger	*Pickled or Spiced Fruits, *Preserves, Jams, Jellies	Broiled, Baked		Pot Roast, Steak, Lamb, *Marinades for Beef, Lamb	Dressing for Poultry, *Marinades for Chicken, Turkey	Candied Sweet Potatoes, Glazed Carrots or Onions, Winter Squash	For Pork, Veal, Fish	Canned Fruit, Gingerbread, Gingersnaps, Ginger Cookies, Steamed Puddings, Bread or Rice Puddings

For:	Appetizers & Garnishes	Fish	Eggs or Cheese	Meats	Poultry & Game	Vegetables	Sauces	Desserts & Beverages
Use: **Mace**	Pickles Fruit Preserves Jellies	Trout Scalloped Fish	Welsh Rarebit	Lamb Chops Sausage		Buttered Carrots Cauliflower Squash Swiss Chard Spinach Mashed or Creamed Potatoes	Fish Veal Chicken	Cooked Apples Cherries Prunes Apricots Pancakes Chocolate Pudding	Fruit Cottage or Custard Puddings
Mustard (Hot)	Butter for Vegetables Seafood Cocktail	Crab		Stew Pot Roast Ham Pork	Fried Chicken	Creamed Asparagus Broccoli Brussels Sprouts Cabbage Celery Green Beans Pickled Beets	French Dressing Mustard Sauce Gravies Cream Cheese and Newburg Sauces	
Mustard (Mild)		Fried Broiled		Beef Stew Swiss Steak		Scalloped & Au Gratin Potatoes Steamed Cabbage Brussels Sprouts Asparagus Broccoli	French Dressing Cooked Salad Dressing Mayonnaise Raisin, White Sauces	
Nutmeg	Garnish for milk, chocolate, and spiced drinks	Baked Croquettes Broiled	Welsh Rarebit	Swedish Meat Balls Meat Loaf Meat Pie	Chicken	Glazed Carrots Cauliflower Squash Swiss Chard Spinach	White Sauce for Chicken Seafood Veal	Ice Cream Cakes	Cookies Puddings
Paprika	Pâtés Canapes Hors d'oeuvres		All Cheese Mixtures	Ground Beef Dipping Mixture for Pork Chops Veal Cutlets	Dipping Mixture for Fried Chicken	Baked Potatoes	Cooked French Sour Cream Salad Dressings White Sauce	
Tumeric		Marinades for Broiled Salmon, Lobster, or Shrimp	Scrambled or Creamed Eggs	Curried Beef or Lamb	Marinades for Chicken		White Mustard	
Vanilla Beans							Fruit	Ice Cream Cakes	Custards Puddings

Courtesy of Spice Islands

Note: All spices are ground except those indicated by an asterisk (*), which indicates whole spice

GLOSSARY

à la Mode—Food served with ice cream

Al dente—The point in the cooking of pasta at which it is still fairly firm to the tooth; that is, very slightly undercooked

Aspic—A jellied meat juice or a liquid held together with gelatin

Bake—To cook food in an oven by dry heat

Barbecue—To roast meat slowly over coals on a spit or framework, or in an oven, basting intermittently with a special sauce

Baste—To spoon pan liquid over meats while they are roasting to prevent surface from drying

Beat—To mix vigorously with a brisk motion with spoon, fork, egg beater, or electric mixer

Béchamel—White sauce of butter, flour, cream rather than milk, and seasonings

Bisque—A thick, creamy soup usually of shellfish, but sometimes made of pureed vegetables

Blanch—To dip briefly into boiling water

Blend—To stir 2 or more ingredients together until well mixed

Blintz—A cooked crêpe stuffed with cheese or other filling

Boil—To cook food in boiling water or liquid that is mostly water (at 212°) in which bubbles constantly rise to the surface and burst

Boiling-water-bath canning method—Used for processing acid foods, such as fruits, tomatoes (with high-acid content), pickled vegetables, and sauerkraut. These acid foods are canned safely at boiling temperatures in a water-bath canner

Borscht—Soup containing beets and other vegetables, usually with a meat stock base

Bouillabaisse—A highly seasoned fish soup or chowder containing two or more kinds of fish

Bouillon—Clear soup made by boiling meat in water

Bouquet Garni—Herbs tied in cheesecloth which are cooked in a mixture and removed before serving

Bourguignon—Name applied to dishes containing Burgundy and often braised onions and mushrooms

Braise—To cook slowly with liquid or steam in a covered utensil. Less-tender cuts of meat may be browned slowly on all sides in a small amount of shortening, seasoned, and water added.

Bread, to—To coat with crumbs, usually in combination with egg or other binder

Broil—To cook by direct heat, either under the heat of a broiler, over hot coals, or between two hot surfaces

Broth—A thin soup, or a liquid in which meat, fish, or vegetables have been boiled

Capers—Buds from a Mediterrranean plant, usually packed in brine and used as a condiment in dressings or sauces

Caramelize—To cook white sugar in a skillet over medium heat, stirring constantly, until sugar forms a golden-brown syrup

Casserole—An ovenproof baking dish, usually with a cover; also the food cooked in it

Charlotte—A molded dessert containing gelatin, usually formed in a dish or a pan lined with ladyfingers or cake

Chill—To cool by placing on ice or in a refrigerator

Chop—A cut of meat usually attached to a rib

Chop, to—To cut into pieces, usually with a sharp knife or with kitchen shears

Clarified butter—Butter that has been melted and chilled. The solid is then lifted away from the liquid, and discarded. Clarification heightens the smoke point of butter. Clarified butter will stay fresh in the refrigerator for at least 2 months, much longer than regular butter

Coat—To cover completely, as in "coat with flour"

Cocktail—An appetizer. Either a beverage or a light, highly seasoned food, served before a meal

Compote—Mixed fruit, raw or cooked, usually served in "compote" dishes

Condiments—Seasonings that enhance the flavor of foods with which they are served

Consommé—A clear broth made from meat

Cool—To let stand at room temperature until food is no longer warm to the touch

Court Bouillon—A highly seasoned broth made with water and meat, fish or vegetables, and seasonings

Crackling Bread—Cornbread baked with chopped cracklings added

Cracklings—The crunchy, crisp bits of pork left after the fat is rendered for lard

Cream, to—To blend together, as sugar and butter, until mixture takes on a smooth cream-like texture

Cream, whipped—Cream that has been whipped until it is stiff

Crème de Cacao—A chocolate-flavored liqueur

Crème de Café—A coffee-flavored liqueur

Crêpes—Very thin pancakes

Croquette—Minced food, shaped like a ball, patty, cone, or log, bound with a heavy sauce, breaded, and fried

Croutons—Cubes of bread, toasted or fried, served with soups, salads, or other foods

Cruller—A doughnut of twisted shape, very light in texture

Cube, to—To cut into cube-shaped pieces

Curaçao—Orange-flavored liqueur

Cut in, to—To incorporate by cutting or chopping motions, as in cutting shortening into flour for pastry

Demitasse—A small cup of coffee served after dinner

Devil, to—To prepare with hot seasoning or sauce

Dice—To cut into small (about ¼-inch) cube

Dissolve—To mix a dry substance with liquid until the dry substance becomes a part of the solution

Dot—To scatter small bits of butter over top of a food

Dredge—To coat with something, usually flour or sugar

Filé—A powder made of sassafras leaves used for seasoning and thickening foods

Filet—Boneless piece of meat or fish

Flambé—To flame, as in Crêpes Suzette or in some meat cookery, using alcohol as the burning agent; flame causes some caramelization, enhancing flavor

Flan—In France, a filled pastry; in Spain, a custard

Florentine—A food containing, or placed upon spinach

Flour, to—To coat with flour

Fold—To add a whipped ingredient, such as cream or egg white to another ingredient by gentle over and under movement

Frappé—A drink whipped with ice to make a thick, frosty consistency

Fricassee—A stew, usually of poultry or veal

Fritter—Vegetable or fruit dipped into, or combined with, batter and fried

Fry—To cook in hot shortening

Garnish—A decoration for a food or drink, for example, a sprig of parsley

Glaze (To make a shiny surface)—In meat preparation, a jelled broth applied to meat surface; in breads and pastries, a wash of egg or syrup; for doughnuts and cakes, a coating with a sugar preparation

Grate—To obtain small particles of food by rubbing on a grater or shredder

Gratin, au—A food served crusted with breadcrumbs or shredded cheese

Grill—To broil under or over a source of direct heat, such as charcoal

Grits—Coarsely ground dried corn, served either boiled, or boiled and then fried

Gumbo—Soup or stew made with okra

Herb—Aromatic plant used for seasoning and garnishing foods

Hollandaise—A sauce made of butter, egg, and lemon juice or vinegar

Hominy—Whole corn grains from which hull and germ have been removed

Jardiniere—Vegetables in a savory sauce or soup

Julienne—Vegetables cut into long thin strips or a soup containing such vegetables

Jus, au—Meat served in its own juice

Kahlúa—A coffee-flavored liqueur

King, à la—Food prepared in a creamy white sauce containing mushrooms and red and/or green peppers

Kirsch—A cherry-flavored liqueur

Knead—To work a food (usually dough) with the hands, using a folding-back and pressing-forward motion

Marinade—A seasoned liquid in which food is soaked

Marinate, to—To soak food in a seasoned liquid

Meringue—A whole family of egg white-sugar preparations including pie topping, poached meringue used to top custard, crisp meringue dessert shells, and divinity candy

Mince—To chop into very fine pieces (about ⅛-inch)

Mornay—White sauce with egg, cream, and cheese added

Mousse—A molded dish based on meat or sweet whipped cream stiffened with egg white and/or gelatin (if mousse contains ice cream, it is called bombe)

Panbroil—To cook over direct heat in an uncovered skillet containing little or no shortening

Panfry—To cook in an uncovered skillet in a shallow amount of shortening

Parboil—To partially cook in boiling water before proceeding with final cooking

Pasta—A large family of flour paste products, such as spaghetti, macaroni, and noodles

Pâté (French for paste)—A paste made of liver or meat

Petit Four—A small cake, which has been frosted and decorated

Pilau or pilaf—A dish of the Middle East consisting of rice and meat or vegetables in a seasoned stock

Poach—To cook in liquid held below the boiling point

Pot Liquor—The liquid in which vegetables have been boiled

Pot Roast—To cook larger cuts of meat with liquid added

Preheat—To turn on oven so that desired temperature will be reached before food is inserted for baking

Puree—A thick sauce or paste made by forcing cooked food through a sieve

Reduce—To boil down, evaporating liquid from a cooked dish

Remoulade—A rich mayonnaise-based sauce containing anchovy paste, capers, herbs, and mustard

Render—To melt fat away from surrounding meat

Rind—Outer shell or peel of melon or fruit

Roast, to—To cook in oven by dry heat (usually applied to meats)

Roux—A mixture of butter and flour used to thicken gravies and sauces; the color may be brown (if mixture is browned before liquid is added) or white

Sangria—A beverage based on dry red wine and flavored with various fruit juices (and sometimes brandy) and served cold

Sauté—To fry food lightly over fairly high heat in a small amount of fat in a shallow, open pan

Scald—(1) To heat milk just below the boiling point (2) To dip certain foods into boiling water before freezing them (also called blanching)

Scallop—A bivalve mollusk of which only the muscle hinge is eaten; also to bake a food in a sauce topped with crumbs

Score—To cut shallow gashes on surface of food, as in scoring fat on ham before glazing

Sear—To brown surface of meat over high heat to seal in juices

Set—Term used to describe gelatin when it has jelled enough to unmold

Shred—Break into thread-like or stringy pieces, usually by rubbing over the surface of a vegetable shredder

Simmer—To cook gently at a temperature below boiling point

Singe—To touch lightly with flame

Skewer—To fasten with wooden or metal pins or skewers

Sliver—A fine thin slice

Soak—To immerse in water for a period of time

Soufflé—A spongy hot dish, made from a sweet or savory mixture (often milk or cheese), lightened by stiffly beaten egg whites

Steam—To cook food with steam either in a pressure cooker, on a platform in a covered pan, or in a special steamer

Steam-pressure canning method—Used for processing low-acid foods, such as meats, fish, poultry, and most vegetables. A temperature higher than boiling is required to can these foods safely. In this method, the food is processed in a steam-pressure canner at 10 pounds' pressure (240°) to ensure that all spoilage micro-organisms are destroyed

Steep—To let a food stand in not quite boiling water until flavor is extracted

Stew—A mixture of meat or fish and vegetables cooked by simmering in its own juices and liquid, such as water and/or wine

Stir—To mix with a steady, circular motion with a spoon, whisk, or beater

Stir-fry—To cook quickly in oil over high heat, using light tossing and stirring motions to preserve shape of food

Stock—The broth in which meat, poultry, fish, or vegetables has been cooked

Syrupy—Thickened to about the consistency of egg white

Toast, to—To brown by direct heat, as in a toaster or under broiler

Torte—A round cake, sometimes made with breadcrumbs instead of flour, which may contain dried fruits and nuts

Tortilla—A Mexican flat bread made of corn or wheat flour

Toss-To mix together with light tossing motions, in order not to bruise delicate food, such as salad greens

Triple Sec—An orange-flavored liqueur

Veal—Flesh of a milk-fed calf up to 14 weeks of age

Velouté—White sauce made of flour, butter, and a chicken or veal stock, instead of milk

Vinaigrette—A cold sauce of oil and vinegar flavored with parsley, finely chopped onions and other seasonings and served with cold meats or vegetables

Whip—To beat rapidly to increase air and increase volume

Wok—A round bowl-shaped metal cooking utensil of Chinese origin used for stir-frying and steaming (with rack inserted) of foods

INDEX

A

O